Praise for *Sea Power*

"No one understands the importance of the oceans and their impact on today's security better than Admiral Jim Stavridis. He is a leader and a sailor who stands out in every way. This is a must-read book."

—Senator John McCain

"Stavridis strikes a perfect balancing tone between the theoretical and the personal; he's read widely in the annals of naval history, and he's also seen years of that history in the making. . . . *Sea Power* is clear-eyed about the dangers of the modern nautical realities, but it doggedly retains this tone of hope throughout. And hope or danger, on one point the book compels agreement: the oceans are still the crucial theaters of this water world."

—*Christian Science Monitor*

"Admiral Jim Stavridis served as a combatant commander for nearly seven years, as NATO Supreme Allied Commander for four years, and knows the world well. In *Sea Power*, he turns his intellect to helping us understand the maritime world in clear, sharp strokes—vital analysis in this turbulent century."

—Robert M. Gates, Secretary of Defense, 2008–2011

"Marvelous and essential . . . [Stavridis] not only describes what his subtitle promises—the history and geopolitics of the world's oceans—but also seeks to accomplish something far more elusive, sophisticated, and significant: to show how service at sea in one of the world's great global navies simultaneously expands tactical, operational, strategic, and policy knowledge and skills in an officer and—most important—develops insights in him or her regarding myriad possible interconnections among those levels of conflict. . . . This is a book for all sailors and policymakers, and especially for those who are both."

—*Proceedings Magazine*

"Admiral Jim Stavridis has sailed the world's oceans and has distilled the journey into a sharply observed geopolitical take on global affairs in the maritime sphere. This is a sailor's view of this turbulent nautical world, and it is a voyage worth taking."

—Admiral Mike Mullen, USN (Ret.), seventeenth chairman of the Joint Chiefs of Staff and twenty-eighth chief of naval operations

"Stavridis, a retired U.S. Navy admiral, summons the collected knowledge of his extensive career as an operational commander to provide insight into navies' routine functioning. . . . It's a stimulating and provocative work . . . a timely reminder that oceans may seem tamed—but that's only true on the surface."

—*Publishers Weekly*

"Fellow Admiral Jim Stavridis spent nearly four decades as a U.S. Navy sailor and is well known as an important geopolitical thinker. In *Sea Power*, both of those attributes come together to create a must-read for anyone seriously thinking about the world's challenges in the twenty-first century."

—Admiral Bill McRaven, USN (Ret.), chancellor, the University of Texas system, and former commander, U.S. Special Operations Command

PENGUIN BOOKS

SEA POWER

Admiral James Stavridis, USN (Ret.), is a graduate of the U.S. Naval Academy who spent more than thirty-five years on active service in the Navy. He commanded destroyers and a carrier strike group in combat and served for seven years as a four-star admiral, including nearly four years as the first Navy officer chosen as Supreme Allied Commander for Global Operations at NATO. After retiring from the Navy he was named the dean of the Fletcher School of Law and Diplomacy at Tufts University in 2013. He has written articles on global security issues for the *New York Times*, the *Washington Post*, and *The Atlantic*.

Also by Admiral James Stavridis, USN (Ret.)

The Accidental Admiral

Partnership for the Americas

Destroyer Captain

Coauthored by Admiral James Stavridis, USN (Ret.)

Command at Sea

The Leader's Bookshelf

Watch Officer's Guide

Division Officer's Guide

SEA POWER

THE HISTORY AND GEOPOLITICS OF THE WORLD'S OCEANS

Admiral James Stavridis, USN (Ret.)

PENGUIN BOOKS

PENGUIN BOOKS
An imprint of Penguin Random House LLC
375 Hudson Street
New York, New York 10014
penguinrandomhouse.com

First published in the United States of America by Penguin Press,
an imprint of Penguin Random House LLC, 2017
Published in Penguin Books 2018

Map illustrations by Jeffrey L. Ward unless otherwise credited.

ISBN 9780735220614 (paperback)

THE LIBRARY OF CONGRESS HAS CATALOGED THE HARDCOVER EDITION AS FOLLOWS:
Names: Stavridis, James, author.
Title: Sea power : the history and geopolitics of the world's oceans /
Admiral James Stavridis, USN (Ret.).
Description: New York : Penguin Press, 2017.
Identifiers: LCCN 2016056758 (print) | LCCN 2017021421 (e-book) |
ISBN 9780735220607 (e-book) | ISBN 9780735220591 (hardback)
Subjects: LCSH: Sea power—History. | Naval history. | Geopolitics—History. |
BISAC: POLITICAL SCIENCE / Political Freedom &
Security / International Security. |
HISTORY / Military / Naval. | HISTORY / United States / General.
Classification: LCC V25 (e-book) | LCC V25 .S73 2017 (print) |
DDC 359/.03—dc23
LC record available at https://lccn.loc.gov/2016056758

Printed in the United States of America
1 3 5 7 9 10 8 6 4 2

DESIGNED BY MEIGHAN CAVANAUGH

For all the sailors on distant voyages.

And for Laura, Christina, and Julia,

who waited patiently for their sailor

to come home from the sea.

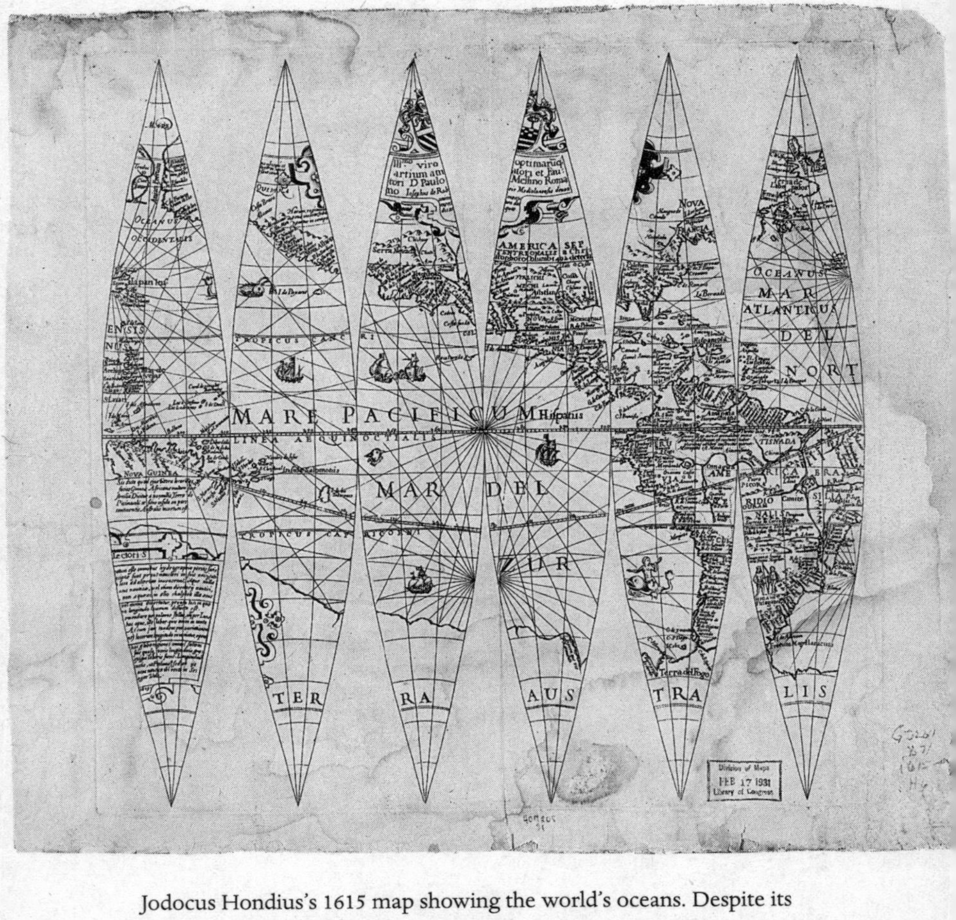

Jodocus Hondius's 1615 map showing the world's oceans. Despite its impressive detail, cartography has come a long way in 400 years.

MARE
ARABICUM
et
INDICUM
ORIEN
TALIS
OCEANUS
Golfo
di
Bengala
Philippinæ
Insulæ
TARTARIA
BEACH
REGNU
I. Hondius
IN COG NIT A
Division of Maps
FEB 17 1931
Library of Congress

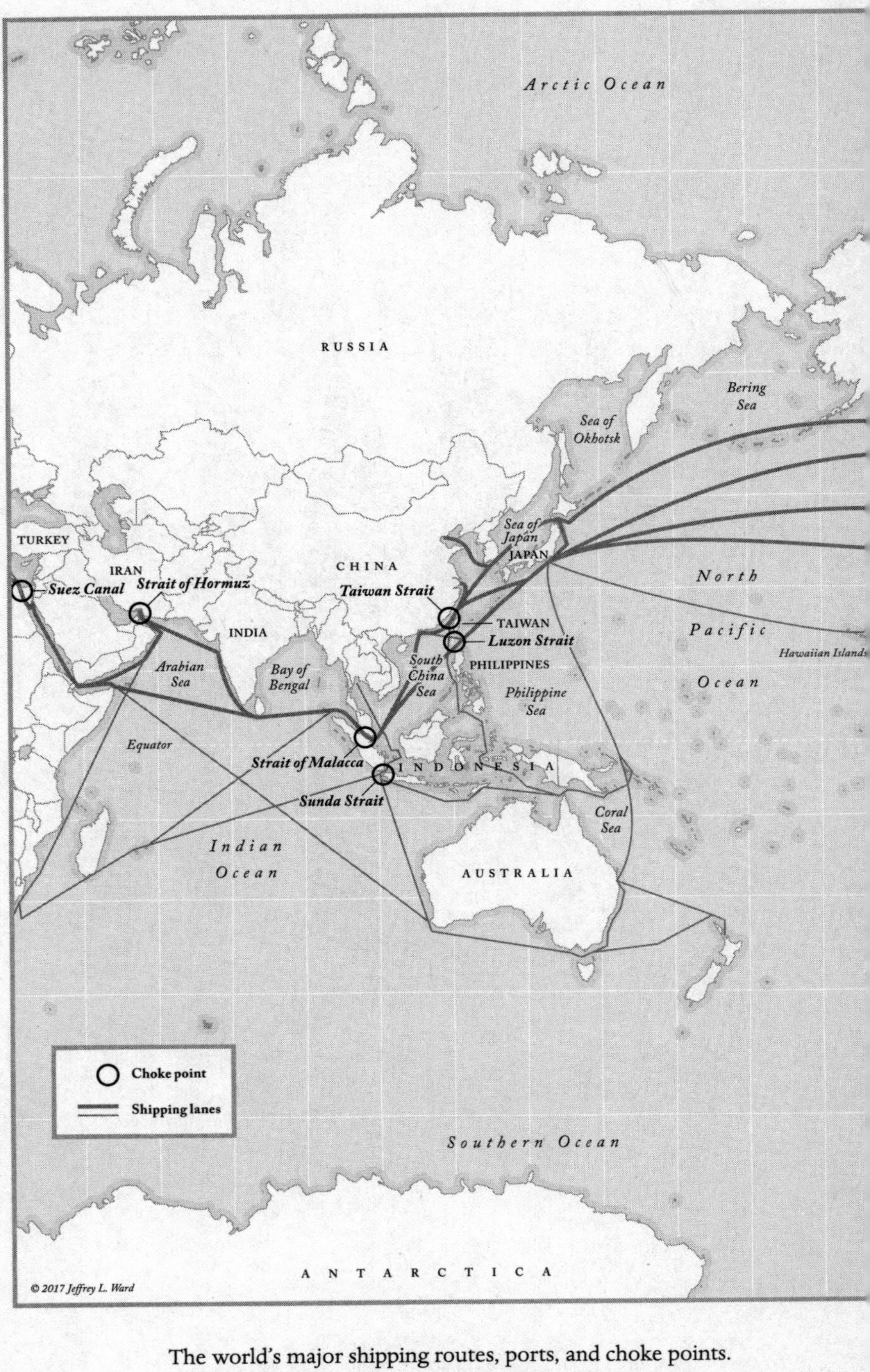

The world's major shipping routes, ports, and choke points.
These routes are the lifeblood of our global economy.

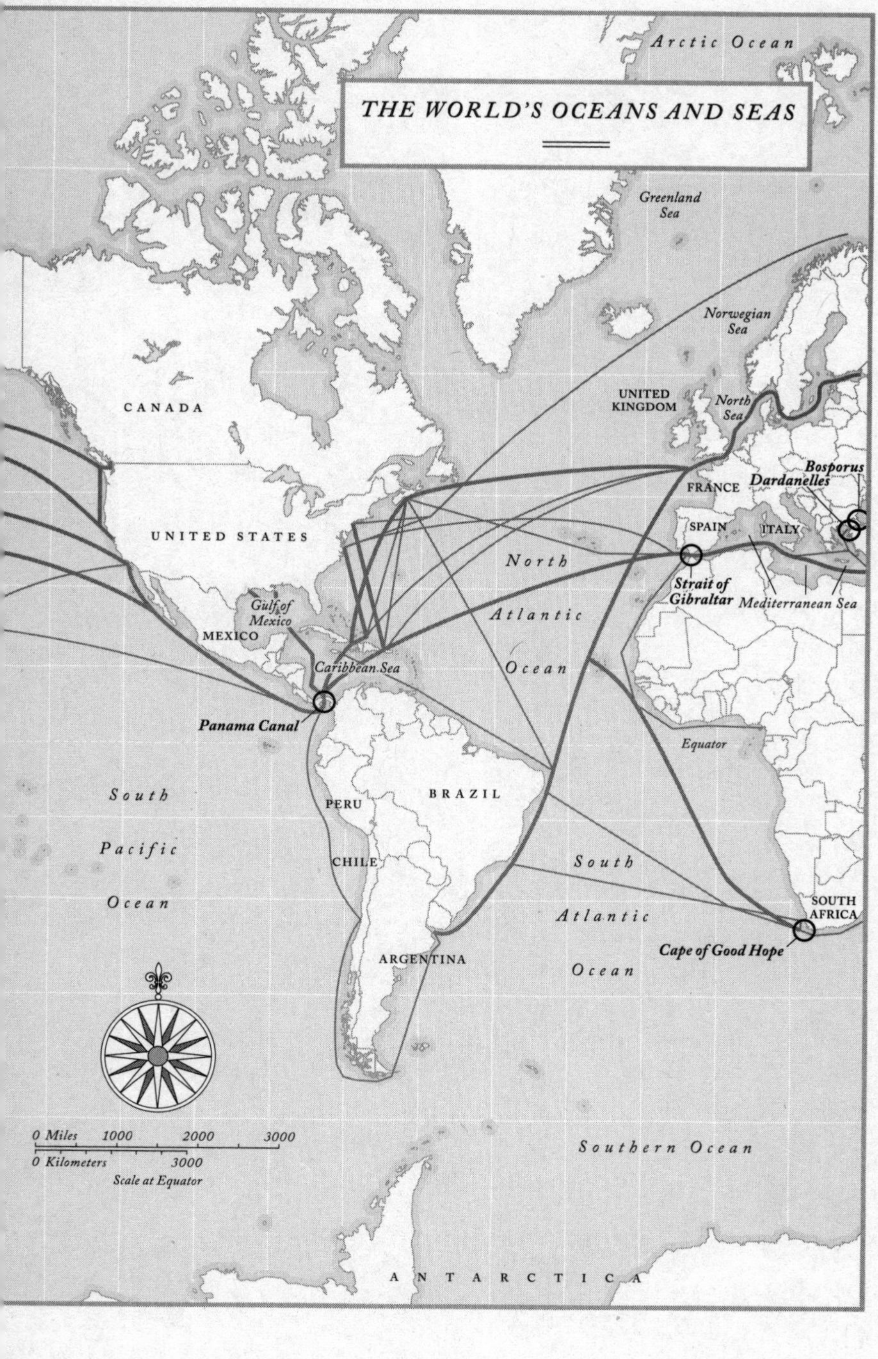

THE WORLD'S OCEANS AND SEAS
Arctic Ocean
Greenland Sea
Norwegian Sea
North Sea
UNITED KINGDOM
CANADA
FRANCE
Bosporus
Dardanelles
SPAIN
ITALY
UNITED STATES
North Atlantic Ocean
Strait of Gibraltar
Mediterranean Sea
Gulf of Mexico
MEXICO
Caribbean Sea
Panama Canal
Equator
South Pacific Ocean
PERU
BRAZIL
CHILE
South Atlantic Ocean
SOUTH AFRICA
Cape of Good Hope
ARGENTINA
0 Miles 1000 2000 3000
0 Kilometers 3000
Scale at Equator
Southern Ocean
ANTARCTICA

CONTENTS

SEA POWER

INTRODUCTION

THE SEA IS ONE

Shakespeare, in his immortal sea drama *The Tempest*, said, "We are such stuff as dreams are made on, and our little life is rounded with a sleep," referring to the small and confined dimensions of our individual lives. It is a haunting passage, and one I have thought about a great deal. The play opens with a massive storm at sea, and the line has always had profoundly nautical implications for me. In my nearly four decades as a Navy sailor, when all the days I spent on the deep ocean, out of sight of land, are totaled, they add up to nearly eleven years. The endless vistas of the open ocean, upon which I gazed for more than a decade of my life, provide quite a setting for such dreaming. And in those days, when I looked at the ocean, I always felt a sense of seeing the same view that millions upon millions of other deep-sea mariners, coastal sailors, and even land dwellers close to the ocean saw. Like the fishermen, traders, pirates, harbor pilots, and indeed sailors of every ilk who went down to the sea in ships of all kinds, we have all seen the same ocean views. In a way, it is like looking at eternity; to gaze upon it for an hour, a day, a month, or a lifetime reminds us gently that our time is limited, and we are but a tiny part of the floating world.

In addition to simply warning us not to overimagine the importance of our own small voyages on this earth, Shakespeare's line also makes us consider quite literally what we are indeed made of. It is worth remembering that each of us is, essentially, largely made of water. When a human baby is born, it is composed of roughly 70 percent water. It has always fascinated me that roughly the same proportion of the globe is covered by water—just over 70 percent. Both our planet and our bodies are dominated by the liquid world, and anyone who has sailed extensively at sea will understand instinctively the primordial tug of the oceans upon each of us when we look upon the sea.

I still dream about being on a ship, and part of why I wanted to write a book about the oceans is in response to those dreams. It often happens as I nod off on my now landlocked bed that I dream of the faint rumble of a ship's engines and feel the rolling of the waves pushing and rocking the hull of my ship. When I rise and head up to the bridge, it is always on a bright day, with the clouds hanging in front of the bow and the ship pushing through the sea. I never know exactly where the dream will take me but I always end up approaching the shore, and when I do, I feel a pang of regret to leave the ocean. The approaches to land are always difficult in my dreams, and the ship often finds herself running out of deep water and becomes rapidly in danger of foundering on a beach or up a river or upon a reef. I always wake up before the ship finally impales herself ashore, and I always wish I had stayed farther out to sea.

The British navy, which dominated the world's oceans for so many years, truly and deeply understood the interconnected character of the global waterways. "The sea is one" is an expression you will hear from a Brit. I heard it first when I was eighteen years old and a second-year student, called a midshipman, at the U.S. Naval Academy in Annapolis,

Maryland. My navigation instructor was a crusty British lieutenant commander, who seemed incredibly old and salty—he was probably in his mid-thirties, and who could imagine being so ancient? This Old Man of the Sea was a crack hand with a sextant, a nautical almanac, and a tide table to be sure, but what he really taught me was the way in which all the world's oceans are at once connected—obvious enough given the continuous flow of water around the continents—but also separate. He would painstakingly discuss each of the great global bodies of water—the Pacific, the Atlantic, the Indian, and the Arctic oceans—as well as the major tributary bodies: the Mediterranean Sea, the South China Sea, the Caribbean. The lieutenant commander could talk for an hour about a particular strait between the Indian Ocean and the Pacific Ocean, and how the water looked in the winter, and why it was a crucial passage. I learned a great deal from him, not only about the science and art of navigating a destroyer, but also about oceanography, maritime history, global strategy, and how the tools of empire so often were dusted with dried salt, like the taffrails of a sailing cutter. You could drop a plumb line from my days as a teenager at Annapolis through the arc of nearly four decades as a Navy officer and finally end up on the pages of this book.

The oceans were the place I spent much of the early years of my career. I sailed through them all, validating the lessons he taught me, improving my own ship handling and navigational skills, and learning to lead men and women at sea. As my understanding and appreciation of the international system increased—accelerated by a PhD at the Fletcher School of Law and Diplomacy of Tufts University, where I am now a very deskbound admiral—I came to understand the influence of the sea on geopolitics. It is no coincidence that so many of the great national enterprises of the past two thousand years were influenced by sea power, and that continues to be true today. The sea is one indeed, particularly as a geopolitical entity, and will continue to exert an enormous influence on how global events unfold—from the high tension of the South China Sea, to the cocaine smuggling of the Caribbean, to the piracy off the coasts of Africa, to the unfortunate reemergence of a new cold war in the Greenland-Iceland–United Kingdom gap in the North Atlantic. Some observers may not be interested in the geopolitics of the oceans, but they will haunt our policy and our choices in this turbulent twenty-first century. The oceans will matter deeply to every aspect of human endeavor.

When we go to sea—whether in a warship for a nine-month combat cruise, or a week on a Carnival cruise liner, or just a day sail out of sight of land—we are launching ourselves into another dimension altogether. The world shudders and shakes beneath us, the wind cuts more sharply with nothing to slow its pace, the weather skims by our unprotected hull, the dolphins sometimes swim alongside for hours—it is a very different world. In a primal sense, we are "an ocean away" every time we go to sea and can no longer see the land. When you are on a hull, however large or small, and come up on the deck and slowly pivot around to see nothing but the ocean stretching away from you, stop and measure the moment in the passage of your life: you are seeing the same view, the same endless ocean that Alexander the Great saw as he sailed the eastern Mediterranean, that Napoleon gazed upon on his long, sad voyage to exile in the South Atlantic, and that Halsey saw as he lashed his Fast Carrier Task Force into combat in the western Pacific. In that sense, as a sailor, you are at once an ocean away from the world of the land, but also connected to a long, unbroken chain of men and women who have set their course for the open ocean.

It is those two important aspects of the oceans that I have tried to capture in this volume: the personal experience of a mariner at sea, and the geopolitics of the oceans and how they constantly influence events ashore. Only by understanding both the individual and personal experiences of sailors and trying to pour that distinct nautical culture into the larger questions of how the oceans drive the international system can we fully appreciate the value and the challenge of the sea. In that sense, this is a book that could have been written by many different sailors at any point in the long, long history of our collective human voyages both over the ocean and through time. Writing it now, in this century, is simply an attempt to take a vivid snapshot of those two tendrils of human experience—a sailor's life at sea and the strategic impact of the oceans—upon the vast water world we call earth.

Let's get under way.

1.

THE PACIFIC

MOTHER OF ALL THE OCEANS

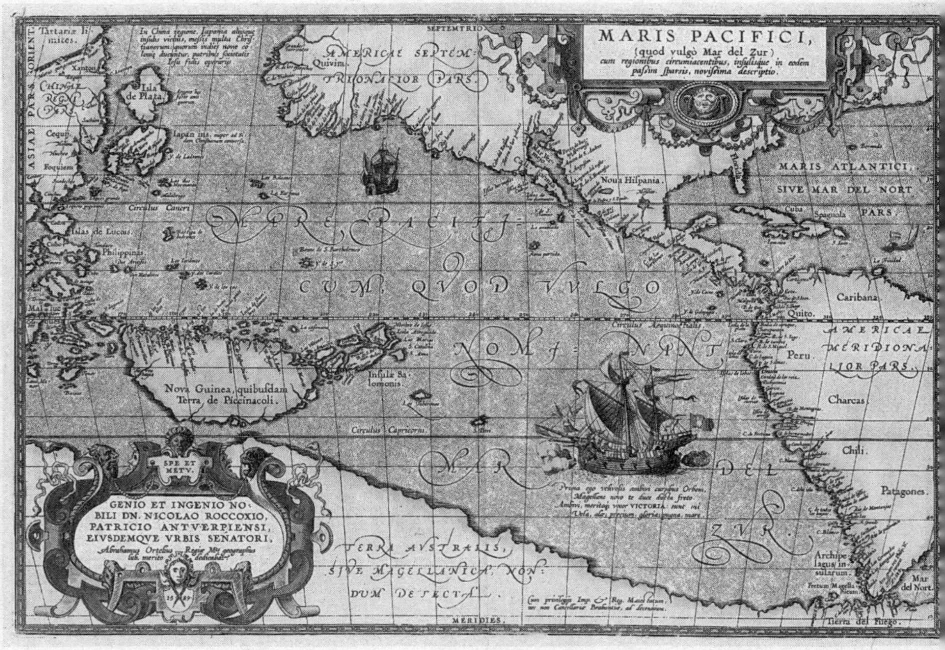

Ortelius's 1589 map showing what was then the Western world's best understanding of the Pacific.

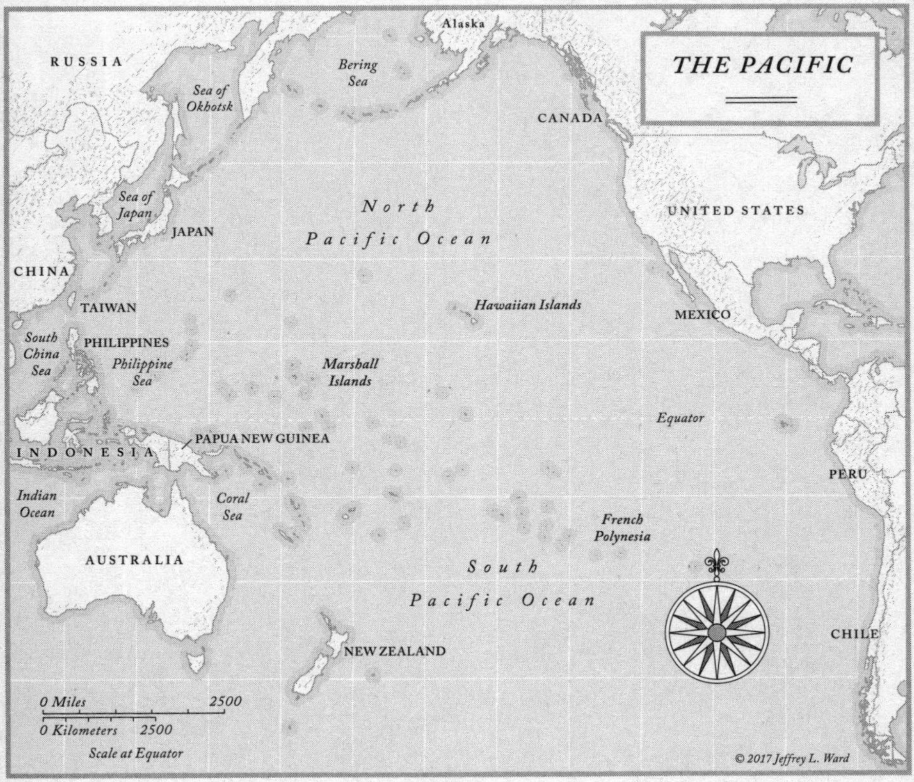
THE PACIFIC
RUSSIA
Alaska
Bering Sea
Sea of Okhotsk
CANADA
UNITED STATES
Sea of Japan
JAPAN
North Pacific Ocean
CHINA
TAIWAN
Hawaiian Islands
MEXICO
South China Sea
PHILIPPINES
Philippine Sea
Marshall Islands
Equator
PAPUA NEW GUINEA
INDONESIA
PERU
Indian Ocean
Coral Sea
French Polynesia
AUSTRALIA
South Pacific Ocean
CHILE
NEW ZEALAND
0 Miles 2500
0 Kilometers 2500
Scale at Equator
© 2017 Jeffrey L. Ward

I vividly remember the first time I sailed into the Pacific. It was in 1972, on a U.S. Navy cruiser, USS *Jouett*. She was a beautiful and modern warship of around 8,000 tons, with a length of about 550 feet, depth of 29 feet, and beam of 55 feet—a lot of ship as a general proposition, but not so much space internally when you considered there were nearly five hundred officers and men manning her.

At the time, I was seventeen years old and a very green midshipman, the lowest officer rank in the Navy, on my so-called youngster cruise out of Annapolis, which is what midshipmen did after their first year of academics instead of taking a summer break. Having grown up in a Marine Corps family (my father would eventually retire as a full colonel of Marines after combat service in Korea and Vietnam), I went to the U.S. Naval Academy with every intention of becoming a Marine infantry officer like my father. And so I went grudgingly to San Diego in the summer of 1972, grumpy about having to go to sea—like many Marines, my father's motto in service was "don't go near the water" (or the Pentagon either, but that's another story).

. . .

JOUETT SLIPPED HER LINES from San Diego's naval station and headed out to sea, past the beautiful shiny buildings of downtown San Diego, perhaps the nicest sea detail (the voyage from a pier to the open sea or the reverse) in the world. We passed under the Coronado Bay Bridge, passing the city skyline of San Diego to starboard and the large island of Coronado to port. I had been given the august responsibilities of "line handler, fantail," which meant that I was to report to the back end of the ship and help haul in the wet, heavy lines after they were slipped off the bollards on the pier. Immediately thereafter, I had been told to report to the bridge of the ship to take a turn learning how to handle the helm.

It was a sunny early summer's day, relatively early in the morning, a crisp Southern California day with a temperature in the mid-seventies, and by the time we were secured from the fantail, the ship was nosing out past Ballast Point and into the Pacific Ocean. Fortunately for my landsman's stomach, the seas were very calm, and as we pointed the bow due west, I made my way up several stories and stepped onto the bridge. As I emerged from the relatively dim passageways of the ship, I was simply stunned by all the sunshine and salt air and the vast ocean in front of me. Like Saint Paul on the road to Damascus, I had an epiphany: I wanted to be a sailor. In all my life, we had not been a family particularly oriented to the water, but the Pacific grabbed me by the throat and said quite simply, "You are home." I've never looked back.

We tend to think of the Pacific as the mother of all oceans because of its size. The Pacific is massive, and I do not use that word loosely. Even the people living along its periphery, from Canada to Chile, from Russia to Australia, and everywhere in between, appreciate only a small aspect of its size. A simple Google search will show a surface area of nearly 64 million square miles. But such a large number obscures its meaning unless you measure it against other benchmarks. The Pacific Ocean alone is greater than the combined landmasses of the entire Earth. In our country, where geography is no longer a widely studied discipline (if at all), it is hard to appreciate that a traveler flying from Washington, D.C., to Honolulu will spend no more time flying to her connecting flight in California than she will from California to her final destination. And perhaps more impressively, there is not a great deal of landmass *inside* the Pacific Ocean. All of the nations that border the Pacific—and there are many—think of the ocean as a kind of endless back porch. The sea dominates the geography of the Pacific more than anywhere else on earth.

But throughout this gargantuan maritime expanse, it is worth remembering that there *are* small and not-so-small islands of all shapes and sizes, both inhabited and uninhabited, each with a distinct culture and often racial group, representing thousands of years of habitation—Tahiti, Fiji, New Caledonia, New Guinea, New Ireland, New Georgia, on and on, an area of the world that is often referred to not by the names of the islands but by the term "Oceania."

In many ways, it is remarkable that these isolated pockets of life have human beings on them at all. To be initially colonized, someone in a distant past had to set sail, cross enormous distances, make landfall, and survive. Conquering such distances requires ingenuity, courage, and an inhuman amount of will. It would have been incredibly impressive if these islands were settled using the technology of a few hundred years ago: large-hulled ships with massive sails and complex navigation equipment like sextants—think of the HMS *Victory*, Lord Nelson's flagship in the 1800s. Instead, humans found a way to conquer these distances *ten thousand years ago*. Using nothing but outrigger canoes with oars, the erratic currents, and the stars, mass migrations from Southeast Asia spread people throughout the saltwater expanse. These Austronesians, the Polynesians, Micronesians, and Melanesians who still inhabit the islands to this day, journeyed as far as Hawaii, more than five thousand miles from what most historians believe was their point of origin on the coast of East Asia. The migrations took many years as Austronesians island-hopped as far as their oars and the sea itself could take them, a drama that would unfold in reverse during World War II as Allied forces followed the island chains back toward the Asian heart of the Japanese Empire.

Soon after I was commissioned as a young ensign out of Annapolis, those primitive voyages were much in my mind when I first crossed the Pacific in the late 1970s. Indeed, what I remember most about my first crossing was simply the length of the voyage. Luckily I wasn't in a *Kon-Tiki*-like boat modeled on the ancient Austronesian vessels. It takes a week to get from the West Coast of the United States to the Hawaiian Islands, and that is merely the front door. From Pearl Harbor on the island of Oahu in 1977, I sailed south to Fiji, New Zealand, and Australia—a long, long haul. We were in a small, three-ship squadron—just two new *Spruance*-class destroyers, *Hewitt* and *Kinkaid*, and a supply ship, the *Niagara Falls*. Crossing the Central Pacific from Hawaii south to the equator was a long, lazy sail with very little to do. There were basic chores in terms of maintaining the equipment and engineering plant on the ship, plenty of drills and practice events, underway replenishment wherein the smaller destroyers come alongside the larger supply ship and receive hoses to refuel—quite exciting at just a hundred feet between the ships. It was calm, hot, and flat, day after day after day.

Although we had access to some rudimentary electronic navigation systems, our principal navigation was done by sextant and paper charts. As the youngest ensign on the ship, I was expected to shoot the stars daily, as well as drive the ship, learn about the engineering plant, and mind my division of sailors (I had charge of the high-tech sailors focused on antisubmarine warfare, who had exactly zero to do in that vast submarine-less expanse). The most exciting thing we had to look forward to was the ceremony of "crossing the line," the day we would finally go past the equator and "enter the Kingdom of Davy Jones."

When U.S. Navy ships crossed the equator in those days, it was traditional to have a pretty rough hazing ceremony conducted by those who had crossed before (Shellbacks) at the expense of those who had not yet crossed (Pollywogs, or usually "slimy Wogs"). The ceremony consisted of being awoken well before dawn and herded up to the forecastle (the forward part of the ship) and sprayed with fire hoses and strewn with garbage. After a few hours of crawling around the rough decks of the ship (called nonskid, very abrasive), knees and palms are quite chewed up. It ends up with a crawl through a few canvas chutes full of very ripe garbage, dosed with this and that, before finally being made to kiss the well-greased stomach of a fat sailor dressed up as "Davy Jones" and being dunked (baptized) in salt water pulled up from the equator. It was quite a memorable day. Luckily for me, my commanding officer had never been across the equator before, so the hazing was sort of adjusted to a more gentlemanly level in his vicinity. I stayed close by his side.

Fiji is an interesting place, and as our ships pulled in, I was struck by its multicultural quality. At the time, about 50 percent of the population were Melanesian islanders, about 40 percent of Indian descent (from the indentured Indians brought by the British to work the sugar plantations more than a century earlier), and 10 percent East Asian or Anglo. The Melanesian percentage has gradually increased over the years, but it remains a multicultural society today. We arrived in the mid-1970s, shortly after Fiji had declared independence from the British crown.

I REMEMBER THE CLUSTERS of islands as we approached Suva, the fairly primitive capital, where we spent several easy days on the beach and playing tennis on the grass courts at the governor general's palace.

Of note, today Fiji has an uneasy political climate, having just emerged from a military coup undertaken by a commodore, of all people (normally it is an army general who takes over a country, not a senior navy officer). But a recent election—largely deemed credible—seems to have put this small, beautiful archipelago back on a relatively stable footing, much to the relief of the Australians, who keep a close eye on the region and worry about refugees streaming out in the case of real violence.

We sailed on to New Zealand, spending time on both the North and South islands. The New Zealand of the 1970s was a lot like the United States in the 1950s—quiet, kind, sensible, and slightly boring but in a very nice way. The two islands that constitute the country are both spectacular and beautiful, ranging from the tropical reaches of the North Island to the high Alps of the South, where the *Lord of the Rings* films were made by Kiwi director Peter Jackson.

After a week or so of liberty and saddled with a colossal hangover from drinking New Zealand's spectacular Sauvignon Blanc at a wine bar, I was given the job of junior officer of the deck, driving my ship, *Hewitt*, out of Auckland's harbor in a hard-blowing squall. It was pitch black and raining sideways, and the conning officer, a lieutenant junior grade who was even greener than I, was noticeably seasick, which did not enhance his already minimal ship handling skills. Our increasingly nervous captain watched us nearly swing the stern into a channel buoy in a too-tight turn and snapped at me to take the conn (drive the ship). That sobered me up swiftly, and with the help and oversight of the ship's operations officer (a very experienced and skilled mariner) we somehow got out of the channel and into the open sea without further incident. The Pacific was hardly pacific that night, let me assure you.

We then pushed on to Australia, thus completing a crossing of both the equator and the Pacific from San Diego to the incredible natural harbor of Sydney. We were all in our dress whites and the sun was shining, with the iconic Sydney Opera House, whose gorgeous architecture to me conjures up white sails at sea, gleaming across the harbor as we tied up on Garden Island, a naval dockyard on a promontory jutting into the harbor. The Pacific Ocean seemed far behind us as we fell into the warm arms of the Australians, who maintain a keen sense of gratitude to the U.S. Navy for our efforts in the Second World War to keep the Japanese from finding their way south. In those days it was a good idea to wear a uniform ashore, perhaps not so much today. But it is worth noting that the Australians continue to be very close to Americans, and in the military context have stood alongside us throughout our missions to Iraq and Afghanistan. I encountered no better fighters than the Aussies in Afghanistan, for example, and they are a serious part of the coalition against the Islamic State today.

After the delights of Sydney, we began to work our way up the Australian coast, stopping over for a few days in Townsville on the Great Barrier Reef. Situated at the foot of the spikelike peninsula on the northeast coast of Oz, Townsville is a laid-back town of around 200,000 today, far smaller those decades ago. It is a gateway to the reef and a significant tourist destination. Drinking a Foster's Lager and looking across the perfectly gorgeous waters of the reef out toward the barrier islands and the Pacific was extremely relaxing, and I felt I was close to the end of the Pacific crossing. Then I remembered what was ahead: the Torres Strait.

The good news about the Torres Strait is that it is relatively wide as international choke points go. It is the body of water between the northeastern tip of the continent of Australia and the big island of New Guinea, and, as a result, one of the busiest sea passages in the world. But the bad news is that it is unusually shallow and filled with a maze of small, nearly submerged islands and delicate reefs. In the mid-1970s it wasn't particularly well marked with navigational buoys, and no one on

Hewitt had ever been through it. Given the risky nature of the passage, the captain elected to take the conn and drive the ship himself, a quite unusual decision. As the sea detail junior officer of the deck, I was supposed to provide tactical navigational advice based on radar sightings, while the ship's navigator used traditional plotting of visual landmarks. Fortunately, we passed through in good weather on a bright day with relatively light traffic, and everyone breathed a sigh of relief as we headed fair from the Coral Sea of the western Pacific into the Arafura Sea of the eastern Indian Ocean.

Thus ended my first crossing of the Pacific, a voyage I have since duplicated many times over.

The first European to cross the Pacific, Ferdinand Magellan, ended up far worse than I did.

To appreciate the voyage of Magellan, you have to look at the globe with eastern Australia and Indonesia at the bottom left part of the circle. It is a water world indeed: you would see only slivers of western North America and Northeast Asia—the rest of the enormous circle is essentially water. Yet despite the long voyages of the Austronesians, there was no real sense of what existed west of the Americas from a European perspective until the beginning of the 1500s, when Vasco Núñez de Balboa crossed the Isthmus of Panama, stood atop a high hill, and both discovered and claimed the Pacific "for God and Spain." The discovery set off a maritime version of the scramble for land colonies in the Americas, and for the next three centuries the Europeans gradually mapped the vast stretches of the Pacific.

It was Magellan, an irascible Portuguese sailing on behalf of the Spanish crown, who actually named the Pacific, deciding that the waves were gentle and calm (which they are decidedly *not* much of the time, by the way) as his ships sailed into the deep South Pacific. He was the first European to sail across the Pacific Ocean, and the five-ship expedition under his command was the first to circumnavigate the globe. (Although Magellan himself did not complete the voyage and was killed in the Philippines in 1521.) Until Magellan, most of the voyages to Asia (in search of spices and gold, principally) were conducted by passing under the tip of Africa; he reasoned that it would be possible to reach Asia by sailing west, particularly as he reputedly thought the Pacific was only six hundred miles wide—he was off by more than ten thousand miles, not to put too fine a point on it. He persuaded the Spanish crown to finance his voyages and they provided him with five ships in 1519.

Magellan's flotilla, consisting of about 250 men, sailed down the coast of South America looking for a gap to sail to the Pacific. Naturally, the weather got worse and worse and the southern winter set in, destroying one ship and requiring the remaining four ships to winter over before finally discovering what would become known as the Strait of Magellan at the bottom tip of South America. The weather continued to be challenging, and the crew of one of the ships refused to continue, but Magellan eventually broke into the southern Pacific after observing the natives along the southern coasts burning big fires—hence the name Tierra del Fuego, or "land of fire."

Getting to the Pacific was exciting, but quickly the enormous length of the ocean ahead of them dawned on Magellan and his men. The sailors gradually pushed themselves farther and farther west from the coast of modern-day Chile without finding themselves in Asia. Eventually, by early spring of 1521, they made landfall on Guam in the Mariana island chain. They worked their way farther west to the Philippines by Easter of that year, where a mass was celebrated on the island of Cebu. Magellan then foolishly became involved in interisland conflict, sailing to a nearby island called Mactan, where his party of fifty Spaniards was overwhelmed by natives and he was killed. His crew chronicled his end: "That [a spear wound] caused the captain to fall face downward, when immediately they rushed upon him with iron and bamboo spears and their cutlasses until they killed our mirror, our light, our comfort, and our true guide."

The two centuries after Magellan's death were consumed in building transpacific trade, with the Spanish Empire in the lead by virtue of its colonies in the Philippines. Spain's flag, the Cross of Burgundy, was the dominant flag, but the Dutch, Portuguese, British, and French were also at play in the Pacific. The Spanish built the first truly international oceanic conveyor of goods, carrying silver mined in the New World to Asia and carting back manufactured goods to European markets. Over time the Spanish influence weakened, reflecting events in Europe (including the wars of the Reformation) that bled the peninsular nation. By the seventeenth and early eighteenth centuries, it was the Dutch and British who were in the ascendance in the western Pacific. In 1743, one of the massive Spanish treasure galleons was seized off Manila by British navy commodore George Anson, striking another significant economic blow against the Spanish. The French explorer Louis de Bougainville was the first of his nation to circumnavigate the Pacific as the French belatedly made their way into the region. While there were many expeditions and increasing levels of trade, there were still vast parts of the Pacific that were completely unexplored. Enter Captain James Cook, perhaps the greatest of all the Pacific sailors in history.

James Cook was born in 1728 to a lower middle-class family from northern England that initially apprenticed him to a shopkeeper; fortunately for the Pacific Ocean, he was obsessed from an early age with boats, rivers, and the sea. He managed to secure an apprenticeship with a shipping firm and began to learn to handle awkward commercial ships in the difficult and constrained waters around Great Britain. Cook also began to develop a true specialization in charting and mapmaking. He was drawn into the Royal Navy by the Seven Years' War and emerged an officer with a series of commands under his belt.

As the British began to think in a truly global way by the mid-1750s, it became apparent that mapping and surveying the Pacific Ocean was a means to develop sea power and leverage global influence. Cook was given command of HMS *Endeavour*, a 106-foot bark—short and chunky, but with a shallow draft to get in close to small islands and over reefs. He sailed for the Pacific in the late summer of 1768. A crucial member of his company was the wealthy, handsome naturalist and scientist Joseph Banks. Together, the two men spent the next several years exploring the far reaches of the Pacific.

One easy way to cruise the Pacific without leaving the comfort of a library is to pull out an atlas and trace the voyages of James Cook. He went out three times on a variety of ships and covered more than 150,000 sea miles. His ships were named *Endeavour*, *Discovery*, *Resolution*, and *Adventure*—all names that quite accurately describe how he spent the years from 1768 until his death at the hands of natives in the Hawaiian Islands (he called them the Sandwich Islands) in 1779. To lay out the courses of the three voyages is to chart virtually every important Pacific port—Cook Inlet and Prince William Sound in Alaska, Nootka Sound in western Canada, the Kamchatka Peninsula of Russia—and all of the important islands: Hawaii, Marquesas Islands, Tahiti, Fiji, New Caledonia, Easter Island, Cook Islands, Friendly Islands, and New Zealand's North and South islands. He also sailed close by Antarctica, circled Australia, rounded Cape Horn at the tip of South America, and cruised both the Atlantic and Indian oceans. In a brilliant and highly readable memoir, *Blue Latitudes: Boldly Going Where Captain Cook Has Gone Before*, Tony Horwitz follows Cook across the many sea miles from Alaska to Tasmania and from Easter Island to Russia. The Pacific was still essentially unexplored and certainly uncharted before this Yorkshire farm boy arrived—his genius opened it up, and his legacy lives today in the hearts and minds of mariners who sail those waters.

The Russians too participated in the great opening of the Pacific to outside powers. Using their bases in eastern Siberia, Russian crews with minimal technology accomplished rugged journeys across difficult distances through what must have seemed to be simply a cold, watery void. They carved out claims to Alaska, of course, being so close to the Bering Strait, but their influence extended south throughout much of the Pacific as well. Lured by the same fur trade that enticed American and Canadian trappers, Russian ships operated from forward operating bases, such as Fort Ross, north of San Francisco, in the early nineteenth century. But overhunting drove down the number of fur animals and made the expensive expeditions less economically viable. The Russian toehold in the Pacific was transitory, retracting from Fort Ross in the 1840s as the weight of its large empire became too burdensome and the czarist façade began to crack. Famously, Russia sold its claims to Alaska to the United States in 1867, just a scant two years after the conclusion of the U.S. Civil War in a deal widely mocked in the United States at the time. Yet despite their transitory physical presence, the Russians made invaluable contributions to the scientific exploration of the region.

The United States came into the Pacific world in fits and starts. Ships from Boston had made the arduous journey to China since the days of the Revolution but never established a permanent presence until the 1840s with the acquisition of California after the Mexican-American War. The fortuitous discovery of gold at Sutter's Mill in 1848 kicked off the California Gold Rush and drove mass migrations west, either by land across the continent, or across the isthmus of Panama (in the days before the Panama Canal), or around Tierra del Fuego as Magellan had done three centuries before. Capitalizing on the use of whale oil, whaling became a boom energy industry that migrated from the Atlantic to the Pacific due to overexploitation. Additionally, the lucrative commercial China trade became more and more important as the decades went on. This mania of interest brought the Pacific world into the minds of those on the East Coast.

The advent of coal-powered ships in the 1860s changed how the United States interacted with its Pacific domain. Coal ships were faster and more reliable than their sail-powered counterparts, but coal is heavy and exhaustible. Ships could not carry an unlimited amount of coal without sinking into the briny deep. They needed dedicated coaling stations at regular intervals in order to maintain their impressive speed. Fortunately, the Pacific for all of its vastness was dotted with islands perfectly situated to serve as coaling stations. It was this impulse that drove the U.S. annexation of Hawaii in 1898, with the beautiful port of Pearl Harbor serving as the fulcrum for its Pacific presence.

In a geopolitical sense, an interesting question to consider is why Japan did not develop much as England did, essentially becoming the Great Britain of the Pacific. There are many similarities in their geopolitical trajectories: each is an island nation that faced threats of invasion early and often (with the British Isles succumbing far more frequently over their first millennia than did the Japanese); both are proud and capable societies with militaristic talent; they both produced skilled sailors and shipbuilders; and each had relatively few natural resources within their natural boundaries, theoretically necessitating a turn to the oceans. Why did the British come to create an empire that held sway over vast tracts of the earth while the Japanese turned inward for the better part of three hundred years, emerging aggressively only in the twentieth century after the opening of their world by the West?

. . .

THE ANSWER LIES AT LEAST in part in the geography of the Pacific Ocean as opposed to that of the Atlantic.

First and foremost, the Pacific is just so much larger than the Atlantic, and the nations on the coast of Asia sit astride a relatively small land littoral facing an enormous sea to their east. Vessels launched to the east would sail away and literally disappear more or less indefinitely given the tyranny of distance. Additionally, unlike the British, who were separated from continental Europe by only a very narrow strip of the English Channel, the Japanese had both a wider distance across which invasions had to be launched as well as fewer and less aggressive geopolitical rivals developing in their littoral. They also keenly felt the size of the Pacific at their back, providing a natural buffer to the east.

The Japanese faced early invasions from the Mongols in the thirteenth century, but defeated them relatively easily by surrounding the invaders on beachheads upon their arrival. Despite having significant internal rivalries, the Japanese were able to set these aside and defeat the Mongols twice in the late 1200s, assisted by the weather in the form of a typhoon (Kamikaze, or Divine Wind) that scattered the invading fleets.

After a long period of consolidation and relative isolation under the various shoguns, the Japanese invaded the Asian continent in the 1500s, attacking the Korean Peninsula around the turn of the seventeenth century. They were defeated by Chinese land forces and the Korean navy, and settled back into the home islands again. This was around the time of the Battle of Lepanto in the Mediterranean, and the change in naval technology in the Pacific was notable as well—the lightly armed galleys heretofore used for grappling and ramming were giving way to heavier platforms capable of carrying larger cannons. After two serious attempts to invade Korea in the final decade of the sixteenth century, the Japanese decided to essentially remain within home waters. Unlike the British, they did not attempt to cross the broad Pacific, but essentially stood watch, protecting their western coastline and relying upon the sheer distances of the Pacific to ensure that there would be no attacks from the east. This became official doctrine; going to sea was seen as "going outside," as one noted Asian scholar, John Curtis Perry, has described it.

Similarly, the Chinese faced resolutely to the west and to their land borders. Why? Because that was the threat vector for them, not from the Pacific. They correctly regarded the principal existential dangers to their civilization as coming from the barbarians of the Asian steppes (hence the building of the Great Wall of China) and to some degree from the infections of European civilization transmitted through trade and engagement. There were abortive attempts at oceanic domination during the impressive voyages of Zheng He in the fifteenth century. But these voyages went west to known entities in the South China Sea, Indian Ocean, and East Africa, resulting in only a transitory impression on the locals and the withering away of the Chinese fleet when political tides turned against exploration. Looking to the east at the enormous range of the Pacific did not engage the Chinese geopolitical imagination any more than it did the Japanese (or that of any other Pacific culture for that matter). In the end, it was the Europeans, ironically, who would well and truly cross the Pacific and seek to connect the two worlds in a fashion beyond episodic trade and missionary work. And no individual act of opening the Pacific world could have been more dramatic than the voyage of American commodore Matthew Calbraith Perry to Japan in the 1850s.

At that point, Japan had held itself more or less aloof from the world for more than 250 years. It had developed a deeply homogenous and intensely internally focused national culture, including limited trade and engagement even in the commercial sphere. But the United States was irresistibly pulled toward Japan. Pacific whaling operations, so crucial to the American economy, shifted from the South Pacific to the North off the coast of Hokkaido. The increasing trade with China made the home islands of Japan very advantageous as logistic bases to facilitate sea lanes of communication. U.S. president Millard Fillmore therefore produced a letter and directed Commodore Perry to deliver it, with the objective of gaining access to Japanese ports.

Although the use of force was authorized, Perry had studied Japan and decided to take another, more diplomatic approach. Sailing in paddle-wheel steamboats, he came loaded with gifts and did all in his power to act the part of imperial representative of a great power. He sailed into Tokyo Bay in July 1853 with the intent to communicate using what we would think of today as a "soft power" approach—sensitivity to culture, avoiding a resort to military force, using economic and diplomatic levers as a first choice, and laying out a compelling geopolitical case to other actors. His ships were deeply impressive to the Japanese, and he augmented the squadron size over the winter. By March 1854, he had managed to execute the Treaty of Kanagawa, the first such cross-Pacific instrument that provided for the rights of shipwrecked sailors and refueling rights at two Japanese ports.

It was the beginning of European engagement with Japan, involving most of the major powers—notably Russia and Great Britain. The internal Japanese debate over modernization crested with a two-year civil war and the return of the emperor in the so-called Meiji Restoration. Suddenly Japan was quite literally on the march—and more important, in terms of naval developments, sailing to sea. Japan's industrial base sprinted into the late nineteenth century, rapidly developing significant military capability in its army and navy. Midshipmen were sent to Great Britain and the United States for naval educations, and the dockyards of Japan began to produce very capable, large warships. The Pacific, after centuries of being seen as a vast empty buffer zone, started to loom on the Japanese geopolitical map as a potential zone of conquest.

In terms of naval strategy, the Japanese, unsurprisingly, began to think like Great Britain. Like the British, they were an island nation hanging off the coast of a huge continent, and they worried about China and Russia, the great land powers. Because Korea was essentially a strip of buffer zone between themselves and the Chinese, it became logical in their eyes that they should dominate and hold it as a means of putting space between themselves and the vastly larger Chinese Empire. This led to the first of two important wars for Japan—both of which had significant naval components—the Sino-Japanese War of 1894. It began when Japan's navy attacked a Chinese troop convoy heading to reinforce Chinese troops in Korea—*before* war was declared, by the way—demonstrating the propensity to seize on surprise that they would again use five decades later in attacking the United States at Pearl Harbor.

The war was short and sharp, and Japanese naval forces comported themselves well. Of note, the naval tactical debate of the period was about whether massive armor or heavy guns were most important in maritime combat, and the Battle of Yalu did not clearly demonstrate the superiority of either. What did emerge was the efficacy of using maneuverability and speed, as the Japanese did under Admiral Sukeyuki Ito. He split his force into a "Flying Squadron" of fast ships and a slower but still capable main squadron, and was able to rake the Chinese ships throughout the engagement with more rapid fire from faster ships. Over the next few months, the war became a rout, and ended in 1895 with Japan consolidating its possession of Korea, Formosa, and various other islands. In terms of geostrategic position, Japan was in the driver's seat in the eastern Pacific. Now it needed to shore up its northern flank, which led to war with Russia.

. . .

The Russians were actually the cause of the Russo-Japanese War. After Japan's victory over China, it was Russia that pushed against the Japanese Empire, demanding the demilitarization of the Korean Peninsula and taking Port Arthur as a warm-weather port. The Russians cooperated with other European powers and pushed hard against Japan's expansion. This led to a war in 1904 for which the Russians were unprepared both militarily and politically. Militarily, the Russian fleet was split all around the periphery of that vast state and needed time to consolidate its forces. Politically, the rumblings that would eventually lead to the Russian Revolution and the fall of the czar were already apparent, and the ruling claque in St. Petersburg could not fully focus on the external conflict that was brewing on Russia's Pacific coast.

The Japanese, although numerically inferior, were able to concentrate their forces and attack early, preventing the Russians from building up strategically to challenge them. Fresh off the defeat of the Chinese fleet, the Japanese fleet again launched its first powerful attack before war was declared—a night torpedo raid conducted by Japanese destroyers that damaged important Russian warships caught in harbor. Despite the arrival of a dynamic new Russian admiral, Stepan Makarov (who died in a mine strike shortly thereafter), and the long sail of the Baltic Squadron to Pacific waters, the Russians never gained the tactical upper hand, and with the help of the interior strategic position and relatively newer technology, the Japanese prevailed. The Russians ended up losing their Pacific fleet and the key base of Port Arthur in January 1905.

The final blow to Russia in the Pacific came when the Baltic Squadron was destroyed in May 1905 at the Battle of Tsushima, losing fifty of the fifty-three ships that had sailed from the Baltic beginning in October of the previous year. Faced with this complete loss of their fleet, the

Russians were forced to settle the war in an agreement negotiated by U.S. president Theodore Roosevelt—for which he was awarded the Nobel Peace Prize. The Russians lost the war because they were outfought tactically in each engagement, but mainly because they failed strategically to concentrate their forces and were defeated piecemeal.

This, by the way, constituted a crucial lesson for the United States on the importance of building a Panama Canal—otherwise the U.S. fleet would be essentially separated for months by the necessity to sail around the southern tip of South America to combine forces. An interesting side note was that the age-old principle of warship captains' "striking their colors" and surrendering their ships was practiced for the last time in the Russo-Japanese War by the Russians. When the commanders came home, they were court-martialed and sentenced to death, ending for all intents and purposes the idea of surrender. Today, in the U.S. Navy and most other naval forces, the philosophy is definitely not one of striking the colors in gracious surrender, but rather "don't give up the ship" and be willing to fight to the end.

It was the occupation and buildup of the Hawaiian Islands that truly vaulted the United States into power in the Pacific. Pearl Harbor, on the island of Oahu, is a spectacular natural harbor, and I can vividly remember the first time I sailed into it in the late 1970s. I was still a very inexperienced deck watch officer, and the captain decreed that I should take the conn into port. It was blowing hard, and the breeze worried me as I tried to line up the ship and glide into the berth, something I'd watched my very salty captain do several times. I had foolishly declined to use an offered tug, and didn't heed the advice of the experienced harbor pilot who was there to advise us: I wanted to do it all by myself, like a defiant toddler.

Unfortunately for me, I simply kept too much "way" on the ship (meaning we were moving too fast) and managed to bang the stern hard against the pier, scraping off a lot of paint and putting a small, insignificant, but deeply embarrassing dent in the after starboard quarter of the ship. My captain sidled over and offered an observation from Admiral Ernest King, the tall, hard-driving Navy leader during the Second World War: "The mark of a great ship handler is never getting into a situation requiring great ship handling"—in other words, use the tugs and listen to the pilot. Lesson learned.

After recovering my composure, I walked around the beautiful naval station later that day and realized that I was in America's gateway to the Pacific, and the heart of the U.S. Navy. So much of the Navy's modern ethos is tied up with the Pacific campaigns of World War II, and when I thought in those long ago days of the legendary officers who led the service through the war, I contemplated how comparatively small and circumscribed my own career would probably be—the cold war of the 1970s didn't seem to offer much chance of massive fleet combat. Admirals like Nimitz, Spruance, Halsey, Kinkaid, and the other giants of the Pacific War had a sense of the vast landscape of the ocean that permitted them to construct the enormous, sweeping, island-hopping campaign that ultimately defeated the Japanese Empire. So much of the Navy's mental map begins at Pearl Harbor and opens out from there to the endless distances of the ocean; so it was fitting and shattering at the same time to be attacked without warning in early December 1941 as war came to the United States.

In order to understand the severity and totality of the Pacific Theater of World War II, you need to imagine the vast scale of the region and pair it with the fact that for the first time in history, military operations would cover the far reaches of the Pacific north of the equator and a good distance south. As the late William Manchester illustrates clearly in his excellent biography of five-star general of the Army Douglas MacArthur, *American Caesar*, the area of operations "covered mileage equivalent to that from the English Channel to the Persian Gulf—twice the farthest conquests of Alexander, Caesar, or Napoleon"—a comparison the ego-driven general would have enjoyed. That vast emptiness, which had taken outrigger canoes decades and steamships months to cross, could now be traversed in weeks. Technology did not just increase the power of ships but added new dimensions to war. Above the water, aircraft and radar altered the calculus of range. Below the surface, submarines could menace military ships and civilian shipping alike with little to no warning. The Pacific Ocean's first experience as an arena of total war came at a time when war at sea was suddenly profoundly different from ages past.

The early morning hours of December 7, 1941, on Hawaii were punctuated by the sound of airplane propellers and air raid sirens. Japanese naval aviation launched what was the largest air attack in history at that time. Planned by the brilliant and colorful Admiral Isoroku Yamamoto, a graduate of Harvard and lover of American culture, the Pearl Harbor raid devastated both the U.S. fleet in harbor and its ground-based aircraft. But the jewels of the U.S. fleet, the aircraft carriers that were the primary target of the raid, were, by a stroke of dumb luck, out of the area when the attack happened and spared destruction. The battleships *Arizona*, *Oklahoma*, *West Virginia*, and *California* were not so lucky—caught in port on a quiet Sunday with much of their crews ashore, they were pounded by the Japanese and sunk.

My wife, Laura, is today the "ship's sponsor" for a new Navy destroyer, the USS *John Finn*, named for a Pearl Harbor Medal of Honor recipient, a high honor of which she is justifiably proud. She christened the ship in 2015 and will be part of the ship's commissioning as well, continuing to have a relationship with the captain and crew throughout the life of the vessel. As a result, we have spent a fair amount of time learning about those terrible hours as an unexpected strike literally blew up the gorgeous harbor before the unbelieving eyes of Navy sailors. Chief Petty Officer

John Finn organized a machine gun nest and returned fire with a "pickup" crew of sailors, receiving many shrapnel wounds in the process. He fought proudly through the rest of the war, and lived to be more than one hundred years old, always remembering the way the world changed forever on that quiet Sunday morning.

That same day, on the other side of the Pacific, 5,500 miles away from Pearl Harbor, Japanese forces assaulted the United States in the Philippines. Just as in Hawaii, ground-based aircraft in the Philippines were devastated by the Japanese air assault. Unlike Hawaii, the Philippines were not one of the world's most isolated island chains. Their proximity to occupied Indochina meant that Japan's air assault could be followed by a ground invasion. Despite valiant resistance by American forces in the mountain redoubt of Corregidor on the Bataan Peninsula, the islands fell and would remain occupied until 1945. The Japanese war machine was churning in high gear and had not lost a battle. Things looked bleak in early 1942 for the United States and its Pacific allies.

American fortunes turned upward at the Battle of Midway in June 1942. The Japanese war plan conceived of surprise attacks across the vast Pacific in order to dislocate American efforts and put Japan in the best position possible to deal with America's demographic and industrial superiority. But in the waters around the small island of Midway, the United States was victorious despite having far fewer ships on hand in the early days of the war. Through another stroke of luck (just as at Pearl Harbor), the American carriers remained hidden from the Japanese because a mechanical failure delayed the departure of a Japanese reconnaissance plane by fifteen minutes. Unsure of the exact location of the U.S. fleet, the Japanese commanders nonetheless decided to switch the weapons carried by their planes from bombs (to target the American fortresses on Midway Island) to torpedoes (to target the American fleet).

The cat-and-mouse game came out in the Americans' favor as the

Japanese aircraft were caught on the decks of their carriers in midtransition between armaments thanks to the fifteen-minute delay. These aircraft were nearly defenseless and were largely destroyed on deck. The result was a catastrophe for the Japanese as four of Japan's carriers, the same ones that had participated in the Pearl Harbor raid, were sent to the bottom of the Pacific along with Japan's hopes of holding out against America's numerical superiority later in the war. As one of the Japanese combatants at Midway, Commander Masatake Okumiya (later a lieutenant general in the Japanese Air Self-Defense Force), said in the book *Midway: The Battle That Doomed Japan*, "The Pacific War was started by men who did not understand the sea and fought by men who did not understand the air."

With the victory at Midway, the Americans could begin to advance across the Pacific in two prongs. The first prong, led by the Navy under Admiral Chester Nimitz, went across the Central Pacific by hopping from island to island, using the islands once coveted as coaling stations as refueling points for ships and aircraft. Meanwhile, the South Pacific campaign was led by the Army general Douglas MacArthur, pushing up from his exile in Australia back toward the Philippines. The people fighting under his command found conditions as brutal as their compatriots in the Central Pacific; the jungles of Indonesia and New Guinea bore deadly traps and virulent diseases. Those same passages of water like the Torres Strait, which one day I would be so nervous about navigating, were then full of Japanese defenses that posed a vastly more lethal threat than simply submerged reefs. The going was hard for both campaigns. But the slow, methodical pace yielded fruit, resources were cut off from the Japanese, U.S. industrial might began to tell, and Japan's strategic options were increasingly foreclosed. Japan's eventual capitulation was inevitable, although the island-by-island defenses were at times fanatical. The prospect of a land invasion of the home islands was predicted to cost enormous casualties on both sides—leading to the decision to use nuclear weapons against Hiroshima and Nagasaki. The long war, culminating in the two atomic bombs, the firebombing of Tokyo, and the subsequent psychological impact of the occupation, headed up by General MacArthur, devastated the Japanese home islands. For Japan, it would be a long period of rebuilding and a withdrawal from global military and security affairs for many years.

It is worth remembering the other two admirals who led the fight in the Pacific, serving under the iconic Nimitz: Admiral William "Bull" Halsey (although he hated the nickname) and Admiral Raymond Spruance. Halsey's life was wonderfully captured in *Admiral Bill Halsey: A Naval Life* by Thomas Alexander Hughes, and Spruance's equally well in *The Quiet Warrior* by Thomas Buell. The two men could not have been more different: Halsey impulsive, tempestuous, and loud, while Spruance was quiet, cerebral, and deeply reflective. But Nimitz harnessed their different personalities and skill sets and together they led the grandest naval campaign in history, equal to the challenges of distance, time, and determined resistance. Their names remain irrevocably bound to the Pacific Ocean, and will remain so as long as sailors go to sea in warships.

Sadly, conflict would not disappear from the region as the Korean War would break out several years after the end of World War II, and of course the U.S. war in Vietnam would follow just over a decade later. But on the vast expanse of ocean itself, the Pacific once again became peaceful. To be sure, there were cold war tensions above and below the waves. The Soviet navy, under the long tenure of Admiral Sergei Gorshkov, expanded its presence in the Pacific for the first time since Russia's defeat in the Russo-Japanese War. Submarines armed with nuclear warheads prowled the oceans to provide a stealthy nuclear deterrent while surface ships on both sides tried their best to find and track their opponents. But the islands and the peoples themselves were largely untouched. The period of U.S.

trusteeship over the islands it seized from Japan in the western Pacific morphed into the Compact of Free Association, an agreement with the Marshall Islands, the Federated States of Micronesia, and Palau, which continues to this day. The return of peace, the economic revival of Japan, and the emergence of new economic powerhouses in Taiwan, Korea, Singapore, and Hong Kong led transpacific trade to overtake transatlantic trade for the first time in the 1980s. That trend also continues.

Are we living in a Pacific Century? It is hard to say. Certainly the Obama administration thought so, announcing a "pivot to the Pacific" several years ago that ended up being more sound than light given events in the Middle East, the resurgence of Russia, and the ideological direction of the Trump administration. But the Pacific region still boasts most of the world's largest and most powerful countries, and economic power is moving inexorably that way. The United States, China, Japan, Russia, and even France all frequently call themselves Pacific powers, and the region is home to a host of other vibrant countries as well, including Australia, Korea, Canada, Mexico, Indonesia, Colombia, and Chile. Almost half of the world's trade happens along the Pacific Rim. And this is just the beginning, especially as India begins to engage in the Pacific in more significant ways. Countries across the Pacific Rim are developing ways to spur economic development of the region, whether through the Trans-Pacific Partnership (an agreement that, after the United States withdrew in 2017, continues to be discussed between the remaining parties) or China's Asian Infrastructure Investment Bank (which I hope evolves into a responsible actor), to unlock the region's potential.

Although the Pacific has a great deal of potential, it is still a region of great risk. Overfishing remains a dangerous strain on the sustainability of global fish stocks, as does the continued increase of illegal, unreported, and unregulated (IUU) fishing. Human pollution is taking a toll on the region's ecosystem with a Texas-size island of plastic circulating both above and below the surface of the Pacific. On the environmental front, the Pacific Ocean experiences terrible typhoons that menace the region, particularly the areas on the front lines such as the Philippines, Taiwan, and Vietnam. The increasing frequency of these storms (regarded by many scientists as the result of global climate change) will be a source of untold suffering and economic backsliding unless the players in the region make sensible investments in humanitarian assistance and disaster relief (HA/DR) capabilities. Military and civilian agencies around the region need to work together to ensure that they are equipped to deal with these challenges.

On the geopolitical and security front, one powerful indicator worth watching closely is the increasingly tense state of the ongoing arms race around the Pacific—which is real and growing. It will have a tendency to increase the possibility of open conflict in the region, and will require delicate diplomacy as military options tempt nations to use the military forces upon which they have spent a great deal of national wealth. And the vast majority of the systems are designed to be used either on, below, or from the sea to attack neighbors around the rim of the western Pacific.

Data from 2013 to the present reveal a preference to modernize systems rather than simply increase the size of the active force within a country. The trends in the macrodata are striking. According to *The Military Balance*, defense spending in Asia broadly (including India) rose 9 percent, from $326 billion to $356 billion from 2013 to 2015. As points of comparison, defense spending over the same period of time in the United States fell 6 percent, from $633 to $597 billion, and in Europe fell 12 percent, from $281 billion to $246 billion. How do we temper this arms race and ensure the security of the Pacific Rim?

North Korea, the most unpredictable and dangerous nation on the Pacific Rim, has more than doubled its military spending to about $10 billion from 2013 to 2015. While it is notoriously difficult to assess the actual spending inside this isolated nation, recent nuclear tests combined with long-range missile testing and road-mobile launchers are obvious causes for concern. The North Koreans will continue to prioritize high levels of defense spending, even in the face of harsh new sanctions and a weakened economic environment—the young leader, Kim Jong-un, knows that only through military might will he retain his grip on power internally and maintain some level of influence in the region.

China is the source of a disproportionately large portion of the increase in Pacific Ocean defense spending. China increased its defense spending by 26 percent to almost $147 billion between 2013 and 2016—and these numbers tell just part of the story; actual defense spending may well be more than $200 billion. The most visible display of China's aggressive approach is the construction of artificial islands that serve as a handful of "3,000-acre aircraft carriers" (a U.S. 100,000-ton aircraft carrier is only 7 acres, by the way) on permanent station in the disputed regions of the South China Sea. This policy decision puts China at odds with many nations throughout the region. Building radar and missile systems as well as airfields on its artificial islands is another key investment.

Other Chinese technological and strategic advances can be seen in China's investment in advanced fighters such as the J-20 and the J-31, the DF-21 antiship ballistic missile known as the "carrier killer," and its own nascent attempts at building an aircraft carrier fleet. These advances, when combined with its focus on offensive cyber, will enable China to push past its current so-called antiaccess/area denial (A2/AD) strategy to a more active defense, which would improve its ability to project offensive power. This will be a game changer in the region.

Strategically, China is by far the biggest military spender in the region, but must also cover more territory both ashore and at sea than other Asian nations. The shift from "peaceful development" to the notion of "active defense" is likely designed to mask internal problems and attempt to shift the focus of its population away from its own contradictions to external challenges. Capable missiles like the DF-21D alter the risk calculation for the United States, especially for carriers. Finally, there is quite a bit of focus on China's aircraft carrier program. Chinese carriers are not competitive relative to those of the United States. However, as a "prestige platform," they are symbolically important and conceivably useful in maritime combat against smaller powers in the region. The irony here is that China's carrier is threatened by the very same A2/AD technologies it champions as Japan, South Korea, and Vietnam all up their game in that regard. Strategically speaking, the Chinese carrier program is not a game changer, but it will unnerve many smaller neighbors.

Given all of this, it is important to think about American capabilities and potential responses at sea. The United States, with its six heavy nuclear-powered carriers and dozens of sophisticated air defense cruisers and destroyers plus long-range bombers operating from Guam, still has a powerful maritime position in the region. The construction of artificial islands in the South China Sea plus the increased capability of the long-range ship attack missiles by China shift, but do not fully reverse, the balance of power in Asia, especially given the strength of U.S. allies such as Japan and South Korea.

Other nations in and around the Pacific are likewise ramping up spending, including Japan, which announced an increase to its 2016 defense budget, the first such increase in more than a decade. The stated policy focus of Japan's drive for security is "seamless integration" with the United States. Japan is adding significant missile defense, airborne surveillance, and advanced aircraft to its already highly capable forces. Another ambitious capability acquisition includes the desire to field an Amphibious Rapid Deployment Brigade by 2017. This capability will integrate ground, naval, air, cyber, and space domains.

Japan's technological edge makes it the second most powerful navy in the world, and its air force and army are quite capable as well. Ensuring that its security policy matches its defense capacity and capability enhances its importance to the United States in a collective defense scenario. Although Japan's record defense budget of $42 billion in 2016 is relatively low when compared with China's, its focus is clear and local and will reduce operational seams to complement its most important treaty ally: the United States.

Japan has reduced spending for its Ground Self-Defense Force and increased both Air and Maritime Self-Defense Forces—clearly showing that its priorities are aligned with its policy shift to support collective defense. These investments are relevant in a confrontational scenario with China. On the other hand, China's spending on defense must cover more territory and focus on internal security. While the exact ratio of external-to-internal defense spending is unclear, we do know that internal defense concerns will continue to act as a brake on its external ambitions.

South Korea continues to invest in technology while increasing the quality (as opposed to quantity) of its personnel. Although the South Korean defense budget increased 6 percent from 2013 to 2015, it shed 4 percent of its manpower in the same period. It is acquiring major systems: upgrading its fleet of F-16 jet fighters, seeking an F-X program to develop a sixth-generation fighter, and developing a new unmanned airborne vehicle for its army and marine corps. While still reliant on the United States for air and missile defense, South Korea continues to pursue a Korean-operated air and missile defense in light of the threats it faces from Pyongyang.

Meanwhile, Australia, another staunch ally of the United States, has increased defense spending by about 7 percent and focused on combat aircraft and ships, including upgrades to its diesel submarine force.

While beyond the far reaches of the Pacific Ocean, India is notable as the only country, besides China, that increased the size of its active military personnel roster between 2013 and 2015 (2 percent, the same as China). This came in tandem with a significant increase to its military budget. A central focus of this increase serves to drive defense production within India's borders in line with Prime Minister Narendra Modi's "Make in India" initiative. New procurement runs the gamut across sectors: new tactical helicopters, new Rafale fighters (despite continuing issues in the negotiations between France and India), and additional heavy airlift transports—with a significant uptick in spending on American systems. Vietnam, South Korea, Taiwan, and other actors are likewise stepping up their defense spending with a focus on a potential war at sea.

This maritime arms race in Asia comes from each state's perception of external threats. A worst-case scenario would see the region falling into the so-called Thucydides trap, where miscalculation of intentions leads to armed conflict—either between the United States and China globally, or possibly between China and Japan in the region.

The best chance we have to avoid conflict rests in maritime diplomacy. This must begin with a continued high-level U.S.-Chinese conversation about points of friction, from artificial islands (and the resultant "freedom of navigation" patrols by the United States) to cyber intrusions to balance of trade disagreements. The United States should encourage cooperation between its allies in the region (i.e., Japan, South Korea, the Philippines, Australia, and others) in a way that does not create an Asian cold war between China and a U.S.-led bloc of nations.

Additionally, Pacific Rim nations should be encouraged to use their militaries for exercises, training, and other confidence-building measures—like the U.S.-organized RIMPAC annual exercise, which has seen solid Chinese participation. This helps build confidence and military-to-military cooperation. And the nations of the region can also work together on soft-power projects using their militaries for disaster relief, humanitarian operations, and medical diplomacy in the coming decades.

The Pacific Ocean arms race is real and it is dangerous. Transparency, cooperation, and diplomacy can mitigate the potential for open conflict. Now is the time to put such mechanisms in place—before nations are tempted to reach for the military instrument and exercise hard power in addressing their geopolitical concerns.

Despite the tensions and the risks in our modern Pacific Rim, the odds are better than even that the region will develop peacefully. None of the societies have a long tradition of imperialist behavior, and most have found ways to cooperate and collaborate in a variety of dimensions, despite the arms buildup. Other than North Korea, which is by far the most dangerous actor in the region, there seems little likelihood of any of the nations' moving to open warfare as an instrument of policy. There will probably be some flash points in and around the South China Sea, but the chances of nation-on-nation high-level combat are low.

The Pacific Ocean that I sailed into in the 1970s as a naïve, young, and unformed officer as the cold war unfolded was a more dangerous place. Today's major actors—Japan, Korea, China, the United States—all know well the devastation of a Pacific war at sea. The strength of commerce, depth of culture, and quality of human capital of the nations in the region all point to the potential for a positive trajectory of growth. While the South China Sea and the Korean Peninsula present challenges and tension, hopefully the Pacific will live up to its name as the twenty-first century sails along; much will depend on the willingness of the actors around its vast littoral to work together around the ocean that binds their fate together in so many ways. On the other hand, the potential for an explosive war—perhaps on the Korean Peninsula, or between Japan and China—looms on the horizon like a tempest headed our way. The twenty-first century in the Pacific has many unexpected twists ahead.

2.

THE ATLANTIC OCEAN

THE CRADLE OF COLONIZATION

Pascoal Roiz's famous 1633 map showing the Atlantic world.

GREENLAND
NORWAY
ICELAND
Norwegian Sea
Hudson Bay
UNITED KINGDOM
North Sea
IRELAND
CANADA
FRANCE
SPAIN
PORTUGAL
UNITED STATES
North Atlantic Ocean
Mediterranean Sea
MOROCCO
Gulf of Mexico
Caribbean Sea
Equator
BRAZIL
South Atlantic Ocean
South Pacific Ocean
SOUTH AFRICA
0 Miles 2000
0 Kilometers 2000
Scale at Equator
THE ATLANTIC
© 2017 Jeffrey L. Ward

Much has been made about the twenty-first century being the Age of the Pacific. And indeed, many metrics would suggest that the Pacific—especially when considered as the Indo-Pacific, to include the waters surrounding South Asia and the Indian subcontinent—will be the dominant sea space of this unfolding century. The Obama administration's famous "pivot to the Pacific" (now tempered as a "rebalance to the Pacific" in the wake of events in the Middle East and Europe) seemed to validate that concept. Recent actions by the Trump administration seem intent on shelving that policy in favor of greater isolation.

Yet no matter where the world is headed in terms of the importance of the oceans relative to one another, there is one inescapable fact about the Atlantic: it will always be the cradle of our civilization as we know it, especially when the Mediterranean is included in its broad remit, and also when we consider that it formed the nexus of exchange between European nations, newly formed North American states, Latin American civilizations, the Caribbean, and Africa.

When I think of the Atlantic Ocean, I am occasionally reminded of Louis Malle's small masterpiece of a film, *Atlantic City*, which came out in 1980. Set in that city, it features an aging Burt Lancaster as a fading mobster named Lou seeking to help a young Canadian on the run, played by Susan Sarandon. Musing on the beauty and power of the Atlantic Ocean when he was a young up-and-comer, Lou says in all sincerity, "You should have seen the Atlantic Ocean back then." Somehow I doubt the Atlantic had changed a great deal over the few decades of Lou's life, but its power to impress has been with mankind for centuries.

The Atlantic Ocean is the world's second largest, after the Pacific, covering more than 40 million square miles (more than ten times the size of the United States*) and about 20 percent of the earth's surface. The name derives from the ancient Greek mythological character Atlas, who in legend supported the world on his shoulders. The ocean is really composed of two distinct regions, often referred to as "basins," one on either side of the equator, and overall forms the letter *S* if viewed from space. Any casual observer looking at the west coast of Africa and the east coast of South America would quickly guess that the two continents drifted apart at some point in prehistory, the space between them creating the landscape of the ocean's sea bottom.

The Atlantic has two key tributary seas—the Mediterranean and the Caribbean, as well as an important strategic gap to the north (the Greenland-Iceland–United Kingdom gap), which was a nautical zone of competition and near conflict in the cold war. To the south, it is connected with its two sister oceans, the Pacific and the Indian, by a relatively small strait, the Drake Passage to the Pacific, and by a broad expanse of ocean water to the Indian Ocean in the east. Including the two tributary seas, it is bordered by nearly a hundred nations and territories,

* Common estimates place the United States at 3.8 million square miles.

ranging in size and economic power from the vast scope and scale of the United States and Brazil to tiny countries like Belize and Montserrat.

MY OWN FIRST IMPRESSIONS of the Atlantic are from the early 1960s, when, as a very small boy, I sailed with my family from New York to Athens, Greece, where my father—an active-duty Marine officer—was headed for an assignment at the U.S. embassy. Sailing in those days on a large cruise liner was a throwback to the great liners of the twenties and thirties—terrific food, small but elegant staterooms, and plenty of open bars. We were on SS *Constitution*, which offered many programs for children, but all I wanted to do was watch the ocean roll by. I was endlessly fascinated by the way the surface of the ocean could form at one moment a smooth skin like a trampoline, and the next be full of chopped whitecaps, and as quickly turn into long but smooth ocean waves. It was the show that never ended, full of colors and light and high-flying seabirds in shades of gray and white. For a very small boy, it was mesmerizing. On the way, we stopped at Lisbon then sailed through the Mediterranean, making a port call near Rome before arriving in Piraeus Harbor, the gateway to Athens in our ethnic homeland of Greece.

I returned to the Atlantic in a serious way just over a decade later, in the early 1970s, when I sailed in the then brand-new aircraft carrier USS *Nimitz*. As a midshipman just over twenty years of age, about to enter my final year at the Naval Academy, I sailed from Norfolk into the rolling, dark blue waters of the Gulf Stream, one of the most distinctive features of the western Atlantic. This current, which forms itself originally off the west coast of Africa, travels across the Central Atlantic as a sort of river within the ocean. It bounces off the northeast coast of South America, splits into two parts, then reforms and heads north through and beyond the Strait of Florida.

The Gulf Stream is typically about sixty to seventy miles wide and almost four thousand feet deep, with a high velocity near the surface, approaching five miles per hour in places. Colonial navigators became very aware of it in the eighteenth century, although mariners argued over the best way to use its speed and pace to best advantage. It has figured in many works of literature and films, and the sense you have of it as a mariner is one of relentless flow and power, moving everything in its path deeper and deeper into the North Atlantic. In a famously long and pedantic sentence, Hemingway laid out a comprehensive if somewhat tedious description of the Gulf Stream, one that would probably require drinking a Papa Hemingway–size daiquiri to get through. It is a feature of the Atlantic that continues to fascinate writers.

THE FIRST EUROPEANS TO VENTURE into the Atlantic were probably the ancient Greeks, although the extent of their travels beyond what is today called the Strait of Gibraltar and was known to them as the Pillars of Hercules is shrouded in legend, myth, and mystery. A central part of the mystery involves the reputed existence of the mythical city of Atlantis. To get a sense of how the Greeks envisioned the physical world, go back to ancient mythology, much of which I learned from my father while a small boy in Greece in the 1960s. According to the myths, the titan Atlas held up the world with arms that never wearied, standing at the very end of the earth before the Hesperides—a collective name for a blissful group of nymphs who resided in a garden at the edge of Oceanus, the ocean that encircled the world. Not exactly precise mapping.

A variety of early explorers began to penetrate the mystery of the Atlantic as early as the sixth century A.D., including an Irish abbot, Saint Brendan, also known as "the Navigator." The voyages of this ecclesiastical character were supposedly in search of converts, few of whom would have been found at sea. Some records indicate his voyages took him to the rest of the British Isles (Scotland and Wales) and possibly across the English Channel to Brittany. The extent of the legends of Brendan the Navigator have him making it to icebergs off the coast of Greenland and possibly the south shore of Iceland. None of what such early explorers managed to learn was made widely available to others, and the Atlantic continued to reflect real mystery and danger to the European world. On the Atlantic's western coast, the widely scattered indigenous settlements in the Americas did not appear to move beyond minor coastal voyaging—leaving a vast tract of unexplored ocean.

Not until the time of the Vikings in the period from A.D. 800 to 1000 is there evidence of recorded voyages into the open Atlantic. The first real settlements in Iceland were probably Viking, perhaps in the late 800s. There are recorded voyages in the late 900s, including one by Bjarni Herjolfsson, who was evidently driven west by fierce storms from the relatively known waters around Iceland and Greenland and reported seeing heavy forests to the west. This voyage has led some observers to credit the Vikings with the first sighting of the New World, linking Europe and North America by the maritime highway that continues to matter so deeply today. By the tenth and eleventh centuries there appear to have been settlements in present-day Canada—Labrador and Newfoundland. Some reports exist of "Viking relics" that supposedly have been found as far inland as Minnesota and the upper Midwest, although the vast majority of serious scholars discount those as urban legends run wild. It is hard to imagine what a Viking would have thought about the fact that in today's world more than $4 trillion passes annually between the two continents, reflecting the largest trading relationship in the world economy.

There is a bit of an academic debate over whether all of the Viking activity constitutes actually "discovering" the New World or merely reaching it. In his seminal work on this topic, Daniel Boorstin makes a distinction between such voyages of exploration and the act of discovery, in the sense that discovery implies providing feedback to European civilization that would cause a real change in its worldview.* What is clear is that the early voyagers like the Irish and Vikings opened the Atlantic world as we understand it today—a maritime bridge of enormous importance. In the end, they were more sailors at sea than colonizers ashore. It was the warmer-weather voyagers in the fifteenth and sixteenth centuries—led by the intrepid Portuguese—who not only explored but also discovered and colonized the Atlantic world both at sea and ashore. In a way, this is the difference between the oceans themselves—which are but glittering passages across which the world's trade, commerce, research, and security are conducted—and the riches of the vast lands that the world of the seas connects.

MY FIRST TRIP ACROSS the North Atlantic as a ship captain was in the mid-1990s. My ship, USS *Barry*, was a brand-new *Arleigh Burke*–class guided missile destroyer with a crew of about three hundred and a huge array of missiles for air defense, land attack, and killing submarines—a so-called multimission warship. Given that the ship was named for Captain John Barry, a Revolutionary War hero of Irish descent, we were sent across the North Atlantic in the early summer of 1994, bound initially for goodwill visits in Ireland. After a brief stop there, we would head into potential combat operations in the Arabian Gulf.

As we sailed across the broad expanse of the rolling Atlantic over that Memorial Day, I was struck by the differences and similarities we experienced compared with early voyagers. We had all the comforts of home—

* Daniel J. Boorstin, *The Discoverers*, 1st ed. (New York: Random House, 1983).

good hot food and showers, pleasant bunk rooms, communications with family and friends back home (although limited compared with today), plenty of fuel brought out to us at sea by wide-ranging oilers (ships designated to act as at-sea gas stations). While our accommodations were not luxurious, compared with a Viking long ship we were living like kings at sea, sailing in a well-heeled palace—a very different world.

But the impetus was the same: we sailed on a mission for our country, left our families for a long, seven-month voyage, faced real danger in our ultimate destination—the volatile Arabian Gulf in the time of Saddam Hussein—and felt between us the same bond that sailors have felt going back two thousand years or more. We were hardly Vikings, nor faced the sea in such a dramatic way, but we were in every sense part of the long story of the Atlantic Ocean. We knew where we were headed, but not what would unfold. In the end, that uncertainty and sense of adventure is a significant part of what draws many of us to the oceans.

THE FOURTEENTH AND FIFTEENTH CENTURIES saw key improvements in sailing technology. The frail, single-mast Viking ship—which was really a simple adaptation of what the Greeks and Romans used in the Mediterranean nearly a millennium earlier—gave way to multiple masts, a bowsprit to carry sail in front of the ship, and a handful of sails. The compass came into general use, as well as simple means of measuring speed using knotted ropes (hence the term "knots" for the speed of a ship). The necessity of "dead reckoning," which is using landmarks ashore to plot a course, was gradually resolved by using celestial means to navigate, which improved gradually. As trade goods—especially spices, gold, jewelry, perfumes, dyes, and gems—began to flow, the appetite for longer and longer voyages increased.

Whether or not we credit the Irish (or more likely the Vikings) with the first significant European voyages across the Atlantic, what is indisputable is the early and enormous impact of the Portuguese. The most iconic of these intrepid figures was Infante Henrique of Portugal, Duke of Viseu, who earned the sobriquet Prince Henry the Navigator. He lived in the first half of the fifteenth century and launched many expeditions throughout the early 1400s that sailed down the Atlantic and explored the coast of Africa. His taste for exploration and profit was whetted early in his life by a crusade conducted against the city of Ceuta, in what is today Morocco—there he discovered spices, gold, silver, and the other potential riches of the Atlantic coast of the massive continent to the south. He also gathered to himself many of the best navigators and sailors of the day in an informal "maritime court" in Sagres, on the southern Algarve of Portugal, which he presided over with enthusiasm. While there is a fair amount of scholarly debate over the degree to which Henry actually conducted regularized meetings of this "court," it seems reasonable to say that upon occasion he brought together maritime experts and drew from their collective wisdom.

Prince Henry sponsored many of the voyages that both solidified knowledge of the world to the south and permitted the expansion of new techniques of sailing and navigation. The caravel, a type of lightweight, lateen-rigged ship (sails fore and aft instead of squared up to the stern of the ship), was crucial to these explorations. While small, caravels could be operated in small flotillas and could sail not only down the coast of Africa, but, crucially, back up the coast by beating into the wind. The expression "sailing close to the wind," implying taking risk and going against the normal flow of events, comes from lateen-rigged sailing caravels.

The Portuguese navigators of the time also perfected the use of the various prevalent winds and currents in the Atlantic to sail first southwest from Lisbon and Lagos to ports on the equatorial coast of Africa, then north and west—actually away from home—but finally swinging back to the northeast around the vicinity of the Azores Islands and catching the so-called Portugal current for home. This huge triangular passage was called the *volta do mar* or the "turn of the sea." A smaller version of it consisted of sailing to a mid-distance port on the African coast, then heading northwest to the Canary Islands before turning for home. Taking advantage of both currents and winds (which were known as the Gyre of the Atlantic) allowed European explorations to unfold with increasing frequency. The technology of the caravels allowed for expeditions via these two routes that thoroughly exploited the vast northwestern coast of Africa, from the ancient port of Ceuta on the southern point of the Strait of Gibraltar down to the first major fort built by the Portuguese off the coast of modern Mauritania on the island of Arguin—which they held for two centuries, until the mid-1600s.

After the death of Prince Henry in the middle of the fifteenth century, the Portuguese voyages continued under a new generation of sailors who had literally grown up in the culture of exploration. Three of the key sea captains were Bartolomeu Dias, Vasco da Gama, and Pedro Álvares Cabral. Dias, for example, departed the White Tower on the River Tagus in the late 1480s and worked his way around the Cape of Good Hope (more or less accidentally, as legend holds it was a storm that blew him east) after a year-and-a-half voyage. Da Gama pushed farther and was the first European to touch the Indian subcontinent at the very end of the fifteenth century. In the first year of the sixteenth century, Cabral discovered Brazil, and continued on the first known voyage to touch four continents: Europe, South America, Africa, and Asia on the Indian subcontinent.

Taken together, the exploits of these and other Portuguese sea captains gradually opened the southwestern coast of Africa, helped build up trading routes, continued the search for the legendary Christian kingdom of Prester John (never found), and eventually rounded the Cape of Good Hope and sailed into the Indian Ocean. Their great voyages of discovery inspired Europeans, exploited Africans (often with extreme brutality), and created the connections between the Atlantic and Indian oceans over the fifteenth and sixteenth centuries. Some have called this the dawn of the Oceanic Age.

My first sea voyage into Lisbon and up the Tagus River was in 1962 on SS *Constitution*, while our family was headed to Athens for my father's three-year tour as the assistant naval attaché. An infantry officer at the time, he was not particularly enamored of sea voyages, but I remember loving the experience of being under way. Our first port after departing Boston was Lisbon, and we sailed up the Tagus on a hot summer day. Even as a seven-year-old boy, I was enchanted by the ships swaying on the waterfront, the wide and beautiful river, the gleaming white tower from which each of the Portuguese captains after the early 1500s departed on the voyages that opened the world. Decades later, I would return to Lisbon as a grizzled four-star admiral with many commands at sea and too many sea miles under my belt to remember—and the magic of that tower felt the same. As I toured the Portuguese maritime museum a few blocks from the waterfront, I was struck by the courage it must have taken to sail away from all you knew—a European and Christian world, a vibrant society, a loving family—to launch into an unknown void to the south. As they watched that white tower—by then known as the Belém Tower, recede from view, how they must have been torn between a longing for home and a thirst for the sea, like sailors everywhere.

COLUMBUS AND HIS FAMOUS VOYAGES of 1492 are discussed in more depth in the chapter on the Caribbean, but it is worth noting that he initially offered his services to the Portuguese and was turned down, finally winning the trust and financing (as well as the affection) of Queen

Isabella and King Ferdinand of Spain. He initially sailed south toward West Africa, but turned westward, taking advantage of favorable winds. In just over a month, he changed the course of world history with his landing in what is today the Bahamas. Eventually styled "Admiral of the Ocean Sea," perhaps the most pompous title in maritime history, he completed three more voyages to the "New World" that would bear his imprint for centuries.

By the sixteenth century, just a few decades later, voyages across the Atlantic were becoming more and more common. Of note, within twenty years of Christopher Columbus's "discovery" of the New World, Ferdinand Magellan, whose expedition would later circumnavigate the earth, sailed on a voyage that resulted in discovery of a passage connecting the Atlantic and Pacific oceans at the bottom of the world—the Strait of Magellan at the tip of South America. Ironically, Magellan was Portuguese by birth, but sailing under commission to the Spanish throne. As we've seen, he would not survive his circumnavigation of the world, but his deeds and the resulting changes in cartography influenced the rising mariners of France and England, who next began to sail the Atlantic waters, especially in the Northern Hemisphere.

While the Portuguese and Spanish led the way across the Atlantic to the Caribbean and South America, the British and the French concentrated on North America. By the end of the fifteenth century, John Cabot—ironically an Italian, sailing for the British crown—explored Newfoundland, but was subsequently lost on a follow-up expedition with five ships. This had a bit of a chilling effect on British exploration, and it was roughly a century before the Brits returned in numbers across the Atlantic. As the sixteenth century unfolded, both the French and the British established colonies in what is today Canada, as well as settlements along the Atlantic coast of the modern-day United States.

In Britain, a nautical tradition emerged in the 1500s under Henry

VIII, who commissioned the building of the first national warships. They featured heavy cannons that were muzzle loaded, and towers fore and aft to afford height from which to shoot down upon opposing mariners. The use of multiple cannons firing together became known as the "broadside," and was used to devastating effect in nautical warfare for the next five hundred years, until the advent of aircraft and long-range missiles in the mid-twentieth century. By the late sixteenth century, the battle for geopolitical supremacy between England and Spain was in full flower, exacerbated by the religious wars that came following the Reformation and Henry's decision to break with the Catholic Church and reject the authority of the pope. English sea rovers, who were essentially pirates formally authorized by the crown and called "privateers," became strategic weapons in the duel between England and Spain. Two of the most feared were John Hawkins and Francis Drake. Their ships, notably Drake's *Golden Hind*, ravaged the coast of South America in the late 1500s.

This led to one of the epic battles of the Atlantic—the attack of the Spanish Armada, sometimes known as the Grand Armada. A massive force for the times, it consisted of well over a hundred vessels, a thousand cannons, and nearly thirty thousand men. All of this was assembled while Spain was simultaneously fighting in the present-day Netherlands, which along with Germany was essentially ground zero of the wars of the Reformation. The English were able to muster more than thirty heavy men-of-war, and by dint of armed merchantmen eventually put to sea nearly two hundred ships. The crucial difference was that the English ships were smaller, lighter, and more maneuverable, and expert sailors manned them. The Spanish ships were heavier (with broadsides more than double in firepower) and had shorter-range cannons. The battle, which took place in the waters off the English coast, was notable for being the first significant clash between sailing fleets, as well as a pivotal moment in the confrontation between Catholicism and Protestantism.

The exchanges included firing many tens of thousands of rounds between the two sides, but without great effect because of the significant distances between the fleets. The Spanish reached their first objective, the French port of Calais, where they were to take on additional troops before crossing the Channel and invading England. Unfortunately for the Spanish, they had expended most of their heavy shot and could not be resupplied from distant armories in Spain, while the English, with the home court advantage, were able to reload. Despite this advantage, the English were not able to crush the Spanish fleet but rather chased them into the North Sea and eventually back to Spain—a voyage that was interrupted by terrible storms and bad navigation, which, between them, account for dozens of sunken Spanish ships. When the Armada limped back into Spain, it was half its original size. "God breathed and they were scattered" is inscribed on the English victory medals.

Over the next century, the remarkable Dutch began to emerge as a competing nautical power with designs on the Atlantic and other territory in the New World. In the 1600s, there were three wars between the English and the Dutch, which did not turn out well for the Hollanders—the British enjoyed a significant strategic advantage by sitting astride the sea lanes over which the Dutch needed to sail to make it into the open waters of the Atlantic. This was the period of the Commonwealth in England, and Oliver Cromwell had a deep distrust of admirals (I am sorry to report) and decided to send his generals (who normally commanded only land forces, of course) to sea in order to take command. This led, of course, to more orderly tactics of columns and the so-called line ahead, which competed with the "melee school" of simply putting your ship next to the enemy vessel with alacrity. By the 1700s, when

England and now France were engaged in Atlantic warfare, command had returned to the sailors—but the general approach of fighting in column and with precise maneuvers stayed central to maritime warfare.

The Seven Years' War in the mid-1700s can be regarded as the first truly global conflict, with France and England fighting in the Atlantic and its tributary seas, the Mediterranean and Caribbean, as well as in the Pacific, the Indian Ocean, and ashore in all of those locations. Britain developed a strategy that served it well for the next three hundred years of aligning with a continental European power to create a geopolitical balance against its major foe—in this case France. The English would hit at various points around the world, including a central campaign against French colonies globally and against France's fleet in the Atlantic, while holding French ships in port by blockading and counting on continental allies (in this case, Prussia) to threaten France ashore. Sometimes known as "Pitt's Plan" after the creative geostrategic genius William Pitt, who conceived it, some variation on this approach continued to be seminal for England for the next three centuries. France tried to respond by defending its colonies and threatening to invade England. In the end, British mastery of the seas was decisive, and Britain ended with possession of Canada and significant gains in the Caribbean Sea. The Seven Years' War demonstrated the power of a global naval force and control of the sea lanes of communication as the key to winning wars.

What is notable in the gradual progress of the Europeans across the Atlantic is the degree to which exploration led inexorably to transformation. In addition to the technical improvements in sailing technique, sails, rigging, and hull form that flowed from the requirement for longer voyages and the urgent need to sail opposing the wind, the other major transformation was the result of the discovery and return to Europe of new agrarian products. Diet began to change in Europe as a result of the flora and fauna hauled back, initially as curiosities, then increasingly as commercial products. This has been called the Columbian Exchange or the New World Exchange.

Just as the Europeans brought "guns, germs, and steel" to Africa and the Americas across the Atlantic Ocean (as writer Jared Diamond describes in his classic work of the same name), the New World sent products back. Tomatoes, potatoes, rubber, vanilla, chocolate, corn, and tobacco came from the New World, while Europe sent onions, citrus, bananas, mangos, wheat, and rice. Livestock sailed largely from Europe to the Americas, fundamentally changing lives there—horses, pigs, donkeys, dogs, cats, bees, and chickens were all introduced as a result of the Atlantic bridge. Discovery of the two new continents created new trade routes for the Europeans, including, over time, the flow of human slaves to the Americas to work plantations (notably sugar, cotton, and tobacco) with finished products then returning to Europe. This "Middle Passage" of human slaves was tragic and horrific, and indeed has come to reflect the worst moments of Atlantic history. Slavery formed but one part of an enormous migration across the Atlantic that has continued to this day, resulting in the eventual settlement of more than a billion people in the Americas today.

All of this helped create the basis in the eighteenth century for the Industrial Revolution, which was enhanced by the trade in raw materials and the flow of humans across the Atlantic. With the increase in trade and commerce, and the attendant rise in industrial capability, came great-power geopolitics. Gradually, the five imperial powers of the Atlantic Ocean—France, Britain, Spain, the Netherlands, and Portugal—embroiled themselves in a series of colonial wars that required the Atlantic to serve as a maritime battlefield, a logistic bridge to support military campaigns in the Americas, and a highway for the economic advancement that fueled the wars. Over the next two centuries, what might be termed the "Wars of the Atlantic" were fought both ashore in the

Americas and in Europe, as well as at sea. Essentially the competition was over the products of the New World—the riches that flowed from gold, silver, slaves, sugar, tobacco, fish, furs, manufactured goods, and the markets themselves. The imperial powers realized that what we would call today "sea control" was an essential element of national power. While a coherent theoretical framework to describe their strategies would have to wait another couple of centuries and the writings of Alfred Thayer Mahan, this was sea power at play on a broader scale than had ever been seen in human history. The rise of great oceangoing vessels—both commercial and warships—created the engine of sea control and power projection that came to dominate global politics for centuries and still exists today. All of that was birthed in the Atlantic Ocean.

In the United States, the relatively small region of New England began to develop as the first truly global maritime hub for the Americas. Rudimentary shipyards began to emerge in the decades leading up to the American Revolution, and the independence and wealth they generated were central to the ability of the colonies to eventually break away from the British crown. Naturally, the disputes at the heart of the revolution fell out of the Atlantic trade, from the imposition of taxation without representation to the growing sense of liberty and freedom owed to men and women who had sailed into the unknown and created a new political entity with increasingly different norms and behaviors. The trading routes grew increasingly complex, to include lumber, meat, grain, tar, resin, pitch, rice, and indigo by the middle of the 1700s; literally thousands of ships were engaged in this trade, with hundreds of warships protecting and escorting them, as well as fighting a series of skirmishes, battles, and wars at sea. Alongside this legitimate trade and military protection, of course, was a flourishing pirate culture centered in the Caribbean, an area that afforded many advantages to piratical activity, as we'll see: many small inlets and bays, tiny islands, temperate weather most of the year, and the natural geopolitical chaos resulting from five national entities competing in a relatively small space.

All of this trade, wealth, and geostrategic competition acted as a complex and combustible mix that was eventually ignited by the ideas of the Enlightenment. This helped create the conditions for the American Revolution, in which the Atlantic again played a major role. Following the French and Indian Wars (the North American portion of the Seven Years' War), the British crown was in a less advantageous position, caught between unrest at home, continued anger and resentment on the part of fellow imperial power France, and a sense in the American colonies that their burden and obligation to Britain was too high a cost to bear. Gradually increasing taxes and tariffs led to significant unrest in the colonies, catalyzed by the Boston Tea Party in 1773—an act that did not go down well in Britain and led to further restrictions on the colonies, including the closure of the port of Boston. By 1775, the northern colonies in particular were in a state of rebellion, and the battles of Lexington and Concord (essentially shootings and skirmishes) led to full-blown war.

No revolution in history has been embraced unanimously. About a third of the American population at the time of the revolution wanted to remain loyal to the crown, about a third were more or less ambivalent, and a third were strongly pro-independence at the outset. But once combat was joined in New England, the tide turned in the colonies and a revolutionary spirit strengthened. While the Americans hardly possessed a significant navy compared with Great Britain, they were aided by the French, still smarting from their losses in the French and Indian Wars and eager to weaken the position of their rival in the Americas. The colonists marshaled their small vessels and attacked British interests where and when they could—afloat on Lake Champlain and ashore into Canada. Surprisingly, they were also able to carry the war into British waters by deploying privateers and the first vessels of the Continental

Navy. Massive British troop deployments to the colonies as well as total control over the Atlantic seaways took a toll on the lightly armed American ships. Americans quickly realized that British control over the Atlantic was a key element they had to overcome to be successful. Only when France entered the war in 1778 were the Americans able to begin to establish some level of what we would today call sea control in the approaches to our shores.

By the 1780s, American naval officers, including the iconic John Paul Jones, had scored real victories at sea in the North Atlantic. Jones sailed into Irish and British waters, first in the *Ranger* and later in the *Bonhomme Richard*, conducting a *guerre de course*, or war against shipping. His small squadron of lightly armed ships attacked a British convoy and captured the heavily armed English ship *Serapis* in 1779. This was perhaps the most famous U.S. naval engagement of the revolution, in which the British captain asked Captain Jones—his ship nearly sunk under his feet—if he wanted to strike his colors (surrender to the enemy). His reply, "I have not yet begun to fight," has been memorized by generations of midshipmen at Annapolis (including a young plebe named Stavridis in the summer of 1972).

John Paul Jones, by the way, is probably the only famous American naval officer many citizens could name from the early days of the republic. He was quite widely traveled across the Atlantic. While he tends to be revered as the "father of the American navy," in fact he was a mercenary who fought for both the United States and the Russian Empire, rising to the rank of rear admiral in the Imperial Russian Navy. He wasn't particularly happy with the way he was treated (he was a prickly Scot) throughout the Revolutionary War and returned to Europe for better pay and larger commands, but was eventually outmaneuvered in court politics. In 1792, he died penniless in Paris and was buried in a French cemetery.

His star rose considerably after his death, however, when Theodore Roosevelt took an interest in him and had him exhumed, and in 1905 Jones sailed once again across the Atlantic, in the American warship USS *Brooklyn*, escorted by three other cruisers. Jones was then buried with enormous pomp and circumstance, first in Bancroft Hall (home of the Brigade of Midshipmen at Annapolis), and ultimately in a gorgeous black marble crypt under the massive chapel at the U.S. Naval Academy in Annapolis. He is probably the only person who crossed the Atlantic over the course of three centuries, from the late eighteenth to the early twentieth.

Luckily for the nascent United States, the French were trying to turn the tide of the battle by helping resupply American forces across the Atlantic, conducting harrying attacks on the British where they could, and drawing up plans for an invasion in the southern colonies. Ultimately, the French Marquis de Lafayette proved to be the reliable ally the colonies needed, conducting a decisive and vital campaign at Yorktown in southern Virginia. The battle—truly a campaign conducted over months—showed the value of sea power. First and foremost, it was enabled by sea control across the Atlantic; it also illustrated the strategic mobility that sea power can confer as the Americans, using French naval power, were able to shift forces smoothly and apply combat power at the point of maximum need. As forces converged via sea on Yorktown in the late summer and early autumn of 1781, the naval fight in the Atlantic turned into a tough, close-in battle between British and French warships. The French mauled the British and forced them to sail north to try to bring more troops to the embattled British general ashore, Lord Cornwallis. But time was against the British, and Cornwallis was forced to surrender as a result of superior sea power—in this case supplied by the French, our oldest and first ally. By 1783, the British had greater geopolitical challenges and turbulence at home, and the Treaty of Paris ended the war and recognized the independence of the new United States, stretching from the Great Lakes to Georgia. The Atlantic seacoast of the United States was our nation's first and most prominent geographic feature, and our doorway to the world opened through it as we achieved our first real degree of independence.

The next great series of campaigns in which the Atlantic played the central role was the long conflict unleashed in Europe by the rise of Napoleon Bonaparte. The long duel between Napoleon's France and the nations he conquered or persuaded to fight with him against the coalition led by Great Britain rumbled along through the end of the 1700s and the first decade of the 1800s. It was a geopolitical fight that ultimately turned upon Britain's use of sea power to maintain its independence, blockade French power, fight over distant colonies, and continue to function economically despite Napoleon's domination of the continent. Perhaps the most iconic sailor in history, Britain's Viscount Horatio Nelson, was a key figure in the long fight. He fought battles on all sides of the Atlantic—in the Caribbean, the Baltic, and the Mediterranean—and crossed it dozens of times in the course of the Napoleonic Wars. His two early successful battles against the French were crucial: in Egypt, the Battle of the Nile probably saved British India from French conquest, and in Denmark, he managed at the Battle of Copenhagen to force Napoleon to the bargaining table. His influence on the British navy is felt to this day.

It is worth knowing that in this age of transparency and political correctness, Lord Nelson would never have passed a U.S. Senate confirmation process. He was subject to violent seasickness and had various other medical challenges. He was a short and scrawny figure, standing well under five feet six inches, who eventually lost both an eye and an arm in combat. Nelson had a long-running affair with Emma Hamilton, who might charitably be called a courtesan, with whom he fathered a daughter out of wedlock. He consistently took delight in countering the tight, regimented tactics of maritime combat at the time, and his ability to weld together a "band of brothers" from among the various sea captains serving under him was instrumental in creating the best fighting force ever to sail the oceans up to that day.

What really mattered about Lord Nelson was his centrality to the fate of his nation in the latter part of the eighteenth century and the beginning of the nineteenth; as a continental land power, France under Napoleon sought to dominate the maritime power of the world, Great Britain. He was fundamental to Great Britain's ability to execute a classic maritime strategy of dominating the lanes of communication across the Atlantic and around the littoral seas of the European continent while maintaining economic vitality from colonies around the world.

By 1805, Napoleon was actively seeking an invasion force to attack Great Britain. Nelson pursued the French fleet (and its Spanish allies) vigorously, knowing full well that defeating it was the key to ensuring the safety—indeed, the sanctity—of the British Isles. The British knew that their strategic center of gravity (which has been described in war as "that about which all else revolves") was the English Channel and the ability to control it via sea power. This pursuit led ultimately to one of the most famous sea battles in history, the Battle of Trafalgar in October 1805. Fought off the coast of Spain in the eastern center of the Atlantic Ocean, it brought together two massive battle fleets. Tactically it was notable for the production of Nelson's memorandum on how to fight the battle, which he promulgated just before the fight.

Nelson knew that he would not have clear and instantaneous communication with his nearly forty major warships, and that the fog of war and the probability of heavy weather would make precise command and control impossible. As he said in the memorandum, "Something must be left to chance; nothing is sure in a sea fight." He lays out the basic direction and tactics of the fight, but then includes the most crucial line, one that is often quoted by sailors headed into combat: "In case signals can neither be seen or perfectly understood no captain can do very wrong if he places his ship alongside that of an enemy." That spirit of independence in command, and the resultant tradition of taking action with real initiative, lives on in the U.S. and British navies—and in those of many allied forces—to this day.

On that October morning, the normally roiling Atlantic was strangely calm. Nelson deployed his forces in two long columns, spreading the nearly thirty ships out and bearing down on the Spanish and French fleets, seeking to force them to fight. Nelson was able to drive into the center of the enemy's line. Just before the battle, Nelson wrote out a will and a prayer, which included the words, "May humanity after victory be the predominant feature of the British fleet." He then launched a signal that any British sailor can quote: "England expects that every man will do his duty." He certainly did, and tragically, he was killed by a sniper's bullet a few hours later while he stood on the quarterdeck of his ship, fully exposed to enemy fire and wearing all his medals and decorations, inspiring his men. He died in agony belowdecks in his flagship, HMS *Victory*, as it rocked on the unnaturally calm Atlantic. The battle was a tremendous success, resulting in the capture of fifteen of the French and Spanish fleets' most capable warships. Thus ended the attempts of Napoleon to invade the United Kingdom, demonstrating the "influence of sea power upon history," as the American naval historian Alfred Thayer Mahan described it decades later in his classic work of maritime strategy.

Ironically, the ultimate loser of Trafalgar, Napoleon, eventually ended his life deep in the southern Atlantic. After successfully escaping from his first exile to the Mediterranean island of Elba, he was defeated at Waterloo and sent far, far from Europe: to the tiny, volcanic island of

St. Helena. A vastly diminished figure, Napoleon's life closed in on him, dampening his exuberant demeanor and saddening his small retinue of loyal courtiers. A superb portrait of both the island and his final days is Julia Blackburn's book *The Emperor's Last Island*, which is as much about the island and the ocean as it is about Napoleon. Bonaparte died there in 1821 after six long years in exile on a tiny rock measuring five by ten miles. He spent much of his final years staring endlessly across the waves of the Atlantic, the one venue he could never conquer.

The next chapter of note in the geopolitical history of the Atlantic was the rise of the U.S. Navy, born of necessity in the turbulent years after the revolution. The two principal political parties of the time, Alexander Hamilton's Federalists and Thomas Jefferson's Democratic-Republicans (who, by the way, were *not* the fathers of today's Republican Party; that party devolved from the Whigs and other groups), were on opposite sides of the "big navy" issue. The Federalists wanted a serious seagoing navy, arguing that American interests would be expanding over time and that the simple existence of the Atlantic Ocean would be insufficient to protect the young nation. Jefferson felt that the real expansion of the United States would be to the south and west, and that agriculture, not nautical concerns, would be at the heart of the new nation's business. In essence, they were both right—and thus the U.S. Navy was grudgingly constructed in stops and starts over the several decades following the revolution. The Navy Department was created in the final years of the eighteenth century in time for an undeclared war with France (the so-called Quasi-War, fought largely in the Caribbean from 1798 to 1800).

Despite Jefferson's aversion to relatively big ships, a declaration of war against the United States by the Barbary pirates forced the by then president to launch a series of expeditions to the Mediterranean to deal with pirates preying on U.S. shipping in the first decade of the nineteenth century. In 1803, young, aggressive naval heroes like Commodore Edward

Preble and Lieutenant Stephen Decatur burnished their strong reputations through their campaigns in the Mediterranean, operating from a base on the island of Sicily. Eventually, this foray across the Atlantic ended in victory for the young United States.

Yet despite this outcome and the seemingly obvious lesson that real sea power was necessary to help guard the nation, the Republicans in office decided that a strategy of small ships—gunboats—and coastal forts could be used to protect the Atlantic coastline. Such forts still exist in a chain running all along the eastern Atlantic seacoast of the United States. They proved quite inadequate, of course, during the War of 1812 with Great Britain. It was lucky that the early construction program for six medium-size frigates—lionized in Ian Toll's brilliant book *Six Frigates*—was completed by this point despite the emphasis by the administration on the gunboat-and-fortress strategy.

Soon the Atlantic was again a battleground for the United States and Great Britain, in a war that stemmed from lingering resentments on both sides after the successful revolution and was catalyzed by the boarding of an American warship, USS *Chesapeake*, by sailors from HMS *Leopard* in 1807. The Brits came aboard after firing on an unprepared *Chesapeake* and forcibly removed four sailors suspected of being British deserters (only one of them was proved to be so). This enraged the American public and, coupled with trade restrictions levied by Britain on the neutral U.S. merchant fleet, led to a high level of tension between the two nations. By 1812, events had spun out of control and the United States—with a navy that numbered a grand total of eighteen seagoing warships—declared war on the British Empire, with hundreds of heavy warships and centuries of nautical warfare experience. Fortunately for the United States, the British viewed the War of 1812 as a sideshow, and never devoted a significant level of sea power to prosecuting it. The British executed largely by blockade, while American warships tried to conduct raids on British maritime shipping. A series of small-scale battles on the Atlantic had some surprisingly successful outcomes for the Americans, with battles coming out roughly a draw over the years of the war.

In the end, while good for American morale, the sea battles were not the drivers in determining the overall outcome of the conflict. The United States fared badly in the War of 1812 because of the combination of the effect of the British blockade on U.S. commerce and the successful invasion of the United States by British troops, who gleefully burned the capital of the young nation, Washington, D.C. While American maritime operations in the North were marginally successful, they did not sway the direction of the war. Fortunately for the Americans, the British had larger matters to deal with than their upstart former colonies. Eventually, given other pressing matters globally and war fatigue in Great Britain, the British were content to come to the negotiating table, ending the war and planting the seeds for the "special relationship" that continues to this day (albeit with occasional subsequent periods of tension between the Atlantic cousins).

From the end of the War of 1812 to the Civil War, the Atlantic was relatively peaceful, and the world saw a period of less conflict after the end of the Napoleonic Wars. Nevertheless, a different type of revolution (that of naval technology) was happening at sea, spurred by inventions and ideas flowing from the war years. Navies began the transition from sail to steam and started to apply serious levels of metal armor to the sides of their ships. Instead of smoothbore cannons that had to be brought to bear at extremely close range, rifled gun barrels led to great improvements in range and accuracy. The initial ideas of fire control, or the way in which guns are sighted using optical targeting systems, were developed and implemented. And instead of hammering home a charge with a muzzle loading system (a slow and ponderous process), the use of percussion-fired projectiles emerged—with significant gains in efficiency and rate of fire. Much of the testing and use of these new technologies happened on training ranges created off the Atlantic coasts of both Europe and the United States. While there were outbreaks of warfare in the littoral seas of the Atlantic—the Gulf of Mexico in the Mexican-American War, the Baltic and Black seas in the Crimean War—for the main part of this four-decade period the Atlantic was not the perennial battleground it had been for the preceding three centuries. However, that changed with the advent of the Civil War in the United States.

The Atlantic became a zone of real conflict again in the 1860s as two American battle flotillas, one from the North and the other from the South (quite small by European standards), squared off on the inland lakes and rivers, the littoral and coastal waters, and occasionally the deep waters of the Atlantic Ocean. The key tactic by the North was the immediate installation of a blockade, which it could put in place because it had the advantage of having inherited a preponderance of ships by virtue of the general loyalty of seagoing officers to the Union. As a result of the disparity in the number of ships between the two sides, the South never matched the North on a ship-by-ship basis. Instead, the South pursued a strategy of privateering and the offering of letters of marque, as well as commerce raiding on a selective basis. The Confederacy also tried to procure ships from a generally sympathetic Europe and attempted to convince other nations that the blockade existed only on paper—something that was true for a year or so before the North became more organized and systematic in enforcing it by putting its assortment of more than two hundred ships to sea over time. New technologies from the "ironclad" armored vessels on both sides (such as CSS *Virginia* and the oddly turreted, low-slung Union *Monitor*) and torpedoes (which are called mines today) were on display. Commerce raiding by the South had some impact (especially the morale-raising exploits of CSS *Alabama* under Captain Raphael Semmes), but could not in any sense turn the tide of the war. As was the case ashore, over time the vastly greater industrial might, employable population, and advanced technologies of the Union made the end more or less inevitable. The North prevailed at sea on the Atlantic as it did ashore, and the blockade was crucial in choking off the South's ability to resist. While it mainly supported the North's efforts on land, the Atlantic nevertheless allowed the North to implement a successful war strategy.

In much the same way that new technologies transformed the fight between the North and South during the Civil War, the Industrial Revolution of the nineteenth century also transformed Americans' relationship with the Atlantic. Advances in shipbuilding techniques expanded the zone of competition between nations beyond naval warfare; commerce in and of itself began to be a tool of statecraft. This was manifested at sea in the rise of various shipping lines and individual packet ships. SS *James Monroe* will sail into history as the first vessel to leave on a schedule regardless of wind and weather, and initial shipping lines included the Black Ball Line, the Red Star Line, and the Swallowtail Line, all of which began to become operational in the third decade of the 1800s. These were of course initially sailing ships, usually called clipper ships, and they competed for speed records. One of Donald McKay's clippers, *Lightning*, sailed 436 miles in a day, the single-day longest distance recorded by a sailing vessel, and a record that still stands.*

The net effect of these new technologies gave a certain psychological power to the growing sense that the seas in general were shrinking. This was especially true for the North Atlantic. As steam vessels became more

---

* Martin W. Sandler, *Atlantic Ocean: The Illustrated History of the Ocean That Changed the World* (New York: Sterling, 2008), 324.

commonplace by mid-century, the ocean appeared further reduced, facilitated by the advent of transatlantic telegraph cables that the increasingly big ships were able to place on the sea floor and operate with reliability by the 1860s. Before the cables became fully operational, normal communications had to be transported in a vessel, a voyage of generally ten to fourteen days. When telegraph cables became reliable, a message could flow across the Atlantic within minutes.

Queen Victoria sent a telegram of congratulations to President James Buchanan to open the line, directed to his summer residence in the Bedford Springs Hotel in Pennsylvania. She said that she hoped the link would create "an additional link between the nations whose friendship is founded on their common interest and reciprocal esteem." The president replied, "It is a triumph more glorious, because far more useful to mankind, than was ever won by conqueror on the field of battle. May the Atlantic telegraph, under the blessing of Heaven, prove to be a bond of perpetual peace and friendship between the kindred nations, and an instrument destined by Divine Providence to diffuse religion, civilization, liberty, and law throughout the world."*

Despite these advances, it is worth remembering how challenging the sea remained for mariners. Even a casual student of the Atlantic knows the story of the doomed *Titanic*, the "unsinkable ship" that was lost after hitting an iceberg. Leaving aside the fairly accurate film and its associated doomed love story paralleling the fate of the ship, the sinking remains a cautionary tale of the hubris of man and the capricious nature of the high seas. As I sailed across the north Atlantic in the mid-1990s, almost a century later, the story of *Titanic* was not far from my mind—even in a high-tech, solid-steel, brand-new U.S. Navy destroyer.

* "England and America United," *Christian Observer*, Aug. 19, 1858, 130; ProQuest, Web, accessed May 14, 2016, http://www.worldmapsonline.com/kr-1858-wotel.htm.

Following the short but bitter Spanish-American War, which saw a few naval engagements in and around Cuban waters, the next significant set of battles on the Atlantic were those of the First World War. The United States tried to avoid being pulled into the war, but eventually was drawn fully into the conflict. Fortunately, by that point in the nation's history our navy had improved dramatically. This was a direct result of the combined strategic thinking of Rear Admiral Stephen B. Luce and Captain (later rear admiral) Alfred Thayer Mahan and the energy and political advocacy of Theodore Roosevelt. Mahan and Luce conducted their collaboration at the Naval War College in Newport, Rhode Island, and Mahan produced a series of seminal books that used the prism of history to describe the importance of sea power. Mahan became a sort of intellectual mentor to Roosevelt, who became the youngest president in American history in 1901 when an assassin struck down William McKinley.

As president, Roosevelt drove a naval construction program that created a true blue-water navy of powerful battleships and cruisers. He pushed through the creation of the Panama Canal, intervened frequently in Latin America and the Caribbean, and used the emergence of new technologies to improve the sea power capabilities of the United States. Big battleships of 15,000 tons and more were able to speed through the waters at nearly 20 knots—a big improvement over sailing ships or more primitive steam-driven vessels that topped out around 12 to 15 knots—and were armed with massive eight-inch guns. Smokeless powder, greater range, and faster, more accurate torpedoes were also developed. The airplane was emerging in that first decade of the twentieth century, and the first flights in America were pushed by Atlantic winds over the beaches of Kitty Hawk, North Carolina. Roosevelt's policy to "speak softly and carry a big stick" specifically envisioned an oceangoing navy as the ultimate big stick. The massive 100,000-ton nuclear-powered aircraft carrier named after him, USS *Theodore Roosevelt*, today sails proudly with the fleet nickname "The Big Stick." Fair enough.

After the collapse of the complex structure of European alliances in the late summer of 1914, "the lights went out in Europe" and the Atlantic again became a field of maritime battle. Both Britain and Germany possessed powerful fleets centered on capital warships, notably the battleship. Indeed, the construction of the German fleet had been one element that raised British suspicions and concerns—logical enough if the long history of British maritime strategy is considered. Most of the German ships had fairly limited cruising ranges, which further convinced the British that they were designed to attack England and cover an invading force.

As the two massive battle fleets of Great Britain and Imperial Germany each sought to bring a "decisive fleet action" off in their respective favor (geopolitical-speak for destroying an opponent's ability to effectively wage war at sea), the scene of potential battle became the North Sea between the two countries. Given that the British home islands are athwart the exit from the North Sea, the German Imperial fleet was effectively held prisoner throughout the war. The two countries fought a series of inconclusive engagements, including at Dogger Bank in 1915, in the center of the North Sea, and at the more important Battle of Jutland in spring of 1916. Several Atlantic battles also took place in the far South Atlantic off the coast of South America, including the Battle of the Falkland Islands. Despite the actions at sea, the land armies quickly bogged down across the center of Europe and the war turned into a slugging match of attrition on land. This led the Allies, especially the British (who were being bled white ashore), to seek alternatives: they seized on the idea of a maritime campaign in the Mediterranean, the "soft underbelly of Europe." With the urging of Winston Churchill, then a very young first lord of the Admiralty, the British launched the Dardanelles/Gallipoli campaign, as he said, "*totus porcus*," or whole hog. It was a fiasco, described more fully in the upcoming chapter on the Mediterranean. Its tragic human consequences are well depicted in the film *Gallipoli*.

Nevertheless, these actions—fought on the periphery of the central theater of the North Atlantic—were of less strategic importance than the war against shipping waged by both sides. The Germans responded to a British blockade with their own U-boat campaign. They began by attacking British blockading vessels with their U-boats, and seeing the strategic effect, added surface cruisers to the mix of ships conducting attacks. By 1915, the U-boat campaigns had increased in strategic importance, and in May 1916 they sank the merchant liner *Lusitania*, a story sharply told in Erik Larson's *Dead Wake*. The killing of 128 Americans helped pull the United States into the war, although not immediately. The declaration of unrestricted U-boat warfare at the end of 1916 both accelerated the British response and forced the Allies to institute a system of convoys.

The United States' increased participation in the form of troops sent to Europe turned the tide of the war. Using the groundwork in the U.K. built by Admiral William Sims, the Atlantic became a bridge across which flowed war materials, supporting soldiers and Marines, and perhaps most important, trade and commerce that fueled the Allied efforts. It was during the First World War that the idea of the North Atlantic community of nations evolved in the writing of geopolitical commentators like Walter Lippmann, who referred to "the profound web of interest which joins together the western world." As he put it, "Britain, France, Italy, Spain, Belgium, Holland, the Scandinavian nations, and Pan America are in the main one community in their deepest needs and their deepest purposes. . . . We cannot betray the Atlantic community. . . .

What we must fight for is the common interest of the western world, for the integrity of the Atlantic powers. We must recognize that we are in fact one great community and act as members of it."*

Tragically, the United States essentially rejected the construct of an Atlantic community after the First World War, declined membership in the League of Nations (the forerunner to today's United Nations), and embarked on an ill-conceived course of isolationism. As I listened to the overheated rhetoric of the 2016 election campaign roughly a century later, I heard echoes of those misjudgments in the words of Donald Trump, who would seemingly have us turn our backs on the larger world, rebuild walls of protectionism, construct a physical wall between the United States and Mexico, dissolve NATO, and repudiate our linkages with allies around the world. This reflects a certain strain of isolationist DNA that has run through our nation's psychology for two centuries. And frankly, we've seen that movie before in the interwar years, and the world reaped a predictable and terrible harvest in the form of the Second World War. Furthermore, the "great wall" of its time, the Maginot Line constructed by France to protect itself from a resurgent Germany led by Adolf Hitler, was a complete failure.

In the run-up to the Second World War, despite efforts to limit naval construction by treaties, the major world nations all rebuilt their fleets. Collective security died a premature death along with the League of Nations, and fascism began its rise in Germany, Italy, and Spain. Britain and France desperately wanted to avoid another world war, and looked away as Hitler annexed various territories and nations in Europe. Appeasement failed, as it always does, and Germany invaded Poland in 1939. The United Kingdom and France both declared war on Germany,

* Bernard Bailyn, *Atlantic History: Concept and Contours* (Cambridge, Mass.: Harvard University Press, 2005).

and Europe was again plunged into war. On the Atlantic, at least, the British had a significant advantage because Germany had not invested in significant capital ships to the degree that it had invested in land forces. This allowed Britain to maintain its independence even after the fall of France in 1940.

Yet even with a relatively small fleet, the Germans were able to strike at British sea power, including sinking both warships and merchant shipping, with their highly capable and technologically advanced U-boats. Even the reconstruction of a strict convoy regime did not stem the losses across the North Atlantic. In addition to the U-boats, German capital warships were engaged in commerce raiding from the northern reaches of the Atlantic down to the coast of South America. By mid-1941, the situation for Great Britain—alone and defiant, but under real threat of collapse—was dire. The U.S. Navy was conducting essentially an undeclared war in the North Atlantic, with Navy destroyers attacking U-boats and torpedoes fired against U.S. ships in turn. When the United States entered the war in earnest after the attack on Pearl Harbor in December 1941, the Battle of the Atlantic was already well under way. Victory at sea in the Atlantic during World War II would turn on the battle to defeat German submarines, and it would be, as the Duke of Wellington said of Waterloo, a very near-run thing.

As the Germans "flooded the zone" with U-boats, the Allies reached back to World War I tactics, techniques, and procedures. The Germans operated in wolf packs, improved their surveillance and targeting ability, and instituted a system of logistics to resupply the raiders at sea from much larger mother submarines. The Allies reinstituted a complex system of convoys, added significant antisubmarine warfare warships to protect them (destroyers and corvettes), and increased the use of new technologies, including surface radar and sound imaging (sonar) to detect the U-boats while submerged. Newer, bigger, and rocket-thrown depth charges were also added to the arsenal of Allied ships to counter the U-boats. U-boat attacks ranged as far as the coast of the United States and deep into the Caribbean. In the summer and fall of 1940, German tactics sank hundreds of thousands of tons of Allied shipping each month, including more than 350,000 tons in October 1940 alone.

Turning the tide after the U.S. entry into the war required cracking the communications code used by Axis powers to target submarines against specific Allied convoys and shipping. It also hinged on improvements in radar and sonar, and the attrition of U-boats, which were difficult to reconstruct as pressures mounted on the European continent. There were also significant operations in Arctic waters as the Allies sought to resupply Russia through northern convoys along the Arctic Circle to Murmansk.

Despite Allied momentum in the Atlantic, the Germans launched a second surge of U-boat attacks across the Atlantic in the spring of 1942, and in May and June of that year managed to sink more than a million tons of shipping. The effects of the attacks eventually peaked in November 1942 with 700,000 tons going down. At the time, Admiral Karl Dönitz had more than three hundred U-boats at play, which he estimated were enough to effectively starve the English people. While the Allies possessed new technologies to combat U-boats, their operators were not experienced, and the Germans had the upper hand. Additionally, a new cipher had been produced and the Allied ability to track the German submarines was again limited. The Allies responded by instituting new tactics, including picket lines to kill U-boats in transit. They also recracked the cipher, and by early 1943 there was improvement (although in March 1943, nearly 700,000 tons were sunk). Two factors were crucial to the Allies' newfound success: first was the Allied ability to more effectively attack U-boats with better technology and tactics; and second was the U.S. industrial machine's production of overwhelming numbers of convoy escort warships. By late spring of 1943, the worst had passed. Despite German hopes of a technological breakthrough of some kind (a new acoustical torpedo, for example), it was clear that the Allies would gradually kill enough U-boats to break the campaign and permit the safe transfer of sufficient U.S. troops to Europe to win the war (alongside the enormously critical Russian campaigns as well). Despite destroying nearly three thousand Allied ships and well over 20 million tons of shipping, in the end the U-boat campaign was not enough.

As Churchill said, "The Battle of the Atlantic was the dominating factor all through the war. Never for one moment could we forget that everything happening elsewhere, on land, at sea or in the air depended ultimately on its outcome. . . . Many gallant actions and incredible feats of endurance are recorded but the deeds of those who perished will never be known. Our merchant seamen displayed their highest qualities, and the brotherhood of the sea was never more strikingly shown than in their determination to defeat the U-boat."* Given that Great Britain needed more than a million tons of food and material weekly, the greatest strategic chance the Germans had to destroy the United Kingdom was to choke it to death. In the end, the battle turned—as battles always do—on a combination of courage, innovation, and communication. The real keys to defeating the U-boats in the Atlantic were longer-range aircraft, radar mounted to the U-boat-seeking aircraft, improvements in depth charges and sonar, British intelligence and code-breaking skills (like Enigma), tactics of avoidance in regard to convoy deployments, and

---

* Winston S. Churchill, *The Second World War*: vol. 5, *Closing the Ring* (Boston: Houghton Mifflin, 1951), quoted in Martin W. Sandler, *Atlantic Ocean: The Illustrated History of the Ocean That Changed the World* (New York: Sterling, 2008), 439.

optical devices like the Leigh Light (a searchlight used in conjunction with radar to help Allied aircraft hunting submarines at night as they surfaced to recharge their diesel batteries).

After the final defeat of Germany and Japan and the end of the Second World War, the United States crucially decided to remain engaged in the world, as opposed to another abrupt withdrawal à la the post–World War I world. The United Nations and the so-called Bretton Woods institutions (the World Bank, the International Monetary Fund) were designed to help ward off another global war. Despite this good news, the Soviet Union emerged in the post–World War II era as a global threat, requiring significant U.S. response and launching what came to be known as the cold war.

This was also the start of my own military career in the mid-1970s, and for the first fifteen years of my seagoing experience I was a true cold warrior, essentially chasing Soviet ships, submarines, and aircraft or being chased by them. These days, given Russia's recent assertive geopolitical behavior in Ukraine, Georgia, Moldova, and Syria, I am often asked, "Are we headed into a new cold war?" The answer is "probably not." I am certainly old enough to remember the cold war, in which I spent a great deal of time on the broad Atlantic tracking Soviet platforms. The cold war was millions of well-trained troops on both sides facing one another across the Fulda Gap in Central Europe; it was two huge battle fleets playing cat and mouse from the High North and Arctic Circle to the bottom of the world off the coast of South America; it was two huge nuclear arsenals on a hair-trigger alert, twenty thousand warheads ready to utterly destroy the world. We are not remotely in that world today, and that is a very good thing, but we do need to be mindful of the geopolitics of the oceans or we risk stumbling back into that late-twentieth-century world.

What was the cold war like in the Atlantic? First and foremost, it was a battle for control—really complete surveillance and the positioning of strategic and tactical assets—in the Greenland-Iceland–United Kingdom (GIUK) gap. This zone of thousands of miles of empty ocean became critical strategically because whichever side controlled it would be able to monitor and channel all the maritime traffic (including subsurface) into and out of the North Atlantic. It therefore controlled the flow of men and material to Europe in the case of a Soviet attack on western Europe. Unlike the Germans in World War II, the Soviets had a huge and capable seagoing fleet; allowing them to break out of northern ports and flow into the GIUK gap would have ceded control over the supply routes to Europe—the precise thing that Germany strove for so mightily with its U-boat fleets.

Thus in the cold war, there was a constant maneuver between the Soviet Union (and its Warsaw Pact allies) and the NATO forces led by the United States for control of the gap. This required significant deployments of U.S. combat power to Iceland, Canada, Denmark, Norway, and of course the United Kingdom itself. Combat power was also stationed at bases in the Northeast of the United States. The operative maritime forces were long-range P-3 Orion antisubmarine warfare aircraft, formidable hunter-killer machines used to find Soviet submarines; nuclear attack submarines of the United States and our allies; satellite coverage of the deep ocean; and occasional deployments of flotillas of destroyers and cruisers (like mine) with significant sonar, torpedo, and other sensors suitable to pursue submarines. The Soviets deployed their ballistic missile submarines (equipped with long-range missiles tipped with nuclear weapons) as well as flotillas of submarines and surface ships. While not exactly crowded up there, it was a "target rich zone" for antisubmarine forces.

The Atlantic was also increasingly a huge trade path for the expansive economies of western (free) Europe and the United States. As the

Europeans moved gradually toward a better state of economic union, it became increasingly clear that this commercial connection across the Atlantic would be vital for the United States as well.

There was a final bloody spurt of combat in the deep southern reaches of the Atlantic Ocean as the twentieth century moved to a close: the Falklands War. In the spring of 1982, over the course of ten weeks, Great Britain and Argentina fought a short, sharp war that cost a thousand lives, sank sixteen ships, and saw more than a hundred aircraft destroyed. It was fought over the Falkland Islands, which had been (and still are) a British protectorate with a British population but are long claimed as the Malvinas Islands by the Argentines. The classic description of the battle from the British perspective is Admiral Sir Sandy Woodward's *One Hundred Days*, his memoir of leading the British flotilla that wrested the islands back from Argentine invaders after a demanding campaign fought as winter drew on in the southern latitudes. While the two nations still disagree over ownership of the islands, another round of violent conflict appears unlikely. The war has been studied by naval strategists and historians and provides a good example of the vulnerability of surface ships to air attack in the era of cruise missiles. As I progressed through my cold war career in the Navy, I would often open up Sir Sandy's remarkable book to help me think through how best to prepare my various at-sea commands for potential combat around the world. It was the final spasm of international violence in the long history of the Atlantic in the twentieth century and, let us hope, the last.

The Atlantic today is, for essentially the first time in its long history, a zone of cooperation and peace from the Arctic Circle to the shores of the Antarctic in the far South. While there are still a few lingering territorial issues to resolve—some African littoral claims, islands in the Caribbean, and the aforementioned Falkland Islands/Malvinas in the South Atlantic—the ocean itself and almost all of its tributary seas are in a relative state of peace. Only the eastern Mediterranean and to some degree the Black Sea present the potential for serious conflict. This is a remarkable change to a body of water that has long been viewed, correctly, as the canvas of war upon which too many admirals have quite enthusiastically painted in blood.

3.

THE INDIAN OCEAN

THE FUTURE SEA

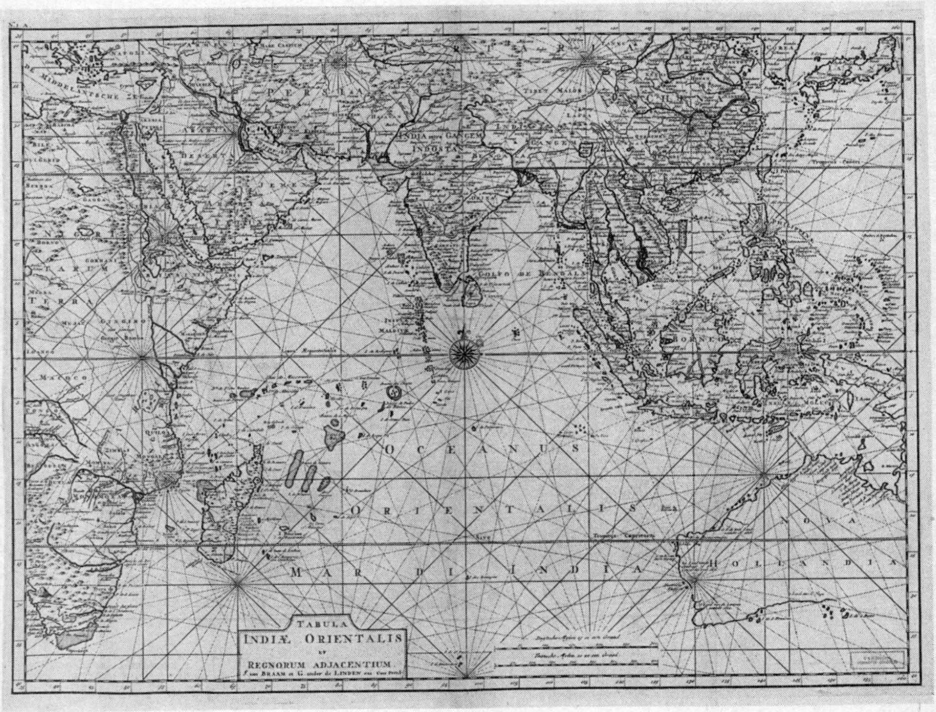

India is the center around which its ocean turns.

Map created by Joannes van Braam, 1726.

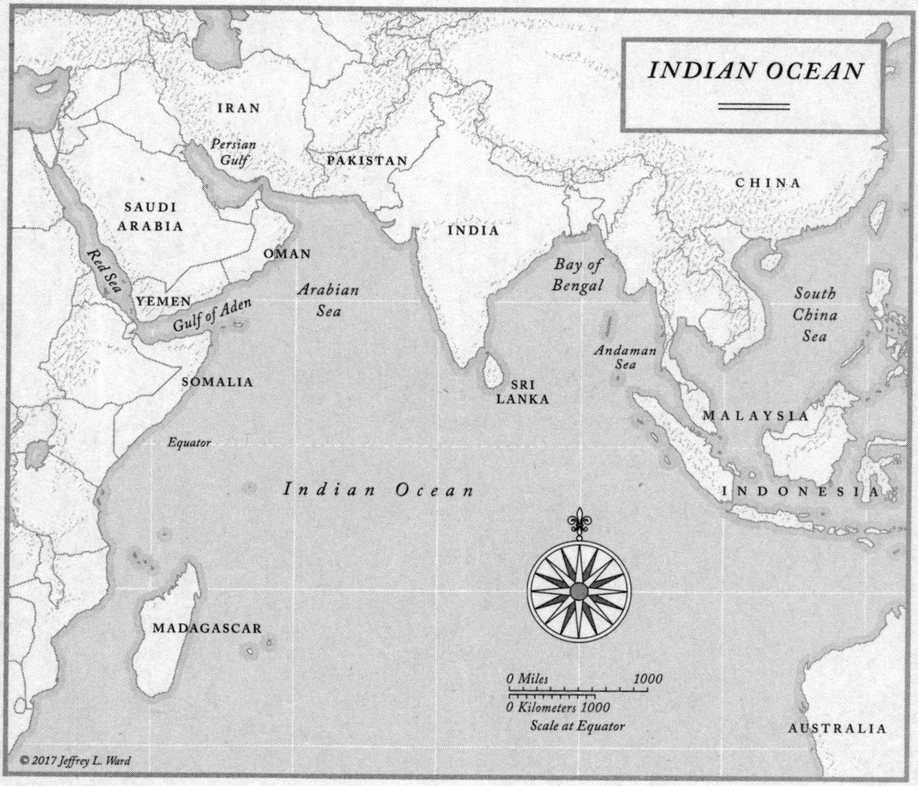

The Indian Ocean will remain a driving economic force in the world oceans for decades to come.

The Indian Ocean is a vast body of water—20 percent of the world's surface and third in size behind the Atlantic and Pacific oceans. If you were to drop the entire continental United States on top of the Indian Ocean, it would fit quite comfortably within its borders as a sort of very large island. In fact, you could probably squeeze three continental United States into the water space and be able to navigate comfortably around them. Yet with all that space—and a sense of real openness for a sailor—the Indian Ocean itself has relatively less human and geopolitical history than either of the other two major oceans, the Atlantic and Pacific. And it is worth noting that even the tributary seas—the Arabian/Persian Gulf and the Red Sea—have become particularly important in a geopolitical sense only in the post–World War II era with the rise of global shipping and the export of oil from the Gulf region. While that absence of global impact is about to change as India rises in its global ambition and reach, it is still relatively a tabula rasa in geopolitical terms.

I first entered the Indian Ocean from the east, through the Strait of

Malacca, in the mid-1980s. I was operations officer in a brand-new AEGIS air defense cruiser, USS *Valley Forge.* AEGIS is a hi-tech, automated command and control and weapons system that can detect, track, and shoot down multiple targets simultaneously. Our mission was to head through the Indian Ocean to the Arabian Gulf at best speed, first taking on fuel and supplies at Diego Garcia, a small island and British possession in the center of the vast ocean space. As the operations officer, I had prepared the charts and set the course, and took the first watch as we drove out between Indonesia and Malaysia and headed toward the Indian Ocean, watching the stars open above us in the unlit sky.

We sped through the long Strait of Malacca after departing Singapore. The night watch was a blur of huge tankers, coastal junks and small boats, and occasionally other warships flashing their signal lights at us. Singapore guards the eastern entrance to the Malacca Strait, one of the busiest in the world, and its multinational character—with Malay, Chinese, Indian, Anglo, and many other residents—makes it a gateway city in every sense of the word. As you get under way from its busy ports and take on speed entering the very crowded Strait of Malacca, you have a sense much like coming through the Strait of Gibraltar into the Mediterranean Sea—yet knowing that unlike the Med, the Indian Ocean is essentially a vast open seaway.

After that long night watch, I was still on the bridge as the sea and anchor detail officer of the deck as we came off navigation detail (additional watches set for close-to-land or very dense traffic maneuvering) and watched the sun rise up as we entered the broad reaches of the Andaman Sea off the western coast of Thailand. Suddenly, we were in an enormous expanse of open water, and we shaped our course for the southwest and the tiny atoll of Diego Garcia.

Sailing across the Indian Ocean, unlike the Med, a sailor is hit by a sense of wide-open space, much like the central and western Pacific.

While you occasionally pass other ships, it is a relatively rare moment to be within visual distance of another vessel. As you stand the long, boring watches, you can easily imagine slipping back over the centuries and seeing, across the horizon, not a smokestack rising where the next ship should be, but instead a set of huge sails as one of the great hulls of the British or Dutch East India Company bears down upon you, the classic northeast monsoons and equatorial currents driving it straight at you. Or so it felt to a very young lieutenant who had probably read too many novels set in the nineteenth century by George MacDonald Fraser, C. S. Forester, and Patrick O'Brian.

But actually it *is* apt to think of a trading ship rather than a warship coming over the horizon. For the Indian Ocean's most salient characteristic is that unlike its massive cousins the Atlantic and Pacific, and as particularly distinct from the perpetual battlefield of the Mediterranean, the Indian Ocean has been primarily a zone of trade. Beginning with the earliest Indian civilizations of the Harappans in the Indus Valley nearly three thousand years before Christ, there have been frequent trading ventures along the coast of modern India and Pakistan, across the Red Sea between the Arabian Gulf and Africa, and indeed between the ancient Mediterranean and the early societies of the Indian Ocean littoral. The engine that drove all of this through the long centuries of the age of sail was mother nature: the monsoon winds, the powerful and perpetual wind patterns that drove ships of trade and of war in the days before mechanical propulsion, coupled with the equatorial currents.

In an oddly named document, the *Periplus of the Erythraean Sea*, written by an ancient Greek of Alexandria whose name is lost to the ages, we see evidence of the commercial potential of the Red Sea, the African coast, and the Indian subcontinent as well. This is matched by discoveries from more than two thousand years ago of Greek amphorae, coins, and other physical evidence of trade in the coastal waters of the Indian

Ocean. The ancient sailors knew of and mastered the monsoons, which provided the ability to transit significant distances. These winds are predictable and therefore recordable. In the fall and winter, the northeast monsoon blows down from Asia toward the Indian Ocean, accompanied by currents that can reinforce voyages in that direction. This is reversed in the spring and summer as southwest monsoons blow back from the Indian Ocean toward Asia and the currents reverse themselves. While their appearance is not always guaranteed, it is sufficiently reliable to have powered the ability for trading across the seemingly endless sea relatively early in the course of human development.

Ancient Indian civilizations probably began sailing the waters of the Indian Ocean as early as the fifth century B.C. As the waters of the Tigris and Euphrates rivers emptied into the northern Arabian Gulf, the conflict between the Persian Sassanian Empire and various Indian empires (Harappan, Mauryan, Guptan) flared back and forth. There is little evidence of major sea battles as was the case in the Mediterranean, largely because the geography is so different. The strategic geography of the Indian Ocean is one of vast, open space—essentially one massive littoral, with the exception of the two inland seas, the Arabian Gulf and the Red Sea. While there were sporadic naval engagements across these two areas, most of the major warfare was focused on the land and the holding of territory.

The ancient Egyptians and Greeks traded with the Indian and Persian civilizations, as well as conducting wars. Trade goods included myrrh, incense, ebony, oil, wood, crafts, crops, livestock, and gold and other metals. The brief but impactful life and adventures of Alexander the Great influenced the rise of trade, opening new cities and extending cultural influence, including the founding of the great Egyptian trading city of Alexandria and even ports on the Arabian Gulf. As a young junior officer ashore for the first time in Kuwait, I was fascinated by the ruins of a Greek temple. The Egyptians and the Greeks both traded across the Red Sea, and when Rome conquered Egypt around the time of Christ, Rome became part of the expanding level of trading in the Indian Ocean. Roman Alexandria became a kind of early hub for the trading runs into the Indian Ocean—the goods included textiles from distant China, glass and crafts, and—as was to be a constant driver in Indian Ocean trade—spices, notably black pepper.

At the same time, on the eastern side of the Arabian Gulf, the various Persian empires opened new ports and began both importing and exporting across the Gulf. In addition to the goods above, pearls, carpets, and horses were part of the mix. The strategic value of the Strait of Hormuz, which guards the entrance to the Arabian Gulf, began to emerge. You can drop a plumb line through the more than two millennia since the Persians established forts and seaports to control the narrow choke point to the present day, which continues to occupy the attention of the world.

The Arabian Gulf and its exceedingly narrow opening, the highly strategic Strait of Hormuz: this seemingly perpetual flashpoint of collision between civilizations was much on my mind the first time I sailed through it in 1984. The USS *Valley Forge* was sent to the Arabian Gulf escorting tankers through the dangerous waters of the Gulf. The threat was from missile strikes or even missile boats attacking tankers bound in and out of the Gulf during the long war between Saddam Hussein's Iraq and Iran under the ayatollahs. Our job was an uncomfortable one: to come close aboard to the massive oil tankers—ten times our size by tonnage—and use our highly sophisticated radar and missile systems to defend them from attack.

It was harrowing work, and I stood long, tension-filled watches as a tactical action officer (entrusted with the authority to launch missiles) in the combat information center, the dark heart of the ship, lit only by the glowing radar screens. Every watch had its inevitable call to general quarters, when everyone in the ship was rousted out to battle stations. Our missiles were in the ready-to-fire position, and fortunately we were being backed up by combat aircraft flying from the rolling decks of a U.S. carrier outside the Gulf in the North Arabian Sea. The real threat was from Iran, which was unpredictable in its intent, although somewhat limited in capability. The other problem was the possibility of a mistake or miscalculation by Iraq, which was trying to export oil under the missiles and guns of archenemy Iran. Our job was to keep the sea lanes of communication open by protecting the U.S.-flagged tankers, while also trying to avoid escalating the situation.

Frankly, not much has really changed down through the centuries in the Arabian Gulf. Just as the geography of the Indian Ocean is one of openness and seemingly limitless horizons, the Arabian Gulf is tight, confined, constrained, and shallow—all things a sailor hates. That trade has crossed the Gulf more or less perpetually has not reduced its fundamental danger to those who would fight in its tight spaces.

The Arabian Gulf has its own history, of course. It is intertwined with the larger Indian Ocean, but has been a distinct Islamic sea since that religion emerged on the landmasses around its periphery. From its northern tip, at the Shatt al Arab delta where the waters of the Tigris and Euphrates flow into the Gulf, to the narrow thirty-five-mile Strait of Hormuz at the south, it is just over six hundred miles: the distance from Washington to Boston. Islamic countries surround it, although they are religiously split between Shi'a and Sunni governance. Iran is a Shi'a nation, and Saudi Arabia, Oman, the United Arab Emirates, Bahrain, Qatar, and Kuwait are predominantly Sunni. Iraq, which has only a small aperture on the Gulf through the Shatt al Arab and the port of Basra, is a mix of Sunni and Shi'a, a source of constant turbulence and disturbance.

. . .

As a result of not only religious differences within Islam but also geopolitical rivalry, the Gulf is today a "cold war" lake between the Sunni bloc led by the Kingdom of Saudi Arabia and the Shi'a world led by Iran. Over the past decade, Iranian influence and power in the region have increased, and today Tehran either directly controls or has significant influence in Iraq, Syria, Lebanon, and Yemen. The Gulf itself has become a place of constant cat and mouse between the naval forces of Iran and those of the Sunni Arab states. In the center of it, of course, is the United States and its Fifth Fleet, one of the largest of all the U.S. global fleets. And this Sunni-Shi'a conflict—both geopolitical and religious in character—gives every impression of being capable of leading to outright conflict between the two nations, which face each other, as Arabs and Persians have done for centuries, across the light blue water of the Arabian Gulf.

The Fifth Fleet is based out of Manama, the capital of Bahrain. It is here that the U.S. Navy has a huge command and control structure, headed up by a three-star vice admiral in one of the truly plum jobs today's Navy offers. It is a large command, both ashore, with thousands of sailors and their families living in Bahrain, and at sea, with at least one aircraft carrier and its attendant escorts under operational control at all times. There are also logistic, patrol, and intelligence-gathering ships and aircraft under the command of the admiral's staff.

All of this seems ironic when you consider the history of the Arabian Gulf—a supremely hot, windy, shallow, and resource-poor body of water that slept its way through the millennia until the rise of oil and natural gas. Even as recently as the time of World War II, "cities" like Bahrain, Dubai, and Abu Dhabi were essentially fishing villages. Dhows plied the waters as they had for centuries, doing some listless fishing, pearl diving, and smuggling. All that changed as the world realized that perhaps two thirds of the earth's oil reserves and a third of its natural gas reserves are in the immediate region, both ashore and at sea. The Safaniya offshore oil fields are the largest in the world, and the shallow depth throughout the Gulf (an average depth of only 150 feet) makes it an easy place to work offshore. Today Dubai is one of the first cities of the commercial world, of course, with Abu Dhabi and Doha, the capital of Qatar, not far behind in sophistication and elegance.

The military technology that resulted from the geography and the political competition reflected more than anything the prevailing conditions of wind and current. Ships within the Gulf were typically dhow-like, with lateen (triangular) sails rigged fore to aft. The term "dhow" covers a multitude of vessels, by the way—African, Arab, Persian, and Indo-Pakistani. They can be very small and coastal—much like the classic dhows that ply the Gulf today—or rather large. A key feature is that they were built "carvel style," which is to say the boards were not nailed or bolted together but rather sewn with rope and then caulked. They almost always have a large square stern.

Because of the nature of the dhows, the use of mounted guns came very late, and the idea of using marines—soldiers specialized in maritime warfare—did not emerge. In the broader Indian Ocean, the winds gave impetus to the rise of sailing over rowing very early on in the developmental process and also spurred the building of more square-rigged sailing ships. Overall, the ships of the Indian Ocean were optimized for sailing and trading, not for fighting—although they were certainly used for all three over time.

My own history in the Arabian Gulf is extensive, as is the case for most U.S. Navy sailors of my generation, officer and enlisted. I went there first in the mid-1980s on the tanker escort operation described above. Shortly after my ship departed following a successful series of escorts, our relief—the ill-fated cruiser *Vincennes*—inadvertently shot down an Iranian commercial airliner, killing 290 innocent civilians in what many in the Navy regard as the worst chapter in our cold war history. It was a terrible mistake caused by the high state of tension in the region, the confusion and fog of war, and a belief on the part of the *Vincennes* crew that the aircraft they saw on radar was an Iranian F-14 carrying either bombs or missiles. If there is any incident that illustrates the danger and confusion of the Arabian Gulf, it is the shooting down of Iran Air Flight 688—which to this day is the number the Iranians always use for the same flight (Tehran to Dubai) as a memorial to the victims.

I have pulled into virtually every open port in the Gulf (obviously not into Iran), and each has its own culture and relationship with the U.S. Navy that shapes the visit. The most open and overtly welcoming is Bahrain, where the Fifth Fleet maintains its headquarters. Here our sailors can enjoy not only first-class hotels and the chance for a cold beer, but also the support of a fully operational U.S. military base with medical, dental, Navy exchange stores, recreation, and all other amenities. Liberty in the United Arab Emirates is a different experience and has evolved over time. Initially, the vast majority of ships were confined to a restricted area in a huge port called Jebel Ali, located in between Dubai and Abu Dhabi. But over time the restrictions have been eased, and today our sailors enjoy themselves in both metropolitan areas.

For me, one of the strange enjoyments of the Gulf is being out at sea, even on the hottest of summer days, when the temperatures can rise to more than 120 degrees and the steel decks nearly glow with latent heat. I always enjoyed going for a (brief) run around the decks, almost like running in a sauna, and the normally flat calm of the turquoise waters is beautiful and quiet. But the operational tempo is the hardest of any spot in the Indian Ocean because of the complexity. At all times, the watch stander is thinking and worrying about Iranian naval ships and aircraft, with which we have a tense relationship (although generally professional). Since the signing of the nuclear arms agreement with the Iranians, there have been some untoward incidents that may be a sign of hard-liners in Tehran trying to ratchet up pressure and perhaps even sink the agreement. Too soon to tell, but it seems clear that the Arabian/Persian Gulf will continue to be a fault line in international geopolitics, and a source of tension that bleeds into the larger Indian Ocean.

All of which brings us to the earliest and darkest forms of trading and commerce along the Indian Ocean and its tributary seas: slavery and piracy. The movement of slaves was a brisk trade throughout the recorded history of the region, persisting to the present day. The transport of slaves from various conquests was part of the shipping routes of the region, including slaves taken by capturing ships at sea in acts of piracy. While slavery and piracy have diminished somewhat, both still exist in parts of the Indian Ocean, albeit with modern tools and sophistication, something I learned a great deal about as the NATO commander charged with eliminating piracy along the eastern coast of Africa, which I will discuss in depth below.

It is worth noting that Indian Ocean trade in the sixth and seventh centuries A.D. dropped dramatically as several of the key trading empires declined in power and influence. Both the Sassanian Persians and the Guptans of India—who had attempted to control trade along with Chinese and Malay entities—shrank significantly in population. This may have been partly due to a global epidemic (paralleled by the bubonic plague in Europe), sometimes called the Plague of Justinian, a disease carried by fleas and rats and well known on ships.

But the energy from the east and west of the Indian Ocean would again reignite the trading regime with vigor. Both from Arabia and from China, the pressure for trading began to put life back into the commerce across the broad ocean. Both gold and ivory were important, as well as the hard woods of Africa; but the rising trade in African slaves was a powerful driver as the religion of Islam appeared, the Arabian caliphate expanded, and much of the Indian Ocean littoral, particularly in the west, became part of the Islamic world. Trade between Arabs, Persians, and the Chinese of the Tang and Song dynasties expanded and drove the trading patterns through the thirteenth century. These included formal trading arrangements, embassies, protected ports, and many advanced mechanisms to expand relations. It also included the expansion of Islam to the littoral of the region, albeit much more slowly in Southeast Asia and much of what is today India. Ports like Calicut and Khambhat became global centers. All of this progressed without significant warfare, at least at sea. But looming from the west was the coming force of Europe as it entered the Age of Discovery and exercised its appetite for trade as well.

Vasco da Gama was a stocky and emotional man of middle-class origin, born around 1460 in southwestern Portugal. He undertook perhaps the most epic and impactful voyage of exploration in world history in 1497–98 when he led four Portuguese ships down the Atlantic coast of Africa (building on decades of exploration led by Prince Henry the Navigator). He then continued into uncharted waters of the South Atlantic, sailed around the Cape of Good Hope at the bottom of Africa, between the island of Madagascar and Mozambique on the east African coast, up the east coast of Africa to an Indian Ocean port called Malindi, and on to the southwestern tip of India, landing at Calicut in the spring of 1498.

The entire length of the voyage was at the time the longest conducted out of sight of land, and was longer than sailing around the earth at the equator. Da Gama returned to Portugal in 1499 to much acclaim, although overall his record is sullied by a variety of massacres attributed to him in India (including burning alive a boatload of hundreds of Muslim pilgrims, among them women and children, who were begging for mercy and posed no threat to his expedition). He returned to India on another expedition several years later, where he was still unable to fulfill his fundamental mission of obtaining a treaty for trade. He eventually died during a third and final voyage to India in 1524.

What began as a spice trade, initially based on pepper and cinnamon, soon expanded as the Portuguese consolidated their head start to India, with England, France, and the Netherlands not far behind. The key for the Portuguese was finding an independent path to the spices, one not dependent on crossing the dangerous Mediterranean and going overland to the Red Sea. This seagoing route was perfect for a small, seafaring nation like Portugal, and allowed it to break the monopoly over the spice trade heretofore held by Venetian, Arabian, and Persian traders. Although there were frequent diplomatic missteps (including by da Gama himself) based on simple ignorance of the cultural mores of the Indian trading culture, gradually the Portuguese were able to insinuate themselves into the trading patterns of the western Indian Ocean.

The nation that soon followed up as more nautical knowledge became available and ships' capabilities improved were the Ottomans, seeking to create a Muslim protectorate over large portions of the Indian Ocean littoral. This was facilitated by the Ottoman conquest of Egypt in the early 1500s, which gave them convenient access to the length of the Red Sea. Soon the Portuguese and the Ottomans were in full competition, each seeking exclusive trading treaties, bases for logistic support, and engaging in combat where they could bring maritime forces to bear. This was difficult for the Ottomans as their sea power was optimized for the more restricted coastal waters of the Mediterranean. In the mid-1500s, the Ottomans launched a fairly large fleet of more than fifty vessels to attack Portuguese positions around the Indian Ocean with a particular focus on Hormuz at the entrance to the Arabian Gulf, sailing this time from bases in present-day Iraq at the northern end of the Gulf. They were crushingly defeated, but the rivalry continued for another century until finally the Ottomans essentially withdrew and the Portuguese turned to face new rivals.

Their legacy at this point included introduction of a kind of patois of Portuguese and local dialects that was used for commerce (often referred to as Portuguese Creole), adapting their ships to long ocean voyages through new sailing technologies, and fusing the power of the state to the commercial interest of quasi-private companies in fairly creative ways. The latter model—of commercial and state interests blending—was raised to its highest level over the next several centuries in the Indian Ocean.

We see this first with the British East India Company in 1600, followed very shortly by the Dutch East India Company. Both used the model developed by the Portuguese as their basis, and both companies existed to create commercial trading opportunities that led to state power. The Dutch began to focus on the eastern parts of the Indian Ocean, including what is today Sri Lanka and parts of Indonesia. They also established a foothold at Cape Town at the southern tip of Africa. Their initial product offerings were traditional spices (pepper, cloves, mace, cinnamon, nutmeg) and, increasingly, coffee. The British, on the other hand, began with a focus on gaining control of as much of the Indian landmass as they could. They built forts and created a string of bases around the periphery of the country in the 1600s and on into the early 1700s.

Despite the increasing level of imperial competition between the Portuguese, Dutch, and British, the fundamental trade routes remained largely in local hands. The Chinese, who had no appetite for colonization and no significant deepwater military capability, were nonetheless involved in all aspects of the trade as well—often providing loans, cooperative arrangements, chandlery, and posted both in China and other parts of Southeast Asia along the trading routes. Each of the imperial competitors created its own string of bases—the Dutch, for example, centered their operations in Batavia (now Jakarta), but with robust capability in Cape Town and present-day Sri Lanka.

While there were occasional indigenous challenges, for example from the Yaarubi regime in Oman, the power of the two increasingly dominant imperial powers—Britain and the Netherlands—gradually consolidated. The big winner as the eighteenth century ended, of course, was Great Britain. Having essentially seized control of Oman, Kenya, and India, the British went on to create a British lake in the center of the Indian Ocean. Neither Portugal nor the Netherlands was strong enough to face imperial Britain, and the defeat of Napoleon in the early 1800s ultimately limited France's ability to play a global role. As a result, much of the maritime history of the nineteenth century in the Indian Ocean is Britain's, upon whose empire the sun never set "because God cannot trust an Englishman in the dark."

While it is certainly fair to say the Indian Ocean became a sort of British lake, it is also quite true that the gaze of the British was ashore, not at sea, once they had established dominance over their imperial and local rivals. There was wide realization on the part of the British that they needed to control the sea lanes to control India, and every English viceroy sent to India reiterated to the crown his need for sea power to ensure dominance. The challenges were from France early in the 1800s, and to some degree from the Dutch, as well as concerns over piracy and slave trading. Each was overcome through a combination of ruthless conquering of needed bases, intricate systems of alliances and commercial trading agreements with littoral states and local rulers, and new technologies—especially the switch from sail to steam power and the completion of the Suez Canal by 1869.

. . .

The Suez Canal is an interesting place for history buffs. There were ancient attempts by both the Egyptians and the Persians to construct small waterways through the Sinai desert and connect the two ancient waters of the Mediterranean and Red seas. It is possible the Persians successfully did so under Darius, but it is difficult to say with certainty. Napoleon expressed a high degree of interest in such a project before his hopes of global empire were thwarted. It was the French who took on the canal as a commercial venture in cooperation with the Egyptian government, interestingly originally vociferously opposed by the British. But by the time it was complete, the British understood its value and eventually took it over as a "protectorate" for decades. In an interesting bit of nautical showmanship, when the canal was to be first opened to traffic, the French empress Eugénie was scheduled to lead a host of international ships down the Canal with the French ship at the lead. But to the horror of the Egyptians and the outrage of the French, a British warship managed to steal a sail on everyone by maneuvering its way through the assembled fleet in the course of the night without lights and managed to be the first ship through the canal—thus presaging the eventual British takeover. The captain was officially reprimanded and unofficially commended.

My first trip of the many I have done both north and south through the canal was in the mid-1990s. I was a relatively inexperienced captain and just thirty-eight years old in command of a 9,000-ton Navy destroyer with a crew of three hundred. I did all the reading I could on the protocols of the canal, and knew that we would have to depend a great deal on the "professional" pilots (former Egyptian naval officers) who would guide us through using their local knowledge. I was told to be prepared to offer some baksheesh, a sort of cross between a gift and a bribe. The usual thing was to offer up multiple cartons of cigarettes. Foolishly, I decided to spare us the expense of a hundred dollars in smokes and offered the pilot instead the "highly coveted" baseball cap of my ship and a hearty handshake. He went immediately into a huge pout, unfolded a canvas stool, and sat passively on the bridge. We were on our own.

Fortunately, my navigator was a brilliant young officer, Lieutenant Robb Chadwick, and he had a crack team of quartermasters who had spent a month learning everything there was to know about the canal and devouring the various charts and descriptions of it, called "Sailing Directions." They managed to get us to the midpoint at the Great Bitter Lake, where the north- and southbound traffic divides up to allow passage, as the canal can handle only one stream of ships at a time. As we maneuvered to our anchorage, the Egyptian pilot finally roused himself and began insisting that we come hard to starboard to a completely different anchorage from the one we had been assigned. Thinking he must know what he was talking about, I started to bring the ship in that direction. Lieutenant Chadwick literally threw himself between me and the pilot and said, "Captain, if we keep heading there we are going to go aground." My choice: follow the advice of the local pilot and fifty-year-old expert, or that of my twenty-six-year-old Annapolis grad on his first voyage through the Canal? I ordered all stop, swung the rudder to port, and headed to where Robb indicated and dropped the hook. The pilot lost his temper and stormed off the bridge. In the ensuing calm, Robb showed me precisely on the chart where we would have gone aground under the direction of the pilot.

Had we gone aground, I would have been a retired Navy commander and probably doing something very different with my life. It was one of those pivot points in life that flashes across the screen when a single decision establishes a very different trajectory depending on the choice we make. So many of our lives and careers depend on others, and very often they are the people who work for us and whom we are mentoring. As an aside, in a cosmic way I returned the favor on 9/11, when I invited then-commander Robb Chadwick to pay an office call on me in the Pentagon. He stepped away from his desk in the Navy Intelligence Center to spend time with me, and thus was out of his office when the plane crashed more or less directly into it. All of his office mates were killed, several of them good friends to us both. Robb and I have had a close relationship since.

It strikes me that the Suez Canal is above all a symbol of the power of connections—between ancient seas, civilizations, rivals, and friends. It became in the nineteenth century a vital interest of Britain's and continued to be so essentially through the late 1960s when the British withdrew their forces from "east of Aden" after Indian independence. With the speed and mobility that the canal provided the mid-nineteenth-century Royal Navy and the East India Company, the British were able to increase their domination over the Indian Ocean.

Indeed, throughout the nineteenth century, the British avoided the kind of major set-piece battles that we see in places like the Mediterranean, but were kept quite busy controlling their rivals, suppressing individual revolts and uprisings (the so-called small wars, although no war feels small when you are in it), weeding out the slave trade, and trying to stop piracy. The heart of nineteenth-century piracy was in the waters between the South China Sea and the Bay of Bengal—essentially in and around the Strait of Malacca. Here again we see the strategic importance of geography, which allowed pirates the ability to build safe havens (much as we will see in the Caribbean) from which to operate beyond the reach of deeper-hulled warships. By 1824, the British and Dutch had reached an accommodation that included a stated intent to work together to reduce piracy and eliminate slavery.

This proved to be no easy task, as many of the pirate regimes were backed by city-states and countenanced by local rulers who would take a cut of the profits. Some operated from fairly large vessels that, when gathered together, could threaten any commercial ship and even some small warships. Some of the pirate fleets boasted hundreds of vessels of varying sizes and required real application of shipboard firepower to suppress. Hence these sea routes continued to be very dangerous throughout the region.

During this period, the British and the Dutch consolidated their colonial control of huge swaths of population and land. All of this had an extraordinary effect on the colonized populations, a phenomenon that is best understood on the British side—the rise of the culture of British India is still part of the DNA of modern India. Reading the superb novels of George MacDonald Fraser, four of which are set in and around India during this period, is not only entertaining but also reasonably historically accurate. Centered on a British officer named Flashman, they show the dark side of colonization in vivid anecdote. The first of the series, *Flashman*, is set in India and today's Pakistan/Afghanistan region as Flashman is an appointed official with the East India Company in 1839. Over the next twenty years, he goes to sea to rescue his wife from pirates (*Flashman's Lady*) and survives the Sepoy Mutiny (*Flashman in the Great Game*), among other adventures. I have read them all over the years, and for a view of how disturbing the colonization of the Indian Ocean littoral must have been for the indigenous populations, they are hard to beat.

The strategic motif of trade as the central focus continued throughout the nineteenth century, with coffee and spices continuing but with the additional inclusion of sugar, cotton, tea, and rubber feeding back to the Industrial Revolution in Europe. The critical ports and territories gradually accrued to the British: Kenya, Somaliland, Sudan, Egypt, Oman, Bahrain, Qatar, Kuwait, Iraq, Mauritius, India, and of course Singapore guarding the gates to the east. France had hung on to a scattering of islands including Madagascar, Réunion, and the Comoros, while Portugal still held Mozambique, East Timor, and the trading port of Goa on the Indian mainland. The Dutch held what is today Indonesia, styled as the Dutch East Indies. Even Italy found its way into the colonial scramble around the Indian Ocean with the acquisition of Eritrea and Somalia.

Throughout the nineteenth century, the advent of new technologies—notably the steam engine—coupled with the opening of the Suez Canal to vastly increase the movement of humans around the Indian Ocean. Indians and Chinese moved back and forth between their regions, and smaller groups of Malays, Indonesians, and Filipinos were moved as low-cost labor: slaves by another name, living under brutal conditions of indenture. Such workers were used on plantations under conditions of complete penury to the benefit of colonial businesses.

In addition to the movement of indentured laborers, another dark side of the trade routes across the Indian Ocean during the nineteenth century was the movement of opium. It was produced in India and Java to feed the markets of China, a trade encouraged by the colonizing powers. This led to the 1839 First Opium War between Great Britain and the Qing dynasty of China. Both Singapore and Hong Kong were central to the highly profitable opium trade.

As the century concluded and the European world headed toward the "dimming of the lights" with the coming of World War I, the changes across the entire Indian littoral were immense. Most important were the movement of workers and the entrenchment of significant colonial regimes throughout the region. Surprisingly, there had not been an outbreak of major great-power combat, and World War I would have little lasting effect on the Indian Ocean—it would be as distant thunder. But of course what lay ahead for the region was the Second World War and its attendant effects—violence, especially on the northeast corner of the

Indian Ocean in Burma and down the Malay Peninsula—but above all the end of colonization.

As World War II loomed on the horizon, British planners understood the vulnerability of the Indian Ocean to Japanese attack, either overland or via the sea. But they thought Singapore would hold, preventing easy maritime access, and the huge distances and the need for Japan to subdue and hold China seemed to mitigate the overall threat. It is easy to understand why the British thought Singapore—the "Lion City"—would hold out against the Japanese onslaught. It has strong geography that ought to favor a determined defender (it lies on an island, for example), and at that point in the conflict, the British still believed that their military simply had better discipline, skills, and technology than the Japanese. They were terribly wrong, and the city fell into Japanese hands on February 15, 1942. It was held until the surrender of Japan in 1945.

I first sailed into Singapore in the mid-1980s, and even then it was a clean, technologically advanced, multicultural city, which used a combination of strong social networking, enlightened racial and educational policies, strict policing, economic incentives, and political control to build a powerhouse city-state out of virtually nothing but raw geography and human capital. Under an inspired leader, Lee Kuan Yew, Singapore has emerged as a showcase city, easily ranking at the top of all social and economic indices in Asia and in the top ten in the world. As I walked around the city looking for a place to play squash (and found one at the "American Club"), I was struck by the incredible contrast with every other major Asian city at that time. It was scrupulously clean, full of public gardens, signed in English (the lingua franca of this most multicultural city-state), and very, very law abiding. Like most tourists of that time, I went to Raffles Bar (named for Sir Stamford Raffles, the founder of the trading post which evolved into modern Singapore) and had a too sweet Singapore sling, a sappy cocktail.

But what is really striking about the city is its geopolitical position. Sitting astride the most important shipping strait in the world, defended by water on all sides, blessed with a fine dockyard and a now-powerful military, Singapore is a good country to have on your side. The United States has a very close relationship with the highly professional Singapore military, and my work with them in the Arabian Gulf on the maritime side over the years left a deep impression on me as to the seriousness with which they take their defense. Given their enviable position, they need a strong military and strong friends as well.

Since that first visit, I have returned to Singapore many times. The most illuminating visit was in the mid-2000s when I served as the senior military assistant to Secretary of Defense Donald Rumsfeld. We went to see the former prime minister, Lee Kuan Yew. It is hard to describe how he is viewed there—sort of George Washington and Abraham Lincoln together, with a little Franklin Delano Roosevelt thrown in. At that point in time he was in his eighties and Secretary Rumsfeld was in his seventies. A former prime minister and nation founder meeting with a two-time secretary of defense, White House chief of staff, and ambassador and having a long cordial conversation. To see these two lions in winter, in the City of Lions, spar about the world was extraordinary. What they agreed upon was that it takes discipline, vision, and some tough decisions to build something lasting. Hard to argue with that, and the nation of Singapore is a pretty accurate reflection of that approach. And the food was a lot better than on my first trip.

All of that modernization came long after the fall of Singapore to the Japanese in 1942, which opened up the broader Indian Ocean to the Japanese war machine. Their naval planners were beginning to think about campaigns—both overland and at sea—that would cut India itself off from the British Empire. Meanwhile, both Italy and Germany mounted maritime campaigns throughout the northern Indian Ocean.

While the Italian forces, operating mainly off the coast of East Africa, were soon neutralized, the Germans continued significant U-boat operations throughout the war. In addition to the German submarines, Nazi surface ships—including the pocket battleship *Graf Spee*—conducted commerce raiding. The strategic theory was to cut off the sea lanes of communication between Britain and its colonies; destroy the general commerce in the region, which benefited not only the United Kingdom but also France and the Netherlands; prepare for further land operations; and conduct harassment against Australia. There were much fewer significant fleet-wide actions in the Indian Ocean than there were in the central and western Pacific, which was the main theater of war, but there were literally hundreds of single-ship and small-group combat operations throughout the region. Overall, operations were a draw, with both the Axis and the Allies having ships "at sea and operational" throughout the conflict.

FOLLOWING WORLD WAR II, the key geopolitical change in the Indian Ocean was the essential departure of the United Kingdom. The Indian Ocean had been largely a British protectorate for more than two hundred years as a result of the "jewel in the crown" of empire, the Imperial Raj of India. The ocean had been ringed by British colonies in East Africa, South Asia, and the western side of Southeast Asia. In today's world it is hard to imagine the power and scope of the British Empire globally in the Victorian era through the end of World War II. By 1968, Britain—which had never truly recovered as an imperial power after the war—made a strategic decision to withdraw "east of Aden" on the southwestern tip of the Arabian Peninsula. In practical terms this meant that a strategic vacuum would be created, just as the cold war began to truly unfold.

Nature abhors a vacuum, and when the British left the waters of the

Indian Ocean, the fleets of the United States and the Soviet Union arrived. Both nations decided to increase the levels of their patrols throughout the region, although their objectives differed. The United States wanted to maintain stability in a vast and now relatively ungoverned part of the global maritime commons; protect the flow of tankers providing needed oil to and from the Arabian Gulf; and ensure a ready, maritime-based supply of strategic minerals and materials—chromium, rare earths, cobalt, manganese, copper. For Russia (which had its own supply of oil from its huge reserves), the objective was first simply to compete with the United States for political influence among the nations of the region and to maintain a strategic partnership with India, which it saw as a potential counterbalance to NATO.

Although today we think instinctively of the Arabian Gulf in terms of the supply of oil globally, it is important to remember that all of those nations did not become major producers until the mid-twentieth century. As other sources of oil ran down, the percentage of oil held in the Gulf region, Iran, and Iraq soared (all this before the advent of a great deal of offshore oil and the use of fracking, of course). This made the region of extreme importance strategically, with tankers departing the Gulf many times an hour and the nations of the region developing OPEC to control the price and quantity of oil on the market. All of this contributed to the strategic importance of the region and in a maritime context to the vital protection of the Gulf region. American war planners were concerned that the Soviet Union might make a play to drive south or at a minimum to achieve warm-water ports on the Indian Ocean—something that history has not shown persuasively to be the case, although it was a commonly held view at the time.

Of note, by the early 1970s neither the United States nor the Soviets had any actual naval bases in the region. The Soviets had a treaty with Iraq that gave them access at Basra, and the United States maintained a very small naval force in Bahrain (only three warships and a generally unhappy two-star admiral, pondering the reasons for his exile). As the importance of the flow of oil increased, the nations in the region began to think about how to improve their geographic and strategic positions. And both nations sought to marginalize China, which for two millennia had been an important player in the Indian Ocean but which neither the United States nor the Soviet Union wanted to see in the region then.

The United States throughout this period cooperated closely with Saudi Arabia and Pakistan (as it does today, of course) as well as with Iran under the shah. Both nations received billions of dollars of training and equipment from the United States (paying for almost all of it from their oil revenues). The United States also exploited the British-owned island in the center of the Indian Ocean, Diego Garcia, where U.S. engineers in the early 1970s built a huge airstrip, massive fuel tanks, significant docks, housing, communications, and intelligence-gathering facilities.

In the mid-1980s, about a decade later, I sailed into the lagoon at Diego Garcia, not quite sure what to expect. A standing joke in the Navy among junior officers was that if you screwed up badly enough, you'd be sent to either Adak, Alaska, or Diego Garcia in the Indian Ocean. From what I had heard, I would have requested Adak. But when we arrived ashore, I found an intriguing and not uncomfortable environment: nice barracks ashore, primitive but acceptable golf and tennis facilities, a small but decent officers' club, and a place of incredible natural beauty. That it was the strategic hub of the Indian Ocean didn't dawn on me, but I sure enjoyed hitting some tennis balls after a few long and boring weeks at sea sailing from Singapore.

The Soviets, on the other hand, worked to conduct frequent "show the flag" cruises throughout the region—to Sri Lanka, Iraq, Iran, Yemen, Pakistan, and of course to India. Over time, the Soviets were able to develop cooperation agreements with India, Yemen, and—on the east coast of Africa—Somalia. As a result, they had access to ports for their warships, with supplies and logistics as well. All of this in accordance with the Mahanian doctrine of sea power both nations followed.

Both nations competed for influence and control over two perceived "treasure houses," as Soviet leader Leonid Brezhnev called them: the energy and oil of the Gulf and the strategic minerals of sub-Saharan Africa. The breakdown for the United States was the collapse of the shah's regime in Iran and the rise of the Ayatollah Khomeini's government, which truly, madly, deeply, hated the United States. This effectively closed off one side of the Arabian Gulf (this was the time we switched to calling it "Arabian Gulf" instead of what we had historically called it, the "Persian Gulf"). It also put a bitter enemy in effective control of the entrance to the Gulf, the Strait of Hormuz.

The Soviets had several successes in this period as well. The Soviet adventures in southern Africa, both in Angola and Mozambique, were initially successful (especially with Cuban troops fighting alongside the Soviets in Angola) and two new client states emerged. And when Somalia and Ethiopia went to war in 1977, the Soviets shifted sides and pocketed a strong relationship with Ethiopia (more than 30 million people) at the cost of betraying the smaller nation of Somalia. Yemen also became a Marxist state. Suddenly, the only major client of the United States was Saudi Arabia, and the Soviets were picking up relationships, bases, and political support around the rest of the Indian Ocean littoral. As a theater of political cold war, the Indian Ocean looked very much like a Soviet win.

In the complex geopolitics of today's world, perhaps the two most dangerous state-on-state confrontations exist around the littoral of the Indian Ocean and the Arabian Gulf. We discussed the Arabian Gulf "twilight war" between Saudi Arabia and Iran earlier in this chapter, but the most dangerous of all—because of the availability of nuclear weapons—is the cold war between Indian and Pakistan. The British departure from the South Asian subcontinent after World War II eventually led to the division of that vast region into three nations: Pakistan, the second most populous Muslim nation in the world; India, which will soon overtake China as the world's most populous state (and possessor of the third largest Muslim population, by the way); and Bangladesh. The Indian-Pakistani hatreds are deep-seated and are partly religious, partly cultural, and partly geographic (with the flash point of the disputed Kashmir region at their tactical heart).

While the divisions between India and Pakistan seem insurmountable at the moment, there is at least a ray of hope in the conversations between Nawaz Sharif of Pakistan and Narendra Modi of India. The United States has a vital interest (as does the entire world) in avoiding a nuclear confrontation between these two states. While their disputes do not typically unfold at sea, it is entirely possible that an incident could cause a flare-up at any point. This is the most dangerous aspect of the Indian Ocean, which has been generally a commercial and not a war-fighting body of water.

One tragic incident that illustrates that not all problems are man-made was the devastating tsunami that struck much of the Indian Ocean littoral in 2004 on the day after Christmas. A 9.0 undersea earthquake off the west coast of Indonesia caused it, and the resulting tidal waves almost instantly killed well over 200,000 people. Some estimates of total deaths rise to nearly 300,000, concentrated in Indonesia, Sri Lanka, India, and Thailand. The waves were as high as one hundred feet in places as they crested across densely populated portions of those nations. I had only recently assumed duties as the senior military assistant to the secretary of defense, and we quickly assembled a crisis action team in the Pentagon to see what the Department of Defense could do.

We put a superb U.S. Marine general, Lieutenant General Rusty Blackman, in charge of the response, and he swiftly marshaled the huge logistic, humanitarian, and medical capability of the department. Conducting daily video-teleconferences with the secretary, he was able to get U.S. hospital ships, big-deck amphibious vessels, and aircraft on scene and dispensing aid and assistance to the various devastated populations. As I watched night after night in the command center in the Pentagon the videos of our sailors, Marines, airmen, and soldiers wading into water to rescue people, moving huge bags of relief supplies, and caring for the wounded and the sick, I was deeply moved. We spend a great deal of time in the military conducting lethal combat operations—that is who we are. But we also can deploy soft power in massive ways that can make a real difference in the world. And the result—a changed view of our nation—is so often the way we can create real security over the long haul. In some ways, the deployment of our massive, 60,000-ton hospital ships, *Mercy* and *Comfort*, can do more for our security than the combat cruises of our nuclear aircraft carriers. Both have a role, and our ability to balance both hard power (combat) and soft power (disaster relief, medical assistance, diplomacy) has been called "smart power." An apt term, and it came home to me in the Indian Ocean during those terrible weeks after a quarter of a million people died on the television screens before our eyes.

Piracy was part of the mission set I inherited in 2009 when I became the Supreme Allied Commander for NATO. The twenty-eight nations of NATO had collectively voted to join the effort to stop the worst of the piracy that was emanating from the largely ungoverned space of what had once been Somalia. Fueled by khat, a soporific drug they would chew, Somali ex-fishermen would mount skiffs and set out to take down large container ships by scaling the sides, overpowering the crew, and then sailing the ships into Somali anchorages and demanding ransoms of millions of dollars. As I took over the mission, there were nearly twenty ships and more than two hundred mariners held hostage, and the number of assaults was rising.

The international community cannot agree on much, but on the view of piracy as an ancient scourge that is punishable by any sovereign nation there is universal agreement. Therefore, my task was to gain additional resources and warships from a broader coalition than just the twenty-eight NATO nations. We cast a wide net, including some traditionally non-NATO-aligned countries: Russia, China, India, Pakistan, and Iran all responded in a positive way—either sending ships, participating with intelligence, or at a minimum providing logistic and refueling support. This was quite unprecedented: a grand nautical coalition that included the United States and Canada from North America, more than thirty European nations, and five aforementioned countries that do not wake up in the morning looking for ways to cooperate with NATO.

Thus we saw in the Indian Ocean a good example of a strategic approach that provides a means to cobble together nations that are normally at one another's throats. That we could in the process significantly knock down piracy was equally good. By 2013, as I was departing NATO, we had just a couple of ships and a small handful of mariners still being held. The bottom had been knocked out of the piracy business, and many of the pirates had been apprehended and remanded to justice. Not a single ship has been pirated at sea off the coast of East Africa in the past couple of years. Partly, this is because of progress ashore as well, fueled by the good work of the European Union. But in terms of reducing piracy in a region of the world that has seen it often, this is a rare good story of coordination at sea, and full of lessons for seeking other zones of cooperation on the world's oceans.

. . .

To summarize: Throughout this book and in our world, discussions about maritime issues tend to focus on the Atlantic Ocean, with its attached Mediterranean Sea; and the Pacific Ocean, with the South China Sea. There are endless discussions about the emerging conflicts, the flow of refugees, and competition over vital hydrocarbons, as well as the geopolitical impact of the two "major oceans." Yet the twenty-first century will be more about the Indian Ocean than either of the other two—and the sooner we fully realize that in the United States, the better.

We cannot forget the facts of the case: The Indian Ocean, while admittedly smaller than the Atlantic or the Pacific, consists of nearly a quarter of the waters on the globe, especially when one counts its major subordinate seas, the Red Sea and the Arabian Gulf. Across its vast expanse move 50 percent of all shipping and containers and 70 percent of all oil, making it quite literally the crossroads of globalization. Nearly forty nations border it, with more than a third of the world's population. And it is the beating heart of the Islamic world, with Pakistan, Indonesia, Bangladesh, Iran, Saudi Arabia, Egypt, and the Gulf States all having coastal access to the Indian Ocean. More than 90 percent of the world's Islamic population is in this massive catchment basin.

And it is highly militarized and constantly in a high state of tension. The highest potential nuclear conflict in the world today is between Pakistan and India—two huge, capable, professional, and nuclear-capable militaries. Iran is an adventurist state with an innovative and battle-trained military force. Many of the other nations along the littoral have internal conflicts and significant chaos along their borders, particularly in East Africa. Piracy, while reduced over the past several years, remains a threat both along the coast of East Africa and in the Strait of Malacca connecting the Indian Ocean with the Pacific.

The history of the Indian Ocean certainly does not inspire confidence in the potential for peaceful governance in the twenty-first century. As we have seen, throughout the centuries its trade routes have inspired competition and conflict since East met West with the arrival of Vasco da Gama in 1497. The British conquest of India and the commercial muscle of the British East India Company dominated the region for a time in the nineteenth century, but the breakup of the Ottoman Empire and great-power maneuvering during World War II led into the long twilight of the cold war when American, Soviet, Pakistani, and Indian vessels played cat and mouse.

There are other flashpoints centered in the Indian Ocean beyond India and Pakistan. There is no love lost between China and India in the region, particularly as China continues to expand its commercial influence and basing throughout the Indian Ocean littoral. There is piratical activity along the East African littoral and throughout the western Indonesian archipelago. In the Arabian/Persian Gulf, the Sunni-Shi'a conflict continues to play out at sea as it does ashore. Yemen is on fire in a manifestation of Sunni-Shi'a conflict as Houthi rebels seek dominance of the poverty-stricken nation. Much of this is well documented in Robert Kaplan's superb treatment of the region, *Monsoon: The Indian Ocean and the Future of American Power.*

The salient question for the United States is simple: What is our role? How can we help create U.S. security and stability in the global oceanic commons upon which we depend for so much of our international trade?

First, we must recognize the vital importance of the Indian Ocean itself. On our maps and globes, it tends to be depicted as split (in order to give primacy to "our" oceans, the Atlantic and Pacific). Our strategic and geopolitical mental map reflects this, and in all of our thinking—from the Pentagon to our Fortune 500 companies to our academic and humanitarian institutions—we should consciously consider the importance of this vast body of water and its littoral nations.

Second, we must consider India. It will soon overtake China as the world's most populous nation, it is led by a dynamic and globally oriented leader in Prime Minister Modi, its lingua franca is English, and—above all—it is a vibrant, legitimate democracy with whom we share fundamental values. Too often in the international conferences I attend all over the world we end up discussing China, the United States, and the European Union—important to be sure—but never even mention India. In this century, the rise of India may be the most important single geopolitical driver, and its engagement in the Indian Ocean will be an enormous part of that.

Third, we must deploy and operate in the region with all of our forces. This most obviously requires a strong and deployable Navy and Air Force, but the Army and Marines have work to do as well. The Department of Defense should be building more exercises in the region like the Exercise Malabar, which brought U.S., Indian, and Japanese forces together in naval exercises.

Fourth, we should continue the global counterpiracy campaign, which has shown real success off the coast of East Africa. When we can bring together not only NATO, European, and Asian allies but also Russia, China, India, Pakistan, and Iran, there are few things we cannot successfully do. Within the turbulence of the Indian Ocean, counterpiracy operations are something almost everyone can agree upon—we can help lead that effort.

Fifth, one enormous key to unlocking the potential of the region is solving two difficult challenges: the Indian-Pakistani conflict, centered on the disputed Kashmir but in reality the result of religious, cultural, and historical differences; and the Shi'a-Sunni divide, which continues to make the Arabian Gulf volatile. These are long-term challenges, but whatever U.S. diplomacy can do to reduce tensions and avoid open confrontation will be helpful.

Sixth, the Arabian Gulf will not simply be a "lesser but included" subset of the Indian Ocean. Because of its particular place as the fault line between the Sunni and Shi'a worlds, it will demand a significant level of U.S. involvement in order to fulfill our objectives there: freedom of the high seas and an open sea lane of communication through the Strait of Hormuz, particularly for oil; capable allies in the Sunni Arab world, led by Saudi Arabia; a functioning modus vivendi with Iran; and an environmentally safe region given the high potential for ecological disasters.

In 2016, we saw several incidents of U.S. warships involved in disturbing scenarios in and around both the Arabian Gulf and the Indian Ocean. There is today a particularly high general state of tension with Iran at sea, in spite of the negotiated nuclear arms agreement. Since the agreement and the lifting of sanctions, Iranian naval forces—and particularly the Revolutionary Guard—have become emboldened. In January 2016, they came upon two U.S. Navy riverine craft operating innocently in their waters (one had broken down, the other was helping, and both had poor navigation and communication equipment readiness). In a violation of international law and seafaring custom, the U.S. Navy sailors were not assisted but instead were disarmed, put into humiliating stress positions, and taken into port. The Iranians used video of the sailors to further humiliate them, in direct contravention of international norms.

Late in 2016, U.S. Navy destroyers operating in international waters off the coast of Yemen were attacked by cruise missiles fired by Houthi rebels, who probably had Iranian training, targeting, and concurrence, considering the staunch Iranian support for the Houthis. Both incidents are harbingers of much more tension to come, particularly in the Arabian Gulf, but also in the northern Indian Ocean.

Above all, we simply need to factor the huge Indian Ocean and the smaller but vital Arabian Gulf fully into our thinking—they must not be forgotten as we sail into the twenty-first century. There will clearly be greater impact from this heretofore less noticed but still enormous body of water, and sailors will find the Indian Ocean far less domesticated than its twin cousins, the Atlantic and Pacific. How the geopolitics of the Indian Ocean unfolds will be a crucial vector for the overall trends of twenty-first-century geopolitics.

4.

THE MEDITERRANEAN

WHERE WAR AT SEA BEGAN

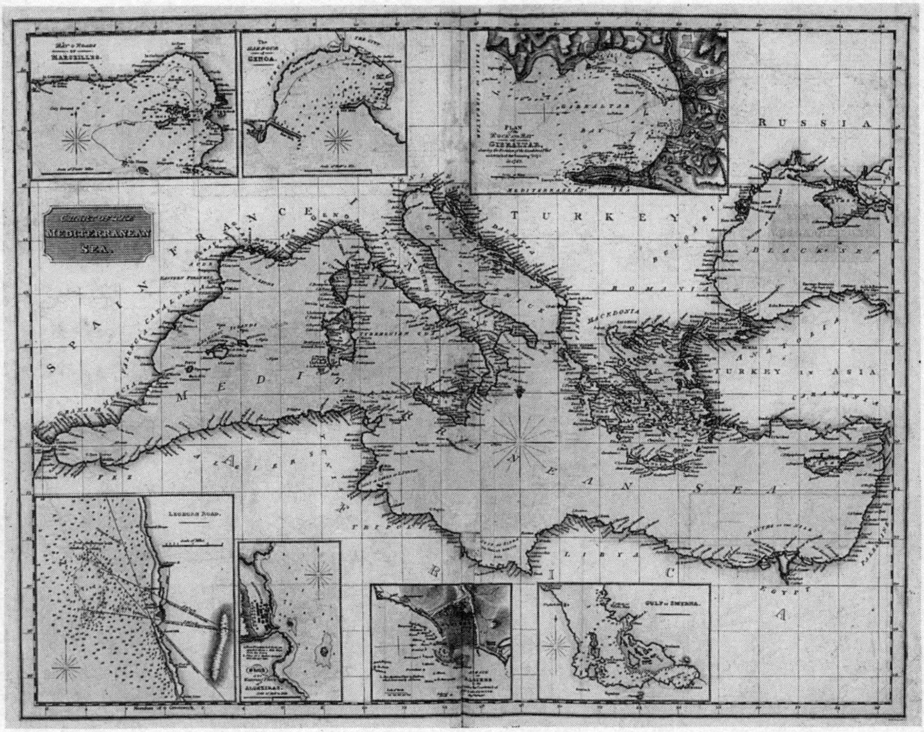

The Mediterranean was the source of the Western world's best sailors for millennia. *Map created by Samuel John Neele, 1817.*

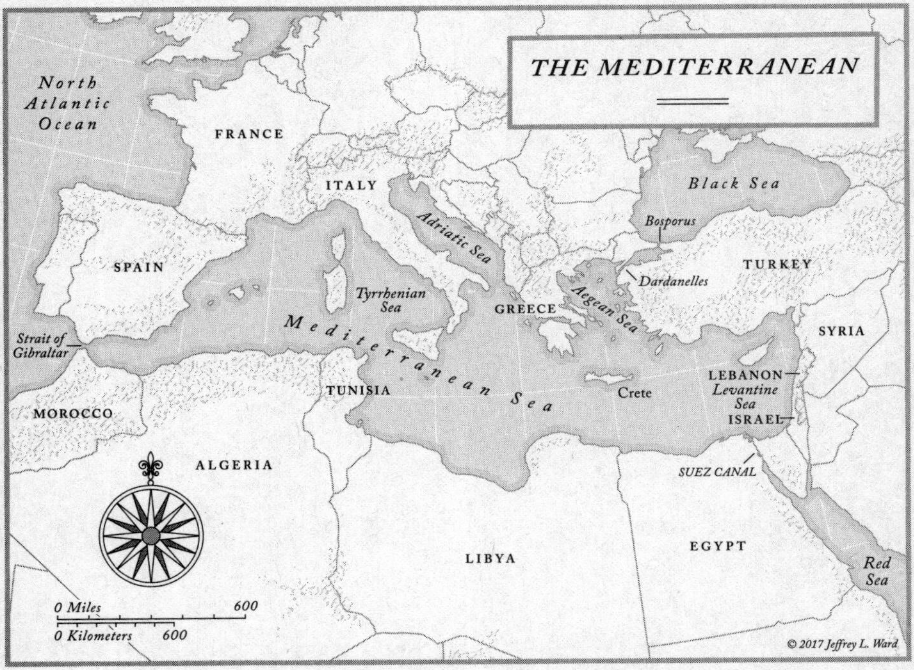

With frictions over natural resources and migration resurfacing, the recent peaceful history of the Mediterranean is under threat.

Mankind's geopolitical journey upon the seas began in earnest on the waters of the Mediterranean. Through the centuries of man's sailing across the ocean's waves, it was in the Mediterranean Sea that sailors created and then perfected the idea of war at sea. As a result, no other body of water can lay claim to such a central place in early global history—at least when it comes to war. If the remains of long-dead mariners were suddenly to float unencumbered to the surface, you could easily walk the length of the Mediterranean over the bones of warriors who died at sea.

The Med is close to a million square miles in area, more than 2,400 miles from east to west, and is spread out along 23,000 long miles of coastline. Yet the opening strait, the only part that links the Med to the vast Atlantic Ocean, is less than ten miles wide at the highly strategic Strait of Gibraltar—which was known to the Greeks and Romans as the Pillars of Hercules.

Another way to think about the size of the Mediterranean would be to imagine the Med superimposed over a map of the United States. The

Strait of Gibraltar would be roughly where San Diego is located on the West Coast. The Suez Canal and the approaches to the Red Sea would be on the northeast coast of Florida, near Jacksonville. The top of the Adriatic Sea would be almost to the Canadian border, just west of the Great Lakes; and the Libyan Gulf of Sidra would touch the Gulf of Mexico. Highway 66, stretching all across the United States, would fit from east to west. This is a big body of water, to state the obvious.

And most important, it has a series of fateful geographic features that appear again and again in the long throw of Mediterranean history: the narrowness of the opening in the west, of course, but also the enormous central importance of the largest island, Sicily—a prize over which nations have fought for more than three thousand years. Likewise, the dagger of Italy thrusting toward Africa and effectively bifurcating the Med is a geographic feature that will continue to make itself known. Its length and central position, with excellent ports both east and west, gave rise to Roman trade and enabled its sea power through the long Pax Romana. And to the south of Sicily, its smaller but almost equally strategic cousin Malta will appear repeatedly in the strategic drama of the Med.

Continuing east, the rocky island terrain of the Aegean has been a maritime battleground that echoes today as Greek and Turkish warships and aircraft conduct a delicate dance of confrontation that seems to belie their common NATO alliance membership and reminds us of Christian and Muslim hatreds from a thousand years ago that drove events through the eastern Med. Here the key islands are Cyprus, dominating the approaches to the Levant, and Crete, long and bulky, guarding the entrances to the Aegean.

To the north of course is the Black Sea, truly deserving of its own place in the books of history, but forever serving as a sort of "Med in miniature" through the millennia, with many of the same conflicts playing out north of the strategic passage of the Bosporus. And to the south, the flat terrain of the North African desert, the rich delta of the Nile, and the harsh land crossing the Suez all play a continuing part in the history, politics, and culture of the Med.

The name of the sea itself derives from the Latin word *mediterraneus*, which can be translated as "inland" or as the "middle place between the land." The Romans thought of it, appropriately, as the mare nostrum, "our sea." From the beginning of recorded Western history, it functioned as a sort of global commons in a relatively confined space, providing a path for trade, an accessible source of protein, a field of transport, a ready battlefield, and a natural barrier.

And it supplied much to the imagination of man as well. As the geography of the Mediterranean gradually revealed itself through the centuries, the legends grew of what lay beyond the Strait of Gibraltar. Dragons, sea monsters, the gates to Hades, the lost city of Atlantis—all occupied a place in popular imagination and culture. Rowing their graceful and reasonably reliable triremes, ancient sailors seldom chose to venture beyond the Strait of Gibraltar, where fear of the unknown held sway.

The Med has also played a central role in both the development of war-fighting technology and the creation of maritime strategy. As the ancients gazed on the Med, they quickly developed seagoing means to do what they already did ashore: fight. The Med gave war the battering rams and multilayered oars of the triremes; the use of marines—essentially specially trained soldiers bred to fight on the waves; accurate cannons and early fire control systems; new means of propulsion, as sailing became vastly more sophisticated; and the application of steam, combustion engines, and eventually nuclear power. Each of the advances in combat at sea was tested, refined, and put to brutal use in the Med.

For a modern Navy sailor, the first sense you feel passing through the

Strait of Gibraltar coming into the Med is one of entering an ancient arena of battle. You feel hemmed in and closed off, something a sailor hates. When sailors part, in addition to wishing each other the common "fair winds and following seas," they will sometimes say, "Godspeed and open water." In the Med, you feel surrounded by history and somehow enfolded by the past, with not much obvious open water around—not a good feeling.

I remember the first time I sailed a warship into the Mediterranean as a junior officer in the early 1980s—on the massive American aircraft carrier USS *Forrestal* (CV-59). Named for the first secretary of defense of the United States, James Forrestal, the ship was a floating city full of planes and bombs. It probably carried as much combat power in the high-performance aircraft on its decks as the entire Roman Empire could bring to bear.

My job as an engineer kept me belowdecks much of the time, but when I ventured up to the hangar deck and then to the bridge as we sailed through the Strait of Gibraltar, I was struck by the small scale of the waterway with land close at hand on both sides. We passed through late on a summer's evening, and the sea was beautiful, flat and calm. The Med is famously fickle in its weather, and it is a wise sailor who remembers the long voyage home by Odysseus to his home island of Ithaca from the Trojan War: a mix of beautiful sailing punctuated by terrible storms and disasters every time he and his crew ventured ashore.

Wherever we went in the Med that summer, we had gorgeous weather; but as the fall descended, the days shortened and the weather chilled. The mistrals of winter—the great storms of the Med—were coming, and you could feel it not only in the surface of the sea and the great clouds above, but in the attitudes of the people in the ancient port cities we visited in the course of that long cruise. The French say a good mistral will blow the ears off a donkey—it will certainly make a ship rock and roll across the Med. The sense of history in every port—Athens, Istanbul, Tel Aviv, Alexandria, Syracuse, Naples, Cartagena, Tunis, and on and on—was palpable. The cold war, in full bloom in those long ago days, seemed a logical enough backdrop to our warship's voyage.

It also reinforced for me the various strategic geographical divisions in the Med. In the 1980s, at the height of the cold war, the United States tried to keep two carrier battle groups on call in the Mediterranean. One was typically in the western Med, with access to allied ports, easier logistics, and the ancient Roman ports on the coasts of Spain and Italy. A series of bases kept U.S. warships well supplied. In the eastern Med, it was another story. There was a great deal of Russian influence in Libya and Syria, and we often passed close aboard Russian flotillas. Our smaller ships would make their way up into the Black Sea, that miniature battle zone, knowing that if hostilities broke out, our strikes against the USSR and its Warsaw Pact allies would make the Black Sea a death trap for U.S. warships. While thankfully we never went to war with the USSR, it was clear that operations in the Med were going to be a very dangerous proposition. We were a long way from home, facing a powerful local opponent—much as the Venetians must have felt as they sailed under Ottoman guns centuries earlier.

The real question that kept occurring to me was simple: Why was the Mediterranean such an early crucible of war and conquest?

First is its location as a watery crossroads between competing civilizations.

Maritime geopolitics was born on the Mediterranean in the early battles between the Greeks and Persians, the Phoenicians and the Romans. As mankind started to ply the waters of the Med, vastly different civilizations came into contact—Europe, Africa, and Asia—and along with the exchange of trade, language, people, and other sources of wealth came conflict. The Med was simply an enabler of it all.

Consider the geography of the Med, sitting as it does in a central position among competing societies and nations. Like spokes on a wheel, the key sea lanes of communication across the Med provided access to invading fleets. As early civilizations found their way to the Med, it was easy for adventurous kings and queens and emperors and pharaohs to envision using the water as a means to transport conquering fleets, ships bristling with soldiers, empty holds aching to be filled with treasure and slaves. And the natural geographic divisions—Italy most of all—create smaller individual zones in which to fight.

Second, the Med is dotted with highly strategic islands. Sicily, Sardinia, Malta, Crete, the Aegean littoral islands—all provide convenient stepping-stones. As various empires consolidated and rose in importance, the battle for strategic landholdings in the Med rose as well. This created a second wave of conflict and enabled bases from which fleets could operate with impunity.

It is worth remembering that even as both trade and war increased across the Med, there were many natural challenges that the ancients had to overcome. For starters, the weather is not easy. While the Med is generally a relatively benign environment in which to sail, it can be unpredictable and unforgiving to the unwary mariner. Second, the technology of navigating deep ocean sailing, out of sight of land, had to be developed over several centuries. Third, the ability to build strong and capable ships that could reliably sail over days and weeks was created over time through trial and error, and much loss of life. But as mankind honed the ability to go to sea, navigate effectively, and fight, the Mediterranean began to function in earnest as a kind of Thunder Dome or fighting cage, where two warring nations entered and often only one emerged.

. . .

THE FIRST TWO CIVILIZATIONS to make their mark at sea have both largely vanished: the Minoan Empire, centered on the island of Crete, which flourished for nearly a thousand years beginning in 2500 B.C.; and the Phoenician/Carthaginian Empire, which was destroyed by the Romans more than two thousand years ago in the world's first fight to the death between two relatively advanced societies.

The Cretans (roughly 2500 to 1200 B.C.) were forced to turn to the sea by a growing population four and a half millennia ago. They were natural sailors, and found many islands north of Crete over which they soon held sway. The relatively less advanced mainland Greek societies were forced to pay tribute to the Minoan kings, including sending tributes of young men and women to perform with the bulls in the capital of Knossos. Their story is part of the enduring legends of Greece, including the killing by the young prince Theseus of the Minotaur, a mythical creature that was half bull, half man, and to whom the tributes were sacrificed. Much of their society was probably destroyed more than three thousand years ago by an earthquake that has given rise to the legend of the destruction of the lost city of Atlantis.

I remember sitting in a small café on Crete several years ago on a lovely summer's night, enjoying a meal of grilled fish and Greek wine in the modern city of Chania, the second largest on the island. My host was a Greek general who led their armed forces as part of the NATO alliance for which I was serving as Supreme Allied Commander.

We chatted a bit about the Minoans, and he opined that if their society had survived, the Greek world would have expanded and dominated the Med much as the Romans later did. When I offered that the Greek mainland city-states could never have banded together to conquer others, his response was simple: that was exactly what the Cretans could have done—forced them to work together. Perhaps. A different twist of the historical DNA, and a Greco-Cretan empire shimmers in the distance, challenging the Romans, perhaps alongside the Carthaginians. Who knows?

At the eastern end of the Med, along the present-day Levant, the Phoenician civilization began about 3000 B.C. and lasted some 2,500 years. Principally traders (as opposed to conquerors), the Phoenicians sailed throughout the known world. Their ships carried tin from Britain, amber and precious stones from the Baltic, as well as spices, slaves, and gold from western Africa. Their intrepid traders sailed beyond the Pillars of Hercules and began the first series of connections between the Mediterranean civilizations and India, operating out of their key ports of Tyre and Sidon. Phoenician trading ports began to dot the islands and the mainland of the Med, and one center began to rise in power on the southern rim of the sea in what is today Tunisia: Carthage.

The Carthaginians, descended from Phoenician stock, eventually created an empire that stretched over the key islands of Sardinia, Corsica, and Sicily as well as much of Spain and great stretches of coastal Africa along the Med. A tough-minded, harsh, and capable people, the Carthaginians competed alongside the early Greek traders (who pushed them out of the Black Sea and the Aegean early on) and finally would end up in a climactic series of wars with the Romans centuries later.

Perhaps the earliest "clash of civilizations" (to take a phrase from the late contemporary political scientist Samuel Huntington) was likewise across the eastern Mediterranean—between the Greek mainland city-states and the world-dominating empire of Persia. Surprisingly, the

Greeks managed to stop their fractious internal wars long enough to face the Persian onslaught roughly five hundred years before the birth of Christ.

The Persians had at this point in their long history conquered much of the civilized world, and had expanded control from their bases in Mesopotamia to the shores of the Med. The Phoenicians in the Levant immediately capitulated and were able to provide ships and expertise in all things navigational to their new Persian masters. The Greeks, of course, pursued a different course and fought hard.

By 492 B.C., the first Persian expedition arrived in Greece, but luckily for the Greeks, it was struck by a massive and disastrous storm. A second try also failed as an amphibious attack at Marathon ended in a significant defeat for the Persians. But the Persians were persistent and determined, and they regrouped over the next decade to finally return with what they considered overwhelming force.

Persian king Xerxes brought nearly 1,500 fighting ships, almost 200,000 foot soldiers, and more than 100,000 sailors, marines, and rowers around 480 B.C.: a seemingly invincible force. The Greeks at this point were able to muster only around 500 ships, and were significantly outnumbered both at sea and on land. When the death stand of the "three hundred Spartans" at Thermopylae failed to halt the marching hordes, the last chance of the Greeks depended on the Athenian fleet, which would fight in its home waters.

Led by the courageous and charismatic admiral Themistocles, the Greeks used the natural terrain of the craggy waters surrounding Athens to position their fleet to best advantage in Salamis Bay, just off the coast of Athens. Civilization in Greece was at stake.

The key, in the end, was freedom. Each of the Greeks was a free man, fighting for his family and his city-state. Virtually all of the Persians were conscripts or slaves. Themistocles gathered his sailors and marines around him the night before the climactic battle and challenged them.

Based on the description of the speech by the Greek historian Herodotus, we believe that Themistocles exhorted his men to row for their parents, to row for their wives and their children, to row for their city, and above all to row for freedom. They did, and their motivation and bravery—coupled with superior technology in the form of swifter, leaner, lighter galleys—carried the day.

I have told that story many times, to many different audiences, and it never fails to create a sense in the room of the power of today's all-volunteer military. At a dinner in New York City onboard the museum ship *Intrepid* a few years ago, I told it in honor of Navy SEAL Lieutenant Michael Murphy, who died in Afghanistan and was awarded the Medal of Honor for his heroic sacrifices on behalf of his men, his family (who were present at the speech), and ultimately his nation. Today a beautiful Navy destroyer, USS *Michael Murphy* (DDG-112), sails the oceans. I like to think you could drop a plumb line from the ancient free Greeks at Salamis Bay to Michael Murphy's ship—having in common their courage, honor, and commitment.

With the Athenian- and Spartan-led Greek victory, a sort of potential golden age shimmered before the Greeks; but they quickly squandered it by returning to what they did with the greatest gusto—fighting with one another. Thus the Greeks, despite all of their access to the Med and their highly capable militaries, were unable to truly push outward on the seas to create a significant empire (beyond conquering parts of Sicily and some other shoreline areas). It was the Romans who truly created the "inner sea" and ruled its complete periphery with extraordinary effect for centuries.

THE ROMANS ROSE IN POWER as the Greek city-states sought to maintain control of the waters between Sicily and southern Italy and as the young Carthaginian Empire was expanding from the North African shore. Rome faced competition from both, and as they consolidated their power in the third century before Christ, the Romans overwhelmed the Greeks who ruled small colonies ashore on the Italian peninsula. Across the Med, the watchful Carthaginians sensed the confrontation to come, and the island of Sicily became the first point of confrontation in what came to be known as the Punic Wars (named for the Latin word for Carthaginian).

Once again, the Med became a massive battlefield as the previously land-oriented Romans recognized the need to build a fleet. Their coasts were vulnerable to the traditionally seafaring Carthaginians, and their seaborne commerce was a rich source of plunder that was highly vulnerable to their enemy's capable fleets. Turning to the conquered Greeks, the Romans were able to acquire a fleet—but they lacked the knowledge of how to fight at sea. They were experts at raising an army and conducting combat hand to hand, but at first were not able to bring their approach to bear against the nimble Carthaginian fleet tacticians, who were masters of flanking, breaking through an enemy's ship line, and above all ramming and sinking enemy ships through superior ship handling.

As would often be the case in war at sea, the answer was to invent a new tactic, technique, or piece of equipment: in this case the *corvus*. This was a kind of gangplank made of iron that could be pivoted and dropped athwart an enemy's deck. It had a gripping hook on the forward end, and soldiers could then surge across it to the opposing deck. In several major seagoing battles of the second century B.C., the Romans were able to use this crude but effective boarding tactic facilitated by the new equipment of the *corvus* to destroy large numbers of Carthaginian ships.

As the Roman-Carthaginian Punic Wars unfolded, over time it was the Roman mastery of the sea that led to the defeat of the Carthaginians. Despite the brilliance of the Carthaginian general Hannibal ashore, it was the ability of the Roman fleet to send a major army to North Africa that sounded the death knell of the Carthaginians in 146 B.C. In the end, it was mastering the Mediterranean Sea that provided Rome first the massive island of Sicily, then the rich raw materials of the Iberian Peninsula, and finally the shores of North Africa and the breadbasket of modern Tunisia. Along the way, the Roman navy swept the seas free of pirates and vagabond maritime states, gaining a strong seagoing culture, a naval officer corps, and the confidence to rule the inner sea of the Med with authority and creativity.

I will always recall a trip to Tunisia in early 2001 a bit after I was first selected for rear admiral. It was with a group of fellow newly promoted one-star officers, both admirals and generals. As I walked along the bluffs overlooking the southern Mediterranean, I was reminded about the destruction of Carthage and it made me wonder how differently Europe and the Mediterranean world would be today if Carthage had been preserved, balancing the Roman juggernaut and creating a vastly different set of geopolitical outcomes.

We always tend to think of history as somehow predetermined—of course the Romans would win—but so often the great twists of history turn on a few decisions, a single battle, an unexpected invention, a visionary or a fanatic's charisma. Carthage faded from history forever, and the Romans won; but what dreams of empire died with them?

What crystallized the Roman domination of the Med following the defeat of the Carthaginians was a series of civil wars that moved Rome from a republic to an empire headed by Caesar Augustus. A series of complex rivalries, the assassination of Julius Caesar, the departure of the legendary general Mark Antony to Egypt, and the rise of Augustus Caesar, then known as Octavian, collectively set the stage for the climactic battle at sea that would decide the fate of the Roman world in 31 B.C.: Actium, a small port off the coast of western Greece.

These were not the largest fleets assembled, but it is hard to find a more pivotal battle in the history of the Med. Octavian, who was closer to his base in Rome, was able to bring just over 250 ships into play; while Antony, operating from Egypt and with the mesmerizing Cleopatra supporting him, brought around 200 larger ships to battle—unfortunately for him, heavy and weighed down with supplies and land troops. Octavian and his admiral, Agrippa, correctly assessed Antony's forces as sluggish and lacking in the ability to maneuver smoothly and swiftly.

The key would be nimble use of sail and rudder to isolate the enemy ships while avoiding grappling actions. Agrippa also used fire projectiles to good effect, and at a crucial moment in the battle Antony and his Egyptian consort slipped away, leaving the bulk of the fleet to destruction. Hardly a proud example of leadership in action, and one of the few times in history a seagoing admiral has simply sailed away and left his fleet to fight to its death.

This battle created the conditions for the Pax Romana, the Roman Peace. The Med, for the first time in its history, was truly an inland sea, controlled and patrolled by the power of one nation: Rome. While nuisance piracy was an occasional hazard, the Med enjoyed perhaps the most peaceful prolonged period in its history. Roman rule continued through most of the next five centuries until the decline and fall of the western empire unfolded in the fifth century A.D., followed by the Dark Ages in Europe and the rise of Islam as not only a religion but an enormous motivating geopolitical force. Beginning with nomadic Arabs, Islam spread around the periphery of the Med, conquering all of the Middle East, then Egypt and the Levant. Using this as a base, Islam spread to conquer the rest of North Africa, eventually taking southern Spain and many of the islands in the central and eastern Med. Frankly, it is not impossible to imagine a world in which Islam had triumphed through much of southern Europe. Yet the Christian armies stiffened their resistance, and Constantinople and the Byzantine Empire held firm throughout much of this period. Over time, the Holy Roman Empire emerged in the West, and by the eleventh century the Christians were preparing to strike back, across the Med, and undertake the colossal misadventure of the Crusades.

During the Crusades, the Med served as a springboard for the Christian zealots of Europe to push their way into the Holy Land, and the newly (and relatively briefly) established Crusader kingdoms depended on the seas for resupply, logistics, and trade. The Crusades also gave great impetus to the rise of Venice and the Italian commercial cities over the course of the 250 years of various Christian campaigns.

Here we see again the political importance of geography. Venice was particularly well positioned in the northern Adriatic, with easy access to the trade coming from Europe over the Alps and superb, relatively safe access to the Med itself. The Venetians were crisp geopolitical actors indeed—rather than seeking to hold huge swaths of territory (with all the attendant headaches of administration), they sought a series of trading bases. They acquired Crete and Cyprus, two of the most strategically positioned islands of the Med. They also built smaller forts and trading stations around the periphery of the eastern Mediterranean. In a way, their sea power strategy anticipated Rear Admiral Alfred Thayer Mahan by some six centuries in systematically pursuing key commercial and trading stations around their world.

All of this was militarily anchored by the great Arsenal of Venice, which was an early technology assembly line construction facility producing great galleys. The Venetians used seagoing technology cleverly and at one time had a fleet of thousands of ships and tens of thousands of seamen—despite having a core population of only around two hundred thousand souls. Their relationships with other kingdoms and empires were based largely on trade, and they were adept at playing off Christian rulers against one another and manipulating them with the power of the Church and the control offered by the papacy. They seemed destined to dominate the eastern Med, and were growing richer and richer—all due to geopolitical planning, excellent use of geography in the Med, and the application of new technologies in construction, weaponry, and administration.

And of course it was not just Venice that displayed power on the waters of the Mediterranean. The great trading cities of Italy and southern France all participated in the rising level of trade. The Italian city-states—Genoa, Ragusa, Pisa, and others—were essentially small maritime nations that developed new types of ships and sails and fueled their wars (and the Crusades) with wealth from trade linen, dye, spices, perfumes, jewels, drugs, and pearls. From the west came oil, soap, wax, honey, skins, and especially wood and metal. Trade was brisk and enormously impactful to the maritime republics of the central Med.

Yet looming on the horizon was a new power—the rapidly rising Ottoman Turks, who came storming out of Central Asia. By exploiting the constant feuding between Arab potentates, they were able to dominate the Levant by 1400. Consolidating their control of modern-day Turkey, as well as large Arab dominions, they truly took the center stage of the Mediterranean in 1453 by doing what so many had tried and failed to do: conquer Constantinople. The Byzantine Empire had been a haven for culture and Christianity for a thousand years, and it finally fell after constricting and losing its ability to protect itself from the sea, as well as simply failing to produce enough resources (people and wealth) to ward off the Turks.

Whenever I am in Istanbul, I try to visit the superb Naval Museum, which is alongside the ferry terminals for commuters crossing the Bosporus in the Beşiktaş district. It is a quiet place full of the relics of the Ottoman Empire, most notably many of the great barges of state used by the rulers and oared by twenty or thirty oarsmen at a time. There is a nice garden outside with various cannons, as is usually the case at such museums. But the thing that always catches my eye is relatively modest—an anchor chain, of which only a few links exist today. It is black and rough, and appears to be made of iron. The placard proclaims it part of the "great chain" made in the eighth century by one of the Byzantine emperors.

In times of war, the chain was used to protect the city from the approach of enemy vessels by stretching it across the entrance to the Golden Horn. It was used successfully many times and appears for the final time in history in 1453 as the Ottomans were besieging the city. Mehmet the Conqueror could not get through it, but instead moved his war fleet of some seventy vessels overland through sheer dint of manpower. In the end, the chain failed to protect the city, just as the city was unable to protect Western civilization from the energy and dynamism of the Ottomans.

With the fall of Constantinople, the Ottomans were able to push into Europe as far as Vienna, and to increasingly dominate large tracts of strategic seacoasts along the eastern and southern Med. Their practices were brutal even by the standards of the day, and included forced conversions to Islam, slavery, and a particular focus on capturing Christian ships and enslaving their crews. The two civilizations—Christian and Muslim—were on a collision course that would bring great strife throughout the 1500s and 1600s.

As with previous conflicts in the Med, geography played an important role. The Ottomans were able to use their sea bases along the coasts and sought to reach out into the island chains of the Aegean and to the west. The Europeans tried to use the coastal bases of Italy as their strategic bastion, while attempting to dominate the same strategic islands. Technologies—cannons, sail, rowing, marine tactics—were roughly equal, although the Ottomans had a better system of administration and training in that it was relatively uniform throughout their growing empire. The West had a collection of different systems at play, which made it more difficult for them to operate seamlessly when fleets from different national entities came together.

The fall of the strategically important island of Cyprus in the eastern Mediterranean to the Ottomans in 1570 finally alarmed the various competing European nations to the point that Pope Pius V formed what was called "the Holy League," principally backed and manned by the Italians and the Spanish, to counter the Ottomans. The Turks continued to push both on land and at sea, and soon it was clear that a significant sea battle would decide the directions of the maritime campaign, and in many ways determine the fate of Europe. That battle occurred near Lepanto, off the western coast of Greece in the Ionian Sea.

The day of the battle dawned clear and bright: October 7, 1571. The Turks brought more than 250 galleys manned by a total of 75,000 seamen and soldiers, while the allied European fleet, commanded by the Hapsburg prince Don John, was made up of roughly 200 galleys manned by just over 70,000 seamen and rowers. Crucially, the Venetians provided half a dozen galleasses—big, heavy, floating forts with terrible killing power. This would be the first great galley battle since Actium, some sixteen centuries earlier and in roughly the same part of the Med. Notably, the Ottomans came to it with overwhelming confidence, not having lost a significant sea battle in more than a century.

But by the time the battle ended around four P.M., the sea was literally red with blood—almost all of it Ottoman. The Turks lost the vast majority of their ships, escaping with less than fifty vessels at a cost of more than 25,000 skilled seamen and marines. The Christian forces lost only 7,000 men and a dozen ships. It was a day upon which history turned, and it marked the high water level of Ottoman maritime ambitions for the broader Mediterranean. The difference was tactical acumen by the Europeans, especially in the use of the galleasses, which forced the Turks to maneuver around them and sustain heavy losses from their large cannons. Almost all the fighting occurred hand to hand, and the commanders were personally involved, with Don John leading the assault that ended up killing his opposite number.

The battle was incredibly decisive in the moment, preventing the further expansion of Islam into the Christian world; but luckily for the Turks, the lack of follow-up by the Christian powers allowed the moment to pass without loss of territory by the Ottomans. The Christians quickly reverted to form with bickering and argumentation that allowed the Turks to hold Cyprus, and their ships continued to rove the Med in force. Despite the setback of Lepanto, the Turks rebuilt their fleet, worked hard to retrain a sailing force, and continued to be a factor in the eastern Mediterranean, where they skirmished with the forces of the Italian states and Spain for much of the next two centuries; but they never again truly threatened to fully dominate the entire inner sea of the Med, which was at one point a realistic ambition for them.

Their failure at Lepanto meant that the Ottoman Empire, as powerful as it would become and as long as it would last, would be bounded. They would not push by the deserts of Arabia to the south, by the Persians to the east, or by the Europeans at sea and in the Balkans to the west. Perhaps most important, as a result of the Battle of Lepanto, the mortal fear of the "invincible Turks" felt by many southern Europeans was shattered. In that sense, it was a critically important battle.

When I was the NATO commander, I went often to Spain, a country I love for many reasons—from the beauty of the language and culture to the excellence of the cuisine to the deep sense of history on the Iberian Peninsula. It is a place that was once an uneasy part of the Islamic world, and the architecture, language, and culture of parts of southern Spain—think Seville—greatly reflect this.

At one of the military summits we held there in Seville, my Spanish counterpart presented me with a beautifully decorated bottle of Spanish brandy in a hand-painted box. The motif on the box was a representation of the Battle of Lepanto, replete with a bloodred sea and the Spanish and Italian flags flying over the victorious Christian fleets. It is a sea battle that changed history across the Med, from the Aegean and the Adriatic all the way to the Strait of Gibraltar, by shutting the door to further Ottoman expansion into the central and western Med.

WITH CHRISTIAN DOMINANCE ASSURED, it was the turn of the British to begin to move in significant ways into the Mediterranean. They consolidated control over key islands and straits—Gibraltar at the Pillars of Hercules, Malta in the center of the Med, and Cyprus, so large and important to the east. And of course Egypt was a stepping-stone on the routes controlling India. British admirals began to be very familiar with the inland sea—especially Lord Nelson.

Throughout the long summer of 1798, Nelson's and Napoleon's fleets played hide-and-go-seek across the broad expanse of the Med. When, finally, the French dropped anchor off the northeast coast of Alexandria in Aboukir Bay, Nelson closed in for the kill after several unproductive weeks at sea. His direction to his captains was simply to put their ships alongside the enemy. His aggressive and motivated captains destroyed Napoleon's armada while it swung at anchor off the mouth of the Nile, and Nelson (a mere rear admiral at the time) was made a baron and became a hero across Europe. Essentially the entire Mediterranean fleet of France was destroyed or captured, and British naval morale peaked, preparing it well for the victories to come. It was the pivotal maritime battle of the Napoleonic Wars and firmly established once and for all British dominance of the Med throughout the nineteenth century.

In the early 1980s, I sailed into the bay of Alexandria on the carrier

Forrestal, not far at all from the site of the famous battle. We went ashore on small boats, rocking through the surf, mooring at a yacht club and enjoying easy hospitality. It was a far cry from the world war that raged in Alexandria in the early 1800s, and the Egyptians were happy to have our U.S. dollars pumping up their economy.

For Nelson, Egypt was an important way station on the voyage to the destruction of Napoleon at Trafalgar; but the months he had spent crossing the Med to find Bonaparte were the pivot point of an extraordinary career—time well spent indeed. For us on an American carrier at the height of the cold war, it was simply a break for ice cream and beer ashore. For all the wonderful Mediterranean nights he spent in the arms of Emma Hamilton, Nelson's destiny lay outside the Pillars of Hercules, in the Atlantic, at the fateful battle of Trafalgar. The Mediterranean was the proving ground that led him to command and glory and death at the pinnacle of British sea power in the early nineteenth century.

Through the nineteenth century, the Med lay more quiet. The height of geopolitical maneuvering shifted ashore to the continent of Europe itself, as successive waves of revolution pushed back against the compromises of the 1815 Congress of Vienna, which had ended the Napoleonic Wars. The "Iron Chancellor," of Germany, Otto von Bismarck, managed to dominate European politics and ensure that other than the battle for Crimea and later the 1870 conflict between Germany and France there was little geopolitical activity happening that involved the Mediterranean. By the time the nineteenth century ended and the twentieth had begun, many major strategic theorists had begun to believe that war between the major powers was impossible given the cultural, familial, and economic ties between them. Sadly, they were wrong, and in 1914, war came again to the Mediterranean Sea as an important part of the First World War, what came to be known as "the Great War."

. . .

The First World War began not far from the shores of the Mediterranean Sea, in Sarajevo, Bosnia, on the periphery of the Austro-Hungarian Empire. In June 1914, Archduke Franz Ferdinand—at the time heir to the empire's Hapsburg throne—was assassinated by Gavrilo Princip, a Serbian nationalist. This led to the triggering of the complex system of European alliances and ultimately to the global war that had at its heart the maritime rivalry between the German Empire and Great Britain.

At sea, much of the war was carried out by auxiliaries, including submarines and distant commerce raiders. And of course much of the fighting between Great Britain (the "Grand Fleet") and Germany (the "High Seas Fleet") was north of Germany in the waters between the two nations, in the foggy, harsh conditions of the North Sea. But a portion of the war found its way to the Mediterranean as well, beginning in that peripheral body of water that has seen so much of war as well, the Black Sea. There two German cruisers joined decrepit Turkish warships and attacked Russia's ports in the Crimean—actions that echo through to the present-day NATO-Russia conflict in the area, albeit with slightly different alliances.

In early 1915, an audacious scheme was concocted by the young Winston Churchill and grudgingly accepted by the canny and seasoned first sea lord, Admiral Sir Jackie Fisher. They sought to break the deadlock on the trenches of the Franco-German front with an attack on Turkey at Gallipoli in the Dardanelles, at the edge of the Mediterranean in the Aegean Sea where it opens into the Sea of Marmara and then to the Black Sea. The idea was to ultimately take Constantinople, the capital of the increasingly unstable Turkish Ottoman Empire (the so-called Sick

Man of Europe) and knock the Turks out of the war. It would also open the southern ports to Russia.

The plan was initially under resourced, and the incremental approach ultimately led to massive losses, especially of British colonial troops, when the Turkish army unexpectedly stiffened and beat back the British attacks ashore on the highly strategic peninsula of Gallipoli. Of the half million Allied troops who began the campaign in February 1915, almost half were casualties by November. The reputations of both Churchill and Admiral Fisher were badly damaged, and the war ended up dragging on for another three years.

I went to Gallipoli—or Çanakkale, as the Turks call it—on a hot summer's day in 2010 as a guest of the Turkish chief of defense, army general İlker Başbuğ. We walked the battle lines where Aussies and Kiwis had fought desperate actions against troops under the command of a young Turkish general, Kemal Atatürk, who went on to drag Turkey into the modern world after the war. General Başbuğ showed me the monuments, which are extraordinary and generous in their respect for the fallen Allied troops. One of them has a famous quote from Atatürk, which is addressed to the mothers of the fallen soldiers: "Those heroes that shed their blood and lost their lives . . . You are now lying in the soil of a friendly country. Therefore, rest in peace. There is no difference between the Johnnies (Anzac troops) and the Mehmets (Turkish troops) to us where they lie side by side here in this country of ours. . . . You, the mothers who sent their sons from faraway countries, wipe away your tears; your sons are now lying in our bosom and are in peace." While there is some controversy about the authenticity of the quote, it is moving and I think has been taken to heart by the Turkish military as part of their culture and history.

Later, we had a glass of good Turkish red wine and a light meal on the battlefield overlooking the strait. I looked out to sea where the ships of the Allied fleet had launched their inconclusive bombardments and tried to supply the troops ashore, and realized that the troops would have looked longingly as well at the ships, wishing they too could have been saved by simply sailing away. There are times when it is good indeed to be a sailor. General Başbuğ and I took note of the difference between the fate of a soldier on the ground and that of a sailor at sea.

In a strange footnote, General Başbuğ—a superb soldier, deeply loyal to his nation—was later falsely charged with undermining civilian control of the military and imprisoned. Fortunately, he was later released and cleared of those trumped-up charges, and today enjoys his retirement. He was a soldier who understood and appreciated sea power, but knew that the men ashore in this battle were the arbiters of the outcome. Our friendship continues to this day.

THE RESULTS OF the First World War were inconclusive. An angry and bitter Germany fell victim to fascism, hyperinflation, and a sense of victimization, and its anger gave rise to Hitler, who dragged his nation into the disaster of World War II. Unlike the First World War—where the pivotal fight ended up being largely ashore in massive trenches on what was essentially the Franco-German border—the Second World War achieved a level of combat in the Mediterranean littoral that rivaled that of the Punic Wars. It is no exaggeration to say that the Med was a heartland battle domain throughout the early years of the Second World War, including the early destruction of French and Italian ships by the British fleet after the fall of France and Italy's declaration of war.

The most important parts of the Med campaigns were in North Africa, where the Allies chose to make their initial attacks against German forces, led by General Erwin Rommel, that were threatening Egypt while seeking to cut Britain off from India, an important source of revenue and resources.

The American-Anglo force landed on the North African shore in 1942 in Operation Torch near Casablanca, and—after initial setbacks—was able to then invade Sicily (Operation Husky) and make its way to Italy (Operation Avalanche). These actions ultimately knocked Italy out of the war and badly distracted Hitler. They were also the making of General Dwight Eisenhower, who emerged from these Med campaigns as the Supreme Allied Commander who would brilliantly lead Operation Overlord and the invasion of northern France a year later.

At sea, as the war began, the Germans and the British launched a series of battles to gain control of the vital shipping routes that would determine victory in the land battles. The fight for Greece went against the Allies, but they were able to ultimately win on the North African coast. Submarine warfare by the Germans was quite effective in these early days, and the situation in North Africa was of deep concern to the British high command. The Med was again an arena of total war at sea.

It was also a period that highlighted the strategic importance of Malta, sitting as it does athwart the key sea lanes of communication in the center of the Med. Operation Torch and the British army campaign under General Bernard Montgomery were able to destroy the North African forces of the Germans, inflicting heavy losses. Rommel barely escaped back to Germany. All of this was enabled by British sea power operating in the central Med and supplying their forces ashore.

Much as during the Punic Wars, the Mediterranean Sea functioned both as battleground—as ships and aircraft sought to destroy one another at sea—and more important as the passage across which moved all the means of war. In all of my voyages through the Med, I was constantly reminded of those long patrols in the Second World War. In C. S.

Forester's riveting novel *The Ship*, he tells the story of war at sea in that arena perfectly, when British ships sailed out of the base at Gibraltar headed to Malta and Alexandria, always seeking to keep open the vital supply lines. As a destroyer captain in the mid-1990s, I sailed those waters often and always felt the hint of danger and the tingling sense of cruising through the scene of those long-ago battles.

THROUGHOUT THE COLD WAR, the U.S. Navy kept two carrier battle groups on patrol in the Med. The idea was to challenge the Russian ability to conduct flanking maneuvers to get behind NATO lines that were dug in along the Fulda Gap in Central Europe. There were constant games of cat and mouse throughout the Med, and Navy ships (especially the massive aircraft carriers) were constantly shadowed by Russian intelligence-gathering vessels. Occasionally, the Navy would send destroyers to shoulder off the Russian AGIs, as they were called (Auxiliary General Intelligence).

The Med served as a sort of venue for training, engagement, and intelligence gathering throughout the cold war. Given its relatively shallow depth (shallow in comparison to the far reaches of the North Atlantic and the even deeper Pacific), the Med was never going to be a venue for a huge fleet action in the age of nuclear submarines, which need to plumb the deep sea for concealment and preparation for attack. In terms of U.S. versus Russian engagement, the Med was not the battlefield it had been for the previous two thousand years, but there was a series of relatively low-intensity conflict incidents alongside the maneuvers of the Soviet and U.S. fleets.

Notable among them in 1985 was the first significant terrorist incident at sea launched against a civilian vessel—a Palestine Liberation Front attack on an Italian cruise liner, the *Achille Lauro*, in which an elderly Jewish-American citizen who was confined to a wheelchair, Leon Klinghoffer, was executed and thrown into the sea. The perpetrators were captured by the United States and turned over to the Italians for prosecution.

Later in the decade there were significant U.S. Freedom of Navigation operations against Libya (resulting in the shoot-down of Libyan fighters whose pilots were trained by the Soviet Union), as well as the strikes against Libya after a terrorist bombing of a German disco killing U.S. servicemen in 1986. Additionally, following the bombing of a Pan American commercial airliner over Lockerbie, Scotland, in 1988, more intense naval operations were undertaken in the Gulf of Sidra. The pendulum of conflict in the Med was swinging from the big-fleet cold war posturing to more complex operations reflecting the fading importance of the cold war ethos.

Throughout this period, I made several deployments to the Med, and on each of them I felt a sense of connection with the many, many sea battles that had gone before. But we never fired a shot in anger, despite many close encounters and provocations. And finally, the dark era of the cold war ended, with all of us thinking we were headed into a brave new world of peace and prosperity with the "end of history" within our grasp. It certainly didn't turn out that way.

After the initial exuberance at the "victory" of the cold war, reality set in as it became clear that knocking off the Soviet domination of various parts of the world would release destabilizing forces. Perhaps the signature conflict in that regard involving the Med in the immediate post–cold war period was in the decade of the 1990s, when the Balkans simply exploded as Yugoslavia broke apart.

Long-simmering religious and ethnic tensions between Bosnian Muslims, Catholic Croatians, and Orthodox Serbs created a vicious war centered in Bosnia in the center of the Balkans. Hundreds of thousands were killed and millions pushed across borders. More than eight thousand Muslim men and boys were slaughtered by Serbians in July 1995 near the town of Srebrenica. This was followed by a second conflict when the largely Muslim province of Kosovo broke away from Serbia in 1998. The international community, after much vacillation, finally intervened both in the air and from the sea. The maritime operations included strikes, an arms embargo, and eventually a significant ground force requiring logistic support from sea. The forces ashore totaled more than 100,000 allied troops between the Bosnia and Kosovo campaigns.

When I was a destroyer captain, my ship, USS *Barry*, had a key role in the mid-1990s as part of the arms embargo preventing weapons from reaching the Serbian aggressors. I remember reading Robert Kaplan's insightful meditation on the region, *Balkan Ghosts*, and thinking that the problems were simply intractable, the well of pain too deep.

And yet, over time, the international community has fashioned a kind of rough peace in the Balkans, and the ships at sea played an important part in it. We had long weeks on station chasing down smugglers and pushing them off the coast under the command of an excitable British commodore. I was glad to put the dark shoreline in my wake and head home. After the Balkan wars of the mid-1990s, things settled down in the Med, but anyone who follows the region knows it was a quiet that would not last—and it has not.

TODAY'S MEDITERRANEAN IS AGAIN a sea of conflict. With Russia's resurgence, we are seeing aggressive patterns of maritime behavior dotting the Med, especially in the Black Sea and the eastern Mediterranean. While the Russian fleet is not the equal of the vast Soviet naval armada, it is quite capable of challenging U.S. interests. Additionally, Israel remains at odds with most of its neighbors, and around Cyprus lie rich fields of natural gas and oil on the bottom of the seabed—with attendant territorial disputes among all the nations of the eastern Med. NATO allies Greece and Turkey still squabble over the Aegean and the islands that make up its beautiful archipelago, and the Black Sea—a subordinate vassal of the Med—has disputes between Russia, Georgia, and Ukraine.

Looking first to Russia, it is clear that Vladimir Putin sees his country as a Mediterranean power and the dominant force in the Black Sea. The annexation of Crimea and the domination of the Luhansk and Donetsk regions of Ukraine in the southeast of the country give the Russian Federation a strong foothold on the necessary strategic real estate. Having had a long-standing treaty with Ukraine to keep capital ships in the port of Sevastopol, it has been easy for the Russians to simply build out the infrastructure there.

In 2013, as the NATO Supreme Allied Commander, I went to the Russian and Ukrainian naval base in Crimea and had lunch on a Ukrainian destroyer with their chief of naval operations. I was there to thank the Ukrainians for their participation in the NATO counterpiracy mission, to which they had sent a ship. After a long, long lunch featuring literally countless toasts with Ukrainian (not Russian) vodka, too much smoked fish, and a half dozen courses based on pork, the navy chief and I went up on deck. He pointed to the Russian ships that were tied up just down the piers as part of the Russian agreement to keep their ships in homeport in Crimea.

I mentioned how it must be somewhat frustrating to have Russian ships in a Ukrainian dockyard now that the countries were not as close as they once were, and that these certainly were not Soviet times. The Ukrainian CNO was smoking a cigarette, and after a long puff, he told me that “Russia will never give up Crimea. Never.” When Russia invaded and annexed Crimea a couple of years later, I was reminded of his words. The need to dominate the Black Sea is primal for Russia, and Crimea is the fulcrum that allows it to do so. As the Ukrainian admiral told me, the Russians will never give it back.

It is interesting to put the Black Sea into the historical context of the Mediterranean. It began as a kind of region of exploration, dating to the ancient Greeks—legend has it that the Argonauts sailed to what is today Georgia to find the Golden Fleece. For centuries, it was disputed between Russia and Turkey, a relationship that has had many twists and turns over the centuries. It was essentially an Ottoman lake at the height of Turkish power, then fell under domination by Russia. During the cold war, it was essentially a Soviet lake, with only Turkey as a NATO ally guarding the entrances and controlling the southern coast.

But with the end of the cold war, the Black Sea has exploded into a sort of Wild West, with new NATO allies Romania and Bulgaria joining Turkey; Ukraine is in a deeply troubled relationship with neighbor Russia, including the annexation of Crimea; and Georgia, a close NATO partner and friend, has two significant provinces occupied by pro-Russian separatists and Russian forces. In addition, today smugglers and violent extremists routinely use the Black Sea as a preferred route into Europe. Russia will continue to regard it as a vital interest, and the potential for exploiting hydrocarbons will also be a key focus for Russia.

Putin has also expanded Russia’s relationship with the Assad regime in Syria. Russia has had naval access and bases along the Syrian Mediterranean coast throughout the cold war and on into the present day, representing at one point the final geostrategic connection between Moscow and the Arab world. Now that Putin has effectively doubled down on Assad—despite the Syrian leader’s vicious and illegal actions against his people during the ongoing civil war—it is clear that Russia intends to maintain its ability to operate in the eastern Med into the future.

This collides with the views of the United States and other NATO allies, which are seeking the overthrow of Assad based on his use of chemical weapons, torture, and barrel bombs in the civil war. The eastern Med, as so often in the past, has become an arena of great-power politics. In today's world, it is eerily reminiscent of the Balkans from a hundred years ago, when the powder keg of Bosnia blew apart the Austro-Hungarian Empire and dragged much of the civilized world into a war that essentially lasted until mid-century.

Even more concerning is the rise of the Islamic State. A group of religious fanatics, they are attempting to rebuild the Islamic caliphate across the Levant and North Africa. Capitalizing on the chaos and destruction in Syria and Iraq, they have dug into the seam between those countries. While they have lost most of their territory in the Levant and do not as yet control any coastal regions, their presence is increasingly felt in Libya, which has a long, exposed coast that is less than a hundred miles from Mediterranean islands and represents a path to Italy and Europe beyond. They have also contributed substantially to the departure of more than a million refugees headed to Europe (as well as several million more distributed throughout southern Turkey, Jordan, and Lebanon). All of this washes up from the shores of the Med, as many of the migrants are coming by sea to Greece, Italy, Croatia, and other coastal regions of the European Mediterranean. At the moment, there is an agreement between Turkey and the European Union to try to stem the flow of refugees and keep them in Turkey. But the fragile accord will probably unwind over time, and the imperative for physical safety and economic opportunity will continue to keep the flow of refugees coming to Europe from across the Med.

. . .

Of particular concern from a seagoing perspective is the threat from Libya. In 1942, Winston Churchill said that Italy represented the "soft underbelly of Europe," and directed the Allied invasion efforts there. Today, we are seeing the nascent flickers of an Islamic State strategy that may try to achieve a similar effect.

Following the brutal decapitation of twenty-one Egyptian Coptic Christians by radical Islamists professing an allegiance to ISIS in mid-2015, the Italian government began to ramp up its efforts to defend its territory from attacks. How realistic is this threat, and how capable is the Islamic state of reaching across the Mediterranean and striking Italy? And what should Italy do?

First, we should listen to what the Islamic State has to say on the subject: From the cover of its *Dabiq* magazine is a story titled "Reflections on the Final Crusade." The general idea is that ISIS will conquer Rome, and the images include a photo of a black jihadist flag flying over St. Peter's Square. The article said: "We will conquer your Rome, break your crosses, and enslave your women, by the permission of Allah, the Exalted. If we do not reach that time, then our children and grandchildren will reach it, and they will sell your sons as slaves at the slave market. Every Muslim should get out of his house, find a crusader and kill him. . . . And the Islamic State will remain until its banner flies over Rome."

Hyperbolic? Of course. Literally possible? Not in the least. But worth considering the sentiment as Europe thinks about the increasing possibility of attacks in its homeland coming across the Mediterranean? You bet.

As Graeme Wood points out in his intellectually smart and historically grounded piece in *The Atlantic*, "What ISIS Really Wants," there is a certain underlying medieval impetus to the Islamic State's rhetoric and its actions. Beheadings of innocents, burnings of captured prisoners, rumors of crucifixions, enslavement and sale of comely women and children, the literal sacking of cities—all of these connote a strong desire to play on the international stage as though the Crusades were still in progress. Thus we come to the importance of Rome, perhaps the most potent symbol of all the Islamic State hates.

In terms of capability, ISIS is not going to launch a conventional attack or strike. But it has two potential routes into Italy by sea. One is by infiltrating the many boatloads of illegal migrants that sail across the short distances from Libya to the southern coast and islands of Italy. The other is by using small craft, much as smugglers and drug runners do to cross the Adriatic Sea, to cross the southern Mediterranean. Both are feasible and easier than working across Turkey and the Balkans and trying to pass illegally into a European Union nation by land.

If ISIS wants to inflame a religious war, what better place in Europe to attack than Rome? A significant strike at a Christian holy site would fall directly into both ISIS's self-stated strategy and its building narrative. Our Italian allies are well aware of this and are responding by taking all the right initial steps, starting with putting portions of both their military and the capable carabinieri paramilitary forces on higher alert; adding more nautical patrols between Libya and their southern islands; sharing intelligence widely throughout both NATO and EU/Interpol channels; and publicizing their measures to appear a more hardened target. All good steps.

What else can and should be done to protect the soft underbelly of Europe across the Med?

First, get NATO into the maritime game in the Mediterranean. Italy should convene an Article 4 discussion at the North Atlantic Council in Brussels within the NATO headquarters. Article 4 of the NATO treaty permits any nation to bring before the council matters pertaining to its individual security concerns. Such discussions are typically used to raise issues considered particularly concerning, and occasionally lead to common action—a decision taken by consensus of all twenty-eight members—under Article 5 (the famous "an attack on one shall be regarded as an attack on all" clause of the treaty). Italy should specifically ask that a NATO task force be established for surveillance and patrol across the Med.

When Turkey felt threatened by Syrian air activity several years ago, NATO responded by sending Patriot batteries to southern Turkey to defend Turkish sovereign airspace. Those batteries remain in place today. In the case of Italian concerns about Islamic State infiltration, the use of standing NATO maritime task forces would be a very real possibility to support the overloaded Italian coast guard and navy.

Second, amp up the maritime intelligence collection processes across the Med. The Italians need access to the highest levels of intelligence being collected today in Libya. This means not only working through NATO channels, but also approaching the Arab nations in the anti–Islamic State coalition (Egypt, the UAE, and possibly Tunisia) for assistance. There is no substitute for on-the-ground assets, and these are thin for the Italians despite their close commercial ties to Libya—so Italy should work it through not only high-tech USA/NATO/NSA sources, but also the Arab networks. Much of this can be sea based, with intelligence collection assets operating from coastal shipping.

Third, focus on the maritime dimension, using NATO navies in the Med. This means sortieing the Italian fleet and coast guard to patrol and map the patterns of movement across the 100-to-200–nautical mile stretch of the central Mediterranean; using long-range patrol aircraft from Sicilian bases; cooperating fully with neighboring Malta, which sits astride the sea lane; and employing high-endurance unmanned drones to maintain a high-quality, real-time sense of maritime domain awareness.

Fourth and most important, develop a strategy for addressing the problem at its source: in Libya. Given the chaos and increasing anarchy in Libya, it is tempting to simply write it off and hope that the revolution ultimately burns itself out. Indeed, many observers express a certain longing for the "good old days" of stability under Muammar Gaddafi. But eventually, Libya will succeed—it has big oil reserves (especially on a per capita basis), an educated population, and enviable geography close to Europe with a huge seacoast.

Europe—our closest ally in the world—needs a stable Mediterranean. This will mean engaging more directly in the coastal regions of the Levant to diminish the threat from the Islamic State and the flow of illegal migrants and refugees. It will also mean a maritime strategy to help move Libya toward a more stable situation. This means exploring a UN or EU peacekeeping mission, supporting the relatively moderate internationally recognized government centered in Tobruk, and cooperating closely with Egyptian efforts to take on the Islamic State in military terms with targeting, intelligence, destroying their financial base by cutting off access to Arab banks and, potentially, air strikes. Here in the United States, we should support Italy in helping lead a European approach to stabilizing Libya.

Just as Churchill looked at Italy as a relatively easy gateway to Europe, the Islamic State has geographic, political, and symbolic interests in sailing across the Med to Italy and across the Aegean to Greece. It will seek to accelerate its reach across the eastern and central Med. And Russian adventurism will continue in and around the eastern Med and the Black Sea. It is clear the Med will continue to be a fickle and changing geopolitical body of water, and one where more security operations at sea loom ahead on the horizon. That sense of being closed in an inland sea will continue for sailors in the Med.

I think back on the first time I sailed in a warship through the Strait of Gibraltar, a young and inexperienced Navy lieutenant. Much of my later career would be spent sailing through the Mediterranean, although I did not know it at the time. I would sail into Cannes for the Fourth of July, hosting an Independence Day celebration for the glamorous citizens of that lovely city, and head from there to shore up an arms embargo in the Balkans, where massacres and bombings were the order of the day.

In port calls to Egypt and Athens and Istanbul I would see the most ancient capitals and what their modern civilizations had become. I dropped into the Iberian ports of the Costa del Sol and saw the mélange of Arab and Spanish culture in the south of Spain. Over time, I would sail by and visit every country in the Med, marveling at the diversity and history, the culture and the beauty. But the overriding impression that stays with me to this day is of the battles fought, the lives lost, the collision of empires, and the throaty shout of war.

ULTIMATELY, THE STORY of the Mediterranean geopolitically turns on the rise of technology in response to the wars of the times; the distinctive geography that allows for miniature arenas of combat while still allowing overall passage throughout the inland sea; and the collision of civilizations fighting over trade, slaves, wealth, and land. Each of those has a part to play in the story of the Mediterranean, but in the end it is the maritime character of the sea itself that has driven so many of these battles.

We sometimes think of the Med as a cradle of civilizations, where nations were born and took to the center of the stage in all their terrible power and ultimate glory—and it certainly was all that—but it was also an unforgiving arena of war at sea, which shaped the course of history down through the centuries as well.

As we look to the future, the security challenges represented by the Mediterranean Sea will continue to be part of the landscape of human history. Sailors on modern warships will continue to ply their trade alongside the tankers, container ships, and gleaming cruise liners. Old ghosts of distant battles rattle still around the Med, and any Navy sailor, walking the decks of his warship at sunset of a winter evening, can feel their haunting presence in the sweep of the deep, uncaring waves.

5.

THE SOUTH CHINA SEA

A LIKELY ZONE OF CONFLICT

John Cary's chart gives little indication as to how crucial this region, only known as the East India Isles in 1801, is to our modern world.

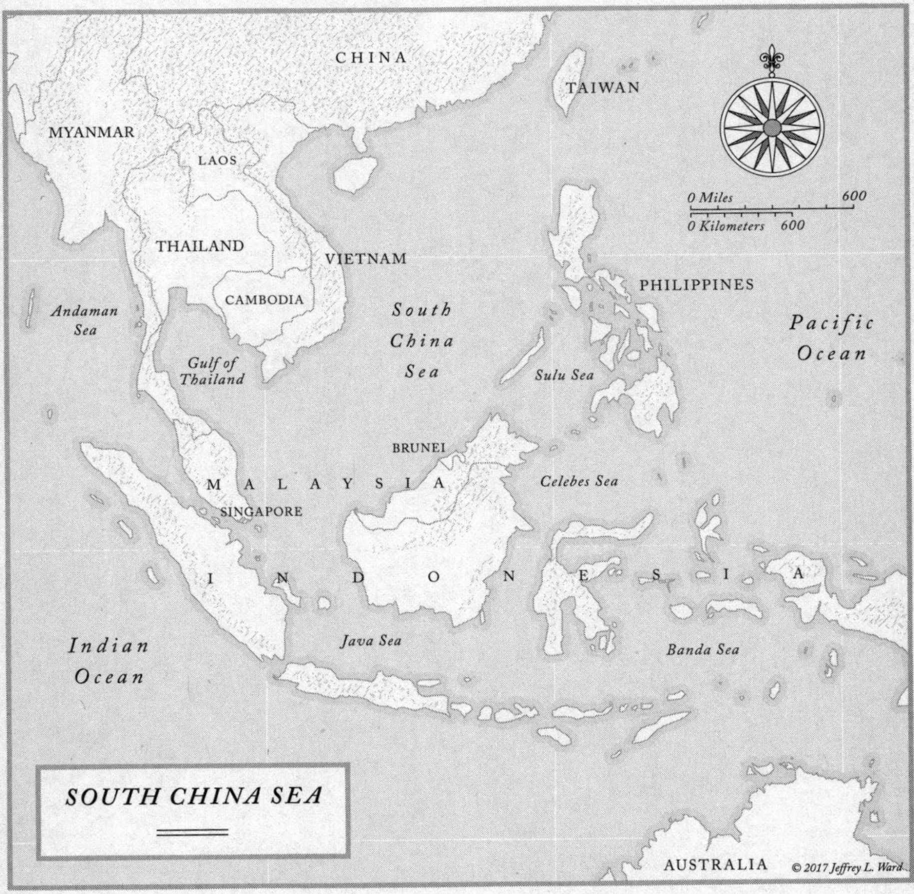
CHINA
TAIWAN
MYANMAR
LAOS
THAILAND
VIETNAM
CAMBODIA
PHILIPPINES
Andaman Sea
South China Sea
Pacific Ocean
Gulf of Thailand
Sulu Sea
BRUNEI
M A L A Y S I A
Celebes Sea
SINGAPORE
I N D O N E S I A
Java Sea
Banda Sea
Indian Ocean
0 Miles 600
0 Kilometers 600
SOUTH CHINA SEA
AUSTRALIA
© 2017 Jeffrey L. Ward

At the heart of the teeming South China Sea is Hong Kong, perhaps the finest natural harbor in the world. The first time I pulled into it was in 1977, as an ensign assigned as the anti-submarine warfare officer on a brand-new *Spruance*-class destroyer named USS *Hewitt* (DD-966). The captain, Fritz Gaylord, foolishly let me drive the ship as the junior officer of the deck for the sea and anchor detail. It was a complex mooring to a buoy, a huge floating concrete hulk anchored to the bottom of the harbor. The idea was to nuzzle the pointed nose of the 9,000-ton warship up to the buoy, hold it steady with the engines and rudder, and allow enough time for a handful of stalwart boatswain mates to jump from a small boat and affix our ship's anchor chain to a kind of connection link on the buoy.

This was a situation that required great ship handling skills which I did not possess, at least not at that early moment in my career. I was dazzled by Hong Kong itself, a spectacular harbor dividing two beautiful landmasses, with thousands of lights glittering on the steep side of Victoria's Peak in the early evening and the bustle of what was then a British crown colony in full bloom. Between my inexperience and distraction, I did a truly lousy job, banging the sensitive underbelly of the ship (where the expensive and somewhat delicate sonar dome resides) against the buoy. Fortunately, the captain *was* a great ship handler, and he took us back off the buoy and coached me through a better landing, despite the brisk wind and steady current.

When it was over, he lit an unfiltered Lucky Strike cigarette (smoking was allowed in those days on Navy ships), smiled somewhat thinly at me, and said, "I hope you're better at finding submarines. Welcome to Hong Kong." It was the beginning of a long and warm association for me with the South China Sea, and the myriad cities, nations, and cultures that surround it.

THE SOUTH CHINA SEA is big—the size of the greater Caribbean—and surrounded by huge economies: China, Vietnam, Malaysia, Indonesia, the Philippines, and others. Through the South China Sea in any given year pass about half of the world's maritime trade, half of its liquefied natural gas, and perhaps a third of its seaborne crude oil. There is evidence of human habitation stretching back thousands of years. Many theories exist as to the origins of the flow of people, goods, and languages across its waters: whatever the truth, we know that an early maritime network quickly became well developed and expansive. It is a sea rich in fish and having plenty of rain, with the access to fresh water facilitating long early journeys of perhaps weeks at a time. There is even scattered evidence of trade between the ancient Mediterranean civilizations and the people of the South China Sea Rim. More recently, in the first centuries A.D., the trade between India and Southeast Asia enriched the people of the South China Sea.

As in the Indian Ocean, the discovery of how to harness the power of the monsoons provided a significant impetus to early trading. Settlements in southern China and the Mekong Delta of the Funan Empire were among the first trading stations in the region. Over time in the first millennium A.D., the rivalry between what are today China and Vietnam first manifested itself as the cultures came into conflict. Also during this period, the South China Sea emerged as the seam between the two great civilizations in India and China, both of which would be impacted deeply by European exploration starting about 1500. Additionally, a trade between China and the Arab world emerged toward the end of the first millennium A.D. Globalization, which we think of as a modern phenomenon, has been alive and well for a very long time.

Across the centuries, various Chinese dynasties dominated the western side of the South China Sea, notably the Tang and Song dynasties, which controlled much of the littoral a thousand years ago. They pressed trade and controlled the ability of individual cities and regions to participate in the lucrative routes. By the time the Ming dynasty ascended in 1368, the DNA of trading, commerce, and seafaring exchanges was embedded in the South China Sea. Even as the Ming leaders looked inward to the land, the sea continued to be a vital part of the region's economy. Illustrating this well are the voyages of the so-called Eunuch Admirals (a term that provides me with a certain amount of personal discomfort to contemplate, I must admit). These were big expeditions, one hundred to two hundred ships, with thousands of sailors and troops. There is a fair amount of controversy about their purpose, but most historians seem to think they were to intimidate, discipline, enforce commercial codes and taxes, and create a sense of awe toward the dominant Chinese. Of note, these voyages were an anomaly; they were discontinued after several decades, and the ships were left to rot. China focused internally for the next five hundred years.

One interesting commodity that flowed across the wide South China

Sea was silver. With Manila as a trading crossroads giving the Spanish Empire in the Americas a toehold in Asia in the Philippines, the Spanish were able to provide much-needed metal currency to the Chinese. While silver also came south from Japan, it was the Portuguese and the Spanish who were largely able to fill China's need for hard currency. This led to the Chinese southern and eastern coasts being integrated into the global economy through access to the South China Sea. What emerged in this period was a trading competition, often verging into open conflict among primarily the English, the Dutch, and the Portuguese. Despite arguments by the Portuguese that they deserved full authority due to their discovery of the sea routes, international law of this period provided the latitude for the intrusion of other trading partners, most particularly the Dutch and British. In the early 1600s, the tiny Dutch state possessed thousands of ships with tens of thousands of well-trained and motivated sailors, and largely dominated global trade with an axis between European Amsterdam and Batavia (Jakarta in present-day Indonesia).

But by the late 1700s the British in the form of the East India Company were coming into their own. This led to the acquisition of Singapore in 1819 and Hong Kong in 1842. The Opium Wars of 1839–42 and 1856–60 were a result of a weak Chinese state colliding with the growing colonial powers. Meanwhile, both the French in Indochina and the Germans on the south Chinese coast were establishing colonial footholds. By the late 1800s, even the United States, traditionally averse to colonial holdings, was seduced into the view of naval strategist Alfred Thayer Mahan that colonies (really "coaling stations" or geostrategic forward bases) provided the foundation of sea power and thus world influence. Mahan's seminal 1890 work, *The Influence of Sea Power upon History*, was taken up enthusiastically by the young American president Theodore Roosevelt at the turn of the century, and the resultant echoes in the South China Sea were profound. And of course increasing in influence and capability, moving along like a shark under the smooth surface of the water, was Japan. The eventual collision of the Second World War was inevitable and enormous, but it began with a relatively mild series of disagreements in the South China Sea.

The key event for the United States in the region was the Spanish-American War, which was precipitated by the sinking of the cruiser USS *Maine* in Havana harbor, in the Spanish colony of Cuba. On a winter day in early 1898, the ship suddenly exploded while swinging peacefully at anchor. Led by William Randolph Hearst's newspaper chain, Spain was blamed for the sinking, the cry of "Remember the *Maine*" swept the country, and the United States declared war on the disintegrating Spanish Empire, leading to the annexation of Cuba as a U.S. territory after the war.

As an aside, I have long kept a painting of the USS *Maine* just before the explosion in my various offices—one hangs today in my Massachusetts office on the quiet New England academic quad of Tufts University, where I am the dean of the Fletcher School of Law and Diplomacy. People often ask me why I keep a painting of a doomed ship on the wall. Why not a valiant and heroic U.S. Navy ship, perhaps the carrier *Enterprise* or the destroyer *Barry*, both of which passed under my command?

The answer is twofold—first, and most important, the painting reminds me that your ship can blow up underneath you at any moment, so you better have a Plan B and, metaphorically speaking, know where the life rafts are located. The second reason is perhaps a bit obscure, but important to me. After the *Maine* was sunk, the Navy salvaged the ship nearly fifty years later, and virtually all of the evidence points to the conclusion that she was not sunk by Spanish saboteurs after all. It appears the explosion was internal, most probably from a boiler or an ammunition storage area. The charge to war was predicated, it would seem, on false evidence. So the second reason I keep a painting of the *Maine* around is to remind me not to jump to conclusions in the heat of the moment. Stop, consider, and above all, question the fact pattern being presented to you—a pretty good reminder.

The reverberations from the explosion of the *Maine*, and the U.S. charge into war, were felt thousands of miles away in the South China Sea. In Manila harbor, the aging Spanish fleet was bottled up and attacked by the superior U.S. fleet under Admiral George Dewey. He pushed his ships into the harbor in a surprise move and caught the Spanish fleet at their moorings. This was on the cusp between the age of sail and the age of steam, and Dewey took full advantage of the maneuverability conferred by his steam engines, passing up and down the Spanish line and hitting them with effective fire that destroyed the Spanish ability to fight. It marked the end of effective Spanish colonization in the Philippines, ending centuries of domination; it also marked the beginning of the engagement of the United States as a colonizing power, something that did not turn out well.

During this period at the tail end of the nineteenth century, the Japanese also were moving south into the South China Sea region. Although they were initially focused on Korea, they also took Taiwan from the ineffectual Qing dynasty in China. This was followed by the Boxer Rebellion, an indigenous uprising that roiled China and affected the colonizing European powers, ultimately causing thousands of deaths. The weakness of the Qing dynasty was an aberration in the long history of Chinese domination of the South China Sea—as Deng Xiaoping was said to have told Henry Kissinger in so many words, China is a great civilization that has had a couple of bad centuries. That weakness, so apparent in the twentieth century in particular, is outside the norm, and current events in the South China Sea show that the pendulum is swinging back strongly toward a policy of strong Chinese activity throughout the region.

By the 1930s, the outlines of conflict were clear. A rising Japanese power needed natural resources and tried to negotiate agreements with a distracted United States just emerging from its own internal economic catastrophe. With Japan rising and increasingly dominating the littoral of the South China Sea—from taking chunks of China itself to Taiwan to moving south into Vietnam—the United States was relatively impotent. The South China Sea, for the first time in a thousand years, was turned into essentially the territorial sea of a single power: Japan. It took four years of war to release it again.

From the very start of the U.S. entry into World War II, the South China Sea became a key objective of our strategy. Why? Because it was the highway over which Japanese logistic support was flowing to their forward forces, which were rapidly overrunning large swaths of the western Pacific Ocean and the East Asian mainland.

As discussed earlier in the chapter on the Pacific, the first blows of the Japanese that landed effectively against U.S. forces after the Pearl Harbor attack in December 1941 were struck against the U.S. garrison in the Philippines on the cusp of the South China Sea. On the island of Luzon, the U.S. commander, General Douglas MacArthur, was forced to abandon his headquarters in Manila and head to the Bataan Peninsula, which could be more easily defended. MacArthur also held the nearby Corregidor Island. The South China Sea was clearly going to be a central objective of both sides, controlling as it does the sea lanes of communication that run athwart East Asia and the routes to the oil and rubber of the south. So the garrison at Corregidor grimly settled in for a siege, with little hope of anything beyond a delaying action and the faint hope of relief in place.

But by early March 1942, it was clear that the position was indefensible and would fall, and President Roosevelt ordered MacArthur to escape; the thought of the most senior general in the U.S. Army falling into the hands of the Japanese, especially after the Japanese success in attacking Pearl Harbor, was inconceivable. Nonetheless, MacArthur tried to stall: after all, he had been a general officer since 1918 and had held four-star command throughout the 1930s. He was a proud and indomitable spirit. But eventually he realized that discretion would be the better course than valor at that point. His departure proclamation is often quoted today: "The President of the United States ordered me to break through the Japanese lines and proceed from Corregidor to Australia for the purpose, as I understand it, of organizing the offensive against Japan, a primary object of which is the relief of the Philippines. I came through and I shall return."

As a young officer in the 1980s, I met the famous retired vice admiral John D. Bulkeley, who as a young lieutenant was given the mission of getting General MacArthur out of the Philippines. He was awarded the Medal of Honor for his command of the torpedo boat squadron throughout the Corregidor campaign and for the safe passage of General MacArthur. By the time I met him, he was an intimidating figure, a crusty seadog who had been recalled to active duty to lead the Navy's Board of Inspection and Survey. His charge was to make sure that our ships were combat ready, and he was a good choice for the job.

At the time, I was a young and untested department head on a "fancy new cruiser," as he styled it, the AEGIS-equipped *Valley Forge*. Bulkeley came down to the waterfront to pick apart our damage control capability, and to stand in front of him explaining why we had failed to correctly align the firefighting water system on the ship was extraordinarily embarrassing. As he quite artfully chewed me out, I kept looking at the single ribbon on his uniform, the Medal of Honor, knowing that he also held the Navy Cross and a slew of other combat awards. I remember thinking that he represented a direct line from the World War II Navy, and his combat runs across the South China Sea dodging Japanese gunfire remain legendary. Would I ever be able to muster the same level of courage and honor and commitment, I wondered?

At virtually the same time MacArthur fled Corregidor, the unchallenged Japanese fleet was moving to dominate the entire South China Sea, headed down the coast of Borneo and building forward operating stations for air and ground troops on the littoral of the sea. The only force between them and domination of the South China Sea was the ABDA fleet of light cruisers and destroyers, which stood for American (our small Asiatic fleet), British, Dutch, and Australian. This handful of ships was truly the "Fleet the Gods Forgot," and it was under the command of a Dutch two-star admiral, Karel Doorman. It was destroyed in February 1942, leading to the surrender of Java and the fall of the entire Dutch East Indies. This provided the Japanese with oil (from the oil wells in Borneo, Java, and Sumatra) as well as rubber, quinine, tin, and other strategic necessities. The South China Sea provided a wealth of riches to Japan's so-called Greater East Asia Co-Prosperity Sphere.

But inexorably, the Allied net began to close. From this point forward, the action shifted to the broader reaches of the Pacific outside the South China Sea. The Japanese, bounded by their limited population base, had taken on an unsustainable task, and the blow at Pearl Harbor made any agreement with the United States impossible. The dual thrust of the U.S. and Allied forces began to hammer back, and by the end of 1943, U.S. forces were headed toward the Philippines again.

The bloody battles of 1943, the island-hopping campaign, and a relentless submarine campaign enabled MacArthur to position his forces by March 1944 to head toward the Philippines and the South China Sea. The most important sea battle—while not fully decisive—was in the Philippine Sea in mid-June 1944. Here Admiral Marc Mitscher was able to take the pressure off MacArthur, who then carried the fight back into the heart of the South China Sea. In October 1944, early in the afternoon, MacArthur climbed down from the cruiser *Nashville* into a landing craft and went ashore onto the Philippine island of Leyte, taking long strides through the knee-deep water after the coxswain dropped the ramp. As promised, he had returned, and the South China Sea became an American lake later that month, after the decisive sea battle of Leyte Gulf, which shattered the heart of the Japanese fleet. The full liberation of the Philippine Islands followed in short order, and not long afterward—deprived of the resources flowing across the South China Sea and faced with a nuclear armed America—the Japanese surrendered.

In the course of my career, I spent a great deal of time in and around the Philippines, which in many ways are the seam between the broader Pacific and Asia proper. They endured centuries of Spanish colonization, experienced the half-hearted attempt of the United States to be a colonial power in the first part of the twentieth century, and finally, as independence appeared assured, fell into the center of a brutal world war. Their nation is also like the Caribbean in that it so often resembles a bull's-eye for the various tsunamis that reoccur again and again in that part of the world. Yet despite so much bad luck and poor governance, the people of the Philippines have a lightness of soul that shines through, a kind of good-humored ability to deal with adversity, and a deep spirituality.

I first encountered the Philippines in the mid-1970s as a young ensign on a destroyer headed into the beautiful natural harbor of Subic Bay, where the U.S. Navy had historically had a large sea and air base. It was a bustling tropical setting, with beautiful beaches, cold San Miguel beer, and very friendly hostesses working across the "shit river" that led to the town and the countless bars, strip clubs, and houses of ill repute.

In fact, as a division officer, I had my hands full trying (and frequently failing) to keep my sailors from falling in love with and marrying the beautiful young local women. We had a "cooling off" period that a commanding officer could impose to prevent premature nuptials, but persistence often found young sailors falling into true love. Many of those marriages, by the way, turned out very well when the young brides made their way back to our home port of San Diego, where they more often than not turned out to be thrifty, sensible Navy spouses. Over the course of my career, I have met many a "deployment bride" from the Philippine Islands, and I would say they fared pretty well.

The strategic value of the Philippine Islands is obvious from a glance at a map, and the U.S. bases there—both the huge naval and air complex at Subic Bay and the even larger air base at Clark Airfield near Manila—were mainstays of U.S. naval and geopolitical strategy in the region throughout the cold war. With "an anchor to windward" in the South China Sea, the United States was able to maintain a strong presence in these waters throughout this period.

While there were numerous skirmishes between the United States and China, especially over the protection of Taiwan, the major set-piece battle of the cold war in the South China Sea was, of course, the war in Vietnam. At the outset of the cold war, with former NATO Supreme Allied Commander Dwight Eisenhower in the White House, there was significant reluctance to get more deeply involved in the region, even given the dangerous and seductive idea of what would eventually be called the "domino theory." This was the idea that if the United States did not prevent individual local regimes from becoming Communist states aligned with either Moscow or Beijing or both, they would fall together, like dominoes, and the United States would have to face a significant Communist bloc in the region. There are many problems with this theory, and President Eisenhower, who had seen so much of war, worked hard to avoid entangling the United States in any sort of land war in the region. While he acknowledged the theory, he managed to avoid a significant ground force engagement in Asia.

Even when our World War II allies, the French, found themselves on the losing end of a vicious insurgency in French Indochina—today's Vietnam, Cambodia, and Laos—Eisenhower refused to either send troops or threaten the use of nuclear weapons. The French were defeated by the insurgent Viet Minh, led by Ho Chi Minh, and expelled from Vietnam after a huge loss at the Battle of Dien Bien Phu in 1954. The United States was deeply worried about this, and many here used the domino theory to begin arguing for more U.S. involvement in Vietnam, which of course came to fruition not on Eisenhower's watch, but on that of his successor, John F. Kennedy.

As the 1960s unfolded, the South China Sea became a principal maritime focus of the United States. While the cold war raged globally, requiring the efforts of the U.S. Navy from the Arctic to the Mediterranean to the Baltic to the deep Atlantic, there was considerable naval activity in the South China Sea. This was because of the increasing tempo of U.S. operations on behalf of South Vietnam as it fought against both the North Vietnamese Army (supported by China) and the insurgency of the Viet Minh and Viet Cong within South Vietnam itself. This required increasing the level of U.S. troops ashore throughout the early-to-mid-1960s under both presidents Kennedy and Johnson.

At the peak, the United States supported more than half a million Army and Marine combat troops ashore, with the Navy fleet in constant support. Maritime activity included complex aircraft carrier strikes ashore against targets in both North and South Vietnam; coastal and riverine operations in direct support of the soldiers and Marines ashore; logistic supply to units ashore and operating at sea for prolonged periods of time; maritime surveillance and intelligence gathering; insertion of SEAL patrols and support of them from the sea; and bombardment with naval guns of targets in the coastal regions. The South China Sea became an American lake throughout much of this period, with hundreds of U.S.

warships in operations throughout. The transit route between Vietnam and the Philippines was a well-trodden path for U.S. sailors indeed.

Throughout the early 1960s, U.S. involvement increased year by year, tripling in 1961 and again in 1962. The relatively young American president, Jack Kennedy, sensed the slippery slope toward the "Americanization" of the war effort. As his date with destiny in Dallas approached, his enthusiasm for the war was diminishing rapidly. After his tragic assassination, Lyndon Johnson felt the need to demonstrate his tough approach toward communism. With a war record that was suspect to begin with, Johnson always seemed intimidated by his Joint Chiefs of Staff and his wunderkind secretary of defense, Robert McNamara.

Perhaps the clinching event that drove further U.S. involvement was the so-called Tonkin Gulf incident of 1964, in which a group of North Vietnamese torpedo boats supposedly attacked two U.S. ships off the coast of Vietnam at the northern end of the South China Sea. The USS *Maddox* and USS *Turner Joy* managed to fire hundreds of rounds of heavy artillery at what most observers have since concluded were "phantom targets" in two highly suspect "attacks." These attacks were used by the Johnson administration to gain congressional approval for direct military action in Vietnam, and the rapid increase of U.S. forces in the country followed, as well as strikes against North Vietnam. Thousands of lives ended and many more were dramatically changed by the events that flowed from the Tonkin Gulf incident.

In terms of maritime operations in the South China Sea, the U.S. Navy was the dominant force. Over the course of the war, nearly two million sailors served in theater. The missions were varied, but on the deep ocean, supply and logistics were critical—more than 95 percent of all the material and personnel that headed in and out of Vietnam sailed at sea on Navy and merchant marine vessels. Two Navy hospital ships were the first destination for many of the wounded.

Additionally, the U.S. Navy spent a great deal of time training the South Vietnamese navy, which, by 1972 when the United States disengaged from active combat, numbered more than eight hundred ships and more than forty thousand men—believe it or not, the fifth-largest navy in the world in that year, albeit mostly composed of tiny riverine and coastal patrol craft. Meanwhile, the U.S. Navy continued a strong effort from the South China Sea. In 1972, it was flying more than 3,800 sorties a month, and Navy destroyers and cruisers fired well over 100,000 long-range shells at shore targets. Mines were used from aircraft to seal off North Vietnamese ports.

As the war ramped up, peaked, and gradually began to falter due to a lack of support in the United States, an aversion to mounting casualties, political disillusionment flowing from Watergate, and bad strategic choices by U.S. military leaders, it was clear that the United States would withdraw. Eventually nearly sixty thousand U.S. troops would die in this war, and perhaps five million Vietnamese. The U.S. Navy continued its operations in support of the South Vietnamese government while it still survived, but when Congress cut off funding in the mid-1970s, the game was over in Saigon. The U.S. embassy was overwhelmed, and the last, sad act of the U.S. Navy was to operate air and sea ferries to save as many U.S. supporters among the Vietnamese along with our embassy and remaining troops. Viet Thanh Nguyen's recent novel *The Sympathizer* is a searing portrait of those final days and the evacuations out of Saigon and captures perfectly the zeitgeist of the moment of failure.

Decades later, in the early part of the twenty-first century, I went to Vietnam for the first time. Not to Saigon (now of course renamed Ho Chi Minh City), but to the north, to Hanoi. I was part of the delegation of Secretary of Defense Don Rumsfeld, who firmly believed that a coherent strategic relationship between the United States and Vietnam was strongly in our interest. We were treated like royalty, and I sensed the deep interest on the part of senior Vietnamese officials in a relationship with us. Why? Because of the economic, political, and military benefits that would allow Vietnam to maintain an independent posture vis-à-vis China.

As our motorcade sortied through the streets of Hanoi, I saw a motorcycle go by with a box of small piglets on the back. In a wire box about the size of a small apartment's refrigerator, they were hurtling precariously through the narrow streets and overtook us before zooming on as we pulled up to the famous prison where Senator (then Navy pilot) John McCain had been held and tortured. The United States and Vietnam had shared a dark chapter, but I hoped the future was brighter for the relationship between the nations than it was for those piglets. It appears that is the case, as the relationship between the United States and Vietnam continues to expand across political, economic, and security dimensions.

So as the United States withdrew once and for all from Vietnam in the mid-1970s, the U.S. focus in the South China Sea continued with our allies in the Philippines and Taiwan, as well as working to improve defense and economic relations farther to the south, with Singapore, Malaysia, and Indonesia. The story of the United States and Taiwan is particularly worth considering for its importance in the region.

IN THE 1950S, the other significant conflict affecting the South China Sea was on the sea itself—between mainland or Communist China, led by Mao Zedong, and the Nationalist Chinese in the Republic of China on the island of Taiwan. Sitting astride the northern entrance to the South China Sea, Taiwan has a long and challenging history of being conquered and colonized over the centuries. Also known as Formosa, the island has been subjected to invading forces numerous times (including Dutch, Spanish, and Chinese), and more recently was a Japanese colony from the end of the nineteenth century to the end of World War II. After the loss of the bloody civil war on mainland China, the republican Chinese, led by Chiang Kai-shek, retreated to Taiwan and for several decades maintained the fiction that they were the "true" government of China. They even held the UN Security Council seat throughout a portion of the post–World War II period until it was turned over to the Communist mainland regime in 1971.

Throughout the cold war, the United States stood with Taiwan, and it continues to provide a great deal of political and military support today. But during the late 1970s, the United States noted a change in Chinese global policy that affected events in the South China Sea—the Chinese shifted their top national security threat from the United States to the Soviet Union. The Chinese began to help the United States diplomatically, and the tension across the Taiwan Strait was visibly reduced. As a result, sadly, the U.S. Navy—which for decades had been visiting Taiwan—stopped pulling into port there.

The two great liberty ports, both cherished by sailors, were Keelung and Kaohsiung. Both were notorious for the beauty of the women, the strength of the liquor, and the inexpensive costs of the clubs ashore—all the things our fearless sailors were looking for on a trip ashore after a month or more at sea. I went out as shore patrol officer on one of the final liberty runs ashore in Keelung, a bustling commercial port at the top of Taiwan. It is a warm and tropical city, with a lot of rainfall, and we had our hands full rounding up sailors who had imbibed a bit too much and returning them to face justice aboard their ship. It was all like an extended scene out of the musical *South Pacific*, and I had a couple of burly petty officers to do the heavy lifting.

But what I remember most vividly the next day was taking a tour of the port and learning about the role of the city during the Opium Wars of the nineteenth century. The British were fighting the weak Qing dynasty and tried three times to capture the city, which was strongly held by the local Chinese admiral. He captured and executed a handful of British sailors, and the city remained a free zone throughout most of the century. It reminded me of how the sweep of history had crossed that island so many times—the Dutch, the Spanish, the British, the mainland Chinese of course, the Japanese, and finally the Chinese republican forces who still held out against the Communist regime ashore.

Like Sicily in the Mediterranean, Taiwan was strategic ground and fought over frequently, with the indigenous people endlessly bearing the brunt of war. As I walked about the port in my Navy uniform, it occurred to me how strategically vital this island remains, plugging like a stopper the great flask of the South China Sea and sitting athwart the sea lanes between Korea, Japan, China, and all the states to the south. Mahan would have advocated planting a flag there and building a coaling station. Those days are gone, but continuing engagement by the United States makes a great deal of sense, it seemed to me on that spring day long ago, and still does today.

The final leitmotif of the South China Sea over the past two decades is the geopolitical contest between an outsize China that is rising inexorably and the handful of small but dynamic nations that share the littoral of the South China Sea with their massive and increasingly assertive neighbor. The history of the waterway is not only about ships passing through it, and the small and great wars on the coasts; it is about the scattered island chains that provide a means for nations to claim chunks of the sea if they can only establish claim. This is the story of the seemingly constant conflict over the Paracel and Spratly islands, for example, as well as over Mischief Reef.

What drives all this, of course, is the presence of hydrocarbons and fish in the South China Sea. While most of the nations would be content with the rules and regulations generated by the United Nations Law of the Sea Treaty, which came largely into force in the 1980s, what is in dispute is access to the region's ample fisheries near the seafood markets of Asia and the seabed hydrocarbons. Some estimates put the total amount of oil and natural gas at levels similar to the Middle East. This is a mother lode of resources, especially for the smaller players along the littoral. So it's no surprise that there has been a constant game of occupying the island chains for nearly fifty years.

What is new is China's strategy to build artificial islands. This has begun in earnest in the past several years, and already the Chinese have built dozens of islands, mostly in the southern and eastern portions of the South China Sea. They are making them large enough to have caught the attention of the U.S. military and political actors in Washington. Admiral Harry Harris, who is Japanese American and the first Asian American four-star officer in the U.S. armed forces, has called the construction of the artificial islands "the great wall of sand." The United States has undertaken a series of Freedom of Navigation missions to challenge China's claims of sovereignty. Admiral Harris has elsewhere called the Chinese claims "preposterous," and most international legal scholars agree. And in mid-2016, the international courts ruled definitively against China, which has thus far simply ignored the ruling and continued to aggressively build artificial islands and conduct its maritime operations as though it owned the South China Sea in its entirety. This situation will grow over the coming decades, and the potential for active combat is not insignificant.

Instead of stone, brick, and wood, this new "great wall" consists of artificial islands strung out across the South China Sea—a region Beijing claims by virtue of historical right. China's claim is encompassed by what it terms the "nine-dash line," a radical demarcation of maritime sovereignty that takes an enormous bite out of the legitimate territorial claims of Vietnam, the Philippines, and other countries ringing the South China Sea.

The crucial context of this behavior is that the South China Sea—Asia's "cauldron," as geostrategist Robert D. Kaplan calls it—is bubbling like the witches' kettle in Shakespeare's *Macbeth*. The South China Sea matters not only because it is contested territory, but because it's hugely important to the smooth operation of the global economy. More than $5 trillion of the world's annual trade passes through the South China Sea, all under the watchful eyes of the (oddly named) People's Liberation Army Navy.

China's aggressive behavior in building these artificial islands tracks with its disregard of other norms of international law. Some of these provocations include lack of clarity on the claim itself—a claim that, again, international lawyers widely regard as preposterous—including an air-defense identification zone over the East China Sea directed at the United States, Japan, and South Korea; the placement of a mobile oil platform in Vietnam's coastal waters; and the widely reported (and massive) cyberthefts of U.S. intellectual property, industrial secrets, and personal data.

The specifics on the construction of these artificial islands are staggering. Thus far—and construction continues—China has created nearly three thousand acres of land out of the ocean. Just consider that the highly touted and massive U.S. aircraft carriers (from which can be launched a wing of more than seventy jets and helicopters) are only about seven acres of flattop. Are these artificial islands similar to hundreds of unsinkable aircraft carriers in the South China Sea? Think that shifts the balance between the two competing militaries? You bet it does.

Besides the obvious geopolitical and military issues, significant ecological damage is also under way, according to many scientists. One expert from the University of Miami, John McManus, called China's building of man-made islands "the most rapid rate of permanent loss of coral reef area in human history."

Add to this the internal tension under which President Xi Jinping's regime is operating: falling real estate prices, an aging population, an imbalance of men (too many) and women (too few), terrible ecological damage requiring significant mitigation, and above all, a sputtering economy that is stunting growth. When authoritarian regimes come under pressure, they tend to look outward to find ways to distract the population. Nationalism emerges. Such is the case in China today. Witness Xi's September 2015 speech at the United Nations—full of barely concealed vitriol directed at the government of Japanese prime minister Shinzo Abe. The tension between Japan and China has been waxing and waning over the past several years. Now it's increasing again.

What is the best approach for the United States? This tense situation is out in the open, and Xi's late September 2015 visit to Washington, and President Trump's trip to Asia in 2017, did not fundamentally change anything.

First, despite provocations, the United States must maintain open communications with China and seek ways to reduce the chances of an inadvertent collision either between the United States and China (unlikely) or between China and one of its immediate neighbors (far more likely). The U.S. relationship with China encompasses economic issues, geopolitical cooperation from Afghanistan to Iran, and global environmental issues—the South China Sea dispute is only one element. Dialogue is crucial. And the agreements on military-to-military contact and cybersecurity that the two presidents discussed during Xi's visit are better than nothing.

Second, the United States needs to strengthen its relationship with existing allies and partners in the region and encourage them to work together better. This applies especially to Japan and South Korea, which, for a host of historical reasons, have long had an uncomfortable relationship. The United States can help build better ties between the two neighbors by promoting military exchanges and exercises, enabling conversations at important events like the Shangri-La Dialogue (an annual gathering of strategic thinkers in Singapore), and encouraging so-called Track II engagement, which is exchanges and dialogue conducted not through government channels (Track I) but instead through academic and research institutions. The Trans-Pacific Partnership, a massive multilateral trade agreement, is a big element: building a network of even stronger trading ties can ensure that America's friends and allies cooperate with one another. And in particular, working more closely with Vietnam makes good sense—and this should include lifting bans on weapons sales.

Third, the fundamental tenets of international law are against China's approach in the South China Sea. The United States should sternly emphasize this in international forums like the United Nations, the G-7, and the Association of Southeast Asian Nations. The intellectual underpinnings of international legal judgments on the South China Sea are very clear: nations cannot simply declare a "historical claim" and take over what other nations regard as international waters. The United States, as a global maritime power, should not miss any opportunity to object. The recent negative ruling against China further buttresses this strategic approach. And frankly, the United States should finally sign the UN Convention on the Law of the Sea, the treaty that governs the world's oceans, to maintain the high ground in these conversations.

Fourth, and finally, the United States should exercise its traditional rights of transit under international legal norms: its Freedom of Navigation operations. That means overflying Chinese territorial claims and sailing U.S. ships through China's claimed water space—the waters within twelve miles of these islands. The United States has a long tradition of countering unjustified historical claims by sailing and flying through international waters and airspace. Now is the time to exercise it in the South China Sea.

None of these strategic prescriptions by themselves will resolve the challenges of the South China Sea. Nor will simply moving U.S. military aircraft and vessels through claimed Chinese air and sea space suffice. Pushing back on Chinese claims in the South China Sea requires a broader strategy that treats this violation of international law in the larger context of both Chinese behavior and Sino-U.S. relations. Above all, it will require U.S. leadership alongside America's many partners and friends throughout East Asia. China's Great Wall was at least partially successful in keeping foreigners out. Its Great Wall of Sand will not be.

Echoes of this argument from five hundred years ago—of the sovereign states' rights in the coastal zone versus the value of mare liberum or the freedom of the high seas—are very much with us today. When I first sailed in the South China Sea in the 1980s, we were only marginally concerned about China. Our ships went pretty much wherever we wanted. But of late, the Chinese—advocating ownership of more or less the entire South China Sea—are vastly more aggressive. Even more disturbing, they are building these artificial islands in a further attempt to solidify their claim to these seas. All of this dates back at least five hundred years, and in many ways a couple of millennia in terms of historical claim to the waters. From the perspective of the United States, acquiescing in these claims will lead to further closure of the high seas, and thus necessitate our Freedom of Navigation operations: short, sharp patrols intruding into claimed territorial seas that we contend are in fact high seas and open to all. To understand this controversy requires looking backward into the long history of the region.

Having spent much of a long nautical career in the Pacific, I am hard-pressed to think of another time of greater military competition in the Asian region, at least since the end of the Second World War. In particular, arms expenditures are rising throughout Asia, especially in the bubbling cauldron of the South China Sea.

Unfortunately, we are merely at the start of an entirely predictable and dangerous arms race as nations in the region increasingly respond both to the perception of a rising military power in China that seems more assertive in a strategic sense and to growing evidence of instability on the Korean Peninsula. All of this happens as the American "Pacific pivot" fails to gain traction in the face of crises in Syria, threats from the Islamic State, and ongoing tension with Russia over Ukraine, and the Trump administration's isolationist instincts.

In terms of military spending, China (which has the second-largest national defense budget in the world after the United States) is on track to double its already significant defense spending by 2020, increasing about 7 percent each year. Meanwhile, the U.S. defense budget and those of European nations in particular have been declining. The Chinese are also buying and building large aircraft carriers, having just begun construction on the first one to be built in China. They are also rapidly improving their offensive cyber capability, which will be central to military operations in the future.

The other nations of the region are responding. Japan has not only increased its defense budget but also passed legislation (not without controversy and protests) that will allow for offensive Japanese military action in defense of allies under attack—clearly strengthening its military alignment with the United States. Vietnam, the Philippines, Malaysia, and virtually every other nation in the region are likewise increasing their defense spending. On average, the East Asian nations are spending at least 5 percent a year more on defense than was the case several years ago. And we should remember that the United States and Russia, the first- and third-largest defense spenders in the world (and the two largest arms exporters), are also Pacific powers.

At a recently completed World Economic Forum in Davos, we saw a bit less public strain between Asian leaders than in the past couple of years, which is good. But in 2014 at Davos, Japanese prime minister Shinzo Abe said that he saw the Chinese-Japanese relationship as reminiscent of the antagonism between Great Britain and Imperial Germany a century earlier, on the eve of the First World War—hardly a reassuring thought. Since then, the two leaders—Prime Minister Abe and President Xi—have managed to appear together at several events and there seems to be less overt tension in the air. But in a variety of conversations I have had with senior military and political leaders over the past few months, it is clear that the subtext remains one of significant competition and indeed potential conflict.

Several of the nations involved in territorial disputes with China are moving closer to the United States. These include Japan (already among the closest of allies of the United States in the East Asian region), Australia (basing U.S. Marines ashore on its northern coast), and Vietnam (which continues to operate closely with the United States in both military and commercial spheres). The Philippines presents a more complicated case. Until 2016 they were moving toward a much closer relationship with the United States. However, their highly unpredictable populist president, Rodrigo Duterte, is now distancing himself from the United States, which has criticized him for violating human rights and encouraging the killing of drug offenders and criminals with impunity. In addition to swearing (frequently) at the United States and President Obama, Duterte has indicated a desire to reduce overall military cooperation with the United States and perhaps align himself with China (and possibly Russia). This trend has slowed under President Trump but Duterte's mercurial nature makes it difficult to predict how this will turn out, but it certainly throws another layer of tension and unpredictability into the already turbulent South China Sea.

The completion of the Trans-Pacific Partnership (which does not include China) would have further aligned the signatories with the United States. But with the Trump Administration's withdrawal from the process, the United States now must watch while China and others take the lead in establishing the new trade rules for the region.

IN ADDITION TO increased Chinese defense spending and assertiveness, there is the North Korean problem. With yet another nuclear detonation, and a 2017 test of an intercontinental ballistic missile, Kim Jong-un has definitively claimed the dubious honor of leading the most dangerous nation in the world. The North Koreans are armed with a small arsenal of nuclear weapons; led by an inexperienced, unstable, emotional, and medically challenged dictator (with a truly bad haircut); possessed of technologically advanced ballistic missiles; and in a virtual state of war with their closest neighbor, South Korea. All of this has an additive effect on the already tense relationships in the region, especially for Japan and South Korea, which must factor into their defense spending the presence of North Korea.

Another fascinating dynamic is the unfolding role of India as a global security actor, which will have knock-on effects in East Asia. India has historically stood a bit apart from East Asian politics, reasoning that it has enormous internal challenges and plenty to do in operating along the vast Indian Ocean littoral. But increasingly we are seeing India under dynamic prime minister Narendra Modi reaching out to engage with the United States and Japan in increased military and security cooperation. This began with counterpiracy operations off the Horn of Africa and now includes military exchanges and joint exercises.

The outlook remains very concerning, and it appears unlikely that there will be any significant reduction in tensions or in defense spending over the next decade and beyond. What should the international community and the nations in the region be doing to help create stability?

First, at the tactical level, the nations in the region should at a minimum encourage military-to-military direct contact. This can lead to defined protocols to minimize the chances of accidental ship and aircraft collisions, misunderstandings that escalate into shooting incidents, and even structuring agreements that would prevent cyberattacks on military command and control systems, which are highly destabilizing and particularly dangerous. Such military-to-military contact can be done bilaterally between the military staffs or organized in parallel to regional conferences.

Additionally, when such regional gatherings do occur—for example the Association of Southeast Asian Nations (ASEAN) annual convocation—having a portion of the event that includes high-level and candid political conversations about security is important and can create a higher level of confidence. Alongside such governmental conferences, private sector engagement (in maritime shipping, commercial air traffic control, cyber agreements, and environmental technologies for example) can be an excellent way for views to at least be exchanged in a neutral forum.

Third, finding ways for the militaries in the region to collaborate operationally, especially at sea, is important. This can be in simple maritime exercises that focus on noncombat operations—such as medical diplomacy, disaster relief, and humanitarian operations. It can also include quasi-military training or operations together for events upon which the nations do agree—piracy, for example, or humanitarian evacuations from a disaster zone.

Fourth, the use of international negotiating platforms to resolve territorial disputes could be key. Putting such disagreements before international bodies like the International Court of Justice in The Hague, another mutually agreed-upon United Nations body, a third-party government, or even an agreed-upon binding arbitrator should be considered. Unfortunately, such international legal activities are not binding, and it appears unlikely that China will accept such outside interference in its "backyard."

OVERALL, THE ARMS RACE in East Asia is simply a reflection of the geopolitical tensions that will remain high in the region for the foreseeable future. While there are ways to reduce such tensions, they are unlikely to diminish as the twenty-first century unfolds, so buckle up.

After putting all of this together, what is the right U.S. strategy for the South China Sea? Can it be separated from our thinking about the broader Pacific and the world ocean? What would Mahan tell us about its importance and our approach?

While it is impossible to pull out a single sea from the whole of the oceans and develop a global strategy based upon it, the South China Sea is unique in its geopolitical significance. Here resources, great and powerful maritime states, and critical sea lanes of communication converge in the most populous region of the world. The United States must retain a presence here. There are several ways we can do this.

We should maintain a network of bases and access agreements around the littoral of the South China Sea. The logical places to consider are in the east (hopefully the Philippines, perhaps even a return to Subic Bay), the west (in Vietnam, Cam Ranh Bay is a logical spot), and the south (Singapore, where we already have a robust presence, makes the most sense). In the north, we should continue to explore a strong refueling and resupply arrangement with Taiwan, even if this makes China upset (which it will). With a package of four bases, or at least four significant agreements for access and resupply, we could operate quite freely in the region.

Additionally, we need to have a strong relationship with each of the nations around the littoral. We already have such relationships with Japan and South Korea, just outside the South China Sea; but we need to pursue exercises, military exchanges, and maritime engagement with Vietnam, the Philippines, and Malaysia. Continuing to pursue good maritime relations with Thailand, Indonesia, and even Cambodia would also be helpful.

The big question over time will be how closely to engage China. It is too soon to tell, frankly, whether or not China's intentions in this region will permit recognition of international norms, and maritime and littoral boundaries. If China truly intends to attempt to claim the South China Sea as its territorial waters, the prospects are slim for an accommodation.

Having said all of that, it is crucial that we maintain an open and constructive relationship with China where we can. Despite our frustrations with their piracy of intellectual property, cyberattacks, unsupportable maritime claims, internal human rights violations, lack of democracy or liberty, and other points of disagreement, there are ways we can find some zones of cooperation. In the maritime sphere, for example, the possibility exists to work together on disaster relief, medical diplomacy, counternarcotics, counter–human smuggling, and environmental issues. The key is recognizing that there will be areas of significant disagreement, but that does not totally preclude working together on specific areas.

And there will be flare-ups between the United States and China. Over the past decade, we have suffered several, including an aggressive Chinese confrontation in 2009 with a U.S. surveillance ship, USS *Impeccable*, operating completely legally in international waters (although within the exclusive economic zone of China); and a Chinese fighter jet collision with a Navy electronic P-3 Orion aircraft in 2001, forcing it to land on Chinese territory. Both of these incidents were eventually worked out diplomatically, but are indicative of the cut-and-thrust of both U.S. and Chinese maneuvering in the South China Sea. And in fairness, we should consider our own reactions if Chinese intelligence and surveillance vessels and aircraft were routinely operating in the Gulf of Mexico, close to U.S. installations and within our exclusive economic zone (EEZ).

Those incidents bring up an interesting aspect of international law that pertains both in the South China Sea and elsewhere. The United States failed to sign the massive 1984 United Nations Law of the Sea Treaty (one of only thirty nations worldwide to refuse, sixteen of which are landlocked). In that treaty, the conditions under which nations can transit another nation's exclusive economic zone (two hundred nautical miles) are somewhat ambiguous. The United States chooses to interpret it as permitting us to conduct national surveillance (a euphemism for spying); other nations (China, India, and others) vehemently dispute this. The text is unclear. This disconnect is what has led to incidents like this involving U.S. spy ships and aircraft operating inside the EEZ but outside the territorial sea (twelve nautical miles). More such incidents will follow, especially in the contentious waters of the South China Sea.

Overall, the South China Sea will be a maritime hinge upon which huge geopolitical issues will ultimately swing. The United States must consider it a crucial zone of maritime activity in the twenty-first century. If we cede it to China—something China deeply desires and would consider inevitable—our global strategy will fail. While we should not push ourselves into a cold war with a rising China, we need to be mindful of our values and the importance of international law. As a young officer sailing these waters nearly four decades ago, I was deeply impressed with the history and civilization of China. We need to respect its culture and importance in this region and upon the dark blue waters of the South China Sea, but not surrender our own participation on international high seas and with close friends and allies. It will be a delicate balance to strike, but a crucial one. Much as with the Russian Federation, we should cooperate where we can, but confront where we must.

6.

THE CARIBBEAN

STALLED IN THE PAST

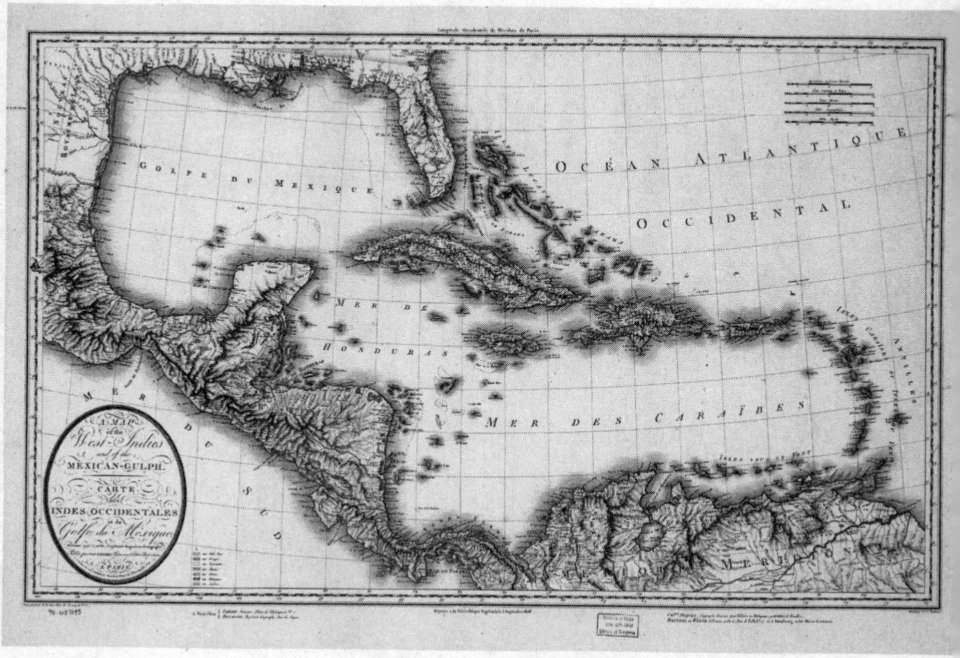

The Caribbean as it appeared to cartographers
Pierre Lapie and Ambroise Tardieu in 1806.

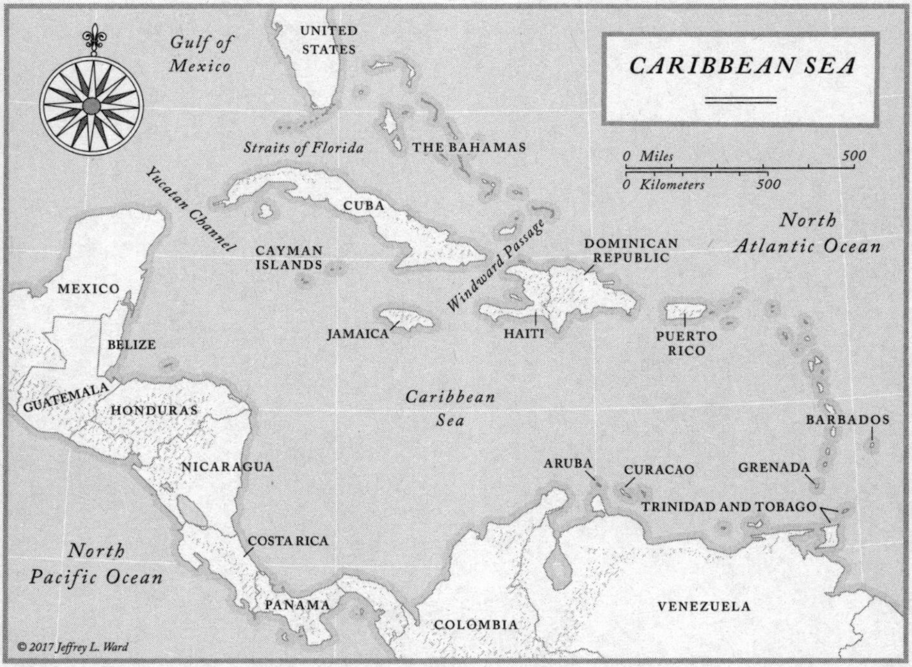

The Caribbean Sea remains the part of America's backyard about which most citizens know very little.

Any understanding of the modern Caribbean actually begins in Madrid, at the Spanish Naval Museum. I went there first in 2009, on my initial visit as the NATO commander. The chief of defense of Spain, an extremely elegant four-star air force general, put me in the capable hands of his chief of the navy for much of the day, and together we spent a couple of delightful hours wandering through the maritime history of Spain—a good deal of which focused on the Spanish conquest of the Americas, centered upon naval operations in the Caribbean.

In the museum I saw the earliest map of any part of the Americas, the chart of Juan de la Cosa, which despite all of its understandable inaccuracies (it was drawn up in 1500 by an experienced sailor but not a formally trained mapmaker), is quite recognizable to modern eyes. Over the part of the map where Central America ought to be located is an image of St. Christopher, the patron saint of travelers—probably an intended homage to Christopher Columbus.

Columbus, as any pre–politically correct schoolchild of the 1970s will remember, was not Spanish, but Italian. He was born in Genoa in the middle of the fifteenth century, probably around 1450 or so. Known in Spanish as Cristóbal Colón, he has come to us in anglicized form as Christopher Columbus. He probably traveled extensively around the western Mediterranean and down the coast of Africa. This was a period in which the Portuguese were daily discovering new ways to harness current and wind to reliably explore beyond the edges of the known world. Some reports indicate that he traveled north as well, perhaps as far as Ireland.

Genoa in the early years of Columbus was like the bar scene in *Star Wars*, with Marco Polo playing Han Solo. It was full of exaggerated tales of the Far East, the riches of trade, swaggering characters and sea captains, and plenty of shady opportunity. The son of a lower-middle-class weaver, Columbus would have grown up with a sense of horizons opening up, and a dream of making it to the richest lands of all—the China of Marco Polo's tales. By the mid-1470s, he had moved to Portugal and set out to find a sponsor for a voyage to the west, eventually turning to Ferdinand and Isabella of Spain (specifically Aragon and Castile, respectively) for sponsorship.

The year 1492 was important in the consolidation of Spain and the removal of the final vestiges of the Muslim world from the Iberian Peninsula—on January 2, eight hundred years of Islamic rule over some portion of modern-day Spain came to a close through the so-called Reconquista. Given the optimism and enthusiasm over these august events, it was not hard to eventually persuade the royal couple (mainly Isabella, a sea captain's daughter and granddaughter) to finance the expedition to the west, through what was called the Ocean Sea.

Columbus demanded and received excellent terms: the title of admiral, significant control over the disposition of discovered lands, and a large share of the profits. The voyage to the Caribbean was soon financed and the expedition was divided among the three famous ships—the *Niña*, the *Pinta*, and the *Santa Maria*—in August 1492. By early October, the "Admiral of the Ocean Sea" is believed to have arrived in the Caribbean on a small Bahamian island today known as San Salvador, the name first given it by Columbus. Thus did Europeans come to the Americas, at least in the case of the Caribbean Sea.

And what a disappointment for Columbus! Far from the glittering palaces and pleasure domes, the gold and silk, the spice and treasure of Asia, he found instead the traditional culture of the Amerindians, who went about mostly naked, built and produced little beyond bare subsistence, and had little idea about gold. Columbus explored and discovered Cuba and Hispaniola without finding anything of conventional value. He departed at the turn of the year in January 1493, bringing a few pieces of gold (he left nearly forty sailors behind to try to develop a gold mine on Hispaniola), some fruits and birds, and several terrified Indians to show at court.

Despite utterly failing at what he actually set out to do—to find a western sea route to the Far East—Columbus put sufficient spin on the voyage's narrative to intrigue many in Europe. Further voyages quickly followed, and investment flowed. On his next voyage in 1493, Admiral Columbus discovered other important islands—Puerto Rico, the Virgin Islands, Montserrat, Guadeloupe, and Antigua. Small bases and commercial entities were established, and more kept coming. There was a haphazard quality to it all, understandable given the depth of geographic misunderstanding that had led to the discoveries.

When I was first a sea captain myself, in late 1993, my destroyer, the *Barry*, was ordered to the Caribbean to conduct humanitarian work and enforce an arms embargo against Haiti. It was a strange first voyage, as this was just after the end of the cold war and the fall of the Berlin Wall. Frankly, I would rather have sailed my brand-new AEGIS combatant up into the Baltic Sea to chase Soviet submarines, but that ship had sailed, so to speak. So off to apply soft power in the Caribbean I went, with an inexperienced crew and all of us trying to find our sea legs on this, the first significant voyage of the newly commissioned warship.

We sailed right by the island of San Salvador at the entrance to the Caribbean, and I called the crew up on deck and gave a very short description of Columbus's first voyage, calling on my excellent fifth-grade history teacher's pedagogy, concluding with the dramatic words, "Just think, here we are just over five hundred years later—half a millennium—sailing in the same waters as Christopher Columbus, the great explorer, headed to help create security in this part of the world. Columbus's legacy continues." I felt pretty good about my impromptu history lesson.

But when I went down to the wardroom for dinner, a couple of my junior officers (who were nearly two decades younger than me and one of whom was African American) pointed out that Columbus's voyages had led mostly to enslavement and death for the locals. Good point, I thought. We should remember that History, with a capital H, is always a throw of the cosmic dice. It seems to provide both the good and the bad in endless measure, and only God can sort it out in the end, I suppose. One man's vaunted explorer is another man's genocidal conquistador, and how those cosmic dice land on the table is so often a random walk.

Indeed, the "Accidental Sea" could just as easily be the name of the Caribbean Sea given the nature of its discovery; but as my younger and wiser junior officers correctly pointed out, before very long, the deliberate and dark scourge of slavery to fuel the production of sugar and other crops would begin to take root throughout these beautiful and pristine islands. Colonization of the Caribbean was also fueled by the desire to proselytize and convert the indigenous populations to Christianity. The Age of Exploration, setting out on the vast oceans of the world, washed ashore on the quiet Caribbean—with explosive effect felt down to the present day. And on reflection it is hard to deny that the ultimate outcome, sadly, was not so much the product of an accident after all, but of a series of acts of avarice and greed that shape the sensibilities of the islands today.

THE CARIBBEAN IS A BIG SEA—if you include the Gulf of Mexico, which we will do for our purposes, it surpasses the Mediterranean as the world's largest body of water that is not categorized as an ocean (after the Pacific, Atlantic, Indian, and Arctic oceans in that order). It is roughly 1.6 million square miles, about half the size of the continental United States.

It is a sort of massive pot-shaped body of water, and it is easy to picture the Caribbean as the rim of a huge volcano. One side is shaped by the long finger of Florida pointing downward on the western side, dropping like the boot of Italy toward the island of Cuba. Americans don't always appreciate the size of Cuba, by the way—if it were laid out on a map of the United States it would stretch from Washington, D.C., to Chicago. Indeed, when President Kennedy was being briefed on the Bay of Pigs operation in the White House in the early 1960s, the commandant of the Marine Corps, a World War II veteran, overlaid the map of Cuba on one of the United States in that fashion to make the point. He then overlaid on the map of Cuba another map with a single dot at its center—it was tiny Tarawa, where in the Pacific War thousands of Marines had been killed to take that small island. Cuba is a big place.

Cuba runs more or less northwest to southeast, and below it is the large island of Hispaniola, shared by the Spanish-speaking Dominican Republic and the Creole- and French-speaking Haiti, probably the unluckiest and certainly the poorest country in the Caribbean. Below them are the long string of islands forming the western border of the Caribbean, which are a mix of nationalities indeed, representing the constant resetting of imperial European ambitions in the Caribbean: British, French, Dutch, Danish, and Spanish are all represented across the centuries, and the present-day culture of each island is a kind of Euro-mélange.

At the foot of the island chain and just north of South America are the twin islands of Trinidad and Tobago. Richer than most of the rest, and representing a curious blend of English and Spanish culture, T & T in many ways has the best of both worlds: a British language and legal backbone overlaid on the warm Caribbean and Spanish island cultures. Because they are blessed with oil reserves (which has been a mixed blessing at times, in truth), they can afford to provide a higher level of resources for social and structural programs than many of their counterparts nearby. My principal memory of my visits there while I was a combatant commander was the exuberance of the motorcycle escorts that accompanied my convoys from the airport to the capital and the government houses. The tall, elegant police motorcyclists would literally stand on their motorcycles and direct traffic without touching the handlebars, moving at very high speed. I have been in motorcades in more than a hundred countries; this was the most dangerous. I described this to the head of U.S. Special Operations Command, a four-star Army Green Beret who had spent his life in combat and danger, and he said, "Those sound like some troopers with a death wish." Yet it all seemed to fit with the energy and the humor of a nation with a love of public theater and plenty of propensity for risk.

Across the north coast of South America, the Caribbean Sea laps against the three Guyanas: French Guiana, Suriname (the former Dutch Guiana), and Guyana (formerly British Guiana). They are sort of three tin soldiers guarding the southern mouth of the Caribbean, representing the three principal colonizing powers that arrived after Spain. Each has its own character, culture, language, and political situation, but the one that sticks in my mind is Guyana, the former British colony that sits farthest to the west. Known principally to Americans as the site of a bloody cult murder-suicide in 1978 known as the Jonestown Massacre after its megalomaniacal perpetrator, Jim Jones, it gave American English the phrase "to drink the Kool-Aid," as in to believe in the cause despite all evidence to the contrary. It is a physically beautiful and relatively resource-rich nation with a quietly defeated air and a political system straight out of the Borgias.

I went there first in the mid-2000s as the commander of U.S. Southern Command, determined to visit all of the thirty-plus nations of the region in the first couple of months on the job. My staff told me not to bother with the three Guyanas because "nothing ever happens there." But I liked the idea of at least setting foot on each of the countries of the region, and after a brief back-and-forth with my doubting chief of staff, we set up a trip after, of course, visiting the bigger, more important countries: Brazil, Argentina, and Colombia. I arrived and was duly shuttled to see the president (or was it the prime minister?), and in his dusty office with the blinds drawn against the tropical sun, I asked him what the greatest challenge he faced was. Poverty? Drugs? Crime? (All of these were pretty obvious problems.)

He shook his head and sighed, admitting that each of those was indeed a challenge; but he said the biggest problem was emigration. "Everyone who can attain a high school degree leaves as soon as they can. Mostly they want to go north to your country, but they will go anywhere to get out of Guyana." It was a sad comment from a sad man, and made me think how lucky we are in the United States—for all our problems and mistakes and challenges, wherever I go people still want to come to, not leave, our country. We talked a bit more, I promised to be helpful in training and equipping his small and relatively docile military, and on I went. In all of the places I visited on the Caribbean Sea, in many ways Guyana was the saddest.

. . .

Colombia is the most beautiful and troubled country in the Caribbean. It ought to work well given the lush beauty, incredible natural resources (gold, oil, rich farmland, gorgeous harbors), and geopolitical position, both commanding the southwestern Caribbean and possessing a long Pacific coast. It sits at the crossroads of North and South America as well as the Caribbean and Pacific, and would also possess the Panama Canal (and Panama) if the United States had not essentially created an independent Panama in 1905 by financing and guaranteeing a revolution and breakaway there in order to build the Panama Canal ("We stole it fair and square").

I spent a fair amount of time afloat in the Caribbean off the coast of Colombia over the years, especially in the first decade of the twenty-first century while charged with the so-called War on Drugs mission as the U.S. commander based in Miami. I had sailed through the waters earlier in my career, mostly en route to or from the Panama Canal, but as a four-star admiral I was responsible for helping our Colombian friends stop the flow of drugs that departed the Colombian ridge—much of it over water routes through the western Caribbean. The volumes of cocaine are staggering, certainly in the hundreds of tons. At one point early in my tenure, we captured a fully formed submarine built in the jungle of Colombia and launched into the Caribbean Sea with a crew of three, diesel propulsion, an excellent communication suite, and—wait for it—ten tons of cocaine in the hold. Street value north of $150 million: an example of powerful innovation and determination. These were the new pirates of the Caribbean, and their remit was law across much of the western Caribbean.

Just north of Colombia is the beating heart of the American economy

(American in the broad sense, encompassing all of the Americas, North, Central, and South): the Panama Canal. Built on what was once Colombian soil after a U.S.-engineered coup and subsequent "independence," it opened in 1914 after much death and suffering among the workers, most of whom came from all around the Caribbean littoral and were directed by American engineers (after a previously failed attempt in the late 1880s led by Frenchman Ferdinand de Lesseps). This is a story of maritime engineering well told by historian David McCullough in his brilliant book *The Path Between the Seas*.

FOR A MARINER, there is no experience quite like transiting the Panama Canal. It is such a specialized nautical operation that even the United States Navy, which famously believes in full accountability for its commanding officers, relieves a CO of his or her command accountability while in the canal. I went through it first in the mid-1980s as the operations officer on a brand-new *Ticonderoga*-class cruiser, the fourth of the class, USS *Valley Forge*. I loved that ship, which I had helped build at a shipyard in Mississippi. When we sailed away, it very much had a "new car smell," and the paint was pristine on its gray hull. As the operations officer, I had charge of the physical care of the exterior of the 567-foot ship, and my boatswain mates took enormous pride in the sides. When we approached the narrow sliver of the canal, I thought my crusty boatswain mate Chief Petty Officer Gene Jones would have a heart attack worrying about scraping our sides on the tight openings, where ships are literally pulled through the locks by mini-trains on both sides. The Panamanians were experts, and the transit went smoothly with hardly a scrape. But that feeling of coming from the open water of the Caribbean Sea into the tiny, vulnerable locks—of giving over responsibility for navigating your ship to the canal workers and the pilot—was an uncomfortable one. I was happy to break free on the southern side and kick up the speed to a full 30 knots, blasting swiftly into the endless Pacific and leaving the canal behind.

UP THE COAST OF Central America you sail past the most dangerous countries in the world—after Panama comes Costa Rica, Nicaragua, El Salvador, Guatemala, Honduras, Belize, and Mexico. Collectively they have the highest violence rates in the world—more violent deaths per hundred thousand in the population than anywhere else, including Afghanistan and Iraq. Tragically, much of the violence is essentially an export of the United States, driven by the vast demand signal of our market for narcotics, armed by automatic weapons and handguns manufactured in our factories, and led by the gang culture created in southern California and sent south with deportees three decades ago. The Caribbean coast of Central America is a kind of Wild West that in places has changed little from the days of the pirates. It has hidden ports and forts that are no-go zones for law enforcement, places from which the drug runners operate with complete impunity.

I FIRST SAILED to the Caribbean in 1975, while I was in my fourth year, a senior—properly referred to as midshipman first class—at the U.S. Naval Academy. Every summer the entire Brigade of Midshipmen, some four thousand strong, dispersed all around the world on their summer cruises.

These were not experiences like going on a Carnival cruise line and enjoying piña coladas in the sunshine while shopping in the ship's arcade.

Summer cruises for midshipmen at Annapolis consisted of flying to some port of embarkation, slinging a huge sea bag over your shoulder, and trudging up a steel gangplank. The idea was to learn something about "the fleet," which at that point in my seagoing career was merely a distant theory.

In the humid summer of 1975, I was bused down to Norfolk, Virginia, where a dozen classmates and I embarked in the brand-new aircraft carrier *Nimitz*. She was a floating city; more than 100,000 gross tons, the length of three football fields, and from keel to the top of her mast about the height of the Empire State Building. After a quick indoctrination we were under way and headed down the East Coast of the United States into the Caribbean Sea.

After a couple of days, we entered the Caribbean through the Windward Passage, the strait that lies between the islands of Hispaniola (Haiti and the Dominican Republic) and Cuba. The captain came on the ship's announcing system, the 1MC, and said we were passing through the same water as Christopher Columbus centuries earlier, a speech I was to duplicate nearly two decades later as a destroyer captain. As a midshipman on *Nimitz*, however, I was having a cheeseburger in the wardroom and decided to forgo the soft ice cream sundae bar in tribute to the no doubt far more rigorous experiences Columbus and his sailors faced.

Our first port of call was not exactly a tourist destination: Guantánamo Bay, Cuba. In those days, of course, it was not internationally infamous as a prison for terrorists but rather as a backwater training facility for ships getting ready to deploy. The main purpose of Guantánamo Naval Station for most of its history was logistic support—a Mahanian coaling station. Over time, because it was out of the main Atlantic shipping lanes and had a ready logistic base, it became the center of training on the Atlantic coast.

In practice this meant that warships would show up for three weeks of brutal training to prepare for combat. Everything a ship could do was exercised, from gunfire to damage control (fighting shipboard fires and flooding after taking incoming fire) to aviation operations and underway replenishment. It was a tight, twenty-hour-per-day syllabus, designed to put the ship's crew under the maximum amount of stress.

The beauty of doing this off Guantánamo Bay was that it provided an opportunity to get the full attention of the crew—who were a long way away from their families and friends. The bars and tattoo parlors of Norfolk seemed a distant memory to the sailors. But realizing that you cannot get the maximum effect by strictly training the crew at sea, the Navy in its wisdom let the sailors come ashore for a couple of days each week to blow off some steam.

So my first chance to set foot ashore in the Caribbean was as a twenty-year-old midshipman on the athletic fields and tennis courts of the naval station under a full-on summer sun. Along with four thousand of my new best friends, I worked out and drank beer for 35 cents a glass with occasional shots of the high-end 50-cent rum to wash it down. Predictably, by the end of the day, the world was spinning a bit, and I went down to the pristine beach with a couple of my Annapolis classmates to sober up and contemplate the world from the vantage point of the sea.

The Caribbean is a gorgeous body of water at night, and that evening the moon hung full and low over the gently rolling waves. As is the case in most of the Caribbean, the landscape of Cuba is dry and rocky once you get away from the beaches; but the beauty of the trade winds and the luminous turquoise water more than made up for it. As I leaned back and watched the moon rise, I thought of all the ships sailing and steaming by that southern point of the long island of Cuba, centuries of history, much of it bloody, passing by me.

The next day we were back aboard the huge steel decks of the carrier and listening to the endless gong of the general quarters alarm.

IF YOU LOOK BACK at the colonial history of the Caribbean, it is easy to be reminded of Winston Churchill's famous description of the traditions of the Royal Navy: "Rum, buggery, and the lash." Indeed, the sea is named for one of the earlier Amerindian tribes, the Caribs, who were effectively wiped out by the intrusion of guns, germs, and steel, as author Jared Diamond titled his magnificent book on why Europe colonized so much of the world and not vice versa.

Pre-European times in the Caribbean are not well understood or documented. The Europeans gave a variety of names to the indigenous tribes they discovered, all of whom they simply saw as candidates for conversion to Christianity and slavery. Some of the terms from those early days of collision include "Taino" or "Tanyo," meaning a native who was relatively cooperative; or "Carib," meaning a warrior and generally a cannibal; or Arawak, who was somewhere in the middle. Cultural anthropology was not a strong suit of the Spanish conquistadores, and the opportunity to preserve the language, history, and culture of the locals was largely squandered.

What is notable is the lack of seamanship or open sea voyaging on the part of the early inhabitants of the Caribbean. Other than some offshore fishing, there is little evidence or record of serious voyages, the use of sails of any kind, or the construction of vessels capable of containing more than a handful of sailors. Thus the monstrous vessels of the arriving Spaniards, although quite tiny by today's standards, were overwhelmingly impressive to the native populations.

These were not entirely unsophisticated societies. The Caribbean natives had probably come into the broad basin of the Caribbean Sea thousands of years before the arrival of Europeans. The best guess would be that they were searching, not for gold and silk like the Europeans, but for land, freedom from oppressors to the south on the South American continent, food, and fish.

At the time of the European arrival, they lived in villages and settlements, some of which were as large as five thousand souls. The overall population of the Caribbean islands is impossible to estimate, but suffice it to say that the overwhelming majority died in the decades after the European arrival. As Mel Gibson's vibrant movie *Apocalypto* depicts, set on the Caribbean coast of Mexico, the arrival of the Europeans was absolutely an apocalypse to the local inhabitants.

THE NEXT ACT in the drama of the Caribbean actually began when a little-known friar named Martin Luther nailed his views to the door of a cathedral in present-day Germany in 1517. The result ultimately was the creation of a pool of gasoline to which the king of England, Henry VIII, put a match in trying to sort out his marital arrangements. Thus emerged Protestantism and the schism in the Catholic faith, resulting in more than 150 years of significant war and bloodshed, with lingering effects far into the nineteenth century.

Overlaid on all of this, of course, was geopolitics and imperial rivalry. Soon Europe was immersed in political and religious wars between Protestants and Catholics that would continue to burn in one form or another for the next five centuries (and sputter along today still in Ireland and the Balkans to some degree). Inevitably, these huge European wars and disputes ashore began to play havoc with the emerging system of societies in the far Caribbean, especially on the oceans.

The principal combatants were, on one side, the Spanish Catholics who over the next several centuries would do all they could to consolidate a massive empire in the Americas; convert and essentially enslave the indigenous populations; extract great treasures of gold, silver, and precious gems; and conduct monopolistic trade in everything the New World had to offer, notably sugar, and—as time went by—tobacco. On the other side were the hardy Protestant English and Dutch, both of whom launched explorers and raiders from the North Atlantic to the Caribbean Sea itself. Somewhere in the middle, and less effective, were the Catholic French and Portuguese, who carved out holdings on the South American continent. Overall, it was an age of sea empires fighting in a relatively small space in and around the islands of the Caribbean and the littoral coasts of the larger land masses that bound it.

One of the main targets of the Protestant sea raiders was the treasure-laden galleons of the Spanish crown. These would sail every year from Spain, carrying trading goods to the New World. The *flota* (fleet), as it was called, would number dozens of significant ships. Upon arrival in the Americas, they would unburden themselves of goods and load into their creaking hulls the precious spoils of empire—silver from the mines of Potosí in Bolivia, gold and emeralds from Colombia, tobacco and sugar, and even goods from China and the Philippines that came across the Pacific. By the latter part of the sixteenth century, the Spanish had created the first global market, and they took enormous rents and profits from it. Such ships were incredible targets, and both the navies and the authorized commerce raiders from the Protestant states gleefully attacked.

Perhaps the most iconic Protestant sea raider was Sir Francis Drake, who made his name in the Caribbean with a series of daring raids and was the darling of his monarch, Queen Elizabeth, with whom he may or may not have had an affair. In the late 1500s, he conducted raids on Spanish ports in Colombia and Florida, burning and pillaging as he went. After a stint of more honest battle in opposing the Spanish Armada in the Atlantic as it sailed toward England in 1588, Drake returned to his first and best love, pirating. He eventually died of disease in the Caribbean in 1596, having made himself rich.

But Drake was hardly the only pirate. There were hundreds of buccaneers (so called supposedly for their habit of roasting both meat and captives over a slow-burning wood fire on frames, called *boucans* in French) plying the Caribbean during the 1500s and 1600s. The Caribbean was not the scene of large pitched battles, but rather a kind of nautical Wild West. There were certainly naval warships, and as time went on and "civilization" descended, they became the dominant force in the region.

But throughout the first century of the Caribbean's colonization, the maritime dynamic was largely that of commercial trading vessels being attacked by opportunistic pirates—all of this fancifully and farcically brought to life, of course, by the swashbuckling and swishing Captain Jack Sparrow in the blockbuster *Pirates of the Caribbean* films. Many of those incidents are loosely based on the exploits of Sir Henry Morgan, a Welsh-born privateer whose life and career are truly the stuff of legend. After a highly successful (and vicious) career as a buccaneer, he returned to England, was slightly reprimanded (wink, wink), then made the governor general of Jamaica, much to the disgust of the Spanish. He milked that gorgeous island for a great deal of wealth by continuing to make it available to sea rovers, and eventually died there in 1688.

I went to Jamaica for the first time in the late 1970s, a period of considerable turbulence in the island's history. Relatively newly independent, Jamaicans were finding their way through a natural transition from reliance on a British backbone of governance to a system (and a set of political choices) more aligned with their culture, history, and proclivities. Not surprisingly, they turned dramatically left. While as a mid-twenty-something Navy lieutenant this was not entirely clear to me, what came across quite vividly was a sense of dramatic, indeed revolutionary, sensibilities that were sweeping the island. This was not a simple land of Red Stripe beer, jerk chicken, joint-puffing and reggae-playing Rastafarians, and gorgeous tourist vistas. Clearly there was much more afoot.

This became clear to my small liberty party of ship's engineers from the carrier *Forrestal* when we decided to get beyond the tourist zone in Montego Bay and tried to go watch a cricket match being played by two all-black teams. With all black spectators. And no welcoming committee. We weren't exactly threatened so much as aggressively ignored, much like the college students in the movie *Animal House* who try so desperately and pathetically to relate to the band in the all-black roadhouse they invade. Needless to say, we pressed on pretty quickly. After experiencing much the same syndrome in a number of other venues, we decided that prudence was in order and we headed back to the beaches of the north shore.

The following evening, I had the bridge watch as we pulled up the anchor and headed fair out to the clear waters of the Caribbean. The evening winds were pushing us hard, and I was struggling to get the ship on course, despite having four huge propellers and a hundred thousand horsepower at my disposal. Finally, I got us straightened out on course and as the sun was setting we turned east and headed into the winter twilight away from Jamaica. As the watch settled into a routine, I tried to put together the little I knew of Jamaican history with all that I had seen and experienced, and I realized the trip had made a lasting impression on me—especially the sense of the overhang of history, the ghosts that rattle our past and somehow exist just beyond the edge of our vision. Since then the Caribbean has always had that effect on me: of being in an edgy dark dream from which I have just awakened, but incapable of really understanding the land in which I find myself—despite enormous sympathy and affection for the islands, coastlines, and people of this remarkable region.

The European land wars of the 1600s inevitably began to bleed over into conflict at sea. The British came late to the Caribbean, but they came to see the power, not only of sugar and tobacco, but increasingly of chocolate, ginger, salt, and indigo. By the latter part of the seventeenth century, their fleet was sailing for open war in the Caribbean, seeking to wrest territory away from Spain. After a complex series of battles, the British ended up with many long-term colonial possessions—Jamaica, Barbados, Nevis, St. Kitts, and other islands.

The Dutch, not to be left out, took and held several islands more toward the southern Caribbean, as well as Dutch Guiana (now Suriname). In one of those absolutely delicious and yet tragic historical ironies, the Dutch traded the colony of New Amsterdam for Dutch Guiana. When that occurred in the seventeenth century, they were regarded as roughly equivalent properties. Today, of course, New York City is worth a couple of trillion dollars, while the capital of Suriname, Paramaribo, is among the most impoverished capitals in the Americas, a city of less than half a million people.

And soon the French began to move in, securing smaller islands and taking a slice of the Caribbean coast of South America, which became French Guiana (which remains today a department of France). Each of the colonizing powers merged private and public efforts by creating maritime trading and commercial companies, which functioned as quasi-official forces to bolster their national claims in the region. These West Indies companies (by various names among the various nations) were akin to the East India companies that would ply the Indian Ocean a century or so later.

. . .

By the 1700s, the economic outline of the next two hundred years was set. It consisted of a slave labor–based economic model that brought African labor to the Caribbean to produce sugar and other agricultural products. These were sent to Europe, which provided the muscle to collect the slaves. The triangular flow of ships went from Europe to Africa to collect slaves, then to the Americas with tradable goods and slaves, then back to Europe to bring the treasure of the Caribbean home.

Sugar itself was well known globally before the colonization of the Caribbean, with origins in the Pacific and Indian oceans, and was once planted extensively in the Levant. But those sources faltered, the European sweet tooth grew, and the appetite for sugar began to drive the economy of the region. There were also Indians and indentured whites involved in the extremely labor-intensive process of growing, cutting, crushing, storing, distilling it into molasses and rum, and transporting. Sugar cane has only about 10 percent sugar in it, and the process of extracting it is brutally difficult work.

In addition to the terrible and obvious human misery involved, the triangular trade also contributed to disease and death. This was not only through the exposure of indigenous natives and African slaves to previously unknown microbes; it was also dangerous for the Europeans, who would themselves face diseases rising from the combination of stagnant water and mosquitoes that resulted when land was fully cleared. Yellow fever was a particular scourge that attacked Europeans, but not Africans (who had a reasonable level of immunity, having been exposed to a variant in Africa). This further drove the demand signal for the "adaptable Africans" and away from using white labor of any kind.

All of this shaped the destiny and demographics of the Caribbean through the 1700s and on into the 1800s, until nations finally began to be repulsed by slavery, beginning with Great Britain, which banned the transatlantic slave trade in 1807; the United States, which fought a civil war to end slavery in the 1860s; and finally Brazil, which abolished slavery in 1888. But the damage had been done, the culture of slavery blighted these societies throughout those years, and its effects continue to be felt today. The numbers are extraordinary and utterly tragic—certainly millions were moved across the infamous Middle Passage, perhaps as many as 12 million, with up to 2 million perishing along the way. But we will never actually know the true numbers.

THERE IS ALWAYS a kind of theater about the Monroe Doctrine, which was issued by President James Monroe in the 1820s and largely ignored by the European powers for the next hundred years or so. The idea was that the United States would not permit any further colonization or manipulation of the nations of the Caribbean, and that our nation would be a sort of guarantor of good behavior. It was paternalistic, condescending, and quite unenforceable by a nation with limited armed forces, a small population, and a confused political culture, and an indifferent approach to international relations generally, to say nothing of being a slave-owning country itself. Over the decades, as the strength and power of the United States grew, the Monroe Doctrine began to have more teeth to it, and would be invoked from time to time to push back against European ambitions in the region. Throughout the nineteenth century, it was mentioned but seldom honored, until the United States burst on the colonial scene more or less by accident as a result of the war with Spain.

The principal connection of the Caribbean nations to the wars of the twentieth century was through the soldiers exported to fight for their colonial masters. During World War I, the British West Indies Regiment, formed from the islands, saw combat in Europe, although the black islanders were often relegated to support and logistic duty, to their dismay. French troops likewise participated with their national elements.

The United States confined itself to a series of interventions throughout the early part of the century, principally by the U.S. Marine Corps, to enforce stability, uphold the banking laws, and keep the Europeans more or less out of places like Haiti, the Dominican Republic, and Central America. The United States also purchased the Virgin Islands from the Danes, a pretty good buy at $25 million, even in 1917, when you look at real estate prices there today. I remember taking my destroyer into both St. Thomas and St. Croix in the mid-1990s and thinking what a wonderful stroke of luck the United States had in three national purchases—the Louisiana Purchase, which gave us essentially the western continental United States; Alaska, which gives us our window on the north and vast natural resources; and the Virgin Islands, which afford us strategic reach into the Caribbean alongside Puerto Rico.

THINGS BEGAN TO really heat up in the Caribbean during the cold war. What set the stage, of course, was the rise of caudillos, a Spanish term for military dictators who came to dominate virtually all the nations of Latin America and the Caribbean by the latter part of the twentieth century. These dictators, naturally enough, gave rise to countervailing freedom movements, some of which were associated with communism, and suddenly the cold war arrived in the sunny Caribbean—with ground zero being on the island of Cuba. After the Cuban Revolution, Fidel Castro came and visited the United States, and it looked as though there might be an amicable relationship. But Castro quickly became associated with the Soviet Union, and in the dynamics of the cold war it was "you are either with us or against us" on both sides. The United States did all that it could to undermine the Cuban regime, most notably with the failed invasion at the Bay of Pigs in 1961. This CIA-supported mission ended up with a thousand Cubans dead, a couple of thousand more jailed by Castro, and bitter enmity that endured for decades.

The height of danger, and the moment at which the Caribbean became the epicenter of the world, was over a ten-day period in October 1962 in the Cuban Missile Crisis. This is a story best told by Graham Allison and Philip Zelikow in their masterful book *Essence of Decision*, about the Kennedy administration's successful effort to avoid a nuclear war. The Navy conducted a significant blockade of the island to prevent more Soviet missiles from sailing to Cuba.

Eventually the crisis was defused after some clever diplomatic maneuvering, but it is extraordinary to think how close the world came to a nuclear exchange and a completely changed and diminished world order in those days.

The cold war hovered over the Caribbean throughout the second half of the twentieth century as a sort of ongoing symphony playing in the background, but the real theme was independence. Most of the islands and other small countries finally broke free from their European overseers, virtually all peacefully: Guyana and Barbados (1966), the Bahamas (1973), Grenada (1974), Dominica (1978), St. Lucia and St. Vincent and the Grenadines (1979), Belize (1981), and St. Kitts and Nevis (1983). Each has its own rich culture and history, although in economic terms most remain relatively poor today.

By the 1980s and 1990s, Haiti had become the center of a great deal of violent activity—both from political turbulence and from Mother Nature. In the 1980s, the dictator Jean-Claude "Baby Doc" Duvalier was forced from power and a series of elections and coups ensued. When elected president Jean-Bertrand Aristide was forced out by his military in

1991, the United States put pressure on the coup leaders to turn over power peacefully. My destroyer, USS *Barry*, was dispatched to Haiti as part of an arms embargo (read: show of force) in the mid-1990s, and all I can remember is steaming placidly up and down the coast, boarding a couple of coastal steamers carrying bananas, and holding barbecues on the fantail for a very bored crew. I remember looking at the dark coast of the island and thinking about all the blood spilled there over the years in the slave times, the heroic but doomed slave revolt, the massacres, the earthquakes and hurricanes. There cannot be a less lucky country than Haiti.

I returned to Haiti roughly twenty years later as a four-star commander in the days after one of the seemingly endless hurricanes had knocked down a great deal of the very shaky infrastructure. I visited with the Haitian president René Préval in the beautiful but poorly maintained presidential palace, toured the city, and tried to be helpful by directed delivery of aid and supplies. The country seemed to be on a bit of an upswing, with significant international aid coming in and a real effort at reconstruction getting traction. Over my three years in Southern Command, I always felt Haiti's luck was changing. But I was wrong.

The really big disaster came just after my time, in 2010, when a massive earthquake killed perhaps 300,000 people (these are highly disputed figures) and completely destroyed the capital of Port-au-Prince, including flattening the presidential palace. The epicenter of that quake was just outside the city, and the destruction was essentially complete. Since then, Haiti has had enormous difficulty mustering the kind of support it needs, as the world's attention has moved on to Syria, sub-Saharan Africa, and many other troubled spots.

One other moment of cold war excitement in the Caribbean was on the tiny island of Grenada, which had suffered a left-wing coup in 1979 and then a brutal countercoup that led to the execution of the prime minister, Maurice Bishop. The newly installed government appeared to the Reagan administration as dangerous to the thousand or so U.S. citizens (including, famously, many U.S. medical students). That the government also had Marxist tendencies was an additional problem. The United States invaded Grenada ostensibly to protect U.S. citizens in a scene reminiscent of the many U.S. invasions in the Caribbean in the late nineteenth and early twentieth century—six thousand U.S. Army, Marines, and Navy SEALs came ashore in Operation Urgent Fury in 1983. They easily restored order and turned over power to the governor-general. Ironically, today you can drive by the monument to the U.S. soldiers killed just outside the international airport—named for Maurice Bishop, the left-leaning leader who was overthrown and executed.

Of note, Operation Urgent Fury further exposed the inability of the various branches of the U.S. military to work coherently together, which was first significantly observed following the failed rescue attempt of the Iranian hostages a few years earlier. The problems were in communications, doctrine, logistics, and tactics; the Grenada invasion led to major overhaul and the implementation of a new joint approach for the armed forces. As usual, it is little remembered in U.S. history, but looms as a significant event in the history of this small, beautiful island.

Indeed, that invasion of Grenada is a sort of metaphor for the lack of U.S. interest and engagement that has been the pattern in the Caribbean. Over my years as commander of U.S. Southern Command, based in Miami (some would say the true capital of the Caribbean and Latin America), I came to know the Caribbean very well, visiting every major island over a three-year period. It is a lovely and vibrant part of the world, dominated by a clear and gorgeous body of water, yet despite its preternatural beauty, it is unfortunately also a part of the world that does not live up to its potential, with poverty, poor growth, corruption, and violence acting as the four horsemen of the tropical apocalypse. It is a part of the world that seems perpetually stuck in the past in so many ways. When I contemplate the Caribbean, I am often reminded of one part of the Pirate's Code in the *Pirates of the Caribbean* movies: "Any man who falls behind is left behind." In the Caribbean, it feels like *everyone* somehow fell hopelessly behind the rest of the world, and the region has yet to catch up.

Let's face it: while physically beautiful, the Caribbean is a sea of nations that by and large don't function terribly well. Central America is the most violent region in the world; Colombia fought a virulent insurgency for sixty years; Venezuela is oil rich and politically poor, unable as a result to even stock goods on the shelves; the three Guyanas (British, now simply Guyana; Dutch, now Suriname; and French, still a very poor department of France) are immersed in poverty; almost all of the islands are poor with weak, corrupt governance; Puerto Rico is in economic default; and Cuba, the "Pearl of the Antilles," is shamefully the last dictatorship in the hemisphere. Even the Caribbean coastline of the United States and Mexico, the two wealthiest nations, has some of the poorest internal states and regions along the Caribbean Sea (e.g. Mississippi, the Florida Panhandle, southeast Texas, and much of the Mexican Caribbean.

Why is this? It is the result of a lethal combination of history and geography, including a legacy of racism, slavery, piracy, anarchy, and small wars. Additionally, the region has a pattern of general physical exploitation with little regard to sustainability. What agricultural development has occurred most often has been conducted to the point of exhaustion, using mono-crop agricultural approaches. Finally, natural disasters (hurricanes, earthquakes, fire) are endemic. Just as a nation like Haiti begins to make progress, for example, it seems there is a devastating hurricane or an earthquake or both. There is no other maritime region that has been dealt such a bad hand of cards, both by history and by nature.

Additionally, the region is a significant transit zone for narcotics flowing largely from the Andean Ridge in South America and up into the United States, the largest drug market in the world. In that regard, by the way, I would prefer to simply park the moral question of whether people should or should not use drugs. All of our societies are grappling with that issue now, and many serious analysts and political leaders are beginning to advocate legalization. My concern here is quite simply about the money.

The cash that comes out of this huge, multibillion-dollar industry is unregulated, and much of it goes into corruption and violence, undermining fragile democracies and stifling growth in other sectors. The idea of a "war on drugs" is limiting and simplistic, and has clearly failed—we need a strategy to fight corruption and violence, which are the root problems.

We need to think holistically about the root causes and what we can do together in the Americas to address them. In terms of causes, it is tempting to focus on the proximity of the United States itself as the heart of the problem. The argument goes that the Monroe Doctrine, dating from the 1820s, made the region into a sort of stifled American lake that was never allowed to achieve its potential. Mexicans have a saying: "Pity poor Mexico, so close to the United States, so far from God." There is a bit of that feeling in the islands as well, where the United States tends to be blamed for everything from the lackluster economy to bad weather when it comes. All of that strikes me as a classic H. L. Mencken solution: clear, simple, and wrong. The situation is far more complex.

The great irony, of course, is that the region ought to work very well. Despite a bloody history early on in the colonial period, there has not been a major war fought in the region between nations for centuries. The Caribbean is nestled in the heart of the Americas, the richest zone of commerce and natural resources in the world. To the north and increasingly to the south are industrialized societies with which the nations of the Caribbean have strong and important demographic connections—think of the Dominican Republic, Haiti, Cuba, Puerto Rico, and El Salvador, all with enormous immigrant populations in the United States on a per capita basis.

While the Caribbean Sea itself can be fickle and bring terrible storms during the hurricane season, it is a natural "tropical silk road" that links all the economies and provides a shimmering tourist industry. Despite the overhang of colonialism, many of the nations in the Caribbean maintain strong links back to advanced nations and economies in Europe, including the United Kingdom, France, and the Netherlands. There is a good deal of material to work with in terms of advancing the societies of the region.

What can the United States do? And perhaps more important, what are we willing to do?

First, we need to begin with a recognition of our responsibilities to the region. Despite our frustration with decades of failure to achieve progress, we have both a moral and a pragmatic set of reasons to expend resources here in the Americas, and I would argue especially in the Caribbean Sea and basin. Given our historical engagement (including multiple military invasions over the past couple of centuries), as well as our penchant for claiming responsibility (the Monroe Doctrine), the moral argument seems fairly clear.

The pragmatic case is equally clear. By building up capable local partners in the region through cooperation—economically, politically, culturally, and in the security dimension—we strengthen our own shared region. The tired and offensive cliché of "America's backyard" has to go and be replaced by a Partnership for the Americas, and the Caribbean—the neediest region of the Americas, encompassing the Central American nations—is a good, practical place to start. If even a tiny fraction of what has been spent in Afghanistan on development had been deployed in the Caribbean, we might have seen extraordinary results. It is never too late to start.

Second, we need to encourage the nations of the Caribbean to work together. The reality is that they are individually too small to achieve real political throw weight. There are some nascent organizations in the Caribbean, but they have never proven themselves effective in moving the global needle politically. We should provide resources, advice, and training to the Caribbean organizations that focus on collective action, and also revitalize the moribund Caribbean Basin Initiative, which has always been a kind of geopolitical afterthought to NAFTA and CAFTA.

Third, our security cooperation has been limited in its approach and effectiveness. Almost entirely focused on the failed "war on drugs," it has not provided the kind of wide-spectrum engagement that might improve the broader security situation in the region. The local forces need training and resources to improve in rule of law, basic investigative work, advanced anticorruption techniques, surveillance, intelligence, and human rights. U.S. Southern Command is the right conduit for this.

A fourth thought would be to build in a constructive and methodical way to draw on the huge diasporas from the region located in the United States today. The Cuban American community, for example, has resources and deep business experience. Each of the other national groups brings different regional strengths within the United States to bear. Connecting the Caribbean diaspora is crucial.

Fifth, we should do this in cooperation with our partners Mexico and Canada, the other two North American economic powers. We all have a shared interest in a successfully functioning Caribbean.

Sixth, the United States should work to develop a collective Caribbean strategy. We have one for the Arctic—why not one for our southern neighbors clustered around the Caribbean Sea?

Seventh, we should think more aggressively about so-called Track II diplomacy, coupling the private sectors in the United States and the region together. This can be done through educational reforms, programs in the arts, sports diplomacy, and medical exchanges. Given that the languages of the region are overwhelmingly English and Spanish, our two core national languages, we have a huge comparative advantage in doing this in and around the Caribbean Sea. When I was the military commander at U.S. Southern Command, we tried a number of innovative things to connect with the region. One was a series of baseball clinics conducted by U.S. troops (carefully screened semipro-caliber ballplayers) and financed partly through donations from Major League Baseball teams. There are many creative approaches in this vein that would help foster human connections.

Overall, this is a region where a little bit of attention and resources go a very long way. There are humanitarian and pragmatic reasons to overturn the Pirate's Code of "fall behind, left behind"—let's work harder to help our Caribbean neighbors sail ahead.

7.

THE ARCTIC OCEAN

PROMISE AND PERIL

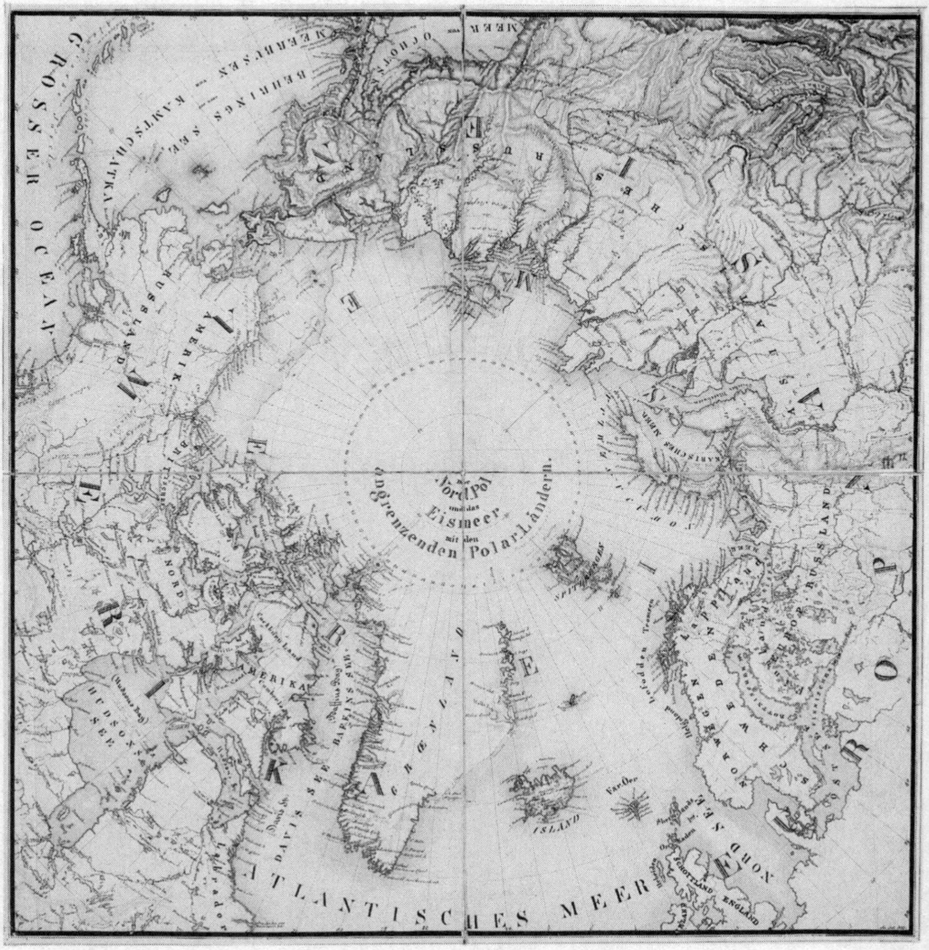

The Arctic Ocean holds a unique place in sailors' lore and explorers' stories. *Map created by Sir John Ross, 1855.*

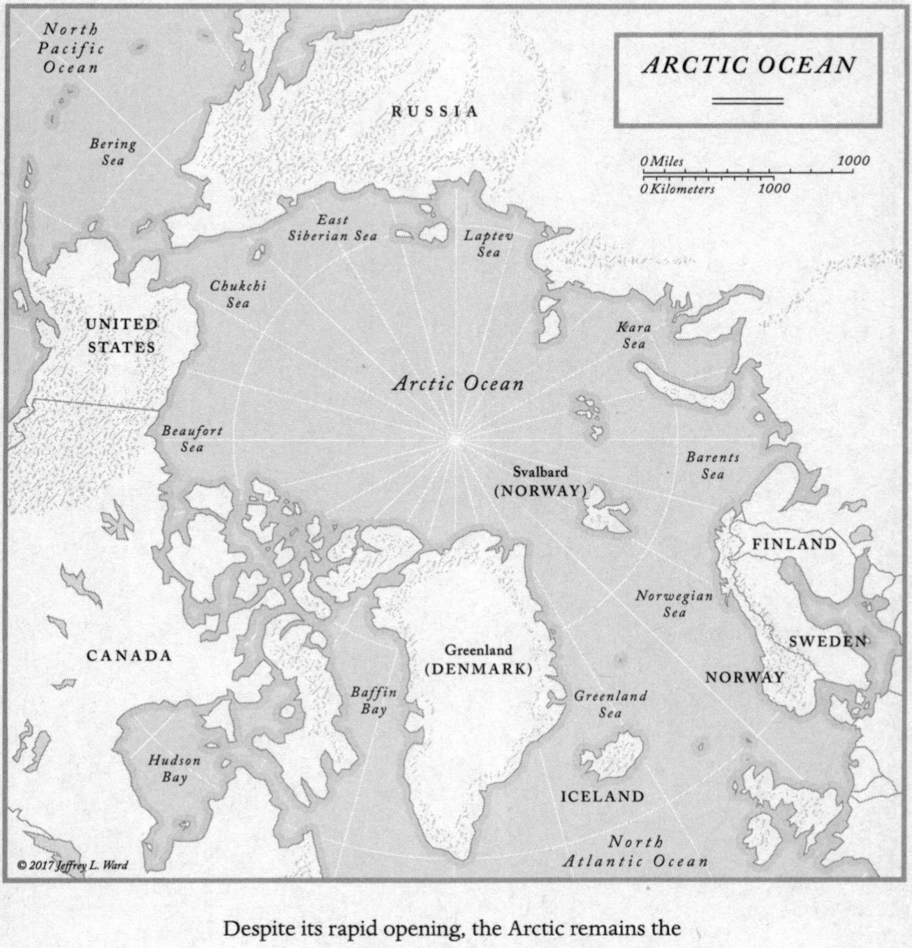

Despite its rapid opening, the Arctic remains the world's least-understood ocean.

THE PROMISE OF THE ARCTIC OCEAN

Almost every one of the world's oceans has been the site of epic battles—some more than others—and there is no well-traveled global body of water that has escaped significant bloodshed. Indeed, it is impossible to estimate how many men and women have died at sea in combat all across the globe down through the centuries that man has sailed the world's oceans. But there is an exception: the Arctic Ocean.

Indeed, with that sole exception, at the bottom of every watery corner of the world lie the rusted weapons of long-dead sailors, their battles ended forever. The last ocean never to have seen any significant level of active combat is the Arctic, existing as it does at the top of the world, far from the reach of mankind. Today it offers the tantalizing chance of becoming a zone of cooperation and peace. But the enormity of its resources represents a prize that will draw increasing attention from many quarters, creating tension and danger.

Today the Arctic world is in a delicate state of tension: between environmentalists who are terrified we will destroy the last pure place on the earth and the developers who want to exploit the enormous natural wealth (albeit responsibly by their lights); between Russia and NATO, which increasingly face off across the Arctic Ocean and are perfectly capable of stumbling backward both metaphorically and literally into another cold war; and between scientists who want to preserve the ocean for science diplomacy and well-intentioned tour operators who want to open a booming ecotourism and educational industry in the last great frontier.

The Arctic Ocean is a place of both promise and peril, as well as mystery.

Above all, as we look at the Arctic, we should consider the place it holds in the collective imagination of the world. The region that even today many in the Scandinavian nations refer to as the "High North" was often thought of as a temperate zone waiting to be discovered. Early maps of the North Pole often showed an area with arable land and a moderate climate at the top of the world, and this misconception persisted for centuries. Early projections by Gerardus Mercator, one of the greatest sixteenth-century cartographers, showed such habitable zones in his 1595 charts. Even as late as the mid-1800s, the theory of mild temperatures and warm climates at the North Pole put forth by serious geographers like the German August Petermann was taken seriously by explorers. And virtually every civilization has a myth or two attached to the Arctic, notably the story of Santa Claus in our own Western canon.

THE SMALLEST OF THE WORLD'S great oceans, the Arctic Ocean (also occasionally called the Northern Ocean) has always been a zone of mystery, shielded from human sight throughout much of recorded history.

Early maps generally depicted it as a huge world of water, replete with gorgeous cartouches on the edges of the charts dominated by dragons and demons; in other cartographic representations it appears with vast oceans but with great hidden temperate land areas in the center of the massive ice fields. Even today, we know more about the moon or Mars, and have mapped them more carefully and fully, than we have the bottom of the Arctic Ocean.

Remarkably, defining the Arctic and the Arctic Ocean remains somewhat difficult, as even the term "Arctic" has varying definitions. It is scientifically and widely accepted to be the portion of the globe north of which there is continuous daylight during the summer solstice—this being 66 degrees, 33 minutes, and 45.9 seconds. Some alternative definitions have to do with temperatures in the region, for example, the portion of the earth with median temperatures of 50 degrees or less in July. Politically, some try to define it as the ocean bordering those countries with Arctic indigenous populations. As always in the human mind, defining a region varies depending on the observer's biases and theories about who should dominate it and how—and the Arctic, despite its shrouded character, is no exception.

It is worth noting in this regard how fundamental the Arctic is to Russia. Fully 20 percent of Russia's GDP and exports come from the Arctic. The Russians, by the way, fully self-identify as an Arctic nation in ways that certainly transcend the feelings of any other sovereign state with the possible exception of Canada. They have just launched the largest and most powerful nuclear icebreaker in the world, the *Arktika*—567 feet long, 33,000 tons, 80,000 shaft horse power, and capable of breaking through up to ten feet of ice. Strangely, for a region that is essentially devoid of human settlement, the Arctic is today the fastest-growing region in the world—each of the Arctic nations is actively pushing for the opening of settlements, increasing military activity, expanding resource exploitations, and generally staking claims with humans in the High North.

In terms of the Arctic *Ocean*, in reality, of course, it is essentially a bounded sea with two major openings, tightly confined at the Pacific end and relatively broadly accessible on the Atlantic side, with long continental shelves along either side. With the warming polar climate, temperatures are higher for both air and water and the permanent ice cover—the central feature to a mariner's cautious and skeptical eye—is eroding year on year. Virtually every reputable scientist looking at the global environment today sees a continuation in this trend, which will provide access for the first time in human history to an enormous trove of treasure in the form of natural resources, geopolitically important terrain, and highly efficient sea lanes of communication.

By 2040 there will be an open passage for essentially twelve months of the year, and another decade later there will no longer be ice over the North Pole. It is ironic that the Western world searched for centuries for the elusive passage to Asia through the Canadian Arctic: the Northwest Passage. Today, with no effort other than pollution and global warming, we have opened it with increasing alacrity. In terms of size, the Arctic is about 5.4 million square miles, covering an area roughly akin to the size of the continent of Antarctica.

This is the promise of the Arctic Ocean: it covers an estimated nearly 15 percent of the world's undiscovered oil (perhaps 100 billion barrels), 30 percent of the similarly estimated gas (some 1,700 trillion cubic feet of natural gas and 44 billion barrels of liquefied natural gas), and possibly a trillion dollars or more of nickel, platinum, cobalt, manganese, gold, zinc, palladium, lead, diamonds, and rare earth metals. In round terms about 25 percent of the proven reserve hydrocarbons (oil and natural gas) are in the Arctic.

It is also a huge incubator for human life–sustaining protein in the form of fish—50 percent of U.S. fish stocks come from the 200-nautical-mile exclusive economic zone off the coast of Alaska, for example. The same is true for many of the other nations that ply these waters, both within their exclusive economic zones and on the high seas (where the competition from non-Arctic nations is robust and rising). All of this takes place in an area that by square mileage is only 2.5 percent of the globe. In terms of geopolitical ownership, it is worth noting that with the full Russian continental shelf claims, nearly 80 percent of the proven reserves of the Arctic will be in Russian hands.

And most important in commercial and geopolitical terms, the fabled Northwest Passage is opening fairly rapidly as the ice cover recedes. Several years ago, over a million tons of cargo transited the Arctic routes and by doing so cut thousands of miles off the traditional sea paths across the lower trade routes. This cargo—which is rising in tonnage each year—falls broadly into three baskets: adventure tourism (the smallest), transarctic shipping (within the port system of the High North itself), and global shipping that has a specific destination around the world but outside of the Arctic itself. There are two key routes that connect Asia and Europe—the Northwest Passage that runs along the North American continent and the Northern Sea Route that runs along Eurasia, essentially along the coast of Russia. Both routes are at present unpredictable and risky, but their use is growing. Obviously, Russia will seek to develop the Eurasian route.

One key sea lane of communication today is the tight Bering Strait off the coast of Alaska, which is the only route between the Arctic Ocean and the vast Pacific Ocean at one end of the Arctic Sea. Taking this as a rude metric of the increase of shipping, the U.S. Coast Guard says that traffic through the Bering Strait increased nearly 120 percent from 2008 to 2012. All of this shipping must move over an area of open sea that is nearly undeveloped in terms of conventional ports, navigational aids, buoy systems, and other supporting maritime systems. For example, Barrow, Alaska—the major U.S. port on the North Slope—is accessible on a reliable basis only by air. Even Russia, which has invested heavily in its portion of the region, has limited coast guard coverage throughout the area.

All of this represents an exciting opportunity for mankind in the form of resources that have heretofore been unattainable given the harsh conditions, ever-present ice, and long distances from global communication centers. The promise of the Arctic Ocean is undeniable, but it sits in the center of a region that presents great peril as well.

THE FIRST TIME I sailed north into the waters of the Arctic Circle, I was in a Navy destroyer in the late 1970s operating in the western Pacific. We were detached from routine patrol around Japan and ordered to head to the west coast of Alaska. Fortunately for us, this was during high summer and while it was not exactly balmy, we were not in unusually uncomfortable seas. The highlight was learning that we would indeed dip our bow inside the Arctic Circle, which would make all of us on the ship "Blue Noses" in Navy parlance. This is usually accompanied by a ceremonial dip in a tub of very cold water on the bow, but because we had no previous Blue Noses in our crew, no one was excited about organizing such a ritual. Thus I earned my Blue Nose certificate without actually taking a dunk in the icy water of the Arctic Ocean.

In geopolitical terms, this was the height of the cold war, and our mission up there was to test the antisubmarine warfare gear on the ship under extreme conditions. We did so without actually stumbling on a Soviet submarine, at least as far as I could tell. As the ship's antisubmarine warfare officer, I was more worried about getting the long towed array cable off the reel on the ship, into the water, and back aboard in one piece than I was about actually finding a submarine. Over the next two decades, there were plenty of interactions between U.S. and Soviet warships in the Arctic, generally under the ice by submarines.

It seems metaphorically sensible that such confrontations were largely conducted in the silent, dark depths of the Arctic, unseen and in many cases unreported. Like those games of cat and mouse, much of what happens in the Arctic, as in Vegas, stays in the Arctic. We dodged a bullet in the cold war and avoided real combat between NATO and the Soviet Union—but looking ahead to the unfolding potential for confrontation around the Arctic Ocean, I often think back on that first voyage and hope that we can again avoid actual sea battles at the top of the world.

THE PERILS OF THE ARCTIC OCEAN

Why do I worry? A variety of perilous conditions will influence the speed with which mankind will be able to exploit fully all of the promise of the Arctic Ocean. Let's examine some of the challenges in the region.

The first and most evident form of peril remains simply the brutal character of the climate. In his extraordinary book (2015) about the doomed U.S. Arctic Expedition of 1879, *In the Kingdom of Ice: The Grand and Terrible Polar Voyage of the USS Jeannette*, Hampton Sides takes the reader deep into the mariners' experiences in the High North. At one point, speaking about the captain of the *Jeannette*, Navy lieutenant George Washington De Long, Hampton says, "He became more and more intrigued by the Arctic, by its lonely grandeur, by its mirages and strange tricks of light, its mock moons and blood-red halos, its thick, misty atmospheres, which altered and magnified sounds, leaving the impression that one was living under a dome." They set sail in April 1879 from San Francisco, and almost all died in the course of their expedition. Today, their bravery in the Arctic is commemorated by a lonely monument in the cemetery at the U.S. Naval Academy in Annapolis. The story is also echoed in Ian McGuire's extraordinary 2016 novel *The North Water*, about a whaling expedition that goes terribly wrong and creates the ultimate confrontation of good and evil—against that most unforgiving environment in the High North.

What makes the harsh conditions even more dangerous, of course, is the lack of facilities for rescue or monitoring of any kind. Taking the U.S. Coast Guard as an example, the closest Coast Guard air station to Barrow—the largest U.S. city on the north shore—is located in Kodiak, about a thousand miles to the south. While there are small commercial airports in some of the northern U.S. cities of Nome, Prudhoe Bay, and a few others, there is very little infrastructure to conduct search and rescue. The Arctic is also famously difficult for the basic transmission of command and control signals. Cellular coverage is virtually nonexistent for obvious reasons, and the general propagation of any form of radio signals is limited. All of this means that if a mariner is in trouble in the Arctic, he or she is in serious trouble.

A second form of peril in the Arctic Ocean today is the confused governance that surrounds the region, especially at sea. Given the confluence of five large key landholders bordering the Arctic Ocean—Russia, Canada, Norway, the United States, and Denmark (by virtue of Greenland)—there are competing national and international regimes at play.

At the international level, there is the United Nations Convention on the Law of the Sea (UNCLOS), which was created in 1982 after more than a decade of negotiation by essentially every nation on earth. It was significantly modified in 1994, and today forms the backbone of the regime of the oceans broadly. Oddly, given its enormous maritime interests, the United States has not signed the convention but instead relies on "customary international law" to gain as many of the benefits of the convention as it can. Most nations believe that the UNCLOS framework is both usable and functional in the Arctic Ocean today, and a 2008 agreement (the Ilulissat Declaration) memorializes that theory.

In addition to the Law of the Sea treaty, there is the Arctic Council, a high-level, consensus-driven forum for the Arctic nations (Russia, Canada, the United States, Norway, and Denmark plus Sweden, Finland, and Iceland). The indigenous people of the region are represented by five nongovernmental organizations that are also permanent participants in the council; they cover the interests of the majority of people living north of the Arctic Circle.

The United Nations has a maritime organization headquartered in London—the International Maritime Organization—that focuses on shipping and its regulation. It has been at work on a so-called Polar Code that would provide agreed-upon guidelines for shipping in the Arctic Ocean. Along with the UN Law of the Sea treaty and the Arctic Council, the International Maritime Organization participates in all the relevant conversations about the Arctic Ocean.

At the national level there are perils as well. Each of the key stakeholder countries has organizations that attempt to provide governance over both its nationals and within sovereign parts of the Arctic Ocean, but that also affect other entities, for example ships in transit.

The third peril of the Arctic is geopolitical competition. It is instructive to look at the alignment of the five key states bordering the Arctic Ocean—four are part of NATO (the United States, Norway, Canada, and Denmark) and one is an uneasy "partner" to NATO: the Russian Federation. As relations continue to deteriorate between NATO and Russia, it is becoming clear that the Arctic Ocean potentially will be more and more a place to revisit the mistakes of the cold war.

Overlaying the geopolitical competition is the warming of the ice, which opens up more and more of the Arctic Ocean for interaction between military forces. The average ice cover in 2012 was 1.3 million square miles below the average of the twenty-year period from 1980 to 2000. In addition, the age of the sea ice is a trend worth noting. Younger ice implies the warming and breaking up of the older caps. The ice caps are both thinning and receding, and the geopolitical impact—opening much more of the open Arctic Ocean—is significant.

There is a growing fear that another environmental danger is not fully appreciated: that the Arctic's permafrost could melt as a result of climate change, releasing massive amounts of methane gas. This would be like dumping enormous amounts of carbon into the world's environment, with potentially catastrophic results. A few numbers to understand this risk: first, the warming trends. Every time the earth's temperature rises one degree, we see the temperature at the North Pole rise about five degrees, largely the result of methane gases.

At the same time, we are globally concerned about the tipping point resulting from carbon emissions, which will occur when around 1,000 gigatons of carbon are dropped into the environment; at the moment, there are roughly 550 gigatons already at play. If we see even a two-degree rise in Arctic temperature, it is possible that 1,700 to 1,800 gigatons of carbon-equivalent methane will be released—immediately overshooting the carbon "budget" that nearly two hundred nations agreed to try to meet at the Paris Climate Summit. While not the result of policy in the Arctic directly, the warming effect on the permafrost there could be the catalytic event that drives global disaster, according to some experts.

Looking at the geopolitical approach of each of the significant Arctic nations is crucial to understanding the complex overlay of relations in the region. While there is nothing inevitable about conflict—or even competition—it appears at the moment that a period of real coordination or cooperation is unlikely. This is the result of the resurgence in aggressive Russian behavior in Europe, which has bled over into relations in the High North. But the view is more complex than a simple "here we are back in the cold war" sigh. Let's look at several of the key Arctic Ocean nations individually.

Russian Federation

The majority of the vast Russian coastline lies above the Arctic Circle, and the High North is a central pillar of the Russian Federation's worldview. It also has by far the largest Arctic population (around four million) and the best infrastructure. Russia sees the promise of the Arctic with great geopolitical clarity, and will maneuver to be a dominant player. The Arctic is also a part of the world that figures deeply in the Russian mind-set and self-image as a nation of rugged individualists who are capable of surviving in the harshest of conditions. Russia will always care deeply about the Arctic Ocean in ways that other Arctic nations (particularly the United States) do not.

This does not presuppose that we are headed into a new cold war (literally and figuratively) in the Arctic Ocean, a sort of zero-sum Great Game of the High North. It is entirely possible that the Arctic Ocean could become a zone of cooperation, not one of competition or, God forbid, one of actual conflict.

However, it is necessary to be clear-eyed about Russian infrastructure bordering the Arctic Ocean. It will remain as it has been for centuries the home of the North Sea Fleet, and provide the bases for the Russian nuclear ballistic missile submarines, many of which will operate from bastions in the Arctic Ocean. Russia is increasing the number of troops it stations in the Arctic region, as well as expanding its bases dramatically.

All of the Russian Arctic-oriented strategies that we have observed over the past five years—both overtly and through intelligence gathering—view overall national Russian priorities as being centered on the region, featured in documents including *The National Security Strategy of the Russian Federation Through 2020* and the even more specific *Principles of State Policy of the Russian Federation in the Arctic Through 2020 and Beyond.*

Much of the Russian focus will be on developing the Northern Sea Route that runs along its northern landmass. Eventually, this route will save 40 percent off the time between Europe and Asia, which will lower transport costs and connect northern Russia to global markets for Russia's hydrocarbon exports. Use of the route will require shippers to develop vessels that can withstand the harsher conditions, and it will be quite hazardous for many years to come. There are currently very few facilities for refueling, repair, navigation, and search and rescue in the event of calamity. The Northern Sea Route will also create governance challenges given the multiple regulatory regimes that will gradually come into play as this new sea lane comes on line.

Russia will also seek to successfully defend its various territorial claims in the Arctic Ocean, many of which have persisted for more than six decades. Famously, the Russian Federation planted a Russian flag on the Lomonosov Ridge (a huge piece of the continental shelf that is entirely underwater and well beyond the 200-mile limit of the Russian coastline) in 2007, and Russia still has significant border disputes with Norway, the United States, and Canada. With the United States, for example, there is ongoing controversy concerning the maritime boundary in the Bering Sea. With Norway, while some issues have been resolved, there remain disagreements over fishing rights in the Barents Sea. There are claims and counterclaims surrounding extended continental shelf disputes involving Denmark, Norway, Russia and Canada.

While there is a great deal of disagreement and controversy, over time there is reason to hope for cooperation in the High North. In spite of the acrimony and the snippy rhetoric both from and directed at Russia, most of the actions Russia has taken in the Arctic Ocean have been fairly pragmatic. The potential for open conflict, while very low, is not entirely absent—all the more reason that the nations along the maritime borders of the Arctic Ocean should work diplomatically for a zone of cooperation.

Canada

With more than 1.2 million square miles of Arctic territory and the world's second-largest land area in the High North, staunch NATO ally Canada has always placed a premium on its role as an Arctic protector, in both the idealistic ecological sense *and* in terms of a realistic geopolitical framework. Canada has the longest coastline of any country in the world, and 65 percent of it runs along the Arctic Ocean. Throughout the first decade of the twenty-first century, Canada has consistently spoken and acted with a central focus on the region in general and the Arctic Ocean in particular.

In particular, the Canadian military has expanded its operational surveillance of the Arctic Ocean and the approaches to Canadian territory. Some of its purchases include a new icebreaker, patrol vessels with some "new ice" capability, a deepwater port in Baffin Bay, and a winter "fighting school" for the army. Canadian work in mapping is also noteworthy. The former Canadian chief of defense General Walt Natynczyk was quite focused on the Arctic Ocean. When I asked him slightly tongue in cheek what he would do if the Canadian High North were invaded across the Arctic Ocean, he said, "Well, Jim, I suspect my first duty would be search and rescue to save the invaders"—his point, of course, being that the conditions in and around the Arctic Ocean are hardly conducive to real military operations supporting an invasion.

And this represents the slight Canadian schizophrenia about the Arctic: while they are strategically aware of potential challenges and are willing to play realpolitik to protect "their" parts of the Arctic and the Arctic Ocean, they are also big believers in a balanced and multinational approach to the region. They have been strong supporters of the Arctic Council throughout its history, as well as key participants in international conferences and proponents of focusing on the High North. In the context of NATO operations, the Canadians are the least enthusiastic of all twenty-eight nations in seeing a NATO presence in the waters of the Arctic, preferring an approach that puts the Arctic Council and its military committee in the driver's seat, not NATO. The Canadians, who are otherwise strong NATO players who participate in virtually every operation, are extremely proprietary about the Arctic. They see a significant alliance presence as somehow undermining their stewardship. Additionally, there is a significant pro–indigenous people and antimilitary bias throughout much of Canadian society, cutting across the political spectrum.

All of this is in marked contrast to the Norwegians, who have a more "lean forward" stance seeking a larger NATO presence in the region—largely the result of their centuries of unhappy interaction with the Russians, whom they perceive as particularly aggressive at the moment. In meetings, top Norwegian military personnel often bemoaned to me the "lack of NATO concern" about their part of the Arctic. They have been adapting their command and control systems to make it easier to "plug and play" with NATO systems so that the alliance can at least have situational awareness of what is going on along the longest border of NATO: the High North.

The Canadians also have a handful of territorial disputes at the moment. They are in dispute with the United States on a fairly large portion of the Beaufort Sea (the body of water just north of the eastern Alaskan/western Canadian border). While not of great significance, there is no quick or easy solution to this argument. Likewise, they disagree with the Danes over some of the boundaries of the Lincoln Sea (a tight body of water between the eastern border of Canada and the western border of Greenland) and ownership of a small island—Hans Island. They are also—along with the EU and USA—pursuing an agreement over the disputed Northwest Passage. This dispute is the most significant and quarrelsome. In essence, the Canadians believe that much of the Northwest Passage lies within their "internal waters," while most other nations believe that the passage is an "international strait," which allows greater freedom of movement for all nations. There are significant equities at play, and this argument is unlikely to be resolved anytime soon. The other two disputes are fairly straightforward and are moving toward resolution. None of the three seriously threaten the peace in the High North, but are indicative of the wide variety of disputed elements in and around the Arctic Ocean.

European Arctic Nations: Norway, Denmark, Sweden, Finland, and Iceland

While the northern European nations all have long traditions of engagement in the Arctic, they collectively lack sufficient resources, geopolitical influence, or populations to make a strong case for deep involvement at the level of Russia, Canada, and the United States. They will pursue their individual national agendas through both the European Union (all are members with the notable exception of Norway), in a NATO context (all are members save Finland and Sweden, which are close partners to NATO), and via the offices of the Arctic Council.

Each of the European Arctic nations has a slightly different set of issues in the Arctic, and at the moment they show little sign of cooperating collectively to establish a European Arctic position on anything.

For Iceland, the Arctic was a zone of danger throughout much of the cold war, when the relatively small island was in the crosshairs of potential Soviet nuclear strikes to blind the U.S. air and maritime defense zones. Iceland was also regarded as an "unsinkable aircraft carrier" in the strategically vital Greenland-Iceland–United Kingdom gap in the North Atlantic. This was the passage through which many Soviet ballistic missile submarines would have to pass in order to attain launch positions against the United States. Thus the Icelandic geopolitical status from those days is as something of a battleground—not a pleasant place to be.

They look askance, therefore, at the deterioration of relations between the United States/NATO and the Russian Federation. Icelandic diplomats are very hopeful of seeing the High North become a zone of cooperation, not a zone of conflict. The Icelanders, who possess no actual territory within the Arctic Circle, see themselves as the potential beneficiary of enhanced trade routes, becoming a kind of hub port on the "Cold Silk Road" across the top of the world. They sponsor an annual conference that is essentially the Davos World Economic Forum of the Arctic Ocean, called, sensibly enough, "The Arctic Circle." This provides a platform for their active approach to peaceful dialogue in the region. They are also highly interested in potential oil and gas fields within their exclusive economic zone, as well as their responsibilities for search and rescue in their "near abroad" in the North Atlantic and Arctic oceans. The Icelanders will try hard to remain relevant in the core discussions of the Atlantic Council, trying to stake out a position alongside the big five (Russia, Canada, USA, Denmark, and Norway).

Denmark is an Arctic nation by virtue of its long possession of Greenland and the Faroe Islands. It has ruled Greenland since 1721, but there is an ongoing political debate about how this ownership will unfold in the twenty-first century. Greenland and the Greenlanders have been increasingly vocal in demanding greater autonomy, and there are voices increasingly raised in favor of independence altogether. Greenland is huge, and there are many military installations dotting the coastlines to which the Danes grant access to NATO and the United States, including the important Thule U.S. air base in the northwest corner of the island. The uncertainty regarding Greenland's future is exacerbated by the discovery of increasing levels of gas and oil beneath its waters, which provides a realistic level of income and encourages the indigenous Greenlanders to consider independence seriously. Finally, the Danes are pushing for a series of very detailed underwater mapping exercises designed to sustain their extensive claims to great swaths of the Arctic seabed, up to and including the North Pole itself.

Overall, we will see the Danes play a visible and aggressive hand regarding the Arctic Ocean. They will seek to hold on to Greenland and will offer higher and higher degrees of autonomy to the inhabitants there while retaining sovereignty. This will require a higher degree of military engagement in the region, especially from new installations in and around Greenland. Copenhagen will not give up its significant stake in the High North willingly.

Norway, a rich country of vast territory and only five million inhabitants, has the resources but not the population to have significant Arctic impact by itself. The Norwegians, more than any other of the NATO/European Arctic states, keep a weather eye on their Russian neighbors. They have several territorial disputes with Russia, some of which have been solved and others of which linger on with little likelihood of resolution. The Norwegian island of Svalbard, high up in the Arctic Ocean, dominates the Barents Sea and constitutes a significant thorn in the side of Russian ambitions in the region. The Norwegians are concerned not only about hydrocarbons, but about fishery rights as well. There are significant stakes for Norway in the High North, especially as easily tapped oil and natural gas along its more southern coasts are depleted in the years ahead.

Most expect Norway to continue to be the nation most concerned about a potential "resource war," or at least an armed conflict of some sort in the Arctic Ocean. This has led Norway to take an aggressive stance on the role of NATO in the High North, constantly pushing it to be aware and informed operationally as to what is moving in the northern latitudes of the alliance. As the NATO commander from 2009 to 2013, I often conferred with my Norwegian counterparts about their concerns and attempted to assuage them as to NATO's interest and engagement.

Sweden and Finland, the two remaining Arctic nations, are part of the Arctic Council by virtue of a small segment of their land territory that lies within the Arctic Circle, but neither has coastline on the Arctic Ocean itself. Nonetheless, Sweden and Finland—non–NATO members both—watch the Russian Federation with concern over its increasingly expansive operational profile in the Arctic Ocean near both nations. Neither nation is looking for disputes with Russia, and of course both were essentially neutral throughout the cold war. Sweden and Finland have drawn closer to NATO over the past decade, including sending significant forces on deployment to Afghanistan. Swedish Gripen jets also participated with great success in the Libyan operations alongside NATO partners. As Russian behavior in the Arctic and in Ukraine makes these two nations nervous, they can be expected to seek even closer ties to NATO. It is possible they will consider membership in NATO, but that step appears unlikely absent yet another dramatic change in Russian activity. In regard to the Arctic, both will be quietly assertive of their prerogatives as Arctic nations, but both are also well aware that without coastline on the Arctic Ocean, their options for operational activity are limited.

The United States

It is striking to imagine how different the United States' and Russia's geopolitical positions would be if Russia still owned Alaska, which the United States purchased from Russia in 1867 under the vision of Secretary of State William Seward. Derided at the time as "Seward's Folly" or "Seward's Icebox," the acquisition stands second only to the Louisiana Purchase as the best deal this country ever made.

The United States has seldom placed a great deal of emphasis on the Arctic. Throughout our history, the country has placed the most strategic importance first on dominating the vast continental lands, then turned to the Atlantic and Pacific oceans as the highways to the rest of world with expanding trade and geopolitical responsibilities. Until 2009, there was literally no stated U.S. policy articulated concerning the Arctic and the Arctic Ocean. The first such document came out as the Bush administration was leaving early in 2009; titled "Arctic Region Policy," it was issued both as a National Security Presidential Directive and as a Homeland Security Presidential Directive. Frankly, the document is pretty thin reading, with little to encourage the U.S. government to devote resources to the High North.

Throughout much of the cold war, the Arctic Ocean was a busy thoroughfare for U.S. and Russian nuclear submarines playing an elaborate game of cat and mouse, best illuminated in Tom Clancy's unforgettable novel *The Hunt for Red October*. The High North was also an air battlefield minded by the North American Air Defense Command, headquartered in Colorado. Teaming with Canada in air defense, the United States built a system of early warning air defense radars across the Canadian and U.S. coastlines that exist today and are still on watch for long-range forays by Russian strategic bombers and reconnaissance aircraft.

In the post–cold war period, there was at first more amity in the Arctic Ocean region, but as relations between Russia and the United States (and NATO) have deteriorated sharply—especially since the invasion of Ukraine and the annexation of Crimea—the cat and mouse and watchful air defense on both sides have resumed with gusto. There is also the emergence of a more significant Chinese intercontinental strategic missile threat to worry about, and more recently the highly unstable North Korean regime of Kim Jong-un has acquired long-range ballistic missiles to marry up with its small arsenal of nuclear weapons. The North Koreans detonated their fourth nuclear explosion in early 2016. Given that these missiles can find their shortest path from Asia to the continental United States over the Arctic Ocean, it is clear that this Arctic path for ballistic missile launches opens a new strategic front from Asia to the United States itself. All of this places a much higher premium on U.S. strategic focus on the Arctic Ocean than was the case even two or three years ago.

Perhaps even more important to long-range U.S. strategic thinking is the enormous amount of natural resources in, under, and around the periphery of the Arctic Ocean. The Arctic zone possibly holds 30 billion barrels of oil and more than 220 trillion cubic feet of natural gas. Such estimates may only scratch the surface as they are generated in a very conservative way by the U.S. government. Additionally, vast levels of timber, fresh water, coal, copper, gold, silver, zinc, and rare earth elements are present.

Fortunately, given the strategic importance of the region to the United

States, the various governmental organizations are now beginning to spend time and resources conducting coherent strategic planning on the Arctic. The Department of Defense via the Navy laid out a reasonable road map in late 2009 and has updated it along the way. The plan includes budgetary line items for strategic planning, operations and training, investments (including weapons, sensors, and installations), strategic communications, and environmental assessments. More recently, in 2013, the Department of Homeland Security via the U.S. Coast Guard promulgated a similar strategic vision, its "U.S. Coast Guard Arctic Strategy." The Department of State appointed former commandant of the Coast Guard Admiral Bob Papp as a sort of "Arctic czar" and designated him the U.S. representative to the Arctic Council until he stepped down in 2017. Even President Obama has joined in and recently became the first U.S. president to visit the Arctic, in the late summer of 2015. What is lacking, unfortunately, is a sense of a coherent, focused national effort despite the nascent efforts of the disparate interagency organizations.

Much of the U.S. engagement under the Obama administration was focused on working through the Arctic Council. This organization, founded twenty-five years ago, has eight permanent members: Russia, Canada, the United States, Denmark, Norway, Iceland, Finland, and Sweden. It also has twelve permanent observers: France, Germany, the Netherlands, Poland, Spain, the United Kingdom, China, Italy, India, Japan, South Korea, and even Singapore. Obviously, many of these nations do not leap to mind as "Arctic family members." But attaining status as an Arctic observer is tied to international shipping activity and physical presence on other strategic shipping points. More nations will apply and gain observer status in the years ahead. For the United States, the Arctic Council represents the best international forum for raising concerns and questions about the behaviors of other Arctic and non-Arctic states. The council also sponsors dialogue among all of the militaries of its permanent members.

Of note, when looking over a list of the number of operational icebreakers in the inventory of various permanent members of the Arctic Council, the shortcomings of the United States are particularly noteworthy:

Russia: 30-plus icebreakers, of which 7 are nuclear powered, including the new *Arktika*, the pride of the Russian fleet
Finland: 7
Sweden: 7
Denmark: 4
Canada: 6
United States: 3
Norway: 1
China: 3 (although not a permanent member, it has more under construction)

It seems quite clear that the "hidden" days of the Arctic are coming to an end. The High North is an emerging maritime frontier with increasing human activity, rapidly melting ice packs, hugely important hydrocarbon resources, and a competing international agenda.

THERE ARE MANY BROAD CHALLENGES facing the United States as we look north to the Arctic waters. First is the rising geopolitical tension with Russia, which has arisen principally out of events in Syria and Ukraine, but will ultimately have repercussions in the High North. We are seeing increased Russian activity with its highly capable and numerous flotillas of ice-breaking ships (such flotillas are strictly Russian in character, and are clusters of icebreakers that operate together), as well as their stated intent to build military bases in the Arctic region. Second is the environmental and ecological damage brought on by the melting polar ice cap, which is straining the entire delicate ecosystem. Third, associated with the melting ice is the growing commercial sense of an oil and gas rush up north. As the principal Arctic nations explore and exploit hydrocarbons, competition and disputes will rise in number and intensity. Fourth, the United States has no serious culture of engagement in the High North, and as pointed out earlier, today we have only a single truly functioning icebreaker (the other two on the list above are out of service at the moment), compared with dozens operated by Russia. We simply lack the idea of an "Arctic identity" that Russia, Canada, Norway, Iceland, and Denmark (by virtue of Greenland in the latter case) have.

WHAT DOES THE UNITED STATES NEED TO DO?

Ensure that the United States remains a leader in the Arctic Council. All of the nations bordering the Arctic Ocean (the six noted above as well as Finland and Sweden) meet frequently to work on issues in the High North. These include exchanging information about military operations, protecting the environment, creating standards for the exploitation of natural resources, practicing salvage and rescue operations, conducting climate studies and other scientific cooperation, and various other activities in the Arctic zone. The United States needs to put real resources behind our participation, sending top government figures to consultations, appropriating significant funds for the activities committed to by the Arctic Council, and driving policy by shaping coalitions within the council.

Build more icebreakers. If the United States intends to be serious about operating in the Arctic Ocean, we need the ability for both military and commercial ships to get through the ice pack. While many of our submarines are hardened and can break through the ice, if we are going to take advantage of the reduced shipping distances, move our oil and gas offshore structures, and support everything from science diplomacy to responsible tourism, we simply need more icebreakers—this is the path to credibility in the Arctic. At this moment, Russia, Canada, Finland, and Sweden all outpace us, and Denmark and China are building more vessels now. Our weak level of response must be reversed.

A good icebreaker costs money—between $800 million and $1 billion. The reason buying one is hard is because they must compete with other high-cost items like Navy *Arleigh Burke*–class destroyers, advanced fighter aircraft, and sophisticated Army command and control systems. But going forward, the necessity and usefulness of such a vessel seems clear, especially when we have such limited capability in that area.

Take a leadership position within NATO on the Arctic. There are varying views of the role of NATO in the High North, which run from Canada's somewhat laissez-faire philosophy of "High North, Low Tension" in terms of NATO involvement, to Norway's desire to integrate national and NATO surveillance systems to cover the Arctic aggressively and thoroughly from an alliance perspective.

The Norwegians often say the High North is the unguarded flank of the alliance, because they fear Russian territorial aggression and a fight over hydrocarbons. The Canadians lean back and don't want NATO engagement; the Norwegians lean forward and want a great deal of NATO in the High North. The U.S. position tends to lie somewhere in between these two views. We should lead NATO to engage more directly and realistically, with exercises, surveillance, overflight, and training in the Arctic Ocean.

Enhance the dialogue with Russia. The reality is that Russia has the most at stake of any nation in the Arctic, and by working with the Russians we can ensure that the region becomes a zone of cooperation—not of competition or, even worse, actual conflict. Despite our disagreements in other areas, we need to maintain the conversation with Russia about the direction of the High North. Russia is building an operations center focused on the Arctic. We should explore how we could be part of that in some cooperative way, sharing our engagement with our Canadian friends and allies, as well as other NATO allies.

In the dialogue with Russia, much of the conversation will focus on commercial and navigational issues. Of note, some scientists are predicting a truly "blue north"—one that has water, not ice, during much of the year—by 2030. Shipping, oil and gas, tourism, science, and many other commercial interests will dominate the agenda over time. Our Arctic czar should spend time with the private sector to fully understand the issues and find linkages with public sector efforts, which can then be translated into a dialogue with the Russians.

Take an interagency approach. U.S. interests in the High North will cut across cabinet departments—Department of Defense, Department of Homeland Security, Department of State, Coast Guard, Department of the Interior—as well as agencies such as EPA, NOAA, and so on. Working hard to make sure that the entire U.S. government is represented will be important. This concept is of course central to the DNA of a Coast Guard officer, making the choice of a retired four-star admiral and Coast Guard commandant sensible—the "Coasties" work with many other organizations and entities within the big tent of the Department of Homeland Security, such as the DEA, Customs, Fisheries, and so forth, and thus are very comfortable in an interagency environment.

In a metaphorical sense, it is worth thinking about Arctic policy in the same way a United States submarine captain approaches the dangerous navigational task of breaking through the ice with his warship—something our attack submarines do with regularity as they patrol the northern seas. Like our Arctic policy, broaching a submarine through polar ice requires careful navigation, delicate planning, and determination.

Sailing the Arctic Ocean is different from sailing any other body of water in the world, and full of dangerous and unique challenges. Any sea captain planning an Arctic voyage will have spent a great deal of time studying the waters, learning about ice and the damage it can do, and seeking advice and counsel from others about the specific difficulties of the intense cold, the crushing ice, the brilliant lights of summer and the deep dark of the winter nights. Any U.S. Navy sailor who has gone above the Arctic Circle is awarded a certificate as a Blue Nose sailor. But very few even of the limited number of Blue Nose sailors have done the most challenging maneuver of all: breaking through the icepack itself in a submarine and bursting to the surface at the North Pole.

Each U.S. Navy submarine that has performed this feat recognizes the significant danger imposed on the boat by the dangling ice keels, large tongues of ice hanging down from the ice pack itself. Avoiding these is crucial, as is understanding the precise thickness of the ice pack at the proposed point of surfacing.

The entire maneuver is controlled carefully by the submarine's captain himself and uses a detailed checklist with two-man control over each step of the standard operating procedure or SOP. Sonar—a pinging of sound through the water that measures distance by listening to the reverberation back—is used to find a flat spot, and the delicate controls of the submarine are used to maneuver the boat just below the surface of the ice. Throughout most of the cold war, most of our boats had hardened sails (the towerlike structure on the top of the boat) for this operation, but even given the hardening, it remains imperative to lower all masts and antennae while situating the boat below just the right patch of "clean" and hopefully thin ice. To make a cheap pun, finding the thin ice feels like "walking on thin ice" above—you know that a wrong step could be disastrous.

Once the thinnest ice patch is located and the ship is positioned beneath it, air is then blown into the ballast tanks, creating the reserve buoyancy and the essential upward thrusting energy needed to break through the ice. Like most submerged operations, this one is quiet and nearly silent throughout most of the boat. But in the conning space—the underwater part of the submarine where all maneuvering is conducted while the boat is submerged—and of course in sonar control, the crunching sound of the ice on the hull is discernible—a low, grinding, pulsing sound until the final breaking of the ice layer.

Once the boat has broken through, the crew can ascend the tower and carefully open the clamshells on the sail of the submarine and check the full status of the hull of the boat as it hangs just through the ice on the surface. Sailors wearing special cold weather exposure suits are initially tethered to the boat as the hull above the ice is checked for damage. Eventually, the goal is to get every one of the hundred or so sailors over the side to walk on the ice, snap pictures, and safely avoid polar bears—which amble right up to the hull.

There are many places in the world a captain can take his or her ship, but only a submarine can sail through the pure, cold water of the Arctic

Ocean, submerge under ancient ice, and ultimately crash its sail up to the sky at the top of the world.

There is a real danger of militarizing the High North. We cannot afford to stumble back into a new (and colder) cold war. There are essentially three choices for the Arctic: a zone of cooperation (best), a zone of competition (probable), and a zone of real conflict (possible but less likely).

At the moment, with Russian versus U.S. and NATO relations at a post–cold war low, I would bet on a deepening zone of competition. We will see Russia aggressively build out its military presence. In one sense, this is quite natural: as the ice "barrier" that protected that northern coast melts, the natural Russian concern about its borders (the result of many bad experiences over the centuries) kicks in and we will see more military activity. This will quickly become a self-fulfilling prophecy as the United States and the other NATO countries respond. What can break the cycle? As discussed above, it will require a multifaceted approach: international (with the Arctic Council as the primary vehicle), interagency (getting the Department of Homeland Security, which includes the Coast Guard, to work with the departments of Defense and State), and private-public cooperation. We need all three.

A good example of the latter would be building emergency response platforms in the High North. The question is whether the United States can provide international, interagency, and private-public leadership in the Arctic, especially with regard to sustainable infrastructure development in the Arctic Ocean. Given our responsibilities, are we prepared to respond to disasters and fully participate in the High North—with search and rescue capability, environmental disaster mitigation, scientific diplomacy, and other activities?

Unlike centuries past, when sea ice covered the north polar region perennially, today there is navigable open water from the Bering Strait to the Barents Sea during the summer. This increasing access to rich resources is awakening all flavors of human activities and associated societal responses, not just from the Arctic states but from our entire world. This leads directly to the hot-button topic of energy exploration, development, and production in the Arctic Ocean.

Oceanic travel across the top of the earth cuts a third off the distance between Europe and Asia, compared with transits through the Panama or Suez canals. What are the implications for new trade routes or trading patterns, which historically have changed the balance of power among nations? How will we use the Northern Sea Route, Northwest Passage, or Transpolar Sea Route into the future?

Vast fishery enterprises are seeking to feed a hungry world, preparing to jump into areas of the Arctic high seas where marine living resources are unregulated beyond sovereign jurisdictions. Can nations collectively demonstrate shared stewardship and commercial restraint to ensure the lasting vitality of Arctic marine ecosystems? There is hope on that front. Nine nations, including the United States, and the European Union agreed in December 2017 to a sixteen-year ban on fishing in the Arctic. This moratorium should give the international scientific community time to understand Arctic fisheries and how to use them sustainably.

Wrapped up in charged dialogues about climate, atmospheric temperatures over the Arctic are rising twice as fast as those in the rest of the earth. Can we turn down the vitriol to appreciate that we are just in our infancy to address climate and other planetary-scale impacts that require coordination among all nations?

So as we conclude this look at the Arctic, where does all this leave us in this vast northern sea? Can we conceive and build sustainable infrastructure in the Arctic Ocean that will resonate with utility and hope, not just for the region but globally?

In this quest, it is important to recognize that economic prosperity, environmental protection, social equity, and societal welfare are all necessary. We have a responsibility to act in the interests of present generations as well as future generations. Moreover, in the Arctic Ocean as elsewhere on earth, we have a shared struggle to balance national interests and common interests.

The challenge for the United States and the other Arctic states, with the central involvement of the Arctic indigenous peoples and the effective engagement of non-Arctic states, is responding in a balanced manner to the opportunities as well as the risks from the opening of the Arctic Ocean.

MORE THAN A CENTURY AGO, in 1879, the United States was seized with "Arctic fever" tied to the later-disproved notion of a temperate land zone in the center of the North Pole—essentially a "land rush" that never materialized. A U.S. Navy expedition was launched onboard the doomed USS *Jeannette*, which voyaged into the Arctic "carrying 'the aspirations of a young republic burning to become a world power.'" It became icebound and was crushed, stranding the crew as winter approached. As masterfully depicted in Hampton Sides's *In the Kingdom of Ice*, most of the brave sailors died trying to bring the United States into the High North. We have largely stayed on the sidelines since then in this vital geopolitical part of the world. But with the appointment of an Arctic Czar, or what I like to call an "Ice King," and an increased focus on the High North, we must again assert our engagement in a challenging but critical part of the globe.

Broadly speaking, the United States is better positioned to take a significant role in the Arctic Ocean than was the case a decade ago, despite shortfalls in leadership attention, interagency cooperation, icebreakers, and other specialized equipment and appropriate infrastructure and installations. The question is whether in this period of constraining resources for the United States there will be sufficient long-term vision to make the key investments necessary. Will agencies of government invest in training personnel to understand and plan for an Arctic Ocean future for the United States? Will our Defense and Homeland Security departments follow through on the road maps they have generated over the past several years? Will presidential leadership go beyond photo-op travel and renaming mountains in honor of indigenous peoples, and truly grapple with both the promise and the peril of the High North?

William Seward had the vision required to ensure an Arctic future for his nation. It was said of him during his lifetime that he was "one of those spirits who sometimes will go ahead of public opinion instead of tamely following its footprints." Let us hope we can sail into the Arctic with his spirit as a guide.

8.

THE OUTLAW SEA

OCEANS AS CRIME SCENES

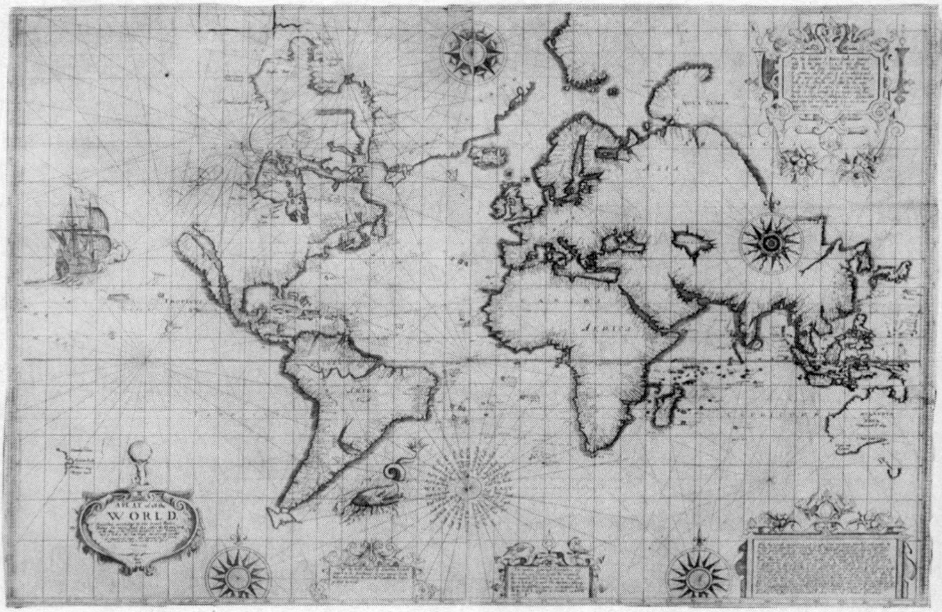

Piracy was a problem in every region from the Americas to Europe and Asia. *Map by Emery Molyneux and Edward Wright, 1599.*

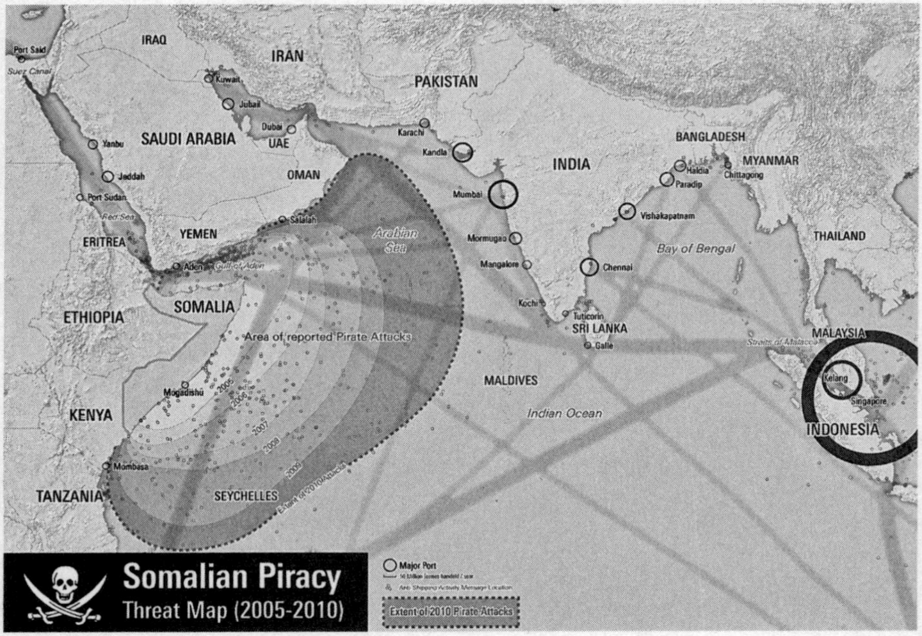

Although the locus of this challenge has shifted to a new region, piracy is still a scourge in our modern world.

Having looked at each of the world's major bodies of water essentially in isolation, we need as well to examine the entirety of the global ocean system. As I mentioned at the outset, the British Royal Navy, perhaps the first truly worldwide force capable of projecting power anywhere on the face of the earth, put it best: The Sea is One, meaning that no matter how large or small a given body of water is upon the oceans, in the end it is connected and a part of the single system.

And it is a busy system indeed. On any given day, it is impossible to accurately measure the number of surface ships at sea, but we can approximate the number of ships generally. By reading through a variety of sources (including Clarksons, the "bible" of international shipping), it is possible to estimate that there are between fifty and sixty thousand large commercial ships—bulk carriers, cargo ships, tankers, container ships, chemical ships, passenger and roll-on/roll-off ships, and liquefied natural gas tankers active throughout the world. These are the ships that I passed thousands of times in my years as a warship captain. The interactions between the world's warships (perhaps five thousand, including many very small coast guard vessels) are generally quite professional. What I felt over the forty years of my career was the way the oceans became more and more full; by some estimates there are four to six times more ships plying the world's oceans than there were some thirty years ago. If you look at a map of the world from space with the high-density shipping lanes marked in red, orange, and yellow, the strategic highways and choke points are quite clear—red belts through the South China Sea, the Mediterranean, clusters around the Suez and Panama canals, long strips around the bottom of Africa, arrows of red in and out of the Arabian Gulf and through the Strait of Malacca. It is a vast and busy universe in which tens of thousands of vessels of all descriptions are under way at any given moment.

The good news is that over the past three thousand years since man began to explore the world's oceans, we have learned a great deal. Mankind has developed extraordinary technology that allows us to accurately map every body of water, to plunge to the bottom of the sea, to track fish, birds, and mammals that inhabit it, to monitor and navigate the thousands of ships that ply it, and to take highly precise measurements of everything about the waters of the world: temperature, acidity, alkalinity, salinity, and on and on. But despite the fact that we are incredibly informed about the oceans in many ways, there are still vast trenches of the oceans that are unexplored, and there remains much we do not know, especially about how the oceans function as a coherent system. In a certain sense we have incredible *knowledge* of the oceans, but little *wisdom* about them.

Nowhere is this more clearly true than when we look at the broad ocean challenges that exist today. Some have called the oceans "the biggest crime scene in the world," and others have referred to them as "the outlaw sea." Sadly, both of these statements are in many ways quite true;

and worst of all, we do not have real granularity in our knowledge of what transpires on the oceans in two potentially very destructive zones: criminal activity and environmental damage.

In terms of crime committed on the oceans, there are many sources, but to name a few that are of particular concern: piracy, a scourge that has been part of the oceans since the very beginning of man's intersection with the sea; narcotics smuggling, an enormous business that moves heroin, cocaine, methamphetamines, and other illicit substances on a huge global delivery network with substantial maritime pathways; illegal dumping of toxic substances, which of course bleeds directly into the environmental challenges we will address below; weapons smuggling, which involves moving all manner of lethal equipment from high-end ballistic missiles to small but deadly handguns; illegal fishing, a business that is destroying the world's fish stocks rapidly; and smuggling of contraband, from the level of nuisance shipping of untaxed cigarettes to the movement of big sums of paper money (both counterfeit and valid). Below we will look specifically at piracy as a case study of the criminal activity on the oceans, and examine the ways in which global security forces, the shipping industry, the insurance industry, and international organizations have tried to address the piracy challenge. There are many lessons learned that can be applied to other criminal activities on the outlaw sea. We will also look quite specifically at the world of fishing, where much abuse of the law occurs that thus far has seen relatively little effective mitigation by the international community.

The other significant challenge to the global ocean, of course, is the environment. Here we see extensive damage that has many sources: global warming that is helping melt the polar ice caps and contributing to the rise of the ocean's sea levels; rising acidification in many parts of the oceans, which is highly detrimental to various levels in the global oceanic food chain; warming of the oceans, which changes migratory patterns and again damages fragile ecosystems; construction damage to delicate coral reefs; pollution that is pumped directly into the oceans either deliberately or accidentally from land or sea; hydrocarbon recovery (both oil and natural gas), which has both deliberate and accidental effects on sea life and coastal ecosystems; higher levels of UV and other forms of radiation; mineral recovery, which will be exacerbated over time by the desire to mine the deep seabed for cobalt, copper, nickel, magnesium, and rare earths; and the simple act of humans populating the coastal regions of the world and inserting large urban centers adjacent to the oceans. When these are taken together, the damage to the global maritime environment may be the biggest threat we face as a species.

In terms of impact on the world's oceans, the three biggest topics that completely transcend not only national boundaries, but also the artificial boundaries between various seas and oceans, are piracy, fishing, and the environment. They are intertwined, and each merits a significant look.

PIRACY

I must admit that as I prepared to take up my duties as the NATO commander in 2009, I did not initially put piracy at the top of my list of worries. Afghanistan, the Balkans, Syria, Russia, and Libya looked like the places that would absorb the lion's share of my energy and attention. But as I began to fully comprehend the extent of the piracy challenges in East Africa—centered mostly on the waters off Somalia—it became clear that I would be doing something very traditional for a Navy admiral: chasing pirates.

Certainly piracy has been a part of the maritime landscape for more than three thousand years, with reports of early piracy taking place in the waters of the Mediterranean in the times of the ancient Greeks by the "sea people," as well as parts of the Indian Ocean and the western Pacific. Julius Caesar was captured and held captive briefly by Sicilian pirates. Much of Viking culture was built on the norms of maritime piracy launched both from and on the sea. Over the centuries, pirate cultures have been very entrenched in a variety of locations, notably North Africa under the so-called Barbary pirates in the eighteenth and nineteenth centuries, the Caribbean in the "golden age of piracy" in the seventeenth and eighteenth centuries, and more or less continually in the Strait of Malacca and South China Sea.

While there was a general lull in piracy in the post–World War II period, by the latter part of the twentieth century it had returned in force in a variety of areas around the globe and continues to the present. Notable zones of pirate activity around the world today include the waters of the Indian Ocean and North Arabian Sea off the northeast coast of Africa, the Gulf of Guinea on the central west coast of Africa, the Strait of Malacca between the Pacific and Indian oceans, and to a lesser degree, in the littoral waters of the South China Sea and Caribbean. The acts of piracy range from small-scale attacks on private yachts to major takeovers of massive international tankers, with the objective of holding the ships and crews for ransom. A variety of observers estimate the cost to the global transportation network caused by piratical activity to be between $15 billion and $20 billion. This includes the cost of increased insurance premiums, ransoms, legal fees, embedded security guards on the ships, inefficient routing to avoid highly pirated zones, additional lookouts, technology and equipment added to ships to prevent successful pirate attacks (e.g., concertina wire and other physical barriers, firefighting water flushing systems on the sides of the ship), and national expenses in sending warships and operational staffs to oversee global counterpiracy operations.

As I took over the job of Supreme Allied Commander at NATO, I reflected on the slightly delicious irony of the need for the military operational leader at NATO to spend a serious chunk of his time learning about piracy, of all things. Many observers had opined that choosing an *admiral* as the sixteenth Supreme Allied Commander was a mistake—after all, there had been a long, unbroken chain of fifteen prior generals, going back to the first Supreme Allied Commander, General Dwight Eisenhower. The concerns of the alliance had always focused on ground combat and high-tech aviation, with a much smaller level of attention paid to things maritime. Indeed, throughout my own career up to that point, I had not paid a great deal of attention to piracy. But finally, I thought, I am going to have a chance to chase some pirates, a mission near and dear to a seagoing officer's heart.

The reason NATO became interested in the piracy mission off Somalia was simple: money. It was beginning to have a very high impact on European companies and indeed on the cost of goods flowing through the East African and North Arabian Sea waters. Additionally, it was increasingly clear that the local terrorist group, Al Shabaab, was beginning to "tax" the Somali pirates and use the funding to undertake acts of violent extremism not only in Somalia but in neighboring countries as well. And we could see flickers of connection between Al Shabaab and Al Qaeda. Indeed, the African group has now pledged allegiance to the so-called Islamic State. So these international terrorist linkages were of legitimate concern.

The roots of Somali piracy lie in a variety of factors. First is the simple difficulty of making a living in any legitimate fashion in Northeast Africa, which has suffered decades of civil war, strife, and depredation. When young, unemployed men find a relatively lucrative (although very dangerous) way to make a living, they are easily recruited. Second, the traditional source of income for many who turned to piracy had been fishing. Due to overfishing and ecological damage in the immediate waters, the ability to make a living fishing had diminished in the latter part of the twentieth century. An excellent explanation of all of this from the point of view of the Somalis (who have some legitimate grievances against the big shipping and industrial companies) can be found in Jay Bahadur's highly readable book *The Pirates of Somalia*. Third, the local water conditions are conducive to pirate activity. Before the real ramp-up in pirate activity, the normal shipping route was quite close to the coast of Somalia as well-laden commercial ships sailed to and from the Suez Canal. The water conditions are calm enough to permit small-boat assaults on the vastly larger commercial ships. And finally, the shipping companies themselves were largely complacent, not having experienced a high level of attacks in recent decades.

By 2009, the piracy situation was at a level demanding international intervention. As I came into office, the number of attacks was rising dramatically, peaking in 2009–10 at more than three hundred. Nearly twenty major ships were being held hostage and worse, more than a hundred mariners with them. While there was relatively little fatal violence, the insurance rates were rising, innocent sailors were held in execrable conditions (usually confined to a small space in a sweltering hulk of a ship anchored in an inlet on the Somali coast), and the flow of resources to local terrorists was rising. Clearly more needed to be done.

A combined maritime force was increased in the local waters, consisting of warships (typically frigates, destroyers, and light cruisers) from the twenty-eight nations of NATO, the European Union, and a loose coalition of Gulf State navies assembled by the United States. Additionally, a very diverse group of nations decided to pitch in, revulsion of piracy being something virtually every nation can agree upon. This led to the deployment of ships from nations that do not normally cooperate with NATO: Russia, China, India, Pakistan, and—quite surprisingly—even Iran. Indeed, this global maritime coalition became an example of what the international community could accomplish if it chose to work together.

I spent a great deal of time working the diplomatic aspects of the coalition, visiting various capitals. It was relatively easy work given the overarching view that the global commons needed policing against piracy and that it was in everyone's interest to participate. In particular, this became a real zone of cooperation between NATO and Russia that paid dividends in everything from sharing maritime tactics to exchanging communication devices to facilitate connectivity at sea between our forces—hardly something that is the norm in terms of working with Russia pretty much everywhere else.

The effort to overcome piracy in East Africa has been relatively successful: by 2013, as I concluded my service as Supreme Allied Commander, attacks were down significantly and they remain so today. The success is the result of a combination of several key factors.

First, the presence of warships has been vital. A frigate or a destroyer with an embarked helicopter or two can cover thousands of square miles of territory and brings the ability to instantly overcome armed pirates, sink their vessels, apprehend them, and incarcerate them (at least temporarily) at sea. They also clearly represent the international community. Over my four years as NATO commander we typically had three to five NATO vessels on station, matched with a similar number for the European Union. Given that the rest of the informal coalition against international piracy also had three to five ships, this became a substantial force. However, despite the presence of those warships, we were often a step behind the pirates. This was because of the sheer size of the operational area off the coast of Northeast Africa, a space roughly the size of

Europe. When people would question why we couldn't catch all the pirates, I would point out that even fifteen warships would be like fifteen police cars trying to cover all of western Europe.

We also supplemented the ships with long-range maritime patrol aircraft. These heavy, wide-bodied, four-engine aircraft lumbered over vast amounts of territory and could remain airborne for eight to twelve hours, operating from bases in Oman, on islands in the Indian Ocean, or from the Horn of Africa. Used throughout the cold war for antisubmarine patrols, these airplanes have the ability to swoop down to the very surface of the ocean, use radar from higher altitude to scan the ocean surface, and provide command and control to helicopters or ships engaged in searching for the pirates. The United States operated P-3 Orion aircraft and the British the comparable Nimrods, and several other allies had similarly equipped planes. Additionally, for overall command of the operation from the air, NATO had available the massive Airborne Warning and Control System (AWACS) E-3 plane, a flying village with extensive radar, communication, and well-trained personnel. These were under my direct command as the NATO Supreme Commander for global operations, and I deployed them on the counterpiracy mission as well.

Tactically, we decided to use an old-school solution: convoys. Rather than letting each of the fifty thousand tankers and commercial ships that transit the area over the course of a year operate on their own, we insisted that for their own protection they be herded into convoys that could operate together. While we did not have enough ships to provide each convoy with an escort, we were often able to keep a warship sufficiently close to each of the patrols to respond to and ward off the pirates. We also debated whether to go ashore and attack the pirate havens, most of which were well known to us, but we were unable to develop the political consensus for doing so given the chances of collateral damage and the difficulty in absolutely identifying the pirates ashore—because their boats and equipment could look a lot like a typical small fishing skiff or a dhow used for legitimate commerce. There was also the lack of a national government with which we could coordinate such onshore action. So much of our tactical execution was done at sea on international waters, where international law gave every nation the authority to respond to piracy.

The hardest part of the operation was actually what occurred *after* we caught a pirate, which we did with increasing frequency. These were young men, ethnically Somalis, most addicted to a mild narcotic called khat that has been chewed in the area for centuries. They have no papers, don't self-identify with a particular functioning government, and thus we had no one to whom we could turn them over for prosecution. Naturally the minute we closed in on them, they would also throw overboard their scaling ladder and guns, so when we boarded their small vessels we would find "innocent fishermen" and have little evidence of their wrongdoing in many cases (unless we had caught them in the act and filmed them on video camera, of course). Eventually several of the local governments proved willing to take them on for trial and conviction, notably Kenya. The pirates were lucky that we couldn't fall back on the centuries-old punishment for such crimes and string them up from a yardarm. While several of the nations in the coalition might have been actually willing to do so, we followed normal mores of Western judicial process throughout the time I was engaged in the exercise.

In addition to the military instruments, both surface and airborne, the shipping industry itself took on the challenge of dealing with the pirates. Initially, this effort focused on routing and convoying, essentially charging captains to work closely with one another at sea and participate in our convoying mechanisms. They also became much better over time checking into the operational centers we established (in the Arabian

Gulf and other littoral areas) over radio when they entered and exited the area. The ships gradually worked harder at sharing observations of pirate activity, and also exchanged ideas for warding them off. This included using the speed and size of the commercial ships; putting up various reasonable effective barriers on the sides of the ships, including barbed wire; tactics to counter a boarding operation, including use of fire hoses at full blast; nonlethal devices such as sonic blast and shock mechanisms; and simply manning the deck and throwing the ladders back into the sea when the pirates attempted to grapple on.

The problem with all of those measures is that they required the merchant crews to do something for which they were neither trained nor particularly well oriented. Mariners today are used to very small crews, good meals, and creature comforts; the idea of fighting pirates does not come easily. Instead, many of the shipping owners developed plans for the mariners to retreat to a citadel inside the ship and radio from there for help. The film *Captain Phillips* about the taking of the *Maersk Alabama* by Somali pirates and the subsequent rescue of the hostage captain provides a vivid and accurate portrayal of a ship takedown and one way the scenario could play out.

What ultimately changed the dynamic altogether and has largely resulted in the dramatic reduction of piracy on the east coast of Africa was the decision by the shipping companies to put security teams on board. This was a new wrinkle in the millennia-old fight against pirates. Initially, the shipping companies wanted no part of this approach due to liability concerns. They were justifiably concerned that any mercenary team they hired might kill an innocent fisherman or other mariner at sea. This actually happened, by the way, and it was not even mercenaries who made the crucial mistake—a well-meaning Italian marine security team on an Italian-flagged vessel managed to shoot and kill two Indian fishermen in 2012. The case occurred twenty miles off the coast of

Kerala, India—on the high seas but well within India's exclusive economic zone (two hundred nautical miles) and is still in litigation, with potentially a significant prison sentence awaiting the adjudication in an Indian court.

Despite legitimate concerns over the potential for incidents like this, shipping companies have finally turned to mercenary firms for protection. This has led to the embarkation of two to six personnel from private contractors, normally well armed and reasonably well trained (at least in the use of the firearms). The host of problems raised by this include how to provide weapons and ammunition, where to base such groups, how they are trained and certified, and what the rules of engagement are for them. Because their activities occur largely on the high seas beyond the jurisdiction of any one nation, this has become a complicated branch of international law. There is a sort of *Mad Max* quality to these forces, despite the efforts of the contractors to train and certify them. While they are not exactly rogue warriors, their presence can make more traditional military sailors nervous, much as police in a city don't like to see armed bodyguards or armed mall guards for that matter. Nonetheless, the results have been striking: no ship embarking an armed security detail has ever been successfully hijacked. This is because the defending team has such a huge advantage in the height of the big tankers and also because the pirates are very lightly armed, untrained themselves, and quite vulnerable during the actual act of boarding. Knowing all of this, the pirates will normally simply sheer off when confronted with consistent fire from a potential victim.

Finally, in addition to national military action and the good work of the industry, there has been additional work ashore by the international community. Let's face it—we are not going to solve piracy solely out at sea. It will require addressing the conditions ashore that lead young men to take up a dangerous and chaotic life. We also need deterrence in the form of local coast guard and police, and a judicial system with real teeth in it. Much of this hard nation building in Somalia has been undertaken by the European Union, and the results—while mixed—are somewhat encouraging. The nascent governmental structures in Somalia, Somaliland, and Puntland—the three "national entities" on the eastern part of the Horn of Africa—are showing increasing capability to respond to piratical acts from the shore side, receive and try pirates, and incarcerate them.

So the good news is that in the pirate waters off the coast of Somalia, there has been a dramatic reduction in successful piracy. But as is so often the case in fighting transnational threats (terrorism, narcotics, human slavery, smuggling), when the international community is able to address it in a given area, it often pops up in another. So it is with piracy, which is showing a great deal of vitality on the other side of Africa in the Gulf of Guinea.

I remember sailing into the Gulf of Guinea on a short cruise as a splinter off operations in the Mediterranean. It is a huge body of water, with many littoral deltas converging as the rivers originating in West Africa run down into the sea, including most notably the Niger and the Volta. In those days thirty years ago, it was a sleepy part of the world. No more, as it has become one of the largest oil and gas hot spots in the world, with much onshore and offshore production in sight. A long history of outlaw operations has coupled with the rise of an Islamic radical group, Boko Haram (which means literally "the Western way is forbidden"). Together, these twin forces are driving up the incidents of piracy to the degree that a variety of Western nations are looking at "getting the band back together" and mounting a mission on the west coast of Africa similar to the one we did several years ago on the east coast. The good news is that there are more capable coast guards, better police and military ground forces, and at least existent courts and judicial systems, albeit highly corrupt and vulnerable to bribes and outside influencers. It seems likely that the next chapter in suppressing serious piracy will take place in the Gulf of Guinea, which looks and often functions like a throwback to the days of Joseph Conrad's *Heart of Darkness*—chaotic, dangerous, and fully in need of a restoration of order. In the end, this particular problem of the outlaw sea will not be solved on the seas themselves, but will require more stability ashore, honest policing, fair courts, legal incarceration, fused intelligence, and above all the "long game" of jobs and education to keep potential pirates from following Johnny Depp's path.

Globally, the number of piracy incidents is roughly flat over the past couple of years, with the caveat that this has always been a relatively underreported phenomenon, especially on the east and west coasts of Africa. The best overall source of information remains the Regional Cooperation Agreement on Combating Piracy and Armed Robbery Against Ships in Asia (ReCAAP), which is a loosely knit group of nations that work together to fight piracy specifically off the Horn of Africa. The directorate also keeps an eye on global trends, and as the piracy meter creeps up on the African west coast, it is likely we will hear from them. As with the other aspects of crime at sea, the key will be cooperative engagement. Hunting pirates is a team sport indeed.

FISHING

A second major challenge to the legal regimes of the oceans involves fishing. Given the size of the world's oceans, which cover 70 percent of the earth's surface and reach depths of more than seven miles, it stands to reason that there are massive stocks of fish. Innocent of all knowledge of territory or international agreement, they are the subject of enormous global activity, valued at well over $225 billion. Europe, the United States, and Japan all have big and growing appetites for fish, as does China—the largest exporter of fish in the world. It is worth noting that this consumption at the industrial scale is largely centered in the developed world, which imports three quarters of the total value of all fish produced.

There is significant downward pressure on fish stocks through overfishing, much of it in violation of nations' exclusive economic zones, international agreements and conventions, and even customary historical fishing grounds. One recent study hypothesized that more than 60 percent of all fish stocks worldwide require "rebuilding," and the literature is replete with warnings of a global fishing collapse. This is borne out by statistics that show a sharp rise in fish caught "in the wild" (as opposed to obtained from fish farms) from the 1950s to the early 1990s, but essentially no growth since then.

From a nonfishing mariner's perspective, there are parts of the world where it is nearly impossible to sail without becoming encumbered with fishing fleets. In my career, the worst of this could be found in East Asia, where massive Chinese, Vietnamese, and Filipino fishing boats were endlessly plying their craft in the littorals of the South China Sea. As we would approach the Philippine Islands in the 1980s, you could smell the fishing fleets—a mixture of gasoline, wood smoke, and the tang of the fish themselves—from miles out to sea when the wind was right. Often operating with small, dim lights, they were highly vulnerable to our massive, 9,000-ton destroyers and cruisers moving at speed through the waters of the fishing grounds. Since the fishing boats were almost entirely made of wood, they would not "paint" clearly on our surface radars, and we would often station additional lookouts with binoculars on the forecastle to try to pick them out of the hazy horizon.

Fishery management is a big industry unto itself, with many sincere efforts made to regulate this global trade. Since the United Nations Convention on the Law of the Sea was essentially ratified worldwide, nations have worked very hard to control the 200-mile exclusive economic zone that provides the legal authority and the concomitant responsibility to manage fish stocks within those waters by each nation. Beyond the EEZ, fishing is regulated by a series of international treaties—by some counts more than seventy in total. The treaties generally address fish, but also include agreements about turtles, seals, polar bears, dolphins, and other species. Most of the treaties have a designated secretariat (a small administrative organization), but little real means of enforcement. Herein lie the problems, and the perception of an "outlaw sea." Despite well-meaning efforts, most observers believe that nearly 90 percent of all fish stocks are "fully exploited, over-exploited, depleted, or recovering from depletion"* Many are declining rapidly, such as tuna—down 50 percent from peak stocks. Indeed, the "oceans are cleared at twice the rate of forests" on land, a chilling prospect.

There are several discrete problems with fishing that are causing the decline in fish stocks, each worth examining quickly. The first is simply our inability to provide accurate measurement metrics. While we can today track total biomass reasonably well (when it is reported, and let's understand that there is a great deal of underreporting happening on the outlaw sea), we are not able to accurately measure the size and level of reproductive capability of fish that are caught. As Professor Bill Moomaw has said, "the artificial truncation" of portions of the fish population over time destroys the productivity of the populations (Moomaw and Blankenship, 14). It is also worth noting that because nets tend to catch the

* William Moomaw and Sara Blankenship, "Charting a New Course for the Oceans," *CIERP Discussion Paper 10*, Center for International Environment and Resource Policy, Fletcher School, Tufts University, April 2014, 14.

biggest fish, the bias of the catch is to remove the larger members of the species, with obviously detrimental effect over decades.

The most blatantly obvious reason for declining fish stocks is simply overfishing. This occurs simply because of greed and economic necessity for poorer fishermen, as well as a lack of concern for the long-term consequences by the big industrial operations. As a seagoing officer, I would often come upon big fishing operations, including the lighter (but still large) long-line fishing platforms, as well as the big net seining operators. There would often be big fish-processing plants located in the same area (Russia and China in particular operate such plants), which were capable of rapidly processing catches and avoiding the probing eyes of inspectors. The key practice contributing to overfishing is destructive fishing practices such as bottom trawling, which not only affects the fish but can be very damaging to the ocean floor as well.

There is also the unfortunate tendency of governments to turn a blind eye to relatively local fishing due to the political impact in the sovereign nation, as well as reluctance to avoid the cost, expense, and inconvenience of an inspection regime (a coast guard) and an attendant court system to rule on charges of overfishing. This tends to go under the header of illegal, unregulated, and unreported fishing, or IUU. Such IUU activities by some measures account for a third of all fish catches, or billions of dollars. Why do we let this happen? As Admiral Hyman Rickover of the U.S. Navy said when asked why he decided to stop naming submarines after fish, breaking a decades-long tradition: "Fish don't vote." Until fish begin voting, unfortunately, it seems unlikely that there will be sufficient political pressure generated to right the ship of overfishing.

Another problem that generates overfishing is one that is quite controllable by governments: the application of subsidies. Governmental monies sometimes directly support the kinds of problems outlined above as national leaders attempt to help local economies. In particular, such subsidies result in the overbuilding of fishing fleets. Some observers believe that nearly $20 billion annually flows to the fishing industry, encouraging the continuation of fishing long after stocks are depleted beyond the point at which such activity remains economically viable.

Shockingly, one out of every four fish (i.e., 25 percent of the world catch) is categorized as "bycatch." This is simply "accidentally" bringing aboard fish and other seagoing species that are not part of the target catch. When vessels use huge, industrial-level trawls—especially when dragged along the seabed—the collateral damage is extreme. The international community has been utterly ineffective in managing this. I think back to my own experience in the Gulf of Mexico watching shrimp boats bring in their big catches with hundreds of sea turtles, ocean fish, and even marine mammals—once you understand the environmentally destructive power of this kind of bycatch, it is hard to watch from the bridge of your warship. Tied to this is a growing trend in using brutally destructive fishing techniques such as explosives and cyanide, which pose a threat not only to the orderly management of fishing but to delicate coral reefs as well. Think of the oceans as a kind of war zone, in which there are daily atrocities, horrifying collateral damage, and no rule of law.

There is an international political component to this, of course: flags of convenience. This is the long-standing practice whereby commercial operators "flag" or register their ships (the way you register a car) in a country that provides, shall we say, a flexible level of enforcement. Not unlike offshore bank accounts, this is merely a means to avoid accountability in the fishing world (and, of course, more broadly in all commercial shipping). In addition to seeking lower standards of enforcement on various practices (fishing, pollution, etc.), shippers also try to find the lowest-priced option. Today somewhere between one thousand and two thousand fishing ships fly a flag of convenience. Many of these are from small Caribbean nations, including Belize (the old British Honduras in Central America), Honduras, and Panama (famous for flags of convenience). The nations profit from the registration fees, and it makes life hard for mariners generally and enforcement personnel (like coast guards) because it is difficult to place effective sanctions on violators—the flag of convenience nation has no real incentive to punish offenders and often has less sophisticated court systems. Indeed, if you look broadly at global shipping, about 55 percent of all ships (fishing, tankers, cargo, passenger, and so on) fly a flag of convenience, and 40 percent are under three nations: Panama, Liberia, and the Marshall Islands. As a naval officer, when I saw those three flags I knew there was going to be a very difficult negotiation if I wanted to send over a boarding party to check for terrorists, drugs, cash, or anything else moving illegally on the high seas.

Taken together, this represents a steady decline in the productivity of the oceans, and the long-range implications for the world's fishing industry are concerning. Unless there is a great deal more regulation and scientific engagement—by private companies, nations, and international organizations—we should fear for the integrity and level of protein we can expect to draw from the sea going forward. After all, in today's world, more than a billion people rely on fish for the protein in their diet, and roughly the same number work on or in the oceans of the world—this despite concerns that fish stocks may have declined as much as 50 percent since the 1970s according to some estimates.

Finally, we should recognize the potential geopolitical tension over fishing that is rising worldwide. Elements of the massive Chinese fishing fleet, for example, consisting of thousands of vessels, have been repeatedly apprehended conducting illegal fishing operations. Indonesia alone has caught and destroyed (by explosion) more than a dozen fishing vessels; Australia has a long record of such apprehensions, as does South Korea. All of this exacerbates the tensions in East Asia and the western Pacific—already one of the most volatile regions of the world.

ENVIRONMENT

Piracy and fishing are sadly very significant sources of illegal activity at sea. But the biggest act of criminal behavior being practiced on the high seas is the willful and preventable damage to the environment that goes on every day. Through the destruction of the maritime world, we are literally watching future generations robbed of their birthright. This is stealing from us all, until and unless we can work coherently together to preserve the riches of the sea for mankind's future. This was a guiding premise in the negotiation of the United Nations Convention on the Law of the Sea three decades ago, but sadly the treaty has not had a sufficient effect on the damage that is unfolding before our eyes.

When I arrived at the Fletcher School of Law and Diplomacy on the campus of Tufts University in Medford, Massachusetts, in the fall of 1981, I was just completing five years at sea on a destroyer and an aircraft carrier. Beginning with my graduation from Annapolis (where we never studied or thought about the environment in any of my classes), I reported to my ships and blithely watched our engineers pump dirty bilge-water, full of black oil, over the side with impunity. We had dumped completely uninspected garbage into the oceans within visual distance of the coasts, and filled the oceans with plastic, toxins, medical waste, slightly radioactive materials, and all manner of utterly unsafe products. I certainly didn't think of myself as a global lawbreaker; everything I just mentioned was "normal underway operations." If I thought about it at all, I would have reflected that the oceans are a huge place, they seem to be able to regenerate themselves, and nothing we were doing was anything other than "the way we always did it."

In my time at the Fletcher School in the mid-1980s, I began to learn about the science, policy, and physical reality of the oceans in ways I never had as a seagoing officer. Sometimes you have to step back from something you love—in this case my seagoing professional life—to really understand it, and especially to be able to judge where it is inflicting harm despite holding no malign intentions. I would have self-identified in those days (as I do today) as someone who "loves and follows the sea." But it took me two years of intensive study and the production of a long dissertation to achieve a PhD in international law with a focus on the Law of the Sea treaty.

Climate change is very real and having increasingly evident effects on the oceans, beginning with the most obvious impact from global warming: sea temperature. As nearly all (more than 90 percent) of the extra heat generated by mankind eventually ends up affecting the oceans, it should be no surprise that temperatures are rising both at the surface and at great depth. There are increases in temperature felt as deep as nearly ten thousand feet, and in parts of the oceans the temperature rise is close to a full degree Fahrenheit. While this does not sound especially significant, it has a gradual but inexorable effect on the existence of life in the sea, and already the migratory patterns of many species are under pressure. There is movement toward the poles, which has knock-on effects, especially on fishing.

Rising temperatures in the oceans also affect ocean currents. There is a complex interplay between salinity, wind, currents, and the resultant upwelling of nutrients from the deep ocean that sustain many of the traditional fishing grounds around the globe. If there is a greater differential between the surface temperature and that of the deeper waters, these upwelling currents are diminished, and it negatively affects ocean life. Additionally, as salinity decreases near melting zones of ice (nearer to the poles), there will be rising levels of acidification and a depletion of ozone—further exacerbating environmental damage.

While such rising temperatures are of concern, it is sea level rise that has potentially the greatest effect on human life over time. The rise in sea level is related to the melting of the polar ice caps and the increase of water volume in the oceans. The numbers are increasingly alarming, and the *rate* of rise is accelerating, with some observers saying that sea levels are rising twice as fast as in the past. This is principally occurring because global warming is causing a melting effect of the glaciers and ice pack at the poles. The potential effects of this are clear: coastal ecosystems are among the most delicate in the world and have important environmental effects such as filtration of water, control of storm waters, and providing nutrients to species in these areas. There would be massive disruption in near-coastal fishing zones and possible knock-on effects in the cycle of global warming. Rising sea levels would also over time claim a great deal of currently arable and habitable land and return it to the sea—meaning coastal living areas would be lost, some small islands would literally become submerged, and current ports would be lost. With nearly three billion people living on coastlines around the earth, all of this will make for difficult adjustments globally.

Two other crucial problems affecting the oceans are oil pollution and resource exploitation. Both are intertwined, especially in regard to liquid hydrocarbons, and both are having deleterious effects on the oceans, despite improvements over the past decades in awareness, regulation, and enforcement.

Oil spills are the most dramatic and obvious, and they can come from offshore rigs, onshore piping systems, or from oil tankers operating at sea. Perhaps the most obvious visually is the offshore oil rigs. Removing resources from the seabed of the oceans is a very complex and difficult business. Throughout my career at sea, as I approached the coastlines of dozens and dozens of different countries, I would be saddened by the proliferation of big, ugly offshore oil rigs. I have passed through significant oil spills a few times, and the obvious devastation—seabirds coated in oil and struggling on the sea surface, legions of dead fish, a sickly, shiny sheen to the waters—is sadly well known. To sail through such a horrible miasma is a memorable experience. I did so in early 1991 during the first Gulf War, when Saddam Hussein's troops deliberately opened risers into the Arabian Gulf from land-based piping and oil rigs and pumped more than 400 million gallons of oil into the northern Gulf, covering some four thousand square miles with oil. They were trying to reduce the operating efficiency of the coalition forces that were marshaling for the liberation of Kuwait following the Iraqi invasion. It had little effect on our ability to operate in the region, but the resulting damage still plagues parts of the Gulf.

The most iconic and highly publicized example of broad area damage from offshore drilling remains the British Petroleum spill in the Gulf of Mexico in 2010 from the *Deepwater Horizon* rig. The short-term effects are well known, starting with the eleven oil-rig workers—essentially mariners—who died and the more than 200 million gallons of oil that flowed into the waters of the Gulf. Following an explosion on the rig, oil was pumping into the Gulf at well over 2 million gallons a day. Engineers struggled to cap the site for nearly three months, and a wild variety of solutions were put forward, including the use of a tactical nuclear weapon. Nearly six hundred miles of pristine coastland was oiled and ruined, and the livelihood of millions of residents interrupted or lost. An enormous amount of remediation and compensation has been accomplished, as well as significant direct fines levied. Unfortunately, the long-term cost is still difficult to assess, as the damage to so many fish and birds simultaneously may have generational effects; there are reports of defects to the circulatory systems of a variety of species.

Most of the top-ranked oil spills in terms of gallons into the water over the decades have been from tankers. As a mariner, I have passed at sea thousands and thousands of big oil tankers over the years, and the vast majority appear to be well operated and professionally handled. We would often exchange friendly signals, and on one or two occasions provided distress relief or medical support. These enormous tankers, some of them three times the size of the U.S. super aircraft carriers, are operated with a tiny crew—just a dozen or so, as compared with several thousand on a carrier, for example. But when something goes wrong, it goes wrong with a vengeance, and nothing is worse that one of these behemoths discharging oil into the sea. As Americans, we tend to remember the *Exxon Valdez* spill into Prince William Sound in Alaska. This came not from an offshore installation but from a ship that was grossly mishandled, and the spill covered 1,400 miles of coast and killed (by most estimates) millions of living organisms including half a million seabirds. Yet this spill is not even in the top thirty in history and put "only" 11 million gallons into the water as compared with more than 200 million from the BP disaster.

These big incidents from offshore rigs or tankers certainly shock the conscience and are remembered decades later, but they are really dwarfed by the steady amount of oil that enters the world's waters year after year through routine pollution. This comes from illegal dumping in the dark of night, accidental inclusion of oil in garbage dumped at sea, and the flow of oil down to the oceans from freshwater sources, largely rivers, which themselves receive automotive effluents or oil-based pesticides. Some experts believe more than 500 million gallons a year of such steady, insidious oil pollution takes place. While the big incidents like the *Deepwater Horizon*/BP or *Exxon Valdez* disaster can be overwhelming in a given spot and of course receive enormous media attention, it is likely that the long-term, underreported but steady oil pollution into the oceans is actually the bigger threat. This quiet but massive input of oil into the sea deserves much greater study for its potential long-term effects.

While it is easy to focus on oil pollution because the effects are so visible, there is also a high level of concern about chemical pollution. This is most typically from broad industrial activities, which end up producing dangerous chemical substances that then find their way into the oceans. An example would be the flow of contaminated silt, essentially dirt, which rolls into the sea. The silt is carried along by deep river currents and over time can include significant levels of pollutants from industrial and residential activity all along the riverbanks thousands of miles upstream. Man's agricultural activities also contribute greatly to this form of pollution, largely from the use of nonorganic fertilizers. Auto activity, in terms of both exhaust and liquid effluents, also ends up frequently in the oceans. Toxic chemicals such as mercury also find their way into the seas, accumulating in the tissues of big fish species such as swordfish and tuna. And of course there is simple, obvious pollution in many low-regulation nations, where factories pump industrial waste, human excrement and urine, and other liquid substances directly into rivers or the sea.

Another concern that I often witnessed over the years was the dumping of plastics and garbage directly into the sea. Certainly the U.S. Navy's hands are not clean in this regard; I vividly remember all manner of plastic-laced garbage being thrown overboard. I would stand on the fantail of my destroyer in the 1970s and watch hundreds of seagulls come and look over the garbage we tossed carelessly over the side. We have come to understand the damage caused by plastics, and the world's navies and responsible merchant fleets, at least, have modified their behavior accordingly. With apologies to Ian Fleming and his immortal novel *Diamonds Are Forever*, as far as the oceans are concerned it is plastics that are forever.

Even as they degrade into smaller shapes and sizes, they still retain their fundamental composition. As a result, when marine animals—especially birds and turtles—ingest the garbage, they consume plastics, which are increasingly found not just in the seas but in the digestive systems of large segments of marine life. As for other refuse, much of it is biodegradable or can be manufactured so that it will disintegrate without harm to the sea, but some vessels and garbage disposal operations continue to discharge highly toxic materials including contaminated medical waste (needles, tubes, stents, etc.), sewage (close to shore), chemicals, drugs, and other nonbiodegradable items.

Looking to the future, there is both good and bad news. The bad news is that the vast array of activities that damage the oceans will only increase—there will be a higher demand for fish-based protein, and for hydrocarbons, and the increasing world population (probably headed to at least 10 billion by the turn of the next century from the current level of about 7 billion) will cause more pollution, including dumping of garbage, plastics, medical waste, and sewage. All of this will damage the oceans, with particular impact close to shorelines, especially on delicate and important coral reefs. And there will be new activities in the oceans, including a likely increase in the recovery of minerals, probably from the deep seabed where plentiful nodules of copper, cobalt, manganese, nickel, and rare earth minerals lie like so many potatoes waiting to be gathered and hauled to the surface. The good news is that we still have time to react and take measures to protect the oceans, beginning with stronger enforcement of the existing accords, negotiation of new international regimes, and a focus on using the oceans in responsible ways in all of our strategic communications globally. We will never fully tame the vast reaches of the outlaw sea, but we can take proactive steps to reduce risk.

WHAT ARE WE TO DO?

What are we to do about the outlaw sea? As citizens of our individual nations, how do we collectively approach this enormously transnational problem, given that most who follow the sea spend their lives and careers focused on national concerns, as I did? In many ways, this is the most important question that mariners and those who truly love the sea must deal with as we sail further on into the twenty-first century.

At the heart of any approach to the challenges of the outlaw sea is the creation of an enhanced level of international cooperation. Only through a high level of integration among international, interagency, and private entities can there be any hope of addressing the challenges inherent in the vast world of the sea. Unfortunately, to date the results of such efforts have been mixed at best. Certainly the development of the United Nations Convention on the Law of the Sea—an international negotiation concluded in the 1980s—has been largely successful. In the early 1980s, there was enormous enthusiasm for the treaty, a massive negotiating project that created the first truly global regime for ocean management. While it has obviously not solved all the problems of ocean governance, it is hard to imagine the level of chaos on the seas without it—even given that the United States, a huge maritime power, has refused to sign it (in a disagreement over deep seabed mining provisions, a foolish position pushed by U.S. neoconservatives). I remain hopeful that using the Law of the Sea treaty as a base, we will be able to negotiate other international instruments and—even more important—enforce them through a combination of sanctions, judgments in national and international courts, and shaming nations that do not follow the rules. So overall, I am cautiously optimistic about international maritime cooperation.

On the other hand, efforts such as the pledge in 2010 by the world's nations to protect at least 10 percent of the world's oceans as protected reserves by 2020 have foundered—to date only 2 percent of the oceans have been so designated. While there have been some successes (the United Kingdom, for example, has created a reserve area in the South Pacific near Pitcairn Island that is three times the size of Great Britain itself), international efforts are lagging overall. Likewise, the jury is still out on a plethora of well-meaning efforts to address fishing, pollution, and the global environment.

In terms of interagency cooperation, again we see a mixed picture. While the Obama administration moved on creating a U.S. government plan against illegal fishing, there has been a lack of sufficient resources placed against the goals. Neither the Coast Guard nor the U.S. Navy has spare capacity to undertake the kind of sweeping tasks outlined in the plan. The good news is that the interagency spirit is willing, but the flesh, so to speak, is weak. This is typical of how interagency projects fail, both in the United States and in other countries. Unfortunately, there is no consistent voice for the oceans in the vast majority of governments.

Another immensely important zone of cooperation will be the intersection of efforts by the public and private sectors. International shipping companies, for example, are increasingly working together with international organizations (such as the International Maritime Organization of the United Nations) to create norms of behavior on the oceans. These run the gamut from agreements on "pumping and dumping"—discharge of anything from a ship—to levels of qualification of crew members, engineers, deck watch standers, mates, and captains. Many fishing companies are likewise working more closely with governmental and international organizations to bring order out of the largely chaotic world of fisheries. The oil and gas companies are cooperating at a higher level with such authorities as well. Getting past a sense of adversarial politics in all of these ocean areas will be crucial.

In Bill Moomaw's superb report on the oceans, he and his coauthor identify seventy-six "treaties, agreements, protocols, and frameworks that address the management of one or more species, fishing practice, or marine resource at global or regional levels" (Moomaw and Blankenship, 39). This sort of international cooperation demonstrates both the hope and the challenge of such an approach: many were lacking a formal secretariat, scientific body, and enforcement mechanisms. Of the seventy-six, only six had all three. This is the case in other areas of maritime management as well. Clearly, much more work will need to be done in the international space to build not only agreements but the right kind of management and enforcement as well. The best way to do this will be under the overarching umbrella of United Nations organizations (especially the International Maritime Organization) and using the principles that guided nearly two hundred nations through the arduous decade-long negotiation of the United Nations Convention on the Law of the Sea.

We must be more innovative and experiment at sea with new ideas of governance and bring more actors into ocean policy. Creating more protected marine areas will be helpful, as will the idea of establishing sanctuaries at sea for fish, birds, and mammals, much as is done on land. Certification programs that clearly indicate to the public which companies are doing business in ecologically thoughtful ways will matter, and encouraging corporate social responsibility at sea will be crucial. Linkages with aquariums, zoos, environmental advocacy organizations, and think tanks all have applicability as well.

The course we must chart for the oceans involves work between and within governments, and above all within the private sector. But underlying all of that effort must be a coherent campaign of strategic communications. Unless we can convince the public of all our nations that the oceans are not a vast, invulnerable dumping ground and an endless source of protein, we will not succeed globally in altering the course we are on. We have a long way to sail before we can feel confident that the outlaw sea has been tamed.

9.

AMERICA AND THE OCEANS

A NAVAL STRATEGY FOR THE TWENTY-FIRST CENTURY

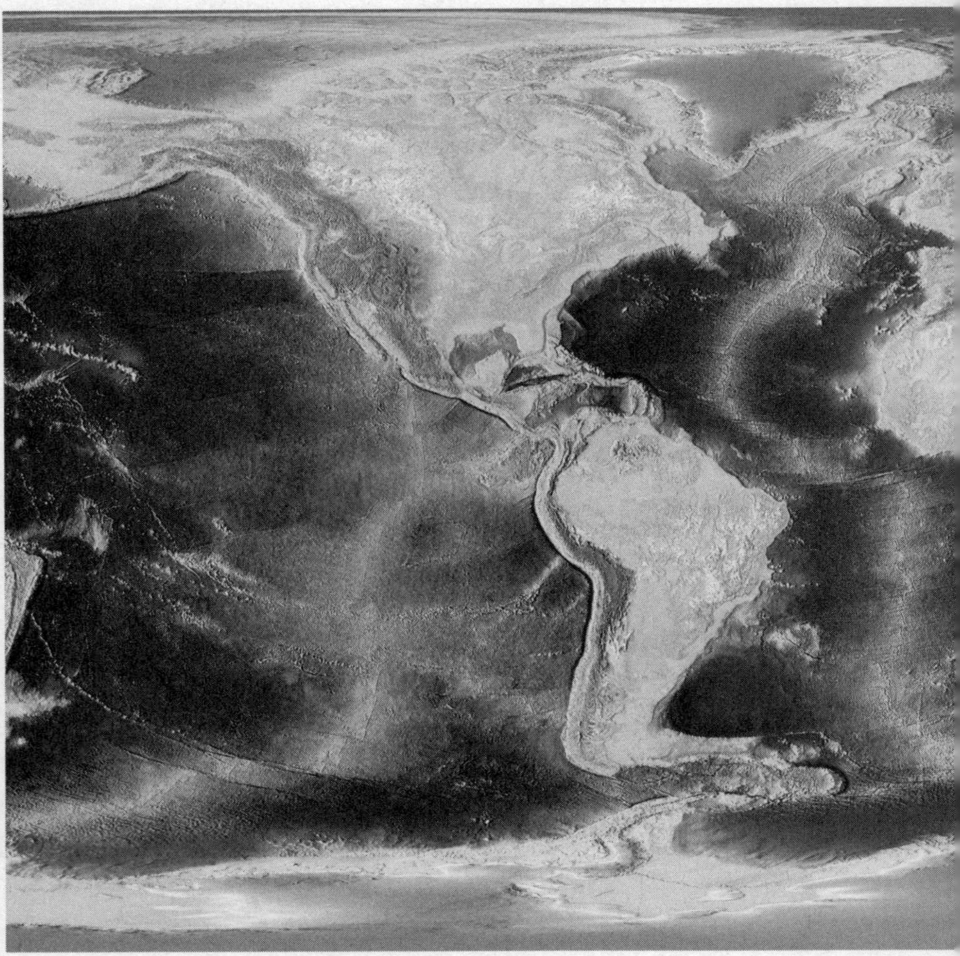

New environmental challenges will tax the oceans in ways never seen in human history. This map displays the world's land and sea elevations.

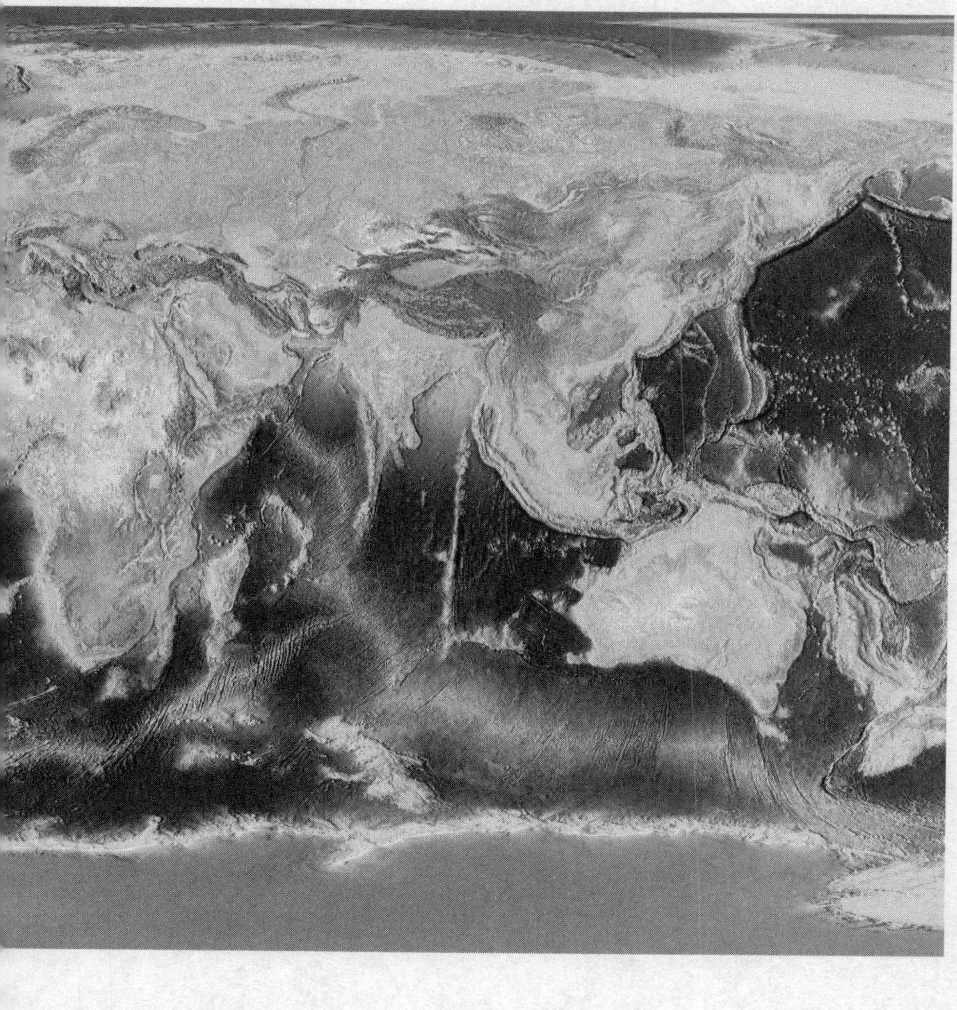

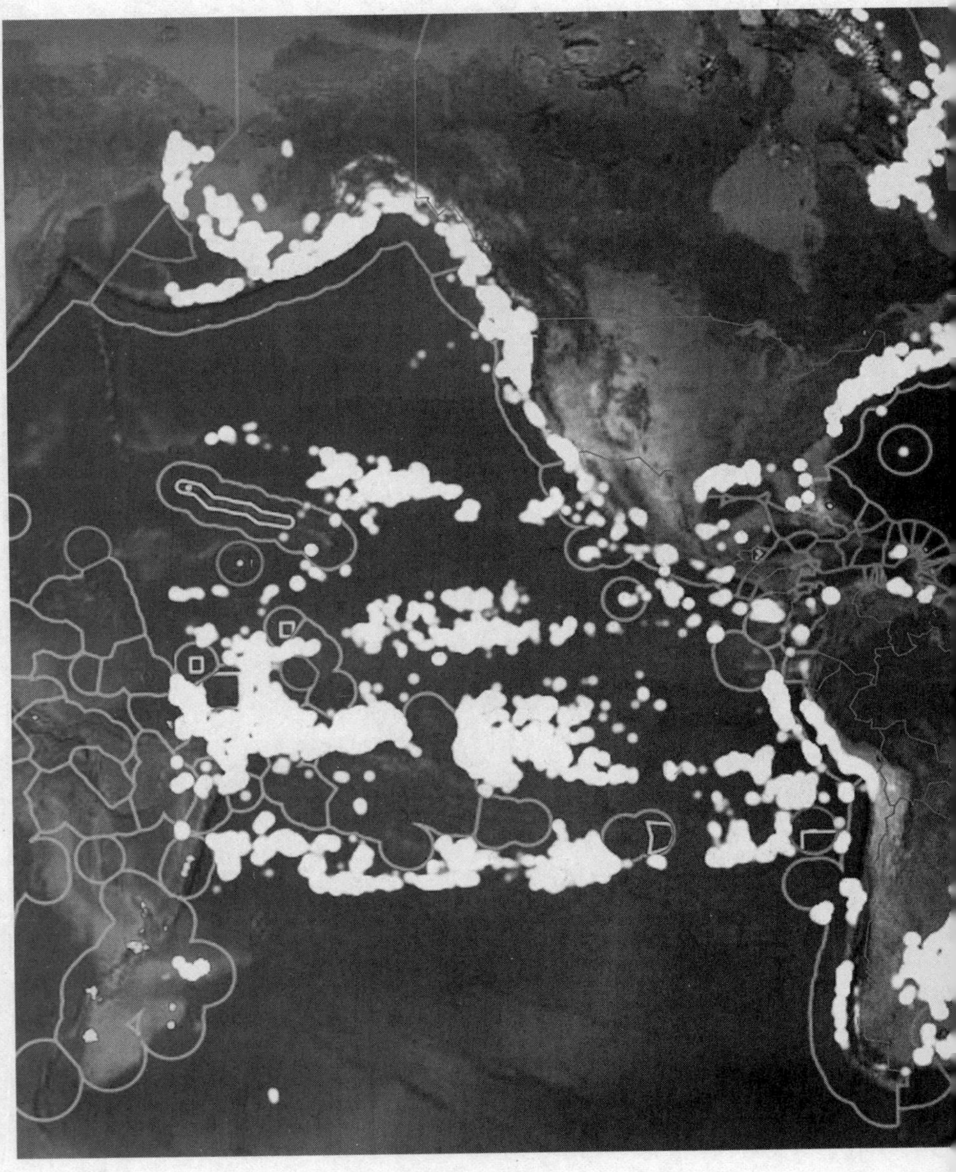

Current global commercial fishing activity.

Courtesy of Global Fishing Watch.

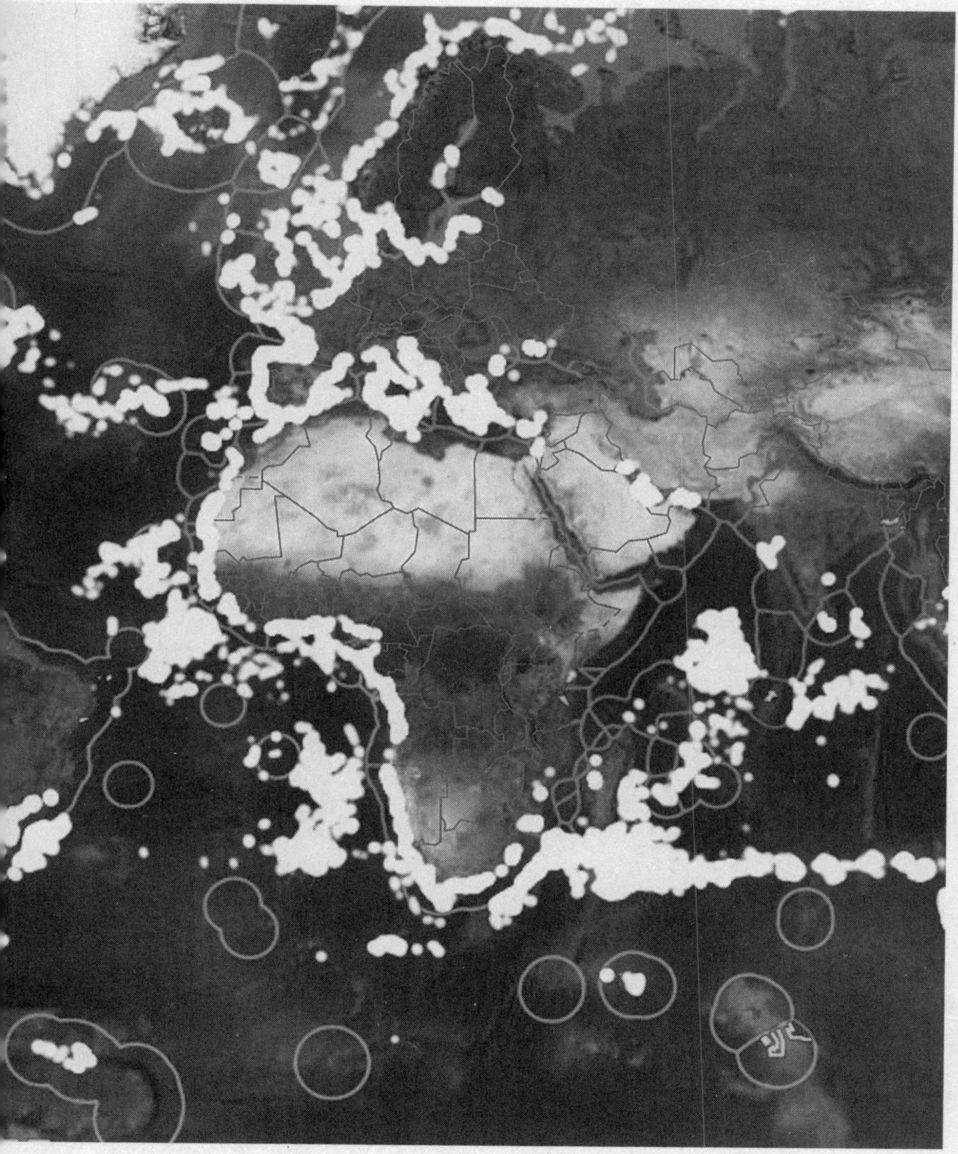

I first heard of Alfred Thayer Mahan when I was seventeen years old and a freshman (a "plebe," as we were not-so-affectionately termed) at the U.S. Naval Academy. Part of the first-year curriculum for the entire thousand-man (and it was all men in those prehistoric days) class was a course titled simply "Sea Power." Some of my wittier classmates dubbed it "Z-Power" to imply that it was boring, but for me it was anything but a sleeper.

The modern version of the course had been created by a venerable historian, E. B. "Ned" Potter, who had also written a classic blue-covered textbook of the same name. Luckily for him, every year he sold a thousand copies of this hardcover text, which no doubt kept him well supplied with the small-batch bourbon of which I am told he was quite fond. I still have my plebe-year copy of the book, a little battered but still very much a text I open from time to time, and of course the title of this work is taken in homage to Potter's course, although the context and approach are entirely different.

The structure of the course was built simply upon the chronological history of man's military journey on the oceans. It began in prehistoric times, moved quite briskly through the age of galleys sailed by the Greeks and Romans, segued into the classic battles like Lepanto in the Mediterranean between the Ottomans and the Hapsburgs, included plenty of material on the American Revolution at sea, followed by a quick nod to the Barbary pirates and the heroics of Stephen Decatur. Then it slowed and began the long sail through nineteenth-century American sea power, with an emphasis on the Civil War, before launching into the real set pieces of World War I and World War II at sea. It was (and remains) unashamedly Western oriented (completing the course, you would have thought that the Chinese didn't build boats). It was unapologetically told from a very American point of view, and was extremely traditional in its outlook. And the high priest of it all was Rear Admiral Alfred Thayer Mahan.

One former secretary of war, Henry Stimson, opined that Mahan manifested "the peculiar psychology of the Navy Department, which frequently seemed to retire from the realm of logic into a dim religious world in which Neptune was God, Mahan his prophet, and the United States Navy the only true church." Mahan was born in 1840 in, of all places, West Point—home of the U.S. Military Academy, where his father was a professor. Mahan's middle name was an homage to the so-called Father of West Point, Sylvanus Thayer. Everything about his early life would have predicted he would become an Army officer, but he set his course early for the Naval Academy and graduated second in his class of 1859.

He was part of the Civil War Union Navy, and over the course of his career spent the requisite time at sea, working his way up to the rank of captain and holding command of a number of ships. Yet he was, by all accounts, an indifferent seaman whose propensity to bump into other ships and navigational buoys was noted by his superiors. But he began writing books early and often, expounding a theory of sea power that would make him perhaps the most influential naval officer of his generation.

Mahan's desire to read, think, write, and publish occasionally landed him in hot water with his superiors, including one famously damning fitness report that said succinctly, "It is not the business of naval officers to write books." (Here I must note that the book you are reading is the seventh I have either written or edited, none at the level of Mahan's classics; but I too found my naval career a bit bumpy at times due to that desire to write. The Navy sometimes retains a level of skepticism toward those who would proffer their views in print, but fortunately I think overall there is a respect for intellectual effort as well as good seamanship in the course of an officer's career.)

Late in his career, Mahan was tapped by Rear Admiral Stephen B. Luce, the intellectual force in the Navy's move from sail to steam in the late nineteenth century, to come to the Naval War College at Newport, Rhode Island, first as a lecturer and later for two terms as the second president of the college, following Admiral Luce. Mahan's lectures, which were deeply admired and absorbed by Theodore Roosevelt among many others, were eventually translated into a series of classic books on sea power and history that are still studied closely today and form the basis for American sea power on into the twenty-first century. He died at the age of seventy-four of congestive heart failure, having finally been advanced to rear admiral (on the retired list) very late in his life and career.

The basic theory of Mahan's body of work is that national power derives from engagement via the world's oceans along three key vectors: production (which leads to the need for international trade and commerce), shipping (both merchant and naval), and colonies and alliances (spread across the globe, forming a network of bases from which to project sea power). All three of these basic concepts still pertain today, although they need a bit of updating as we will discuss in more depth below.

In addition to these three key vectors, Mahan also returns again and again to a handful of principal conditions that affect a nation's ability to develop and wield sea power effectively. The first is the most straightforward and immutable: geography. As he says, "The seaboard of a country is one of its frontiers; and the easier the access offered by the frontier to the region beyond, in this case the sea, the greater will be the tendency of a people toward intercourse with the rest of the world by it." In the case of the United States, our vast coastlines afford immediate access to the Atlantic, Pacific, and Arctic oceans, as well as the Gulf of Mexico and Caribbean Sea to the south. This is an enviable position for developing and exploiting sea power, as we have seen repeatedly in our history. Coupled with enormous natural resources and relatively temperate climate, the geography of the United States features perhaps the best set of circumstances to build the nation into a sea power.

A second factor cited frequently by Mahan that remains important today is the actual size of the seacoasts. Mahan's comments here are quite specific: "As regards the development of sea power, it is not the total number of square miles which a country contains, but the length of its coast-line and the character of its harbors that are to be considered." The United States has 133,000 kilometers of coastline as measured along the tidewater boundaries—an enormous stretch, virtually all of it easily accessible from the land and situated in temperate zones. This is among the largest coastlines in the world (measuring coastlines, by the way, is a tricky business, and the numbers used here are from the World Resources

Institute). Only Canada has a larger coastline by this measure, and much of it, of course, is inaccessible much of the year.

Mahan also cites the importance of the native population in determining a nation's ability to use sea power. As we increasingly see in this century, demography is destiny in many ways for nations. Mahan's view was that it is not only the number of the population, but their fitness to conduct the business of using the oceans—shipbuilding, working on ships, propensity to join the Navy and Coast Guard—that is critical. As he says, "the number following the sea" matters. Closely associated with the number is the "character of the people." In this regard, Mahan (like Theodore Roosevelt as president) believed in an activist philosophy of life, with an aggressive commercial approach to seas—specifically the economic incentive of the people to want to engage in trade globally.

As he said, "The tendency to trade, involving of necessity the production of something to trade with, is the national characteristic most important to the development of sea power." In terms of the characteristic that drives all this, he also said, "It seems scarcely necessary, however, to do more than appeal to a not very distant past to prove that, if legislative hindrances be removed, and more remunerative fields of enterprise filled up, the sea power will not long delay its appearance. The instinct for commerce, bold enterprise in the pursuit of gain, and a keen scent for the trails that lead to it, all exist; and if there be in the future any fields calling for colonization, it cannot be doubted that Americans will carry to them all their inherited aptitude for self-government and independent growth." No shrinking violet, Mahan, but rather an unabashed capitalist (and imperialist, frankly) who also would have been happier to see the United States more aggressively pursuing colonies abroad like our European counterparts.

A final factor upon which Mahan lays emphasis is the "character of the government." Consistently throughout all his writings he calls on the U.S. government to fully understand the importance of sea power—a national imperative in the view of Mahan. He says, "It would seem probable that a government in full accord with the natural bias of its people would most successfully advance its growth in every respect; and, in the matter of sea power, the most significant successes have followed where there has been intelligent direction by a government fully imbued with the spirit of the people and conscious of its true general bent." Mahan—aided by Rear Admiral Luce and truly energized by Teddy Roosevelt—preached this doctrine religiously throughout the senior part of his career. And his ideas caught the attention of policy makers not just in the United States but across the Atlantic as well, including in both England and Germany.

All of these underlying factors are important to his thesis, but at its heart, Mahan's siren call is for a big, muscular fleet: think of the Great White Fleet of Teddy Roosevelt, sailing the globe, refueling at well-selected coaling stations (which we would call forward bases today), and inspiring fear and awe in the nations of the world. This is the relevance of the expression "Speak softly and carry a big stick." The key was being able to overmatch your opponent in terms of fleet fighting capacity—essentially using the inherent mobility of naval forces to concentrate and defeat an enemy at sea in a decisive battle.

But there is a strategic concept behind all of that: the ability of a nation to use sea power to ultimately contain powerful nations that have concentrated their use of forces ashore, ignoring the sea out of lack of interest, or an inability to see the force of the sea power argument, or simply because they lack the geography, character, and political will to exploit the oceans. Let's begin with the ancient Greeks: Athens was a sea power (with a good deal of land force character as well). With both land power and sea power, Athens was initially able to hold off Sparta (an essential land power) in the Peloponnesian Wars. Sparta, with its center of gravity deep inland on the southern peninsula of Greece, was a "heartland" power. Over time, the Spartans realized they needed to create a navy to compete effectively with Athens, learning the lessons of sea power.

Flash forward to the age of Britannic majesty, the British Empire. How did a small island nation, devoid of most natural resources, come to dominate much of the world's land surface? Through the effective use of sea power, building a colonial empire "upon which the sun never set." Mahan seized upon British mastery of sea power to set up the case for the United States to build a similar fleet, and a colonial empire, taking advantage of its coastlines, maritime DNA, and naval approach to have real influence in the world. The British, according to Mahan, were able to challenge continental (heartland) European powers like Germany/Prussia because they were able to dominate the sea lanes of communication around the world.

Many analysts posited this same dynamic in the cold war between the United States and the Soviet Union. The USSR was a classic "heartland power," with huge land-force capability, the advantage of an interior position geopolitically, domination of its near abroad (through the Warsaw Pact), and a mind-set forged in the great land wars against Napoleon, Kaiser Wilhelm, and Nazi Germany. Against the USSR stood the USA, a maritime nation—essentially an island nation—protected by its great oceans and geographic position, underwritten by a strong navy, and perfectly capable of combining with continental allies (via NATO) to ensure that the heartland nation was unable to attain its ultimate desire—to dominate the "world island," as geopolitical analyst Halford Mackinder styled the entire Eurasian continent. As Mackinder said, "Who rules East Europe commands the Heartland; Who rules the Heartland commands the World Island; Who rules the World Island commands the

World." This quote sums up the concern Mahan had about domination by a strong land power, and why sea power was so important as a counterbalance.

The interesting question in the twenty-first century is whether or not shifts in power, international norms, or technology have substantially altered the Mahanian approach. Personally, I believe his message still rings true for the United States. As we seek to craft an international maritime strategy for the nation, Mahan's point of view—adapted somewhat for today's world—still presents a timeless message.

Taking his principles as a starting point, what advice can we imagine Mahan presenting the president today?

First and foremost, he would emphasize the need for the United States to regard itself as a maritime nation. This means supporting a reasonably sized civilian merchant marine; a powerful, capable navy; a robust shipbuilding industry; a competent fishing fleet; efficient ports and infrastructure; ice-breaking capability for the Arctic; and the ability to conduct broad area surveillance of the ocean approaches to our nation.

Mahan would also emphasize to today's president the importance to the United States of defending the concept of an open global commons—the rights of high seas passage and transit, the importance of the UN Law of the Sea treaty (which he would support, as virtually every active-duty admiral in the U.S. Navy does today), and safe passage free from piracy, political interference, or natural barriers. The open flow of free goods on the oceans (95 percent of global trade moves by sea) is crucial to a geopolitical power like the United States. This means challenging attempts to close the global commons by nations such as China, which is building artificial islands and declaring much of the South China Sea a "historic claim."

A third key element in Mahan's prescription would be a strong system of alliances and partnerships around the world. He would have thought in terms of colonies, which are—praise the Lord—things of the past. In their place today, we need strong alliances, with NATO at the top of the list. By working with NATO, the United States has reliable and immediate access to bases and logistic support all around the periphery of Europe and up into the Arctic. Our warships can pull into port in Rota, Spain; Souda Bay, Greece; Portsmouth, England; Toulon, France; Bremen, Germany; and essentially anywhere within the twenty-eight nations of the alliance. Over my time as a Navy commander, I have frequently made port calls, refueled, sent my crew on liberty, conferred with close colleagues from allied navies, and generally found support and sustenance in our alliance. Similarly, in the Pacific, we have formal alliances with Australia, New Zealand, the Philippines, Thailand, Japan, and South Korea—all of equal value in ensuring a global system of operating locations.

In addition to alliances, the United States needs an active network of partners and friends—nations that we are for a variety of reasons not ready to engage with a formal alliance—but with which we have warm relations nonetheless. Nations in this category include Saudi Arabia, Bahrain, Kuwait, Israel, India, Malaysia, Singapore, Finland, Sweden, Colombia, Brazil, Argentina, Chile, and Peru. I have made port visits to each of the nations mentioned above and have found a welcoming committee in each place. These partners and friends are an essential part of our global maritime network as well, and part of our maritime strategy would include embracing them. When you put all the capability of our allies, partners, and friends together, it is a formidable naval force indeed—that approach toward international coalitions must be central to our global maritime strategy.

Fourth, Mahan was keenly aware of the importance of the private sector in ensuring that the United States maintain a robust maritime capability. In his view, the primary key was supporting the maritime industry and the global trading capability. In today's world, both of those are necessary, but they are not sufficient. Another key component of an effective global maritime strategy for the United States must be a high level of private-public operational integration and cooperation. One key example is in the world of sharing intelligence and information on ship movements at sea, both passively through the Global Positioning System and associated beaconing systems, and through active shared reports. This is crucial to ensure an open and free global navigational system, especially in the face of potential piratical activity in places like the Strait of Malacca, the east and west coasts of Africa, and the Caribbean Sea. Another example is specific to piracy, and that is exchanging operational protocols—embarked security teams, convoy operations, distress reporting systems, and countermeasures on individual ships. And all facets of global shipping systems—ships, ports, loading cranes, buoyage systems—are now vulnerable to cyberattack and are therefore a shared responsibility between the U.S. government and the U.S. operators.

Mahan was very focused on the rise of competing sea powers, and in today's world he would signal concern about two: Russia and China. Russia has rebounded from a period of decline in its military capability and is today using a highly targeted program of rebuilding its fleet. While in total ship numbers slightly smaller than the United States, the Russian fleet is very actively focused on the undersea world. While Mahan was not writing about the incredible advancements in submarines, by the end of his life he would have been aware of their growing potential to influence war at sea. The Russians have certainly taken the idea of submarine capability to heart and continue to expand the number, technology, and operational reach of all their submarines—both nuclear and diesel powered, and including both attack and ballistic missile versions. Likewise, the Chinese are improving all aspects of their oceangoing fleet, with an emphasis on technology, undersea capability (both offensive and defensive), long-range surface-to-surface missiles used to attack American aircraft carriers, and long-range land-attack precision cruise missiles. This is in addition to their very capable nuclear-powered ballistic missile submarines. Mahan's advice would be to keep a weather eye on the rising power of both of these potential competitors at sea and maintain the ability to defeat both.

What would Mahan have missed or gotten wrong?

I think the biggest surprise to Mahan would have been the rise of undersea warfare as a critical (some would say dominant) element of naval and maritime strategy. Coupled with this, of course, would be the advent of nuclear propulsion, which gives these undersea warships the ability to submerge for long periods of time (months), limited only by food supplies on board—they can propel themselves and create both water and breathable air. And he would have been stunned at the size and capability of today's submarines—while some small diesel-powered boats were in existence by the end of his life, to think of a 19,000-ton, 560-foot-long warship with missiles capable of destroying large cities and creating nuclear killing zones around the world all while being under the water and essentially invisible would have been too much even for a man used to ranging freely across the oceans of the mind.

A second surprise: it would have been hard for him to conceive of the way in which warfare has gone from service-specific to joint, meaning highly integrated among the land, sea, and air components. The way in which the United States would fight a war today depends utterly on seamless command and control between the services (Army, Navy, Air Force, and Marine Corps), integrated munitions that can be shifted between them, and operations that use all branches to create shock and awe—missile strikes, aircraft attacks, naval gunfire, Marines landing and flying to an objective, heavy Army units right behind, all of it collectively creating a sense on the part of the enemy that defeat is inevitable. For Mahan, naval forces would have generally operated within their watery domain, fought a great battle with an enemy fleet, and been tasked with sea control, logistic resupply for forces ashore, and occasional power projection from cannons and Marines over a beachhead. But the essence of the fleet was to find and destroy the enemy fleet, thus ensuring control of the vital sea lanes of communication.

He also, naturally enough, would have had no conception of the importance of cyber. The world of information, command, communications, and cyberwarfare simply had no existence in the period of time in which he was writing. It is hard enough for us to keep up with the latest changes in information warfare, let alone expect Mahan to imagine them. Perhaps the biggest technological change on ships would have been the use of computational power to direct weapons, giving them a distance, accuracy, and lethality he could not have imagined. The major cultural change, of course, would have been the advent of instantaneous communications, meaning that a captain's decisions in battle are far more subject to "helpful advice" from a fully informed chain of command. I suspect the latter would not have been good news, as Mahan was someone who prized the initiative, verve, and confidence of the American naval commander at sea. But all good things must end, and in today's world a captain still maintains a certain amount of tactical control over operations, even if he (or she!) is receiving a great deal of broad operational and strategic guidance.

Additionally, it is hard to imagine that Mahan could have predicted the integration of space and unmanned systems into the nautical battle world. The vast expanses of the ocean always provided a sort of natural hiding place for ships, and the challenges of navigating across the trackless oceans challenged even the best of navigators. Electronic aids to navigation emerged in the middle of the twentieth century (radio beacons, for example), and radar deployed from aircraft began to shrink the unknown spaces of the sea. Once satellites were launched, and the Global Positioning System put in place, the world of the oceans was finally effectively mapped and tracked from on high. This has changed the character both of navigation itself and of how combat is conducted—virtually all naval weapons today depend on guidance obtained at least in part from GPS systems.

One final surprise for Rear Admiral Mahan would have been the emerging importance of undersea cables in linking the world together and creating a sort of undersea sea lane of communications (quite literally) upon which we all depend. One other important aspect of thinking through a maritime strategy for the twenty-first century is what lies at the *bottom* of the ocean. In addition to a formidable geography—just like the surface of the earth, with high mountain ranges, valleys, plateaus, plains, and on and on—there are critical cables, man-made of course, that carry much of the world's knowledge and commerce.

At the bottom of the world's oceans, like so many snakes surrounding the globe, are the standard commercial fiber optic cables that carry 99 percent of the world's international telecommunications daily. They move information at a brisk clip: two terabits of data every second, including nearly $5 trillion every twenty-four hours in financial transactions. About two hundred of them carry the vast majority of all that vital information.

As one observer recently commented, "Though often mentioned in passing, the fact that the overwhelming bulk of Internet activity travels along submarine cables fails to register with the public. High-flying satellites orbiting the crowded skies, continent-spanning microwave towers and a million miles of old 20th Century copper phone wire all carry but a fraction of the Earth's Internet traffic compared with deep-sea fiber-optic cables." As we consider the role they play today and what the potential might be for further enhancements, there is both promise and peril to consider.

First, the peril—as strategists are increasingly aware, these cables are vulnerable. While their extreme depth protects them up to a point, advanced industrial nations—including the United States, the Russian Federation, and China—all reportedly have significant ability to monitor, exploit, damage, and destroy the cables. During the cold war, both the USA and the USSR were believed to have attacked antisubmarine systems and arrays at similar depths.

As Steve Weintz wrote recently in the *National Observer*, "If you wish to practice hybrid warfare—disruption and degradation with little overt engagement—then the ability to cut submarine cables at will and at depth gives you a very powerful weapon. Cut up undersea hydrophone networks and you deafen your adversary. Cut Internet cables and you have the ultimate denial-of-service cyber weapon."

There have certainly been plenty of incidents of accidental cable cuttings and losses of data resulting from such activities. In 2006 and 2008, accidental destruction of cables effectively shut down Internet services to several large countries or parts thereof, including, among others, Egypt, India, China, and Pakistan. Fortunately, the cables are fairly substantial: typically, a couple of inches thick and well insulated with galvanic padding. But they are quite vulnerable, especially at cable heads when they emerge from the water. In Egypt just a couple of years ago, swimmers were caught while trying to cut through a major 12,500-mile cable. Internet speeds throughout Egypt plummeted by more than 60 percent.

Overall, the cable system is fairly robust in facing routine challenges—

accidents, anchors dragged over them, corrosion, low-level attacks. The challenge will come as nations and transnational groups (criminal cartels, terrorists) find ways to disrupt them on a massive scale. Even with the 285 cables on the bottom of the world today and the 22 "redundant" or "dark" cables in reserve, the vulnerabilities are clear. Both individual nations and international organizations should collectively be thinking through disaster scenarios and considering how best to use collective defense of these cables going forward.

So much for the peril; but what about the promise of this system? Are there new technologies coming that can leverage and improve this capability? The good news is a resounding yes.

First, the information technology itself is improving—and it has to. Just a couple of years ago, the Internet moved about five gigabytes per capita. It will hit fourteen gigabytes per capita in 2018. And with billions more devices connecting to the Internet in the next decade, the problem is obvious. Fortunately, we are able to use new phase modulation and also improve what is called submarine line terminal equipment (SLTE). This will boost capability by more than fifty times. Additionally, the prosaic ability to lay, adjust, repair, and maintain the cables is improving through the use of unmanned systems, big data analysis, and better materials.

Additionally, there are increasingly creative ideas about how to leverage the cable system to improve access to high-speed Internet around the world. Satellites—at least for now—are just not the answer. Their signals capacity is severely limited by latency and bit loss, whereas underwater fiber optic cables deliver signals at nearly the speed of light (they are optic, after all). So what can we do to amp up their contribution?

One idea is to create mobile networking hubs, both airborne and on the surface of the sea. The airborne vehicles could operate at forty to fifty thousand feet in altitude, which would enable broadcast to 250 nautical miles in all direction while receiving data from as far as 500 nautical miles. The surface hubs would be a system of "risers" above the cables to move the data to the surface and make it accessible to the mobile airborne hub.

Such a system could have serious commercial viability, of course. It could also be very advantageous to military planners seeking another means of moving data. The key is the relatively low cost of moving data compared with satellites—this system, even considering the added cost of the mobile airborne hubs and the risers, would be orders of magnitude less expensive than satellite systems, and vastly faster. From a military perspective, this would be a redundant system to the backbone satellite systems in use today. This is also an idea rife with potential for public-private partnerships, as the risers could be connected via the systems that oil and gas industry platforms are using today.

As with any system for communications, there is both risk and reward possible. In the case of submarine cables, we should increase our ability to protect this vital portion of the global communications grid and seek innovative ways to leverage its capability.

So if all of that reflects Mahanian thinking, where are we today? Are these classic ideas and principles important today, as well as the new technologies that are all part of our idea of twenty-first-century sea power? The short answer is yes—up to a point.

In March 2015, the chiefs of the nation's sea services—Navy, Marine Corps, and Coast Guard—unveiled "A Cooperative Strategy for 21st Century Seapower," charting a forward, engaged, ready course to meet the nation's global maritime strategic responsibilities. Then–chief of naval operations Admiral Jonathan W. Greenert, then–Marine commandant General Joseph F. Dunford Jr. (he has since been promoted to chairman of the Joint Chiefs of Staff), and Coast Guard commandant

Admiral Paul F. Zukunft underscored the growing importance of increasing cooperation among the services to achieve the maximum forward presence and war-fighting capabilities required for national defense and homeland security. I enjoyed leading a conversation among the three of them at the official rollout of the document in Washington in 2015.

This is *not* about diminishing the criticality of our nation's air and ground forces: far from it. The document is about how the maritime world fits into the broader geopolitical context out of efforts to create twenty-first-century security.

A bird's-eye view of the shipyards, port facilities, Navy ships, Marine Corps, Coast Guard, and Special Forces bases and stations in and around the nation certainly reminds us that the United States is a global maritime power. This is as true today as it has been since the beginning of the Republic. What is often forgotten is the critical importance of a *maritime strategy* to go with all that capability. The sea services have developed such strategies for three decades, and they have been largely successful in driving the size, deployment patterns, and impact of our maritime forces.

In 1986, with the fast-growing Soviet navy as the potential adversary, the U.S. Navy and Marine Corps published "The Maritime Strategy," aimed at using maritime power, in combination with the efforts of our sister services and forces of our allies, to bring about war termination on favorable terms. This flowed from presidential guidance. As then–secretary of the Navy John Lehman once reminded, President Ronald Reagan, when asked to summarize what his policy toward the cold war would be, replied: "We win and they lose." Pretty simple.

As a newly selected lieutenant commander (still a *very* junior officer), I was in the Pentagon as a special assistant to the chief of naval operations and had a chance to play a small role in the formation of "The Maritime Strategy." Because I had a brand-new PhD, it was assumed that I was at least marginally capable of thinking and writing. This translated mostly to getting coffee for the actual authors, senior captains not only with comparable degrees but in possession of actual experience as strategic planners. But in hanging around the process, I learned a great deal about how these strategies are put together that I was able to use when I was more senior.

In a nutshell, it begins with a political idea that "now is a good time" to put out a fresh strategy. This normally comes either when a high official (a secretary of defense or the Navy, or a chief of naval operations or Marine Corps commandant) comes into office. Or occasionally when a distraction is needed from the negative flow of events. A small team of bright officers is selected, several of whom will have had experience doing such work in the past. They will be given office space, a small support staff (such as Lieutenant Commander Stavridis), and will put together a draft concept.

This will then be vetted through the enormous staff groups in the Pentagon, a process that can take months. Various offices will attempt to drive their particular areas of emphasis to the top of the priority queue, for example subsurface warfare, the threat of cyber affecting seagoing operations, tactical strike operations with aircraft, unmanned vehicles, and so forth. Lots of horse trading goes back and forth at increasingly higher levels in the food chain, until the leader of the drafting group—having done his or her best to synthesize all the "helpful input"—will take the melded draft concept to the decision maker, say the chief of naval operations. This august leader will provide a blessing, and now the true hard work begins—writing the actual words that will be part of the strategy.

No one should ever underestimate the passion that goes into the heart and mind of a human being offered the chance to edit another's prose. Once the drafting team produces an actual draft—sentences, paragraphs, a title, and so on—it must be sent around not only to the Pentagon staff, but to the various fleet elements as well. *Lots* of "helpful input" comes back, and is again considered (and mostly rejected) at this point. Finally, a smooth draft is completed that can go "outside the life lines of the Navy (or Marines)" and be presented to the Department of Defense (the boss) and informally to think tanks, influential thinkers and writers, retired august figures, and the like.

All of this will typically have taken about nine to twelve months, but incredibly the product is usually pretty balanced and often contains some basic, useful guidance. "The Maritime Strategy" of 1986 was big and bold and really captured the imagination of the Naval Service. Subsequent strategic road maps would be published in 1992, 1994, and 2007. The massive blue-water threat of the USSR faded and the sea services became more skilled at littoral warfare as guided by the strategy titled ". . . From the Sea" in 1992. (Note: the three dots in front of the words "From the Sea" were intentional, meant to imply the flexibility of the Navy.) The world economy—largely dependent on sea transport of commerce—was becoming more interconnected. The challenges to national security were evolving to include wars between major powers, regional conflicts, international terrorism, piracy, and response to natural disasters. There was one constant. Whenever a new international crisis faced the nation, the president then in office would continue to ask, "Where are the carriers? Where are the Marines?" Why? Because they form the ready strike forces that are sustainable from the sea.

"A Cooperative Strategy for the 21st Century" addresses the challenges and opportunities before the sea services from 2015 to future horizons, framing the strategic discussion in terms of:

- Global security environment
- Forward presence and partnership

- Sea power in support of national security
- Force design: building the future force

World changes since 2007 are presented in summary and then examined in detail: "Today's global security environment is characterized by the rising importance of the Indo-Asia-Pacific region, the ongoing development and fielding of anti-access/area denial (A2/AD) capabilities that challenge our global maritime access, continued threats from expanding and evolving terrorist and criminal networks, the increasing frequency and intensity of maritime territorial disputes, and threats to maritime commerce, particularly the flow of energy."

Chinese naval capabilities, the longer reach of that navy into the Indian and Pacific oceans, and China's growing territorial claims are highlighted, as are China's participation in international exercises and disaster response missions. In the strategic context, these are understood as both challenges and opportunities. But of course it is not all about a Pacific pivot: Europe still matters deeply.

More U.S. ships, aircraft, and Marine Corps forces will be operating in the Indo-Asia-Pacific region. In broader terms, if the sea services' global forward presence is imperative, the expansion of naval and Marine Corps planning and operations with allies and other friendly nations on seas around the world goes hand in hand. Such partnerships provide increased international stability in peacetime and increased combined-force capability in time of conflict. In parallel, the Coast Guard, as a regulatory and law enforcement agency, and one of the nation's five armed services, is expanding combined operations—with more than sixty bilateral agreements already in place with foreign governments—countering international illegal operations and further enhancing maritime stability.

The sea power now required to protect the homeland, provide national security, and provide sea control includes:

- The Navy's powerful carrier strike groups, centered on a massive U.S. nuclear-powered carrier with its embarked air wing, accompanied by a brace of cruisers and destroyers
- Amphibious task forces with their embarked Marines
- Surface warships and submarines operating independently or in small tactical groups
- Cutters of the U.S. Coast Guard, which have reasonable warfighting capability

If the maritime strategy is to be implemented and succeed, it will be essential to have all-domain access—that is, access allowing both protection of U.S. operating forces wherever they may be and effective projection and mission completion by those forces in areas contested by foreign powers. In the words of the chief of naval operations, "We must be able to create access in any domain. That means altering how we plan and coordinate actions in the air, sea, land, space, and cyberspace domains, identifying and leveraging the right capability mix to assure access and freedom of action."

Against the current background of budget constraints, flexible, agile, and ready forces and the most highly trained and capable sailors, Marines, and Coast Guardsmen—"our greatest asymmetric advantage"—will be required. This will include a balanced force of submarines, aircraft carriers, amphibious ships, and surface combatants for deterrence, sea control and power projection, and maritime security needed to combat terrorism, illegal trafficking of people, drugs, and arms, piracy, and the safeguarding of freedom of navigation.

There is one top-priority, underlying message throughout the new maritime strategy: *the need for sea power is greater than ever.* Again, this does not diminish the need for other forms of national power—land, air, special operations, cyber. But make no mistake: there are extremely difficult international threats and challenges in the years ahead. It is essential that we provide the forces and the people the sea services require, and this new strategic vision does a commendable job articulating the case.

Throughout the nearly four decades of my long career on active service in our Navy, I worked on many strategic plans. The Navy, along with the other services, is constantly tinkering with a new version. Sometimes it truly laid out big visions ("The Maritime Strategy" and the associated six-hundred-ship Navy of the 1980s come to mind) and other times the "visions" are somewhat incremental and timid. As we head for the turn and conclude two decades of this incredibly turbulent twenty-first century, it is high time for some "blue sky" (some would say "blue water") thinking. The oceans remain largely ignored as much more than a convenient highway for our goods. If the United States is to prosper and lead in this century, we need a coherent national strategy, of which a significant component should be based on the timeless strategic principles of Mahan as adapted for today's world—the power of our geography, national character, and a keen sense of the potential of the oceans.

One final thought to consider is how we should look geographically at each of the world's oceans from a *strategic* sense. While the essence of sea power is the connective power of the unity of the oceans into a single global commons, there are historic, cultural, political, economic, and military reasons to think about each from a strategic perspective.

Let's begin with the "twin towers" of the world's oceans, the North Atlantic and Pacific. Like two massive guardians, they flank the continental United States, providing distance—which translates into time and insulation from the rest of the world. U.S. strategy throughout our history has been to ensure that we have benign neighbors to north and south, and we have achieved that, enjoying an excellent relationship with both Canada and Mexico. The Caribbean is largely harmless, and the prospects of war in the Americas are remote. All of this translates into three key strategic elements: maintaining a cordial relationship in the Americas, especially with Canada and Mexico; ensuring that we have sufficient sea power to maintain sea control in both the North Atlantic and North Pacific; and controlling the Panama Canal to provide the ability to "swing" the U.S. fleet as necessary. In practical terms this translates into approximately 350 significant battle force ships, divided into at least twelve carrier battle groups. There have been multiple studies over the past thirty years that have validated these numbers again and again. Time will tell whether the promised fleet-size increases under the Trump administration will come to be and, if so, whether they will meet the needs for our international interests.

During the 2012 election, President Obama mocked Republican presidential candidate Mitt Romney when Romney suggested that we needed a set minimum number of ships. Obama pointed out, correctly, that we don't need cavalry units anymore when Romney accurately said our fleet was the smallest in decades. Romney was right—quantity has a quality all its own when it comes to ships, and the enormous distances of the Atlantic and Pacific testify to the need for a formidable U.S. fleet. Events since 2012—the rise of China's navy, a much more assertive Russia with a significant naval building program, distributed threats around the world—make the argument for higher numbers of ships even more salient. U.S. maritime strategy must be built on an absolute ability to control the ocean approaches to our nation. We are not seriously challenged today, but if we neglect fleet size and military spending, the day will come when we cannot take for granted the sea lanes of communication to and from our continent. This is the basic building block of our strategy.

The Third Fleet in the Pacific is commanded by a three-star vice admiral reporting to the overall commander of the Pacific fleet. The old Second Fleet, which patrolled the East Coast, was decommissioned in 2011 and has been taken over by the four-star commander of the Atlantic fleet. Both fleets have two key missions: protecting the coasts of the United States and the territorial seas, as well as the high seas; and conducting training and exercising to prepare the Navy ships that will go forward and operate on deployments to the Sixth Fleet (Mediterranean), Fifth Fleet (Arabian/Persian Gulf), Seventh Fleet (western Pacific and Indian Ocean), and Fourth Fleet (Latin America and Caribbean). This structure remains viable at the moment, although over time the United States should consider an Eighth Fleet for the Indian Ocean as operations increase there. We do not need a fleet for the Arctic (yet), but we should reserve the number for a Ninth Fleet for the High North. Interestingly, the Navy has designated a numbered fleet for cyber operations, the Tenth Fleet.

After the North Atlantic and Pacific, the closest ocean space is, of course, the Caribbean. Not only is it the "soft underbelly" of the United States, but it is also the waterway that controls the Panama Canal. The vast majority of trade transiting the Americas goes through the canal, and we must control the approaches to its passage. In 1962, the United States almost went to war with the Soviet Union when it sought to emplace nuclear-tipped missiles on the island of Cuba. While there was legitimate concern about the presence of such weapons so close to U.S. borders, the geostrategic reason for the confrontation was simple: the United States cannot cede control of the Caribbean to anyone else. Today when I think about the Caribbean, it is even clearer than ever that we need to invest there in the broadest terms.

This region—the Caribbean and the waters of Latin America—is the purview of the Fourth Fleet. The newest of the modern U.S. fleets, it has its headquarters in northern Florida and reports to the combatant commander in Miami. When I arrived as commander of U.S. Southern Command in 2006, there was no designated fleet controlling the area. I had to requisition forces from the Atlantic Fleet commander, who had many missions of his own and was not always fully attentive to the needs of the region. Working with the chief of naval operations at the time, an old friend and fellow captain of destroyer *Barry*, Admiral Gary Roughead, we were able to stand up a small but symbolically important new command: the Fourth Fleet.

This was not without controversy in the region, and some of the nations perceived it as a return to U.S. imperialism. Cartoons of me appeared in various publications around the region in the left-leaning countries like Argentina, Nicaragua, and especially Cuba (of course) showing an admiral with a battle helmet and a long spear through the heart of South America. I kept making the point in all my visits that the Fourth Fleet was focused not on combat but on the real missions of the region: humanitarian assistance, disaster relief, medical diplomacy, training and exercises, protection of the Panama Canal from sabotage, and counternarcotics. Over the past decade, that message has landed and the protests have faded away. However, I still treasure the fact that I was personally condemned in *Granma*, the official publication of Cuba, on the front page by Fidel Castro himself.

This is why the naval station at Guantánamo Bay is a very important U.S. installation. We need to reimagine Guantánamo Bay in strategic terms, getting away from the idea of it as a prison colony for terrorists—a failed construct from a geopolitical perspective. The base serves today as the logistical, training, and naval hub of the Caribbean and South Atlantic. It is where the U.S. military stages and operates its extensive program of humanitarian activity, medical diplomacy, and disaster relief—swinging into action after the frequent hurricanes, earthquakes, and other natural disasters of the region. Guantánamo Bay is leased from Cuba (although the Castro regime disputes the legitimacy of the agreement and doesn't cash the rent checks).

The "normalization" of relations with Cuba is a good thing on balance, as it will probably end up creating more pressure for liberalization of the regime in Cuba than the embargo had accomplished across the decades. Over time, it will gradually have the effect of helping the people of Cuba achieve their potential. And—*ojalá*, as is said in Spanish, "God willing"—it will ultimately strengthen the democratic movement there and resolve the last remaining dictatorship in the Americas in a positive way.

Over the next five years, the United States will come under serious pressure from the Castro regime and its partners in the Americas (Venezuela, Nicaragua, Ecuador, Bolivia, and others) to close the naval station and return it to Cuban sovereignty. They will say: you gave back the Panama Canal, closed bases elsewhere (in Ecuador, for example), and generally do not deploy forces without the consent of a host government. If relations with Cuba are "normal," why would Cuba not get the same treatment?

One answer would be to begin using the base as the hub of a U.S.-led international effort to address the challenges of the region. Naval Station Guantánamo, with the cooperation of Cuba and the United States, could be used for:

- Large-scale disaster relief efforts as the inevitable hurricanes and earthquakes devastate the region
- Humanitarian relief work, cooperating to build clinics and schools and develop sources of clean drinking water
- Basing hospital ships and training vessels focused on civil improvement projects and education
- Storage of relief supplies—major facilities for this already exist

- Collective counternarcotics efforts, partnering with the Joint Interagency Task Force in Key West

All of this would require a delicate negotiation with the Cubans, agreement from the United States to continue providing the lion's share of the funding, and cooperation from other partners (Brazil, Colombia, and Mexico all have capacity). It would probably also require closing the detention facility as other nations are unlikely to participate without the departure of Joint Task Force Guantánamo (the detainee command). All very complicated.

But the idea of essentially internationalizing Naval Station Guantánamo has real possibilities and would allow the United States and Cuba to work together on a positive project going forward. The odds of the United States' needing the base for combat operations are essentially nil—luckily we enjoy peace here in the Americas. We should explore the possibilities for collective use of Naval Station Guantánamo in addressing the real problems in this hemisphere: poverty, natural disasters, development, and narcotics.

Moving a bit farther afield from the continental United States, it is the two "forward seas" that matter most: the Mediterranean Sea and the South China Sea. Each is ringed with U.S. allies and friends, and each faces a variety of challenges both internal and external.

For the Mediterranean, it is the pressure of violent extremists, at the moment surging principally from the so-called Islamic State, that is the most dangerous element, from the Syrian seacoast to the long stretch of Libya. Additionally, there is pressure from Russia, which seeks to maintain bases on the Mediterranean and continues to press south from its

Crimean bases in the recently annexed region of Ukraine. Our NATO friends and allies need our support and presence in the region.

The job of patrolling the Mediterranean falls to the Sixth Fleet, which is based out of Italy. It has a flagship and a handful of surface combatants (typically AEGIS guided missile destroyers and cruisers) and also can access aircraft carriers and amphibious readiness groups that are in transit or swung north through the Suez Canal from the Indian Ocean and the Gulf in times of need. As events over the past several years have demonstrated, the eastern Mediterranean is a zone of conflict akin to the South China Sea. We should therefore increase the size of the Sixth Fleet and have a permanently deployed flotilla of at least ten ships to the Mediterranean (today we typically have two or three).

In the South China Sea, we should likewise be working closely with allies (the Republic of Korea and the Philippines, as well as Japan just to the north of the region) as well as with friends (Vietnam, Taiwan, Malaysia, Singapore). We currently have an aircraft carrier strike group permanently stationed forward in Japan, and that should continue. We need to increase the number of our submarines in the region, basing them out of Guam or Japan. Forward naval presence in the South China Sea will be necessary to maintain a balance in the region.

North of the South China Sea, we will also need a maritime-based plan to deal with North Korea over time. Let's start with why we care. North Korea is arguably the most dangerous nation in the world—they have a small arsenal of nuclear weapons, a budding ballistic missile capability that will soon be able to deliver them at range (as evidenced by their November 2017 long-range missile test), and they have continually demonstrated the propensity to use military force while occasionally conducting an actual nuclear weapon test. The nation has significant malnutrition, a huge prison population on a per capita basis, no democratic means of succession, and territorial disputes with its southern neighbor, the

Republic of Korea. The North Koreans also regularly threaten the United States, Japan, and other countries that they perceive stand in the way of their economic and political objectives. Taken together, the pattern of behavior and basic fact pattern on the ground in North Korea demand a plan for dealing with this pariah state.

First, the international community should be increasing sanctions dramatically. Given the level of sanctions leveled on Iran for merely pursuing a nuclear weapon, why would there be any fewer sanctions applied to a state that has such weapons and detonates them in unnecessary tests? The U.S. Congress just passed a revised, tougher set of sanctions that will begin to go after international cash accounts and penalize banks that do any kind of business with North Korea—this is an important step that other nations should follow. Japan is likewise imposing new, stronger sanctions. Other nations in the region—especially China—should follow suit. Initial sanctions to North Korea's weapons tests in 2017 were a step in the right direction, but more action is needed to slow North Korea.

Another important element is preparing appropriate levels of missile defenses, especially in South Korea and Japan. For example, adding the state-of-the-art Terminal High Altitude Area Defense (THAAD) system to the arsenals of both countries. Given that there are tens of thousands of U.S. soldiers and their families in both countries, this is in the interest of both the host nations and the United States. The United States, South Korea, and Japan should work together to finance and put in place this highly capable system, which has a range well over two hundred kilometers and flies at Mach 8-plus to effect terminal kills of incoming ballistic missiles. China will not like this (seeing it as at least partially directed against Chinese systems), but will need to accept the need on the part of the other nations. Perhaps the Chinese concerns will lead to a more aggressive stance toward Pyongyang, which would be helpful.

Indeed, much depends on Beijing in terms of reining in Kim Jong-un. While the young leader's attitude toward China is ambivalent at best (he killed his uncle, the central interlocutor, early in his regime), the Chinese have real economic leverage. They should be encouraged to use it, and if necessary, the sanctions regime against North Korea should apply to Chinese banks and businesses conducting commerce there.

In addition to THAAD, more advanced Patriot Air Defense and AEGIS maritime-based air defense systems should be deployed to the defense of South Korea and Japan. Both nations have versions of Patriot, and Japan has AEGIS ships; but these systems can be modernized, and all three nations should conduct exercises and training together to link them into a coherent regional missile defense system.

Additionally, there is more that the United States and its allies can do in the cyber world. While North Korea is notoriously difficult to penetrate (because it carefully screens its links to the Internet), it does use portions of the Web for specialized security functions, and its military rides on a computer-based backbone that can be accessed, albeit with difficulty. Working closely with our South Korean and Japanese cyber counterparts, we should use cyber aggressively to sabotage the North Korean weapons programs, insert monitoring devices in their critical infrastructure, and generate the means to attack their electrical grid if necessary and in response to a North Korean attack against the South. The North Koreans have already lashed out at a U.S. company, Sony Pictures, over cyber circuits, destroying millions of dollars in equipment and doing significant business damage to Sony's interests by releasing thousands of embarrassing internal e-mails.

In terms of additional military preparations, the United States should do all it can to link South Korea and Japan in the air defense area, as well as in maritime cooperation. Working together in the air and at sea can help provide a deterrent effect on North Korea, balancing the strong

U.S. ground forces on the Korean Peninsula already. Conducting a large, annual, U.S. Joint Staff–sponsored exercise in the region specifically focused on North Korea and the danger it poses would make sense. It should have a strong cyber component as well.

Finally, despite all the frustrations and dangers, we need to do what we can to keep a means of communication open with North Korea. While fruitful negotiations seem unlikely, we should be generally open to dialogue—but careful not to fall into the familiar trap of North Korea: bad behavior, negotiations, concessions on food, fuel, and sanctions, and no change in overall behavior. It is a depressingly familiar cycle. This is where working with China over time might have a helpful effect—without Chinese engagement and economic clout, any attempt at negotiation will be unlikely to succeed.

As in the film *The Interview*, which mocked Kim Jong-un and was the motivation for the Sony Pictures attack, it is easy to laugh at the chubby young leader. But he is a clear and present danger to the region, and we will need determined collective action—economic, military, and diplomatic—to counter his growing potential to provoke a major crisis in the heart of the world's economy, East Asia.

ALL OF THIS WILL BE the purview of the U.S. Seventh Fleet, historically the largest and most capable. It will need the most advanced weapons systems, to include antimissile technology on AEGIS combatants, significant carrier presence (at least two, one permanently in Japan and the other roaming the Pacific), strong Marine Corps elements (on Okinawa and Guam), ballistic missile submarines as the most survivable leg of the triad to deter China, and strong special forces and cyber support. The Seventh Fleet should remain headquartered on the islands of Japan, our strongest ally in the region, and will also require a string of bases around the Pacific. Some of the key nodes are on the home islands of Japan, the South Korean Peninsula, and Okinawa. Additionally, we should explore at least cooperative arrangements to base a light footprint in the Philippines (the legislature there appears poised to approve a return to historic Subic Bay), on northern Australia (probably in Darwin), and—over time—in Vietnam. Access to bases in Singapore is essential, and the defense relationship there is very strong.

The major body of water the greatest distance from the United States, literally on the other side of the world, is the Indian Ocean. Here our strategy must first and foremost take into account the emerging superpower India. We should do all we can diplomatically, culturally, militarily, politically, and diplomatically to strengthen our ties with India. This should particularly include cooperating in the maritime realm, including a new series of exercises and training with the Indian navy; promoting sales of advanced naval hardware, notably the AEGIS combat system on surface combatants; cooperating on operating nuclear submarines; working with India and Japan on naval exercises focused on counterpiracy in and around the approaches to the Indian Ocean; and developing a program of maritime science diplomacy for the Indian Ocean.

In addition to working closely with India, our two major Anglophone allies New Zealand and Australia are important as well. Australia is of major geostrategic importance given the size of its coastline, which includes a huge coastal "waterfront" on the Indian Ocean. Great Britain continues to own Diego Garcia and deploys internationally to the Arabian/Persian Gulf as well, and our involvement there will be crucial.

The Arabian/Persian Gulf will continue to be a vitally important waterway for the United States, and the linkages between the greater Indian Ocean and the Gulf will be a "hot" seam in maritime affairs. The United States must continue to maintain a significant naval fleet (numerically, the Fifth Fleet) in the region. It is mandatory to maintain a carrier strike group (a nuclear-powered aircraft carrier and a handful of AEGIS guided missile escorts) in the region 24/7. Additionally, having a Marine Expeditionary Unit (also known as an Expeditionary Strike Group) in the area will be advisable. The latter consists of three large amphibious ships that carry a specially trained and reinforced Marine Expeditionary Unit (about two thousand Marines, aircraft, and the ability to move them with extreme speed). We should also have a strong minesweeping and special forces capability. Clearly the region will continue to be contentious, and given the high level of global hydrocarbons moving through it the United States will need to work with coalition partners to keep it open.

Finally, there is the Arctic. The strategic terrain at the top of the world will be increasingly important to U.S. strategy, and our approach in the High North must include first and foremost ensuring that we have sufficient icebreakers. This means a strategic program to purchase (or lease) icebreakers. At an absolute minimum, a coherent U.S. maritime strategy should have four heavy and four medium icebreakers. Fortunately, pretty much everyone in Washington agrees with the idea that we need icebreakers, and we need them now. Our global maritime strategy should have an icebreaker component built into it.

Additionally, we need more transportation and exploration infrastructure (roads as well as ports and airstrips) in the High North. While we have some in place and plans for others, the fall in oil prices in 2015–16 has slowed the pace of construction. In addition to shore-based infrastructure, we also need sea-based structures that can be used for emergency search and rescue, environmental disaster response, and scientific research. These can be built on the basic structures of offshore oil and gas platforms and—when hydrocarbon prices rise again—can be built into the tax base levied on the companies exploiting the natural resources of the region.

There is not a U.S. Navy fleet assigned to the Arctic, and at the moment one is not necessary. The best approach would be to make this an area of focus for the U.S. Coast Guard, with the Department of Defense acting in support.

What remains? Both the far South Atlantic and the South Pacific are relatively secure and can be considered theaters where an "economy of force strategy" can be used. This simply means that we do not need permanently deployed ships or permanent bases in either region. We will need to make occasional cruises to support presence and conduct basic military-to-military contacts, but no significant forces will be required.

Taken together, it is clear that many of the principles of Mahan apply—we still need forward bases, extended fleets, and secure logistics (although not so much coal anymore). But what we can add to the Mahanian construct is international (both alliances like NATO and informal coalition partners), interagency (especially with the Coast Guard), and private-public cooperation. This twenty-first-century global maritime strategy is the right one for our nation, requires a fleet of around 350 ships, is affordable, flexible, and provides the nation both hard-power and soft-power options—a smart-power approach for the seas.

THE UNITED STATES CONTINUES on a voyage that is both personal to the mariners who sail it and of vital geopolitical importance. In the end, we are an island nation, bounded by oceans and nurtured on the global commerce, international markets, fishing expeditions, hydrocarbon offshore rigs, and strategic waterways of the world's oceans. Without the oceans and our ability to sail them, we would be enormously diminished as a nation. Our ability to navigate, both literally and figuratively, through the oceans will be a determinative part of the voyage of our nation in this century. I began this volume with the thought that there is both a deeply individual component to sailing and understanding the oceans and a key geostrategic element to the idea that the sea is truly one. Taken together, it seems clear that the nautical character of our nation will continue to be vital, indeed essential, for all that the future promises to our country and the world. Let us continue to sail in our ships, which take our sailors daily out of sight of land, and leave us gazing at the eternal vista of the deep sea, where we stand on a narrow hull, rolling before the waves and the wind, knowing we are at heart a nation that will forever depend on sea power and our sailors for security and prosperity.

ACKNOWLEDGMENTS

First, my research assistants during academic year 2015–16, Matt Merighi and McKenzie Smith, contributed to chapters 1 and 2 on the Pacific and Atlantic, respectively. My research assistant for 2016–17, Colin Steele, added content and edits for this paperback volume, and Commander Jeremy Watkins helped with ideas for chapter 9 on strategy and contributed data for the arms race in the Pacific highlighted in chapter 1.

Some of this material was published in previous public writings of mine, mostly in *Foreign Policy, The Wall Street Journal, Nikkei Asian Review, Signal* magazine, and *Proceedings* (U.S. Naval Institute), and is reprinted with their permission. All of it is original work of mine, of course. In particular, some of the material at the end of chapter 1 on the Pacific is based on a column I wrote for *Nikkei/Financial Times Asia* in 2015. At the end of chapter 3 on the Indian Ocean is some material from a column in *Foreign Policy* written in 2014. The final paragraphs of chapter 4 on the Mediterranean are based on material published in *Foreign Policy* in 2015. Chapter 5 on the South China Sea has several paragraphs based on articles from *Foreign Policy* and

Nikkei Asian Review from 2015. Chapter 6 contains some material from a column in *Foreign Policy* in 2015. Chapter 9 includes material on undersea cables and the new maritime strategy that appeared in *Signal* magazine.

Captain Bill Harlow, a close friend and colleague of more than three decades, has been a superb supporter, adviser, and sharp-eyed editor of this manuscript.

My friend and agent Andrew Wylie supported this idea and helped persuade Penguin Random House to take the plunge (pun intended) to publish such a watery book.

Scott Moyers, a gifted agent and now an editor at Penguin Press, conceived the idea and persuaded me to take on the challenge of crafting this broad and deeply personal book.

My wife, Laura, as always, has been a stalwart and patient source of love and support, even when our weekends were a bit curtailed as deadlines loomed.

All errors of fact, content, or imagination are mine alone.

I dedicate this book to all the sailors at sea: Godspeed and open water to them all, wherever the wind and waves have taken them.

SOURCES AND RECOMMENDED READINGS ON THE WORLD'S OCEANS

NONFICTION

Admiral Bill Halsey: A Naval Life by Thomas Alexander Hughes (Cambridge, Mass.: Harvard University Press, 2016)

America and the Sea: A Maritime History edited by Benjamin W. Labaree, et al. (Mystic, Conn.: Mystic Seaport Press, 1998)

The Anarchic Sea: Maritime Security in the 21st Century by Dave Sloggett (New York: Hurst, 2014)

Arctic Dreams by Barry Lopez (New York: Scribner, 1986)

Asia's Cauldron: The South China Sea and the End of a Stable Pacific by Robert D. Kaplan (New York: Random House, 2014)

Atlantic by Simon Winchester (New York: HarperCollins, 2013)

Atlantic History: Concept and Contours by Bernard Bailyn (Cambridge, Mass.: Harvard University Press, 2005) (Web)

Atlantic Ocean: The Illustrated History of the Ocean That Changed the World by Martin Sandler (New York: Sterling, 2008)

Bitter Ocean: The Battle of the Atlantic, 1939–1945 by David Fairbank White (New York: Simon & Schuster, 2006)

Black Sea by Neal Ascherson (London: Jonathan Cape, 1995)

Blue Latitudes: Boldly Going Where Captain Cook Went Before by Tony Horwitz (New York: Picador, 2003)

Box Boats: How Container Ships Changed the World by Brian Cudahy (New York: Fordham University Press, 2006)

"Charting a New Course for the Oceans: A Report on the State of the World's Oceans, Global Fisheries and Fisheries Treaties, and Potential Strategies for Reversing the Decline in Ocean Health and Productivity" by William Moomaw and Sara Blankenship (Medford, Mass.: The Center for International Environment and Resource Policy, The Fletcher School of Law and Diplomacy, Tufts University, 2014)

Cod: A Biography of the Fish That Changed the World by Mark Kurlansky (New York: Walker, 1997)

The Cruise of the Snark by Jack London (New York: Macmillan, reprint, 1961; 1939)

The Discoverers by Daniel Boorstin (New York: Vintage, 1983)

Dreadnought: Britain, Germany, and the Coming of the Great War by Robert K. Massie (New York: Random House, 1991)

Facing West by John C. Perry (Westport, Conn.: Praeger, 1994)

Gift from the Sea by Anne Morrow Lindbergh (New York: Pantheon, reprint, 1991; 1955)

Globalization and Maritime Power, edited by Sam J. Tangredi (Honolulu: University Press of the Pacific, 2011)

The Great Ocean: Pacific Worlds from Captain Cook to the Gold Rush by David Igler (New York: Oxford University Press, 2013)

The Great Pacific Victory from the Solomons to Tokyo by Gilbert Cant (New York: The John Day Company, 1946)

Great Wall at Sea: China's Navy Enters the 21st Century by Bernard Cole (Annapolis, Md.: USNI Press, 2011)

Guns, Germs, and Steel: The Fates of Human Societies by Jared Diamond (New York: Norton, 1999)

The Indian Ocean in World History by Edward A. Alpers (New York: Oxford University Press, 2014)

In the Heart of the Sea: The Tragedy of the Whaleship Essex by Nathaniel Philbrick (New York: Viking, 2000)

Inventing Grand Strategy and Teaching Command: The Classic Works of Alfred Thayer Mahan Reconsidered by Jon Sumida (Baltimore: Johns Hopkins University Press, 1997)

The Log from the Sea of Cortez by John Steinbeck (New York: Penguin Classics, reprint, 1995; 1951)

Longitude: The True Story of a Lone Genius Who Solved the Greatest Scientific Problem of His Time by Dava Sobel (New York: Walker, 1995)

Maritime Economics by Martin Stopford (New York: Routledge, 1997)

The Mediterranean and the Mediterranean World in the Age of Philip II, 2 vols., by Fernand Braudel (New York: Harper, 1972)

The Mediterranean in History, edited by David Abulafia (London: Thames and Hudson, 2003)

Mirror of Empire: Dutch Marine Art of the Seventeenth Century, edited by George Keyes (Cambridge: Cambridge University Press, 1990)

Monsoon: The Indian Ocean and the Future of American Power by Robert Kaplan (New York: Random House, 2010)

Ocean: An Illustrated Atlas by Sylvia Earl and Linda Glover (New York: National Geographic Press, 2008)

The Oxford Encyclopedia of Maritime History, edited by John Hattendorf (Oxford and New York: Oxford University Press, 2007)

Pacific Ocean, by Felix Riesenberg (New York and London: Whittlesey House, McGraw-Hill, 1940)

The Pacific Theater: Island Representations of World War II, 8 vols., by Geoffrey M. White and Lamont Lindstrom (Honolulu: University of Hawaii Press, 1989)

The Polynesian Journal of Captain Henry Byam Martin, R.N., by Henry Byam Martin (Salem, Mass.: Peabody Museum of Salem, 1981)

The Price of Admiralty by John Keegan (New York: Viking, 1983)

Principles of Maritime Strategy by Julian Corbett (Mineola, N.Y.: Dover Publications, 1911)

The Quiet Warrior: A Biography of Admiral Raymond Spruance, by Thomas Buell (Annapolis, Md.: USNI Press, reissued 2013)

The Rise and Fall of the Great Powers by Paul Kennedy (New York: Random House, 1987)

The Sea and Civilization: A Maritime History of the World by Lincoln Paine (New York: Alfred A. Knopf, 2013)

The Sea Around Us by Rachel Carson (Oxford and New York: Oxford University Press, reprint, 1991; 1951)

Seapower by E. B. Potter (Annapolis, Md.: USNI Press, 1972)

Seapower: A Guide for the Twenty-First Century by Geoffrey Till (New York: Routledge, 2013)

Seapower as Strategy: Navies and National Interests by Norman Friedman (Annapolis, Md.: Naval Institute Press, 2001)

The Sea Power of the State by S. Gorshkov (New York: Pergamon Press, 1979)

Sovereign of the Seas by David Howarth (New York: Atheneum, 1974)

Villains of All Nations: Atlantic Pirates in the Golden Age by Marcus Rediker (Boston: Beacon Press, 2004)

Voyage of the Beagle by Charles Darwin (New York: Penguin Classics, reprint, 1989; 1839)

FICTION AND LEGEND

The Caine Mutiny Court Martial by Herman Wouk—the stress of men at sea in a small minesweeper during World War II.

The Cruel Sea by Nicholas Monserrat—convoy duty in the North Atlantic during World War II, with lessons in leadership and coping with tragedy.

Lord Jim by Joseph Conrad—mistakes made at sea and their impact on a young life.

Master and Commander, the Novels of Patrick O'Brian by Patrick O'Brian—a series of twenty brilliant sea novels that take the reader deep into the lives of Captain Jack Aubrey and his seagoing surgeon, Stephen Maturin.

Moby-Dick by Herman Melville—in Captain Ahab's fevered search for the Great White Whale, we find the greatest sea story of all in the ill-fated voyage of the *Pequod*.

The Odyssey by Homer—a journey across the wine-dark sea from victory at Troy through a long decade returning home to Ithaca.

The Old Man and the Sea by Ernest Hemingway—Santiago the fisherman's fight with the huge fish and then the sharks is the stuff of legends, and a metaphor for life itself.

The Open Boat by Stephen Crane—survival at sea in the most challenging circumstances.

The Secret Sharer by Joseph Conrad—a sea captain's imaginary stowaway; or is he real? The sea can make men and women mad, especially those with the loneliness of command as part of their burden.

The Ship by C. S. Forester—a day in the life of a World War II destroyer in the Mediterranean, full of timeless observations of the sailor's life.

Toilers of the Sea by Victor Hugo—fishermen, salvage crews, battles with creatures of the deep.

Two Years Before the Mast by Richard Henry Dana Jr.—a weak-eyed college student ships out and discovers the life of a sailor in the nineteenth century.

INDEX

Praise for Serhiy Zhadan's *Mesopotamia*

"One of the most astounding novels to come out of modern Ukraine. *Mesopotamia* is seductive, twisted, brilliant, and fierce. It brings to mind our own fiction from a time when we still felt like we had something to fight for and a chance we could win."—Gary Shteyngart, author of *Little Failure* and *Absurdistan*

"To say that Serhiy Zhadan is a poet, a novelist, a rock star, a protester, a symbol of his country's desire for freedom and change, is to say the truth—but what is truth? Zhadan is a literary master of enormous force. At times he combines the energy of Jack Kerouac and atmospheric spell of Isaac Babel, at other times he is a balladeer of his country's struggle. 'Such strange things have been happening to us,' he writes, of the streets where 'winters are not like winters / winters live under assumed names.' In *Mesopotamia*'s nine stories and thirty poems we find ourselves in the newly independent Ukraine, stunned by its grit, its rough backbone—and its tenderness. What do we discover here? That 'Light is shaped by darkness, / and it's all up to us.' We also discover that Serhiy Zhadan is one of those rare things—almost impossible to find now in the West—a national bard, a chronicler. This is a book to live with."
—Ilya Kaminsky

"To know Dublin, read your Joyce, for Macondo, García Márquez, and for Mesopotamia, Serhiy Zhadan. Of course this Mesopotamia is not the Birthplace of Civilization (or is it?), it's Kharkiv, the Ukrainian Center of Nothing, located smack-dab on the Russian border, which, in Zhadan's brilliant vision, is smack-dab in the middle of life lived beyond the fullest because any second could be your last, creaming with joy, madness, war, orgasm, stupidity, and a blinding light that smells like the essence of human spirit. We need to learn from Ukraine. Zhadan is a masterful teacher. The use of poetry as Notes—so far as I know, this has never been done before and is positively Nabokovian. This book is world-class literature."—Bob Holman, author of *Sing This One Back to Me*

"To say that Serhiy Zhadan is a great Ukrainian novelist of whom you might not have heard does not begin to cover it. Serhiy Zhadan is one of the most important creators of European culture at work today. His novels, poems, and songs touch millions. This loving translation is a chance to see Ukraine in terms other than the familiar, but more importantly a chance to allow prose to mend your mind."
—Timothy Snyder, author of *On Tyranny*

"Unlike Joyce's Dublin, the cradle of Zhadan's civilization is a place of refuge for young people fleeing hardscrabble lives in the provinces, and a hardscrabble home for natives buoyed by desire yet adrift amid the flotsam of a spent empire. The men and women in these comic and heartfelt pages endure the dynamic paralysis that comes over those who are all dressed up with nowhere to go. They aspire, struggle, fight, fail, drink, fuck, and then they fight some more. Amid the city's detritus, they refuse to become part of it by continuing to love and dream. There is nothing marginal about them. They insist on being seen, heard, understood. They will charm and madden you. They will haunt your dreams, and you will never forget them." —Askold Melnyczuk, author of *House of Widows*

"Zhadan is the rock star of lyrical melancholy, and *Mesopotamia* is not just a book of short stories but a cosmos with Kharkiv-Babylon at its center. We meet its lovesick citizens at weddings and funerals; their visceral, fantastical lives unfold in the intensely prophetic atmosphere of the upcoming war." —Valzhyna Mort, author of *Factory of Tears*

"With tales at once earthy and phantasmagorical, sentimental and anarchic, Zhadan is an exhilarating chronicler of a new kind of borderlands." —Sana Krasikov

"Serhiy Zhadan's dazzling novel—here fantastically well translated—evokes voices that get under our skin and take us into the rich inner life of people about whom we have long known nothing."—Marci Shore, author of *The Ukrainian Night: An Intimate History of Revolution*

"*Mesopotamia* offers a sublime experience of taking you right to the middle of a very specific world, where you eat and drink and love and fight and die with the characters, until you notice that that world has transcended the time and place and became part of the eternal human story."—Lara Vapnyar, author of *Still Here: A Novel*

"*Mesopotamia* finds poetry in the most unlikely places—in the bars, tower blocks, and concrete boulevards of a Ukrainian city. By turns funny, shocking, and touching, weaving between the lyrical and the grotesque, Zhadan's stories provide a lesson in belonging."—Uilleam Blacker, University College London

"*Mesopotamia* is a portrait of post-Soviet Ukraine's lost generation, of people who came of age in the disorienting conditions of crumbling Soviet order and stagnating social transformation. Serhiy Zhadan gives voice to his generation from Ukraine's eastern regions bordering Russia. These are the people who have been missing from contemporary literature, whether in Ukrainian or in any other language. To understand the background to the crisis in this region, which has had such a major impact on the world recently, perhaps no other writer can provide insights as powerful as Zhadan."—Vitaly Chernetsky, University of Kansas

"Serhiy Zhadan has written a love song to contemporary Eastern Ukraine—vices, passions, and ghosts included. His Kharkiv is filled with gritty stairwells, red nightgowns, raw love, and a bit of magic. Costigan-Humes and Wheeler have brought Zhadan's evocative prose to life for the English reader."—Amelia Glaser, author of *Jews and Ukrainians in Russia's Literary Borderlands*

The Orphanage

BOOKS BY SERHIY ZHADAN IN ENGLISH TRANSLATION

The Orphanage
What We Live For, What We Die For
Mesopotamia
Voroshilovgrad
Depeche Mode

The Orphanage

A Novel

SERHIY ZHADAN

TRANSLATED FROM THE UKRAINIAN

BY REILLY COSTIGAN-HUMES AND

ISAAC STACKHOUSE WHEELER

YALE UNIVERSITY PRESS ■ NEW HAVEN & LONDON

A MARGELLOS
WORLD REPUBLIC OF LETTERS BOOK

The Margellos World Republic of Letters is dedicated to making literary works from around the globe available in English through translation. It brings to the English-speaking world the work of leading poets, novelists, essayists, philosophers, and playwrights from Europe, Latin America, Africa, Asia, and the Middle East to stimulate international discourse and creative exchange.

Yale University Press books may be purchased in quantity for educational, business, or promotional use. For information, please e-mail sales.press@yale.edu (U.S. office) or sales@yaleup.co.uk (U.K. office).

Set in Electra and Nobel types by Tseng Information Systems, Inc.,
Durham, North Carolina.
Printed in the United States of America.

Library of Congress Control Number: 2020939623
ISBN 978-0-300-24301-7 (paper : alk. paper)

A catalogue record for this book is available from the British Library.
This paper meets the requirements of ANSI/NISO Z39.48-1992 (Permanence of Paper).

10 9 8 7 6 5 4 3 2 1

The Orphanage

"Go pick him up!" Pasha's dad yells.

"He's her son. She oughta pick him up," Pasha retorts.

"He's your nephew," the old-timer reminds him.

"So what?"

"And he's my grandson."

And the television is on the whole time. He never turns the television off, even at night. It's like their very own eternal flame, burning to commemorate the dead rather than entertain the living. The old-timer watches the weather report like he's expecting they'll mention him by name. After it ends, he just sits there, like he can't believe what he's heard. Pasha doesn't really watch TV, especially this past year—the news has been just plain scary. Pasha sits in his room on a couch by his desk, surrounded by textbooks, until he can't stand it anymore. Then he jerks to his feet, goes outside. Springs protrude from the couch like twigs from a Boy Scout's campfire. The furniture in the house is old, yet full of life—it'll probably outlive its owners. Pasha's sister suggested they at least get some new chairs, but he simply brushed her off. What's the point of hauling stuff around? That's like doing pull-ups when you're seventy. Yeah, sure, go right ahead, just make sure you take some ibuprofen first. His sister hardly comes by anymore, so nobody's talking about hauling furniture around anymore either.

Pasha liked their house; he'd lived here his whole life and

planned to keep on living here. It was built by German POWs shortly after the war—a rather spacious duplex on the second street back from the train station. Their densely populated settlement, which was mostly home to railroad workers, was built around that station, so they'd often refer to their whole town as "the Station"—it gave them work, it gave them hope, like a heart blackened by locomotive smoke, pumping the blood of the local gullies and windbreaks. Life still revolved around the station, even now, with the depot as empty as a drained swimming pool and the repair shops unused, if you didn't count the bums and swallows that slept there. There just weren't any jobs now. Sure, maybe they lived in a so-called workers' settlement, but they were the first to find themselves out of work. The shops were shut down, and the people scurried off in all directions, hiding in crowded apartment blocks with wells dried up by the scorching summer and cellars where the supplies had already run out by Christmas.

Pasha didn't have anything to complain about, though—he was on the government payroll. "Yep, yep," Pasha thought as he shut the front door, insulated with hospital blankets, behind him. "I'm on the government payroll, even if I'm not actually getting paid all that much." The snow—blue-pink with deep, dark pores—reflects the evening sky and the approaching sunset. Sharp to the touch, smells of March water, conceals black, viscous earth, renders weather reports unnecessary—the winter will last long enough for everyone to get accustomed to it, suck it up, and learn to cope. And then something else will begin. For the time being, the world feels like a lump of snow in someone's warm hands; it melts, releases its water, but the longer that goes on, the colder their hands get, the less warm motion they retain, the more icy stillness seeps into them. The water remains lethal, even as it melts. The sun drowns in an intricate system of watery mirrors and reflections. Nobody can really get warm—right after lunch, once the wet blaring of horns announcing shift changes at the station subsides, twilight sets in, and that illusory sensation of warmth, of a thaw, disappears again.

Pasha skirts the building and takes the soggy path through the trees. They had always shared the duplex with a railroad worker. Half the building belonged to him, half to Pasha's tight-knit family—mom, dad, Pasha, and his older sister. About fifteen years ago, when Pasha's family still all lived together, the railroad worker burned his half down. They put the fire out before it got to their half. The railroad worker didn't feel like rebuilding—he went to the station, caught a train heading east, and disappeared from their lives forever. They knocked down his half of the building, whitewashed the burned wall, and went on with their lives. From the outside, the structure looked like half a loaf of bread on a store shelf. Pasha's old man always bought those half-loaves so he wouldn't have to pay too much or have too much left over. Living by the railroad taught him that.

Black trees in the snow, biting boughs against the red backdrop of the sky, their street on the other side of the fence, the neighbors' little white houses, yellow lemons of electric light scattered here and there, gardens, fences, fireplaces emitting smoke like the warm January respiration of weary men standing out in the cold. Empty streets, no one in sight, train cars being coupled together, metal on metal, like someone rearranging iron furniture. And from the south, from the direction of the city, sporadic blasts have been coming in all day, since morning—sometimes intense, sometimes diffuse. An echo ripples high up in the air. The acoustics are distorted in the winter; you can never really tell where one is coming from or where it's hitting. Fresh air, the smell of damp trees, tense silence. It only gets this quiet when everyone pipes down and starts listening. Pasha counts to a hundred and heads back. Ten. There were six last night. In the same interval. I wonder what they'll say on the news.

Pasha sees his dad in the kitchen. He's standing hunched over the table, packing an old duffel bag.

"Long trip ahead of ya?" Pasha asks.

What's the point of asking, though? He's going to pick up the kid, obviously. He makes a big show of tossing things into his bag: a newspaper (how can he reread old newspapers like that? It's like looking at a completed crossword), glasses (Pasha's always hassling him about those thick glasses that warp every image—"you might as well wear sunglasses, you can't see a damn thing anyway"), pension card (he'll get a free senior citizen bus ticket if he's lucky), his cellphone, worn smooth like a rock in the sea, and a clean handkerchief. The old-timer washes and irons his handkerchiefs himself, doesn't pass it off on his daughter. He takes out the ironing board once a month and smooths out his handkerchiefs, grayed by the passage of time, like he's drying out devalued hryvnias that have been through the washing machine. Pasha's always getting his old man tissues, but he keeps using his handkerchiefs—has been since the days he worked at the station, when tissues just flat out didn't exist in this part of the world. He can hardly even use his cellphone, but he still takes it just about everywhere—beat-up frame, faded green button. Pasha puts minutes on there for him; he's never learned how. Now he's folding everything meticulously, rooting around in his bag, silently taking umbrage at something or other.

It's getting harder and harder to deal with him—can't even talk to him without hurting his feelings. He's like a little kid. Pasha walks over to the stove, begins drinking right out of the teapot. All the wells dried up in the summer. They're too scared to drink from the tap—who knows what's floating around in the pipes now? So they boil their water and steer clear of lakes and rivers. The old-timer is rooting around in his pockets, refusing to respond to Pasha.

"Fine," Pasha says. "I'll go get him."

The old-timer isn't just going to roll over, though. He takes out the newspaper, unfolds it, then folds it in four, and sticks it back in his bag. Dry yellow fingers anxiously tear the paper; he's all hunched over the table, not even looking at Pasha, like he wants to prove something, take on the whole world.

"Did you hear what I said? I'll go pick him up."

"You don't have to."

"I said I'd pick him up," Pasha repeats, a bit anxiously.

The old-timer makes a big show of picking up his newspaper and leaves, flinging open the door leading to the living room. A strip of soft light from the television reaches the dark hallway. Then he shuts the door abruptly, as though he's locking himself inside an empty fridge.

DAY ONE

A January morning, long and motionless, like a line at the hospital. Morning briskness in the kitchen, slate twilight outside. Pasha walks over to the stove, and his nose instantly catches the sweetish smell of gas. For Pasha that smell is always associated with vigorous mornings—getting up for work, tossing textbooks and graded assignments into his briefcase, ducking into the kitchen, breathing in sweet gas, drinking strong tea, following it with black bread, assuring himself he's living the good life, and running off to work once he's fully convinced. That smell has been with him his whole life; any time he wakes up somewhere outside his own home without the morning stove, its aged burners crusted with ash, he has no appetite. Pasha peers out the window, considers the black snow and black sky, sits down at the table, and shakes his head, trying to gather his wits. Six a.m., January, Monday, one more day with no job to go to.

He grabs some assignments off the windowsill, leafs through them, puts them back immediately, gets up, goes over to the main room, peeks in. The old-timer's sleeping in his chair. A blood-drenched man is crying out to him from the screen, to no avail—the sound's been off since last night. Now you can't get to him, no matter how loud you yell. Pasha stops for a second, looks at the blood. The yelling man shifts his eyes toward Pasha and starts yelling at him—don't turn it off, listen, this is important, it involves you, too. But Pasha quickly finds the remote, squeezes the large red button like he's trying to get toothpaste out of the tube, tosses the remote on the table, slips outside, and shuts the door carefully, so as not to wake his dad. But the door still creaks menacingly in the morning twilight. The old-timer wakes up immediately, finds the remote, and turns the TV back on. It's showing something horrible, something that involves everyone. Pasha's already running up to the station.

"Something's off," he thinks. "Something's definitely off around here." Not a living soul, not a single voice. No locomotive noise. No peddlers. It's just above freezing, and water is leaking from the dark blue snowbanks—clouds in the sky, moisture hanging in the air, sometimes turning to barely perceptible drizzle, fog settling on the far-off tracks, no voices or footsteps coming out of that fog. "It's still early," Pasha thinks, anxious. "It's still early, that's all." In the south, over there, by the city limits, a suspicious silence has settled. No blasts, no shredded air. A bus comes around the corner. Pasha exhales in relief. The buses are running, everything's fine. Yeah, it's just early, that's all.

He nods to the driver, who tucks his head deeper into the collar of his leather coat, then walks through the empty bus and takes a seat on the left side. He sits for an instant, fidgets, then gets up and moves over to the right. The driver observes all this warily, as though he's afraid of missing something important. Pasha locks eyes with him in the rearview mirror, which pushes him to look away, fire up the engine, and ease out the clutch. Disgruntled metal crunches, and the bus gets moving. The driver takes a victory lap in the empty fog, leaving the station behind. “They drive dead people to their funerals in buses like this,” Pasha thinks for some reason. “These same buses, just with a black ribbon running along the windows. I wonder if there’s any room for passengers? Or does the widow have to sit on top of the coffin? Where’s this hearse gonna take me, anyway?”

The bus passes one empty street, then another. The market should be up ahead; old ladies are always selling some kind of frostbitten food there. They turn a corner—no old ladies, no pedestrians. Pasha’s starting to realize that something definitely is off, that something’s gone down, but he pretends everything is just fine. Come on, don’t freak out. The driver takes great pains to avoid making eye contact, goading the hearse through the fog and water. “Guess I should have checked the news,” Pasha thinks, his anxiety mounting. The thing is, there’s this silence—after all those days when the sky in the south, over the city, looked like scorched rebar. It’s quiet and empty, as if everyone just hopped on the night train and skipped town. Now Pasha and the driver are the only ones left. They pass two high-rises built on sand, then an auto repair shop, then they drive on out of the workers’ settlement. A long row of poplars leads out to the highway—the poplars peek out of the fog like children from behind their parents. The sun is moving somewhere up high, it’s already appeared somewhere up there, even though you can’t quite see it yet. You can feel it, though. You can’t feel anything else. Pasha’s watchful eyes consider the dampness all around him, trying to figure out what he’s missed and what that blood-drenched character was trying to communicate to him. The driver carefully dodges some cold potholes, reaches the highway, and turns right. The bus steals up to the stop, like usual. Generally, at least one person gets on here, but not today. The driver stays put, probably out of habit, without closing the doors, and then looks back at Pasha, as if asking for his permission to continue. The doors close. They get going, pick up speed—then there's a checkpoint right in front of them.

"Motherfucker," the driver mutters.

The place is packed with soldiers. They're standing behind some cinder blocks, underneath some frayed national flags, wordlessly looking toward the city. Just how many times has he driven through this area over the past six months, since the government returned after brief, intense fighting? When he was heading into the city or coming back home to the Station, he had to wait for them to check his papers—wait for trouble, that is. But they always let Pasha through, without saying a word—he was a local, with the papers to prove it. The government didn't have a bone to pick with him. Pasha had gotten used to the soldiers' apathetic eyes, smooth, mechanical movements, and black fingernails, and to the fact that you had to hand over your papers and wait for your own country to verify your standing as a law-abiding citizen. The soldiers would give Pasha his papers back, and he'd stuff them in his pocket, trying not to make eye contact with anyone. Rain had washed the color out of the national flags. It dissolved in the gray autumn air like snow in warm water.

Pasha looks out the window and sees a jeep wrapped in dark metal armor streaking past them. Three men with assault rifles hop out of the jeep and run toward the pack of people clumped together up ahead, paying no mind to the express hearse. The soldiers are standing there, yelling back and forth, grabbing binoculars out of each other's hands, scanning the highway, straining their eyes, red from smoke and sleepless nights, framed by deep wrinkles. But the highway is empty, so empty it's unsettling. There's generally always somebody driving through, even though the city's been completely surrounded for a long period of time and the ring is tightening, someone or other is always making a run for the city or coming back along the only road. Mostly soldiers transporting ammunition or volunteers taking all sorts of useless crap like winter clothes or cold medicine from here, the north, where there isn't any fighting, to the besieged city. Who needs cold medicine in a city getting pounded by heavy artillery, a city that's going to fall any day now? But that wasn't stopping anyone; every once in a while, a whole convoy would leave the mainland and make a run for the besieged area. Sometimes they'd come under fire, which was to be expected. It was obvious that the city would fall, the government troops would be forced to retreat and take the flags of Pasha's country with them, and the front line would shift to the north, toward the station, and death would come a few miles closer. But did anyone actually care? Even civilians mustered up the courage to make a run for the city over the crumbling asphalt of the highway. The soldiers tried to talk them out of it, but nobody around here really trusted the soldiers. You just couldn't tell people anything, they all thought they knew best. You'd see some old-timer hiking all the way into town in the middle of a mortar attack to file some paperwork for his pension. Well, if it comes down to death or bureaucracy, sometimes death is the right call. Sometimes the soldiers would get irritated enough to block off the crossings, but long lines would form at the checkpoints as soon as the shelling abated. Then they'd have to let people through.

Now the highway is completely empty. Seems like something's happening over there, in the city, something scary enough it's even deterring the taxi drivers and speculators. A pack of unshaven men, pissed off from sleepless nights and fighting without gaining or losing ground, are standing by cinder blocks and barbed wire, and they're all yelling to vent their hatred. One tall soldier emerges from the group and heads toward their bus, frenzied eyes beneath his oversized helmet, frenzied and open, wide open with fear, probably. He thrusts his hand forward. Stop, don't move. They aren't moving, though—they're standing still, holding their breath. Suddenly, there's so much space inside the bus, and the air is so thin. Gulp down as much as you can, it still won't be enough. The soldier walks over to the doors and smacks the metal with his hand. The bus echoes like a sunken submarine. The driver opens the door a bit too abruptly.

"Where the fuck are you goin'?" the soldier shouts as he ducks into the bus. He's forced to hunch over a bit, so his helmet slips down over his eyes, and Pasha senses something familiar about him. Where does he remember him from? "Where have I seen him before?" Pasha asks himself. The soldier gives him a dirty look, comes over, adjusts his helmet, rubs his eyes, and yells right in Pasha's face.

"Papers! Papers, for fuck's sake!"

Pasha rummages through his pockets and suddenly, there are pockets everywhere. He gets lost in them, can't find anything except junk—the wet wipes he uses to clean the mud off his shoes when he gets to school, printed lesson plans, and a slip informing him that his package is ready for pickup at the post office. "Yep, yep," Pasha thinks, looking into the soldier's eyes in terror. "Gotta pick up that package, package, package. I completely forgot." His skin is instantly cold and clammy, as if it's him, all of him, getting scrubbed with a wet wipe.

"Well?" the soldier yells, hovering over him.

The thing is, Pasha can't seem to figure out what language he's speaking. The words are bursting out of him, choppy and broken—no intonation, no detectable accent—he's just hollering, like he's trying to cough up some mucus. "He must be speaking the official language." Some unit from Zhytomyr was stationed here a month back. They were Ukrainian speakers, so they laughed at him for sliding back and forth between languages. "Are they those same guys? They've gotta be," goes Pasha's frenzied line of reasoning as he looks into the soldier's enraged eyes that reflect his fear back at him.

"Forgot 'em . . . ," Pasha says.

"What?" The soldier doesn't believe him.

The driver leaps out of his seat, still unsure what to do with himself. Run for it or stay put? Pasha doesn't know what to do with himself either. He's thinking, "How could this be? Just how could this be?"

Somebody's shouting outside, a sharp, prolonged shout that makes the soldier shudder. He turns around and bolts off the bus, shoving the driver, who falls down into his seat and then springs to his feet again and darts after the soldier. Pasha darts off the bus too, and all of them run over to the pack, which suddenly falls silent and makes way for them. Then men—one at a time, two abreast, large groups—start emerging into view from the south, the direction of the besieged city, like they're pushing out of an invisible patch of turbulence. They're coming this way, plodding away from the horizon and moving toward the pack that stands and waits wordlessly. Barely visible at first over there on the horizon, they grow gradually, like shadows in the afternoon. Nobody's looking through binoculars anymore, and nobody's yelling—it's like they're afraid of disturbing this procession as it slowly strings out to fill up three hundred yards of highway. The men are moving at a measured pace; at first they seem to be in no rush, but it soon becomes apparent that they simply cannot go any faster: they're exhausted and this last stretch is taking too much out of them. But they have to keep going, so they do, forging on doggedly, moving toward their flag, out of the valley, toward the checkpoint, like people walking along the highway because they got kicked off the bus for trying to get a free ride. It's as if time has sped up, and everything's happening so quickly that nobody even has a chance to feel scared or happy. The first group is approaching the paint-stained cinder blocks, while more of them continue appearing on the horizon, descending the slope and then moving upward again, heading north to join their buddies. The closer they come, the more distinct their features become, and the quieter it gets, because you can see their eyes now, and there's nothing good in those eyes—just exhaustion and frost. Their breath is so cold that you can't even see it rising from their mouths. Faces black with dirt, the bright whites of their eyes. Helmets, torn black winter hats. Handkerchiefs, gray from brick dust, wrapped around their necks. Weapons, belts, empty pockets, bags hoisted over their shoulders, hands black with motor oil, shoes smeared with pulverized brick and soggy black earth. As they approach, the men in the first group glare at the ones standing and waiting for them, their eyes reproachful, mistrustful, like they're the ones at fault. It's as though everything should have played out differently—the men who've just arrived should've been standing under the low-hanging January sky, looking toward the south, at the horizon, where there's nothing but dirt and death. The first guy to arrive walks over to the pack, thrusts his fist into the air, and starts yelling, like he's berating the gods for their bad behavior, the fury of his curses and threats mounting. Tears trickle down his face, washing his skin. The pack makes room for the newcomers, who blend into it, like dirty river water blending into the clear ocean. The pack can no longer fit between the cold cinder blocks; the first guy keeps standing in the middle of the crew, clamoring about injustice and revenge, about surrendering the city, about abandoning it and everyone who lives there, just handing it to them, backing down, buckling under the pressure, retreating, and escaping from the trap. The ones who got out are doing fine. But what about the guys stuck back there on those blasted streets? What should we do about them? What about them? Who's going to get them out of there?

"So we just hung them out to dry? We just ran and gave up the city? How can you do a thing like that? Who's going to answer for it?" he yells, without lowering his fist. "Olezha, my pal Olezha . . . I didn't even have time to throw some dirt on his body or drag him into the snow. He's still lying there, all burnt up, by the gas station. I just left him. Who's gonna drag him out of there? Who's gonna take care of him?" he yells, threatening a raincloud with his fist. He keeps carrying on until a newcomer squeezes past and knocks him upside the head. Shut your goddamn trap. We're already hurting here without your bullshit. Then everyone starts talking at the same time—asking questions, answering, being led over to the bus to warm up, getting wrapped in old burnt blankets. Suddenly, yet another group pops out by the checkpoint, carrying a stretcher on their shoulders, and on the stretcher is a guy who's so ripped up and bloody that Pasha just averts his eyes. Some officer type starts yelling that they need an ambulance. An ambulance—around here? The fresher soldiers from the checkpoint intercept the stretcher and take it over to the bus. "Take him to the Station. Come on, get a move on," they yell at the driver. Pasha thinks that may be his best bet—heading back home—so he steps toward the bus, but there's already a soldier standing by the doors. Without a glance, he shoves Pasha, who sees the stretcher being carefully carried into the bus; Pasha glimpses sticky hair, a sugary white bone, like someone sliced open a melon and dumped out its sweet insides—he glimpses a contorted hand latching on to the stretcher, clinging to it like only someone clinging to life can.

The driver tries to turn around, but the pack is swaying back and forth; everyone's yelling and getting in the way, getting in the way and yelling, and mostly yelling at others for getting in the way. Eventually, somebody issues a command; the pack shifts and creeps off to the side. The bus turns around and disappears. Pasha's jostled to the side of the road; he's trying, fecklessly, to break out of the pack when somebody standing behind him says, "Gimme a light." It's a soldier with no helmet and dirty silvery hair.

"Don't have one," Pasha replies.

"What do ya got?" The soldier's not letting him go. Pasha automatically reaches into his pocket and produces his papers.

Pasha stands on the shoulder, the dirt torn up by truck tires and tank treads, and tries to recall where he's seen those fingers before. Contorted, lifeless, but clinging to life. He remembers immediately—a week ago, on the last day of classes. It was just a week ago. Everything was the same as it is now—brisk wind, pale January sun. Somebody is calling him into the hallway. He steps out. Teachers are herding their students back into their classrooms. The kids bolt toward the windows to see what's going on. He glances back at his kids.

"All right now, keep it down. I'll be right back," he yells. But nobody's listening to him. The principal, her sickly body swaying laboriously, rushes past Pasha. He runs after her; they go out onto the front steps and stop. A jeep full of soldiers is parked by the school. No license plates. Just a military motto, painted white on black. Pasha's no expert on military mottoes, so he doesn't really know who these guys are. They could be with one of the volunteer battalions, or maybe the National Guard. The flag on the jeep is the same as the one on their school. The town hasn't changed hands.

The feverish soldiers are running around and making some calls; the man in charge walks over to the principal, takes her firmly by the arm, leads her away from the entrance, and starts talking, his voice cold. Pasha catches fragments of their conversation. The soldier's laying out his terms, not asking for permission.

"No. Can't go anywhere else . . . has to be here . . . where you are . . . it's you we're here to protect . . . call whoever you want . . . get Kyiv on the line for all I care." The principal slumps in her black suit, and her face goes gray, which makes her look even older. She'd like to object, but she just can't do it. She turns toward Pasha, seemingly expecting him to back her up. The soldier pats Pasha on the shoulder as he passes, and school chalk dust rises from his scholastic blazer.

Then an old army ambulance, brown like a soggy meatloaf, pulls up to the school. Soldiers start unloading the wounded, heave them over their shoulders like merchants handling bags of goods—apparently, there aren't any stretchers—trudge up the steps and down the empty, echoing hallway. They turn left, and their clay-smeared combat boots kick open the first classroom. The Ukrainian language classroom. Pasha's classroom. The classroom where Pasha teaches kids. The wounded are placed right on the floor, in between the desks. Shortly thereafter, Pasha sprints in after them and dismisses the class. The scared kids step over fresh blood and then jostle in the hallway. Pasha steps out, too.

"Go home, quit standing around." He's speaking Russian, as he always does in the hallway, outside of class. Then he opens the door apprehensively. The classroom smells of mud and blood, snow and earth. Soldiers bring in blankets and warm things, shove the desks into the middle of the room and the wounded toward the walls.

Another soldier walks into the classroom, a machine gun on his shoulder, lips clamped around a cigarette. Black hair, eyes dark, which makes them look mistrustful, dust eating into the wrinkles on his face; the only other guys Pasha has seen that looked like that were coal miners coming up to the surface. He casually surveys the wounded, notices Pasha, nods, and says hello. He speaks with a thick Caucasian accent and mixes up Ukrainian and Russian, but he tries to be friendly, as if he really cares whether Pasha believes him. He translates some words from Russian to Ukrainian as soon as he gets them out, trying his best, like he's taking a language exam. Hey, Teach, don't be scared. We won't let 'em take your school. We'll protect you, so you can keep teaching your kids.

"Who are those guys?" The machine gunner nods at the portraits on the classroom wall.

"Poets," Pasha answers, tentatively.

"Poets, huh? Well there you go. They any good?" The machine gunner asks in a doubtful tone.

"They're dead," Pasha answers.

"Perfect." The machine gunner chuckles. "The only good poet's a dead poet."

He carefully opens the window as though he wants to air out the room and deploys his weapon on the sill. Pasha gathers his students' assignments and tosses them into his briefcase. As he's about to leave, his eye is drawn to one of the wounded men who's been placed by the recently painted radiator—two fuzzy blankets with crusty bloodstains, an old tattered sleeping bag, head facing the wall, only his greasy hair and unshaven face visible, the torn sleeve of his army jacket lying right there, patches of dirty skin marked with little cuts between bandages, left hand poking out of the sleeping bag, exposed; just like when a passenger in a sleeper car stretches his hand out from under the blanket that encases his motionless body. That blanket re-creates the protrusion of his knees and the indentation of his stomach like the Epitaphios re-creates Christ's body. The nakedness of this battered male body stands out among the bundles and warm clothing tossed on the desks nearby.

"Here and now," Pasha thinks. His skinny, pale hand, dotted with sparse hairs, looks so out of place against the classroom floor with its new coat of paint from the summer, against the desks and the blackboard, clinging to the sleeping bag, too afraid to release it, as though that sleeping bag is the last thing linking him to life. Pasha can't look away from the long, black fingers—all cut up and roughed up and tinted a gasoline blue. Then a brisk, wintry breeze rushes inside, shaking the window frame, but the machine gunner holds it open. Pasha remembers where he is and quickly steps out into the hallway, straight into the principal's embrace.

"Pasha, Pasha," she cries, grabbing him by the arm. "How could this be? Tell them to go."

It hits Pasha that even her tears are fake. "She doesn't know how to cry," he thinks. "She just doesn't know how it's done. Well, she doesn't know how to laugh either."

"Tell them to leave, you have to tell them to leave," she's using the formal "you," as though she's addressing a tram conductor.

"Yes, yes," Pasha assures her. "I'll tell them. I'll tell them right now."

He walks the principal back to her office, helps her get settled, leaves, shuts the door, stands there for a bit, and hears her sniffle, then instantly regain her composure, take out her cellphone, dial, and start making a stink.

"Take care of this one without me," Pasha says in a whisper, and heads for the door. There are soldiers standing on the front steps, smoking. They fastidiously wipe their dirty boots with a clean rag whenever they come inside. Blood doesn't come off all that easily, but it does come off.

In the damp wind, you perceive smells more distinctly. The heavy smell of wet clothes fills the air immediately. People coming from the south give off a burnt smell, like they've been sitting by a campfire. They keep coming, most continuing on foot, toward the Station, while one group piles into a jeep, and another helps a guy into the back of a truck. There isn't enough room up front. A soldier walks by, his bulletproof vest grazing Pasha, who cringes, takes a step back toward the side of the road, then another, his high boot crunching in snow mixed with yellow clay, then another step, and then one more.

"I wouldn't go over there if I were you," someone says.

Pasha turns toward the voice—man standing nearby, dark

Wolfskin jacket, hiking boots, laptop bag, meticulously groomed facial hair. His expression is condescending, even disparaging. He carries himself well, but if you look a little closer, his chin, too small for the rest of his face, and the finicky wrinkles around his mouth make you think he's letting his beard grow out to seem tougher than he is. He looks about fifty, and he sizes Pasha up like he's his commanding officer. The same way a passenger who got on at the first stop views someone who's gotten on later—yes, both of them have tickets, but the few extra hours spent in the train compartment give him an odd kind of authority. His name is Peter. That's how he introduces himself, in passable Russian, making no apparent effort to conceal his accent.

"You shouldn't go over there," he says, nodding toward the roadside ditch. "You'll get your legs blown off. Let's get out of here—pretty soon they're gonna get all riled up and start shooting each other."

He turns around, starts making his way through the crowd. Pasha glances back, sees a thick heap of mushy snow down below, and runs after Peter.

They shove through the thinning crowd, away from the checkpoint. Peter cautiously circumvents a group of soldiers engaged in a heated argument and steps over some wounded guys placed smack-dab in the middle of the road on some blankets and old civilian coats. Pasha sticks close to him, trying not to make eye contact with the soldiers. That's how he'd walk by stray dogs as a kid—just don't look them in the eye; if you do, they'll sense that you don't belong here. Pasha just couldn't get used to all the soldiers around, even though it'd already been a few months; he'd always avoid them. Whenever they stopped him by the station, he'd answer their questions flatly, looking past them the whole time. There are so many of them here, and there's this odd smell—dirt and metal, tobacco and gunpowder. Pasha skirts past another group apprehensively, sees the soldiers' mistrustful eyes, and hurries to catch up to Peter, who's approaching an old blue Ford encircled by soldiers. They have spread out a hand-drawn map with trails marked and slopes outlined in red pencil. Soaked by the rain, the map looks like a tablecloth doused with wine at a train station restaurant. Peter squeezes through the group of soldiers, pats one of them on the back, shakes another guy's hand without taking his eyes off the map, and immediately starts arguing with them, running a pink, neatly cut fingernail along the disintegrating paper, yelling and working himself into a frenzy. The soldiers are yelling, too, running their own fingers—black and frozen—along the map, disagreeing with Peter. Eventually, one of them, apparently the guy in charge, a short, stocky man with a gray crewcut, spits, pulls a black ski hat over his large skull, slings an assault rifle over his shoulder, and orders everyone to pile into the car. A tall old soldier, frail and hunched up, scoops up the map and sits in the driver's seat. The gray-haired man in the ski hat takes a seat next to him. The rest of them cram in. Peter manages to stuff himself inside, though nobody seemed to invite him. He even tries to shut the door, but then he suddenly realizes he's forgotten something. He leans out of the car and yells to Pasha:

"Well, are ya coming or what? We aren't going to wait around all day! Get over here!"

Pasha's taken aback at first, but then he runs over to the Ford. There are already about four soldiers sitting in the back. They all seem absolutely massive in their bulletproof vests. Well, and Peter's taking up some room, too. Just how on earth did they all fit back there? Pasha's shifting around tentatively outside, but Peter's not letting up.

"Come on, let's go," he yells, patting the black denim over his skinny thigh invitingly.

So they set off—the hunched-up driver and the commander who's doggedly trying to find something among the remaining clumps of map are up front, the armored soldiers, Peter, and Pasha on his lap are in the back. Pasha's uncomfortable. He's never sat on anyone's lap before, except when he was a kid. The soldiers are uncomfortable too, on his behalf. Silence sets in—nothing but the sound of vests knocking together dully.

The Ford glides down the highway slowly, passing an endless chain of soldiers making their way toward the Station. The soldiers look back hopefully, but upon seeing how many passengers are in the car they turn their heads back, clearly disappointed. The trip isn't all that long. The driver veers right once they get to the settlement, steps on the gas–the tires skid and make deep incisions in the yellow snow—and pulls into a motel parking lot. Pasha's shoved clear first, and then the rest of the passengers pile out into the damp air.

Two-story building, a sign with the word *Paradise* spelled out in Cyrillic letters hanging over the front entrance. Café to the right, carwash to the left, reception desk in the middle. The shockwave of an explosion has knocked out the windows on the second floor, so the owners have put plastic over them. Up on the roof, a satellite dish pierced by shrapnel looks like a sunflower in the morning, facing east toward the sun.

The parking lot's packed with military equipment and cars—heavy special-purpose vehicles, sedans with Polish license plates (the drivers clearly haven't paid any customs duties on them), and a bunch of beat-up shabby junkers—no windshields, slashed-up doors, missing hoods. A tank, still intact, buried under all sorts of colorful things, is parked off to the side. Blankets, sleeping bags, sacks, and hiking backpacks have been tied to the armor with ropes; somebody has even slapped a pull-out bed to the side of the tank. A pack of soldiers stands by the café, smoking, yelling, arguing. The guys Pasha arrived with head toward the group by the entrance. Peter considers the sign skeptically.

"Paradise," he says, smiling. "More like the first circle of hell. Well, are ya coming?" He nods at Pasha and walks over to the group.

Pasha can't think of anything better than tagging along. "Why am I following him?" he thinks, continuing to follow him. "What am I listening to him for?" he asks himself, trying not to lose Peter's assiduously unkempt hair in the crowd. He pushes past some soldiers, steps into the café.

A few tables, a bar with the spoils of a hunting trip—a stuffed pheasant, deer horns, and something's severed head (Pasha figures it must have belonged to a dog, but he could be mistaken)—hanging over it. Restroom door off to one side, a plasma TV on the opposite wall. No empty seats; soldiers are sitting around and looking at themselves in the screen. A woman is bartending; she looks at the customers scornfully, though her scorn is kind of listless. She's kind of frumpy and not all that well put together; blond hair sprouts out of her black roots like fresh blades of grass through a field that was burned last year. A bottle of Coke and heaps of chocolates lie on the shelves behind her. Dried fish looms on the counter in front of her. The woman pulls out the most important stuff from deep down, underneath a heavy hatch from a compartment loaded with more fish, and pours a round. Everyone's talking at the same time, hardly listening and constantly interrupting each other, and the fish odor is so strong you'd think this was a wake that had dragged on for three days.

Peter strides up to the bar and nods at the woman, who feigns a smile and keeps pouring. Peter asks a question. The woman nods in response, still not concealing her scorn, still carefully scanning the room. Peter opens the side door, and Pasha slides into the next room after him. There are tables here, too, it's packed with soldiers, too, and there's the same chaos of voices fusing into a menacing din. There's a little table on the far side of the room by a staircase, and Peter heads that way, giving a soldier—black from smoke and alcohol—an offhand greeting. The guy waves back at Peter without looking in his direction, says something, continues talking, and nods; it's as though he's having a conversation with an invisible person. Peter has already crossed the room and plopped down in a plastic chair. Pasha takes a seat next to him. Fish and alcohol in plastic cups instantly materialize. Peter grabs his disposable cup, toasts carelessly with someone at the next table, lifts it to his mouth, and disposes of the alcohol. Or appears to . . . the cup in his buoyant hand is still full. He dumps its contents out under the table, onto the cold stone floor, with one inconspicuous movement, then produces a small brown leather flask from an inconspicuous pocket, unscrews the cap, and pours himself a drink more to his liking, without bothering to offer Pasha any. Pasha bends forward to grab a cup with his lips, empties bitter, burning fluid into his body, and then coughs violently; somebody basically shoves a piece of fish in his mouth, and he starts chomping on it to cover up the taste of local knock-off booze with the deathly smell of fish. Peter looks at all this with tenacious, attentive disgust, although it's unclear what disgusts him, Pasha or the fish. Nevertheless, Peter soon regains his composure, smiles, yells something into the crowd, answers somebody's question, comments on a conversation going on at the next table, sips his drink, and starts grilling Pasha.

"What do you do?" he asks.

Pasha hesitates, unsure of what language to use. Eventually, he answers in Russian.

"I'm a teacher."

"Gotcha," Peter says with a chuckle.

He reaches into his pocket, takes out two packs of cigarettes in succession, the first unopened (the cheap, strong ones), the second already going (the light ones with almost no nicotine in them). He puts the cheap ones back in his pocket, takes out two lights, and offers one to Pasha, who turns him down, so he assiduously tucks the extra back into the open pack, sticks the other one offhandedly in his mouth, takes a brand-new Zippo out of an inconspicuous pocket, flicks it smoothly with his thumb, places it back in his pocket, and takes a drag. He winces painfully, as if he's smoking homegrown tobacco.

"So where are your students?" Peter asks, blowing smoke, which makes his voice sound hoarse and confidential.

"On break," Pasha answers.

Peter nods eagerly.

"Gotcha," he says again. "On break . . . People only go to school so they can go on break. I'd always go fishing with my old man."

"In a river?" Pasha asks.

"Nah, in the ocean."

"What ocean?"

"The Pacific."

Pasha isn't sure what to say next.

"Where were you planning on going?" Peter asks.

"Into the city." Pasha squirms in his chair. Peter's tone is so friendly that you immediately start to distrust him.

"Gotcha. Got things to do?"

"Yep," Pasha replies after a moment's thought. "My nephew's staying at the orphanage. I want to take him home . . . for his week off."

"Seems you have every day off around here."

Pasha doesn't care to respond to that.

"Guess I'll pick him up some other time," he says after a short pause.

"Gotcha. That'll be about two months from now."

"Huh? Two months?"

"Well, they'll have to establish a new front line and set up new checkpoints, that'll be about two months. Why didn't you pick him up earlier, right at the beginning of break? Don't you read the news?"

"I don't," Pasha admits.

"I don't either. I write it," he adds, takes an artificially short pause, chuckles, and blows tobacco smoke all over the place.

"What should I do?" Pasha clearly has no idea. "He has some health problems. I'm scared something'll happen to him."

"Go pick him up now," Peter suggests, still smiling. "It'll take them a few days to move on out." He points at the soldiers around them. "You'll be the least of their concerns. The city's changing hands. Who knows what'll happen to the orphanage. The new government," he nods in the direction from which he supposes the new government is coming, "won't be messing around with orphanages. After your boys pull out, they're gonna clean house."

"Your boys" rubs Pasha the wrong way, but he refrains from getting into it with Peter.

"There's shelling over there, yeah?" Pasha conjectures.

"There sure is! I wouldn't want to spend my break getting shelled."

Pasha's mind is racing feverishly. He can't come up with anything better than calling his old man. He produces his cheap Nokia, starts dialing.

"Two months. Then you'll have service again," Peter comments. "That's if your government gets on it." Once again, he emphasizes the word *your.* "They haven't been trying all that hard so far."

Pasha looks at his screen—no bars. Everything was fine last night, though.

"They've got jammers, you know? So your boys," Peter motions to the area around him, "won't know what's going on. Nobody knows anything and nobody trusts anybody. We're back in the Middle Ages," he adds, and fastidiously stubs out his half-smoked cigarette in a makeshift beer-can ashtray. "Do you teach history?" He scrutinizes Pasha.

"Nah," Pasha answers.

"That's a good thing," Peter says, praising him for some reason. "Teaching history in your country is like going fishin', you never know what you're gonna pull out. I appreciate the way you love history in these parts, though," Peter says, taking out another cigarette, flicking the lighter, and blowing some more smoke up at the ceiling. "Keep picking, keep digging around. Good work. Keep it up.

You know what advice I'd like to give you?" Peter continues, kicking back in his chair and clamping his cigarette between two fingers. As he's listening to him, Pasha spots four soldiers barging into the room—their faces particularly dark, their movements heavy and anxious. Their eyes, red with anger and smoke, scan the room with exacting precision and unerringly pick out the two civilians. They head in their direction, weaving through the tables. Their relentless movement is felt throughout the room, and the conversations hush; everyone's eyes follow the four men moving toward their table. Everyone's tense and dead still. Everyone except Peter, so consumed with his pontificating that he's completely oblivious, sitting with his back to the room, considering Pasha through strands of smoke, and inserting such serious pauses that you'd think he was listening raptly to his own voice. "I'd encourage you to be careful about your history. You know, history's one of those things . . ." He goes quiet for a second, seemingly groping for some fresh insight. Suddenly, he takes note of the silence now prevailing in the room and stares at Pasha, transfixed—Pasha can't seem to figure out why. Suddenly, it dawns on him that Peter's looking into his glasses, seeing the reflection of those four bearing down on him. Panic scampers across his face. The corner of his mouth jerks up, and his spasmodic desire to turn around makes a vein in his neck twitch, but he composes himself and takes another drag—it's a nervous drag, though—releases a neat puff of smoke, and finishes his thought: ". . . one of those things nobody has the right to take away from you!"

"Who are you?" The first guy speaks at the back of Peter's head. Pasha's scared eyes consider his combat boots with last year's grass stuck to their worn toecaps, beat-up kneepads, heavy side pockets stuffed with something sharp and metallic, an AKM he's holding like an infant that can't seem to fall asleep, assault vest holding several extra magazines, clumps of colored tape on his sleeves, and, most important, a knife jutting out of a special pocket near his heart—it has a black handle with deep grooves. Pasha unconsciously starts counting those grooves, but then the soldier repeats, "Who are you?"

The second and third guys come over, cutting off any possible escape routes. "Escape routes?" Pasha says to himself in his head, desperation rising. "Think again!" The fourth man peers out from behind the first guy's shoulder, his gaze full of such suspicion that Pasha tips his glasses up onto his forehead, like he's rubbing the lenses clean, just because he doesn't want to see any of this. Peter turns toward the voice and flashes a carefree smile.

"I'm a journalist," he says, stuffing his hand into a deep pocket—apparently reaching for his press pass—and all four of them instantly tense up. But then Peter takes out his hand and proffers the necessary papers. "Everything's fine." He's trying to speak in a light, simple manner. "I'm a journalist. Here's my pass."

"Hans," the soldier says, "check this." Hans takes the pass and runs his fingers over the paper, line by line—frosty red fingers with black earth under the nails. Peter smiles and extends his hand. Come on, give it back already. We're in the middle of a real interesting conversation here. And Hans hesitates, goes to hand the pass back, but then stops short and looks at it one more time.

"When did you cross the border?" he asks unexpectedly.

"A month ago," Peter says after a pause.

"Uh-huh." Hans doesn't really believe him. "I've had my eye on you since fall."

"That's rich," Peter says defiantly.

"I have," Hans says, his tone just as defiant, and hands Peter's pass to the first guy, who looks at Peter without saying a word.

"Listen guys," Peter says, rising from his chair. All four of them tense up once again. "I was here in the fall, too. Here's my passport. Take a look at my stamps."

He produces his passport and thrusts it at the first guy, who passes it along in silence, his eyes fixed on Peter. He tries to calm himself down and puts his hand in his pocket, which causes everyone to tense up yet again, but he just takes out his cigarettes.

"Want one?" he asks, his eyes darting from one guy to the next.

But none of them says anything. Hans leafs through the passport, hands it to the first guy, leans in, and whispers something in his ear. The first guy nods and gives Peter his papers back.

"So what's the problem?" Peter asks, affecting a relaxed tone.

The first soldier doesn't say anything for a while, looking at Peter the whole time, until the latter breaks down and looks away.

"The problem is that somebody's been snitching," he says. "I mean, somebody's leaking intelligence information. And it looks like it's one of the civilians."

"What makes you think that?" Peter asks, still smiling.

"Because we know everybody else," the soldier answers. "Somebody's been snitching. Do you know who?" he suddenly asks Peter.

Then all four of them encircle Peter, who turns white as a sheet.

"No, I don't."

"You sure?" the soldier asks.

"I'm sure," Peter answers without hesitating.

"All righty then. You're free to go," he says to Peter and turns toward Pasha abruptly. "Now you."

Pasha lowers his glasses onto the bridge of his nose, visibly flustered, digs around in his pockets, locates his papers, and hands them over, but he can tell that's not enough. He has to give them some assurances that everything's fine and he's not going to cause them any trouble.

"I'm with him," he says feverishly, turning in Peter's direction—but Peter's gone, disappeared, vanished into thin air, leaving the unopened pack of strong cigarettes on the table.

Pasha's sitting in a cold, spacious room with a computer and a black safe in it—the accounting department, apparently. He didn't get a good look at the little sign by the door. Hans had led him up the stairs and pushed him into the damp darkness of the hallway softly yet persistently, so he wouldn't even think about resisting. Thing is, he wouldn't have anyway—he groped his way down the dark hallway, reacted to a command issued behind him, stopped. Hans walked over to the door and tried the handle; it creaked in his hand. Busted. The door wouldn't budge. Then he rammed his shoulder against it and crashed right into an empty room. He took another step inside, examined the locked safe skeptically, left it alone.

"Sit here," he yelled in Pasha's general direction. "And wait."

"Until when?" Pasha asked, just in case.

"Until we check your documents," Hans replied abruptly.

Pasha walked across the room, sat down on one of the three chairs by the wall, thought for a second, and then slid over. Hans watched, not saying anything.

"Stay here," he said eventually. "Don't even think about escaping."

"Okay," Pasha acquiesced instantly.

Hans left, carefully closing the broken door behind him.

Pasha's sitting and waiting. It's chilly in that room, the plastic sheet over the window isn't keeping the wind and moisture out. "How'd I let myself get caught like that?" he thinks. Before this, he'd kind of just gotten by. He'd occasionally cross paths with soldiers, purely by accident—at the store, on the street, at the station. Whenever they started asking questions, he'd say he was a teacher. That generally worked, regardless of who the soldiers were fighting for. During times of war, people leave priests and teachers alone. They really shouldn't, though. Pasha thought back to the first time armed men had spoken to him—it was back then, last spring, right after it'd all started, right after they'd come to the city, started taking over police stations and tearing flags off public buildings. Most of the locals didn't know what to make of them, what to expect of them. Pasha didn't know either, and he didn't care to. He was walking home from school—he'd decided to cut through the park—just minding his own business, plodding down a sunny May path. The academic year was coming to a close, summer was just around the corner, and he wanted to lock himself in his room and not come out again until the first autumn bell rang. And then two guys with assault rifles blocked his path. Well, actually, Pasha, oblivious and nearsighted, ran into them. The guns in their hands made them feel obliged to react somehow, so they stopped him, quite delicately, no tough-guy stuff. Pasha remembered that some of them, especially the ones who weren't local, the guys who'd come in from out of town, behaved like that—markedly cordial, constantly smiling at the civilian population. Giving children candy, giving up their seats on the bus for elderly people, courteously waiting like everyone else, no line-cutting: we're here for your benefit, we're just like you, we'll protect you so you can keep teaching your kids. You want everyone to like you, especially when you're holding a weapon and you don't know who you'll have to use it on. Those two guys adopted a markedly cordial tone, like they were talking to an old friend. What's the big rush? Watch where you're going next time, all right? One of them, with a soft, round face, started chuckling, his laugh childish and carefree. It seemed as though the other guy wanted to laugh, too, but nothing came of it—crooked lips, evasive eyes. Pasha immediately latched on to those eyes, the eyes of a fisherman who could wait because he knew what awaited him. And that nose—knocked into his face, squished between his cheeks, like he was an old syphilitic, the nose of a boxer. Round Mug was already patting Pasha on the back, jovially poking fun at his glasses. Pasha didn't like that; he distinctly remembered that—it was so stilted and artificial, as though this was all some kind of performance. They looked unnatural, like actors who'd left the theater to make a cigarette run: their fresh camo had a faint warehouse smell to it, pirate bandanas, the ones beachgoers in Crimea wear, sunglasses. Old AKMs they'd apparently taken from the local cops and brand-new white sneakers they'd probably just bought—maybe just for this country, just for this war—the dust from the street hadn't burrowed into those sneakers and the grass hadn't stained them; they were brand new, solemn, completely clashing with the guns and camo. Pasha stood there and looked at their sneakers, not knowing what to say. They kept laughing, and then No Nose casually asked: "So, uh, what do you do?" He kept smiling crookedly—I'm just asking, you don't have to answer, but, of course, you probably should.

"I'm a teacher." Pasha swallowed hard. "Just as long as they don't ask what subject," he thought.

"What do you teach?" No Nose seemingly heard his fears.

"Little bit of everythin'," Pasha answered.

He stood in front of them, gaze downcast, so they thought he was afraid. Their tone grew less cordial, more condescending, like they were talking to a wimp who was afraid to make eye contact. Actually, Pasha was just examining their new sneakers.

"Some fuckin' education you got around here," No Nose said, and they started laughing again.

Pasha nodded as a goodbye of sorts, stepped around them wordlessly, and began walking away nice and quiet, nice and slow. "Just as long as they don't yell anything at me," he thought. "Just as long as they don't yell any insults." He kept walking, holding his breath so they wouldn't hear his heart pounding. "Why didn't I say anything to them?" he asked himself later. "Why?" He walked ten, twenty, fifty, a hundred yards. Behind him, the laughter ended abruptly. Pasha turned on to a path to his left. It was all over.

Pasha takes out his phone and checks the time. Twelve o'clock. He's been sitting here for about an hour, but nobody's come for him, nobody's let him out. "I'll wait a little longer," Pasha tells himself. He waits and then waits some more, and the longer he waits, the colder it gets, since the plastic sheet is doing nothing to keep the place warm. Waves of brisk air burst inside. At first, Pasha tries to ignore the cold, then he starts to feel sorry for himself—just had to leave the house today of all days—then he gets angry at the soldiers for holding him here in a cold room, even though they have no right to do so. The colder he gets, the more justified his indignation seems.

"What the hell?" Pasha says to himself. "What do they want from me? I'm gonna go give 'em a piece of my mind." He stands up resolutely, walks over to the door, and pulls on it just as resolutely. But the door gives a menacing squeak and his resolve flutters away instantly. He stands there, still holding on to the handle, and apprehensively listens to the silent hallway, listens hard but can't make anything out. Now he's afraid to go out into the hallway—might see someone out there. He's afraid to shut the door, too. What if it squeaks again? What if someone emerges from the damp gloom and heads toward him? He stands there, not knowing what he should be most afraid of. But just standing there is scary, too, so Pasha timidly sticks his head out into the hallway. It's empty.

"I'll come right back," he says to himself. "Lemme find someone, tell 'em I'm still here, and then I'll definitely come back." He leaves the door open and advances blindly down the dark hallway, tries one door, then the next, then another, and eventually the fourth one's unlocked. Pasha pushes it and finds himself in a motel room. After the dark hallway, the diffuse, glimmering light coming through another plastic sheet on the window instantly blinds him. Feeling like he's underwater, Pasha examines an unmade bed and a table cluttered with empty champagne bottles, the local brand. Television in the corner. The news is on, and for Pasha it feels like he's seen the news in real life outside, just a few miles from here. He stares blankly at the moving picture, only noticing the clothes scattered across the bed a little later. Black skirt, dark stockings, and weightless lingerie. And a blouse. And a vest. There's a badge on the vest, and the word "WAITER" has been printed on the badge. "ANNA" has been added in blue marker. "I guess Anna's in the shower," Pasha deduces, hearing water hitting the plastic doors of a walk-in shower, crashing against a woman's warm body, flowing down her long legs, and vanishing down the drain. Anna will have a fit if she catches Pasha in here. "They might even shoot me," Pasha thinks. "Gotta get outta here." But he looks at the lingerie on the bed and realizes that it might still be holding some warmth from her body, that it'd be nice to wait for her to come back, hand her her clothes, wait for her to get dressed. He'd like to meet her.

"Well, her name's Anna. Anna," Pasha thinks. "What more is there to know? I should find her after all this is over. Find her and talk to her about everything. Will she want to talk to me?" Pasha asks himself incredulously, listening to the water flowing off her. He turns around and unexpectedly sees his face in the mirror on the wall across from him. Fair hair that hasn't been cut for a while, glasses with thin, inexpensive rims, bags under his eyes, two-day stubble that makes him look more slovenly than rugged. Birthmark on his right temple, scar on his neck—got it as a kid. He fixes his glasses and looks at his fingers. Yeah, and that hand he hates. He finds himself thinking that he doesn't like the way he looks. And he finds himself thinking that he wants to like himself. He goes out into the hallway and quietly shuts the door.

There are more people downstairs. Or maybe they're just yelling even louder. Pasha slides between their backs and sneaks toward the door, trying not to call any attention to himself. A large group is sitting in the corner, hovering over the table, whispering about something, occasionally kicking back in their chairs and laughing anxiously. One of them turns halfway around and surveys the room languidly yet very attentively, and his gaze snags on Pasha. Hans—Pasha recognizes him and freezes, too terrified to move a muscle.

One of his sharp eyes narrows for a brief moment when his gaze bumps into Pasha; a wrinkle under that eye of his twitches almost imperceptibly, just for a split second. Then his gaze keeps moving; he turns around and slaps the guy next to him on the back. Then that guy turns his head, locks his eyes on Pasha, and gets up slowly. Pasha stands completely still, too afraid to fix his glasses even. The soldier lazily walks toward Pasha, making little effort to sidestep the tables and people in his way, and gives him a sharp look, not saying anything. Then he takes Pasha's papers out of his pocket and sticks them in his crippled hand. He turns around and lazily walks back. It takes Pasha some time to collect himself; then he quickly heads to the next room over; he wants to go around the bar, but an incredibly young rifleman tugs on his sleeve. Helmet dangling from his hand, swaying like a cooking pot, high taped-up boots—looks like he pulled them off someone's feet and just cut the laces, so he had to tighten them up with whatever he had. The tape squeaks with his every movement. The rifleman, who's not even looking at Pasha, tugs him over to the bar. One sec, don't get your panties in a bunch. Pasha stands behind him and watches. The rifleman flashes the woman behind the counter what looks like a V sign, but actually it's just him ordering two more. While the woman's pouring their drinks, he roots around in his pockets, takes out a handful of small bills, scrutinizes them discontentedly, reaches into his pockets again without letting go of Pasha's arm, and then suddenly produces a hand grenade. The woman freezes; the rifleman places the grenade on the counter and keeps rummaging through his pockets as the grenade starts rolling down the counter, rolling and rolling, very slowly. The woman can't take her eyes off it, the cup runs over, and the other people standing around also notice the grenade, but they can't get anything out. All they can do is watch it roll slowly, very slowly, toward the edge, pause, roll over the edge, and plunge to the floor.

"Get down!" Somebody shouts in Pasha's ear and charges through the crowd.

The woman shrieks, too. Pasha tears away from the rifleman and dashes toward the door, to the light. There's hardly any light left at this hour and what light remains is chilly and damp.

"Where we headed?" the taxi driver asks him.

"Home," Pasha answers.

"You military?"

"Nah, I'm a civilian."

"Gotcha." The taxi driver pulls out discontentedly, yanking the wheel like he's wringing out a wet sheet.

He doesn't say anything for a bit, but then he breaks down and starts talking. He's pissed off and anxious. Well, if you disregard all his anxiety and anger, you can glean that he's talking about how there aren't any decent roads around here. They fucked the roads up, really fucked the shit out of 'em, and now there aren't any left, not that there were any to begin with. He's more and more anxious. And it's unclear what bothers him the most—that there never were any roads to begin with, that they're gone, or that there probably won't ever be any. So he's getting all pissed off and anxious. Well, soldiers and roads, and they fucked the shit out of everything. My brother's hunkering down in some basement in the city with his family, he doesn't wanna crawl outta there.

"I keep telling him," he says to Pasha. "'Get outta there, I'll take you to the other side. At least there's work here, nobody knows who's gonna be running things over there. The new government might shoot ya.' But he's still hunkering down, too scared to leave his house. I mean, who the hell cares about that house of his? The roads, man, they just fucked the shit out of them—"

"What was that about getting to the other side?" Pasha interrupts him.

"Huh?"

"Your brother, can you take your brother to the other side? Everything's blocked off."

The taxi driver explodes. And he launches into angry arguments, his basic point being—all his rambling aside—that there are one hundred and twenty-five ways to get in and get out. You can even take freight trains out of there, which a lot of people have been doing. And he's already made two trips today, skirting all the checkpoints and putting one over on all those sucker generals. And what they show on TV is all wrong, and he doesn't watch TV at all because there's nothing worth watching anyway.

"So," Pasha interrupts him again. "You really can cross over?"

"Yeah." The taxi driver nods.

"To the orphanage, too?"

"The orphanage?" The taxi driver's expression turns dark. "In theory, yes. It got walloped yesterday, though. Seems like it got . . ."

"Fucked?"

"Yep," the taxi driver concurs. "I think it got fucked up, but I don't know for sure. Haven't been there for a while. What's there to see at that orphanage anyway?"

They sit there, looking at each other. Pasha—kind of chubby, so unshaven as to almost be bearded, ski hat, and, most important, those glasses that immediately make you distrust him. The driver—an oversized leather jacket, shabby and cracked; it's as if he sleeps in it, as if it's his own skin, like an old iguana at the zoo. Worn into his skin, won't even be able to peel it off his carcass. And the peaked cap on his head is made of leather, too, and it's all worn, too, like a soccer ball that's been kicked around for a long while on asphalt. Round fish eyes, a mustache that conceals his torn upper lip. He looks at Pasha, trying to figure out what he's getting at, while Pasha looks at him, too, through the lenses of his white-collar glasses and thinks, "That worn look of his, it's not because he's poor. He's got a decent car, sure, it's not brand new, but it looks like it was in good hands in some place like Holland. And he smells fine, doesn't reek or anything, at least. But that worn look of his . . . It's like he's been rubbing up against something, like a cat against his owner's leg. Or a cow against a telegraph pole."

"Ready to go?" the Iguana asks.

"Sure you'll get me there?" Pasha involuntarily fixes his glasses, then jerks his hand back. "I hate myself," he thinks. "I just hate myself for that. Why am I constantly touching them like that?"

"Doubt we'd make it to the orphanage," says the Iguana. "I can do the train station, though. You'll figure it out from there."

"All right," Pasha agrees hesitantly.

"Do ya even have any money on ya?" The Iguana asks, just in case. He squints, but one round fish eye, as watery as morning air, doesn't quite shut all the way, still pierces Pasha.

The driver swings around in front of the motel, right at the feet of some soldiers who are standing around, puffing on their cigarettes, and looking at them in their customary fashion, the way they'd look at any other moving target. The mud-caked Opel bashes through some puddles and bounces down a narrow strip of asphalt, away from the main road, into the gray dampness of the winter panorama that opens up before them as soon as they crest a little hill and turn behind a row of trees. Over there, fields drop off and stretch as far as the eye can see; over there—where you can no longer make anything out—beyond the fog and the low-hanging clouds that look like cargo planes, something is breathing, burning, and glimmering. Pasha surmises that it's the city. The driver bounces in and out of potholes, getting more and more angry, and then he loosens up once the motel disappears behind the trees, slows down—"lemme wipe down the windshield," he tells Pasha—pulls onto the shoulder, scoops up handfuls of hard, darkened snow, and begins wiping the glass with it. Pasha watches the snow snap and slide down the glass, eroding the space, watches the driver blow on his icy fingers, clearly in pain, and press his worn skin against the dirty hood as he reaches for the glass and rubs little clumps of ice into it. Pasha gets out of the car and looks to the south, trying to kill time—he doesn't have all that much to spare, though.

A field, black with last year's unharvested sunflowers. Gray in certain spots, almost blue even. Shreds of snow. Damp, thick soil. Deep ruts from the vehicles that have driven into this dark sunflower armhole, either to fend off an attack and then keep going, or to let a passing convoy through. Pasha takes a step forward; grass pokes sharply through the hardened crust of the snow. "Stay outta there," he reminds himself and steps back, closer to the car that's making its presence felt behind him with its warm gasoline smell. Beyond the frigid sunflowers, transmission towers stretch out like a row of fishing-rod holders. Black metal supports the heavy horizontal lines of wire slicing through the sky and extending into the rain. Down below, far away beyond the fields, the wet fur of barren trees looms among a group of dachas. There's something different about the trees this winter—as sensitive as animals, trembling with every blast, retaining all their heat to combat the cold, and warming little black cavities around themselves, where old grass grows a dark green. The bark is damp and vulnerable; you touch it and dark painful sap stains your hands like paint, like blood from an incision. And beyond the dachas, which stretch along a shallow industrial stream overrun with cattails, you can barely make out the wall of the maintenance depot in the gully. The gully, filled with rain and fog, bends toward the city, and the air becomes so dense that you can't see any farther, but there's something over there. That's where it starts, where the city begins. And there's one last thing. Off to the side, on the horizon, where the sky has a milky, tin sheen to it, the factory smokestacks loom—tall, cold, dead. And there isn't a single bird around, as if there's been a great famine and all the birds have been eaten. The front line should be somewhere in there. A real front line. Before, while the city was under siege, Pasha never had to cross it, but today it looks like he'll be crossing that line. "Well, here we go," Pasha thinks, trying to put himself at ease. "Well, here we go."

The last time Pasha took a taxi was a month ago, on his way back from the city. The road was constantly coming under fire, yet everyone thought that their chances of dying weren't as high if they drove fast. They stood there, a dark, frightened pack—Pasha and several women weighed down by bags like they were sins—by an empty gas station at the edge of the city. They were heading back home to the Station. Nobody wanted to pick them up for the longest time.

Eventually, a guy in a Zhiguli slammed on the brakes, coming to a stop right in the middle of a puddle; one of the women motioned at the driver. Pull forward, you expect us to slog through the water? But the driver started yelling with such desperation that everyone wordlessly traipsed through the puddle. He tore away from the gas station, turned into a field, and goaded his car across the black, coal expanse between the city and the Station, not slowing down for a second, not turning his lights on for a second. He blazed ahead, yelling the whole time, laying into those hapless women. They just nodded wordlessly in reply, seemingly agreeing with everything he said. They were like pilgrims at a church—they'd come all that way to repent their sins, so why wouldn't they just go ahead and repent? Pasha wanted to interrupt him and protect the women's dignity, but he didn't interrupt the driver or stand up for them. He even tipped the guy.

The road's in such bad shape that people mostly use it out of respect for its past. They might as well have been driving through black soggy mud. But it seems as though the iguana taxi driver knows this road as well as his own body—he scratches where it itches and rubs where it aches. He crosses himself vigorously when a large wooden cross comes into view on the shoulder and glares at Pasha. Well, are you gonna cross yourself or what? Pasha pretends to be oblivious. Down below, at a fork in the road just before a bridge, are several abandoned checkpoints that look like ravaged birds' nests. Clothing, dishes, newspapers, smashed military supply boxes, sandbags mauled by the wind—all of it lies out in the open, orphaned, burrowing into the ground and mixing with the snow and silt. The Iguana tenses up every time they pass a checkpoint.

Guys have been rotting away here for the past few months, and nobody knows what they've left behind, what surprises might still be in their burrows. Now it's impossible to tell who controlled those checkpoints because everything's burnt out, shredded with shrapnel, and the trees look like the masts on fishermen's ships—sharp, tall, stripped of their branches. Driving over the bridge is particularly scary, since bridges are strategic targets. Each strategic target elicits one desire, first and foremost: to blow it up and send anyone who's decided to cross it flying into the air. The Iguana even shuts his eyes as they pull onto the bridge. Seeing that, Pasha winces, too. They ride like that for a bit, completely in the dark. Fear is an invisible yet all-encompassing thing. You can't see any apparent danger, everything's quiet, and the sky up above is glimmering like a sheet of metal, but the mere realization that you're in the crosshairs and that someone can fucking waste you at any moment, regardless of what color the sky is and what's moving around up there, makes the whole situation unsettling. So you just want to keep sitting there with your eyes closed and count to a hundred, until all the monsters around you recede.

The Iguana cracks first—he steps on the gas, snakes between some cinder blocks with warnings painted on them in red, and surges ahead, down a streaked coal road. Then, before they reach the next hill, he abruptly turns the wheel as they approach a row of low black trees—packed tight with mulberries and sharp acacias—that stretches off to the right. The Opel flops into a snowy pit like a dog into a foamy wave, skids hard, spitting up black earth and ice, and then keeps moving, moving forward. It gradually crawls out of the snowy mush, kicks some up on the grass sprinkled with gravel that conceals an old, barely visible path, gets firm ground under its wheels, keeps slipping on the wet clay, and then pushes ahead, along a row of mulberries as black as newspaper headlines.

"Where are you going?" Pasha asks, frightened. "What if there are mines?"

"Mines? You gotta be kidding," the Iguana replies wrathfully. "Nobody's been out here for two years, look how tall the grass is."

The grass is smacking the undercarriage of the Opel and poking at the windows; there would've been no getting out of this thicket if someone hadn't thought to sprinkle the road with gravel, unseen, yet felt—it crunches under the tires, like an apple in your mouth, dully turning over under the rubber. The Iguana steps on the gas with relish; the translucent afternoon sun dangles right above them in the sky.

"Used to be able to get back to the dachas this way," the Iguana explains with relish. "Now the road's all overgrown, see?"

They ride down the invisible path for a while, squashing dry weeds and hugging the trees so nobody can spot them, even though there are so many gaps that the January gusts blow right through. Hide all you want—you'll still have some serious explaining to do at the first checkpoint. The first dachas are up ahead, their fences visible through the mulberries. The trees end abruptly—then comes a flat field that's been ripped up by moles, followed by a street as quiet as death. Once again an inexpressible fear overcomes Pasha; once again he wants to close his eyes and hide under the covers. Meanwhile, the Iguana decides to go for it; he steps on the gas and turns off, right into a ravine, where a stream should be flowing. And the car slides down the field, bouncing up on every molehill; the dachas remain up above, while they nearly slide into the stream, and there are cow paths running alongside it, and the Iguana heads down these cow paths, going faster and faster, farther and farther away from the empty dacha windows. Pasha can't help but look back, and he spots smashed, angry shutters, but those shutters are no longer relevant to him and the Iguana. They fly past a patch of cattails, pull onto a concrete surface, whiz down the lousy yet hard road for a long time, an inexpressibly long time, and then they're driving through the high entrance of the maintenance depot.

The road gets better, but the Iguana doesn't speed up. Instead, he slows down, starts listening intently and looking all around. Pasha rolls down his window. Outside it smells faintly of a swamp and dead grass. They push on. The outer wall keeps going and going; eventually, a gate—blue, metal, wide open—appears up ahead. The Iguana pulls up carefully. It's quiet and empty—feels like somebody has just stepped out but will be coming back. That kind of silence, it scares them, presses down on them. And there's something over there behind the gate, right on the ground, between torn work overalls and a stained rag. Something that doesn't belong. The Iguana slows down and looks over there, transfixed. Pasha sticks his head out the window; he wants to catch a glimpse, too.

"What is it?" he asks, frightened. "Huh? What is it?"

"Dogs," the Iguana answers, swallowing hard. "Somebody shot 'em."

"But why?"

"Who the fuck knows?" the Iguana explains. "Maybe so they wouldn't make any noise."

There are two dogs. Big, dark, unknown breed. They lie there in the dirty water, one next to the other. The blood underneath them has soaked into the snow and asphalt; red fur has clumped together around their wounds. Scowls hardened by death, sharp yet now completely harmless fangs, glass-button eyes, black paws. Empty lot, open gate. The Iguana drives on wordlessly. The sun comes out for a brief instant. Pasha looks at its rays, shielding his face with his hand and then looks over at the Iguana—it seems like the Iguana's eyes are moist. Probably the sun.

To their left, the concrete wall stretches on and on, and a gas pipe painted yellow runs on their right. The pipe's broken in a few places. It looks like a bone that needs tending to. There's nobody to tend to it, though—empty street, not a single person on the main road, just burned metal up ahead; it looks like somebody chewed a piece of overcooked meat for a while and then set it aside to cool. The Iguana carefully skirts the burned heap.

"That's a tank," he says. "A T-64. Those things burn like firewood."

"But how'd it get that way?" Pasha asks.

"What's the difference?" the Iguana answers. "You shoulda seen it before. There were two corpses inside. I kept coming over here all week. You'd think somebody woulda taken 'em away."

"Why didn't you do it?" Pasha suddenly turns toward him.

"What fuckin' good would they do me?" the Iguana answers harshly, his cap sharply and menacingly aimed straight at Pasha.

Pasha doesn't know what to say. He turns toward the window. The Iguana looks at the road, not saying anything either.

"It's scary," the Iguana says unexpectedly. "Holding something that's dead is scary. What don't you get?"

Pasha just nods, discreetly rubbing his hands together, as if they're cold. They keep going. The wall keeps going, too, eventually running into the main road that leads to the city. There are two-story houses behind the main road; mostly workers from the maintenance depot live here. Pasha scans the windows warily; half of them are smashed, half of them are covered with plywood or plastic sheets. They're all dark. No people. Pasha thinks about how the last time they saw real, living people was by the motel, but those people were so damn angry that they weren't like people at all. There was Anna, too, but he didn't even catch a glimpse of her. "I wonder what she looks like," Pasha thinks. "Would I recognize her if I saw her?" There was Hans, too. Pasha thinks of Hans—his heavy eyes, the lazy movement of his shoulders—shudders, and starts looking around. The Iguana pulls up to the main road and hesitates. He rolls down the window, sticks his leather head outside, and listens tensely. It seems as if he's sniffing the air, but the air has a burned, dead smell to it, so he can't do too much sniffing. So the Iguana sticks his head back inside and retreats into his burrow, rolling the window up quickly and anxiously.

"Looks clear," he says to Pasha, mouthing the words. "Wanna try?"

"Okay," Pasha replies, also mouthing.

They carefully crawl up the hill. The wall stays behind, while a panorama of a wide road and a low-hanging sky opens up to the left. There's so much sky that it's all you can see, but your eyes adjust to the sheer abundance of air. The Iguana and Pasha spot a white-and-gray bus with busted windows and soldiers crowded around it. It's unclear who they are: no flags, can't make out any insignia from the car, and Pasha doesn't know much about insignias anyway. Dark and apprehensive, they stand there, holding their guns and looking straight at them. Straight at their Opel. Their expressions are intent and surprised, seemingly asking, "Who are you? Where'd you come from?" The Iguana even crouches at the wheel, slowing down involuntarily, and all he wants to do right now is put it in reverse and roll back, behind the wall, but Pasha realizes that there's no going back. Just don't go back, anything but going back.

"C'mon," he hisses at the Iguana. "C'mon, step on it." And the Iguana steps on it obediently, yet timidly, turns, and then advances forward slowly, very slowly, the way kids walk to the bathroom in the middle of the night—carefully, slowly, groping ahead, afraid they're going to bump into an open door. And both of them, Pasha and the Iguana, look in the mirror, scared, and see one soldier break away from the group and aim his Kalashnikov at their Opel, which is slowly receding, and they see one of his buddies touching his arm. Forget it. Don't. But he shrugs his friend's hand off and raises his Kalashnikov again. And Pasha thinks to himself, "Maybe I should get out of the car, talk to him, explain everything, and show him my papers? But who is he? Who are those guys? How do you talk to them?" At this point, there's nowhere to hide; the Iguana's practically paralyzed, and Pasha's head is sinking into his shoulders. "Should've gone home," he says to himself, eyes fixed on the soldier, who's looking at them with thrilled disdain. But behind the soldiers, somewhere out there, beyond the hill, the silence suddenly shatters—there's an explosion, soldiers drop to the ground like ripe apples onto wet grass, the guy who was aiming at them drops to the asphalt, too, and scurries to the side of the road, and that's the last of it Pasha sees, since the Iguana rams the gas pedal into the depths of the Opel with his foot. They fly down the empty road under the wet skies—afternoon sunlight bursts through in blinding spots like pools of thaw water, and all the water around them flares into a thousand sparkles, the way it does in March. But then the skies close like elevator doors, and once again everything's damp and silvery.

When they get down to the traffic circle, the Iguana goes the wrong way, dodges a barricade made out of wooden pallets, and whizzes down a wide, empty street. He whizzes along and whips into the square next to the train station. It's empty, too—it seems like everyone who wanted to leave did so a long time ago. He slows down.

"That's it," he yells at Pasha. "Hop out." Pasha does hop out, paying as he's lunging out of the car. He even has enough time to take umbrage at the fare. He's always paid what they've told him to pay, he's never taken umbrage before, but something stings him this time—they were scared, together, they were on edge, together. "What are you rippin' me off for?" Pasha thinks indignantly. But he pays the full fare, goddammit, he always pays what they tell him to pay.

The train station is painted yellow, but the paint has become dark and heavy in the rain. The national flags have been prudently taken down from the columns—the army's leaving the city, don't want to agitate the newcomers. The wastebaskets attached to the columns are filled to the brim with bright wrappers and plastic. There are several bloody bandages on top, draped over empty Coke bottles. The blood's bright, too. Nobody has emptied the wastebaskets in a while. Even the pigeons are steering clear of them. "Yeah, where are they?" Pasha thinks, squinting all around. "Where is everybody?" Remnants of snow on the roof, gnarled trees nearby, the skies settling frigidly. Pasha's eyes slide up and then down, and he suddenly notices them—hundreds of warm clumps of birds are clenched like fists, hundreds of bird beaks are aimed down at him, hundreds of round eyes, frozen from constant fear. Pigeons are huddled against one another, perched high up above the columns, under the awning of the station, nestling into one another like they're cold. But they're scared, not cold: scared of the racket behind the factory, scared of the silence of the surrounding streets, scared of the mercury gleam in the sky, scared that nobody's around. Scared of Pasha, who appeared out of the blue and is hanging around outside the station, yes, scared of him, too. They're keeping their eyes, as round as the sun, fixed on him. Pasha immediately feels uneasy, standing there with all the birds' exacting eyes on him. "I wonder how many of them there are up there. How'd they all cram in there?" he thinks. "What if something happens to the train station? What if it burns down? What then? Where would they go? Where would they hide?" Suddenly, he starts to feel so sorry for them, as well as for the kid—what the hell is he still doing at that orphanage? Should've picked him up ages ago. His mom's an idiot, just dumping him off there like that, but does that mean Pasha and his old man can't look after him? Of course they can. Should've started a while ago, especially considering the state he's in. "I'm always putting everything off, never have enough time for the most important things, I'm always avoiding everything, stepping aside. I don't have the guts to say what I think and think what I want. When's this all going to end?" Pasha asks himself. And he starts to feel so sorry for himself, too, as sorry as he feels for the birds that are looking at him the way they would at a hunter—their expressions doomed yet intrigued. And just as Pasha's starting to really feel sorry for himself, he lowers his eyes and sees the windows. Through the windows he sees dozens of eyes with that same bird look—exacting and doomed. They vigilantly track his every movement, his every step, watching through the unwashed station windows, transfixed and mistrustful. And at this instant, Pasha realizes that the station is packed with people; they're hunkering down inside, like it's a church in a besieged city. They think that nobody can get to them there, looking through the windows at a world that's implacably narrowing, shrinking. When spurts of fire snap dryly on the next street over, Pasha finally comes to his senses. He darts toward the station door, rams his shoulder into it, pressing himself into it, but it won't budge. Then another spurt crackles in the air, and Pasha panics, scratching at the door like a drowning man at the bottom of a steamboat, until a hand, a tiny child's hand, pushes the door in his direction. "Pull, not push," Pasha says to himself, yanking on the door. The scent of hundreds of frightened, sleep-deprived people, the smell of fear and sweat, the heavy blend of hysteria and sleeplessness hits him in the face. Pasha lunges inside and finds himself amid warm bodies and wet silence. "They can all see," Pasha thinks. "They can all see how scared I am, how freaked out I am. They're looking at me like I'm some sort of clown. Well, I am a clown. Why the hell did I come all the way down here anyway?" He takes off his glasses (coming inside made them fog up), wipes them with his sweater sleeve, puts them back on (he always seems to be fixing them), and looks around cockily. Yes, I'm listening now. Anything you wanted to say, huh? And he notices, with a certain degree of disappointment, that nobody, nobody at all, is paying any attention to him, that nobody's even looking at him, that everyone who could get a spot by the windows is peering out at the big, wide world. It's as if they've run in here to get out of the rain and now they're gazing at the sky, waiting for the storm to pass. Everyone who couldn't get a spot by the windows is balled up on the benches and in the corners, anticipating something, who knows what. Pasha's standing in the middle of this frightened, fragrant crowd, and he realizes that he has no particular reason to stay put, either, that he has to keep moving. So he starts moving, starts making his way through the viscous crowd like he's wading through autumn water without taking off any of his clothes.

Just women and children—no men. Pasha's the only person with a beard. It feels like he's just stepped into a women's prison. "Where are the men?" he asks himself. "Maybe men aren't allowed in here? Maybe they're all out doing something important, and I'm standing here with my dumb-ass beard like I'm waiting for a train? Maybe the men are already gone and they left their women here in the luggage rooms?" At this moment, somebody shrieks wildly in the corner, and everyone looks over; the room freezes for just a second. Then it starts buzzing and yelling incoherently—the women peel away from the window, lifting their drowsy heads off their neighbors' shoulders, popping out from behind the columns. The outcry doesn't abate; moreover, some distinct words and tones come through, and Pasha understands, not with his head but with his lungs, that this has to do with a child. So he darts into the crowd, trying to push his way through. He catches the women's all-encompassing scent, the breath and smell of a hundred women, the smell of abandoned homes and hastily gathered bundles, the smell of outbursts and grievances that can't be addressed to anyone. He pushes forward. "Let me through," he says. "Let me through, I'm a teacher, let me through." But nobody is really listening to him. Also, you can't hear all that much amid the wailing and shrieking that keeps coming and coming from the corner, never relenting. Pasha basically hops on some woman's shoulders, and she gives up her spot right away, glaring loudly at him. But he doesn't care; he barrels into the corner and sees a woman on the floor. She's wearing nice—well, expensive—clothes: a pink leather jacket and high-heeled boots. She's sitting on the floor on a folded piece of cardboard, squeezing a little girl, about two years old. She's squeezing her hard, like somebody's going to take the girl away from her, and she's hollering so everyone understands that's not going to happen. The thing is, everyone's more than willing to protect the woman in pink, but they can't understand what they're supposed to protect her from. The child can't understand what's going on with her mom, why she's hanging on to her like that, what she wants from her. She isn't used to seeing her mom like this, so she lets out a frightened scream. And the women gathered around start yelling like somebody's being strangled. Pasha realizes that if this goes on any longer somebody really is going to get strangled, so he sits down beside the woman and begins talking to her. But she just looks at him, her eyes dead with fear, and keeps wailing. Then Pasha snaps, grabbing the woman's head with his left hand and yanking her toward him.

"What?" he hisses right in her face. "What? Well?" The woman focuses her deathly eyes on his glasses and suddenly says—it's more of a forced sob, actually:

"Took it right off my hand . . . while we were sleeping."

"What'd they take?" Pasha asks, bewildered.

"The gold," the woman howls. "They took the gold."

"Who did it?" Pasha asks, trying to take her daughter out of her arms.

"I don't know." She just squeezes the girl even closer to her chest. "I don't know. We were sleeping."

"Who took it?" Pasha gets up and looks around. "Who?"

He's speaking quietly, but he can tell that everyone's listening to him. They listen, not even bothering to hide their staring. They watch him, their eyes heavy, sticky, yet devoid of fear. They're watching. Who are you? Where'd you come from? What are you doing here? Pasha watches them, too, his eyes sliding across their faces—drowsy, embittered, wet with tears—and he realizes that he really is the only man here, and he doesn't elicit any trust, just suspicion and irritation. It's as though he's herded them in here into this building and locked it from the inside so nobody can get out, so everybody knows that he's caused all the problems around here, that it's all his fault, that he—bearded Pasha, the teacher in the warm jacket who wormed his way into the crowd, sniffing around and probing for information—will have to answer for everything. Pasha can't take their eyes on him and the silence any longer; he can't take the wailing behind him and the child's sharp, wet shrieking.

"Who took it? I'm asking you, who? Why won't you answer me?"

The women won't answer him, but they do step aside. Two figures emerge from behind them. The first guy's stocky, like he's been stomped down—coarse hair and light, sun-faded eyes. He looks like a supervisor—well, an ex-supervisor, a guy who doesn't have anyone reporting to him—in a camo jacket with a collar made of some dead beaver and ironed pleated pants tucked into his blue rubber boots. Walking behind him is this really young, snotty-nosed guy with red, angry, swollen eyes; it looks like he was playing a computer game all night, and he lost. Jerky movements, jagged gait, jacket with some sparkles on it, kid's footwear, dark green sneakers that have gotten even darker from all the water. "Guess there still are some men here. Not all of them left. The best ones stuck around," Pasha thinks.

"What's going on here?" Stocky asks.

He's talking, mixing the two languages, standing in front of Pasha, not looking straight at him, addressing his question to someplace off to the side, like he's talking to spirits. He's talking, his stomach solidly and skillfully pushing Pasha into the corner, toward the woman and the girl, who's quieted down, intrigued by these new characters.

"So," Pasha begins explaining. "Basically, this woman was sleeping . . . next to her child, and they took their gold." He's involuntarily mixing the two languages, too. "Yeah, basically, she was sleeping, and they took their gold . . . ," Pasha says, his tone less assured.

"And who are you?" Stocky asks him, even though he's looking at the woman, whose face has several band-aids on it—either somebody hit her or she fell. So Pasha doesn't know if he should answer or let the woman answer for him.

"Me?" he asks, just in case.

"Yeah, you," says Stocky. "Maybe you're the one who took it?"

"Me?" Pasha asks with a flustered sigh.

He chokes on the warm, stale station air, about to give Stocky a piece of his mind, but somebody beats him to the punch.

"Yeah, it was him all right," a lady with gold teeth says quietly yet firmly.

Pasha turns toward the voice. Rage takes the wind out of him; he wants to see that lady, get a good look at her. He searches for her eyes but only sees her teeth shining dimly in the crowd. Pasha finds himself thinking that he's never seen so much gold. "Maybe that's the gold that got taken," he thinks. "Maybe she took it and hid it under her tongue. Yeah, it's gotta be hard to talk with it in your mouth, but nobody'll take it from you at least." He lurches forward, looking to give her a piece of his mind, but Stocky flings his hand out. Pasha runs into this barrier, bounces back, and then charges into the crowd again, but this time Stocky flings out all five of his chubby splayed fingers covered with fair, seemingly bleached hair. Pasha looks at those fingers and steps back, scared.

"Freeze," Stocky says. "Freeze. Who are you?"

"A teacher," Pasha answers.

"A teacher? Oh, please!" yells another woman, who, incidentally, also has gold teeth. "He took it!"

"Quiet down," Stocky replies, lifting his heavy hand. "We'll sort this out. Papers," he says, turning toward Pasha.

"Gotta ask who he is," Pasha thinks. "Don't even think about handing him your papers." And then he reaches for his papers right away. Stocky interprets that in his own way, intercepts Pasha's arm, wrings it like a wet sheet, and spins Pasha toward the wall. The ladies all start carrying on at once.

"It was him!" they yell. "It was definitely him! He's been bumming around here. It was him!"

"Quiet down," Stocky interrupts them and then turns to the side and issues an order to the young guy. "Check his pockets."

"Who do you think you are?" Pasha eventually forces out a question, shaking his head.

"Shut your trap," the young guy advises him and begins rooting through his pockets. He takes out a pack of gum, some tissues, then some coins, then some paper clips. Then all of it slips out of his hands and spills across the sticky floor. Then he reaches into the pockets of Pasha's jeans, takes out his wallet, makes a big show of opening it up in front of everyone—to clear himself of any suspicion—picks through it with obvious interest, takes out some old receipts, a shopper's card, and package slips from the post office. He counts the bills, pauses for a split second—"C'mon, c'mon," Stocky says, nodding at him—stuffs the wallet back into Pasha's pocket, pats him down with his hands, as bony as the Grim Reaper's, and then reaches into Pasha's backpack. He digs around in there as if he owns the place, pulls out some sandwiches, a bottle of water, and a shabby old detective novel. Pasha's just standing there, looking down into the corner at the woman pressing the girl against herself, while the woman's looking at Pasha as if she's never doubted, not even for a minute of her hapless life, that it was him, Pasha, this bearded, bespectacled geek, who took her gold. Then Pasha gets spun around abruptly, so now he's facing his peers.

"Why the fuck are you roaming around without your papers?" the young guy asks, seemingly speaking not to Pasha but rather to the whole gold-toothed pack of women. "Huh?" he says in a theatrically pushy tone.

"I have my papers," Pasha answers, aggrieved, and he feels like he's about to burst into tears, and everyone will see him, a real big dude with a beard standing there and crying, and they'll all laugh at him.

They don't let him cry, though. Stocky turns around with Pasha, shoves him forward, and they cleave through the sticky margarine of the crowd. "Take it easy," Stocky yells up at the ceiling, seemingly addressing the birds. "We'll sort everything out." The birds don't answer.

The train station attendant's nest looks like a death row inmate's cell, cramped and poorly ventilated. The curtains are drawn, so you don't know what's going on in the main hall. The screen of the computer on the desk is all taped up, and last year's calendar is taped to the glass. A cup filled with coins and tacks, a calculator, several trade union newspapers. It's hard to like your customers when your work space looks like this. Oh yeah, and there's a portable television, too—red, caked with dust, as if someone's sprinkled ashes on it—it looks like a mini gas chamber. Pasha's led inside, over to the wall. Stocky locks the door and tucks the key into his pocket. "At least he didn't swallow it," Pasha thinks as he observes all this. He goes to sit down in an office chair, but the young guy beats him to it—he plops down and immediately turns on the TV. Nothing's really on—just some shadows walking through smoke, bleeding profusely, and showering the camera with curses. Stocky sits down, too, right on the desk, ass on the calculator. He tosses his camo jacket to the young guy, who just sits there with his arms extended, like he's holding the bread and salt at a welcoming ceremony. Stocky crosses his arms on his chest and occasionally scratches his jaw—that's him sorting everything out. He's wearing a dark green vest under his jacket; it goes with his boots. Pasha eventually reaches into his inside pocket, takes out his papers, and hands them to Stocky, wordlessly. He flips through Pasha's little blue threadbare passport wordlessly, stops when he gets to the picture (Pasha quickly takes off his glasses and aims his weak eyes at nothing in particular), and finds the line listing his place of residence.

"From the Station, yeah?" he asks calmly.

"Yeah," Pasha answers.

"You're a teacher?"

"Yeah."

"Why didn't you say so?"

Pasha is on the verge of tears again, but he can't cry here. He starts making excuses—there was no time, I was confused, should've repeated myself, you didn't hear me, you didn't get what I meant. He keeps talking and talking, thinking to himself, "Who am I even talking to? Who are these guys? What are they doing in this office? Should ask 'em, really should."

Before he can ask, somebody knocks on the little window built into the wall of the office. The young guy spins around in his chair like a weathervane, opens the narrow embrasure, leans forward, listens and listens, hearing someone out for a while, for an eternity, while they cry and gripe for a while, for an eternity, and then he begins answering. His voice is hollow; half of what he's saying is unintelligible—and that's from inside the office. One can only imagine what those craving information, those on the other side of the window, are making out. He's speaking resolutely, as if he's been containing himself for a while because he didn't have an audience, but now he has the floor—now he has the chance to say whatever he wants.

"No," he says. "There won't be. And there won't be tomorrow either," he adds. "Or the day after that," he says, getting all riled up. "There won't be one going there, or one coming from there, either. Nothing's running." He paints a pretty sad picture. "He's gone," he declares. "Him, too. They're gone. Everyone's gone!" he exclaims, robbing the passengers on the other side of the window of any hope.

But they aren't retreating, aren't giving up. They keep trying to squeeze something out of him, anything at all. But he isn't about to reveal his railroad secrets just like that. "Where?" he asks, surprised. "Fucked if I know." Viewing that as an exhaustive answer, he shuts the embrasure, and turns toward Pasha and Stocky. There's a timid knock on the window. He slams his fist against the glass without even turning around. Silence falls on the other side.

"So are you station attendants or something?" Pasha asks, flustered.

"Yep," Stocky answers him. "Hey, Teach, hope you're not mad at us for twisting your arm and dragging you on the floor like that. There's all kinds of shady types floating around in here with our people. You know what it's like. Our bosses just fuckin' took off. They left us in charge. No hard feelings, right?"

Pasha's not mad anymore. He just kind of loosened up after "Teach." He fixes his glasses with his pointer finger and hates himself for doing it.

"Where do ya need to go?" Stocky asks him.

"I just wanted to duck in here and wait it out. Then I'll get going," Pasha replies.

He finishes talking and hears a trembling outside. You might think it's about to rain—that is, if you don't look out the window. Stocky hears the rumbling, too; he hears the rumbling coming closer and closer, so he's in no hurry to pump Pasha for answers. He simply says: "All right then, you can go. Just don't step on any mines."

"Where are they?" Pasha asks, flustered.

"All over the place," Stocky shouts cheerfully, and starts laughing, giving the young guy a playful punch on the arm. But the young guy isn't laughing; he's moving his jaw muscles up and down, his expression malicious.

"I gotta get to the orphanage," Pasha interrupts him eventually.

Silence sets in immediately. Stocky exchanges a meaningful glance with his colleague, who just whistles in reply.

"Oh man, for real?" Stocky asks.

"What's the big deal?" Pasha answers anxiously. "My nephew's over there."

"Wow." Stocky nods. "Wow."

"Yeah, what's the big deal?" Pasha asks in a slightly combative tone.

But they just nod, still not saying anything. The young guy stops moving his jaw muscles; he sits there, sullenly examining his green sneakers. One might think that for him those sneakers are the problem—if he had different sneakers he'd be in a much better mood.

"So?" Pasha cracks first.

"All right," Stocky finally ventures to say something. "All right, Pasha," he says, calling Pasha by his name for the first time. "So in about an hour, Alyosha," he starts, pointing at the young guy, "is going to take a group past the retention basin and out to the edge of town. He'll take you to the fork in the road, by the meat-packing plant. You know the spot, right?"

"Yeah."

"Head out with the group. You'll just peel off by the plant. Go down into the gully and then up the other side. The orphanage's over there. Got it?"

"Got it. Where's he taking them?"

"Out of the city," Stocky explains. "How are you planning on getting out, huh?"

"Getting out of where?"

"Out of here."

Pasha doesn't say anything, and they let it go—the answer's obvious. "I'm trapped," Pasha thinks frantically. "God, I'm trapped."

"So? Are you in?" Stocky asks him. Pasha weighs his options.

"Yeah," he agrees, his voice tense. "Yeah," he repeats with more conviction.

"Well, come back here over to the window in an hour," Stocky replies.

"Okay. Will do."

He wants to leave, but Stocky isn't opening the door. He gives Pasha an inquisitive look, seemingly waiting for a specific response.

"How much?" Pasha asks, when he figures out what it is.

"Nothing at all." Stocky flashes a kind smile. Then he pulls the calculator out from under his ass, presses some buttons, and adds in a confiding tone. "Well, what do you got on you? You probably got a hundred, right? I'll just take that."

Pasha pays what they tell him to pay. Stocky takes out some keys, opens the door, warily peers out into the hallway, quickly lets Pasha out, and locks the door from the inside. "Feels like I just went to confession," Pasha thinks as he walks back to the waiting area.

It hits somewhere close by. Thing is, you can't ever tell where the next one will hit. There are explosions all over the place—behind the tracks, behind the main avenue in town. Everyone huddles by the walls; muffled howling follows the blast and then it gets quiet again. After that, the silence outside snaps and wailing follows.

"It's on fire!" someone suddenly yells by the entrance, and everyone runs over to look out the window. Pasha peers out, too; he stands next to the crowd that nearly ripped him to shreds with its gold teeth just half an hour ago and sees greasy black smoke behind some high-rises—so greasy and so black that it looks like they've been burning corpses back there. "Where's the fire? Where?" asks a short little woman in a black coat. Her red, frozen hands keep fixing her hair as it spills out from underneath her beret. Where? Eventually, she realizes where and she releases a wild, full-throated scream, frightening the already frightened birds and children. "What? What's over there?" the women standing behind her ask one another, and the petrified children ask, "What? What's going on?" And everyone realizes what's going on over there—clearly she lives in one of those high-rises, and clearly there's a fire somewhere over there. So let her yell, let her yell it all out. There's nothing you can do. Pasha turns around, walks across the main hall, turns down a corridor, passes black bodies lying by the wall, huddled by the radiators—it's safer by the radiators—and ducks in response to every flash in the sky, to every sound outside. He squats down when a blast goes off nearby, right behind the train cars, and he scurries over to the luggage room, hunched over, squeezes between some bodies, finds a little crevice by a column, plops down, curls up, shuts up.

Somebody's nestling against his shoulder, slipping under his arm. "That lady," Pasha figures. "That lady with the gold under her tongue." She sits there, afraid to move a muscle. "Let 'er snuggle," he thinks. "Let 'er warm up. When's the last time I lay next to a woman like this?" He thinks and thinks, trying to recall, and thinks some more, but then gives up. "It'll come to me later," he thinks. "It's nice and warm. I'm safe here and it smells like a woman." Granted, the woman smells kind of funny, like someone who walked around in the rain in a fur coat and then slipped under the covers next to you. Now there's this canine smell—something living, something from the street, something stray. Pasha casts a sideways glance—yep, it's a dog. Just how on earth did he get in here? Wet, gray fur, dark, frightened eyes. Pasha wants to nudge him over; he touches the dog's spine and feels him tremble resignedly. C'mon, get outta here. But the dog resists, turns his muzzle toward Pasha, and looks him in the eye, hinting that he doesn't have anywhere to go. Just like Pasha. "This just isn't right," Pasha thinks. "Dogs should be protective, dogs should snarl. This one's lying here, burying his head under my arm, like he doesn't want to see anyone."

He's just like the rest of the bunch here—averting their eyes, wrapping themselves in blankets, burrowing into their clothes like fish in silt. An old guy's sitting on a chair in the far corner. Old woman's coat, soggy fur hat. He clearly brought the chair from home. He's holding some taped-up pillows. Everyone who ran away took something; they're lugging whatever it was around now. Apparently he decided that there was no point in setting off without his pillows. Pasha looks around, studying the crowd. People sleeping on blankets or on the bare floor. People who've hung their bags all over themselves so not a single one gets stolen. Some people have even rolled their suitcases all the way here. But generally, their belongings are sparse. Makes sense—they were in a rush, so they grabbed whatever was at hand. Documents and valuables, mostly. Now they're sitting here and suspiciously surveying their surroundings—when you have gold earrings in your pocket you're a bit reluctant to make friends with strangers down by the luggage room. Pasha catches those glances, the glances of people who might be about to have something taken away from them, which makes them so vulnerable, defenseless. There's no finding their bracelets and cash in their homes. Just try it. But here, just root around in their pockets or under their shirts—you'll find everything, you'll take everything away. They realize that, so they have this hounded look about them; their eyes slide down other people's bodies, and when their eyes rest on you, fear and animosity immediately appear in those eyes. The dog can sense that, too—nobody wants him here, nobody's keeping him here, and the most he can count on is someone's weakness, not their magnanimity. Maybe that's why he unerringly chose Pasha.

This time, the impact is right over his head. So close the lights go out. In the darkness, the women start wailing again. The dog buries himself even deeper under Pasha's arm. Pasha would be more than glad to hide under someone's arm, too, but there's no arm like that in the station. After a while, the lights come back on—the lamps flicker, faintly illuminating the hallway. The women immediately regain their composure—they take out their food, root around in their bags, check their pockets. Pasha can't stand it anymore; he gets up and heads for the exit. The dog slinks after him, obviously. They pass through the dark waiting area and look out the windows. The smoke behind the high-rises has settled in the rain. It's quiet outside; seems like the shelling is over. Now it's even harder to breathe in the main hall. Outside the window the dark silver of the January sky has spilled all over. Pasha pushes his way toward the window. The women track his every move discontentedly. Pasha feels like a criminal who's come back to the scene of the crime. "What am I standing here for?" he thinks. "What am I waiting for? Something's gonna come flying in here and knock all the tiles off these walls, and I'll get smacked right in the head, and nobody'll ever dig me out. When's Alyosha gonna take us outta here?" Pasha produces his phone and checks the time. Another half hour. "Where's he going to take us? Traipsing down the railroad tracks through an industrial park with a bunch of women—what kind of idea is that? Don't see us getting far. C'mon, get the hell out of here," Pasha says to himself and walks decisively toward the door. He freezes in front of it, feeling weakness and indecisiveness sweep through his body, starting from his lungs. But he exhales deeply, pushes the door, and steps outside. The door shuts behind him immediately. But the dog manages to slip through first.

So Pasha's standing in the doorway; once again, he hears the pigeons breathing overhead and contemplates the sky as dark threads of intermittent smoke float by. "I'll run across the street," he figures. "Go past those houses and get to the high-rises that way. Seems like they're done shelling this place. If I get stopped, I'll tell 'em I'm going home." He runs his hands through his pockets—papers, wallet, keys, phone. He can leave now, but he isn't leaving. He's just standing there. Something's wrong, but he can't put his finger on it. It's too quiet. Incredibly quiet. Unfamiliarly quiet. Over the past few months, he's grown so accustomed to the air quivering. It was quivering just an hour ago. The lights disappeared just half an hour ago. But now it's quiet. And empty. And smoke flows across the sky quietly and sorrowfully. In this silence Pasha suddenly starts to discern a rumbling of sorts. Something's moving by the main avenue, moving in his direction. That something isn't visible, but the rumbling's becoming more expressive, more threatening. And it'd be nice to hide somewhere from that rumbling, curl up under someone's arm, and wait it out in the corner, eyes shut in fear. Panic overcomes Pasha. "What should I do?" he thinks.

"Where should I run?" And the pigeons overhead begin rustling their wings anxiously. And the women behind him are glued to the windows, peering outside, yet not understanding what's going on—what's that rumbling? Where's it coming from? Pasha's standing, turned to stone on the empty, soggy steps, and he feels all these eyes on him: the tense eyes of the women, the mistrustful eyes of the birds, and another set of eyes—the eyes of something unknown that's staring at him from nowhere. And when there's too much anticipation, so much that his heart starts to ache, a tank—dirty, green, logs attached to the back, three passengers on top—barrels around the corner and into the square. It turns sharply and careens toward the train station. It pulls right up to the steps with the columns, releases some menacing smoke, and comes to a sudden stop. "A T-64," Pasha thinks automatically, connecting the dots. The turret's moving slowly, very slowly, aiming the gun right at Pasha. "It's gonna fire," Pasha thinks, too afraid to even swallow. "It's gonna nail me." He feels cold sweat soaking his T-shirt, feels like he can't feel his feet, and feels like he can't feel anything at all. He's watching the gun, mesmerized. And the three guys sitting on top are watching Pasha with genuine interest—where the hell'd you come from, Four Eyes? They're yelling back and forth cheerfully; Pasha can't hear what they're saying, but it's obvious they're talking about him, and it's obvious that they don't have anything nice to say. Dirty uniforms, smoke-stained faces, heavy, crusty deposits of earth on their shoes. And the flag hanging over the turret—dark and soiled, like a bandage that's been pressed against an open wound for a long time. Pasha can't even make out the color, but it's not the same flag hanging over his school. "Just don't move," Pasha cautions himself. "Stay put."

And then the tank stalls, and it gets really quiet. And the birds nestle against one another. And the women on the other side of the windows watch, quiet. And the dog hides between Pasha's legs, timidly scanning the strangers. One of the soldiers, the guy sitting right by the turret and hugging the gun, yells:

"Hey, c'mon, c'mon!"

Pasha looks around, not knowing what to do.

"Come over here, c'mon!" the soldier yells cheerfully.

At this point, Pasha realizes that the soldier's not yelling to him. He's yelling to the dog. "He's mine," Pasha decides. "I'm not gonna give him up, no matter what." The soldier's already rooting through his pockets, though. He produces a mushed-up Snickers, rips it open, takes a bite, and tosses the rest onto the asphalt, right in front of the tank. The dog immediately springs to his feet and walks down the hill, tail between his legs. He grabs the Snickers, greedily devours it, and lies down next to the tank, trying not to look at Pasha. The soldiers laugh, and Pasha gives them a flustered smile. What's so funny, though?

Then the guy who yelled stands up and jumps down onto the asphalt. Chunks of dirt fly off his heels every which way. He fixes his rifle sling and pulls a gray keffiyeh off his face. Tall, well-built, athletic. The left half of his head is gray, which makes him look like an arctic fox. His gaze is foxlike, too—predatory and mistrustful. Black kneepads, shabby bulletproof vest, fingerless leather gloves. The two other guys jump down after him. They're dirty, too; one of them is in a warm coat, the other in a leather jacket, camo underneath. They go up a few steps, stop in front of Pasha, and look up at him from below, but he doesn't forget, even for an instant, who's in charge.

"Who are you?" asks the guy with the keffiyeh, the Arctic Fox. He's speaking Russian, but he has a strange accent, like he's only heard the language spoken on television. The sun emerges from the fog for an instant, gleaming on his gray hair.

Pasha delivers his usual spiel: school, winter break, orphanage, nephew. He takes out his papers.

"Local guy?" the Arctic Fox asks, surprised. "Why aren't you fighting?"

"Health problems," Pasha replies and looks at his papers in the soldier's hands—is he gonna give them back?

He toys with Pasha's papers, flips through the shabby pages again, fixes his keffiyeh again, shuts Pasha's passport, pauses briefly, and hands everything back.

"What's wrong with you?" he asks.

Pasha shows him his right hand, desperately trying to spread his fingers.

"What?" The soldier's confused.

"He's got a problem with his fingers," the guy in the leather jacket says behind him. "See?"

Pasha keeps showing him his hand, just in case, seemingly to confirm what the other man said—yeah, I got a problem. The Arctic Fox scrutinizes Pasha's hand mistrustfully and then quickly loses interest in Pasha and in his problem.

"Who's in there?" He nods at the train station.

"Women and children," Pasha says, tucking his papers into the inside pocket of his jacket.

"Any soldiers?"

"I didn't see any."

"Are you armed?"

Pasha doesn't reply.

"You gotta be kidding me. Him?" says the guy in the leather jacket, laughing. "Let's get going."

The Arctic Fox turns around and whistles for the dog to come over. He runs over obediently, not raising his eyes to Pasha, and tags along with the soldiers. The Arctic Fox walks up to the door and pulls on it resolutely. All four of them, including the dog, disappear into the building.

"You can all go to hell," Pasha says, and shuffles off to the first platform.

In the winter, he always remembers his childhood. Black trees buried in the snow, a line of workers trudging away from the station like hunters coming home. The golden commuter train, the blue shadows at dusk. It's winter now, too, and the holiday season has yet to come to a close. Rain and fog fill the ground with water, and the sheer abundance of moisture makes the sky look like a drowned man brought ashore—bloated body, blue tint on a gray backdrop. You don't even want to look at a sky like that. And Pasha isn't looking; he's sitting on a bench and incredulously examining last year's grass—it's poking through the sidewalk tiles, shivering in the fresh air. Pasha lifts his hood; his coat is nice and thick, and his bag warms his back. You can just sit here like this for an eternity, experiencing the early, January twilight descending from the sky, seeping through the surrounding area like purple dye, eroding objects away, and blurring lines. "Why'd the dog leave me?" Pasha thinks. "Why didn't he stay with me? It's a strange time—can't hold on to anyone, can't hang on to anyone." He felt this for the first time several months ago, in the spring, when the vise started tightening around the city. The trains stopped running, the Station grew calm. The younger students weren't talking about that—they were afraid, they didn't have the vocabulary. The older kids didn't either, but they weren't afraid of anything. They argued, yelling over each other and paying little attention to Pasha. He didn't get involved when the students asked him to settle their disputes. He'd laugh everything off and start talking about their homework assignments. "That's not your job," he said. "Being good students, now that's your job." But they were bad students. And they behaved badly. And they simply ignored whatever Pasha said. One time, when the rumbling started particularly close by, Pasha tried taking them out of the classroom, to what he called the shelter. The kids laughed in his face; they were glued to the windows, searching intently for traces of smoke in the sky. Pasha stood there, waited around a little while longer, and then headed to the shelter. In the hallway, he bumped into the principal—thick layer of makeup, drawn-on eyebrows. She looked like a clown that'd been drinking hard for a long time.

"Are you all right?" she asked.

"Yeah, everything's fine," Pasha said with a nod.

"What about your kids?" she asked, clearly uninterested.

"They're doing fine, too," Pasha assured her.

After that, the kids didn't even want to talk to him; it was like he didn't exist. It was like his subject didn't exist. When school let out, Pasha would breathe a sigh of relief and head home. When he had to leave for school, he'd breathe a sigh of relief. He felt his best during the quarter-mile walk from his house to the school building. Sometimes on his way home in the evening, he'd sit down on the bench and pretend he was waiting for a bus. He'd tuck his chin into his collar, sit there, and look at the dark apple orchards with flashes and rumbles beyond them. In the spring the sky is so resonant; everything bounces off it, makes it reverberate, like an empty tanker. "What could I tell them?" Pasha thinks. "What could I teach them besides grammar rules? Everyone has to decide for themselves what to do and who to be with. It's every man for himself," Pasha thinks, and wraps his coat even tighter around his shoulders to protect himself against the thick fog, against the twilight encompassing the train station, and against the blasts that are starting up again somewhere behind the high-rises.

"Hey, mister," says a surly voice. "You still breathin'?"

Pasha springs up, still not fully awake, the sweet taste of sleep and tranquillity lingering in his mouth. Alyosha is standing in front of him: jacket zipped up to his throat, which makes his head somewhat birdlike, and he has bird eyes, too. Vulture eyes. He stands there, his green sneakers pattering in the cold water as he shifts from foot to foot, takes his red hands out of his pockets, blows cold air on them, sniffles, his frozen nose quivering, and looks ahead, the whites of his eyes bloody.

"You comin', mister?" he asks. "Or you gonna stay here and freeze your butt off? You already paid, so let's get rolling."

"Yeah, I'm coming, gimme a sec," Pasha replies, stands up, and sees that Alyosha isn't alone.

A group about a dozen strong is plodding along behind him through a fine spray of rain. A woman—around forty, dark, puffy jacket, short skirt, high heels—is out front. Well-dressed, self-confident, nice haircut. You might think she's walking home from the office. In her regular life, she's probably a government official who knows how to take bribes. The only thing is, now she's carrying a large bag from the hardware store on her back, and something's jingling heavily, something like metal dishes or copper utensils. "Looks like she ransacked a church," Pasha thinks. Following her are two other women, one very young and the other much older—clearly a mother and daughter—their arms intertwined. The older woman keeps affectionately calling the younger one "Annushka," but the younger one doesn't even respond. Annushka speeds up a little, like a runner trying to pull away from her closest competitor as she goes around a bend. Her mom won't let her, though. She's hanging on her daughter's arm like an old winter coat, holding a duffle bag in her free hand. Behind them, a young girl is pushing a stroller. Pasha thinks that she could pass for someone in his class, he could teach her. "But do I really need to teach her anything?" he asks himself. "Seems like she's doing just fine without me." The stroller's packed with clothes and bottles of water—just a big, damp heap, not packed in bags. The local sidewalks have done a number on the wheels. You can tell that the stroller is used often, that it's simply indispensable around the house. But there's no child in the picture, and you don't even want to ask where it is. Next in line is a little woman in a fur coat. The fur coat is all she has—no suitcases, no bags, no bundles. It seems as if that fur coat is her family's sole valuable possession, so she isn't taking it off, she's fused to it. "She looks like a squirrel," Pasha thinks. Her worn-down shoes stomp through the puddles. The heels are uneven, so from the back it looks like she has two hooves. Behind them an old man's pressing a teenage girl—either his daughter or granddaughter—against his side, under his down jacket. She's wearing a gray spring jacket and holding a bloated backpack in her right hand. A self-assured, young blonde woman is walking along behind them, one hand clenching a pack of cigarettes, the other loose on the handle of a wheeled suitcase. She's wearing sneakers, ripped jeans, and a little orange jacket. If they decide to shoot, they'll start with her, obviously—she's the most radiant of them all.

Pasha lets this whole bizarre procession pass and falls in behind them. "This is gonna take a while," he thinks. "I'll walk with them as far as the meat-packing plant and then peel off." The procession walks slowly, as if nobody's in any rush to get anywhere, as if they all have truckloads of time, a whole train car filled with time—one of the hundreds lurking here in the fog like drowsy animals. Most of them are battered and burned out, some are riddled with holes, but a few are more or less undamaged. They're waiting for their turn—nobody'll make it out alive. The procession advances down the platform slowly, stopping and crouching with every bright flash in the evening sky. When the platform ends, Alyosha stops and turns toward the group. Everyone freezes. The teenage girl cranes her neck at her grandpa and asks a question, but he puts a finger against his lips—Be quiet, listen, not now. Alyosha resolutely wipes some snot from his nose and scans the group.

"First, some ground rules," he says. "Turn off your phones, no smoking."

"It's like we're at the theater," Pasha thinks.

"Follow me," Alyosha continues, his tone surly. "Keep it down and keep up. You're on your own if you get caught."

"Who the hell am I even listening to?" Pasha thinks. But he doesn't say anything; they told him to keep quiet, so he keeps quiet.

Alyosha hops off the platform, right into the fog. The woman with the bag waits—is he going to offer her his hand, help her get down? He doesn't, so she hops down too. The something metal jingles inside the bag. Alyosha hisses threateningly somewhere in the darkness. Then Annushka jumps into the darkness, taking her mom with her. She jumps gracefully; the old lady flies after her like ballast dropping from the basket of a hot-air balloon. The girl with the stroller goes to jump, but then balks. Pasha can't stand to look at her like that, so he pushes his way to the front, jumps down, takes the stroller, and gives the girl his hand. Once the girl lands on solid ground, she yanks her hand away warily, grabs the stroller, and disappears into the fog. After that, the blonde girl charges toward Pasha and tosses her suitcase down. Pasha catches it, scraping some skin off his hands in the process, and puts it on the ground. Then he catches the blonde girl.

"Watch it," she advises him coldly, and disappears, too.

After that, Pasha carefully lowers the granddaughter and then reaches up to give her grandpa a hand. His hand is bony and unyielding, the hand of an old teacher at a bad school grabbing a naughty student by the ear. Hoof Lady is the last one remaining on the platform. Pasha extends his hand; she accepts it, steadying herself—her touch is nice, dry, like she's just left a warm apartment—hops down with surprising finesse, crashes into Pasha, pushes off of him with equal finesse, and tucks her hair back with one quick movement. Her face is wet from the rain, but she's smiling, like she's enjoying a nice stroll. Maybe she just doesn't want to reveal how scared she is.

"What's with your fingers?" she asks Pasha. "You break your hand?"

"I'm good," Pasha answers reluctantly.

"All right," she replies incredulously, turning around and shuffling her worn-down hooves along the railroad gravel.

Pasha glances back at the station one more time. He sees men with rifles stepping out of the building onto the platform. Stocky's running after them. No camo jacket—clearly, he didn't have time to put it on. Pasha's dog is running after them, always getting in the way; he's holding something in his mouth, something dark, something it's best not to look at. Pasha doesn't look.

The gravel crunches under their feet; they see the occasional empty bottle or supermarket bag on the ground; the snow along the tracks was melted away some time ago by the same fire that charred the train cars. Alyosha's walking like a zombie. With determination, that is. The women can barely keep up. The blonde is having a particularly hard time. She's dragging her suitcase, which bounces on rocks and flips over repeatedly, dragging it like an anchor, just can't drop it. Pasha catches up to her and offers to pull it for her, but she recoils from him, accentuating just how terrified she is and thanking him stiffly, even though it would've been better if she hadn't thanked him at all. Pasha stops and lets the rest of the solemn procession pass.

"You get the cold shoulder?" says the one in the fur coat with a laugh, nodding at the blonde woman.

"Yep," Pasha answers and waits for everyone to get some distance on him before he starts moving again.

At first, everything's going just fine. Alyosha runs, and everyone runs after him. Alyosha crouches in the wet weeds, and they all crouch down as best they can. Alyosha tells them to shut their traps—who could ignore Alyosha? They quickly leave the side tracks behind, crawl under a tanker ("the power lines are down, don't get shocked," Alyosha says), and walk along a corridor of busted and burned train cars. And then the corridor comes to an end, and up by the switch the tracks start heading north. Alyosha veers left, takes a path only he knows, moves through tall, dry cattails, skirts a burned truck, hops over a ditch, and ducks under a crooked concrete wall. Everyone else follows suit. The old man's panting by this point, his granddaughter, tucked under his warm jacket, is starting to cry, the blonde woman is anxiously twirling her cigarettes, glancing warily at Alyosha. They were ordered not to smoke, so she isn't lighting up. Hoof Lady takes some pieces of candy out of her pocket and offers the girl one. She pauses mistrustfully, yet eventually accepts it. Hoof Lady tries pushing one on Pasha. Pasha refuses automatically.

"You really don't want one? Just take it," Hoof Lady says. "What's your name? Mine's Vira."

Pasha tells her his name but still doesn't take the piece of candy.

"All right, fine," Hoof Lady—Vira, that is—says with a laugh and tucks the candy away in her pocket.

"So," Alyosha says. "Down there, on the bridge, they could start shooting. Walk fast, don't make any noise. Ready?"

"Need a smoke break first," says the blonde woman.

"You can smoke when you get home," Alyosha answers, gets up, and quickly sneaks along the wall.

"Asshole," she mutters at his back. Alyosha hears her—his shoulders even twitch—but he keeps going, so she has to keep going, too.

The going's tough. Their shoes keep landing on crushed bricks and rebar. Alyosha pauses sometimes, takes out his phone, cautiously turns on the flashlight, and hops over yet another ditch. At one point the blonde woman can't take it anymore, sits down on her suitcase, and starts griping about something. The column stops. Alyosha's standing up ahead in the darkness; he doesn't circle back. Vira leans in to say something to the blonde woman. Hey now, don't get all bent out of shape. Vira takes her by the hand and helps her up. C'mon, gotta get going. She nods at Pasha. Quit standing around and help. Pasha picks up her suitcase and feels that it's empty. He starts dragging it anyway, though, dragging it behind everyone.

A little later, Alyosha slides through a hole in a fence; everyone follows him reluctantly. They plod across an empty lot under a sky that flickers a fiery white. Those lights are somewhere in the east. When they flash, you can see every bush along the nearly imperceptible path. It looks like they're walking back to the locker room after losing a soccer match. How does their guide know where he's going? Nobody has a clue. He doesn't appear to know any better than they do. He stops abruptly at one point. The woman with the bag crashes into him in the darkness, the girl with the stroller crashes into her, and Annushka and the old lady crash into her. Everyone stands, waits.

"Hold on," Alyosha says. "Quiet. Gimme a sec."

"We're lost," Pasha thinks. He takes off his glasses and cleans them—like that'll help. The teenage girl slips out from underneath her grandpa's jacket and puts her backpack on. Vira walks over and starts patting her on the head. The blonde woman can't take it any longer; she takes out a cigarette, roots around in her jacket pockets, finds her lighter, and flicks it. A small, distinct flame escapes. She tries to catch it with the tip of her cigarette, tries again and again, but can't.

"Are you out of your mind?!" Alyosha turns around, sees the

flame, and darts toward her. “Put it out!” he shouts in a whisper. “Put it out, now!”

A short, piercing whistle comes out of nowhere, then something explodes off to the side, about fifty yards away. Chunks of earth go flying every which way, everyone drops to the grass, the teenage girl screams, her grandpa lets out a shriek, a terrified sigh of sorts. It’s as if he wants to hold all his fear inside but can’t. Everything stands still for several seconds, and then something whistles by and rips up the grass.

“Follow me!” Alyosha yells. “Get moving.”

Everyone gets up and runs across the field, as if this is a game they’re playing. They’re struggling, though. Annushka’s dragging her mom; she’s dangling behind her daughter, trying to keep up. The woman with the bag disappears somewhere up ahead. The old man’s lagging behind, panting, dropping back. Pasha runs up to him, tosses the suitcase aside, picks up the girl, takes the old man by the arm, and begins carrying them. There’s a third blast, somewhere nearby. Pasha thinks he feels a hot breeze grazing his face, but that’s probably the fear talking, just the fear talking. Run away from here, get to a safe place. The sky lights up again; the black silhouette of a building surfaces up ahead. Alyosha’s bitter scream comes out of the fog—over here, god fuckin’ dammit, get over here! Everyone runs toward his voice. In the very back, Pasha’s carrying the girl and the old man. He can feel his knees buckling—he’s nearly spent. “Almost there,” he reassures himself. “C’mon.” The building’s close, very close. There’s another flash, up in the air. Pasha runs forward, carrying the girl and the old man, and reaches a wall. He sees a broken doorway and tumbles through it, his elbow clipping the jamb.

He charges inside and crashes onto the floor, still pressing the girl against his side. She lets out a desperate cry, Pasha tries to calm her down, but how can you calm someone down when everyone else is yelling? The old man is lying on the floor, off to the side, groaning. The blonde woman runs, nimbly diving toward the wall.

"Against the wall," Vira yells. "Against the wall, now!" Everyone bolts into the darkness, sprawls out on the floor, and holds still. One lands very close by, on the other side of the wall. It's scary when that whistling starts, then things ease up. Basically, it's scary while you're listening to that whistle, in that instant. Then you start thinking about what to do, then you don't have time to be afraid. After that, bursts of automatic gunfire crackle dryly. They aren't coming any closer, though. "All right, that was the worst of it," Pasha thinks. He takes off his backpack, places it under his head, takes out his phone, and checks the time. "It's only five. Feels like New Year's Eve," he thinks. "You're celebrating and celebrating, then you look at the clock and it's only five. How long am I gonna have to lie here?" The floor's wet. Pasha immediately feels it on his back, but he's afraid to lift his head, so he keeps lying there, trying not to think about anything. "Just can't fall asleep. I won't ever wake up," he thinks and falls asleep right away.

He sleeps briefly and anxiously—no dreams, like always, just some pictures on the tips of his sleep, as though somebody's showing him something, but as soon as he tries to get a closer look, they retreat into the shadows, taking the pictures with them, laughing maliciously, glaring at him from those shadows. "What's depicted over there?" he thinks. "What is that?" A freshly whitewashed hallway, dark spots showing through, like on a dead person's skin. A metal staircase is attached to the wall; there's an opening at the top.

If you climb up, you get to the roof. There's a wet stone floor. "No, the wet floor's here, where I'm lying with my head on my backpack," Pasha thinks. "What's up there?" The attic, packed with his old things, is up there. And in the middle of everything are two big suitcases. "I have suitcases in my attic?" Pasha asks himself. "No, I don't," he answers his own question. "I don't." And he walks over to the suitcases. He walks over, and goes to open one, but a heavy canine scent hits him and he balks. Then the person showing him all this steps away from him into the shadows. C'mon, follow me. You have to see this. You'll be scared stiff, you'll be scared numb, but you'll look at it anyway. C'mon.

"Where's my suitcase?" Pasha hears but doesn't recognize his own voice. "Where is it? Huh?"

Somebody's kicking him in the shoulder. Pasha takes out his phone and turns on the flashlight, without getting up. The blonde woman is standing over him. Her sneaker is kicking his shoulder like he's a dog that's been hit by a car.

"Where's my suitcase?" she repeats coldly.

Pasha sits up, his back resting against the brick wall.

"Out there," he says, pointing toward the opening.

"What the fuck? Where exactly 'out there'?" she asks.

"Well, uh, out there." Pasha points into the darkness. "You started running, I was carrying the old man."

"What fucking old man?" She's starting to get riled up. "Did you just leave it there?"

"Well, uh, you started running." Pasha fixes his glasses with his whole hand, a bit awkwardly. He's still picking up this faint wet-dog smell, and it feels like several pairs of eyes are looking at him from somewhere in the darkness. And there's Blondie here, too.

“Are you a complete idiot?” she yells, kicking him even harder—in the leg this time. “Are you a complete fucking idiot?”

“It was empty,” Pasha says, trying to defend himself.

“And you went through my stuff, too?” she replies, growing more enraged.

“No, uh . . . ,” Pasha answers, frightened.

“You idiot!” she yells. “Go look for it!”

Pasha gets up, like an idiot, looks for his backpack, puts it on, and goes to leave.

“Sit down!” someone yells at him from the darkness. Pasha recognizes Vira’s voice. “And you sit down, too!” Vira yells, probably at the blonde. “Sit down, both of you! You got a death wish or what?”

“You’re the one with a death wish. That goes for all of you!” the blonde woman hisses ferociously, turning around and groping her way toward the exit. “Idiots,” she says in parting, and disappears through the doorway.

“Gotta stop her,” Pasha says. It’s unclear who he’s talking to, though.

“Come on.” Vira scoots over, very close to him, finds his hand, and pulls it toward herself. “Just sit. You can go out and look once things settle down. For her and her suitcase.”

Pasha sits down obediently. Vira huddles against him, as if she’s cold, and Pasha feels as though his train station dog has come back to him. The only thing is, he smells like refreshing water and a woman’s warmth. It’s obvious that she isn’t the least bit cold. They sit there, leaning on each other. Pasha wants to say something, but he’s afraid everyone will hear him and misunderstand him, so he keeps quiet. Her hand unexpectedly slides through the wide sleeve of his jacket, slips under his sweater, touches his frozen wrist, touches his skin silently; she doesn't say a word. And Pasha decides to go for it; he wants to find her hand and touch her wrist, too, but suddenly he hears a woman's voice in the darkness, right above them.

"Where's our guide? Has anyone seen him?"

Vira instantly pulls her hand back like nothing happened at all. She gets up quickly. Pasha gets up, too, and turns on his phone's flashlight. Annushka's standing in front of him, her mom peering out from behind her. They stand there, giving Pasha a demanding look.

"Where is he?" they ask Pasha.

"I don't know," he answers.

"Who does know?" Annushka asks coldly. Her mom isn't asking any questions, but her expression is cold and demanding.

"He's been gone for a while." Everyone turns toward the voice—the woman who was at the front of the group is sitting up against the wall, her bag next to her. Pasha aims the light in her direction and sees that her heels have broken.

"Quit shining that light at me," the woman says, and continues: "He's gone. He got the fuck out of here."

"What now?" Now Annushka's demanding an answer from her.

"Couldn't tell you," the woman replies.

The old man and his granddaughter emerge from the darkness. He isn't looking good—leaning on her shoulder, holding his chest, breathing heavily.

"We have to get going," the old man tells Pasha.

"He needs a doctor," the granddaughter adds, also addressing Pasha.

"Where are you gonna find a doctor out here?" asks the woman sitting in the dark.

Everyone's quiet for a bit. Pasha can feel his phone dying.

“We have to get out of here,” Annushka tells him adamantly, as if she’s worried Pasha doesn’t understand the importance of what she’s saying.

“Well, what am I supposed to do?” Pasha asks.

“You’re the only man here,” Annushka points out.

Her mom doesn’t object. Pasha does, though, nodding at the old guy. What about him? The old guy merely coughs despairingly and waves in reply—nah, nah, you’re the only man here, count me out.

“We have to get out of here,” Annushka repeats.

“Yeah, we have to get going while it’s quiet,” Vira agrees.

It really is quiet on the other side of the wall. Not even the blonde woman is making any noise. Pasha thinks about going out to look for her, but everyone’s formed a tight circle around him—there’s no escaping. And he’s standing here, like a priest taking questions after his homily, and thinking, “This is some responsibility, real responsibility—leading a group of people I hardly know, in the dark, who knows where.” Pasha isn’t used to this kind of thing. He doesn’t even take charge in the classroom; he generally just lets the kids run the show. At home he wasn’t in charge of anything either. At home his sister was in charge of everything. And when his sister was gone, there really wasn’t any need to take charge of anything. But now he’s suddenly got a whole bunch of women, children, and sick people that he has to take somewhere.

“All right,” Pasha ventures. “Where were you going?”

“Who the hell knows,” the woman in the corner with the broken heels answers hoarsely. She gets up, picks up her bag, and approaches Pasha. “That guy said he’d get us out, so we went with him.”

"I need to get home," the girl with the stroller responds, her quiet voice coming out of the darkness. "Everyone's expecting me. They don't know where I am."

"Where do you live?" asks the woman with the broken heels.

"By School Number Five," the girl replies.

"That's in the other damn direction," the woman with the broken heels says comfortingly. "Why the hell did you tag along with us?"

"I don't know." The girl starts crying. "He said he'd get us out and I thought he would. I need to get home," she reminds everyone.

Pasha looks at her stroller packed with winter clothes and bottles of water.

"Okay," he says. "We walk to the fork in the road by the meatpacking plant, then go our separate ways. Yeah?"

"Yeah," says the woman with the broken heels, hoisting the jingling bag over her shoulder.

"Yeah," says the girl with the stroller, quietly and timidly.

"Yeah, yeah," says the young girl impatiently. "Let's get going already."

"Yeah," says Vira.

Pasha turns around and sets out, shining his flashlight ahead.

"Hey!" Annushka yells at his back.

Pasha stops.

"Aren't you going to turn the light off?"

"But then I won't be able to see anything . . ."

They climb out through a smashed window. First, they pass Annushka's mom down the line, from person to person. Pasha holds her at the top and Annushka catches her outside. Then Pasha lowers the stroller. The old man keeps coughing, but he looks at Pasha like he's a hero. They venture out to some tram tracks and walk down them. That's safe at least—who would lay mines along a tram route? The tracks bend toward the main avenue a little later, though. And here opinions diverge. Pasha suggests steering clear of the avenue—they're shooting everything in sight over there. Better turn right, there should be a footbridge across the train tracks over that way. And then there's some houses, nobody'll get us over there. None of this sounds all that convincing; Pasha realizes that he's advocating for crossing the bridge mostly because it's closer to the orphanage. And he isn't any good at lying—he's a teacher, after all.

"Where?" the woman with the bag interrupts him. "You wanna go where? There were tanks by the bridge just yesterday."

"What are you talking about? There aren't any tanks over there," Vira counters. "There's no way."

They're standing around arguing about tanks, and Pasha doesn't really know what to do. "All right," he says. "Do what you want, I'm heading for the bridge." "That might get them off my back," he thinks.

"Good thinking," Vira says unexpectedly. "Good thinking. I'm with you."

"We are, too," Annushka and her mom reply. "Let's go."

"So are we," the old man and his granddaughter add. The girl with the stroller doesn't say anything, but she keeps standing close to Pasha, just in case.

"Have it your way," the woman says matter-of-factly, heaves the bag over her shoulder, and sets sail down the tracks toward the avenue.

The rest of them start walking in the opposite direction. There are intermittent flashes in the sky; where they came from, it sounds as if the sky is caving in on them. Everyone freezes and then turns around.

"That's by the train station," Vira says quietly, but nobody responds.

So they keep walking like that—not talking and not turning around, seemingly afraid they'll see something horrible if they do.

"Almost there," Pasha whispers to himself—everyone can hear him, though. "Just a little farther. The park's just past this building, and then the bridge. I know the way." Everyone knows the way, actually. They're all locals. Nobody can guarantee that they won't step in somebody's brains along the way, though. Suddenly, desperate assault-rifle fire breaks out somewhere by the avenue. Pasha darts ahead, everyone else in tow; they run over to a dark five-story apartment block.

"C'mon, go inside," Annushka yells. "Go inside!" They string out along the wall, running to the blasted front door. Pasha dives into the black pit of the apartment block and then suddenly stops. Annushka rams into his back, dragging her mom along like she's on a leash.

"Well?" Annushka hisses. "What's going on? Keep moving."

"Hold on," Pasha suddenly says, his voice quiet.

"What's going on over there?" Annushka asks, still confused.

"Shh," Pasha whispers.

The rest of the group barrels into the apartment block, breathing heavily. The old man's gasping for air, as if somebody was just holding him underwater. Everyone figures out what's going on right away, though. Something's up. They stop dead in their tracks and listen hard.

"Shh," Pasha repeats. "Hear that?"

Everyone listens. And they hear the wind going from room to room, somewhere above them. And drafts sweeping in one smashed window and out another. They hear drops of water trickling in a broken pipe and the wind dragging old newspapers across the steps. Most important, they're standing transfixed and listening. Somewhere between the third and fourth floors, on the landing, someone's cautiously blowing on their fingers, rubbing their hands together, putting on fingerless gloves, and quietly, very quietly—so nobody, nobody at all, can hear—picking up something metal. They hear him standing up cautiously, very cautiously, crouching, looking outside, nimbly stepping over shards of broken glass, surveying the space with a trained eye, looking all around, sniffing all around, and sensing someone's presence nearby, an uninvited presence.

"Hurry," Pasha whispers, gasping with fear. "No talking. Follow me."

They skirt the building, one after another, and run over to the first trees, moving from trunk to trunk. From off to the side, from the rotten grass, a potent stench hits them—something poisonous even. "Don't look, don't look," Pasha repeats to himself. He keeps running. He can hear the women's labored breathing behind him. They run over to a playground with a burned swing set and find themselves out in the open. Pasha looks around—the apartment block looms in the distance like a whale that's beached itself out of sheer despair. Black windows that look like they're stained with coal, no movement, no voices. This makes things even scarier. They dart toward the park and run between the trees, blending in. They're as dark as the trees, so it looks like the crooked acacias are running alongside them. Then the park ends abruptly; Pasha runs onto a strip of asphalt, his heavy shoes pounding resonantly, runs the remaining distance, and stops right in front of the bridge. More precisely, in front of what's left of it. Even in the pitch dark, you can see that there is no bridge, that what hangs above the dark, overgrown gully is emptiness. And there's no bridge. There's nothing. And descending into that gully is just like voluntarily descending into hell—you should have a really good reason. Pasha doesn't have a really good reason, though, so he just stands there, resting his hands on his knees, breathing heavily. And the women stand behind him, not saying anything, breathing heavily.

"So, what now?" Annushka asks after she catches her breath. "Huh?"

"Dunno," Pasha answers honestly.

"Well, where were you headed? There's somewhere you're going, right?" Annushka pressures him.

"Over there." Pasha nods at hell. "I was headed over there."

"Dammit," Annushka replies angrily. "Frickin' clown. All right, let's go." She grabs her mom's hand and starts dragging her back to where they just came from.

"Where are you going?" Pasha yells desperately at her back, but Annushka doesn't answer. Her mom could've said something, but she didn't know the right answer.

"I'm gonna get going, too," the girl with the stroller says after a short pause.

"Wait." Pasha catches his breath and tries to adopt a serious tone. “Let’s go around the other side.” He points at the black fog. “We’ll go out that way.” He waves his hand in the air, vaguely depicting something, which makes things even scarier.

“Nah.” The girl pushes the stroller farther away so she isn’t tempted to argue. “I’m gonna get going. Everyone’s expecting me.”

Nobody stops her. They’re all so confused that they don’t even know what would be worse—her staying with them, here at the beginning of hell, or her going someplace where she’ll probably get shot.

“It sucks when women leave you,” Pasha thinks. “I should’ve stopped them. How can you stop women, though? Who can stop them?” Pasha can’t, he doesn’t know how. He can’t now and he couldn’t last fall. Last fall, not all that long ago, sometime in September, when things got really tough and trains loaded with military vehicles started arriving at the Station every day, when people suddenly started shooting right on the main road, Maryna came over to his house—ran over, actually—and started carrying on. Gotta go now, otherwise it’ll be too late. Gotta drop everything and get out. The way it went embarrassed Pasha in front of his old man, who was sitting in the kitchen and could hear everything, and his sister, who sat there, consoled Maryna—she loved her—then started carrying on, too, and yelling at Pasha. What kind of man are you? What are you sitting around waiting for? Take her and get out of here! Pasha tried calming everyone down, explaining everything; he said something about his employment record (to hell with your employment record!), about how the school year was just starting. He said that they had nothing to be scared of, that they didn’t have anything to do with this, that they weren’t taking sides. Pasha was “just a teacher, just a teacher,” he kept repeating, seemingly apologizing for being just a teacher. He didn't really care about anything else. Where would he go? What use would he be anywhere else? They don't have anything to be afraid of. Everything's fine. He's just a teacher. Eventually, Maryna snapped and ran out of the house. Pasha went after her, but he stopped under the trees in their yard. Fall was just starting—spiderwebs were getting tangled and lost in the trees, the grass was heavy, saturated, the evening sky looked like molten metal that would soon be poured into a mold and made into something useful. Pasha's dad stepped outside, feigned surprise when he saw Pasha but didn't say anything, went down the walkway toward the gate, and peered inside the mailbox.

"There's no mail on Saturdays," Pasha reminded him. He went back inside without saying anything. "He's really lost it," Pasha thought. "He's turning into a freak. I'm not going anywhere."

"He's really hurting," the girl says, reminding everyone she's still here.

Pasha turns around. The old man really is in a bad way; he's doubled over, coughing and rubbing his temple.

"He needs a doctor," the girl says.

"What about going to a hospital?" Pasha asks, with some hesitation. "Do you think any hospitals are still running?" he asks Vira. "Or did everyone already take off?"

"I think they all took off," Vira replies. "That's if they could get out."

"So what are we supposed to do with him now?" Pasha asks, confused.

"I know a vet."

"A vet?"

"Yeah. He treated my dog a year ago. Well, that was when I had a dog," Vira says. "He worked out of his apartment, I remember that. He's not exactly a doctor, but he has something. Aspirin, analgin, or something like that."

When the old man hears "analgin," he starts coughing violently—a sign of approval, clearly.

"Is it far from here?" Pasha asks.

"How should I put it . . . ?" she answers, and Pasha realizes it's a long way.

He heaves the old man over his shoulder like a knight's cloak and carries him, stopping several times along the way to catch his breath. The girl runs alongside him, and Vira keeps pace, too. They cross the street, duck between some buildings, pass a day care center, reach the next street over, and walk along a row of linden trees. Something starts burning on the horizon again. It seems like they're bombarding the city in a circular pattern. The sky goes from dark to blue-tinged pink; it hollowly snatches every explosion. You can hear intermittent bursts of automatic gunfire coming from the avenue. Not a single person, empty city, colorful sky, black lindens growing out of the dark fog. Pasha finds a bench, lowers the old man onto it, and collapses next to him. Vira stands nearby; the fog wraps around her, so it looks like smoke is rising off her fur coat. The girl is crying, holding her grandpa's hand. Suddenly, there's some movement at the end of the street. A vehicle. No headlights, obviously. It's heading in their direction, though.

"Quick!" Pasha yells, grabs the old man, runs under an archway, and looks back to make sure everyone's with him. Then he cautiously peers around the corner and sees a swamp-colored minibus tear down the street. Lacerated metal sides, like the flanks of a battle-hardened dog, smashed windows. It seems like the passengers are jumping out while it's still going full speed.

They get to the vet's building around seven. A nine-story prefab apartment block. Half the windows are gone. Shadows, silence. The bench outside the building is all bashed up. Pasha looks at it and realizes that it was like that before the war, in peacetime, as they say. The building had an intercom, but now the door's wide open. Gloom flows out of it like black water.

"You remember what floor?" Pasha asks.

"Third, I think," Vira answers hesitantly. "Or maybe fourth."

"Damn." Pasha lowers the old man onto the ground. He slumps over into the fog; his granddaughter scampers over and grabs his hand. "Wait here," Pasha says, and goes inside the building.

He takes out his phone once he steps inside and turns on the flashlight. Smashed bricks, a thick layer of broken plaster, somebody's shoe, some scraps of something. He goes up the stairs, carefully stepping over everything. Vira follows him. They go up to the third floor. Vira examines the doors.

"Nah," she says. "This isn't it. He had a metal door."

They go up to the fourth floor. No metal doors.

"Are you sure it was metal?" Pasha asks.

"I don't know," Vira answers, beginning to doubt herself.

They go up the stairs and go up some more. And then head back down to the third floor.

"Well, I think this is it," Vira says, pointing at a black door with no number on it.

The door is metal—but it's been charred black, so it takes a minute to figure that out. Pasha walks over and delicately bangs his fist against the metal surface. A heavy echo rings through the building. This frightens Pasha at first, but then he summons his courage and starts pounding on the door, not holding anything back. No response.

"Maybe they can't hear us?" Pasha asks.

"You gotta be kidding," Vira answers in a surly tone.

They go back outside and turn off the flashlight. The old man doesn't even acknowledge them. His granddaughter's been standing on her tiptoes, looking up, waiting for them.

"Nobody's home," Pasha informs her.

She starts crying. Vira tries to console her. But it's not like that's going to do any good. "What should I do?" Pasha thinks. "What should I do?"

"Who are you?"

Suddenly, someone's standing in the darkness, but there's no telling who. It's as if the darkness is talking to them.

"We wanted to see the vet," Pasha answers the darkness.

"What vet?" the darkness asks.

"In the apartment on the third floor," Pasha says.

The darkness mulls over what it's heard, not saying anything for a bit.

"There's no vet on the third floor," it says. "One apartment's empty, some businessmen lived in the other one. But somebody threw a grenade in there last summer."

"Listen," Pasha says and takes a cautious step toward the darkness. "Don't be scared. I'm a teacher."

"Huh? Whose teacher?"

"I'm just a teacher. We've got an old man with us. He's really hurting. He needs a doctor."

"Why are you asking for a vet then?" The darkness is confused, once again.

"Is there anyone else around?" Pasha asks.

"Nope." The darkness starts moving. A small woman breaks away from the wall and heads toward Pasha. Long jacket, warm hat, can't make out her face. She's wearing glasses, though. She's blind as a bat, just like Pasha.

"How'd you wind up with him?" she asks, nodding at the old man.

"We were coming from the train station," Pasha explains. "Trying to get out. And then he started to feel real lousy. Is there a hospital around here? Or a pharmacy at least?"

"A pharmacy?" the woman asks indignantly. "A hospital? We've been living in the basement for the past two weeks!"

"All right, all right," Pasha says, trying to calm her down. "There's no need to yell."

He turns toward Vira. "Gotta get going," he says. "Keep looking." The old man gets up, Vira holding him on one side and his granddaughter on the other.

"Hey!" the woman yells at their backs. "What are you doing dragging him around? That'll kill him. Leave him here. I have a first aid kit and some water, too. If he dies, at least it won't be out on the street."

Pasha heaves the old man over his shoulder again. They walk along a wall, turn a corner, and go down into the basement. Up ahead, the woman is walking resolutely, even though it's pitch black—the moon or something like that should be hanging overhead, but the fog's lying so low that there isn't any sky. Once again, there's a blast somewhere on the other side of the city—dull and deep, stretched to steady, drawn-out intervals. Pasha moves in the dark as if he's walking along a riverbed; he's afraid he'll lose his balance and topple over, along with the passenger on his back. They go downstairs, and the woman opens a door. They walk down a hallway, and then the woman gropes for another door and opens it. Stale, stagnant air hits them immediately. Pasha can't see anything, but he can hear a lot of people breathing.

"Come on in," the woman says. The door closes behind them. Then, in the darkness, someone turns on a flashlight and shines it right in Pasha's face.

There are about two dozen people stuffed into a small room. They're sitting against the wall, leaning against each other. Mostly women and children. There's one guy, though—about forty, winter coat, deerskin hat. He looks at Pasha and then averts his eyes. There's a gas camp stove and a grocery bag off to the side. But everyone has their own food with them, something homemade. They're dressed warmly and wrapped up in blankets, rugs, and coats, too. Have they been here for a while? Can't tell. Based on the heavy scent and red eye-pits, it's been several days. Or maybe it's pushing two weeks already. Pasha takes a look around and then lowers the old man onto the cement floor. Several women spring up; the man in the winter coat burrows even deeper into the wall. The women pick the old man up, toss a gray winter jacket on the floor, lower their patient onto it, lean over him like myrrh bearers, and begin noisily deliberating over how to save him. His granddaughter is standing next to them, crying. Pasha's listening intently to the sounds outside. Two hits—can't tell what side they came from, though. "If one lands here, there'll be no digging us out," he thinks. He takes out his phone. It's almost eight.

"OK," he says to the woman who brought them here. "I'm gonna get going. Could you look after him?"

"Yeah, may as well, since he's here and all," the woman says calmly.

"Why don't you take my number?" Pasha suggests. "Just in case."

"Well, how'm I supposed to call you?" the woman inquires. "A paper cup on a string?"

"All right, all right," Pasha says. "I'll try and come back tomorrow. With a doctor."

"Uh-huh," the woman says unenthusiastically. Then she adds, "Where are you going this late?"

"Well, I have to get to the orphanage."

"The orphanage?" the woman asks in a frightened tone.

"Yeah, the orphanage" Pasha repeats, irritated. "Gotta pick up my nephew."

"Damn," is all she says in reply. "You better just stay," she offers again.

"Maybe I really should stay?" Pasha thinks, hesitating. "I'll spend the night and then push off in daylight. Don't want any run-ins with anyone tonight." He scans the room: damp walls, low ceiling, doors that open outward. "If it hits in the hallway, there'll be no escaping. It'll be a mass grave," he thinks.

"Nah," he says, more or less decisively. "I'm gonna get going. I'll try to stop by on the way back."

"Uh-huh," the woman answers, stepping aside.

"Wait," Vira says as he's leaving. "I'm gonna get going, too."

Nobody keeps them there any longer.

As soon as they step outside, they start inhaling the air deeply. Because there's finally some air to breathe. They start walking, hugging the buildings and hiding between the trees. The rain picks up, the air turns frigid. A fireworks show starts off to the north. The sky blazes unwaveringly, and Pasha realizes that even if he does make some headway, it's highly unlikely he'll want to come back this way. Vira wordlessly tries to keep up. They walk with their heads down. Have to watch your step. When Pasha lifts his eyes, he spots some figures—two or three, can't make them out in the dark—at the end of the street. Pasha yanks Vira's sleeve and pulls her down. They crouch, tumble up against the wall of an apartment block, and steal over to the entrance.

"Is it locked?" Pasha thinks frantically. He cautiously pulls on the door—it gives. They slip inside, run up the steps, stop between the second and third floors, freeze by the window, tensely examine the oily darkness down below. Time passes slowly, very slowly. "Are they gone?" Pasha wonders, and instantly sees the first figure down below, standing right in front of the building, looking up, right at the window—right at them. "Yep," Pasha thinks. "He saw us all right." But the figure down below turns to the side, waits for his buddies. His buddies come over, walking quickly. Three of them? Three of them. Armed. One of them has an RPG on his shoulder. The first one takes out a map, shines a flashlight on it. They all stand around him. The broken light snatches his black gloves, the heavy tactical goggles on his helmet, and the insignia on his uniform out of the darkness. Pasha tries to get a better look, but the flashlight turns off and all three of them dissolve in the black rain. Nothing to see but still, sodden silhouettes. They look like drowned men floating along a riverbed with a map in their hands. Eventually, the first one points off to the side. Everyone starts moving. Pasha exhales with relief. But one of them suddenly stops, turns around, looks right at Pasha again, like he discerns him in the darkness, unerringly sees him in the blackness, and heads toward the building. Pasha jerks to his feet, stands straight up, but Vira intercepts his arm.

"Sit still," she whispers. "Sit where you're sitting." The first one steps into the building. Broken glass crunches dryly under his boots. He doesn't turn his flashlight on. He moves through the gloom. With caution, with skill. One step, two, three, four, five. He tries the door of the first apartment, then the second. Everything's locked. Everything's quiet. He stands there for a bit, listening hard. Pasha's heart is pounding so loudly that it's impossible *not* to hear it. "He can hear it," Pasha thinks. "He can hear everything." Metal quietly taps against metal. "The RPG," Pasha thinks. He goes up one step, then another, stops between the first and second floors—directly below Pasha and Vira. He listens hard again. "Run for it," Pasha thinks, panicked. "Run upstairs and hide somewhere." He tries getting up again, but again Vira brusquely pulls him back down.

"Sit," she mouths. Pasha can't see that in the dark, but he can feel her hissing: "Sit, sit where you're sitting." The guy down below goes up one more step, freezes, hesitates—should I keep going or not? Suddenly, the door opens down below.

"Where are you?" a surly voice calls to him from outside. "What's taking you so long?"

"I'm coming," he replies. He turns around and stomps down

the stairs. The metal door squeaks sharply. Two shadows run past the window and disappear into the night.

"They gone?"

"Think so."

"Wanna get going?"

"Wait," Pasha says judiciously. "They're still somewhere nearby. Let's wait a little."

"Are you actually a teacher?" Vira can't help but ask.

"Yeah."

"What do you teach?" she probes.

"I'm just a teacher."

"Who're you going to meet at the orphanage? Your nephew?"

"Yeah."

"So he doesn't have any parents?"

"It's just his mom. Well, my sister. We're twins."

"Really?"

"Uh-huh."

"Well, why isn't she picking him up then?" Vira asks.

"Her job's . . . ," Pasha explains reluctantly, and then tries changing the subject. "What kind of coat you got there?"

"It isn't mine. I grabbed it from the office."

"Where do you work?"

"At a massage parlor."

"Huh?"

"Well, it's this parlor," Vira says, choosing her words carefully. "Officially, it's called a massage parlor. Do you know the big new office building downtown?"

"Yeah."

"Well, um, that's where our office is. There's a sign outside for a travel agency, too. A lot of people think that we actually are a travel agency. So I woke up there this morning. Well, in the parlor. I mean the office," she corrects herself again. "There really hadn't been much shelling in our neighborhood before that. And then it really started coming down. We just threw something on and ran to the train station. I grabbed someone's fur coat. All I got underneath is jeans and a bra. Damn, if I could just get home somehow, change my clothes."

Pasha wants to say something encouraging, but he can't come up with anything, so he just keeps quiet.

"I can see me not picking him up earlier, sure. With my job and all." She can't help but say something. "But what about you? You saw perfectly well what was going on. Don't you watch TV?"

"I don't," Pasha says. "I don't like politics."

"Well, now you're stuck sitting here," Vira tells him angrily. "Some fuckin' teacher . . ."

She gets up a little later. C'mon, get up, quit sitting around. Pasha gets up obediently, grabs his backpack, fixes his glasses (good thing she can't see that in the dark), and follows her. They stop when they get outside.

"Where should we go now?" Pasha asks, hesitating.

"Let's go back to those guys in the basement," Vira suggests. "It's late. How far do you think you're gonna get? To the first checkpoint?"

"Nah, I don't wanna go back to the basement. It's too crowded."

"Have it your way," Vira says stiffly.

"Want me to walk you back?"

"You don't have to," she says, reaches for him, squeezes his hand, lingering briefly on his hardened fingers.

Even though it's dark, and even though all Pasha wants to do is hide his hands deep in his pockets, he can still feel her thin bones, thin engagement ring, and her nails—so chipped that you might think she just finished doing some hard work. Like cleaning fish. Or digging herself out of her own grave. Pasha suddenly feels uncomfortable. He yanks his hand away, tucks it into his pocket, turns around, and starts walking. Vira starts walking, too, trying not to click her worn heels too loudly.

Pasha gets to the Palace of Culture and finally begins to recognize the area. Not much farther—cross the square, take the main road to the tram ring, go past some houses, then cut through the park. And then the orphanage will be somewhere up there. Better not cross the square, though. Actually, better go back to the basement and chow down on their food. But there's that old guy who's dying. And Vira wearing someone else's fur coat. So Pasha keeps walking under the trees, crouching down, looking in every direction. When there's an explosion behind the apartment blocks, he squats down in the tall grass, sits there for a bit, then musters the resolve to keep going. "TV," he thinks, irritated. "What does the TV have to do with this? And what does politics have to do with this? Who even needs politics?" Pasha thinks back to the election last fall. Some guys from the city who worked for one of the candidates rolled into the Station, asked him to campaign for them. Pasha turned them down. They weren't planning on paying him.

"You aren't just all about the money, are you, Pasha? This is about something bigger!" they said.

"I'm nonpartisan," Pasha replied.

They didn't pressure him, but their parting words weren't exactly kind, either. Then, on Sunday, during the election, Pasha had to sit around at the school—it was a polling place, and he was on duty—until late at night. People were reluctant to go to the school. Some came, though. Pasha greeted childhood friends he'd lost touch with, greeted his students' parents, who he didn't really care for and who didn't really care for him, greeted his former teachers, who didn't recognize him. They trudged off, as if possessed, to booths draped in blue, where they cast their ballots for a brighter future. "I'll be just like them one day, as soon as I retire," Pasha thought. The soldiers who kept coming by to make sure everything was going smoothly didn't even look in Pasha's direction, like he wasn't even there. He acted like that, too, like he wasn't even there. He was one of the first to vote. Which box did he check? He couldn't tell you. In the early evening, one candidate's representatives—the same guy Pasha decided not to campaign for—made a real fuss, started pressuring the election commission, argued with the voters, and kicked their competitors' representatives out of the school. Soldiers arrived. The candidate's representatives and the soldiers locked themselves in the principal's office. They were talking for a while. "It's a good thing I didn't campaign for him," Pasha reassured himself. Then, a month later, the candidate, who, for some reason, didn't even wind up winning, stepped on a mine. They gave him a hero's funeral. It suddenly turned out that everyone in town loved him. Even though, for some reason, nobody had voted for him. “Well, how could I have helped him?” Pasha thought, as he stood there at the farewell rally. Pasha stood far away and looked at his face, tinged dark by death, looked at the white cloth covering him, at the red casket, at the soldiers standing off to the side and looking at all the men like they were murder suspects. Then the casket was taken from the Station to the city. And then, several weeks later, things got really bad.

“Yep,” Pasha thinks. “All right now, just climb this hill and then you’re there.” It’s past nine already. At home, Pasha is usually sitting in his room by this time and his dad’s watching the news. Pasha adjusts his backpack and starts walking up some stone steps. There are a lot of them. Pasha’s struggling—he’s worn out from running around all day and chilled to the core. The fog grows thicker at the top. It looks like he’s going up into a raincloud. He counts the first fifty steps, stops, catches his breath. Then keeps going. His shoes get heavier and heavier, his movements slower and slower. Another fifty. The steps are all cracked. Have to be careful, have to watch where you’re going. Don’t listen to the explosions, don’t pay them any mind. Something bursts somewhere far behind him. Another fifty. Here, up on the hill, it’s calm, not scary. Don’t have anything to be afraid of. Another fifty. He can hardly breathe—doesn’t exercise, rarely walks anywhere, used to run. Running just isn’t safe anymore. They might think you’re trying to escape. Another fifty, and another, and another, and he finally crawls to the top of the hill, stops, turns around, and sees the whole city laid out below. The rain’s let up, fog’s settled in the valley, like milk that’s been boiled for too long. Pasha looks at the city, yet can’t see it. All he can see is a black pit. Hovering above it is thick black smoke with long tails, like the strings on kites. And it's as though somebody's pumping souls out of the city. And those souls are black and bitter, snagging on trees and taking root in basements—you just can't rip them out. And over there, far away, on the other side of the city, something's blazing, sprawling across the horizon, like scalding lava coming out of the ground. There's the sound of automatic gunfire coming from the city itself. The bursts aren't that frequent, though. Seems like that's it for today, time to sleep. That's if you have someplace to sleep. Pasha calms down a little. "Just had a tough day," he says to himself. "No big deal. Good thing it's all over." And he spots some grocery bags in the grass, something neatly folded. He walks over, kicks it with the tip of his shoe. Something supple, yet springy. Feels like chopped meat. Pasha lurches back and runs away. One more black kite rises behind him.

There's a new lock on a long chain attached to the metal gate. *Children* is painted on the gate. Pasha looks for an intercom, but there isn't one, so he has to hop the fence. He lands on some wet grass, twists his ankle, hisses in pain, but gets up and goes to look for a living, breathing person. There aren't any living, breathing people in sight, though. The main building's surrounded by small apple trees, as dark and crooked as the back of a woman who's toiled in the fields her whole life. No lights, no voices. The sign is still intact, but the flag over the front steps is gone. "Yeah, makes sense," Pasha thinks. "Why provoke them?" He suddenly realizes that he didn't see a single flag in the city today. Except for the one on the tank. A tank is a movable object, though—here today, gone tomorrow. But the train stations and schools stand still—until they get blown up. And there they stand: no lights, no heat, no flags.

Sheets of plywood cover the windows. Chairs from the auditorium are blocking the main entrance. "Where is everyone?" Pasha thinks, growing anxious. "Did they all up and leave or something?" He climbs the steps, approaches the door, peers through the cracks. He can't see anything, though. His fists pound on the windows, but the plywood muffles the sound. Down the steps, around the building, over to the gymnasium—big, white, with broken windows and a caved-in wall, like someone's taken a bite out of a burnt sugar cube—up to the door. He tries it. Locked. But there's someone on the other side, someone over there who's shuffling their feet, blowing warm breath through the cracked door, but not opening it. "I'm so sick of all this," Pasha thinks, getting angry at God knows who. "Traipsing around in the rain all day, having to explain myself, being afraid. I'm so damn sick of this."

"Open up," he says in a commanding tone, surprising himself.

"Who's there?" asks a woman's voice, frightened, yet still firm. She'd stand in front of a tank before letting him in, if it came to that.

"I'm here for Sasha," Pasha explains. "My nephew."

The door opens. Standing behind the door is Nina, the director: about thirty, pointy nose, attentive eyes, skinny, sickly, discontented. Warm, knitted leggings, black sweater, gray vest, also knitted. She looks like a gray crow. She's known Pasha for a long time, so she isn't surprised.

"Pasha?" she asks discontentedly. "Is that you?"

"I'm here for Sasha," he explains.

"Are you alone?"

"Huh?"

"It's just you, no soldiers, right?"

"No," Pasha answers. "Just me."

"Come on in," Nina says, and takes a step back.

She lets Pasha in, locks the door, nods for him to follow her. In the wall behind the basketball hoop, there's a hole from a mortar shell. Drafts seep in and out through the hole. There are unwieldy plastic jugs of water along the wall.

"Haven't had water for a while," Nina explains, without stopping. "The lights come on in the morning, for an hour or two. Why didn't you call ahead of time?"

"Didn't have service," Pasha answers.

"Really? We still do."

"You're up higher. How're things here? Been much shelling?"

"Not in the past few days. The gym got hit before that, though. There was smoke everywhere, enough to cover a whole city. Everyone probably thinks we got cooked."

"Where's Sasha? Is he sleeping?"

"Sleeping?" Nina asks, stopping. "Nobody's slept in a while, Pasha. Well, they do during the day," she adds. "When it isn't so scary."

They leave the gym, walk down a dark hallway. Nina turns on a heavy-duty flashlight, shines it ahead of her. The windows on the first floor are covered with blankets and political posters that have been ripped off the walls. It's cold and damp. Frozen flowers. Dirty footprints in the hallway—guess there's nothing to wash the floors with. Besides all that, it's just like any other educational institution. Visual aids, pictures of the local flora and fauna. Pasha catches a glimpse of wolves' silhouettes in the snow and a fossilized fern. "Ferns," he thinks. "What do ferns have to do with this?" Sheets of plywood with dust-caked national symbols on them. Fairy-tale characters on the walls, looking like straight-A students. Smells like something's burning.

"We haven't run out of food yet," Nina explains. "Have to cook it over an open fire, though. Like we're camping," she adds. "Yeah, here, take a look. You'll find this interesting."

The door to the far room is resting against the wall. The sign on the door reads, "Library." Pasha peeks inside. A blast knocked out a window, the roof's sagging. Books lie in the middle of the room in a big, wet pile. They just lie there, getting all mushy, like food left out in the sun.

"Good thing the kids don't like reading," Nina says. "Nobody was in here when it got hit. Everyone was in the kitchen."

"Any of the teachers still around?" Pasha asks, bewildered.

"The gym teacher, Valera," Nina answers. "And me. Everyone else took off. Same for the kids—the ones who could, left. The locals bring us groceries. They used to help us get water, too. Now they've stopped coming around—they're afraid."

"They have reason to be."

"Yeah."

They go downstairs and reach a long, dead-end hallway. There are old Soviet civil defense posters on the walls. Gas masks that look like the heads of anteaters are scattered across the floor. It's warmer and cozier down here. The only thing is, there are just a few too many pictures of nuclear explosions on the walls.

"We're lucky the basement was designed as a bomb shelter," Nina says. "Especially for us. Well, and for World War III."

They peer into the first compartment.

"Is Sasha in here?" Nina asks quietly, turning off the flashlight so as not to wake anyone. Nobody's actually asleep, though. Quiet voices start coming from every direction.

"He's in the third one," a voice says eventually. "A little girl," Pasha notes to himself. "He was in here," the invisible girl says. "He started scaring us. We kicked him out."

"Uh-huh," Nina replies. "Well, his uncle's here. Pasha."

Then she shines her flashlight right in Pasha's face.

"Take him away," the girl pleads in the darkness. "He keeps scaring us."

"Will do," Pasha promises, flustered.

They leave, close the door, walk over to the third compartment. It's locked from the inside.

"Damn," Nina curses quietly, and begins delicately knocking on the door. It's made of heavy metal. Apparently, you really could wait out WWIII in there.

"Sasha, open up," Nina requests.

"Does he give you a hard time?" Pasha asks—his way of encouraging her.

"They all do," Nina answers. "And he does, too. Sasha, your uncle's here. Uncle Pasha," she adds, just in case.

At first, nobody responds. Then the door trembles heavily and opens. Sasha's standing there: boxers, warm sweater, baseball bat in his hands. "He's grown," Pasha notes to himself.

"Pasha?" he asks, surprised.

"Been practicing?" Pasha answers a question with a question. "Where'd you get it?" He points at the bat.

"The locals brought it here," Nina explains. "And he took it. Sasha, I asked you not to lock the door."

"What are you doing here?" Sasha asks, ignoring her.

"Came to pick you up," Pasha says.

"Ah, what took you so long?"

He turns around and goes back into his room.

"I'll go get you a sleeping bag," Nina says in a tired voice, leaving Pasha alone with his nephew. "Spend the night, then go."

"Yep, that's what we'll do, yep," Pasha says.

He steps into the compartment. Dry, dark basement, bare pipes along the walls. Concrete floor, concrete ceiling. You could live through a nuclear attack down here, all right, though you wouldn't live all that long or all that happily. The kid's set up his own little nest in the corner: mats tossed on the floor, a down blanket on top, and then a sleeping bag. Several pillows, pots, plates, bottles, crusty leftover ramen. Books. Pasha walks over, takes a closer look. Mayne Reid, Conan Doyle. All of them have library stamps on them. There's a pack of filtered cigarettes on Mayne Reid. Pasha looks at the cigarettes in surprise, the kid sees where he's looking, even jerks to grab them, but then he restrains himself and sizes Pasha up with an air of independence.

"You've put on weight," he comments.

"That's just my jacket," Pasha says defensively.

"It's a crappy jacket."

"Been reading?" Pasha tries changing the subject.

"They're for rolling paper." The kid's mocking him.

"Gotcha. I read those books when I was a kid, too. Read them out loud to my sister. To your mom, I mean," he adds, just in case.

"How's she doing?" the kid asks, his tone growing more serious, yet softer.

"All right," Pasha replies tentatively. "Working."

"How'd you get here?" the kid inquires.

"Took a taxi," Pasha answers. "Then walked."

"How you gonna get back?" the boy inquires. "A taxi?"

"We'll see."

"OK. We'll see. You should get to bed."

"What about you?"

"I'm gonna stay up a little longer," he says, chuckling. "And have a smoke."

Nina comes in with the sleeping bag, little girl in tow: about twelve, tar-black hair falling in her eyes, curious, yet mistrustful gaze. She's carrying a pillow and a blanket.

"You should sleep here," Nina says. "That'll put us all at ease. You'll help bring in the water tomorrow."

"Okay," Pasha agrees.

"Good night." Nina leaves, not even looking at him or Sasha. It's as if they've offended her somehow. The girl, though, looks at both Pasha and the kid with genuine interest. But she has to leave, too.

Pasha sheds his backpack, takes off his shoes and coat. His shoes are as heavy as corpses. And they smell like corpses, too. Pasha takes some sandwiches out of his backpack.

"Want one?" he asks the kid.

"You make them yourself?"

"It's all fresh," Pasha says, aggrieved.

"No, thanks," the kid says in a conciliatory tone. "They feed us. Get some sleep."

"Where do you go to the bathroom?" Pasha asks, crawling into the sleeping bag.

"See those?" The kid points at a row of empty bottles. "Pick the biggest one. Make sure it's empty, though."

“They aren’t all empty?” Pasha asks, surprised.

“Get some sleep,” the kid replies.

“He’s angry with me,” Pasha thinks. “He’s mad. Mad that we didn’t come for him earlier, that we don’t call him often enough, that we don’t visit. Most of all, he’s mad that he’s here.” Pasha didn’t want his sister to send him away. Why? Let him live with us, I’ll keep an eye on him at school. His sister and his old man haven’t talked in two years, though. They started fighting when she was still living with that guy, Aram, away from Pasha and his old man. After that, when Aram took off and it was just the two of them in their one-room apartment in that prefab building, she and her old man entered a state of trench warfare. The kid was a bad student, but his behavior was even worse. He was bound to run into some trouble with the law—his dad was on the run, his mom was a train stewardess, always on the road, she hardly ever saw him, and the world was filled with temptation and challenges. How could he restrain himself? It’s not like he really tried to, though. He didn’t heed Pasha’s advice, and he flat-out ignored his grandpa. Just the way it ought to be, basically. Well, and he was sick, too. Pasha immediately regrets thinking of that. Best not to think about that. But it is what it is. What is it? It feels like the sign of death has been hanging over the kid for a while now. And his death is just a matter of time. Then his sister just sent him here, to live with orphans and the children of drug addicts, without warning Pasha or her father. That’s when her dad stopped talking to her altogether. Pasha took some serious flak from him, too, even though Pasha had nothing to do with any of this—he, too, was against the idea of the orphanage. He argued with his sister, paid the director a visit, talked to the kid.

But then he eased up, gave up, retreated. The kid could see that. He probably held it against Pasha. That wimp couldn't get me out of here, he didn't have my back. Pasha couldn't really say anything to that. Well, yeah, I am a wimp. I couldn't do it. I didn't have enough patience to take on the whole world. That's just how it goes sometimes. I'll take him home tomorrow, make sure he's fed and bathed. Won't send him back. He can read Mayne Reid at home. And urinate in bottles, too.

There's one more thing, though. Pasha remembers it well. Last year, in the spring, when all of this was just getting started, when nobody understood anything, he and the kid got into a really intense fight. The kid kept grilling Pasha, asking him whose side he was on, what he was going to do, who he was going to shoot at. Pasha reluctantly replied, like always, that none of this had anything to do with him, that he couldn't get behind anyone, that he wasn't on anyone's side. Then, completely out of the blue, the kid came back with something about not wanting anything to do with him, about being ashamed, about his uncle being a one-of-a-kind douchebag. At first, Pasha didn't know what was going on. Later on, he found out that one of the kid's classmates lost his dad—he was tortured to death a few weeks after it all started. Pasha hadn't known about that. He should have, though. Then he tried to explain what he'd meant, but the kid was set on seeing things his way. And Pasha couldn't seem to find the right teaching method to change his nephew's mind. That's how they left things. They still talked and all, but it was obvious that the kid had distanced himself, stepped away, stopped trusting his uncle. Pasha was worried about this, obviously, but what could he do? "What could I have actually done?" he thinks as he's falling asleep. "What could I have done? What?"

Where'd she leave her clothes? Where's her house? When's she going to get there? Half of them don't have homes—they've dispersed across the nearby cities, escaped from here, riding in an endless line of rail cars, drifted all over the world. How much time must pass before they return? And when they do return, will they recognize their homes? After all, everything used to look completely different. Nowadays, it's hard to recognize anything at all here: dwellings with no voices, streets with no lights, squares with no birds. A heavy gray building sits atop a hill. The windows are all boarded up. There are some signs and warnings written on the boards—about what's already been done and about what will be done. And about what will be done to everyone who lives here for what has happened and what will happen. And about what will be done to those who've never been here before. The foggy sky hangs low over the building, like the fog's getting sucked right out of the windows. It rises, twists into knots and loops, lets the wind carry it south, to the sea. Black apple trees stand around the building; they keep standing where they were put, even though they went barren a long time ago. Wet yellow grass, dark sticky clay, damp air that smells faintly of burnt rubber. Creeping from the trees to the building are stray dogs, three skinny and wary dogs, their eyes so desperate and so hopeless, as if they've been feeding on corpses for the past few days. And they know that it can't get any worse, that it won't be any worse, that it just won't be anything really. So all they can do is hide in the grass and rocks and warm themselves, hoping that everything will end quickly and painlessly. They drag themselves through the grass to the patch of broken asphalt in front of the building, sniff out the voices inside, sniff out the smell of helplessness. They come even closer, sticking their canine snouts into the holes between the boards. Suddenly, they detect another smell, a new, unusual one. The smell of an outsider. They detect that this smell is completely different, that something is seeping through the fatigue and apathy, something menacing that truly frightens them. The smell of strength? The smell of love? And the longer this smell persists, the more uneasy they become. They even begin to howl, taking in wet air and exhaling warm breath out of their mouths. Then they crack, turn around, and run back into the grass between the rocks.

Sometime in the early morning, the city really starts burning.

DAY TWO

They wouldn't even fight. She'd just get really quiet whenever she didn't like something. And he'd just leave the house whenever he had a problem with something. Then he'd come back. They'd sit in the kitchen like nothing had happened. Pasha would purposely check his students' homework very slowly, while Maryna would keep sending these short texts, one after another, like she was taking some endless test. She'd go to bed first, and he would only follow after he'd delayed long enough for her to fall asleep. He'd get into bed carefully, so as not to wake her. She wouldn't really be sleeping, of course. He knew that, obviously.

Two years ago, after many long months of talking and getting to know each other, after taking several breaks and feeling strange surges of tenderness, Pasha proposed to her. Maryna took offense. She didn't move out of his place, though. They kept living like that—with this concealed and inexplicable resentment. Maryna didn't want to marry him, but Pasha didn't have the guts to kick her out—he was the one who'd suggested she move in, after all. So they slept in the same bed. The worst thing was that Pasha could no longer hide anything from her. She watched him from up close, she could see everything very well. She saw his body in the morning, his face, his skin, which was getting less supple, growing dimmer, fading like a newspaper left out in the sun. She saw how he treated his dad, the way he was always bickering with him. She saw how afraid he was of his sister. She saw how he hid from his nephew, how he secretly hated his principal, how he ignored his students. She saw that he just didn't know how to act around her, how to talk to her, how to sleep with her. He lived like someone who'd committed a crime right in front of a witness who'd file a merciless, cold-blooded report, not omitting a single detail, not missing a single incident. "I set myself a trap. And I took her along for the ride. Why would I do that?" Pasha thought despairingly, as he looked at Maryna. Things got downright bad last winter. Something had changed in the air, like it'd been electrified. It felt like everyone had gone crazy—only talking about politics, watching news reports, sharing them. Pasha talked but didn't watch anything. His words lacked conviction, though, which pissed Maryna off, just infuriated her. Something had broken in his language, cracked, like ice on a reservoir in March, and it was on the verge of splitting into countless heavy, prickly shards. Pasha didn't even try to fix anything—how can you fix ice that's snapping and sinking into frigid water? "It's a real shame," he thought. "But what can you do?" He kept sleeping next to her. He'd just delay getting into bed more and more to let her fall asleep. And he'd sleep in workout clothes so he wouldn't have to feel her warmth.

In the morning, he'd wake up and lie there for a while, completely still. So there was no way she could tell he'd already woken up, so there was no way she'd even try to ask him about anything, so she wouldn't touch him by accident, so there was no way he'd touch her. He'd gotten into the habit of waking up and lying there for a while, completely still, thereby tearing a few extra minutes of peace and quiet away from the world. A few minutes when he didn't have to talk to anyone, when he didn't have to listen to anyone. Like now. He takes out his phone, checks the time before the screen goes black again, examines the concrete floor. His shoes, heavy and hefty as kettlebells, lie next to his sleeping bag. Seven a.m., the screen goes black, it gets dark again, his winter jacket has a damp smell to it in the darkness—that's smoke and yesterday's rain. It didn't dry out all the way overnight, now it's filling the space with the scent of rain and the chills. Pasha catches a whiff of wet clothes and fishes the scent of crushed plaster and bricks out of the moisture, along with frozen, crushed stone and the thick grass that he trudged through, and all of yesterday with its smells, glints, and voices pounces on him, shaking him so hard, like a late-night tram shakes the last passenger, that Pasha props himself up on his elbows, listens hard to the darkness, and rubs his face with his numb hand.

"You're finally up!" says a voice in the darkness.

He takes out his phone again, turns on the flashlight, looks around. The kid's sitting on a blanket, like the Buddha—calm and listless from being alone for so long. Turtleneck sweater pulled up to his nose, sweatpants, knitted women's socks. A death row prisoner in solitary.

"What are you doing up?" Pasha crawls out of his sleeping bag and feels a chill immediately rise through his body. The cold doesn't faze you when you're sleeping, but it gets to you as soon as you crawl out, like when you're approaching an unseen body of water at night.

"You kept me up," the kid says calmly. "You kept talking to yourself. No wonder Maryna left you."

"Nobody left me," Pasha replies, his tone a little too harsh. He digs around in his sleeping bag, finds his glasses, plants them on his nose, fixes them with his dead fingers. "We weren't married," he adds, just in case.

"Gotcha," the kid says. His voice is filled with such contempt that Pasha's whole body shudders.

"Man, it's cold," Pasha says, finds his jeans, tries pulling them on, gets all tangled up trying to keep his balance. "What was I saying?" he asks cautiously, so as to elicit a straight answer but not make the kid think he cares all that much.

"Something about conferences," the kid says.

"Conferences?"

"Parent-teacher conferences," the kid adds. "Oh yeah, and you were calling out to some girl named Anna. Who is she?"

"A waitress."

"Hehe. So you were calling some waitress over. When's the last time you ate?"

"When was it?" Pasha asks himself; he's standing there, frozen, on one leg, like a crane, thinking. Then he pulls on his jeans and sweater wordlessly, picks up his jacket, as wet and heavy as a fisherman's net, and puts it on. "When was it?" he repeats.

"Let's go," the kid says.

Sasha gets up, finds a pair of adult-sized rubber boots, takes a large knife out of one of them and a flashlight out of the other, tosses a green jacket over his shoulders, and steps out into the hallway first. Pasha takes a while to tie his shoes, hastily rolls up his sleeping bag, and runs out after the kid, who's standing at the end of the hallway and looking at him reproachfully.

“Shoes,” Pasha explains.

“Yep,” the kid replies. “They reek, I know.”

Pasha is about to say something, but the kid is already up ahead, turning the corner, so Pasha decides not to continue this strange exchange.

They go up to the first floor. The kid turns around.

“Wanna see a demolitions guy?” he asks.

“What kind of guy?”

“A dead one,” the kid explains succinctly, and keeps going.

They go up another flight of stairs; the kid opens a window between floors, steps onto the sill. Wet wind whips through the open window, along with the distant sound of explosions and automatic gunfire, particularly alarming in the rarified morning air. Pasha hesitates, since he can’t figure out where they’re shooting, where the danger is. But then the kid extends a calming hand.

“C’mon,” he says. “We can’t go through the gym anyway. Nina’s there. She won’t let us.”

Pasha ventures out onto the windowsill, leaving behind heavy tracks, black as seals on documents. The kid goes right from the windowsill onto the canopy, then onto some sandbags that are blocking the back entrance, and finally hops down into the thick morning fog. Pasha hops down after him. The kid’s jacket flashes in the fog, a bright green splotch. Pasha heads toward it.

They walk down an asphalt path, go behind a building, and enter an orchard. Leaves that never got raked up shine yellow in the fog; they bounce wetly when you step on them, so it feels like you’ll get sucked into them on your next step, sink in up to your waist, fall into a pit or an open manhole. Then the path just disappears, but the kid knows where he's going. He confidently navigates the terrain, steers clear of the rebar sticking out of the grass, steps over a concrete stake lying between some apple trees, and dodges some wet, taut branches. Pasha is soon short of breath, but he tries not to show it—he doesn't want the kid to see that this morning run between the wet apple trees is wearing him out.

"Almost there?" he asks the kid, trying to calm his breathing.

The kid doesn't answer, though. Or maybe he does, but Pasha just can't hear him. They're suddenly stopped by a metal fence. "Looks just like the ones at the zoo," he thinks. His school has a fence just like this one, too. The kid finds two bent rods, squeezes between them, slides over to the other half of the apple orchard. This all takes Pasha a little longer—he tries, gets caught, panics, backs up, sheds his jacket, and only then squeezes between the rods. The kid's gone.

"Sasha," Pasha yells into the thick fog. "Sasha, where are you?"

He takes off his glasses, cleans them, puts them back on—that makes no real difference, though—slips into his jacket, trying to warm himself up. The rain let up last night and the fog's settled, like snow that's slid off a mountain and into a valley. He takes a step forward, stops. Then another step. In the fog, he bumps into the kid, who's standing at the edge of a ravine, craning his skinny teenage neck, staring down warily. Down below, the fog is just as thick. At their feet, the ripped armholes of a valley open up before them; they can see yellowed grass and wet bushes—the fog snags on them, wraps around them like a spiderweb. Then the dense, milky expanse continues—dusky silver, endless. And somewhere over there, in that dense milk, is a constant rumbling and the gleam of yellow lights; exhausting bursts of automatic gunfire crackle, mortar shells explode—often, not like yesterday—but they can't see anything, so they get this feeling that they aren't exploding here, in this life, next to them. Smoke rises out of the valley, smoke weaves into the fog like a dark strand into a dead man's gray hair, as fear and danger immediately return.

"Watch out," Pasha says. "Step back."

"You scared?" the kid asks without turning around. He's looking down, into the fog, mesmerized.

"Where are those explosions?" Pasha decides not to continue this unpleasant line of conversation.

"That one was on the edge of town," the kid says, listening hard. "And that last one was by the train station," he adds after a pause.

"By the train station?" Pasha asks, surprised. "But it's just women over there. I was there yesterday," he explains.

"You were on the prowl?" the kid inquires. "How would they know who's where? Maybe they think there's a unit posted over there. So they're hittin' 'em hard."

"Like they didn't know who was there," Pasha retorts. "Those guys," he hesitates, trying to figure out what to call them. "Those soldiers," he clarifies. "They stopped by yesterday. I talked to them."

"That right?" the kid asks mockingly. "You talking to soldiers . . ."

"All right, knock it off. What are we doing out here?"

"Wait a sec," the kid replies.

They're standing at the edge of the ravine, listening to what's happening down in the fog. Pasha realizes that the city's over there: thousands of houses, thousands of trees, thousands of burrows and basements with thousands of residents hiding in them right now. Just try and find them down there in the fog. Try and track them down. Can't hear their breathing, their hearts beating, can't hear anything. This thick fog filling up wrecked apartment blocks and mutilated manholes—that's all there is. "And there's nothing you can do to help," Pasha thinks. Even if he wanted to get them out of there—try and pick them out of that stew. All he can do is stand here and listen to everything around him give way to destruction and death.

"It's seven-fifty," the kid says suddenly. "Listen."

Pasha takes out his phone. It really is seven-fifty. He listens hard but can't hear anything besides the crackle of gunfire and rumble of mortars. Soon a sound emerges out of the fog, barely audible at first, then more and more persistent—a dry, metallic buzzing, a stubborn, rhythmic drone. Endless, hopeless.

"What's that?" Pasha asks, confused.

"A phone," the kid explains.

"Whose phone?"

"The demolitions guy."

"What's he doing here?" Pasha's trying to comprehend all this. Meanwhile, the droning sound doesn't go away; someone's stubbornly trying to reach the demolitions guy.

"So there are mines everywhere." The kid points at the fog. "The security forces wanted to get all their vehicles out, so they could leave the city. They sent some demolitions guys in. One of them got blown up. About five days ago. Somewhere down there." The kid points ahead. "And someone calls him every morning. At seven-fifty."

"Why seven-fifty?"

"Are you dense or something? They call right before school starts."

"Who?"

"Isn't it obvious?" the kid asks, surprised. "His son. Or daughter. Guess nobody told her that her dad's gone, so she keeps calling, like she promised she would."

"Promised who?"

"Her dad. Before he left."

Pasha thinks of how he gets ready for school every morning, drags himself down the hallway, sits in the kitchen. It makes him feel so bad, like someone's calling him and he can't even pick up.

"What's with his ringtone? Couldn't he pick something more interesting?"

"Whatever," the kid replies. "What, do you want him to use the national anthem? Well, maybe you should. You are a teacher, after all. A government employee."

"What for?"

"To instill patriotism," the kid says, laughing. "Do you even know the words?"

"Listen." Pasha changes the subject again. "Gotta go get him." He nods in the direction of the fog. "Him just lying there like that . . ."

"Are you dense or something?" the kid asks again. "Wanna get blown up too? Spring'll come, the snow'll melt, and they'll take him away."

"There isn't any snow down there," Pasha replies.

"No, there isn't . . ."

Meanwhile, the ringtone quiets down. All they can hear is the explosions. The wind's cold—feels like the fog is flowing up their sleeves and into their pockets.

"Let's head back," the kid says, turns around, and starts walking toward the orchard.

"You promised to help get the water, Pasha," Nina says.

She's standing in the hallway, a woolen shawl wrapped around her back. It's as if she were waiting just for them. She looks like a security guard at a dorm, a men's dorm, no less. She'd die before letting any outsiders in. The kid, head down, slips into the basement, back to his burrow. Pasha stays, hides his eyes.

"Where were you?" Nina asks. She's trying to speak in a severe tone, but her voice is too tired, like a wife who has been waiting all night for her husband to come home—she really should give him hell, but she just wants to go to bed too badly.

"Nowhere," Pasha answers. "What about the water?"

"Go to the kitchen." Nina decides not to give him hell. "Valera, the gym teacher's there. Grab some breakfast while you're at it," she adds.

Valera the gym teacher is sitting in the cafeteria next to a lit potbelly stove, drinking tea and reading some old newspapers. Pasha walks in, gives him a curt greeting. The cafeteria is big, gloomy, and cold. Fog hovers outside the windows, peering through the glass like kids looking at snakes in a terrarium. Foodstuffs are neatly piled in the corner: grains, pasta, canned goods. A fire-blackened teapot that looks like the burnt remains of the Reichstag is heating up on the stove. Valera nods. Sit down, take a load off. He's sitting there wearing a black coat—it's worn, yet still nice. There's a hat on the table in front of Valera, as if he's planning on having it for a snack. Greasy hair, hasn't been washed in a while. His gaze is firm, yet somehow muffled, broken. It's obvious that he's a confident man with principles. It's just that he's been put in tough circumstances lately, so he hasn't really had grounds to stand up for them. Wash that hair of his and he'll get his firm look back. And there's his mustache, too—trimmed, yellow, nicotine stained.

Pasha sits down, picks up a mug with coffee in it, thinks about where to dump it, gives up on that idea, sprinkles some black tea right into the coffee, and tops it off with boiling water.

"Nina asked us to go get some water," Pasha says.

"Uh-huh," Valera answers skeptically, as if he wants to say, "She didn't have to remind me."

Pasha doesn't like that. Nina doesn't exactly elicit warm feelings, but this gym teacher guy in the black coat doesn't really elicit any feelings except disgust, maybe. Valera cracks, averts his eyes. He sits there drinking his tea with an air of independence. Pasha swallows his swill, burning the roof of his mouth, and decisively sets his mug aside.

"Let's go," he says, standing up.

"Lemme finish my tea." Valera's trying to speak calmly.

"C'mon, let's go." Pasha ignores him.

"Like I'm gonna wait for this asshole," he thinks, heading toward the gym.

Valera grabs his hat discontentedly, gets up, starts walking, keeping his distance, asserting his independence. Something about him pisses Pasha off. Maybe it's his showy superiority. Maybe it's his helplessness.

They pick up empty water jugs in the gym. The jugs are tied

together with a rope, looking like a bunch of exotic plastic fruit. Pasha picks up one bunch, slings it over his shoulder. Four barely seaworthy six-quart vessels in front, four on his back. Valera tosses some jugs over his shoulder, too, and steps outside first.

They pass the main building, get to an open area. Fog instantly encompasses the black coat, the blue plastic. Pasha walks toward the sound of the empty jugs resonantly bumping together; he's like a shepherd who's more concerned about sticking by his animals than anything, more than rounding them up, even, a shepherd afraid of getting lost in the thick, compacted air. They eventually reach the gate. The gym teacher takes a key out of his coat pocket, opens the lock, and uncoils the chain. They leave the gate open, keep going. The cracked asphalt has been split here and there by mortar shells. The grass on the side of the road is faded, burnt rebar lies nearby. Something suddenly emerges out of the fog—a bus stop. Or what's left of it. A black, charred wall, a heap of fallen bricks. The national flag—also charred—has been painted on the wall. A sign, white on blue, peers out from underneath the bricks—ORPHANAGE. Valera stops, puts the jugs down, takes out his cigarettes.

"Want a smoke?" He proffers one to Pasha.

"No, thanks."

"It got taken out a month ago," the gym teacher says. "Nina was heading to the city that day. I don't let them out anymore. And I have the key to the gate," he reminds Pasha.

"Gotcha," Pasha replies, his tone somewhat mistrustful.

The gym teacher finishes his cigarette. They pick up the jugs, push on. Soon some houses appear. Through the fog, they can discern gray roofs, dark fireplaces. The sliced slate of the fences, the black hollows of the windows, the tree trunks trimmed by mortar shells. There's a store—a large, one-story building with a metal door—at the fork in the road. And in front of that a well. A well meticulously covered with blankets and old padded jackets so nothing gets inside. They approach, look around. In the fog, the houses are nearly invisible, like they're taking shape on photographic paper. Valera removes the blankets with practiced yet cautious movements, and begins retrieving the water. Pasha holds the jugs, while the gym teacher pours from the bucket. Holding the jugs is awkward; they keep slipping out of Pasha's hands. He keeps holding on to them—doesn't want Valera to notice his crippled hand—and occasionally blows on his stiff fingers. They fill up the last jug, wrap the blankets around the well again. They stand there, breathing on their clenched fists. The water's freezing, burning their skin, deadening it, numbing it. Valera tries to knock a cigarette out of the pack, but his fingers won't cooperate. Cigarettes spill out, fly into the black water at their feet, sink to the bottom like torpedoes. Valera curses, tucks the pack into his coat pocket, picks up the jugs. Pasha slings the jugs over his shoulder and turns around to head out but bumps into the gym teacher, who's standing completely still. His back has tensed up—it doesn't seem to be from the heavy load, though. Pasha looks around him impatiently. There's something in the fog, a few steps away from them—three men. Or maybe four even. They're standing there, not coming any closer, so you can't make out who they are. Valera slowly lowers the jugs onto the ground.

"Listen, pal! What'd we fuckin' tell you about taking water?" one of them says. He's speaking Russian, emphasizing the curse to sound more convincing.

"You fuckin' listen, pal." Valera gives him attitude right back. "You need a whole well to yourselves?"

“Who the fuck are you? Could be anybody,” one of them persists.

“I’m from the orphanage,” Valera explains.

“Fucked if I care. Should’ve blown you to hell ages ago.”

“Fucked if *I* care,” Valera replies coldly, picks up the jugs, and heads right at the voices.

Pasha rushes after him, following the heavy bunches of water jugs dangling from his back. The guys in the fog step aside, oddly enough. As Pasha slips past them, he catches a whiff of tobacco and a whiff of fuel oil. It’s as if they ate the oil and rubbed the tobacco into their hair. No time to pick up any more smells. Or catch a glimpse of anything else. Then, as they’re walking away, once the store and the well have dissolved in the fog, someone yells:

“Hey you, from the orphanage!”

Valera hesitates, stops. Pasha runs into him again.

“You’re fuckin’ . . . uh . . . dead meat!”

Valera isn’t listening, though. All you can hear in the fog are his high boots stomping through the cold puddle water.

They walk in silence. The fog has blanketed everything on the orphanage grounds—feels like you’re walking through a wall, leaving behind the world of the living and groping ahead until you run into something horrible. Pasha’s walking along, just listening to the jugs softly knocking against each other, and he suddenly realizes that he hasn’t felt this good in a while. Well, no, not exactly good. What’s so good about trudging through some place where, in all likelihood, they’ve been burying corpses for the past several months, where, in all likelihood, they’ll keep doing so for the next several months? Anyway, you’re walking through the fog, carrying water, and at least there’s something to keep you busy, at least something in all this has meaning. You don't have any doubts while you're walking—you know you have to carry the water back. And then you'll have to make the walk again, with empty jugs, to fetch more water.

Valera plods along, all hunched over. You can hear his stride, his coughing. But you can't actually see him. It's like a dead man's walking alongside you. Pasha speeds up, pulls even with him.

"You know them?" Pasha asks, nodding, even though Valera can't see him.

"Yep," the gym teacher answers without stopping.

"Local guys?"

"Yep."

"What do they want?"

"They don't want anything." The gym teacher spits angrily, puts the jugs on the ground, and takes out his cigarettes. Pasha puts his jugs on the soggy earth. His shoulders are aching. He sighs heavily, taking in a mouthful of thick fog. "Everyone around here's mad at Nina. Last summer, when it all started, they wanted to hand her over to the commandant. I stopped 'em."

"How'd you do that?" Pasha asks.

"I just up and stopped 'em," the gym teacher explains. "Well, and then the army came. And then all of this started." Valera waves, as if he's referring to the fog. "All right, let's go." He tosses his cigarette butt into the water, picks up the jugs, starts moving.

"He's a good guy," Pasha thinks as he's picking up his jugs. "What the hell's my problem?"

The kid's already waiting for Pasha in the gym.

"Where've you been?" he exclaims. "Let's get going already."

His backpack and things are on the floor in the corner. "I'm all packed. How much longer are you gonna make me wait?"

"All right, all right. We'll get going soon."

And then Nina walks up to him.

"Are you really leaving?" she asks.

"Yes, we are." Pasha fixes his glasses and immediately adopts a stilted tone, the same tone he uses with the kids at school.

"You're going out there now?" Nina asks anxiously. "Can't you hear the explosions? You should at least wait until after lunch. It generally quiets down after noon."

The kid's standing next to them, listening intently to their conversation.

"What?" he yells impatiently. "C'mon, let's go, already!"

Pasha hesitates. On one hand, he wants to get as far away from here as possible; on the other, he remembers what it was like walking here from the train station yesterday, so he isn't too eager to leave.

"Wait," he tells the kid. "Let me call your mom."

"What for?"

"To see what the situation is like down there, at home," Pasha explains.

"Whatever," the kid drawls, clearly disappointed. "See what the situation is like . . ."

But Pasha's stopped listening. He walks over to the corner, takes out his phone. The kid and Nina stand nearby, waiting and occasionally glancing at each other. Nina looks at the kid with concern, and he looks at her with hostility and unconcealed irritation.

The phone keeps ringing and ringing. Pasha's just about to hang up.

"Hello," he suddenly hears his sister saying. Well, yelling, actually. She's used to yelling. She yells at work and at home, too. She thinks people understand her better that way.

"Yeah, Zhenya," Pasha says. "Are you home? How are things down there?"

"Yeah, I'm home! It's a fuckin' shitshow. The army's attempting a breakout. The Station's packed. Everyone's leaving. They're afraid the Station's gonna get attacked."

"I'm here with Sasha," Pasha interrupts. "I want to take him home."

"With Sasha?" his sister yells, surprised. "How'd you get there?"

"I want to take him home," Pasha explains. He can hardly hear her, so he, too, starts yelling.

"How ya gonna do that?" his sister shouts indignantly. "There's no getting through. There are soldiers everywhere. Just sit tight at the orphanage. At least they'll feed him there."

"He's sitting tight down in the basement," Pasha yells in reply.

"In the basement? Why's he down there?"

"There's been fighting over here," Pasha explains.

"Well, just sit tight then. At least he won't go hungry!"

The call drops, but Pasha doesn't want to call her back. What can I even say to her? He's standing there with his back to Nina and the kid, tensely looking at his black phone, stalling, pretending he's waiting for her reply.

"Well?" The kid cracks first. "Get ready, c'mon."

"Pasha?" Nina tries to pull him out of his trance.

"Here's the deal." Pasha turns around abruptly and starts talking, looking between Nina and the kid, not making eye contact with anyone. "So, what's the deal? They aren't letting anyone into the Station, the checkpoints are blocked off. The army left." He nods at the window. "Those guys," he says, nodding again, "are just coming in."

"Well, let's roll then!" the kid interrupts him. "Or are you planning on hanging out here, like the gym teacher?"

"Sasha!" Nina yells at him.

"Go to hell, both of you!" The kid turns around furiously and runs down the hallway.

Pasha stands there for a bit, not knowing what to do, then dashes after the kid. He runs down the hallway, turns the corner, sprints past classrooms as empty as hotel fridges, reaches the end of the hallway, runs down the stairs, and stomps along the cement basement floor. He runs to the compartment, pulls on the door. The kid's locked himself inside, obviously. Pasha starts pounding on the metal door. "Just so long as he's okay," he thinks. "Just so long as *that* hasn't started. Just not now." A group runs out of the first compartment to see what all the commotion is about. Pasha's anxious, worried about the kid; he wants him to open up, so he keeps banging on the metal door, pounding and jolting loose ten-year-old rust that settles in the hallway twilight. "Go to hell," he thinks, repeating after the kid. "All of you. Why'd you crawl out of your burrows? Haven't you ever seen how big, happy families settle disputes? Yeah, how would you know? When's the last time you even saw your parents? You're sitting around here like rats in the hold of a ship, waiting for them to smoke you out with poisonous fumes. What do you know about a normal family that's trying to live a normal life? What do you even know about living a normal life?" Pasha's yelling to himself, then he turns around, and suddenly sees all of them. All three of them. He saw the oldest girl, around twelve, yesterday—she came by with Nina last night, carrying the sleeping bag. Her hair that keeps falling in her eyes—that's how he recognized her. And that mistrustful glare. It seems to have filled up with even more mistrust overnight. And more fear, too. She's standing there in her faded pink down jacket, hiding her hands in her pockets. Knitted socks and warm slippers. The slippers are too big—they probably belong to someone else. The girl who's peering out from behind her shoulder looks younger, about ten or so. She's mistrustful, too, and frightened: fair hair gathered in a ponytail, several boys' sweaters, one on top of the other, dull jeans, worn sneakers. She's holding a plastic mug with something hot in it—guess she didn't want to leave it in her room. Who knows when she'll be back. Hot things get cold, so it's best to keep them at hand, just in case. And there's a third girl. She's peering out from the doorway, not venturing out. Buzz cut—looks like she just got home from the hospital. But she's afraid they're going to send her back. And all of them have this heavy look in their eyes, and the shadows under them are so black, so deep. And at first Pasha doesn't realize what's going on. Then suddenly, it hits him—all three of them are wearing makeup. Thick, showy makeup, just like the older women around here wear. At first Pasha's surprised, but then he starts to understand—well, what else are they supposed to do all day down here in the basement? They sit around and do each other's makeup so things won't be so scary. But they still are. "I scared them," Pasha thinks. "I was the one who scared them." But he looks at them, looks at the makeup under their eyes, at the fear they're trying to cover up, and he realizes that he has nothing to do with this—their fear runs too deep, it's constant, it's part of their lives. And Pasha wasn't the one who scared them. They were scared before he came along. Down here in the basement, Pasha's probably just like all the other assholes around them, like their parents, who abandoned them like rabbits locked up in cages—you're on your own, let's see how long you live. Do whatever you have to. They're standing there, looking at Pasha wordlessly. The girl with the ponytail lets slow tears trickle down her face, washing away the makeup, forming distinct grooves. And all of this looks so strange here in the basement hallway: Pasha with his dead fingers, the kid hiding from the whole world in a bomb shelter, these girls with unnatural, clownlike makeup standing here and whimpering like young clowns who've come to see an old clown and gripe about the struggles of their profession. The old clown's on the verge of tears, only holding it together because he's too embarrassed to cry in front of these painted children. So he just sits down on the cement floor, rests his back against the metal door, takes off his glasses, and starts wearily rubbing his eyes, which are tearing up from all the dust, sleeplessness, and despair.

Then Nina comes downstairs. She sees all this, but she doesn't say anything. She immediately ushers the girls back to their compartment yet doesn't close the door all the way, so Pasha can hear everything. He can hear Nina wiping someone's tears away, washing the mascara off her face, giving someone sugar for her tea, asking someone to bring her some wet wipes. She's talking about her sister—younger, more confident, more successful—about how she'd always wear hand-me-downs from her older sisters, friends, and cousins. And Nina's hand-me-downs, too. She just had so many clothes; they looked so good on her—everyone, even the girls who'd given her their clothes, was jealous of her. "Because it's not about the clothes you wear, it's about your sense of dignity," Nina says. "And about not being afraid." Well, she didn't actually say all that, obviously, but Pasha knows that's what she meant. "Yeah, that's it," he thinks. "That's right. It's not about the clothes you wear, not about how you look. If you think about it, it's like we're all living in an orphanage. Abandoned by everyone, wearing too much makeup and whatever clothes we come by. Thing is, that makes no difference. You can wear clothes stolen from the thrift store and feel like the king of the world or you can have a nice warm jacket and be a fat prick nobody wants anything to do with," he thinks. "And why don't I ever talk to my kids about stuff like that? I give them all those dumb-ass dictations, make them do difficult and confusing exercises, teach them grammar rules that they'll never need. I teach them to speak properly. But just speaking, speaking so people hear and understand you—I don't teach them that. Well, I don't know how to do it myself."

"Yeah," Pasha thinks. "Why do they listen to her? Why do they stop crying? Why does their fear recede when she's talking to them? Maybe it's because she has a calm, quiet voice. You don't make threats in a voice like that. You don't even defend yourself in a voice like that. You say that there's nothing to be afraid of. It's just that everyone else around here yells. Constantly. At home. On the street. In public places. In public recreational areas. Just like my sister. Yeah, my sister." Pasha thinks back to their telephone conversation, and he gets this bitter taste in his mouth, as if he's swallowed a metal spoon. He thinks back to his last train ride with her—two winters ago, before all this started. It turns out that it isn't all that great when your sister's a train stewardess. Especially when she's the stewardess on your train. When she's checking your ticket, bringing you your sheets, locking the bathroom door right in front of your nose—I'm sorry, sir, but the restroom is closed when the train is approaching a major station. Well, she didn't check his ticket, obviously. He didn't even have one—he rode in her compartment. That was nice, but overall the trip was endless and exhausting. His sister started yelling on the platform, back at the Station. And she kept yelling the whole way: at Pasha, at the stewardess from the next car over, at the policemen assigned to the train, at the trainmaster. Not to mention the passengers, who didn't even put up any resistance. In fact, some of them even liked it. Some people like women who yell a lot. They view their outbursts as them being feisty. She even burst out yelling a few times throughout the night, seemingly frightened by her own protracted silence. They slept sitting up, on the lower bunk—his sister let some guy without a ticket hop onto the top bunk and made herself some extra cash on the side. They sat there until the early morning, watching snow flashing gold in the station lights that flew past the window. Exhausted, she'd occasionally doze off, resting her head on her brother's soft shoulder. Pasha sat there, trying not to disturb her, but whenever the train jolted, his sister would shriek and wail in her sleep, scaring the sick passenger on the top bunk. Come morning, when they were crossing over to Kyiv's right bank approaching the station, Pasha was sound asleep, curled up on some blankets. His sister, who'd already torn all the passengers out of bed and chased the sick traveler from the top bunk out of their compartment, came back, leaned in toward her brother, and gave his shoulder a gentle, sisterly touch. And when Pasha opened his eyes and recognized her, she calmly said:

"All righty now."

"All righty now," Nina says, standing over him. "All righty now."

Pasha shakes his head, quickly gets up.

"Go to the kitchen," she tells Pasha. "Grab something for the road. I'll talk to him." She points at the compartment door.

"I'll do it myself," Pasha replies. "I'll talk to him myself."

"You'll get to talk to him. You'll have plenty of time to talk."

Pasha gets up, goes upstairs, walks down the hallway.

The gym teacher is sitting by the window, reading some newspaper. The fog outside the window begins breaking into pieces, and when another piece comes off and is carried away by the wind, the cafeteria lights up—and he can read the next page. Then a new patch of damp gloom creeps along, and the gym teacher sets his newspaper aside. He sits, waits. He looks as if he's mulling over what he's read. He's extended his legs toward the potbelly stove, trying to warm up. His black coat, still so damp, hangs above it. The coat dangles from an old broom, the sleeves drooping, empty and hopeless. It looks like the outlaw who was hung on the cross about thirty-three years or so after the birth of Christ. His wet hat hangs nearby, too. A teapot smokes on the kitchen stove; the gym teacher occasionally pours some more hot water into his mug of strong tea. Pasha enters, stops in the doorway, thinking he may have come at the wrong time, but the gym teacher immediately waves him over amicably. C'mon, take a seat by the fire. Pasha walks over, smiles at him like they're old friends, and rests his foot on an upside-down crate. The firewood crackles dryly, the fog outside the window hovers whitely. One might think that they're simply snowed in at a hotel in the mountains. And they have plenty of time and firewood to warm up and steady themselves for their long journey. Only thing is, the explosions somewhere out there, beyond the fog, won't abate. And when you turn your head, your eyes land on a mountain of unwashed dishes that have been in the sink for who knows how long. But if you don't look at them, if you don't listen to the artillery firing into the city, if you only look at the stove, for instance, you feel a sense of serenity and security. The only thing that can scare you is the crucified coat looming up above. Death's somewhere nearby, just biding its time.

"Want some tea?" the gym teacher asks.

Pasha nods. He finds his mug—the brewed tea has gone cold—pours some hot water into it, and wraps his hands around the mug, trying to warm up. The metal is instantly hot, making Pasha's hands hot, too, yet he keeps holding it, not wanting to let go of this metal hunk of heat. The gym teacher's stroking his mustache somewhat comically, like they do in the movies, and he invites Pasha to sit down again. Pasha waves preemptively. Nah, I'll stand. Let's hear it.

"Where you from?" the gym teacher asks. "The Station?"

His Russian is strange: proper, more or less, and with no Ukrainian mixed in, but it isn't homegrown. Around here, foremen at mines, Party organizers at meetings, or cops at police stations talk like that. It's the language of not particularly well-educated people who speak about important state matters, and since they're afraid of saying the wrong thing they mostly speak in clichés. Pasha's used to this kind of Russian; he can speak it too. Nonetheless, Valera makes bureaucrat-speak sound pretty nice, like a retired general telling his grandchildren heroic tales of his life, taking some parts from general staff data and embellishing the rest.

"Yeah, from the Station," Pasha says. "I'm from the Station."

"I was born here," Valera continues, with satisfaction. "Near the hospital for employees of our local railroad station. Twenty minutes from here at a brisk walk. I remember when they built this orphanage. It was in the early to mid-seventies. We were attending secondary school at the time. We'd run over here and steal building materials."

"Why?" Pasha asks, confused.

"We didn't have any toys," the gym teacher explains.

He's in a warm gray turtleneck sweater and black dress pants, which he apparently wears to work, with blue sweatpants sticking out (he probably wears them to work, too). He's kicked off his boots and slipped on some rubber sandals. "It's a shame we don't have a gym teacher like him at our school," Pasha thinks. They weren't blessed with a great gym teacher. For starters, she's a woman (yells all the time, never listens, same old story), and she fled last fall, too, when the city was being surrounded. Pasha was even forced to fill in for her a few times, but nothing good came of that. He wore his heavy winter boots to gym class, didn't have any athletic shoes. This made the high schoolers mad. Pasha could sense that, so one time he went down to the principal's office, showed her his hand, and said that he was going to file a complaint, that it just wasn't right they were making him, a guy with a health problem, spin around on the pull-up bar. The principal got scared, but not for Pasha with his stiff fingers who was forced to risk his life on the pull-up bar. She was covering her own ass, since Pasha really could file a complaint. "Basically, it's a shame that we don't have a gym teacher like him," Pasha thinks, the hot water burning his lips. "Going to the teacher's lounge wouldn't be so bad then."

"Been here awhile?" Pasha asks.

"I started immediately after receiving my degree in physical education," the gym teacher replies. "I'm a seasoned educator. I've outlasted them all," he adds, now using his own words. "Everyone took off, you see. Nina's the only one who stuck around. I'm committed to giving my younger colleagues the benefit of my experience."

"Gotcha," Pasha replies approvingly. "Some good kids you got here, too."

"Yeah, we have a good crew here. Broken homes, juvenile delinquency, falling in with the wrong crowd. Parents suffering from alcoholism, unfavorable societal circumstances. Nobody wants anything to do with them," Valera adds, using his own words again. "They get dropped off here like puppies at a shelter. Responsibility is reassigned to the teaching staff."

"Like that only happens here," Pasha chimes in. "That's how it goes at every school. Nobody wants anything to do with them. Who takes care of them? Couldn't tell you. Why did their parents have them? Nobody knows."

"They had them to continue their lineage," the gym teacher explains, then pauses to think. "We had it good. Like, back in the seventies, when they charged us with theft of the people's property."

Pasha looks at him, confused. Whose property?

"I mean the building materials," the gym teacher explains. "We faced a jury of our comrades. In an auditorium at the warehouse complex. They dragged our parents down there. Our teachers and Party leaders came, too. And they really started laying into us, with the gloves off. Threatening us, blackmailing us, saying they were gonna lock us up for a long time. After all, we weren't kids anymore. We were going through a rebellious phase, adapting to the demands of society. We weren't afraid, though. It's strange—I'm thinking back to what I felt. We weren't the least bit scared. We knew that nothing bad would happen to us. They'd give us a little scare and then let us go. Because the whole country, with all its factories, mines, and Party program, was behind us. And nobody would turn us in. Knowing that is very important. Especially when you're a teenager. Don't you think?"

"Yeah," Pasha agrees.

"Well, we all just got lucky. We had a good country and a good childhood."

"But no toys . . ."

"Yeah, we didn't have toys, but we had a country. A good country. Not the worst one out there. At least it raised kids. It raised me, for instance. And I wasn't afraid of anything. I grew up here and came back after receiving my degree in physical education," the gym teacher reminds Pasha. "I'm committed to giving my younger colleagues the benefit of my experience. Just so you know, I'm not going anywhere. That's how I was raised. In that other country. Everyone took off, but I stuck around."

"Nina stuck around, too," Pasha reminds him.

"Yeah. Why'd I stick around? Why didn't I run away? Because I don't have anything to be afraid of. I don't stir things up. I just do my job. Why should I be afraid? Right?"

Pasha nods silently. Obviously, he agrees. Naturally, he agrees. He's the same way. He's always done his job; he didn't run away. "Why should I be afraid?" Pasha asks himself. "I have nothing to be afraid of, I didn't do anything wrong, it's not my fault," he answers himself. "I didn't ask anyone to come here, I didn't kick anyone out. I just do my job. I just teach kids how to write properly. I'd say that's much more important than standing around at checkpoints. Checkpoints get taken down, but grammar rules remain. So don't direct your complaints at me. Or at him," Pasha thinks. "He stuck around. He's definitely not going anywhere. He really will outlast everyone. He'll live forever. I love people like him," Pasha thinks, getting all emotional. The hot tea and the cozy afternoon fire have made him sentimental. He hasn't felt this calm in a long time.

Nina comes in. She frostily wraps a blanket around herself, sticks her pointy nose in the bowls and mugs, counts the canned goods, walks over to the stove, extends her arms, and warms her red hands. Valera notices her but doesn't really pay any attention to her, like she isn't even here. And she isn't saying anything; it seems as if she isn't listening to them either. She's thinking her own thoughts, warming her hands. When Valera stops talking, the explosions and crackling gunfire out the window become more distinct. It's as if someone has opened the doors of a warm, sleepy train compartment on to the noisy hallway. Valera is impatient for the conversation to resume.

"Who's gonna answer for all this?" he asks, waving his hand around. "Nobody. You'll see, they won't find the guilty parties."

"They'll make us the guilty parties," Pasha contends.

"No, they won't," the gym teacher objects, confidently. "Don't think so. Whoever started all of this has to answer for it. Personally, I'd like to see how they get themselves out of this one. I'll be really interested to see how they get themselves out of this one."

"It's not the first time for them," Pasha says.

"Sure isn't." The gym teacher takes his pack of cigarettes out of his coat pocket and lights one in the stove, leaning in sharply and nearly burning his eyelashes off.

"You're right, though. Obviously they're gonna try and pin it all on us, on the people who stuck around. Yeah, that's how it'll play out, for sure. But no way in hell are they gonna pin anything on me!" Valera says heatedly, and all his impenetrable canned phrases disappear instantly. "Not gonna happen! I don't have anything to do with all this! And they don't either!" He points at some place behind Pasha. He even looks around, but nobody's there, obviously: hallway twilight, the cafeteria walls painted blue. But it's clear that the gym teacher is talking about the kids, about the ones who took off and the ones who stuck around. "They don't have anything to do with all this either. I feel sorry for them, Pasha. You believe me?"

"I do."

"Yeah, I do feel sorry for them. They were born at the wrong time and in the wrong country. They're not like us. We have something to remember." The gym teacher enjoys a kind, carefree laugh, and Pasha can't help but crack a smile. "We had a real country, we didn't have to be afraid. Thinking about my childhood always makes me smile. I'm serious. You believe me?"

"I do."

"What about you?" he asks Pasha contentiously.

"Me too. It makes me smile, too."

"What about you, Nina?" The gym teacher finally acknowledges his boss. "Does thinking about your childhood make you smile?"

Nina keeps looking at the fire, as if she didn't hear the question. And then she answers.

"No. It doesn't. All I remember about my childhood is that hungry feeling in my stomach."

"Well, everyone had it rough—" the gym teacher counters.

But Nina curtly interrupts him.

"Not everyone did. Far from everyone. I had it real rough. I didn't have anything to eat. And my mom didn't have anything to eat either. Even though she was growing up when you were out stealing building materials. He told you about that, right?" she asks Pasha.

"Yeah," Pasha says, flustered.

The gym teacher sneers but doesn't say anything.

"Don't sneer at me." Nina continues to talk in a calm, flat voice, as though she's confessing to mortal sins and knows perfectly well what awaits her. "Nobody died of starvation, as you can see, but I don't have any nice memories of my so-called childhood. Do you know what my nickname was at school, Valera? As a gym teacher, you'll find it interesting. 'The Athlete.'"

"Why?" Pasha asks, surprised.

"Because I always wore sneakers. Summer and winter. One of my neighbors gave them to me. My father was out of the picture, and I won't even tell you what my mom did for a living. She didn't make much money doing it, though. And she grew up without a father, too. And she wore hand-me-downs all through her childhood, too. And she didn't have any nice memories about her so-called childhood either. You know why you weren't afraid? It wasn't because you lived in a wonderful country, it was because somebody was always covering for you—whether it was your parents or the Communist Youth League. Thing is, nobody covered for me. And nobody'll cover for them," she says, pointing at the blue walls behind Pasha and Valera. "Nobody besides us. But that doesn't mean they should be afraid. They shouldn't have to be afraid. All of our experience and all of our grown-up knowledge isn't worth a penny if they are. Not a penny."

Nina quiets down. Flustered, Pasha and the gym teacher keep

silent, too. They don't have anything to say, they aren't ready. The firewood cracks off dry shots in the stove, and once again the explosions in the foggy mush become more distinct.

"And one more thing," Nina adds. "Valera, you say that you don't have anything to do with this. When's the last time you voted?"

"I don't do that, Nina," the gym teacher replies defiantly.

"And do you know who our deputy is?"

"I have no clue."

"And you don't have any idea what side he's fighting for, do you?"

"No," Valera answers honestly. At this point, Pasha still likes what he's hearing.

"Then how can you blame anyone for this? On what grounds?" Nina asks. "What right do you have to air your grievances? Do you know your students' parents, or what's going on in their heads? Do you know where their parents are right now? What they've been doing? Who's been buried this past year? Them passing their physical fitness tests—that's what you care most about, right?"

"What do physical fitness tests have to do with this?" Valera asks, a little flustered.

"Everything. Yeah, you're always reminiscing about when things were good, nice and calm, when you weren't afraid. Then why are all of you so scared now?"

"I'm not scared."

"You are, though. You might not be afraid of getting blown up, but you're afraid of telling it like it is. And you're afraid of telling them the truth," Nina says, pointing at something behind Valera and Pasha. "That's a lot harder than reminiscing about your happy childhood."

"That's not what Valera was talking about—" Pasha tries to stick up for the gym teacher, but Nina interrupts him quietly yet firmly.

"That's exactly what he was talking about—about fear and irresponsibility. And you, Pasha, do you talk to your kids about the war?"

"I'm a language teacher," Pasha replies.

"Do you realize that half of their parents are fighting? Do you have any idea about that?"

"Well, yeah," Pasha says tentatively.

"And do you have any idea that some of them are fighting against you? Against us," she corrects herself.

"Nobody's fighting against me," Pasha objects coldly, beginning to enjoy this conversation less and less. "I'm not on anyone's side."

"Well, when they're shooting at your nephew—are you still not on anyone's side? When shells hit the orphanage where he lives? Who are they fighting against, then? Against me?"

"I don't know who's doing the shooting."

"Really?" Nina's surprised yet calm. "I do, though. Want me to tell you? Do you know what direction the gym faces? Valera knows, he's the gym teacher."

"I don't know," the gym teacher answers just as flatly.

"I do, though," Nina says. "The gym faces south. And the shell came from the south. And what's to the south? Valera, what's to the south?"

"Well, how am I supposed to know?" the gym teacher replies, irritated.

"You know, you know perfectly well. The border is to the south. The national border. The former national border," Nina corrects herself. "And the shells are coming from down there. And what don't you get about that? And what's so confusing about that? And if you don't want to admit that to yourselves, who's going to tell you?"

"There are shells going the other way, too," Valera snaps back.

"Yeah," Nina agrees. "But you don't talk about that either. Like it has nothing to do with you. Even though you should've made up your minds and picked a side a long time ago. You're so used to hiding. So used to staying out of things, letting someone else decide everything for you, letting someone else take care of things for you. Nobody's going to decide for you, nobody's going to take care of things. Not this time. Because you saw what was going on, you knew. But you kept silent, you didn't say anything. Nobody's going to judge you for that, obviously, but don't count on your descendants' appreciation. Basically," Nina says, standing up resolutely, "what I'm saying is, don't delude yourself—everyone's going to answer for this. And those who aren't used to answering for anything will be the worst off. I'm going to make lunch, Valera. You can help me, if you want. Yeah, Pasha, you can stay for lunch, too. Sasha's waiting for you, though, so you might want to get going. Just make sure you take something for the road."

Pasha thanks her, bewildered, stuffs several cans in his pockets, and leaves without another word.

The kid's sitting in the hallway, his back resting against the wall. He sees Pasha, gets up, wordlessly walks across the gym toward the exit. Green autumn jacket—wrong season—black jeans, leather backpack, and in his hands the baseball bat. And sneakers on his feet.

They walk around the outside of the orphanage. The gym teacher's coat looms in the window. It almost looks like Valera's waving goodbye to them. Just can't see his face, though. Or his hand. The clothing's still there, but there's no person.

It's 2 p.m. The fog has settled; it's getting dragged down the streets, thickening in the trees and slowly trickling down into the valley, into the city. They approach the gate, hop the fence, walk across the grounds. The kid confidently dodges piles of leaves. Pasha tries to keep up. They aren't talking to each other. In the wet air, steps ring resonantly, like someone's hammering nails into a tree. Pasha stops at the edge of the grounds; the kid hears this, stops in his tracks. He keeps quiet, though, waiting for Pasha to say something.

"We aren't going through the city," Pasha says. "Gotta get to the road that runs around it."

"All right," the kid answers, a little condescendingly.

"Do you know where that road is?"

"Yeah, I do," the kid says reluctantly. He hasn't decided how he's going to act around Pasha.

"Let's try and get out of here before the sun goes down," Pasha replies. "Sound good?"

The kid hesitates—should he keep being mad or loosen up? The wind is blowing away from the city, pulling scraps of fog up out of the valley. The sweet taste of something burning instantly appears in the air. The taste of metal and wet dog. Pasha twitches; the kid cringes, gripping his bat even tighter.

"All right," he says. "We gotta head through this neighborhood, then there's a fork in the road. We should steer clear of it, there used to be a checkpoint there. I know a shortcut, though."

Pasha stands still, weighing what he's heard. The trees overhead start making noises. Pasha lifts his head. Something is up. Eventually it hits him—he sees trees, fog, and the sky somewhere up above. No birds, though.

They move swiftly down a broken road, pass charred rebar and the destroyed bus stop, then the store, leaving the well behind. Here a street starts. Long, endless. Brick houses, garages, additions stacked on top of one another. Slate riddled with shrapnel. Gas pipes running on both sides of the street. One of the pipes is broken and bent. Looks like there's no gas here. Or electricity. There aren't any people in sight either. Not a single person. Only trees. Their bare branches tap against one another overhead. A metal gate squeaks somewhere nearby. But behind them, in the valley, in the city, things are just getting started. Lunch has just ended, probably, and now they're feeling refreshed, so they've gotten back to work. The explosions grow more intense; soon something hits very close by, right here in the fog. Pasha and the kid speed up. They're hurrying, nearly running. But the faster they go, the scarier it gets, as if somebody is chasing them down the dead street. Pasha even starts to think that someone really is following them, right on their heels, keeping pace. "Just calm down," Pasha tells himself. "There's nobody here." But he looks around from time to time, trying to make something out, anything at all, beyond the fog, which is making everything invisible, suspicious. Suddenly, he actually spots someone over there. Someone's moving. He can hear someone's heavy breathing. Pasha tries to put it out of his mind. He just speeds up, but the kid notices the crazed, frightened look on his face and realizes that something's up, something's going on.

"What?" the kid asks.

"We're fine," Pasha answers, but he can't help but look back again.

The kid follows his eyes and looks back, too. There's no escaping out here, though. They stop, stand, look into the fog, wait. One second, two, three. It gets colder, which scares them even more. Someone's definitely over there, someone's standing there, trying to catch their scent. It's just that they can't see anything beyond all the pieces of fog. Then Pasha crouches. And notices the dogs. A dozen, maybe more. Skinny strays, abandoned by everyone, standing several yards away from them, extending their skinny, soaked necks, listening intently. The kid crouches too. He sees them too. The cautious, careful dogs. They aren't the least bit frightened, though. It's immediately obvious who the outsiders are, who's out of place here. Their eyes are heavy, ferocious, but their voices are silent. They're waiting.

"Let's go," Pasha says, almost inaudibly. "Leave them alone."

They stand up straight and keep walking, trying not to panic, not to rush. Pasha gives in first. He turns around, crouches. The dogs immediately freeze, keeping their distance. Pasha stands up straight again and takes a step back. The dogs retreat reluctantly. But as soon as he turns around, they hurry to catch up.

"Ignore them," the kid advises. "They can feel that you're scared of them."

"I'm not scared of them."

"Yeah, sure," the kid says quietly. "Even I can tell you're scared of them. I'm scared, too. Who knows what they've been feeding on out here. Keep walking. Stay calm."

They keep walking, faster and faster, more and more anxiously, almost breaking into a run. But they realize that running isn't an option—that would be a signal, a sign for those stalking them. Pasha's on edge, soaked with sweat. He scrambles to come up with something, feels panic creeping up to his throat. "Why'd I drag the kid out here?" he thinks. "How could I? How am I going to protect him now?" The kid has a more confident air about him, though. He is holding a baseball bat, after all. But the fingers gripping that bat have turned completely white. Probably from the cold. Pasha notices some crushed bricks on the road. "This is ridiculous. Gotta do something," he thinks. "Can't keep running like this." And he's just about to pick up a chunk of brick when the kid suddenly says to him, quietly yet clearly:

"Look to the left."

Pasha looks to the left. He sees a green gate that opens into a yard. The kid grabs his sleeve and drags him toward the gate before he can figure out what's going on. Pasha's boots hit the wet asphalt hard as he races after the kid. The dogs bolt after them, a dozen hungry, cold throats responding, growling with thrilled despair, so loud the whole world can hear. They lunge at them, their teeth snatching thick pieces of air. The kid leaps into the yard; Pasha stumbles through the gate after him. "Hope it closes all the way," he thinks. "Just hope it closes." He yanks on the gate from the inside. For an instant, just a brief instant, it's stuck, won't move. Then it budges and swings shut with a bang. The dog closest to them, the leader, pounces, his front paws landing on the gate, but Pasha manages to close it in the nick of time. Bang on it all you want—they're in the clear now. The dogs realize that; disappointed, they rub their muzzles against the gate, snarl, bark out all their disappointment, and try to crawl under the metal fence.

"Hurry up," the kid yells and darts away from the gate.

Pasha runs after him. There's an asphalt walkway in the yard. A truck has smeared red clay across the asphalt—must've been loading possessions. Their own or someone else's. The lock on the front door of the house has been removed, but the door itself is closed. Right behind the house, the garage door is wide open. Inside, cardboard boxes, tools, and pieces of metal are scattered all over. There's an outdoor shower behind the garage; the water tank's in a dampened, darkened flowerbed. Then there's a fence and a vegetable garden behind it. The kid pushes the crooked gate, runs down a soggy path. Pasha can feel the mud sticking to his boots, weighing them down, making it hard to run. But he has to run. They run through the black unharvested garden, past soaked cornstalks, past heavy, rotten vegetables. And they run straight out to a scorched clearing. The kid races out and then freezes—frightened and mesmerized. Pasha runs after him and his eyes immediately land on a bloody heap of mush in the middle of the scorched grass: scraps of cowhide, bones, tendons mixed in with mud. "They butchered the cattle," Pasha figures. "And smoked the meat." The kid's stopped dead.

"Don't look!" Pasha yells. "Don't look."

He covers Sasha's eyes. The kid suddenly goes limp, doesn't resist, doesn't say anything. He lets Pasha drag him away from the mountain of rotten innards, stumbles through the thick grass, shakes Pasha's hand off him, keeps running, not looking back, not exhaling. "That time was just like this," Pasha thinks. Just like right now—the kid, pale and limp after an attack, the teary-eyed doctor standing over him, not knowing what to say. Best not to think about that.

Behind the gardens is a dirt road that's been ripped up by tank treads. They move through the deep ruts, viscous masses of clay sticking to their boots, and run across a wet pasture toward what used to be a farm. Two wrecked cowsheds, concrete slabs lying in the grass, a rusty water tower off to the side, a low-hanging, silvery sky poking through the fog up above. The locals took the doors off one of them. The structure itself looks like the skeleton of a large animal, a large, horned animal—walls whitewashed by rain, beams bent by the snow. Everything else has been cleaned out, taken to another house or burrow. No windows, no doors, just black holes and cold drafts. They run inside. There are two large straw nests in the corner. Looks like someone was here, lying low. There aren't any shell casings around, so they didn't do any shooting. They were just waiting things out. They were probably wounded: straw soaked with dark blood, empty vials stomped into the dirt floor, disposable needles, sodden bandages. The nests are wet. Clearly, whoever was lying here left a few days ago. The place smells sharply of urine and mud. Pasha walks over to a smashed window and tries to discern something, anything, in the fog. It's just before dusk. The fog gleams and settles in the fine rain. The neighborhood's roofs, tall trees, and dark rows of corn loom beyond the rain. Farther along, to the right, the horizon hovers and then drops off, and down there in the valley lies the city. They can't see the city, but long black streams of smoke are rising from over there. They have been since yesterday; it's as if the ground has been ruptured and now something truly terrible is coming out of the earth, and nobody knows how to stop that something, the worst thing, since nobody knows how it happened, how the earth split and released all its blackness, which is now creeping across the January sky and filling up all its cracks and openings. "Who's going to put out the smoke?" Pasha thinks. Everything around here will burn, like in a medieval city, the flame skipping from house to house, from street to street. Give it a few days, and nothing will be left.

"That's the warehouses burning," the kid says.

"What warehouses?" Pasha asks, confused.

"By the railroad," the kid explains. "See that?

The kid points at something in the rain. Pasha looks intently. Beyond the corn and the rain, he can make out gray smoke that's settling heavily, pressed down by the rain, unable to rise.

"Can you imagine how much stuff is gonna burn?" the kid says with some sort of delight in his voice.

"Yeah," Pasha replies. "Let's take a break. Are you hungry?"

"Nah," the kid answers. "Not after seeing those guts."

"Nina . . . ," Pasha says and then pauses. "She's kinda harsh."

"No, she's okay."

"Why does she have to lecture everyone? Like she's a teacher or something."

"Well, she is a teacher," the kid reminds him. "What's she supposed to be like? That's what she always says. That's why people don't like her. Because she lectures everyone."

"Well, there's no need to lecture me," Pasha says, aggrieved. "I'll figure things out on my own."

"You've really got things figured out, huh?" the kid asks.

Pasha doesn't say anything. He thinks of Nina, gets angry with himself. Why didn't I say anything to her?

"Seems like she never feels sorry for anyone."

"Who's she supposed to feel sorry for?" the kid inquires. "The gym teacher? You?"

"Well, I don't have anything to do with this." Pasha is trying to be more straightforward. “It’s just that you can’t blame everyone. Everyone’s different.”

“Yeah?” the kid replies skeptically. “I’d say you’re all the same. The flag at the orphanage got torn down. Do you know how it happened?”

“How?”

“Basically, they wanted to tear it down, but Nina didn’t want to let them. Everyone else just stood there and watched.”

“So what?” Pasha still doesn’t see what he’s getting at.

“Well, basically, only two guys wanted to tear it down. Against one Nina. And everyone else just stood there and watched. And didn’t do anything. About a hundred people—they just watched, didn’t do anything. Everyone’s the same. I don’t feel sorry for anyone.”

“All right,” Pasha replies. “Let’s go.”

“Okay.”

They go out into the rain and walk, cowering from the cold, sinking into the wet earth. An empty lot stretches out beyond the farm. Then a row of trees comes into view. They walk toward it. They’ve lost all sense of time. It’s tough going at first, and it doesn’t get any easier or any harder. They plod along mechanically, heavy mud caked on their shoes, tucking their freezing hands into their pockets. The kid warms one hand at a time, switching when the one holding the bat gets cold. They trudge up to the trees. Pasha fights through the prickly branches, the kid in tow. They reach an open area. A deep basin, a ravine stuffed with fog like a pillow with feathers, sprawls out before them. It feels like the fog has been dragged down, as if it’s flowed down there to hide for a moment.

"Go around?" Pasha asks.

"Can't," the kid answers. "That'd tack on a mile or two."

They stand there and look down skeptically. The ravine's wide. Can't see the bottom. Just a white, eerie feeling flowing over the edges, treading up to their feet. One step and you come out on the other side of life. Don't feel like going all the way around, though.

"Let's go, okay?" Pasha takes several steps forward.

The kid holds his hand, following his every step. The ground gives way; Pasha skids down, grabs the sharp blackthorn and briar bushes with his free hand, cutting himself. Blood starts trickling over his fingers, but he doesn't have time to wipe it off. He has to hang on tight to keep himself from tumbling right into hell. Pasha's getting angry, but he doesn't say anything. He doesn't want to scare the kid. He's dragging him along, feeling the warmth of his hand. It's nearly impossible to make out the kid, but he is here—Pasha can hear his breathing, the ground rustling under his sneakers, but can't actually see him. Pasha talks to him, keeps repeating himself. Careful, careful. Watch your step. But what's there to watch when you can't see anything? They grab on to each other, on to the wet grass, on to the prickly blackthorn, ripping their skin up and sliding down into the endlessly long and endlessly deep ravine. They slide to the bottom, landing in a knee-deep pile of last year's snow—December snow. It's colder down here. The snow lies unmelted. Pasha touches the crust, pressing his lacerated hand with its dead fingers against it, cooling the blood flowing down his wrist. The kid tosses his backpack next to him and falls into the snow, face up. He lies there, catching his breath. Pasha picks up some prickly snow with his uninjured hand and starts devouring it.

"Is it good?" the kid asks.

"It's cold," Pasha replies.

"Don't eat too much. You'll catch a cold," the kid says without irritation—a first—his voice tinged with concern. Pasha may have just imagined that, though.

Going uphill is even tougher, but they keep trudging along. Pasha's out front. He's carrying the kid's backpack on his chest as he drags him along. The kid's straining, trying to push through, but it's clear that he's exhausted. What isn't clear is how much they have ahead of them. Climbing and climbing, latching on to taut grass, on to cherry roots. And when you don't have any energy left or any certainty that you're headed in the right direction, when the kid's hanging down below like a warm, dead weight, when your injured hand is starting to go numb, you suddenly grab a cherry branch and realize that this is it—it's the edge, the other edge of the abyss, the opposite bank of the river, the River of the Dead. He boosts the kid up, climbs out after him. They sit on the grass, their breathing labored, not saying anything for a while.

"Which way now?" Pasha asks, once he's worked up the nerve.

"Straight," the kid says with a nod. "The road's straight ahead."

A field of sunflowers looms up ahead—last year's ungathered harvest. The dark sunflowers, dried out by the summer heat, look like a scorched forest. Another row of trees is visible beyond the sunflowers. And then there's the road. Just have to walk through the flowers.

Pasha goes first. The kid follows, as usual. The sunflowers part, whipping their hands. Water flows up their sleeves. "They're just going to stand there," Pasha says to himself, thinking about the sunflowers. "Like zombies. Cursed and forgotten. Until somebody plows all this up."

They keep moving—slowly, but they're still moving. The sky grows dark, the black mass of the trees bears down on them. Two hundred yards to go, one hundred and fifty, one hundred. Distinct trees gradually appear in the air at dusk, ducking out of the darkness. And meanwhile, military vehicles emerge plainly and translucently from behind the trees—a column of trucks, tanks, and APCs. They roll along leisurely, without beginning or end—the first ones have disappeared around the fork in the road, the last ones are unseen in the evening twilight. They keep going and going, rolling along the half-frozen road. "They're coming from the south," Pasha finds himself thinking. "From the national border. The former national border," he corrects himself. "The former border."

"There are so many of them," the kid says, mesmerized.

"Bad timing," Pasha replies.

"Yep. Could've hitched a ride if we'd left half an hour earlier, you know?" he scoffs.

"What are we gonna do? Wait it out?"

One of the trucks suddenly peels away from the column and comes to a halt; three soldiers hop out of the cab. They walk down a hill, go over to the field, and stop. Pasha instantly crouches, pulling the kid down with him. Shh, don't move. They're coming. The soldiers wade into the sunflowers, lazily moving in Pasha and the kid's direction. The distance between them grows shorter; Pasha hears sunflowers snapping underneath them, someone bursting into loud laughter, someone else cutting him off, hears them get quiet, stop, and listen warily to the afternoon silence. They examine the fog, examine the smoke on the horizon, consult each other briefly, turn around, and swiftly head back to the truck. The vehicle sets off, wedges itself into the column, dissolves into it.

"Let's go back," Pasha says quietly. "Now."

And he runs, crouched over, toward the ravine. The kid obediently runs after him.

They get back to the neighborhood after dark, at around six, taking some barely visible paths to the main street. Pasha picks up some hunks of brick along the way in case he needs to fend anyone off. The street's empty, though; their steps echo resonantly, the city trembles somewhere out there in the dark, like a tormented man in his sleep. The earth's slightly frozen; breathing in the cold air is painful but nice. "We'll warm up at the orphanage," Pasha thinks. "We'll spend the night and try again tomorrow."

"You cold?" he asks the kid.

"No," the kid lies.

"Yeah, right," Pasha thinks. The cold numbs your hands and face. You want to get to a warm building as quickly as possible, even if it doesn't have any running water or electricity. Just get out of the cold, warm up.

They pass the well. Even though it's dark, Pasha spots fresh tracks all around, left by the treads of a heavy vehicle. It's as though somebody was hanging around here, at the intersection, not knowing which way to go. Pasha tenses up but doesn't say anything to the kid. They keep walking. The worst part is that the tracks lead straight to the orphanage. The clumps of clay and black mud on the gray wet asphalt are fresh, left recently. Apparently, the kid's spotted them, too, and he knows what's going on, but he isn't saying anything. He's hiding his head in his shoulders, warming his hands in his pockets, and keeping quiet. Pasha's been carrying the bat for a while now, tucked under his arm like a baguette. They walk past the wrecked bus stop and get to the orphanage grounds. Going inside is scary; the space between the trees feels particularly empty—step into that emptiness and it'll suck you in for good. The kid ventures onto the path first. He walks between the wet trunks, his eyes fixed on the twilight at his feet so he doesn't trip on someone's severed head. They eventually make it across the grounds to the gate.

"The lock," the kid says quietly.

"What about it?"

"They busted the lock," the kid explains.

Pasha takes a closer look. The lock really is busted, but the gate has been shut neatly. The kid takes a step forward.

"Stop," Pasha says, firmly latching onto his shoulder. "Where are you going?"

They stand there and look straight ahead, not knowing what to do. They see someone approaching—coming out of the darkness from the orphanage, right at them. "The gym teacher," Pasha thinks. "Going on a water run. He was the one who opened the gate. He's the only one with a key." But it's someone short and unremarkable, a gnome holding a box, coming right at them out of the darkness. Pasha is taken aback. It seems like the gnome is, too. Pasha quickly turns on his phone flashlight; the light from the screen snatches sharp angles and deep cavities out of the darkness for several seconds. Autumn jacket down to his knees—probably someone else's—track bottoms with white stripes, ragged winter boots. Black hat, heavy face, sliced up by wrinkles. Black circles under his eyes—must have health problems. Clearly has bad breath. Pasha doesn't want to check, though. The gnome's holding a bag of pasta. He catches a glimpse of Pasha's beard, heavy boots, and baseball bat during the several seconds while the screen is on and immediately tenses up. But then he glances at the kid and relaxes again. Oh, good, they're locals, from the orphanage.

"Where you goin'?" he hisses, his voice low and hoarse.

"Where's Valera?" Pasha replies. He doesn't know who this guy is or how to talk to him.

"Who the fuck is Valera?" the gnome hisses anxiously.

"The gym teacher."

"They took your gym teacher away." The gnome wants to push his way past, but Pasha won't step aside, so he has to explain further.

"Where'd they take him?"

"To the hospital."

"What happened?"

"They stabbed him."

"Who?"

"Fucked if I know!" The gnome can't take it anymore. "They just stabbed him. Then they loaded him into a bus and took him to the hospital."

"Where is everyone?"

"Everyone's gone," the gnome mutters nastily. "And you should leave, too. It's just not safe around here."

"Where you taking that?" the kid asks, pointing at the pasta.

Pasha wants to ask about the pasta, too, but before he can, the gnome shoves him, squeezes his gut past him, and runs away. Pasha considers darting after him, but the kid restrains him.

"Where you going?" he whispers. "Leave him alone. Let's get out of here."

"What do you mean? We have to see what's going on."

"There's nobody in there," the kid says, his tone insistent. "He just told you."

“You’re gonna listen to that guy? Maybe someone stuck around. Gotta check it out.”

“There’s nobody in there,” the kid insists.

“What’s wrong?” Pasha asks him.

“Everything’s fine,” the kid answers. “There’s nobody in there. Let’s go.”

“He’s scared,” Pasha figures. “The gnome with the pasta freaked him out. Oh, Lord, what did you expect from him? He’s only thirteen. Obviously he’s scared.”

“Come on, Sasha,” Pasha says in a calm tone, like everything’s just fine. “Maybe someone stuck around. Gotta check it out.”

“What if one of them, one of the locals, is in there?” the kid asks.

“Well, what if Nina’s in there? Or one of the other kids?” Pasha insists. “We can’t just leave without even looking.”

“Well, what if they’re gone? What if they actually took Valera to the hospital?”

“I don’t believe him,” Pasha replies. “I won’t believe it until I see it.”

The kid thinks.

“All right,” he says. “Let’s go. Just be quiet.”

They push the gate, and it opens with a piercing squeak. Pasha hesitates for an instant but then steps inside. The kid follows closely. They pass the main building and approach the gym. Dark, dead quiet, door opens inward. Pasha takes a cautious peek. He turns his phone flashlight on. There are tracks all over the floor—the distinct imprints of army boots and a wide, dirty streak. It’s as if someone’s dragged bags of cement across the gym. Pasha’s already beginning to suspect something is wrong; he quickly walks down the hallway, runs toward the basement, and bursts into the first compartment. Scattered things, rumpled sheets, mats. They packed in a hurry, leaving their clothes and belongings behind—even their toothbrushes are still neatly arranged in a dry cup. Pasha runs over to the third compartment, Sasha's compartment. The sleeping bag's gone, the books are still there. They weren't interested in books. Pasha and the kid run back upstairs, walk over to the cafeteria, go inside, and look around. Dishes all over the floor, trampled metal bowls, bent forks. The corner where the food was—empty.

"Damn, they cleaned everything out," Pasha says.

"Who did?" the kid asks.

"Well, those guys, the locals. Those bastards."

"What'd you expect from them?" the kid asks. "They hate Nina. They would've burned the place down a long time ago. They were too scared, though."

"Not anymore, I guess."

"You got that right," the kid says. "Pasha!" he calls suddenly.

His voice makes Pasha spring up and come over immediately. The kid's looking at the corner, and Pasha follows his eyes. Cold stove, overturned chair, trampled newspapers with dried bloodstains on them. And a winter coat. Pasha lifts his phone, shines it ahead. Several barely noticeable bullet holes in the fabric—have to get close to spot them. Pasha walks over and touches the coat. It's still wet. He counts the holes. Four.

"What'd they do that for?" the kid asks, almost inaudibly.

"I don't know," Pasha answers. "Don't know."

"Did they kill him?" the kid queries.

"Maybe," Pasha answers. "Maybe. They don't have any pity for anyone," he says, sticking his dead fingers in the punctured fabric. "Anyone at all."

His heart tightens; he feels his head spinning, his body tipping to one side. He tries to center himself. It feels like this spring—big, cold, steel—has been tightening inside him for the past two days. It's been tightening this whole time. Every minute, every second. It's been tightening all the way, to the limit. It's been tightening, pressing on his chest, not letting him breathe, cutting off his airway. And when he starts to suffocate, when the lack of oxygen numbs his chest, Pasha slowly counts in his head:

ten

nine

eight

seven

six

five

four

three

two

one

that's it—

and the spring loosens up, squeezing his heart hard. Pasha gasps for air, deeply and abruptly, chokes, doubled over by a violent cough, resting his hands on his knees, struggles to catch his breath, senses that the spring is still loosening up, repelling him, spinning him around, and giving him the energy to keep going.

"Hurry up," he says to the kid. "Hurry up, let's go."

His voice, dry and demanding, surprises the kid; he's surprised, but he doesn't object. All right, let's go. They turn off the flashlight, head outside, slip through the gate, and dissolve into the trees.

"You're all the same." Pasha repeats Sasha's words as he rushes through the darkness. "Everyone's the same." At least everyone he knows is. They're all one and the same. Pasha thinks back to two Septembers ago: the first week of classes, sunny day, still feels like summer, the sun's lazily drifting over the slate roofs of the Station, chains of train cars, dark red like wet bricks, rolling along behind a row of dry pines. The students are messing around in the flowerbeds in front of the school, cleaning up the grounds, swinging old spades at the robust steppe weeds that have overrun the surrounding area. Off to the side on the athletic field, the younger kids are raking, gathering something up, working away. This is a good chance for the teachers to get some sun. Pasha's standing in his classroom—the window's open—taking in the warm air turned slightly bitter by the smoke, and lethargically watching the kids. Vadik, the shop teacher, a friend of Pasha's you could say, is the guard on yard duty. Workmen's jeans and a dark dress shirt, anxious and inattentive. He doesn't like kids and doesn't really bother hiding it. The kids don't like him either, and they don't bother hiding anything. Kids don't hide anything at all. Compulsory education is designed to break them of that habit. The upperclassmen aren't doing much of anything, mostly just keeping each other from working—the boys are yelling over each other and the girls are watching it all with poorly concealed admiration. The guys in eleventh grade are hassling Dimka—lives by the train depot, skinny frame, narrow shoulders, yellow unkempt hair. Dimka's a bad student and a bad dresser. And he doesn't talk right either. So they're giving him a hard time, treating him like a punching bag. Much to his credit, he is fighting back, but he's just kind of going through the motions. He's yelling and trying to fend them off, but then four or five come after him at once, so he doesn't stand a chance. Pasha realizes that it's gone too far. They've already taken one of Dimka's shoes off and now they're trying to toss it into a sorrowful September maple, but Pasha doesn't feel like getting involved. After all, the shop teacher's down there. It's his responsibility, let him handle it. But the shop teacher is just standing there, his back resting against a tree, smoking inattentively, and watching. And it's abundantly obvious that he doesn't care what happens to them. Let them kill each other for all he cares. That's precisely what they're doing, actually. They knock Dimka down and start burying him in the flowerbed. The blade of a spade glistens in the sun. "I should step in," Pasha thinks, but he doesn't. And Vadik the shop teacher doesn't step in either. And then the spade strikes Dimka, who's been buried by this point, right on his skull. The hollow sound of metal on bone is followed by a desperate, overpowering, dizzying wail. Dimka lies in a half-finished grave, furiously smearing blood across his forehead. And blood runs into his eyes, blinding him and mixing with the mud. Only then does the shop teacher dash toward Dimka, throw the upperclassmen off him like they're little puppies, grab him, and drag him back to a classroom. And then the rest of the teachers flock to the wailing, wounded student. Pasha runs over, too, scurries around, doles out some advice, and keeps getting in everyone's way.

Then they had parent-teacher conferences. It turned out that Dimka only had one parent. Well, he had two, but his father couldn't come—he was in prison. His mom came and made a real stink. The students kept quiet, froze her out. At first the teaching staff was freezing her out, too, but then they all started talking at once, first blaming the victim himself, then blaming the upperclassmen, and then they gave Dimka's mom some flak. You didn't raise your kid right, didn't give him enough attention. Pasha wanted to speak up, tell everyone what had actually happened, but he didn't speak up or tell anyone anything. Instead, he got up, went outside, and had a smoke. The shop teacher followed him.

"That bitch," he said, clearly referring to Dimka's mom. He asked Pasha for a cigarette.

"It's my last one," Pasha replied.

The shop teacher took that as an invitation, fished Pasha's last cigarette out of the pack, quickly smoked it, and then went back inside to keep arguing. Pasha quit smoking after that. For good.

That was a year and a half ago. Just a year and a half ago. Tranquil times, things were steady. A year and a half ago, Pasha would go to work and teach private lessons in the evenings and on weekends. He made more than enough to get by. He shopped at thrift and wholesale stores; you could almost have called him well dressed. His jacket was shabby, though, and he bought defective boots—he had to get them repaired. They were brand name, though. Basic cellphone, Chinese-made backpack. He didn't really need anything more than that. Maryna shopped for herself. They didn't eat out. Well, there weren't any restaurants at the Station.

A year and a half has gone by. Nobody needs tutors anymore. The kids are gone. Maryna left him. The shop teacher is on the other side of the front.

They run to the steep steps that lead down toward the city. The kid's tired; he's dropping back and spitting a lot. Pasha takes his backpack and slaps it on his chest like it's a parachute. It's not too heavy for him because his own backpack is almost empty, except for the canned goods, tapping together hollowly. The kid's clearly hurting, though. He really needs to get warm, but where is he going to get warm out here? The fog has lifted completely, and a round moon the color of slightly stale cheese with a glint of red at the bottom—as if it's been dipped in warm blood—hangs above the city. The sky's as empty as can be: no stars, no movement, just the fatal sheen of a full moon hovering over this valley of death that they'll have to cross, from beginning to end. Farther off, beyond the railroad tracks, a high, white flame is blazing. Settling smoke is smoldering nearby. And you can hear the businesslike crackle of automatic gunfire all around the city. You can feel movement in the city. It's as though somewhere over there under the full moon unseen swarms of people are racing down the crumbling streets, searching for warmth and food. You can't see them from here, but you can easily hear them, which makes things even more unnerving.

"Are we going down?" Pasha's mostly asking himself.

The kid gives him a barely perceptible nod, yet keeps standing still, not moving at all. Then Pasha grabs his hand as firmly as he can. The kid grasps his hand back, latches on to his dead fingers like they're the only thing in this world he can trust, and the two of them head out. First fifty steps. The wind blows the smell of stagnant water, the smell of pharmaceuticals, out of the valley. Another fifty. Under their feet, the steps crumble. They must've taken a real beating last night—chunks tumble down the hill, cracking right under the soles of their shoes. Another fifty. A tree trimmed by shrapnel, a neat imprint from a shell on the asphalt. Another fifty. And another. The city is coming closer. The smell of smoke is coming closer. Fear is coming closer, helplessness is coming closer. Another. And another fifty, the last fifty.

They go across the grounds to the street, walk crouched over along a row of linden trees and get to the tram circle, run in little spurts out to the main road, trying not to stop when they're out in the open, and reach the square. They stand under some spruces and hide. On the other side of the square is the Palace of Culture. Black, burned out. A shockwave broke all the windows. It looks like a television with a missing kinescope. There are clusters of apartment buildings behind it. They can slip through the neighborhood and get to the main avenue. Just have to run across the square first. Pasha looks all around. Coast is clear. The square's empty and quiet. Running across it shouldn't take longer than a minute. It's still scary, though. Nobody can see you, but you can't see anyone either. The moon hangs right above the Palace of Culture, seemingly prompting them. C'mon, don't waste any more time, run straight at my dead light.

"Let's go," Pasha whispers, still not releasing the kid's hand, and they charge forward. And as soon as they move away from the merciful spruces, the ones they were hiding behind, they hear this sound coming from somewhere behind the square, from off to the side, from the road—the irreversible clatter of treads on asphalt. It isn't that close—a block away—but Pasha identifies a T-64. There's no mistaking it. "Is it following me or something?" Pasha thinks in a panic, and desperately runs forward, dragging the kid along with him. Fifty yards. The tank is very close, behind the building closest to the square. Another fifty. It's going to pop out any second now. Pasha can already feel it. Another fifty and another. It's already here, it's already barreled around the corner. Another few yards and it'll be rolling right at them. Pasha speeds up, the kid's starting to whimper. Another fifty. His boots are heavy and hot, the kind of boots that are only good for drowning in. The moon draws things closer, outlines them clearly, adding a yellowish tint and otherworldly shadows. The rumble of the T-64 is already behind them. "Don't look back," Pasha yells to himself. "Just don't look back, don't look back." Several more steps, and they fly around the corner, fall onto the asphalt, onto crushed bricks, onto the empty plastic of bottles, onto dog shit and ripped playbills, tumbling and skinning their palms on sharp stones. Pasha immediately shields the kid with his body, as if that will help, as if to make sure they don't spot him. Actually, they don't spot him. The T-64 rolls toward the tram circle, toward the place they just came from, without even stopping. "Just missed each other," Pasha thinks. "Got lucky." He stands up, lifts the kid, who rubs his aching elbow. His jacket is ripped at his shoulder and his left sneaker is coming apart. His tears have dried, though. Just like that.

"Now where are we going?" The kid's embarrassed about crying. He's trying to speak calmly. But it's obvious that he's still scared—his voice is quivering, and he wants to find some crevice to hide in.

Pasha's scared for him, too. "Will he make it or not?" he thinks, with a tinge of doubt. "Maybe we should go right to the doctor. Well, the vet."

"There's a basement close by." Pasha's thinking out loud. "We can run over there and spend the night. It's close by."

"Sure you can find it?" the kid asks skeptically.

"It's about fifteen minutes away," Pasha reassures him. "We'll go through the neighborhoods. Two blocks that way, then there's a construction site, and some high-rises. They're camping out in the third one from the road. Or the fourth one," Pasha adds hesitantly. "We'll find it," he says confidently.

"Well, all right."

Pasha takes out his phone. It's only eight. It feels like they've been running around for days already. The thing is, his phone's dying. That's the thing.

There's an open area running between two long, looming rows of five-story buildings that stretch from south to north. Old, run-down workers' dormitories. The local factories built them for their people, but nobody has ever repaired them. Their people clearly haven't gone anywhere; they're clinging to their burrows, not letting any outsiders in. At any rate, they aren't a wealthy bunch—most of the windows have wooden frames, only a few apartments have insulated glazing. No intercoms, only every other balcony is glazed. A lot of satellite dishes, though. Basically, it isn't high-end housing. A mangled playground, detached swings. Pasha and the kid are walking, trying not to make any noise and apprehensively glancing at the empty windows in the steady moonlight. They're in plain view. Like targets on a shooting range. They pass one dormitory. Another one follows and then a few more. Pasha exhales with relief when they get to the next street over. They reach an intersection, look all around, run across the road, and walk another block. Everything's going according to plan so far. Up ahead there's an empty lot with traces of construction work: a pit, a fence, concrete slabs. They feel sand under their feet; they have to take the path the locals made straight through the construction site so they wouldn't have to go around. They come to a row of nine-story buildings.

"Everything's fine," Pasha says. "We made it."

It's mostly quiet. There are some shells hitting behind them, coming from where they were half an hour ago. First building, second one. They approach the third one. Pasha can tell that something's wrong, something's out of place. But he can't pinpoint what it is. They turn a corner and bump into a crowd. About twenty people. They're standing outside an apartment building. Pasha wants to duck back behind the corner, into the darkness, but he realizes that it's too late for that—the crowd has already noticed them. The crowd may have noticed them, but nobody's paying any attention to them; everyone's standing there, tensely watching the door to the apartment block, seemingly expecting something terrible to come out. Pasha and the kid approach the group and stop, standing off to the side.

"This it?" the kid asks quietly.

Pasha takes a closer look. Nine stories. Dark holes instead of windows. Bashed-up bench. Something looms by the bench. Looks like a dead dog. Pasha shudders but stands there, doesn't step back.

"This is it . . . I think," he says tentatively. "What are you standing around for?" he asks the guy in front of him.

He turns around—wide, peaked cap, shabby, girly jacket, track bottoms, fake leather shoes with wing tips. He's about fifty or so, but you can tell he has some health problems, which makes him look even older.

"We want to get home," he says angrily. He's speaking Russian, but every third word is in Ukrainian. "They liberated the city, the new guys," he says, pointing at the apartment block. "They're already here. Now we can go back home."

"So?" Pasha asks, confused.

"They said there's mines in there," the guy says, spitting on the asphalt.

"Who said that?" Pasha asks, still confused.

"Well, they did, the new guys," he explains, pointing at a group of soldiers standing by the door. "Why the fuck would you plant mines here?"

Pasha surveys the crowd and finally realizes that they're locals, from this building. They all scattered when the shelling started in their neighborhood. Now these new guys have taken the city, and they've come back like nothing ever happened. They're standing here wearing autumn jackets, winter coats, holding sacks, one guy with a television set. They clearly grabbed their most valuable things when they were leaving. Soldiers—these new guys—are standing by the bashed-in door to the apartment block: astrakhan hats, strange uniforms, unfamiliar insignias. Pasha's never seen ones like that. There's a good chance they were riding in the column Pasha and the kid saw earlier today.

"Who are you?" The guy suddenly addresses Pasha. "Do you live here?"

"My brother does," Pasha answers. "The vet."

"Ah, I know him. Lives on the third floor."

"Fourth floor," his neighbor contests. Lanky, wet hat, ravaged leather jacket, enormous, oversized felt boots.

"You're full of shit," the guy argues. "He lives on the third floor."

"Yeah, third floor." Pasha tries mediating.

"Yep," the guy says with satisfaction.

"So," Pasha ventures, "some people from this building have been camping out in the basement, right?"

"In the basement?" the guy asks.

"Yeah."

"Our basement's been flooded since before New Year's," the guy says.

"Those cocksuckers broke the water pipe, flooded everything," Lanky seconds him. "Fuckin' bastards," he adds firmly.

"Wait a sec. It's all flooded?" Pasha can't believe it. "But there are people down there."

"You got the wrong place," the guy replies. "There's nobody down there."

"Yeah," Lanky seconds him, coming over. "There's nobody's down there."

Hearing their conversation, a few more men turn around and come closer, looking at them mistrustfully, listening in, studying them.

"You hear that?" Lanky addresses a young guy—about twenty years old, down blanket on his back. "He says there's some people in the basement."

"There's nobody down there," the young guy replies hoarsely.

"Nobody," the others second him.

"Nope, nobody," somebody in the darkness says hollowly. "Who are you?" he asks Pasha.

"The vet's brother," Lanky explains. "Know him? He lives on the fourth floor."

"I know him," comes a reply from the darkness. "He lives on the third floor."

"Gotta get out of here," Pasha thinks. "Right now. Go somewhere, anywhere." But how are you supposed to leave when twenty pairs of eyes are watching you, watching you intently, watching you with suspicion?

"Coast is clear!" someone shouts.

Everyone forgets about Pasha and turns toward the voice. Two guys come out of the building. One of them looks like a teenager: skinny, a high schooler's busted stride. Kuban Cossack hat on his head, AK across his chest, hands ostentatiously resting on the barrel and stock. The second guy is obviously in charge: Kuban Cossack hat, too, AK, too, but he's got all kinds of daggers and pistols hanging all over him, like in the movies.

"Coast is clear!" the young guy repeats and makes a big show of taking out a cigarette, tossing it in his mouth, whipping out a lighter, and flicking it.

It won't catch, though. Sparks merely fly into the blue evening gloom. He's getting anxious; everyone's watching him with unconcealed aggression, seemingly saying, "Quit showing off."

"Go on inside, c'mon," the guy in charge adds, and steps aside.

The locals are in no rush to go inside, though. They stand there, thinking, waiting. Pasha inconspicuously pulls the kid to the side. But something's been set in motion, something's restraining him; he turns around, walks over to the bench, and probes what's on the ground—the thing that looks like a dead dog—by giving it a little kick. Turns out it's a fur coat. A woman's fur coat. It's wet and stained with clay. One sleeve's been ripped off, lying nearby. For an instant, Pasha thinks he recognizes the coat. But does he? How can he be sure out here?

"Hey," he calls to the guy. "Whose coat is that?"

"Fucked if I know." The guy turns around and gives Pasha a heavy, unfriendly look.

Pasha puts his hand on the kid's shoulder; they walk down an asphalt path, pass the second apartment block, the third one, the fourth one. "No pity for anyone," Pasha says. "Anyone at all."

They get to a day care center that's behind the row of linden trees, crawl through a hole in the fence, walk up onto the front steps, and sit down.

"You hungry?" Pasha asks.

The kid shakes his head.

"Now where are we gonna go?" he asks.

"We'll try to get out," Pasha suggests.

"In the dark?" the kid asks skeptically.

"Looks like things have calmed down. No more shelling."

"They wiped everyone out, that's why the shelling stopped."

Pasha's frantically considering something.

"Stay here," he says suddenly. "Wait for me."

"Where are you going?" The kid's scared.

"Just stay here," Pasha yells to him.

He gets up, sheds both backpacks—first the kid's, then his own—picks up the bat, and approaches the door. Push. The door gives easily, opens with a squeak. It smells like a cafeteria and several days' worth of moisture. Pasha takes out his phone, goes to turn on the flashlight, and remembers that his battery is almost dead. There's enough light in here as it is—the windows in the hallway have been smashed, a heavy moon hangs low beyond their frames. "It's as bright as day in here," Pasha thinks and walks down the hallway. There's a threadbare rug on the floor; it's been torn in several places. Pots with frozen flowers in them on the walls, cast-iron radiators painted white under the windows. Pasha feels like he's gone back to his childhood, which immediately makes him want to hang himself. He opens the door to the next room. Toys are scattered across the floor: cars, planes, teddy bears with their extremities ripped off. The toys look like they died recently. And not of natural causes. The next door's already open. Pasha warily stares into the dark hallway—no windows, the moonlight can't get in here, can't tell what's farther down. Suddenly, something under his foot lets out a high-pitched shriek, which terrifies Pasha. He lurches to the side and holds the bat out in front of him. Silence. Stare. He sees a squeaky toy—just stepped on it. He curses, quickly walks down a dark hallway, and gropes his way forward, holding his dead fingers out. Next he reaches a sleeping area. Two dozen beds with shredded mattresses, torn pillows, and dirty sheets. It looks as though someone performed a long, thorough search. But didn't find anything. "Where are they going to sleep?" Pasha thinks. Yes, like that's the most important thing right now—"where are the kids going to sleep when they come back? Where are they going to sleep? They can't sleep on shredded mattresses, can they? And they can't sleep on empty pillowcases either. And these gray, trampled sheets—they won't do. Where are they going to sleep? Where?" Pasha realizes that he has to leave, has to grab the kid—he's waiting for him down there, on the steps—and get going, that there's nothing for him here, that sleeping here on these contorted mattresses just isn't safe, that he has to get out of here, get out of here as quickly as possible, as far away from here as possible, but he keeps standing there, looking at the wrecked room, unable to move an inch. He's just staring at the black aperture of the door that leads to the next room and saying to himself, "Don't go in there, no matter what, just don't." And slowly, like a dead man in a movie, he heads toward the door. He walks, his boots crushing the torn pillows, trampling the sheets, leaving footprints on squashed sketch pads. "No matter what," he says to himself. "Just don't." And he keeps walking, stepping over tiny blankets and sharp pieces from a construction set. "Don't go in there, don't go in there," he repeats, holding his hand out, and his hand plunges into the darkness—up to his wrist, up to his elbow, up to his shoulder. "Just don't," he says to himself for the last time, and plunges into blackness. And he comes out the other side, in the next room; it's probably the cafeteria's storage room: empty shelves that clearly once held canned goods line the walls, empty cookie boxes are piled up on the windowsill, salt is strewn across the floor. An industrial-size refrigerator looms gray in the corner. Pasha approaches the refrigerator and listens to it intently, as if it's a gigantic dead heart. And it, as befits a dead heart, is showing no signs of life. Then Pasha grasps the handle—don't open it, just don't open it!—and pulls it toward himself. And such an unbearable, heavy, lethal stench hits him right in the face. Something so finely chopped, so shredded, and so rotten, something so finely cut, cleaved, and amputated that Pasha doubles over abruptly so he doesn't puke his guts out, and then he dashes off headlong. Empty pillowcases, displaced beds, black hallway, dead toys, open doors, cast-iron radiators, the moon out the window—unbearably close, so close that Pasha practically feels the stench coming right at him, feels that the moon hovering over the crushed city is spreading the smell of a body chopped to pieces. He bursts outside, exhales deeply, gasps for fresh air, coughing violently and frightening the kid, who runs over, not knowing what happened, but clearly knowing that something terrible happened, something that he'd better not ask about. He can ask, but he'd better not listen to the answer. Pasha thrusts his hand out, his fingers frozen stiff. Don't ask, don't ask, just don't. The kid nods wordlessly in reply. I won't, okay, I won't.

And suddenly it turns out that they're trapped. And they've backed themselves into the trap. No telling how they get out now. "Why didn't I pick him up earlier?" Pasha asks himself in despair. "Why didn't I leave the city last night? Should've grabbed the kid and gotten the hell out of here while I had the chance. Why'd I stay there for the night? Where should I go now? Heaven forbid something happens to him—what would I tell his mom? What would I tell my old man?" The kid isn't asking any questions, but him not saying anything makes Pasha want to justify himself. But what can he say in his defense? That he's an asshole who waited until the last minute, until the door of the trap opened, and then he guilelessly strolled right on in, and dragged the kid along with him to boot. But now that the city's fully besieged, now that all the possible openings and cracks have been closed up, all he and the kid can do is dart from corner to corner, like two rats that can't flee their ship.

Then the kid says quietly: "Hey, how'd you get here? You remember?"

"Uh, I came from the train station," Pasha replies, after a moment's thought.

"Well, let's go to the train station then," the kid says. "That's if they haven't burned it down yet."

"Are you for real?" Pasha's skeptical. "How do you know who's there now?"

"Pasha." The kid's starting to get mad. "You're a local guy, you've got health problems and a kid. What do you have to be afraid of? We can spend the night at the station. Can you find the way? Just not down the main avenue. They'll definitely be shooting there."

"I think I can find it," Pasha answers. "I'll try."

"There's no way in hell I'll find anything out here," he thinks, growing angry with himself. He stares at the row of trees tinted silver by the moonlight. But he keeps walking, trusting his inner voices to lead him through the dead city.

They reach the remnants of the footbridge. Boards and rebar hover over a black pit, like a ski jump for suicides. "The bridge," Pasha whispers confidently. "I was here yesterday." He nods to the kid and cuts between some trees. He walks through the park, touches crooked acacias, feels the frozen spring in his heart loosening up even more, pushing him forward, not letting him stop. They plod out of the park and walk through the thick grass, right up to the black frame of an apartment block that rises over them like an ocean wave at night. Playground, charred swings, cellar hatches with busted locks—someone cleaned out everything they could get their hands on. "Any second now," Pasha says, to himself more than anyone. "It should be somewhere around here." And there it is. He comes across the tram tracks, gleaming in the tall grass. "Everything's fine," Pasha assures the kid. "Now we can get out." They walk at an even pace, not rushing. A little while later, they bump into something big, something that's lying right on the tracks.

"What's that?" Pasha asks.

"A cow," the kid says.

Pasha comes closer, cautiously touches the supple carcass with the tip of his shoe. The carcass appears to still be somewhat warm.

"Yeah," Pasha says. "It's a cow."

Detached horns, right rear leg twisted unnaturally.

"What happened to it?" the kid asks.

"Maybe they were hauling it behind a car, and they drove too fast," Pasha suggests. "So they broke its horns and twisted its leg."

"But why'd they just leave it here?" the kid asks, surprised.

"Who the hell knows?" Pasha replies. "They were in a rush. Anna fuckin' Karenina," he curses, walking around the carcass through the wet grass.

The kid doesn't say anything. He doesn't even ask who Anna Karenina is.

At around ten, they get to the run-down building where Pasha and the group of people were hiding out during the shelling.

"Through the window," Pasha commands curtly.

The kid obediently starts crawling through the opening. Pasha gives him a boost from behind and then crawls in after him. They jump down onto the floor one after another and sit, their backpacks resting against the wall. The kid takes his pack of cigarettes out of his pocket. He flagrantly takes one out, not hiding anything, rolls it between his fingers to warm it up—he's clearly done this before—sticks it in his mouth, and takes a lighter out of his other pocket. Pasha reacts to the lighter more than anything; he grabs the kid's cigarette, rips it right out of his mouth, crumples it, and tosses it aside. He takes the lighter, too.

"What the hell!" the kid yells, aggrieved.

"The light," Pasha says in a conciliatory tone. "They'll start shooting if they see it."

"Yeah, sure." The kid still looks aggrieved, but it's mostly just an act. He tucks his cigarettes away and doesn't ask for the lighter back.

They sit for a while, not saying anything. Pasha feels bad about his outburst. The kid realizes that he really doesn't have any reason to be mad. They don't say anything for a while. Pasha cracks first.

"You hungry?"

"Do you have anything?" the kid asks, incredulously.

"Some canned stuff," Pasha replies. "I don't have a knife, though."

"Gotcha." The kid smiles crookedly, rummages through his pockets, and takes one out—foldable—blade on one end, spoon on the other.

"Where'd you get that?" Pasha asks.

"From the locals," the kid answers. "Traded some cigarettes for it."

"Where'd you get the cigarettes?" Pasha's surprised.

"From the locals, too," the kid explains.

Pasha realizes that he'd better not ask any more questions. He takes out a can, pierces it with the knife, and begins ferociously slicing through the metal in the dark. He cuts his hand right away. For the second time today. He smears blood all over his jacket and jeans, then tries to stop the bleeding. The kid takes a handkerchief—clean, ironed, neatly folded—out of his backpack. Pasha awkwardly wraps it around his hand.

"Where'd you get that?" Pasha asks, pointing to the handkerchief.

"It's grandpa's," the kid explains. "He gave me a whole bunch of them. I used them to clean my shoes. This is the last one."

Pasha thinks of his dad. "Should call him," he thinks. "He's all worried, probably."

"I forgot to call him," Pasha says.

"You forgot or you didn't want to?" the kid asks.

"Didn't want to? What's that supposed to mean?" Pasha says with affected surprise.

"Do you call him a lot?"

Pasha considers arguing with the kid but then eases up. "Come on," he thinks. "Who am I kidding?" He hands the kid the can. Drops of blood shine duskily in the moonlight.

"Want some?"

"Not anymore," the kid answers.

Pasha folds the knife up, gives it back to the kid, and puts the cans on the windowsill.

"I bought him his first phone a while back," he says, referring to his dad. "A basic Nokia. I put in our numbers, mine and my sister's. Uh, your mom's. I tried to teach him how to text. Didn't pan out. He didn't like writing. He sent me a text once, though. You know when?"

"When?"

"On the anniversary of mom's death. Uh, your grandma's death. He texted to remind me. I asked him later on, 'Why didn't you call?' He said, 'I was afraid I'd start crying.' Can you imagine that? I think that's why he doesn't talk to us—he's afraid he'll start crying."

"Well, I think that he doesn't talk to you two because you don't have anything to say."

Pasha's quiet for a bit. They stand up, head toward the exit. Pasha suddenly turns around, grabs the cans off the windowsill, and puts them on the floor.

"What for?" The kid's confused.

"For the dogs," Pasha explains.

They set off into the moonlight and across the field, and find a hole in a concrete wall. Next comes a little ditch, a path, a burnt-out truck—there's no telling how it got here. They walk through high cattails for a while; the path bends toward a railroad switch. Train cars. Pass through an endless corridor of burnt metal, crawl under a tanker black with soot, clamber onto the platform, and get to the station building.

There are even more people here, even though this is supposed to be where the shells were coming down. Those who came earlier look at the newcomers with mistrust. We don't have enough room as it is. This whole place looks like a ship that's going down in the open sea. The passengers are sitting and watching the water rise; meanwhile, passengers from another ship that has already successfully sunk are emerging from the depths of the ocean. They climb onto the sides of the ship and cling to the ropes and life preservers, overjoyed that everything's working out so well. The people sitting at the top, on the deck, are fuming, looking at them with hatred in their eyes, showering them with curses, not showing any sympathy, not a single drop of empathy. Even though they're all going to drown, obviously.

A two-man patrol immediately identifies Pasha in the waiting area. Two young guys wearing brand-new, spotless uniforms, like they just came from a parade. They fish Pasha and the kid out of the motley, mostly female crowd. They come over, offer a markedly polite greeting, turn on their flashlights, and ask to see Pasha's documents. While he's rooting around in his pockets, they suspiciously eye the blood on his jacket sleeve, the fresh clay on his boots, the dark bags under his eyes, and his gaze, inflamed by the cold and his overwhelming fatigue. They take no interest in the kid, but their eyes catch the baseball bat sticking out of his backpack. But when it comes to these locals, who knows? Maybe they just like baseball, we'll have to ask our bosses about that one. They flip through Pasha's passport, scoffing when they see the flag on the first page. They still aren't used to the fact that all the locals have passports with enemy flags in them. They check Pasha's address and hand his papers back to him.

"What about the trains? Are they running?" Pasha asks, once he's mustered the resolve. He's speaking proper Russian, like they are, even trying to replicate their accent. That doesn't make much of an impression on the soldiers, though.

"Nothing's fuckin' running in your town," one of them replies reluctantly. The second guy has turned his back on Pasha so he doesn't have to answer.

"How can we get out of here?" Pasha isn't giving up.

The soldier sizes Pasha up. He considers retreating, but then he sees the kid looking at the soldier like he's a toad—looking at him with hostility, that is. Then Pasha's eyes slide over him, from bottom to top. He notices his neatly trimmed nails, notices the cut he got on his neck while shaving, notices that the soldier is sniffling—caught a cold during a military campaign, clearly. "He's a kid," Pasha thinks. "Just got called up."

"You're representatives of the new authorities, right?" Pasha asks, with overt sarcasm. "I have a kid on my hands."

"You're completely safe here." The second guy turns toward him. Wide cheekbones, narrow, somewhat swollen eyes. He's a kid, too.

"Okay," Pasha says. "Can the new administration provide the temporarily displaced persons with food?"

"What persons?" Narrow Eyes asks, confused.

"The temporarily displaced persons," Pasha repeats. "We," he says, pointing at the kid with his dead finger, "are the temporarily displaced persons. We're only going to be here temporarily, isn't that right? You're the new administration, aren't you?"

"Yeah," Narrow Eyes confirms. "Why don't you go talk to the commandant?" he says in a confidential tone.

"Where is he?" Pasha asks, all business.

"In the train station attendant's room. You know where that is?"

"Yeah," Pasha replies flatly, takes the kid by the hand, goes around the patrolmen, and walks across the waiting area, stepping over the drowsy, temporarily displaced passengers who have sprawled out in every place imaginable: on the floor, on the windowsills, against the columns.

The newcomers didn't bring a lot of stuff with them. It doesn't seem like they had any time at all to pack or change their clothes. They just grabbed whatever was at hand and ran. Sleeping on their coats, sleeping on their bedspreads, using their winter boots as pillows. No suitcases, no bundles, faces dark with fear and sleeplessness, laden eyelids, wrinkles around their eyes. They're sleeping, their children pressed up against them—shielding the children from the cold with their warm bodies. Pasha treads carefully; he doesn't want to bump into anyone. The kid hops over the drowsy bodies with care, too. There are two guys with Kalashnikovs by the train station attendant's room—they're sprawled out in office chairs. One of them is dozing off; the other guy is looking at some pictures on his phone. They don't even look at Pasha—one of them just blocks the entrance with his rifle. That doesn't stop Pasha, though.

"In his office?" he asks.

"In his office? What?" The armed man looks up from his phone.

"The commandant, for fuck's sake. Is he in his office?" Pasha repeats his question.

"What are you swearing in front of the kid for?" The armed man sounds aggrieved.

"I'm a teacher, I'm allowed to," Pasha explains.

For a second, the armed man tries analyzing what he's heard. Nothing comes of this analysis.

"Yeah, he's in his office," he says. "He's busy, though."

"Sure," Pasha says, opening the door.

The commandant's well over fifty. Large frame, red mug. Clearly has high blood pressure. He's anxiously spinning in an office chair. Stripes on the sides of his pants, officer's boots. A strange tunic with some curious epaulettes. Crosses on his chest. He looks like a small-town opera singer. He's tossed a peacoat with a beaver collar over his shoulders; Pasha's seen that style before. Standing next to him is another soldier—his adjutant, Pasha immediately deduces—portly, chubby cheeks, shaved head. Wearing camo, holding a Cossack whip. "He punishes those who violate fire safety regulations at the station," Pasha thinks. The room's very stuffy. The curtains have been resolutely ripped off, the window's covered with plywood. The television in the corner has a smashed picture tube. Trampled calculator on the floor. Next to it is a gas generator humming laboriously. There are cables running away from it; a large lamp is shining. The commandant tenses up when he sees Pasha and the kid. A pink splotch, like a tender burn, immediately spreads across his face.

"Who are you?" he asks severely.

He's speaking Russian; his accent comes through in the interrogative.

"I'm a teacher," Pasha answers, and proffers his hand.

Flustered, the commandant shakes it. And the adjutant does, too—he has no other choice.

"I'm here on behalf of the citizens," Pasha says, without releasing his hand. "Their authorized agent."

The commandant doesn't like the phrase "authorized agent." If he were acting in good conscience, he'd put Pasha against the wall for that. He jerks his hand back.

"What's with your hand?" he asks severely, nodding at the bloody handkerchief.

"Oh, that," Pasha answers casually. "It's nothing."

Then he meaningfully touches the bandage, seemingly demonstrating—uh-huh, it's nothing, things get a lot hairier out on the battlefield. The commandant gives Pasha an understanding look, but he isn't saying anything, which makes him nervous.

"So what do you want?" he asks.

"The citizens would like to know how you will provide food and transportation," Pasha says. "Many of them have children on their hands."

"Children," the commandant replies discontentedly, wiping his sweaty neck with his sleeve. "You see what's going on. The city's under bombardment. And you're talking about children."

"What actions will the authorities take with regard to the temporarily displaced persons?" Pasha can feel that he's adopted the gym teacher's manner of speaking. That immediately makes him sound more convincing.

The commandant tenses up again. He shifts his gaze from

Pasha to the kid and then back to Pasha, as though he's thinking about who he should shoot first.

"All right," he says. "Here's the deal. Alexei, you take care of Comrade Authorized Agent. I have a call with the command center."

He takes out his phone, turns his back on them. Chubby-cheeked Alexei makes a sweeping gesture with his hand, as if he's shooing some butterflies away. "C'mon, everyone out, no eavesdropping on his conversation with the command center." Pasha leaves. The kid follows him. Alexei's next. He's walking, lazily tapping his whip against his thigh. He steps out into the hallway, stops, and looks around. Pasha and the kid stand next to him, waiting. A crowd of women and old people immediately gathers.

"Comrades," Alexei says in a choppy and official-sounding voice. "I ask that you not succumb to panic. The authorities are handling the situation that has arisen. A field kitchen will arrive in the morning. We'll send one bus to the factory and another one to the main residential area. Got that?"

"Yeah," says an elderly woman in a wet wig. "What should we do until morning?"

"Suck dick," Alexei answers irascibly, turns around, and disappears behind the door.

The crowd mulls that one over, then disperses. Pasha takes out his phone. He tries to call his old man. He doesn't have service, obviously.

They find a spot by the luggage room. The kid takes out an extra sweater, tosses it on the floor, sits down. Pasha sits next to him. He can feel that moisture has seeped through his jacket; it can't withstand the local climate. Pasha shrivels up and huddles into himself, trying to capture some remnants of warmth. It's just like when you wade into the sea in the morning—you search for a warm current, cling to it. You can't quite get warm, though, like when you can't quite fall asleep. The kid's dozing off, hat pulled over his eyes, head resting against the wall. It's painted blue. Pasha pulls his hood over his head, tries to forget about the cold and the dampness, tries and tries, but he can't. He scans his neighbors from underneath his hood. Most of them are sleeping, but one small woman is telling her neighbor something in the corner. The woman looks about forty: gray coat, dark boots, short hair. She's pressing a folder against her chest. "A bunch of important documents," Pasha thinks. "They were in a drawer. She grabbed them on her way out. Nobody'll have any use for her if she loses them." Her neighbor—older than her, portly—is sitting on some bundles that have sprawled out underneath her. It looks like she's sitting on top of someone, almost done strangling them. She's only half listening, keeps crying. Short Hair realizes she should stop, calm her friend down, but she can't. She's going on and on, in a hollow, insistent whisper. Everyone around her can hear; they listen in, catching some words here and there. So nobody's sleeping, and this lady sitting on the bundles is crying, crying so bitterly that nobody would even think of saying anything to her.

"I'm leaving the apartment this morning," Short Hair says. "And he's lying there on the bench. They put him there this morning, so everyone could see."

"Are you for real?" Her neighbor's crying. "You can't be serious."

"Yeah, black, purebred. No head," the woman continues.

The lady bitterly wipes her mouth with the corners of her handkerchief.

"Thing is, he wasn't from our building. I know that for a fact. Someone dropped him off."

"Black," Pasha thinks. "Purebred. No head. I'm really hungry. Really hungry." He tosses his head back. His eyes shut; cold is pooling in his lungs like water in a clogged drain. Someone gets up in the corner, slowly walks toward the exit. Skinny, darkened. Suitcases in his hands. And when he passes by, the suitcases give off a wet dog smell so potent that Pasha turns around. It's like someone's come to take him away. He huddles into the wall, closes his eyes tight, so tight, but that only makes things scarier, so he frantically lifts his head, drowsily looks around, and takes in the dead dog smell that's gradually diffusing around him. He looks at the ladies. The one who was crying is sound asleep, head drooping onto her chest. Short Hair's nodding anxiously, though, seemingly agreeing with someone invisible. Beside her, a family's sleeping—a boy and girl with their mom. Some guy on crutches is next to them, followed by some more women. Quiet, choked. So hungry.

"I'm hungry." The kid gives Pasha a little shove.

Turns out he isn't asleep either. He's waiting.

"Want a can?" Pasha asks.

"Nah, you'll start bleeding all over the place again."

"I'll be right back. Hang tight." Pasha gets up, looks around, and trudges off to the waiting area.

The room is sorrowful, like the hold of a ship packed with captives. Everyone realizes that they won't all be saved, but everyone's hoping to save themselves. The patrolmen spot Pasha from afar, turn around, and quickly head toward the exit. "Well, okay then," Pasha thinks, watching them walk away. Then he goes up the stairs to the second floor, steps over a body, and bumps into a bag. The body lurches awake, emerges from a heavy sleep as if it's rising from the bottom of a river. Eyes linger on Pasha for an instant, then blur, flicker out, and sink to the bottom. Pasha finds a sign—Snack Bar—in the corner on the second floor. He can't find the entrance, though: barricaded windows, an advertising stand, a heap of scaffolding, drowsy women on the floor. Everything's closed, everything's dead. Just as he's about to turn around and head back, he hears footsteps and cheerful voices behind him: a woman in a short down jacket and high-heeled boots, purse in hand. Two soldiers—unarmed—are following her. "Those staff officers," Pasha thinks. They walk, yelling back and forth and paying little attention to the drowsy people all around. The first one pulls the stand aside, revealing a door; he pushes it, and it squeaks open. The other one gently pushes her; she laughs ostentatiously, doesn't resist, disappears inside. The door squeaks shut. "There's gotta be something at the snack bar," Pasha thinks. "Some chips at least. Or chocolate. Just have to ask someone." He approaches, carefully pushes the door, and peers into the darkness. Empty, expansive room, several tables with overturned chairs on them. There are layers of paper on the windows so the glass can withstand a shockwave. There's a bar in the corner—it's empty, too.

"Hey," Pasha calls. No answer.

He walks over to the bar, lifts the board, and finds himself behind the counter. A hallway leads farther back, to the next room. Pasha pokes his head inside. It's dark in the hallway. He takes out his phone—the battery's almost dead—and turns on the flashlight. Several chairs, last year's calendar on the wall, a mountain of dirty dishes. A partially open door at the end of the hallway. Pasha advances toward it. He sees a down jacket on a chair, though. And a light-colored women's sweater. And an undergarment. And he hears something over there, behind the door. Voices—rushed and raucous.

"Anna," someone yells. "What's wrong, sweetie?"

Pasha turns off his phone, gropes his way out of the hallway. He walks across the room, goes downstairs, finds the kid.

"Well?" he asks.

"Try to get some sleep, all right?" Pasha requests.

The kid looks at him attentively, agrees.

But the suitcases, where'd the suitcases come from? They never had any suitcases. When they were younger, his parents didn't travel, didn't vacation. Pasha remembers this one summer, though, in the early nineties. He's in seventh or eighth grade, he and his sister are in the same class, his parents are on vacation—actually, no, his parents' jobs have just disappeared, stopped providing them with anything, yet they still go to the station every morning, like they're possessed, like they're wind-up toys. The station stands empty, the tracks are quickly overrun by grass. The country changed rapidly, but all of them—its citizens, the residents of this particular railroad town—weren't able to change; they just didn't have the right mechanisms in place. They kept going to work, work they weren't getting paid for. Just because they'd been going their whole lives, gotten used to it. You wake up every morning and you trudge off to work, as if you're going to toil like a galley slave when you get to the depot. But the depot's come to a standstill, like a sailing ship that's been raided by pirates. Walls and the Party slogans on them—

there's nothing else left. And the workers stand under the slogans, and they're eager to fulfill and overfulfill the plan, meet their coworkers halfway, and take on extra duties, yet nobody has any use for their duties and nobody's going to meet them halfway anytime soon, and there are just these tight-knit flocks of pigeons—there are suddenly so many of them—flying from the station to the city, from the plant to the residential area, searching for happiness and free grub. In the summer, his mom somehow gets awarded a trip to the sanatorium in the next town over, in a pine forest, by a river, and this all looks so unreal. They haven't gotten anything in a long time, even though they're still hoping they will. Break their backs at work and get something in return—that's what they're used to. But they haven't gotten anything for the past few years, even though they're still willing to break their backs, and this has crushed their long-held notions about how things should be, about basic fairness. Oh yeah, and then there's this trip to the sanatorium, and at first the whole family's planning on going, and Pasha's looking forward to it, getting ready, like a real adult—well, he thinks he's all grown up. How old is he? As old as the kid is now, about thirteen or so. And he's packing his things. And obviously, he doesn't have a suitcase—just some shabby sacks that his old man uses when he goes to the makeshift market downtown. Pasha is given one of these sacks and told to think about what he'll need on vacation, to make sure he doesn't forget anything, to act like an adult. Pasha methodically moves his things from the wardrobe in his parents' room into his room; he places them on the bed, sorts through them. He's going to work out; he'll need athletic clothing. But he's also going to go for walks in the woods, so he'll need something comfortable and practical. And he shouldn't forget to bring a warm sweater, too. And he's meticulously packing all of it, tossing some T-shirts and socks in, taking his favorite detective novels. Then, ashamed of himself, he stuffs one last thing in, on the very bottom, under his sweater and socks. Sunglasses—his dad's old pair. He found them in a drawer; his dad hasn't worn them in a while. Pasha's ashamed of himself, but he still tucks them in his bag, just in case. After that, pleased with himself, packed and pleased, he goes to the kitchen and sits down at the table. He sits there listening to his elders' conversation with an air of importance. The conversation is a somber one: the family doesn't have any money, they have no idea how they're going to pay for this vacation. The next town over isn't the Black Sea coast, obviously; it's just as much of a dump as the Station is. But you still have to pay extra for children, for food, for lodging.

"Where are we going to get the money for that?" his mom asks. "Huh? I'm not going anywhere," she says firmly. "I'm staying home. There's no point in going there anyway." But his dad insists because he loves her. No, you definitely have to go, you need this, you need to get healthy. Pasha doesn't understand all this health talk; he doesn't even think about that, health problems don't exist for him, they just don't, everyone's supposed to just be fine. He doesn't understand any of this. But he does understand that his dad's an amazing guy, that he's deeply in love with his wife, Pasha's mom, that is, and that this is real, grown-up life. Pasha understands that since he's acting like an adult, too—he gets it. And he's sitting there, admiring his own maturity and his old man's maturity. And how helpless his mom is, her inability to deal with troubles, touches him. And he doesn't even understand that they won't be going anywhere, that he, his sister, and his dad will have to stay home, tend the garden, and skip ice cream to save money. That his mom will go to the sanatorium by herself, share a room with some lady from accounting, and race over to the phone every two hours to make sure dad's heating up all the food she left for them. He doesn't understand that yet; his parents call them into the kitchen again—his dad sits down at the table, his sister's chattering on about something, not taking any breathers, not stopping. And then his mom starts saying something about the trip being called off, about how they'll have fun without her, just the three of them. She hasn't even finished yet, and Pasha still hasn't fully grasped what she's getting at, but his sister gets this intuitive feeling, as only a child can, that she's being deprived of something very nice and important and she starts wailing, loudly and uncontrollably. His dad doesn't even bother trying to console her; there's so much despair in her wailing that all he can do is wipe away a meager tear with a barely noticeable movement. Pasha notices everything, though; he suddenly understands everything and starts wailing, too, finally realizing that he won't get anything: no workouts, no walks in the woods, no nothing. And that nobody has any use for his maturity, nobody has any need of it, that all this is so ridiculous and so hopeless that, once again, everything has already been decided for him, once again he's been put in his place, and there is no point in hoping he'll get anything at all. Then his mom, completely bewildered at this point, suddenly flies off the handle and starts yelling at his old man. It's all your fault, this is all because of you, you did this. His sister's wailing even louder because she feels sorry for her dad. But she feels sorry for herself, too, so she's wailing for herself and for him. And Pasha's wailing for himself and for him, for his old man, who couldn't do anything, couldn't ward off their cries, just like he couldn't ward off mom's illness, mom's death.

Pasha didn't unpack until the fall.

The days are so short this time of year, and there's so little light that it takes you a while to get used to the darkness once the sun goes down, like you can't believe that that's it for today—no more sunlight, just twilight. Pasha's always out of sorts in the winter: doesn't have enough daytime, can't get settled in the evenings, mixes up the hours, mixes up his desires. It seems like it's time to go to bed, but he's sitting there, leaning against the wall, slipping into a slumber, but something keeps pushing him out of it, as if there are some guards on duty nearby who won't let him relax, won't let him drift off. A moan wakes him up once again. He lifts his head—Short Hair, resting up against the bundles, is talking in her sleep. Pasha catches some words here and there. Something about wiping your feet, about shoe covers, about the schedule. "Yeah, the schedule," he thinks. "What time is it? How much longer until morning?" For the past two days, he's been hovering in the damp air, not having anywhere to go yet afraid to stop. The kid is on his conscience, too. "It's a good thing we managed to get clear of the orphanage. We'll be home tomorrow if everything works out. And the kid'll stay with us. I don't think Nina will mind. Yeah, gotta find her when all of this is over. And the gym teacher, too," Pasha thinks, immediately remembering everything: the executed coat, the dude with the pasta, the voices by the well. He remembers the crowd outside the apartment building, the soldiers, the darkness, the bashed-up bench, the torn fur coat. "Wonder how Vira's doing," he thinks. "Should've gotten her number, at the very least. What could've happened to her? Did she get home, or is she still hunkering down in some basement? In the basement that I never wound up finding. I'll find her when all this is over, I definitely will. Office building, massage parlor, travel agency. I can always find her through her friends. Through her friends," he repeats. "Yeah, through her friends." Pasha turns toward the kid, who's sleeping without a care in the world. Next to him on the floor is the bat—it looks like a child's toy. Then Pasha stands up carefully, so as not to wake anyone, fixes his glasses, goes to the waiting area, and then makes his way to the second floor.

The snack bar door is half-open. Pasha slides inside. He shines his flashlight ahead, walks behind the bar, emerges in a little hallway, stops in front of a door, hesitates briefly, and then knocks carefully. Silence. Then he hears some rustling and the crackling of couch springs.

"Who's there?" a dry voice asks.

"It's her," Pasha surmises, and opens the door.

There's a small kitchen in the corner: sink, microwave, knives on the table, sugar spilled all over the floor, shelves with spices and kitchenware on them. Oil, vinegar, ketchup. No alcohol. There's a couch against the wall, and there she is, sleeping on it. She leaps up and turns on a little flashlight as soon as Pasha comes in. At first, Pasha shields his eyes with his hand, but then he decides not to hide—he looks, examines. Pink hair tangled like wires from sleeping, warm sweater. Apparently, she was sleeping on the couch, wrapped up in a down coat and some sort of tablecloth. She quickly fixes her short skirt, but not before Pasha gets a good look: black stockings, gray sweater, no makeup, tired and vulnerable face. Her expression is wary yet devoid of fear—she doesn't really understand who he is, but she can see that she doesn't have anything to be afraid of: slightly blurry gaze through his glasses, beard, blood on his jacket sleeve, boots covered in clay. Pasha looks haggard and like he's in the wrong place at the wrong time. Probably woke her up at the wrong time, too.

"What?" she asks dryly.

"I'm just ducking in for a second."

Pasha adjusts to the abrasive light, surveys the room, and thinks about where to sit. She notices that, so she immediately pulls a bag toward herself and covers up with the tablecloth. This spot's taken. Don't even think about it. He isn't thinking about it, though. He sees a beer crate in the corner, places it in the middle of the room, sits down.

"Did I wake you up?" he asks.

"What do you think?" she asks in reply.

"Well, sorry. You're Anna, right?" Pasha switches to the informal "you" to sound more convincing.

"Yeah, and?" She's still shining the flashlight right in his eyes.

"I saw you come in here. With those two."

"What else did you see?" she asks angrily. "Who are you?"

"A representative of the citizenry," Pasha answers.

"Huh?"

"A representative," Pasha repeats. "Of the citizenry," he adds. "Forget it," he says finally. "Turn off that flashlight."

Anna listens, placing the flashlight aside, at a safe distance. It gets dark in the room.

"I'm looking for someone," Pasha says. "You might know her."

"Who?" Anna grows apprehensive.

"You work at the travel agency, don't you?"

"What agency?"

"At that big office building downtown," Pasha explains. "Right?"

"Yeah." Anna scrutinizes him, then snickers. "You're a client, yeah?"

"Not exactly. I'm a representative of the citizenry," he reminds her. "I need to get ahold of Vira. You know her?"

"Vira?"

"Yeah."

"What does she look like?"

"Well, uh." Pasha tries to describe her. "She wears worn-down heels and a fur coat."

"What kind of fur coat?"

"Don't know," Pasha admits.

"Well, I don't know either," she says with a tired laugh.

"She wears an engagement ring!" Pasha suddenly remembers.

"An engagement ring?" Anna laughs. "Really? We don't really do engagement rings at the travel agency." She keeps laughing.

"She told me that she works there," Pasha says, his tone aggrieved.

"Is she a cleaning lady?"

Pasha gets flustered and stops talking, so she goes quiet too, stops laughing. They sit, not talking.

"Got any smokes?" she asks eventually.

"I don't smoke," he answers.

"I smoked all of mine," Anna says discontentedly. "With those two. The bastards showed up with no cigarettes."

"Where are they?"

"How am I supposed to know?" Anna replies. "They ran off somewhere."

"Why'd you stick around?"

"Where could I go? I'll wait until morning, then head out. What's going on with you and Vira?" she asks after a moment's thought.

"Nothing. We met yesterday."

"You like her?"

"I didn't get a good look," Pasha admits. "I'm just worried about her. I want to find her when all of this is over," he adds.

"What makes you think that all of this is going to end?" she asks.

"Well, it has to end at some point."

"You think so?"

Pasha doesn't answer. He doesn't want to say anything bad, but nothing good comes to mind. She doesn't say anything either—just fixes her hair and wraps the tablecloth tighter around herself. It looks like he's come to visit her at the hospital. And she's sitting here—cheerful, all smiles, sure that she's getting better. He's trying really hard to be cheerful, too, but he, unlike her, knows her diagnosis.

"Well, the engagement ring?" Anna asks again.

"What about it?"

"Well, she wears an engagement ring. Maybe she has children, a husband. A fur coat."

"I don't think she has a husband."

"And the ring?"

"Who the hell knows," he says. "Half our teaching staff are divorced women. But they keep wearing their rings. To look more presentable."

"Are you a teacher or something?"

"Well, yeah."

"What'd you teach?"

"Ukrainian."

"I see," Anna says. "A real promising career path. Why aren't you fighting?"

"For which side?"

"For any side."

"Got a bum hand," Pasha says, showing it to her.

"So what? I've seen much worse. One guy was missing half of his head, for real. He got in a car accident sometime before the war. But he'd still come by and see us . . . at the travel agency."

"And how is he?" Pasha asks incredulously.

"What do you mean?"

"Missing half his head—how is it for him?"

"Ah, you mean *that*. Well, he doesn't come by to play soccer. What does he need a head for? I felt sorry for the guy."

"Why?"

"He was handsome," Anna explains. "Well, before the accident. Now he's like the Terminator."

Anna's all chipper, like a child whose parents have been talking her ear off, distracting her, drawing her attention to something else, and at one point, she really does forget about the pain and the doctors and remembers just how many treats await her once she gets out of here. If she ever gets out. Pasha suddenly finds himself thinking that everyone around here speaks as though they haven't talked to anyone in months—quickly and incoherently, trying to confess everything, not wanting to take anything with them. They say so many unnecessary, unimportant things, raising their voices, lecturing, accusing, justifying themselves. Abandoned, neglected, forgotten. Aggrieved. "Yep," Pasha thinks. "They're aggrieved, obviously. And abandoned. No pity for anyone," he thinks. "Anyone. Anyone at all."

"Sorry?" Pasha asks. "You feel sorry for everyone around here, yeah? You'll sleep with them all."

"Yeah, so what?"

"Never mind," Pasha replies. "Don't feel sorry for anyone. Anyone. Sleep with whoever you want."

Noticing that his voice has changed, Anna tenses up. She pulls the tablecloth up to her throat, waits, and then says:

"Listen, Teach. Do you know that all professions deserve respect?"

"Uh-huh." Pasha sneers. "And they're all useful to society."

"Well, what's so useful about what you do?"

"Knowing languages is useful," Pasha replies.

"Yeah, you don't even speak the language outside the classroom, though," she hisses, and Pasha notes that her voice has changed, too, become snakelike, threatening. She continues before he can show his surprise. "At least I don't play mind games with people. I just do what I do."

"Don't get angry," Pasha suggests.

"Don't get angry? Yeah?" she says angrily. "Some dickhead comes in here and starts telling me what to do. He doesn't feel sorry for anybody. Well, I do. I feel sorry for the kids you teach."

"The kids are fine." Pasha's growing anxious.

"Sure they are," Anna says with a dismissive wave. "You don't feel sorry for them either, do you?"

Pasha doesn't say anything. She looks at him, waiting for him to respond, but he keeps quiet, so she figures it's best to change the subject.

"I bet you don't like kids either," she says.

"Why's that?" Pasha's aggrieved.

"I can see it in your eyes," Anna says. "And you don't have your own kids either."

"Well, actually, I'm here with a kid." Pasha's still aggrieved.

"Whose kid?"

"My nephew," Pasha says. "I picked him up from the orphanage." He's speaking in a weighty tone—the kind people use when talking about something serious, important. He speaks, then waits for a reaction.

"From the orphanage?" Anna gets all chipper again. "The one on the edge of town?"

"Yep."

"That's my orphanage," she says. "When were you there?"

"Tonight," Pasha says reluctantly.

"How's everything over there?"

"Fine."

He averts his eyes, but she doesn't notice that.

"Nina still working there?"

"You know her?" Pasha's surprised.

"I have since I was seven." Anna nods. "We went to the same orphanage. But she went to the teachers college and I went to the travel agency."

Now cheerful, she's even set the tablecloth aside. She finds her jacket, tosses it over her shoulders, and starts speaking differently—without that lazy irritation, her tone simple, trusting.

"The kids in our class didn't like her. I didn't like her either," Anna admits with a smile. "Neither did the teachers. Well, they didn't like anyone. But they really didn't like her. She was always going against everyone. That's a lousy habit."

"Yeah," Pasha agrees.

"You aren't like that, though, are you?" She's speaking with the same smile, and Pasha eagerly nods in reply.

"You agree with everyone, don't you?" She keeps smiling, but Pasha isn't sure whether he should be enjoying this. "Nobody really cares if you agree with them or not, though. Is that right? Well, this one time," she continues, losing all interest in Pasha, "one of the kids got a pair of shoes from their parents. A pair of cheap, Chinese sneakers. They were new, though. Do you know what it's like to get new sneakers?" Pasha is about to answer, but she cuts him off. "Nah, you don't know anything. Well, we get up one morning and see that someone's dumped brilliant green dye all over those fuckin' sneakers. For real. Well, everyone started saying she did it. They went to the director's office and told her. The director believed them. Actually, everyone believed them." Anna automatically begins rooting through her pockets, looking for her cigarettes. She's worried, all anxious, and then she remembers that she doesn't have any cigarettes. "Well, and I stuck up for her. That caused a lot of problems."

"How do you know she didn't do it?" Pasha asks skeptically.

"We were roommates," Anna replies. "And I know for a fact that she didn't go anywhere that night. But nobody believed me. You know what they're like at orphanages? They'll devour you. Especially over a pair of sneakers."

"Well, you stood up for her . . . then what?"

"Then what? I stood up for her, and that was it. Then I regretted that, obviously."

"How come?"

"I took some flak, too. It was an orphanage, after all. They stopped liking me, too. That doesn't feel good. You get what I mean?"

"Yeah," Pasha says.

"I think you get it. What's wrong with your hand?"

"Got problems," Pasha explains.

"I can see that," Anna says. "You've probably taken a lot of flak for your hand over the years."

"Nah, not really."

"Yeah, right." She doesn't believe him. "You definitely have. Kids are cruel. Like puppies. And they're as trusting as puppies, too. Then they grow up, become more mature, more confident. Their cruelty doesn't go away, though. Neither does their trust. And you say you don't feel sorry for anyone."

Pasha doesn't say anything; he looks at his hand. It's as though he's letting the meager beam from the flashlight through his fingers. And she's looking at his fingers, too, seemingly mesmerized, as if she's never seen anything like this. Actually, she hasn't. Where can you see something like that?

"You know," she says to him. "Since I've got you . . . Come here. Do you want to?"

Pasha freezes and immediately wants to tell her that he does. Obviously he does. He wants her, with her pink hair. Wants her warmth, wants her voice. He can feel just how cold these last two days have made him, how chilled to the core. Obviously he wants her. Then he thinks of the kid. "What if he already woke up?" he thinks. "How long have I been up here?"

"I want to," Pasha admits. "But I haven't showered in two days. I doubt you'd like it."

"I haven't either, if I'm being perfectly honest," she admits.

"I'm gonna get going." Pasha gets up laboriously, hiding in a shadow. "I really should find something for the kid to eat," he says, his tone making it a request.

"Well, look around." She loses all interest in him again, covers up with the jacket and tablecloth, turns off the flashlight, and faces the wall.

Pasha walks over to the shelves in the dark, opens a cabinet by touch, begins carefully studying what's there inside, seemingly not believing his eyes, needing to touch everything with his own hands, feel it. Tin cans, plastic containers, dishes filled with grain. Bags of sugar and pasta. And then, unexpectedly—chocolate! That's it. Chocolate. Pasha unerringly recognizes a flat bar under some sort of canned food. He carefully plucks it out, stuffs it in his pocket, and leaves.

Sasha's sleeping deeply, the way only kids can: head buried in his sleeve, all curled up like a puppy, warming himself with his own body heat. He's clearly dreaming. Maybe even about something nice. Why not? Pasha's hovering over him but can't bring himself to wake him up. Behind him, the lady sitting on the bundles begins talking in her sleep. Seemingly warning him. Pasha shudders and carefully slides the chocolate bar up the kid's sleeve. He returns to the main hall. "Wait until morning," he reminds himself. "Wait out the night, then get out of here. We'll be home tomorrow. Everything's going to be fine. Everything'll work out." Hundreds of women's drowsy bodies, warm clothing, winter footwear, children on their hands, kitchenware tied to sleds, bags, and cardboard boxes. One woman is whispering in the corner, another's wrapping a blanket tighter around her shoulders. A truck's powerful headlights are punching through the darkness and onto women's pale blue faces. Basically, this all feels like the theater before the beginning of a performance: the lights are off, everyone's quieted down, yet someone's still trying to finish a thought, whisper the most important thing. Something's missing, though. "The actors," Pasha thinks. They'll appear any second now, though. They definitely will—there's no getting by without them. It's a little after one. Another few hours. The bus will appear. Everything's going to be fine. The shelling's shifted to the north, toward the town; it's quiet around the station, but nobody's leaving. Nobody believes that it's all over. They think it's a trap. They think that over there, behind the station doors, something scary still awaits them. So it's best to camp out here, behind the sturdy station walls. They huddle together like the animals on the ark, whispering calming words to themselves that they don't quite believe. Pasha notices the patrolmen who recently checked his papers; they're at the other end of the hall, by the doors. They notice him, too. They stand there and watch his every move. One of them whispers in the other guy's ear, and he nods. "I should get going," Pasha decides. "I shouldn't wait for them to decide to come over." He turns around slowly, without making any abrupt movements, carefully examines the schedule on the wall, as if he's really counting on taking the first morning train out of here, nods with an air of importance, pretends that he's committing something to memory, and fixes his glasses so he can see better. Then quietly, step by step, he sets out for the exit, leaving the patrolmen with nothing. But when a few steps remain, he overlooks a drowsy passenger who's lying on a sheepskin coat right at his feet. She's placed two metal buckets near herself—one full of apples, the other full of golden onions. He overlooks her, hits a bucket with his foot; it clings to his boot, turns over, and then rolls resonantly across the stone floor, as though someone's ringing a bell to warn everyone about a fire or the advance of enemy troops. And the toll of the bell bounces off the high windows and cold ceiling, and everyone jolts up, emerges from their restless slumber, sticks their frightened heads out of their dreams, squinting into the twilight to see what all the commotion is about, what all the ruckus is about, where they should run. The children immediately begin whimpering. The women cry out, not yet understanding what's going on, but still wanting to draw attention to themselves, just in case. The apples roll between other people's things; soles trample them, and they disappear forever among the women's frightened bodies. Everyone looks at Pasha like he's a demon who's appeared out of the darkness and broken the prevailing silence, shattering it with a terrible ring and ruckus. A demon who's come to bring them some kind of message. Pasha stands there, feeling everyone watching him, waiting for him to say something, to communicate something important. The children are scared of his big, dark figure, and he's making the women tense. But nobody dares ask him who he is, where he's come from, or what he bears. At this point, Pasha's thinking about making something up, but then he sees the patrolmen coming straight at him—confident, leisurely. He realizes that he has nowhere to go, he's completely at their mercy. Then Pasha bends down, picks up several apples, and puts them in the woman's hand. She's oblivious, just sitting there and looking at him like he's an anomaly of nature.

Then he fixes his glasses again and disappears down a hallway. The patrolmen stop. "Follow him, find him, and shoot him behind the columns or let him live? Let him live," they think. And Pasha lives.

Feels like March. Restlessness and alarm. And knowing that everything can work out, everything can come together, makes it painful to breathe. That as soon as you ride past the closest railroad signal, a new way of life, nothing like his, nothing like what he's used to, begins. He always loved the Station, though—the dry greenery of summer, the grass turned black by fuel oil, the side tracks that wander among tenacious blades of grass until they get lost. He loved the voices of the Station, its smell. The sky above the maintenance buildings. The train cars that look like buildings whose residents just can't ever get settled; they move from one place to another, trying their luck. He loved fall, too. Fall at the Station was serious and severe. In the fall, everyone would come together after the long summer months, after all the dust and sun, and you could see how everyone had grown, how they'd changed over the summer. Then smoke would float out of the nearby gardens and dachas, from yards and little parks—first they'd burn weeds and then the leaves that had fallen from the high trees. The air would turn cold, bitter, winter clothes would be unpacked, the rainy season begin, the ground fill with water, and moving around become difficult. Not that there was anywhere to go around here. The winter made life at the Station cheerful and sunny once again: snow buried the moats behind the warehouses and the paths along the river, the river itself froze over, and a cold current moved under the gray ice slowly, like blood when you're sleeping. In the morning, locomotives coated with snow and hoarfrost rolled in after their nighttime journeys, after fighting through fog and snowdrifts—exhausted, yet implacable, eager to continue hauling their endless chains of cars. The sun hung over the roofs and the tracks, railroad men argued cheerfully, they—schoolkids at the time—cut class, clambered up the embankment, and ascended the hills that stretched along the frozen riverbed. The sun hovered at the highest point in the sky; in the winter there was never enough sun. You had to hunt it down, fish it out of the frosty landscape. Trains would occasionally barrel out of the snow and cross the horizon in weary bursts, leaving golden swirls of hoarfrost in their wake, connecting the known with the unknown.

But in the spring, everything would change, one way or another. The air would be different. It would creep along, mixing above the Station, and in the stagnant, solidified space, currents of something unknown, something that would thrust you forward, force your heart to beat faster, would flow by, one after another. The evening streetlights would shine desperately, torridly. Fog would rise from the river. Locomotives move cautiously through the dark, like dogs. In March, he always grew restless; in March, he wanted to get out of here, toss his things in a bag and take the first evening train in an unknown direction—disappear into the green twilight, follow floods of sunlight until he dissolved. In the spring, everyone was drawn to the station, to its travel smells and transient lights. Rowdy groups of teenagers hung around outside by the station walls, reacting sharply to the adults' admonishments and defiantly sticking their young, buzzed heads toward the winds and drafts. Vapid talk, frenzied laughter, unwarranted happiness—just the way things ought to be in the spring when you're fourteen, and that's exactly how things were.

And there was nothing beyond that. No flags over the station, no anger in adults' conversations, no borders, no portraits of outstanding employees on boards of honor eroded by time. No empty shelves in cold stores, no dark faces on black TVs, no lying press, no vile slop that his family had to eat every morning just to subsist. The March air, as brisk as water in the morning—that's all there was. Air that heated up after winter ended, and it consisted of sweet faith in the idea that everything was just getting started, that things would only get better and better as they went along. At this moment, right now, here, in this crummy little park, amid mounds of black snow, in the blackness filled with birds' cries and locomotives' horns, everything's good, too, incredibly good, everything's just how it should be, so you can feel currents of happiness mixing with currents of hunger in the air.

The world's simple, and it makes sense. There's just enough of it—no more than you can feel and your memory can encompass. It has a defined outline and steady borders. These borders lie somewhere nearby, behind the closest row of cold trees. Over there, farther off, beyond those visible borders, something different begins, something alien that doesn't make much sense and therefore isn't very interesting: people you don't know, circumstances that don't pertain to you, a country that seems vague to you. But here everything's where it's supposed to be: you can recognize it by touch, you can recognize its voice. Your house, filled with a thousand objects—it's compact and committed to memory, down to the last button in the top drawer. Your family that you've gotten used to like someone gets used to their own body. Your parents, still alive and well, who you keep growing apart from, who understand you less and less. That doesn't worry you one bit, though. It's enough that they're around somewhere, somewhere nearby, watching over the thousand familiar objects from your childhood and simply belonging to the thousand voices you've known ever since. Sure, you might be growing apart, sure, they might not understand you, but they'll still have a place in this world. There's enough time to fix everything, enough space so you aren't getting in each other's hair. There's enough room for school, with its deathly scent of microwaved food, its resonant evening hallways, its intimacy and estrangement. There's enough room for friends and casual acquaintances, inconsequential conversations, fleeting crushes, unconscious fear. There's enough room for your enemies, too, for hurt feelings, for shame, for the last teenage tears shed into your pillow—no one will see them, yet you'll never forget them. There's room for everything, since that's how everything was designed. Everything fits, nothing is superfluous. Just don't go beyond the borders, hang on to this fragile March light that's running out so quickly, peer into the station windows as if they're glass boxes filled with monsters, and only take what life has prepared especially for you.

His sister grew up, his peers matured, and high school receded into the past. For the first time, he had to leave that world for a longer stretch, head out—to the city, for college. And this step beyond the boundaries of his cocoon, beyond the boundaries of what made sense, wound up being the first catastrophe, a trauma that subsequently accompanied him for a long time. It wasn't just his address or circumstances that had changed; his conception of the world, of its boundaries and capabilities, had changed too. Suddenly it turned out that the world was much bigger than you'd imagined, and much more dangerous. Suddenly, it turned out that it consisted of countless unfamiliar objects that didn't make any sense, that its language consisted of a thousand unfamiliar words, and that you had to memorize all those words, memorize and use them, otherwise you wouldn't survive, you wouldn't be able to get back home. Extracted from his shell, his cocoon unraveled, he stands amidst an empty country that's alien to him, and he can't understand where to go from here, how to withstand the invisible pressure that's thrusting him out of reality. Shock and despair overwhelm him; now what he wants more than anything is to go back about ten years, into his old clothes, to his childhood things, to his hiding spots. Well, fear passes all on its own when you're seventeen; you overcome it due to your natural desire to survive, to devour your portion of justice. He gradually gets used to the big city, to strangers, to his new circumstances. The only thing is, as soon as he gets the chance, the moment the opportunity presents itself, he escapes back home, transferring multiple times along the way. It's as if a cold metal spring is pushing him out of his new life—back to his cocoon, back to where he was at peace. He comes back and locks himself in his room, not saying anything to anyone, ignoring his parents and sister. He's like a young kangaroo that's grown a lot but is still trying to cram himself back into his mom's pouch. He simply can't fit, though, which is obviously making things a little tense at home.

On the weekends, everything was just like it used to be: the same trees on the horizon, the same sky above the roofs, the same smell of the past. But the shell had been hopelessly cracked; the world had been cracked, and piecing it back together was impossible.

He suffered through his college years, then came back to the

Station and began teaching at the school. For a while, he couldn't take the smell in the school cafeteria. Then he decided that from then on it would be his smell—the smell of bitter, overcooked food, the smell of apathy and detachment, the smell of someone else's life that you're trying to pass off as your own. The world shrank back to its familiar size. The door closed behind him. He was safe again. Don't look beyond, don't talk to strangers, know where all the objects you need are located. The sweet smell of gas in the morning kitchen, the rustle of rain outside the window, like the faint working of the ocean—in March, he always felt this odd draft, as if that cold metal spring was pricking his heart. There was a completely different, alien world nearby, as sublime as it was dangerous, and its unavoidable presence nearby, just around the corner, beyond the horizon, unnerved him, threw him off balance. Then Pasha would go out to the porch, walk over to the garden, and listen to the rain above the trees, listen to it surround him, cave in, snag on the thin apple branches, fall right at his feet—the way it can only fall in March.

Pasha stands on the black platform and notices that the rain that started last night isn't even thinking about letting up—it's spilling onto the city, slanting down and hitting the metal freight trains, the busted tankers. Pasha puts his hood up and steps under the awning, pressing against the station wall. It's 2 a.m. He doesn't feel like going back inside, but the rain's growing more persistent; it starts somewhere beyond the main avenue and stretches to the north, toward the Station, spilling out of the nippy nighttime sky. "It's a good thing we can wait it out here until morning," Pasha thinks, catching chilly drops with his lips. "Where could we even go? Nowhere. Just sit here, wait, and hope that you don't drown, that you'll pull through. What's next?"

The station doors squeak open; a passenger is squeezed out. Squeezed out like toothpaste. Bags first, followed by a peaked cap, then a foot holds the door. All of him wrings out; he pops outside, cowers from the rain, spots Pasha, plods toward him. An old officer's peaked cap with the insignia ripped off, the dark overcoat of a train steward—more like stewardess, actually—grocery bags in his hands, it appears there are more bags inside, a bunch of empty bags, coiled up and twisted like intestines. And he's wrapped see-through bags around his feet, over sneakers that are black with dust. Black nails, black teeth, a lingering smile. And deep wrinkles on his cheerful face. Oh, yeah, and his beard. Makes him look like Karl Marx. And little hairs poke out of it, rest on his shoulders, shed like needles off a Christmas tree that stands in a warm room until spring. He places his bags filled with bags on the ground, takes a cigarette butt out of his pocket, clamps it in his black teeth, and gets right in Pasha's face.

"Hey, Soldier boy!" he yells. "Gimme a light."

"I don't smoke," Pasha answers disdainfully, and backs up, pressing himself into the wall. "Gotta get going," he thinks. "All right, gotta get going."

This old guy isn't just going to roll over, though. He's padded himself with his bags filled with bags; the rain shines coldly in his beard, like dew in September. He points a black nail at Pasha and shouts cheerfully:

"Gimme a light, Soldier boy!"

He says it with such confidence that Pasha involuntarily reaches into his pocket and finds the lighter he took away from the kid. The old guy is still right in Pasha's face, like he wants to kiss him. Pasha leans in, catches a deathly whiff of rot and infirmity, and raises his hands, shielding the lighter. A brief, fiery flash snatches his face out of the nighttime expanse: chapped lips, bloated skin, like that of a dead man, and an insane yellow eye, watching him from under a lowered brow. But the wind blows out the flame in the next instant. Nevertheless, the old guy manages to take a deep drag, seemingly sucking in all the surrounding warmth. He holds his breath, exhales laboriously, and then points his black nail at Pasha once again.

"Our boys really are givin' 'em hell!" he says with a laugh.

"Yeah, they are," Pasha answers inattentively. He doesn't know how to ditch this crazy guy with the bags.

"Really givin' 'em hell," the old guy says with satisfaction. "Our boys know what they're doing."

"Yeah, they do." Pasha doesn't argue with him.

"Yeah, they do." The old guy laughs cheerfully.

"Yep." Pasha agrees again.

"Why aren't your boys hitting back?" the old guy suddenly asks him.

Pasha shudders, looks at the old guy, and realizes that he's perfectly sane, he knows exactly what's going on, he has everything all figured out. And he can see right through Pasha. And the old guy can also see that Pasha knows exactly what's going on, so he's looking at him carefully, scrupulously, with yellow hatred in his eyes. Pasha grows anxious, not knowing what to do, fixes his glasses with his finger, and huddles against the wall. "I should pick something up and knock him out," he thinks, looking at the old guy. "Just knock him right out." And his gaze gradually gets heavier, cooler, like the earth soaked with winter rain, and he puts the lighter back in his pocket, slowly, very slowly, but the old guy catches that movement and notices the change in Pasha's eyes, even in the dark, and when the silence between them becomes absolutely unbearable, he suddenly throws his head back and bursts into a hoarse laugh.

"Yeah, Soldier boy!" he says, choking with laughter. "Just like that! Yep!"

He laughs so desperately that Pasha breaks down and starts smiling. But then the old guy starts coughing—a deep-seated, poisonous cough—which makes Pasha huddle into the wall again. The old guy stops coughing, catches his breath, regains his composure.

"It's really pouring, isn't it?" he asks, his tone still cheerful. "Where you headed?"

"To the Station," Pasha answers.

"It's over there." The old guy resolutely points a fingernail into the darkness. "See that over there? That's the North Star."

Pasha looks into the darkness. It's moving, throbbing. And there aren't any stars over there, obviously. Yet he can see all the murk that's been hanging over the city for days now, weighing it down, filling it up. "How much more time needs to pass before all this ends?" Pasha thinks, contemplating the slanted streaks of water. "How much more time needs to pass before all of this disappears underwater? Time has stopped, nothing's left, don't feel sorry for anyone. I'll never be able to get out of here, nobody'll ever get out of here alive, everyone'll stay here, everyone'll lie down under this lethal water." Pasha thinks of everything that he's seen over the past two days: all the exhausted eyes and faces contorted with anger, all the voices hoarse from dehydration, all the silhouettes shaken by sleeplessness, all the cold and all the dampness, and he suddenly gets this queasy feeling—because he's chilled to the core, because he's really hungry, because of this old guy who smells like death and seems to be decomposing right here, in the streams of rain.

"You see?" he asks. "Can you see it?"

"No," Pasha answers.

"Exactly," the old guy continues. "Exactly. There's nothing over there." And he's speaking like he's delirious, pointing into the darkness. "Two freight trains filled with bodies. Two whole cars, Soldier boy. I saw them. With my own eyes. There's nothing over there. Don't feel sorry for anyone."

He picks up his bags, pulls on the door, sticks his head out into the rain, and disappears around the corner.

DAY THREE

Looks like a fisherman who didn't wind up catching anything all day: raincoat, camo underneath, rubber boots. His gut hangs down like a mailman's bag. A Cossack whip sticks out of his bootleg, so everybody knows just who they're dealing with. He shakes his large buzzed head, shouts, snaps orders. Nobody's listening, though. The soldiers are scurrying all around—not to accomplish anything, just to keep warm. A field kitchen, black with smoke, rolls up to the station steps; they get it going and heat up the food. The rain hasn't abated since last night. It persists, douses the flame. The soldiers haul over a large tent with an ad for a local beer on it, set it up above the kitchen, and cram themselves inside. Alexei stands under the cold January sky, not knowing where to go from here—step under the tent and sink to his subordinates' level or keep waiting around out in the rain and get absolutely soaked. Cold heavy drops flow down his chubby, unshaven cheeks. He stands there and berates the soldiers. They berate him in response, and it becomes abundantly clear that that's just the way they interact with each other, always getting too emotional or something, like a married couple that's been living together for decades. They used up all their cordial words a long time ago, so they communicate with curses and maledictions. Well, it's not like they're going to sit there in silence.

Pasha and the kid make their way to the waiting area, pushing through the crowd to get closer to the windows. Outside the windows, facing the soldiers, Alexei is hollering his head off. You can't hear what he's shouting, but he's gesticulating so vigorously that you understand exactly what he's getting at. The smoke from the kitchen, broken up by the rain, drifts over the ground. The last thing they want to do is leave the train station, go out into the rain. The women stand around, huddle against one another, draw closer to the windows. It's as if they're watching a movie with no sound. Starring Alexei. He's big, silent, waving his arms, threatening someone with his fist, menacingly directing his gaze at something beyond the horizon. He suddenly turns around, falters for an instant when he spots a group of spectators, dozens of women's frightened faces carefully tracking his every move and gesture, surveys them all with the severity of an ataman, focuses his eyes, and begins yelling again, invitingly, spiritedly. Apparently he hasn't adjusted his language, yet he instantly sucks in his gut, and his cheeks, too. He's a military man, through and through. Pasha watches him and finds himself thinking that Alexei's expression is so piercing, so sincere that it seems like he's directly addressing Pasha, sharing something remarkably intimate with him. "Damn, that's because he is," Pasha eventually realizes. "He's yelling something at me." Pasha shoves a couple of small women aside, forces his way toward the doors, and opens them.

"Representative," Alexei says, his voice discontented, "of the cocksucking citizenry." Pasha walks down the steps, puts his hood up. The kid is at his heels, holding the bat. They approach. Pasha proffers his stiff hand. Alexei tenses up, yet shakes it. He mechanically shakes the kid's hand, too. Apparently he doesn't know how to talk to them. He has to strike the right tone. He clearly can't talk to

Pasha like he does to the soldiers. First off, Pasha is a representative of the citizenry. Second, there's a child around. So he gathers his thoughts, wipes some raindrops off his face, and nods in the direction of the kitchen, making one chubby cheek flap.

"So here's the deal," he says hoarsely, with the authority of a commander. "Just like we promised." He points at the kitchen. "We're providing . . . ," he pauses, "food for the civilian population," he concludes, businesslike. "So, you, Mister Esteemed Representative of the Citizenry, take care of this. So those were the instructions," he says. "From the command center," he adds.

The soldiers look at Pasha with hatred in their eyes. If it weren't for this asshole, we'd still be sleeping. Wouldn't be getting soaked outside this godforsaken train station. Pasha can feel their eyes, filled with justified indignation, fixed on him, yet there's nothing he can do about it. If you're going to call yourself a representative of the citizenry, oversee the smooth delivery of their meals. That's exactly what he's doing. He goes back to the main hall, where a crowd of soaked and mistrustful women surround him, listen to him wordlessly, and Pasha can already hear their grievances in their silence. But he raises his hand resolutely and begins speaking.

"So here's the deal," he says. "Instructions, just like they promised," he says. "Meals," he adds. "For the civilian population," he explains. The women listen without interrupting. Pasha feels as if they don't understand him, as if he's not using the right words. He lowers his hand, fixes his glasses.

"Listen," he says wearily, "there's food over there." He points out the window. "Walk on over, put some on your plate."

"Are they going to send some buses?" a woman wearing a mournful black headscarf asks, just as wearily.

"Promised they would," Pasha answers.

"That came from the command center?" a woman asks.

"Yep."

The women slink outside, shielding themselves from the rain with whatever they can, surround the tent, and hold out empty plates. A soldier in a dirty white apron and rubber gloves is heaping on generous portions of porridge with pieces of dark-colored meat in it. Another guy is serving them tea in mugs and thermoses.

"There's enough to go around," he says with a laugh. "There's enough for all you little ladies." The women don't react; they don't even cry. Cold, wet, hungry. They grab their rations and run back through the streams of water to the building. Pasha stands on the steps, pretending he's overseeing the process. The kid runs through the crowd, somehow digs up a disposable plate, and runs over. He devours half of his meal quickly and greedily, like a duck, and hands the rest to Pasha. He declines at first, as if he's not hungry, but then he breaks down, picks up a spoon, and quickly finishes what the kid's left him. He immediately realizes just how long it's been since he last ate, just how hungry he was. Pasha wearily rests his back against a column and surveys the crowd out in the rain. As the women pass, some of them nod at him like he's an old friend. We're good, thanks, we're eating. They look at him like he's in charge. They might think that he's actually responsible for something. Moreover, Alexei makes a big point of talking only to him. He comes over, frostily rubbing his hands.

"As per our instructions, we're now finishing meal service," he says.

"Yes, you've carried out your assignment," Pasha replies. "That's a wrap. When's the bus coming?"

"It's coming," Alexei answers reluctantly, his chubby cheek twitching, "at the scheduled boarding time."

"Well, that's good," Pasha says. "Well, that's just terrific."

The soldiers are standing off to the side, looking at the drenched, all-female line, trying to boost their morale, defuse this shitty-ass situation, cracking jokes, and making fun of each other. This scares the women, though—they don't expect anything particularly nice from the soldiers here, so they grab their food and run back to the building. The soldiers keep giving Pasha nasty looks. A local guy who isn't fighting, who's hiding behind a bunch of women. They're whispering to each other, laughing and showing their young, strong teeth. Pasha adamantly pretends that none of this has anything to do with him. He stands leaning against the column and listens to the freezing pigeons cooing up above him. Out of the tent comes one of the soldiers—young, about twenty, light brown hair, well groomed. Scrupulously polished combat boots. Even his nails are nicely trimmed. He's a bit chubby, though. White ghillie suit, black puffy jacket. "Looks like a penguin," Pasha thinks. "Black top, white bottom." And an old officer's map case rests on his shoulder. He looks like an old-time political officer. He walks up the steps toward Pasha, slings the map case over his shoulder, takes an apple out of his pocket, and offers it to the kid. The kid looks at him with disdain, yet accepts the apple and immediately begins munching on it. He purposely doesn't say "thank you." The Penguin looks at him, yet can't withstand his gaze, so he turns toward Pasha.

"So how's the situation, Pops?" he asks in a businesslike tone.

He's speaking proper Russian, with no accent. It's immediately obvious that he isn't from around here. He wants to see how the civilian population is feeling.

"It is what it is," Pasha replies. Well, what else could he say?

"Was it rough?" the Penguin asks.

"What do you mean?"

"Well, under those guys." He nods to the north. "Was it rough under them?"

The kid lifts his head toward Pasha. Well, did you have it rough, huh? And up above, it seems like the pigeons have stuck their beaks out so they can hear his answer.

"There are women and children here," Pasha says cautiously. "They have it rough."

"Gotcha." The Penguin nods in understanding. "Well, we'll push through, rebuild. Your son?" He points at the kid.

"Nephew."

"Where's your dad?" The Penguin leans in toward the kid. His tone is friendly, but he's scrutinizing everything, doesn't want to miss anything.

"He burned up in a tank," the kid says, crunching on his apple.

"Whose tank?" The Penguin's eyes light up.

"His," the kid answers without blinking. "His dad, my grandpa, brought it back from the war," he explains.

"He's pulling your leg." Pasha can't help but interrupt. "His dad walked out on them. He was staying at the orphanage."

"So he's an orphan." The Penguin nods sympathetically. "Is your mom still around?"

"Yeah," Pasha explains. "She's on the road. She's a train stewardess." And then he immediately bites his tongue.

"A train stewardess?" the Penguin asks warily. "Well, where is she now? What route?"

But then Alexei calls to him. Perfect timing, actually.

"Vasya," he says, "quit fucking pestering the civilians." Vasya gives the kid another discontented look, but he continues imperturbably munching on his apple and gives him a look right back. Yeah, Vasya, quit fucking pestering us. Vasya turns around, runs back to the group. The pigeons dejectedly huddle closer together to stay warm.

Two LAZ-model buses pull up a little after nine—beat-up, one blue-green, the other gray . . . well, just dirty. They were being used by soldiers, too; frayed flags hang on the blue-green one, and a military slogan that's now indecipherable was spray-painted on the side of the other one. The dirty gray bus has broken windows with wet curtains like ripped sails sorrowfully drooping out of them. The headlights are busted, too. And to be perfectly frank, it doesn't have a license plate, either. And soldiers are driving both buses. They're military vehicles. The dirty one even has several holes in the side. It's taken a beating. The women immediately spill outside, carrying their bags and bundles and dragging their children and kitchenware along. They dart toward the buses, yelling and carrying on. At first Alexei doesn't know what to do with the civilian population, but then he quickly regains his composure, shoves his way closer to the buses, raises his hand, and waits for everyone to calm down. Once they all do calm down, more or less, he angrily starts telling everyone to calm down and listen to what he has to say or they aren't going to get anything done, and that he's getting pretty fucking sick of them. He tells them that he had to take these vehicles off the front line, where blood is currently being shed for a just cause, and that his superiors have given him explicit instructions to tell them all to fuck off and send the vehicles back to continue the fight for their bright future unless they all take a few steps back. When they all quiet down, Alexei says with an air of importance, his chubby cheeks flapping, that the blue-green bus is going to the plant and the dirty one's going to the residential area.

"And that's it?" a young woman wearing an elegant hat and holding a down blanket asks dejectedly.

"What else do you want?" Alexei snarls at her. "You want us to walk you home? I'd be glad to!" he promises threateningly and begins pushing his way through the crowd, back to his guys.

The woman starts to cry, while everyone else storms the buses—it's better to go to the plant than sit here at the train station with this chubby-cheeked bastard. Alexei summons Pasha with a commanding gesture. He reluctantly walks over.

"So here's the deal," Alexei says. "You'll be in charge of the lead vehicle."

"What vehicle?" Pasha asks, confused.

"Uh, that one." Alexei points. "The dirty one that's going to the residential area. You'll be responsible for the noncombatants. Got it?" he asks. Actually, he's giving an order, not asking.

Pasha and the kid are the last passengers to cram into the bus. The only spots left are on the steps, down below, by the front doors. The driver's getting angry, yelling at the women to keep going, move down the aisle. But how are they supposed to do that when the bus is packed with pillows, mattresses, and jars of preserves? The women sit by the smashed windows—two or three to a seat, all on top of each other. They're packed together, arguing and crying. Children are whining; feathers fly out of ripped Chinese down jackets. The driver tucks his AK away and yells to Pasha:

"Calm them down already."

"How am I supposed to do that?" Pasha yells in reply. "Get moving. That'll calm 'em down."

The driver spits. Pasha shuts the smashed doors, even though that's pointless. Since the windows are smashed, too, closing the doors is like putting a newspaper on your face to stay warm in the winter. But rules are rules—the doors shut, the LAZ heads out, Alexei rubs his cheeks in relief. The field kitchen cools off like a lover's heart after a torrid romance.

The ride is cold and uncomfortable. Pasha and the kid are pressed up against the doors; a woman has rested her large leather suitcase right on top of Pasha. At first he tries to distance himself from her, scoot over, but there's nowhere to scoot to, so he stays put. The rain flies through the windshield; the driver's put on yellow tactical goggles, but they aren't helping much. In the north, at the edge of town, there's a series of explosions. They can't see the flashes through the rain, but they can hear something coming down behind the quiet residential neighborhoods. The women begin wailing again, all at once, all together. The kid's bewildered, huddling into Pasha's jacket. He might be cold or he might just want to cry. He holds it together, though.

They pull away from the station, turn to the right, to the south, dodge a fallen road sign, then a bullet-riddled bread truck, and then a heap of discarded furniture: a couch, a wardrobe, a chair with ripped upholstery. Guess someone was shedding their dead weight as they fled. Morning city, apartment blocks singed like fireplaces, shattered grocery store windows. It's dark inside. The bars on the windows are bent—looks like somebody tried stealing stuff but couldn't pull it off. The owners took almost everything with them, leaving behind empty shelves and old, dead fridges that the thieves were too ashamed to take. What does anyone need an old fridge for? Maybe for hiding corpses, but that's about it. The driver sees a newly built church behind the stores, and he automatically crosses himself, as do some of the women. They look at those who don't cross themselves defiantly, disdainfully, like beachgoers standing in cold water up to their throats look at people who're afraid to get wet.

They bear right at the intersection, skirt past the black courthouse, the savings bank with boarded-up windows, and the pharmacy: the cold apertures of windows, the twisted bars. Somebody tried to find something, anything, but did they? Can't tell. Then there's an empty school, a destroyed newsstand, a bullet-riddled obelisk, scraps of metal, burnt bricks, bloody clothes. There's hardly anyone out—just a few soldiers standing by the newsstand, smoking, talking, not paying any attention to anyone. And an elderly lady is dragging a sled loaded with cardboard across the wet asphalt. She might be going to burn it or she might use it to patch up the windows. Other than that, it's just empty and damp. No movement, no voices. And here at the intersection a car nearly crashes into them. The driver's so surprised that he only hits the brakes at the last second. The LAZ screeches, freezes, the driver's chest hits the steering wheel. And the car, unmoving and dead, freezes, too. Pasha peers out the window, and what he sees renders him speechless. Right in front of them is an Opel, meticulously smeared with mud. And at the wheel is the Iguana, gray from sleeplessness, frightened, angry. He's sitting there, his eyes wide, not knowing whether to berate the bus driver or apologize. And next to him, in the passenger's seat, sits a guy in a muskrat hat and a gray winter coat, also frightened, also gray. But that's not important. What's important is that there's a coffin tied to the roof of the Opel. Pasha doesn't believe his eyes at first. “This can’t be for real,” he thinks. “Where’d they pick it up?” It really is a coffin, though. The women see it, and they watch it, mesmerized. And the driver even takes off his goggles to check. Yeah, it’s a coffin. And Pasha realizes that the guy in the muskrat hat has probably just ordered the coffin, that he’s taking it home to bury someone. Public transportation isn’t running in the city, so he’s taking a taxi. And it seems that the Iguana will carry just about anything. A coffin? Well, a coffin it is. Knowing the Iguana, there’s a good chance that the coffin isn’t empty—there’s already somebody in there. All this lasts only a few seconds. Nobody has time to say anything; the women whimper, and the driver looks at the Iguana like he’s the captain of a ghost ship. The Iguana recognizes Pasha, and his eyes—always round, fishlike—become as round as the moon. He looks at Pasha like he’s a dead man who’s returned from the cemetery for his own wake. The Iguana’s fear passes quickly, though; he steps on the gas, the Opel jerks forward, races to nowhere, disappears into the rain.

The neighborhood ends. Then the road stretches along an empty field—concrete structures started in the eighties yet never finished, abandoned forevermore and now finished off by mortar fire. Beyond the field is a little ditch with a bridge running over it, and right in front of the bridge a checkpoint. It’s obvious that they were fighting for control of this area for quite a while. How’d the bridge remain intact? Couldn’t tell you. It’s still standing, though. They pull up, stop. Mortar fire has slashed the asphalt around the checkpoint—it looks like someone’s been hacking at it with a shovel. The cinder blocks have been slashed, too, and blackened with smoke. Soggy clothes, empty water bottles, and medical kits are scattered all around. A broken tree, torn paper, bent metal.

There are caution signs off to the side, on the ground. Three or four soldiers—anxious, angry—are in charge. They've clearly just taken over, the checkpoint's just been vacated. They're steering clear of the dugouts—don't want to risk it—standing out in the rain, inspecting the vehicles. The driver pulls up a little closer, looks out the smashed window. A soldier approaches him: red beard, winter footwear, a tourniquet wrapped around the stock of his Kalashnikov. The driver cheerfully asks a question or two, cracks some jokes, but the bearded guy merely grimaces in reply as he peers inside the bus. Pasha slowly turns away from the window so as not to draw any attention to himself, and notices in the cracked rearview mirror that another soldier is swinging out from behind the LAZ. He's walking, swaying heavily, steadily thumping his fist against the side of the bullet-riddled bus. Slight, short-legged, heavy, high boots, short hair, gray, even though he looks very young. Mirrored sunglasses. Fresh scar along his skull. Fingerless leather gloves, dark-colored, with shreds of blood on them. It's as if he's been in the kitchen, trying to tenderize meat with his fists. He's walking, approaching, not paying any attention to the women. They don't interest him. He can tell that what's most important is up ahead, next to the driver. He comes closer and immediately locks eyes with Pasha. And Pasha can see his expression change, his gaze begin to drift, his right eye give a deathly twitch, as if he's taking aim at Pasha. And putting two and two together, his jaw locks up, and he furiously grinds his teeth. Pasha goes as stiff as a board. The kid, who's standing with his face buried in Pasha's stomach, can sense, just with his back, that something's up, but he can't turn around because he's pinned between Pasha and the doors, so he just looks up and asks in a whisper:

"What?"

"We're fine," Pasha answers, also in a whisper, without taking his eyes off the soldier. "Everything's fine."

But the soldier thinks Pasha's talking to him, that he's addressing him, which makes him grind his teeth even more furiously.

"What?" he says, swallowing lingering saliva and resentment. "What the fuck is fine?"

"Pasha?" The kid questioningly tugs on Pasha's sleeve.

"We're fine, we're fine." That's all Pasha can say, and his stiff fingers squeeze the kid's shoulder firmly, very firmly.

"What?!" The soldier's getting all riled up. He yanks his gun off his shoulder. "What?!"

At this point, a very young soldier, who can see what's going on, moves away from the cinder blocks, his stride powerful. Black slightly askew winter hat, dark hair, skinny, smiling, hand resting confidently on the stock of his gun. He walks over, peers over his buddy's shoulder, sees Pasha, smiles, and realizes that he knows him—can't remember where he's seen him before, though. But he knows him, he definitely does. And Pasha knows him, too. And he can't remember where he's seen him before either. And they look at each other briefly, for a split second, but that's long enough for the soldier to put his hand on his buddy's shoulder—earnestly, with authority.

"Everything's fine, Rustem," the soldier says. He's still smiling, yet it looks mechanical. "Everything's fine. Let 'em go. It's cool."

Rustem's shoulder twitches. It's as if he wants to shake the hand off, but the bearded guy isn't letting go. He keeps smiling, his grip firm. Rustem, overcome with hatred and suspicion, merely narrows his eyes and grinds his teeth, but he restrains himself, doesn't say anything. He isn't saying anything, so no one else around him has anything to say either. The driver waves goodbye to the bearded guy; the LAZ heads out, slips between the cinder blocks, and rolls onto the bridge.

Only now does Pasha feel just how scared he is. How sticky and cold he is. It feels like someone just came up to him, took his death out of a sack, showed it to him, and then tucked it back into the sack. He's seen it, though, so he realizes that someone can take it out again, anytime, anywhere. But how does he know that second guy, the young one? Who is he? Who was that?

"Who is he?" the kid asks him. "Who was that?"

"Dunno," Pasha replies. "Don't remember."

"Yeah, sure." The kid gives him a doubtful look. "Maybe he was one of your students?"

"Maybe," Pasha answers, and it starts coming back to him.

Two years ago? Or three? When was it? Springtime. Must've been April. Or May? Yeah, May. So many smells—new, fresh smells. The city, the high-rises, the cold apartment block, the elevator as cramped as a coffin, the last floor, the freshly whitewashed hallway, the dark stains showing through the plaster, the metal stairs attached to the wall, the gaping opening. What's he doing there? Who has he come to see? Pasha tries to recall, but before he can the sky lights up above their heads. Bright, horizontal flashes slice through the gray, rainy expanse. Grad rockets are soaring from the factory, right over their heads—pale shadows whiz over them and fly to the north, to the other side of the city. And once again, Pasha can feel the metal spring digging into his heart, speeding it up, pushing him forward, forward, pushing him farther away from here, before something hits in retaliation, before the flashes come crashing to the ground, flooding everything with metal and death. The driver tenses up and tries to squeeze everything he can out of the LAZ. There isn't much there, though. The bus continues through the industrial park, passes one factory, followed by another, then a depot, followed by some warehouses. Just get out of here. Poplar trees along the road, gate arms, closed metal gates. Just get past the industrial park, where there isn't a soul in sight. If anything happens, nobody will find out, nobody will come help. The spring inside him tightens, making his blood pump faster. "Just get out of here," Pasha thinks. The driver looks frightened; he wasn't expecting rockets flying right over him. Now he's clutching the wheel, not hiding anything at all—not his fatigue, not his anger or fear. "Just like that soldier at the checkpoint," Pasha thinks. "The young guy who kept smiling. He wasn't hiding anything either, everything was right there on his face, everything was in his smile." Pasha thinks of the soldier, thinks of his victorious smile. That guy really wasn't hiding anything. It was like he was telling Pasha, "I stormed this shitty-ass city, took over this checkpoint, drove everyone out, wiped 'em out, I'm the one in control around here, I'm the one calling the shots, I can hand you over, all of you, right down to your guts, bitch, but I won't, run along now, you're fucking worthless to me, get out of here, scram, you'll be dead soon anyway." "Something else, there was something else," Pasha thinks frantically. "But what was it?" Freshly whitewashed hallway, metal stairs, last floor. Something from a previous life.

When it gets so cold that the kid wraps his arms around him, trying to get warm somehow, when the driver stuffs his hands in his pockets, leans against the wheel, and starts steering with his stomach, and when the women, all padded with pillows and blankets, stop shouting, they finally roll past the last factory wall, cross a black plowed field, and roll into the neighborhood. Pasha has tucked his head into his shoulders and turned his side toward the windshield so he doesn't feel the draft as much, but soon enough he can't help glancing at the road, checking out what's up ahead. What's up ahead is a long street, lined with houses. Many houses with signs of shelling, holes in the slate, black marks on the walls and fences. A local guy, frightened, enraged, peers out from behind a green metal gate. He looks at the newcomers with suspicion. Who are you? What've you come for? And most important, is the shelling going to start again? Pasha came here several times as a kid, with his old man. That's to say that he doesn't remember anything. Or anything good, at least. A mining town that merged with the city in the eighties, even though an endless industrial park has always separated the two. A certain degree of autonomy, separation. Nevertheless, everyone works in the city. They used to, that is. Before the war. The neighborhood's been cut off; they were fighting for control over it in the fall, but then stopped a while back. When the city was getting shelled, the people here were already patching up their roofs and putting up new fences. Fences are an absolute must, obviously. The LAZ continues down the main street, reaches the end—apparently this mining town's historic district—and pulls up to the bus stop. Pasha's frozen fingers open the doors; he and the kid spill out like two paratroopers with one parachute between them. Stiff bodies, numb feet, damp clothes, heavy heads. Ten a.m. It's a nice January morning.

Pasha immediately notices what's changed over the past thirty years, since he was here last. Nothing. A new church was built. And a supermarket. That's it. The old town council building doesn't have a flag on it—apparently, they tore down the previous one, the national flag, but haven't had time to put the new one up. The old cultural center—showing no signs of life. The nearby school is empty, too; rain hovers over the soccer field. Stores stretch along the street: the white brick, darkened by time, the blue paint of the window frames, the Coca-Cola ads taped to the doors. And a crowd, black, taciturn, tracking them tensely, suspiciously. Just watch—the crowd'll charge and rip 'em to shreds. The women begin disembarking, tossing their bags and pillows out the windows, step out into the rain, mill around near Pasha, continuing to view him as the guy in charge, staying near him, assigning responsibility to him for whatever happens to them. As everyone's disembarking, the driver eyes the crowd that's been standing by the store. Then he shifts to Pasha, who's now getting soaked along with his expeditionary force, flashes a crooked smile, starts up the bus, and puts it in reverse. And the two groups are standing opposite each other—two packs of fierce wet passengers at the empty bus stop, and just a hundred yards of thick damp January air separates them. They stand there, not knowing what to expect from each other, what to say to each other. Pasha doesn't know what to say either; he stands there, surveying the crowd opposite him, discerns several older men in black jackets and a woman in a raspberry down coat and two girls about ten years old, standing by themselves, no adults nearby, backpacks slung over their shoulders. He can't make out anyone else—just blurs of faces under headscarves and warm hats, deep cavities of eyes, makeup smeared by rain, strands of hair that poke out from under hoods, hastily applied lipstick. Women, mostly women. Harsh expressions. It's as if they can tell something bad is brewing. Nobody's smiling.

Pasha remembers the driver's crooked grin, remembers that guy who recognized him but didn't say anything, smiling at the checkpoint, and suddenly he remembers everything.

A year before the war, a previous life. Pasha's been tutoring a happy-go-lucky sixteen-year-old kid all spring, prepping him for his entrance exams. The kid's dad is a highly regarded and quite disagreeable businessman—sells coal. He wants to send his son to the capital. And then he's planning on moving there himself. He finds Pasha. Have to know Ukrainian, for the future. Pasha's a good, affordable teacher. And he hardly ever talks. He doesn't talk more than he should, that is. He only speaks Ukrainian during their lessons. It's as if the language consists solely of medical terms that simply have no practical application in everyday life. The kid knows his future is riding on this. And he wants to move to the capital. What could he even do in this town? Sell coal? His dad's the one who sells the coal. So he has to study. The only problem is that he hates all this: Pasha, coal, his dad. His dad more than anything. And he isn't Pasha's biggest fan either. He doesn't even bother hiding that. So twice a week, on Wednesdays and Saturdays, Pasha takes the train to the city and walks the fifteen minutes from the station. The kid lives in his own apartment. Two rooms, not very big. Prefab building, last floor. Ninth floor. Every lesson ends with a fight. With the kid throwing a fit, actually. Pasha just sits there, hears him out. He considers dropping the kid several times—calls his dad, who insists that Pasha continue the lessons. He even starts paying him more. Not much more, but still. One time, in May, probably—warm days, clear, high-hanging sky—the dad shows up unannounced, right in the middle of a lesson, decides to pay his son a visit, which throws him off for some reason. He flat-out ignores

Pasha, gets all riled up, starts yelling; his dad stops playing nice, too. Turgenev's fathers and sons, basically. Pasha tries to mediate, calm them both down, but first the kid tells him to go screw himself and then the dad does, too. When the kid, swept up in the moment, tells his dad to go screw himself, he cuts loose and nails his son right in the head. The kid falls back into a chair but springs right back up, saliva dribbling out of his mouth, wipes the tears away, grinds his teeth helplessly, wildly, and runs out of the apartment. His dad follows him; Pasha, sensing that something's up, also runs after him. He even catches a glimpse of the kid scrambling up the metal stairs, to the roof, his dad laboriously following him, and them disappearing through a hatch, one after the other. Pasha stays down below, looks up, at the bright blue square of May sky, and keeps repeating to himself: "Just don't jump, just don't jump."

Summer passes. The kid doesn't get in anywhere. He fails his entrance exams. Passes Ukrainian, though. Pasha's still all worried, beating himself up; he thinks that he's partially at fault, too. He's worried the kid's dad is going to give him trouble. But nobody hassles Pasha. He never sees the kid again and he quickly forgets about him. Now this has made him remember. "Man," Pasha thinks, surveying the dark crowd in front of him. "How'd that happen? My students fighting against me—how did I not notice that? How'd I miss that? Well, not really against me." He tries to reassure himself. "Not against me. Why bring me into this? Yeah, fine, they aren't fighting against you." Then he immediately disagrees with himself. "But they are against you, directly against you. Against everything that has anything to do with you. But what has anything to do with you?" Pasha asks himself, confused. "All of it," he answers himself. "Your subject, your school, the flag outside. They're fighting for that. Against it, actually. Why didn't he turn me in?" Pasha thinks. "Why'd he let me go? He could've turned me in. He had reason to, after all. Then what would've happened to the kid?"

And Pasha gets scared again. Very scared. And very cold.

This is how they take the dead to the cemetery. They're walking down the street at a leisurely pace, in no rush whatsoever, carrying the coffin, passing the last houses, reaching the end of town. It's like they're discarding useless things. Away from prying eyes, away from their homes. Just like now. The group sprawls down the street like a fire hose, stretching through the rain toward the city limits, away from downtown. The people out front are now lost behind a sheet of rain; those in the back are milling around here, by the stores, arguing, deliberating.

The two groups just came together. Everyone was asking each other where they've come from, where they're going. Several well-informed individuals emerged right away and started talking. They're definitely going to try and take the town back in the evening. Convoys kept arriving at the Station all night, coming from somewhere by Kharkiv, and they're all going to head this way today, to take the town back. But why try and take it back? An exhaustive answer followed that question. First off, there are mines and coal here, second, it's a straight shot to the city from here, and third, nobody wanted them to come in the first place. Those guys who rolled in yesterday—they're all in the city, none of them are in the town. So just come on by and hang the national flag on the town council building. The men held meaningful pauses, letting the women interrupt them, and they unabashedly interrupted the women, too, saying that nobody would come anywhere near here, that the Station, along with all the military equipment there, got hit yesterday, but that staying here still wasn't an option. There'd be a battle to retake the city and those new guys, the ones who rolled in yesterday, would probably retreat through the town, so not a stone would be left standing. The women yelled in protest, referencing relatives they'd spoken to just yesterday who'd talked to some people in the know who said that nobody would be retreating, that the new authorities would be here awhile, so it was time to flee, no matter what. The men sneered in response. Yeah, yeah, they'll be here awhile. Sure . . . They'll cut a deal, the new guys'll leave the city, the other guys'll come back, but still, we really ought to get the hell out of here. Needing to get the hell out of here—that's what everyone is talking about. Some voices are sharp and resolute, others quiet and confused. Nobody wants to stick around. Pasha tries to make sense of where they're all planning on going, how they're going to escape, what route they'll take. He calls for order, asks for permission to speak. But nobody's listening to him anymore; they aren't paying attention to him anymore. They merely look at him mistrustfully when he approaches, talk in hushed voices so he can't hear them, turn their backs on him, hiding something important from him. Eventually, the kid can't take it anymore.

"What are you even talking to them for?" he asks. "Let them go wherever they want. Leave 'em alone."

Pasha suddenly notices the kid. He's been kind of quiet since morning, not saying anything, not smoking, not hassling anyone. Hands tucked in his pockets, back turned to the rain. "Is he all right?" Pasha thinks, worried. "Last thing we need is another attack."

"Are you all right?" he asks.

"Are *you?*" the kid answers. He really does want to hear the answer, just like Pasha.

"So." Pasha sits down on a wet step and tries to speak calmly, yet with conviction. "So, we gotta get out of here. Can't stay here."

"But where should we go?" the kid asks him.

"Home."

"Through the fields?"

"We'll go with everyone else," Pasha says, after a moment's thought. "They're looking to leave the city by the railroad crossing. They say the checkpoint's empty over there. Our guys left yesterday, but those other guys haven't come yet."

"Your guys?" the kid scoffs.

"All right, don't start with me," Pasha says angrily. "Basically, there's no front line over there. We can just cross on over, go someplace, and call a taxi. We'll be home tonight. That's if they haven't blown everything up by now."

"How long are we gonna have to walk?" the kid asks. "To get to the railroad crossing," he adds.

"Five or six miles," Pasha says. "And then it's another five or six from the railroad crossing to the closest village."

"Man." The kid's surprised. "How're we gonna swing that?"

"We'll swing it," Pasha says. "If we want to."

"What if they actually did blow everything up?" the kid asks quietly.

"There's no way," Pasha reassures the kid. "Nobody blew anything up. Don't worry."

"You don't worry," the kid replies. "All right, nobody blew anything up. Get up," he says, setting off after the group. Pasha gets up, surveys the city. In the north, behind streaks of rain, the air trembles now and again, as if someone's using power tools behind thick curtains.

The street's empty. The sky looks like a mountain of sheets piled outside the train stewardess's compartment by passengers in the morning—heavy clusters of clouds all the way out to the horizon, scattered and twisted inside out. The procession sprawls down the street. They walk as if they truly are accompanying a body to its final, sorrowful resting place. The women carry their bundles, sidestepping potholes filled with water, but that doesn't help much. Water, cold wintry water, is everywhere. "For three days now, I've been trying to escape," Pasha thinks. "For three days now, I've been running around in circles, like a circus bear. And there's no end in sight. For three days now, I've been walking with some people I don't even know. Like some metal spring in the air is pushing me forward, goading me along, not letting me stop. Just like them," Pasha thinks, looking around. "Something's goading them, too, pushing them farther away from their homes. Half of them have no homes. No relatives. So they're wandering along the edge of town, with no chance of escaping. They're walking in circles, walking around their city. And I'm walking with them, for some reason. And I'm dragging the kid along with me, too." Pasha's most concerned about the kid—his shoes aren't made for this weather, and they're soaked—have been for a while. Just how are they going to make it? Pasha could turn to one of the locals, ask for a ride, but there simply aren't any locals around. It's like a ghost town, and they're the last ones left. They're walking down a long, empty street, their wet shoes kneading a gruel made of snow, mud, and sand, moving in a dark stream past other people's yards.

Steppe begins beyond the last fence. The snow is almost blue from all the moisture, with black melted spots on higher ground. There's a row of prickly, barely visible trees on the horizon. Up to its belly in snow, an old ambulance sits by the side of the road. The driver's side door is gone and its insides have been ripped out; they lie nearby in a snowbank. The back doors stick up. Empty inside. Dirty rags, camo jacket, spare tire. The group walks by, examining the abandoned vehicle fearfully. Several women cross themselves. It looks as if they're crossing themselves because they're passing the red cross on the ambulance. Pasha walks, his hand resting on the kid's shoulder, which is probably weighing him down, but he keeps it there—it's warmer that way. "Really should dry his feet," Pasha thinks uneasily. "Change his socks. He might not make it otherwise. I'd have to carry him." That wouldn't be easy—he realizes that right away. Just beyond the town, the road starts going uphill. They're moving at a decent clip at first, trying to pass each other or keep pace, at the very least, but just a mile or two later, in the middle of a field, the women stop, sit down on their bundles along the side of the road, to rest, catch their breath. They're trying to stay warm in the rain—fine, invisible, implacable. One of the women—headscarf concealing her face, yellow winter coat, high boots—is sitting on an upside-down bucket, hanging her head, looking at her feet, not moving. Pasha can't help but go over, try to do something. The woman lifts her head abruptly—abscesses, bloody, cracked lips. Pasha takes a step back, involuntarily averts his eyes. Eventually, he works up the nerve.

"Everything all right?" he asks. "Need any help?"

The woman looks at him, not understanding anything. And

not saying anything, obviously. Pasha stands there, hunching over her and trying not to look her in the eye. The kid timidly peers out from behind him.

"Do you need any help?" Pasha asks again.

The woman thrusts her hand forward—no. She has abscesses all over her hand, too. Pasha grips the kid's shoulder, nudges him forward.

"What could you do to help?" says an irritated voice behind him.

Pasha turns around. Some teenager, about fifteen or so, not very tall, though, only about a head taller than the kid, black Adidas hat, spring jacket—isn't keeping him warm at all—wet sneakers that sink into the snowy mush. Frozen to the core, hands tucked in his pockets, carrying an old, sun-faded hiking backpack. He gives Pasha a contentious look, sniffles. Where'd he come from? Who knows.

"Do you know her or something?"

"What's there to know?" the teenager asks, surprised. "She lives here, everyone around here knows her."

"Here?" Pasha's confused. "Like in town?"

"Well, yeah."

"What's wrong with her skin?"

"Fucked if I know," the teenager answers honestly. "She's sick, don't get too close to her."

"But why's she running away?" Pasha's still confused. "If she lives here . . ."

"Everyone's running away, so she is too," the teenager explains. "I'm telling you, she's sick. Don't get too close to her," he reminds Pasha.

He lifts his hood and goes around Pasha and the kid, hopping through the puddles and running ahead.

The road slopes downward, into the valley. There's more snow all around. Cattails line the road. Sharp, deathly stalks show what direction the wind's blowing. The women stop more frequently, wrap headscarves around the children, toss their clothing on the children's shoulders, walk slower and slower, their arguments growing quieter and quieter—all this jostling around in the snowy slop is taking a lot out of them. It's best to keep quiet. The descent into the valley is long; then they climb back out, ascend a hill. When they reach the top, they see a freshly made path that runs off the road. Over there, off to the right, about two hundred yards away, several structures loom: a small hamlet. Poplars around the buildings, barns. Looks like someone's farm. One line of travelers heading away from the road. And another line heading back, away from the buildings, toward the road. They approach, their expressions somewhat empty, and scared, seemingly regretting that they spent time there, that they went there in the first place.

"What's over there?" Pasha asks the women who are making their way out of the deep snow, back to the road.

One of them immediately hangs her head, turns away, and keeps walking, as though she didn't hear him. Another woman runs into Pasha, then goes around him, which makes her trip on her fur coat. While she's lifting the flaps and stepping onto the asphalt, she says:

"You can get warm over there. They made a fire."

Hurrying to catch up to her friend, she's not looking at Pasha either. "Who are they?" Pasha thinks. "No bags, no things. Where are they going?"

"Let's go warm up, all right?" he says to the kid.

The kid nods wordlessly. All right, let's get moving. Quit standing around.

They walk down a narrow path as a wet crust coats the snow right before their eyes. Don't want to veer off the path—the snow's pretty deep here. The closer they come, the stranger things get: large house with a slate roof, apple trees by the windows, sheds, small fence, people scurrying around the yard. Can't tell what's going on. A man who was toward the front of the pack heading away from the town emerges from someplace outside, walks over to the fence, knocks down part of it with a kick. He picks up the broken boards, carries them back to the house. Bricks and slate are scattered across the yard; the remnants of a broken couch poke through the snow.

"What was this place?" Pasha asks himself.

The kid doesn't know what to say. They turn the corner of the building. It looks like a stage once the colorful curtains have been taken down—now you can admire the bare brick walls and the disgruntled stagehands wandering around, not knowing what to do with themselves. One of the walls is completely gone—probably a direct hit. The house has been split in half; furniture spills outside, like someone's guts after they've been cut open. The house is large, yet destitute. There's hardly anything left inside: dishes filled with snow, broken plates, sauce-covered curtains stomped into the wet floor, jagged shards of brick, newspapers, rags. And a lot of folks inside, clearly freezing. They're sitting by the stove, burning the fence, trying to get warm. It looks as though the place was cleaned out a long time ago, and there's nothing more to take—no food, no valuables. The owners might not even know how many walls they have now; they might be hoping nobody breaks in, worrying about someone busting the lock. Well, nobody's busted any locks, it's just that one of the walls is missing. Oh, and the porch is gone, too. And the front door. Pasha steps inside, under the roof. It's full of holes, but there's hardly any rain inside and it's even warm by the stove. Granted, pushing his way over there won't be easy. Men in black jackets have occupied strategic positions. They're the ones who keep an eye on everything, determine who to let near the family hearth and who to chase out into the rain. They look at Pasha like he's their enemy. Who's this character with the glasses and beard? Where'd he come from? They instantly sense competition. The women who were with Pasha at the train station avert their eyes, acting like they've never seen him or the kid before. But Pasha unabashedly steps over some bundles, approaches the fire, and gives one of the men a gentle punch.

"Let the kid get closer," he says.

The man looks at Pasha with defiance and disgust, yet his disgust doesn't last long, and his defiance lacks conviction, and he can't say anything to Pasha, so he merely looks at him in silence.

"C'mon, c'mon," Pasha adds severely. He says it quite firmly, so the man's compelled to answer, yet rather amiably—last thing he needs is to get into a brawl here, in the ruins.

"Well, c'mon," the man mutters. He's about to say something else, but Pasha isn't listening to him anymore.

"Sit down," the man says to the kid. He comes over, sits down on a pile of bricks, and extends his frozen hands toward the fire.

"Take off your shoes," Pasha advises him. "Put on some dry socks."

The kid complies: takes off his shoes, peels off his socks, roots around in his backpack for a dry pair. Pasha steps aside so he won't agitate the serious-looking men in the black jackets. He finds a busted chair missing one leg, places it against the wall, gets situated, more or less. The men, seeing that Pasha has stepped aside and isn't laying claim to anything else, ease up, leave the kid alone. They're just like dogs—ward off the danger, then relax. The women stay away from them; they're afraid, sitting off to the side and catching some warmth.

"So where should we go?" one of them—dark face, yellow teeth, shabby hat, looks like a beaver—asks. "How far can you get?" It's unclear who he's asking.

"We'll cross the front line, get to the Station," another guy—slight, mouse eyes, high-pitched voice—answers him.

"Well, what's the point?" the Beaver asks him. "They'll take the Station any day now. You think they're just gonna let up?" He points at the ceiling. "They'll chase those guys." He points in Pasha's direction. "All the way to the Dnipro. So where are we supposed to go?"

"Where are you headed now?" asks the guy with the high-pitched voice.

"If only I could get to the motel," Yellow Teeth says. "My daughter's there. She's a waitress. I'll camp out at her place. She has her own room."

"The motel?" someone asks him. "At the edge of town?"

"Yep, that's it," Yellow Teeth says with satisfaction. "I could camp out there until summer. Nobody'll be trying to blow up a motel. I know the owner, too. He's a good guy."

“What’s your daughter’s name?” Pasha interjects loudly.

The group’s dead still; they all turn toward Pasha.

“Anna?” Pasha asks, just as loudly.

“Huh?” Yellow Teeth forces out a response.

“I’m asking you, what’s your daughter’s name?” Pasha repeats clearly. “Anna?”

Yellow Teeth’s somewhat flustered; he turns toward his pack and smiles somewhat timidly, seemingly apologizing to them for something. Like for leaving himself exposed. Then he hastily roots around in his pockets, produces an old cellphone—all dirty and beat up, looks more like a shoe brush than a phone—presses a button, runs outside just as hastily, and disappears around the corner. His friends are sitting around, their silence oppressive, looking at the flame, not knowing how to act. Eventually, one of them gets up, goes out into the rain, disappears. Then someone follows him. The small guy with mouse eyes is the last to leave. He stands up, looks into the kid’s eyes obsequiously, tosses several boards into the stove, and runs out without saying goodbye.

“Did someone call him or something?” Pasha asks loudly, turning to the women. But the women avert their eyes, not saying anything either.

Pasha takes out his phone. No service, obviously.

Wonder who could’ve lived here. Pasha scans the wrecked house. In the kitchen, above the table, last year’s calendar. In the large room, where they’re sitting around getting warm, faded wallpaper dangling loosely. Wooden floor. In the corner a bent metal bed. Three women, as dark as trees in the winter, lying on it. Several small, shredded pillows scattered around it. Clearly, children slept in that bed. Some people come inside, make their way closer to the fire. Others head out into the rain once they've warmed up a little and eaten something out of their bags. "I wouldn't ever want a bunch of people to gather in our house and be all warm like this," Pasha thinks. Examining someone else's domestic life is like flipping through someone else's porn magazines—you never know what not to touch. Here someone else's whole life has been turned inside out like pockets. Actually, it's like an orphanage. You can't hide anything, everything's exposed. The wallpaper and the pillows. And hundreds of strangers pass through your life, not leaving a single trace. They burn someone else's furniture, not knowing who's living in their houses now. Maybe someone's fueling the stove with their library. "Gotta get out," Pasha thinks. "Gotta get home fast. Dad's probably scared out of his mind. Yeah, and the kid really shouldn't be seeing all this."

"All warmed up?" Pasha asks.

"I'm fine," the kid answers.

"Time to go," Pasha says. "It's almost one. Don't want to be walking in the dark."

The kid gets up, tosses a painted board into the fire. The flame immediately licks the old, cracked paint. The women sit there, their eyes fixed on the fire. And not saying anything, afraid they'll say too much. No one's listening to them, though—everyone has had enough as it is.

Soon enough, their clothes are wet again. Their shoes squelch, it's tough going, and there's nowhere to stop and get warm. Endless rainy fields that drop off in the south, turning into heavy, soggy slopes that roll all the way down to Azov. They're white from the snow and black from the dirt on the bends. A low, twisted row of trees that's supposed to block the wind and snow stretches along the road. It doesn't actually block anything. Wind crawls under their clothes, clutches them, constricts their movements. Discarded belongings occasionally loom in the snowbanks: an empty bag, an extra pair of shoes, a woman's sweater. Travelers shed what they don't need. It's a long, arduous trip—ascending past the chalk quarry or sliding down to the empty steppe lakes surrounded by cattails. This one hill is particularly tough. Their feet slip, the wind cools their blood, an endless expanse of white stretches to the other side of life. It feels like you'll never get out of this valley, this trap, like you'll be trudging on among these wet, frightened travelers until you lose consciousness. On his way up, Pasha notices that a crowd's gathering at the top; they're standing around, discussing something, in no hurry to move forward. "Might have to turn around," he thinks, scared, and picks up the pace. He's dragging the kid along. He asks the kid if he's all right every once in a while, and the kid nods wearily in reply—I'm all right, just fine. They crest the hill. The wind's particularly nasty up here. The rain has let up, though. The air smells like wet snow. The next snowy valley opens up before them; a cold forest sinks into it blackly. And the road under their feet falls sharply, weaving between some trees into a cold, frozen thicket. On the other side of the forest, the path shoots up a hill. Spoil piles from the mines and the gray blocks of buildings come into view beyond. It seems as though a whole new life begins over there. It's really close—just go down the hill, walk through the forest, head up the next hill, and you're saved. The only problem is that a black tail of smoke—thick, ominous, like someone's burning casualty lists—hovers high and crooked over the forest. The thing is, the road leads down there, to where they're burning them, and there's no going around the forest. Unless you want to wade through knee-high snow for who knows how long, who knows how.

"Where's the fire?" Pasha asks the men who are standing around and anxiously smoking.

"By the tracks," answers one of them, turning around. It's the Beaver. He immediately recognizes Pasha, bites his tongue, but it's too late. "At the railroad crossing."

"In the woods?" Pasha asks incredulously.

"Well, yeah. The front line runs along it. There's some guys on one side," he says, giving Pasha a confidential glance. "And some other guys are on the other side. It's like a border."

"What about the trains?" Pasha's still confused.

"Well, they let some through," the Beaver explains. "And stop some others. It's just like a border," he reminds Pasha.

"What's burning?" Pasha inquires.

"Oh, I don't know." The Beaver grows anxious, choosing his words with care, and turns toward his friends. They avert their eyes, though, not saying anything. "It might be a stronghold."

"What now?" Pasha walks right up to him, looks him in the eye, not letting him step aside.

The Beaver realizes that Pasha has no grounds to get tough with him, but something forces the Beaver to keep standing there, on his tiptoes, and keep answering his questions. He can feel something inside Pasha that he knows he should be wary of. And his friends, wet and smoke stained, are just biding their time, not getting involved. They're smoking out in the wind, tucking their cigarettes in the sleeves of their black winter jackets.

"Well, I don't know," the Beaver says. "Hafta go back, maybe."

"Go back?" Pasha's surprised.

"Well, there's smoke everywhere." Pasha's reaction scares the Beaver. "How are you gonna get through?"

"Yeah," adds the small guy with the high-pitched voice and mouse eyes. He's standing somewhere down below. "Gotta head home and wait. We'll come back tomorrow."

Then they all suddenly turn toward Pasha and the kid, seemingly on cue, and start talking. "Yeah, yeah, gotta go back home and wait. We'll come back tomorrow. And you can wait with us, too," they hint cautiously. "Don't be afraid. Just wait it out with us. What do you have to be afraid of?" And the Beaver notices that everyone's turned toward Pasha, walked over to him, and they keep repeating, seemingly to each other, to no one in particular, yet actually to Pasha, first and foremost: "We'll come back, yeah, just have to wait it out." And the Beaver lowers his head and looks at Pasha defiantly, feeling he has his friends' backing. We'll wait it out, we'll all wait it out. And you'll come along with us. Pasha senses his gaze on him—and not just his. Mouse Eyes with the high-pitched voice tries to block Pasha's path with his chest, but he doesn't have much to block with. Pasha easily pushes him aside, pulls the kid along, and then turns around.

"Yeah," he says. "We'll come with you. Be right there," Pasha says. "Let's go," he whispers to the kid.

They head downhill, trying not to hurry, getting farther and farther away from the group. Pasha can hear the men having an anxious discussion that quickly turns into a fight. Why the fuck did I have to tell him? You should've stopped him. Why were you just standing around? And so on. "Faster, faster," Pasha whispers under his breath, more to himself than to the kid. "Faster, faster, they won't run after us, they don't have the guts." The afternoon sky hangs low over the forest itself. A dark rope of women, just women, both young and old, walking down the road cautiously, afraid they'll slip. But the closer they get to the forest—smoke splits above it—the hastier their movements become, the more anxious their strides become. Pasha and the kid speed up; they walk, not looking back, hurrying to distance themselves from the group on the hill. They pass some women, now nearly running. The women see that they're hurrying, so they speed up, too. Those two, they might know something, maybe we should go hide in the woods right away, maybe, back there, behind us, on the hill, something terrible, something that you just can't run away from, something you just can't avoid, is going to appear any second now. Pasha and the kid can hear the women conscientiously splashing through the puddles, trying to keep up. The string shuffles along, runs to the first cluster of trees. They don't even cast any shadows under the gray January sky. And it doesn't get any easier when the forest encircles them. It gets worse, scarier: trees battered by shells, trenches stretching along the side of the road, and snow, the snow!—a dark yellow, like it's rotten or something, like someone died a few days ago and is now rotting out in the fresh air. In a few spots, the yellow stains have spread and turned completely brown. In others, dark clumps show through faintly, like birthmarks on someone's skin. But it's all like this, touched with rot.

"What's with the snow?" the frightened kid yells, running, gasping for air, yet not stopping. "What's wrong with it?"

"I don't know!" Pasha exclaims, not stopping either. "Run for it."

"What's wrong with it?" the kid demands.

Horror and hysteria cut through his voice. It's as though he's on the verge of bursting into tears, but he realizes that he can't cry, he shouldn't cry, even though he really wants to. So he holds it in, but he can only hold it in for so long—that's obvious. "That's obvious," Pasha thinks, immediately understanding what's going on. "That's obvious. He can only hold it in for so long." This is just like that time. Just like when he had his first attack. When he turned his stomach inside out, and he ran out of the house, into the night, and Pasha had to run after him, chasing him between the trees, like he was trying to catch his own shadow. "The same thing's going to happen now," Pasha says to himself. "That's obvious." So he picks up the kid, along with his backpack, and heaves him over his shoulder. He immediately feels all the weight of this thirteen-year-old kid and all the weight of his winter clothes, and he feels all three days' worth of fatigue. "Just stay on your feet," Pasha reminds himself, and he keeps running, hearing the weary women's labored breathing alongside him. He runs past the yellow, dead snow and the slashed trees, down a long, very long winding road littered with boards ripped out of something, pieces of metal stomped into the snow, dirty rags. The farther he runs, the darker the snow becomes. Then suddenly it's just gone. There's only black burned earth between the trees. And the trees are all burned, too. And smoke and fire seep through everything around them. And then they reach the railroad crossing.

Looks like a big dumpster that someone's carelessly set on fire: metal beams, a shattered tree, clothes stomped into a ball of soot. Melted glass, destroyed foodstuffs, sandbags ripped like pillows in a child's room. Off to the side, between tree trunks slashed by shrapnel, a gate arm lies on the ground. A busted-up booth, trenches all around—also burned out and packed with frigid sand. The cold steel of train tracks, white as bone. Marks left by mortar fire and a bunch of military equipment. Shredded, blood-stained camo scattered across the embankment. The blood hasn't frozen yet—looks like the garment was just cut off someone's body, just a little while ago, and it looks like whoever cut it off is somewhere nearby, hasn't gone far, could come back any minute now. But that's not it. It's just that there's a Ural-model truck, loaded with dark crates, parked behind the booth, on the other side of the embankment. The cab's burned out, the wheels reduced to scorched scraps. For some reason, the crates aren't burning, though, just smoldering, and smoke rises off them, like the truck bed is a crematorium, methodically filling the winter sky. "Guess this is where the smoke's coming from," Pasha surmises. "This is what's burning." Pasha lowers the kid onto the ground; they stand there, apprehensively eyeing the Ural. The women who were following them come running over, wheezing wearily. A woman carrying a large plastic bag slings it off her shoulder, collapses on top of it. She doesn't have the energy or words to gripe about anything.

"What is that?" a frightened woman—roughly fifty—yells to Pasha. Heavy fur hat with black-dyed hair sticking out, dirty sheepskin coat, winter boots with broken heels. Her makeup has been washed away like a drawing in the sand.

"It's on fire," Pasha explains. "Shrapnel, probably."

"I mean what's the smoke coming from?" she continues, still yelling. "What's in the crates?"

"Dunno," Pasha admits. "Food, maybe?"

"Food?" she yells. Terrified, she covers her mouth so as not to scream and then darts forward, over the embankment, across the tracks, far away. Just get away from here.

The kid yanks on Pasha's sleeve.

"C'mon," he yells. "Quit standing around. It's gonna blow."

He darts forward, too. Pasha runs after him. They cross the tracks, slip through some bullet-riddled cinder blocks, dodge trenches, coils of barbed wire, tumble behind the last dugout. Out of the corner of his eye, without turning his head, Pasha sees a black army boot on a breastwork—right foot, cut shoelaces, blood everywhere. Pasha even thinks there's a foot inside, the remnants of a foot, with bloody mush inside it. He wants to stop and move closer, wants to get a better look, but the kid, still running, shouts piercingly. C'mon, c'mon! Keep moving, follow me! And Pasha runs forward, down the ripped asphalt, through the black, broken forest and the wet afternoon air, running, grabbing the kid by the shoulder and dragging him along. He wants to give the woman in the fur hat a hand, but she lurches back, as if she's just seen her death at the front door, and Pasha and the kid abandon her, leaving her on the black road. They run, not looking back, racing farther and farther down the winding, wooded road, charging ahead, only thinking about one thing. Now, right now, any second now, at this very moment—it's gonna blow, wipe everything out, implode this wet, wintry space, implode the sky above them, stop time, now, right now, right here.

They reach a row of trees, collapse into the snow, gasping for air, breathing laboriously, like they've just taken the stairs up to the top floor.

"Hear that?" the kid asks once he's caught his breath.

Pasha listens intently. Engines. He lifts his head, glances at the main road. Way up there, atop a hill, beyond the fog, two jeeps are creeping, crawling along. They descend apprehensively, as though they're afraid of bumping into something unpleasant. Haven't turned their headlights on, though—they're too afraid.

"What should we do?" It's unclear who Pasha's asking. "Are those our guys? Hope they're on our side."

"What if they're not?" the kid asks him.

"That's bad if they're not," Pasha answers. "Really bad."

"You know, Pasha," the kid says to him, his tone serious, judicious. "If those guys aren't on our side, they're gonna kill you. I have no idea why they haven't killed you already."

"Haven't given them a reason to," Pasha replies, aggrieved.

"Uh-huh, haven't given them a reason to, sure. You know what I'm getting at . . ."

"Yeah." Pasha unexpectedly agrees with him. "Got to stay off the road. Who knows who's over there."

That's exactly what the kid wants. He gets up and runs toward the road. They race across the asphalt, skid onto the shoulder, dive into the snow, and make their way down a barely visible track that shoots off to the side. It seems like nobody's driven along this track for a while, but the frozen imprints of treads crisply come through the freshly fallen snow, like a scar through a thin T-shirt. They run along them, reach higher ground, and then quickly go down a hill, gradually fading out of view. The kid, still running, pulls the bat out of his backpack and hurls it into a heap of snow. "He's all grown up," Pasha thinks as he runs after him. "So mature, so serious. He's absolutely right—they might not kill me, but they'll throw me into some pit. And I'll sit there until they pull me out. It's all so obvious, who I am, where I work, what I do." And Pasha realizes that he hasn't actually seen the kid for a while. And that when he did see him, they didn't have real conversations. They'd just exchange a few words about something trivial, something neither of them found interesting, and go their separate ways. Back to their respective corners, until the next time, until the next conversation. "Until the next fight," Pasha adds to himself, and thinks back to how he found the kid among the trees, how he dragged him along, how the kid resisted, didn't want to go with him. How he eventually bit Pasha's hand. How he screeched in surprise and grabbed the kid by the scruff of the neck like a naughty puppy, how the kid squirmed and howled—just like a puppy, actually—fearfully and maliciously. How later on, at home, in the kitchen, everyone was yelling, their voices angry, like they were at someone's funeral, like they were blaming each other for someone dying—no chance of forgiveness, no hint of leniency, letting their voices get loud and uncontrolled, not listening to anyone. That time the kid curled up into a ball. He started shaking, all shriveled up and huddled with convulsions. But everyone was yelling so loudly; they wanted to scream it all out, so they weren't even paying attention to the kid. They only started when he let out a screech and began rolling across the floor, as though demons were crawling out of him. Pasha was the first to notice, but his voice just snapped. He darted over to the kid, turned his head toward him. Pale face, eyes rolled back in his head, a string of saliva dangling from his lips. Pasha picked him up and placed him on the bed. After that, his sister, the kid's mom, that is, began wailing, howling as loud as she could, and then rushed over to the kid's side. Pasha's old man stopped short before he could get out his most cherished curse. Everyone was hovering over the kid, not knowing what to do with themselves or how to act; they stood there and watched warily as the kid got really quiet, as if he was falling into a warm, deep sleep. And Pasha rushed to call the ambulance, still not knowing what he would say or how to explain what was going on, while his sister was hovering around the kid and wailing—despondently, as loud as she could—scaring Pasha and his old man. "How old was he then?" Pasha thinks, trying to remember. "Nine, ten? How many more times did it happen after that? Twice, three times?" That went on until his sister started talking—quietly at first, on the phone, to her girlfriends, and then loudly, more firmly, with conviction, with authority to Pasha and his old man. The kid's not doing well, need to do something, need to get him treated before it's too late, even though, in all honesty, it's already too late. There's no real point, what's done is done, it'll be easier to just send him to the orphanage, save myself the hassle. Pasha's old man was indignant, obviously. And Pasha was indignant, too. But his sister did as she pleased. Neither of them, not Pasha and especially not his old man, could deter her, stop her. Maybe they actually started believing that the kid had something really wrong with him, and things would be better that way. But actually, they probably just didn't feel like fighting for the kid. They surrendered him, didn't protect him. Maybe they thought, "The kid's just a kid, he doesn't understand what any of this means anyway, we'll see once he gets a little older." But it seems that the kid understood everything; he understood everything perfectly well. "That kid, he really does understand things, and now he understands everything perfectly well, and he's absolutely right," Pasha thinks as he stomps down the snowy slope. "He's really matured since then. Why am I such a wimp?" he thinks, wheezing. "Why didn't I protect him? He'll never forgive me for that. Never," Pasha agrees with himself. "No matter what."

The track runs along the foot of a hill. People clearly used it to avoid the checkpoints on the main road. Their feet slide, a brisk wind wafts in from the steppe. It's getting even colder, even more foul. In one spot, where the track veers to the right and goes uphill, they can see that some tanks stopped and lingered for a while, long enough for their treads to plow up the ground all around. The snow has sunk by the track. It's as if someone did some digging and then filled up the pits, and the earth has sunk under the pressure of heavy rain. Pasha stops and looks, trying to figure out what this is, what's buried here, what it could be. The kid comes over, catches Pasha's eye. They stand there, not daring to speak. And then a phone rings. Right in the middle of the field, in the gray, wet, snowy field. Pasha twitches. He immediately thinks of the demolitions guy by the orphanage. "From underground," he thinks, terrified. "They're calling from underground. Buried him with his cellphone." And the kid cowers, tucking his head into his collar, not saying anything. Then he can't take it anymore.

"C'mon," he says. "Pick up already, someone's calling you."

Pasha slaps at his pockets, pulls out his phone. Someone really is calling him! His dad. He holds the phone against his ear, tries to make something out, anything. Mechanical noise, crackling, then some sort of cold echo, like the call is coming from a barrel that's been welded shut. The call drops. Pasha tries to call back, but he doesn't have any service. There's no knowing how his old man got through.

"Dad called," Pasha says. "I've got to call him back."

"Yep. And what are you gonna tell him? That you're hiding from tanks out in some field? Let's go."

He starts moving again, tucking his hands into his jacket

pockets, not saying anything. Pasha's breathing heavily, but he's keeping pace. Suddenly, behind them, where the woods are, something explodes. Pasha slumps onto the snow, the kid crouches. One, then a second, then another.

"What's that?" Pasha yells.

"It's coming from the woods," the kid answers intently, adamantly, seemingly afraid that Pasha won't listen to him. "Run, hurry up."

They get up, run down the track, sliding on the hardened, snowy crust, go down into a gully, and dodge some thornbushes. There are more and more of them as they go. The track snakes between black, twisted branches, and they suddenly pop out by some people's yards. Back there, amid the thorns, in the field, Pasha heard dogs' voices—chilled, hoarse—but he thought he was just imagining things. But no, he wasn't. There's a village up ahead. They've popped out right on someone's property, and a dog—somewhere over there, in the early twilight, beyond the snow and trees—is tearing through the air with his teeth, sensing their approach, wailing, warning everyone that outsiders are approaching, snapping the sonorous afternoon silence.

"Stop," Pasha yells.

The kid stops, discontentedly. Pasha walks over, places his hand on his shoulder. The kid's wiped out, wheezing, his eyes red with fatigue, scanning the area for any possible danger. He waits wordlessly.

"What are we gonna do?" Pasha asks, looking the kid right in the eye.

"Well, isn't it obvious? Let's find someone who's still alive and get the scoop."

"What if they turn us in?" Pasha asks quietly.

"What if they don't?" the kid asks in reply.

"It's risky," Pasha says.

"It's cold," the kid reminds him. "Get with the program, Pasha. Let's go look for some people already."

The street starts abruptly, seemingly coming out of nowhere, out of the air. And the air all around is like a boot someone's kicked off after coming in from the snow and placed by the radiator so the cold water can drip off it. It starts raining again. The first yard is spacious. An old brick house hides behind a lopsided fence. There's a pile of firewood by the porch—somebody clearly stocked up that morning. Moisture seeps into the fresh notches on the wood. The windows are dark. But everything around here is dark; there aren't any lights on in the house across the street either. Just dogs erupting in some barns nearby.

"It's dark," Pasha says, nodding at the house.

"Clearly it's dark," the kid answers. "They cut the power lines."

Farther down the street, a fallen pole lies on the ground. The wires around it look like hair that's been brushed with a rough comb. Beyond the trees, at the end of the street, they can hear a powerful engine. Sounds like a tank. There's no knowing where it's going, but it's best not to wait around.

"C'mon," the kid says, slipping through a hole in the fence.

Now the kid's telling Pasha what to do, and he's listening. "Well, why not?" he thinks. "He's absolutely right, knows what he's talking about." They walk through a little garden. Garage to the left, smells like gasoline, rickety addition to the right, a soggy path between them. They walk, watching their step, past the garage. And here, bursting at their backs, comes a dog's heavy bark. The kid leaps forward, Pasha instinctively ducks—a dark German shepherd with yellow spots is thrusting all of its muscular body at a wobbly barn fence, extending its hind legs like a ballerina in pointe shoes, trying to break out of its open-air cage, its mouth grabbing air spitefully, viciously barking at these two outsiders, sticking its snout out into the rain. The smell of wet dog. The front door swings open; on the threshold, warily hunching over and peering into the twilight, stands a man. Track bottoms, shabby sweater, bare feet. He's curling his toes, like he's stepping into the cold sea. He's shivering, can't make anything out.

"Who's there?" he yells and breaks into a coughing fit. He's holding on to the door with one hand so it doesn't shut and he's holding an ax, which he apparently used to chop the firewood just before this, in the other. "Who's there?"

The dog's going wild, lurching at the fence, banging his tense body against it, trying to break free somehow and devour them.

"Cool it!" Pasha suddenly yells. "We aren't going to hurt you!"

They move closer. The man is about fifty. He gives them a frightened look, still not lowering his ax.

"We're from the Station," Pasha yells over the dog. "I have a kid with me. We just want to get warm real quick."

He squeezes the kid's shoulder. I'll do the talking, you just keep quiet. The kid plays along, slouching and sniffling out in the rain. The man keeps coughing; then he turns around and disappears into the house. Without closing the door behind him. Pasha walks up the steps, the kid in tow.

There's a table heaped with apples on the porch. The apples are as chilly as the extinguished meteorites that kept falling in the steppe all through autumn. The place smells of dampness and rot.

They walk into a room. Bed in the corner, winter coat instead of a blanket. A lightbulb dangles like a disconnected studio microphone. The lights are out, the owner's got a gas lamp burning. He's sitting at the table, his expression surly. He's placed the ax next to him, on the table. Two mugs, two plates, gray bread. One might think he's planning on slicing it with his ax. There isn't much light, but his face is still visible. Yellow skin, heavy bags under his eyes, bald spots. "Heavy drinker," Pasha thinks. "Or he used to be." His bare toes tap across the dirty rug. Pasha and the kid stand in the doorway, in no rush to come in, yet not intending to leave.

"Excuse me." Pasha's tone makes it sound like he's telling the owner to go screw himself. "I've gotta dry his clothes, otherwise he'll catch a cold."

"Who are you?" the owner asks gloomily. He's clearly trying to sound tough, but he lacks natural toughness. And the bags under his eyes make him look hungover, not intimidating. He's speaking Russian, but it's far from flawless. He's stressing the wrong syllables and such.

"I'm a teacher," Pasha explains. "From the Station. We were in the city. Heading home now."

"You're coming from the city?" he asks, surprised. "How'd you get through? They closed the checkpoint over there, at the railroad crossing."

"There's no checkpoint there," Pasha replies, and then wordlessly begins peeling his jacket, heavy with moisture, off his body.

The owner looks at him morosely, yet doesn't say anything; he restrains himself, observes. The kid pulls off his shoes—also wordlessly, without waiting for an invitation—squelches over to the table in his wet socks, and sits down, opposite the owner. And then a woman peers out of the next room. Fat, frightened. Short hair dyed chestnut brown, heavy chin, wet eyes. She sees her husband at the table, the ax next to him, two strangers—one an adult with a beard and glasses, the other just a kid. Who are they? No clue.

"What do we have here?" she asks discontentedly, primarily addressing her husband, as if he just invited them in off the street to have a nice chat. "Well?"

"Where can we hang our clothes?" Pasha interrupts her.

He walks over, his eyes red behind fogged-up glasses. The woman gives in, averts her eyes, and then looks at the kid, but he has red eyes, too, from the rain and sleeplessness.

"What are you sitting around for?" she yells at her husband. "Huh?"

The owner anxiously springs up and grabs Pasha's coat out of his hands. Let's go, the stove's over there. They walk into the next room. Bed, chair, torn photo wallpaper. Lit stove, dry firewood on the floor. They hang up their clothes; Pasha moves two pairs of shoes, his and the kid's, closer to the fire. They come back. The kid's already sleeping on the bed. The owner walks over, gently covers him with the coat. He comes back and sits down at the table, closer to his ax.

"What's going on in the village?" Pasha asks severely.

The owner looks at him, waits, doesn't answer. There's no apparent reason for him to be afraid of this teacher, but something still compels him to exercise caution. "There's something off about this teacher," the owner thinks.

"I don't know," he says. "I haven't left the house in three days. There was some shelling over there."

"Is public transportation running?"

"Is public transportation running?!" he repeats, aggrieved. "Did you hear what I just said? There was shelling."

"Well, how can we get to the Station?"

"How am I supposed to know?" the owner answers wearily.

He sits there. His eyes wander, his fingers drum on the table. Pasha's bearing down on him, not stepping back.

"So what are we gonna do?" he asks.

The owner strokes his ax, contemplates, deliberates, and runs his hand through his thinning hair.

"What's going on over there, at the Station?" he asks.

"Everything's fine," Pasha replies, growing a bit anxious. "If he tries to kick us out," he thinks, looking at the owner. "I'll knock him out. With his own ax." "Everything's under control. The situation is stable."

Hearing that, the owner warily lowers his eyes. "Something's up," he thinks with a tinge of doubt. "This teacher, he's hiding something."

"Well, all right then," he says, eventually. "Are you gonna tell me what side you're on, at least?" he asks hopefully.

Pasha walks over to the table, rests his fists on it, and looks the owner right in the eye, his gaze persistent and draining.

"Well, what do you think?" he answers.

The man thinks, hanging his head. It looks like he's thinking with the bags under his eyes.

"I see," he says eventually. What do you see? What the fuck do you see? Pasha only says that to himself.

"Okay," he says to the owner.

"So," the man says anxiously, "why don't I give you a ride out of the village? If the checkpoint's gone."

"And?" Pasha's bargaining with him.

"I'll try to slip out to the main road. I'll drop you off there. Then you'll call a taxi and head home. Don't have to pay me anything."

"Why's that?" Pasha asks severely.

"Listen." The man's growing even more anxious. "I'm not asking you any questions. Just let me give you a ride, all right? Maybe you'll bail me out one day."

Pasha doesn't reply. He looks at the owner like he's a piece of spoiled meat.

"I'll bail you out," he says harshly. "I'll give you a medal."

The owner gives him an aggrieved look. The bags under his eyes twitch. But he restrains himself, doesn't say anything.

"Let the kid sleep," he says, standing up. "We'll leave in an hour."

He gets up, turns off the lamp, leaves. Pasha stands there in the dark for a bit. He looks at the kid, at his face, as tranquil as a dead person's, at his jacket, which he's sleeping in—didn't bother taking it off. At one point, it seems as though the kid has stopped breathing. Pasha breaks into a cold sweat at the thought of that. The kid's saying something, though, incoherently, in his sleep, so Pasha calms down. Everything's fine, he's still alive. He gropes for a chair, sits down, rests his head in his hands, and sinks into a deep sleep. In his sleep, all he sees is snow that he has to wade through. He steps through this snow, sinks into it, pulls his leg out, sinks into it again, takes one step after another, struggling, like he's walking through a river. He wades through the snow, continuing to do what he's been doing all day, just in his sleep, though—trying to escape, trying to get somewhere, feeling that spring inside him compressing, feeling it compel him to take step after step. Feeling someone's breath—

heavy, animal—at his back. He turns around. He doesn't see anyone, though. Just white snow stretching to the horizon. He occasionally wakes up, sees the damp moonlight through the window, hears raindrops pattering against the glass, catches the sweet smell of gas, and sinks into his snow again, wades through it again, shivers in it, gets lost in it, tries to escape death. But how are you supposed to do that in this snow? You won't escape, don't even try. The snow makes you helpless, vulnerable. You sink into it. It burns you down to the bone, and then you'll never cast off the touch of death, you'll feel it for as long as you live. But how long will you live, huh?

It hadn't snowed for a while that winter. All December, cold dry air was coming up from the south, from the sea, chilling the trees and rivers. Then, sometime around the holidays, before New Year's, it snowed. And it snowed for a few days straight, without letting up. On New Year's Eve, they—still the whole family—sat in the main room, endlessly flipping through the channels, seemingly expecting to receive some good news. How old was he then? Fifteen, going on sixteen. His sister went to bed. She couldn't take it anymore. His parents weren't saying anything, and it felt like something had been taken from them, they'd been deprived of something, something important had been stolen from their home. And everyone knew that, but for some reason they weren't saying anything. At some point, Pasha went to bed, too, but he didn't lie there for long. He stood by the window, looking at the snow that kept falling and falling and listening to his parents switch off the television and begin clearing the table. He listened to his mom rattling the dishes in the kitchen, his dad going outside, grabbing something from the yard, coming back inside, and the brisk breath of the blue nighttime snow flowing through the house, touching your skin. And you instantly feel the entirety of winter, just how much of it there is, how it begins right here, outside the window, between these trees, how it fills up the space around you: their snowy yard, the street lined with sleepy houses with smoke rising out of them into the sky, the road they'll have to shovel come morning, the footbridge that's also been coated by nighttime snow, the stores and library, the school, the local businesses, the railroad buildings, the train station, empty at this hour. The route that he could walk with his eyes closed, the route that he got used to as a child, the route he associates with his childhood. Winter is at every intersection, reflected in every dark window, making itself felt on the roofs and hillsides. And everything that he's used to, that he knows so well, is filled with winter, like a mailman's bag with newspapers. Have to embrace this winter, live it, have to get used to it, have to learn to derive pleasure from it, feel joy. "I'm gonna start learning right away, tomorrow morning," he says to himself. "I'm going to work long and hard at it." Winter shouldn't scare you, you shouldn't be afraid of it. It's like a dog that you let into your home, make a part of your life. Then, for the rest of its life, it'll be willing to die for you, it'll recognize your voice and scent, follow you wherever, wait for you, no matter where you go or when you come back. "I'm gonna learn that," he thinks. "I have so much time ahead of me, it'll all work out." And with that, he falls asleep.

In the morning, he runs over to the window and doesn't see anything! Just snow—deep, shiny, its crystals wounding his eyes, blinding him. And he quickly gets dressed and slips outside. Before anyone else gets up, before anyone notices that New Year's Eve is long gone and a new day filled with light and snow has begun, he runs outside and drowns himself in the snow, jumps in it, tramples through it, wades under the trees, white and laden. He makes his way out to the street, the empty street of the new year—no one's out, no one's moving around—walks at random through the fresh, untrodden snow, reaches the school, passes the stores, pops out by the train station. It's empty here too this morning. Everyone's asleep. Nobody's aware that a new year has started, that a new life has started. Nobody's aware of anything. Nobody's around. And he trudges across the railroad tracks, plunging into knee-high snow, climbing the embankment, a white expanse now hovering over the tracks, and an entire world opens up before him, one filled to the brim with snow. And he immediately wants to cross it, from beginning to end. And he slides down the embankment, runs through a row of trees, wades through the snow, which is getting deeper and deeper. He descends into the valley, passes some snowbanks that faintly outline the foundation of an unfinished factory, plods into an open field that stretches all the way up to the sky, as far as the eye can see. He's walking endlessly, losing all sense of time and space, feeling only the snow around him and the sun that's rising higher and higher in the January sky. When he's worn himself out, he just falls onto the snow, his face sinking into it, his lips touching it, burning himself. Then he rolls onto his back and looks up at the sky—endlessly high, immaculate. And then he spots a cloud—the first and only one in this immaculate, shining space. "Where'd it come from?" he asks himself, annoyed. He turns his head and sees clouds rolling in from the south, from the sea, covering the horizon. They'll be here soon, above him, right over his head. He shrugs frostily and feels that lying in the snow isn't all that cozy: his fingers are frozen, the snow on the lapels of his coat has turned into an icy film. "Time to go back," he says to himself. "Screw that," he replies to himself. "Don't think so," he adds less firmly. "Just not today. Today, nobody can stop me, no matter what. Today, I'm going to learn to love the world and take it as it is. And have the world learn to love me."

He gets up and keeps going, through the deep, untouched snow. It's getting harder and harder to move, though. And his feet in his short winter boots are freezing, aching. "Gotta head back," he reminds himself somewhat anxiously. "Don't think so," he sharply answers himself again. "Well, all right." He begins bargaining with himself. "Walk to those trees over there, and then turn around. We'll see," he says to himself in a dismissive tone. He walks, pulling his legs out of the snow. The trees float forward, slowly, unhurriedly. It's getting even colder. Eventually, the clouds roll into his valley, blocking out the sun. Suddenly, it's so gray and gloomy. But he's already reached the trees; he victoriously stands on the slope, looking at the frozen river below. "The river!" he yells to himself cheerfully. "I made it to the river!" "That's great," he answers himself anxiously. "Now head back home. Wait a sec," he disagrees with himself. "I'll go down to the river and then turn around." "Don't, go home," he objects. "Whatever," he says, not listening to himself. "There and back, that's it."

He rolls down the slope, reaches the bank dotted with cattails, and runs out to the middle of the river. He victoriously throws his arms up toward the leaden sky as snow starts to fall. "Ye-e-a-h!" he shouts and then crashes through the ice. Under the thick layer of snow, he didn't even notice that the ice was very thin, especially in the middle of the river. It all happens before he can get scared. It's a good thing that the river's so shallow and silty. So he's up to his waist in icy water. Frightened, helpless. And he instantly realizes that it'll be dark by the time he gets out of here, by the time he gets home. And he's wet and frozen. Will he make it through the deep, dark snow? Now that's a big question. And at this point, he starts to panic.

He plods through the snow for a long, very long, endlessly long time, his hands and feet numb, expending every ounce of energy to keep himself from stopping, to push through another snowdrift, to trudge to the top of another hill. Walk, walk, don't stop, just don't stop. He looks back and sees a flat, gray expanse sprawling out, encircling him, robbing him of any chance of escape, and this all-encompassing gray is so eerie that it somehow gives him new strength, and he starts running, running and crying, occasionally looking back, fearfully discerning black dots emerging over behind him on the horizon—one, two, three, four, five—and they're growing in size, moving in his direction. He still can't make out what they are, but he clearly, lucidly understands that he has to escape, no matter what, run far away from those dots on the gray backdrop, because that's his death heading toward him, and he just can't let it catch him. Don't let it catch him, break out of this deep, gray mush, get home, try to outwit his own death—that's all that needs to be done.

Then, through a whole night of feverish heat and chills, feeling his body burning up and his heavy head exploding from exhaustion, he curses everything in this world, curses himself for being so foolhardy, curses himself for being so naive, curses the world for its deception. He curses and realizes that the wintry tinge of mortality, the icy breath of fear and nothingness will accompany him until the day of his death, the death that's missed its target this time around, yet probably hasn't waived its rights. No, death hasn't waived anything, it knows how to wait, and it'll catch him at this time of year—in the deep snow, under the leaden skies, among the cold rivers. One of these days, it'll do it, as soon as he lets his guard down and forgets about its presence, its lingering resentment. So he'll have to go through his whole life with this fear of the snowy unknown, the icy wasteland. But for now, he still has to try and survive. Because the dead aren't afraid. At all. Of anything. With that, he falls asleep.

"Pasha," the kid says. "Wake up."

Pasha springs to his feet. The kid produces some matches, lights the lamp, all business. He's already got his shoes on. Pasha drowsily rocks his head back and forth, finds his glasses, which slipped off his nose while he was sleeping, and puts them on.

"Where's the owner?" he asks.

"He went out—" the kid begins.

"He went out?" Pasha interrupts him, springing up. "He's gonna turn us in," he thinks in a panic. "That's gotta be it."

"He went out to the garage," the kid says, seemingly hearing his thoughts. "To warm up the car. He's gonna take us to the bus station. Grab your stuff."

He steps outside. Pasha goes into the next room, finds his clothes, retrieves his boots. His jacket's dry, and so are his boots, more or less. He puts them on, laces up, picks up his backpack, leaves the room. He bumps into the lady of the house in the hallway. Frightened, she presses herself against the wall. Pasha cautiously walks past, taking in the smell of hard soap. It's as if she was eating it. Pasha leaves without saying goodbye.

A blue Zhiguli, Model Three. Rotten fenders held together with playdough. There's a layer of paint on top, but it still looks like the Zhiguli is made of playdough. The passenger's seat is gone. Clearly, the owner uses the car to haul vegetables or something, so he just threw one of the seats out. Pasha and the kid hop into the back. The owner has pulled on his rubber boots and put on his peacoat. He isn't looking at Pasha. He walks on, opens the gate, gets behind the wheel, roots around in his pockets awhile, seemingly trying to delay their departure, but eventually gets going. He pulls out, cautiously enters the street fog. Pasha sits behind him, examining the wrinkles on his neck, the gray, unwashed hairs poking out from underneath his black hat. The kid's sprawled out beside him, extending his legs all the way up to the driver's seat. He's peering with great interest at what's happening out the window. And out the window, absolutely nothing is happening. The street's empty, dark, the fog merely accentuating the darkness. The driver isn't turning on his headlights. He gropes ahead slowly, yet confidently—he apparently knows the way—moving down the street like it's the hallway in his own home. He even tries to dodge the potholes. They reach an intersection, slow down. The driver warily peers into the fog, practically sniffing it, deliberates for a moment, then turns left. He drives a hundred yards, slows down again, crosses himself.

"What are you doing?" Pasha asks him, surprised.

"There's a church over there," the driver explains, nodding at the darkness.

Pasha peers out the window. But he can't see any churches, obviously. The kid turns toward him and winks cheerfully, seemingly saying, "Well, aren't you gonna cross yourself?" Pasha smiles in reply. They drive into a field. The fog comes apart like an old boot. The driver steps on the gas.

"They took down the checkpoint," the driver explains. "It was there, on the edge of town."

"Whose checkpoint was it anyway?" Pasha asks.

"Well, uh . . . ," the driver hesitates. "Your guys,'" he finally musters. "They pulled out two days ago."

"I see," Pasha replies coldly, seemingly saying, "That's what they had to do—guess nobody bothered asking you."

That's how the driver interprets what he's said, too. He rides on in silence, his eyes fixed on the black asphalt. The rain's calming down. It gets very quiet, spacious—everything's filled with blackness, flooded with it. They actually get to the main road a little later. A bent metal sign protrudes somewhere off to the side. The driver stops, turns off the engine, gets out, walks forward.

"Where's he going?" Pasha inquires.

"Who the hell knows," the kid replies. "Maybe he's running away."

"What about his car?"

"He's so afraid of you, he'd think nothing of just leaving his car here," the kid says, laughing.

Suddenly, in the surrounding blackness, the moon—big, bright yellow—comes into view. It's been hanging over them the whole time. They just couldn't see it behind the clouds. But now the clouds have parted, and it's spilled out, right at them, and suddenly everything's translucent, so close. It's like somebody's switched on the light in a child's bedroom to ward off their fears and make sure there weren't any monsters under the bed. Pasha and the kid start paying attention to the driver; he's flustered, stopped on the main road and looking in every direction. Emptiness all around, nobody's going anywhere, nobody has anywhere to go. There's just the bent sign reminding them that the former border isn't that far from here. A one-hour drive and you're there. But what can you even do there? The driver comes back, plops heavily into his seat, sighs and moans, trying to elicit sympathy. But he can't. So he pulls out onto the main road and turns right. Then he turns on his headlights and pushes his Model Three to the limit, seemingly afraid he won't make it on time. He goads the car forward, squeezing the last bit out of it and paying no mind to the potholes. Shortly thereafter, out of the darkness drifts a spoil pile.

Pasha recognizes this area. The mine they're passing now hasn't been shut down, so there's still some life here. The Station is close by—about twenty miles if you take the main road. It's longer if you stick to the back roads, naturally. They pass the spoil pile, empty dachas. Five-story apartment blocks emerge up ahead. The driver stops.

"That's as far as I go," he says.

"You can't be for real!" Pasha says cajolingly.

"There are soldiers over there." The driver shakes his head. "That's it."

"I'll talk to them," Pasha says. He's full of it, though. "Don't be afraid, those are my guys over there."

"Nah." The driver shakes his head resolutely. "You're gonna have to walk from here."

"Just leave him alone," the kid suddenly interjects. "He still has to make it back. Let him go."

The driver jerks to say something in reply but can't muster anything—he just tucks his head into his shoulders, patiently waits in silence. Pasha suddenly loosens up. "Yeah," he thinks. "What am

I hassling him for? What do I even know about him? He could've taken us right to the commandant's office. But he didn't, he didn't hang us out to dry. Why'm I getting into it with him?"

"All right," Pasha says to the driver. "No need to get all bent out of shape. Things happen."

The driver nods. Uh-huh, yeah, they do. Get out already.

"Here." Pasha produces his cans, holds them out to the driver.

He grabs one with his big hands. He doesn't know what it is, but he grabs it anyway.

"What for?" He's perplexed. "You don't have to."

"Take it," Pasha insists. "We'll settle up after the war ends. If we make it . . . ," he adds.

The kid reaches into his pocket, takes out his chocolate bar, and hands it to the driver.

"Here," he says condescendingly. "Don't get bent out of shape."

The driver is unexpectedly flooded with emotion. His eyes even become moist. Deeply moved, he shakes the bags under his eyes and tries to smile, but nothing comes of that.

"Good luck with everything," he says to Pasha and the kid.

"Same to you," Pasha answers. "Same to you."

The kid gets out of the car. Pasha follows him, shuts the door. Once they've taken a few steps, they hear tires screeching behind them. The driver turns around sharply and steps on the gas.

"Why didn't you eat the chocolate?" Pasha asks.

"I wanted to share with you," the kid answers.

"He's kidding," Pasha surmises. "Or maybe he isn't."

They pass the first apartment block. And then a school, and then the black cube of a mall. They squat, frightened, when an APC, packed with people and things, pops out behind the mall.

But the APC disappears around the next apartment block, like it was never here in the first place. Now what should they do? They don't know. They have to head toward the bus station, follow the APC. Or stay here, in the middle of the street. They don't want to stay in the middle of the street, so they turn behind the apartment block and stop, stunned.

The street's packed. Cars dark with dirt, frozen armor, multifarious military vehicles—there's no end to the column, the cars are parked next to each other in two rows, so you can't walk between them, can't squeeze your way through. The APC they just saw is now off to the side; soldiers hop out of it, splashing into puddles, and trudge along the street, shoving through a crowd of soldiers just like them who are standing around, not knowing where to go from here. They're standing in groups—some large, some small—building fires, warming up, standing by some buildings, sitting or lying on benches, hiding in the darkness. The buildings are dark, devoid of life, but if you look a little closer, behind the curtains and the blankets hung up instead of drapes, you can spot some apprehensive gazes, some faces that immediately recede into the depths of their apartments as soon as they sense another gaze from outside. Pasha and the kid stand at the beginning of the street, and they realize that they'll have to pass through this frigid crowd, and that it's best to stick close to the soldiers instead of continuing to wander through the black empty city on their own. "What could they even do to us?" Pasha reassures himself. "After all, I have the same flag in my passport that they have on their tanks. I'm a teacher, after all. I could be their kids' teacher. Yeah, their kids' teacher," he thinks and moves forward. Sasha is at his side.

"You haven't lost your passport, have you?" he asks. "And what if they want to check your address?"

"You think that'll help?" Pasha follows with a question of his own.

"It might," he says tentatively. "Or it might not," he adds calmly.

Pasha notices that the kid's voice has changed over the past few days—he speaks calmly, unhurriedly. Like he actually trusts Pasha. "Now I just have to get him home," Pasha thinks, as he peers at the soldiers through the darkness. The soldiers aren't paying any attention to them; they're talking among themselves, asking questions, offering explanations. Occasionally yelling out each other's call signs and then quickly going quiet, as if they don't want to talk about that anymore. Occasionally arguing, getting all riled up, debating in hoarse voices. Then they grab their riled-up buddies by the shoulders, take them aside, grasp their heads, look into their eyes, say some soothing words. And everyone—the ones doing the soothing and the ones being soothed—is speaking loudly, shouting, like they're at a soccer match. "Why are they shouting?" Pasha thinks, confused. "What for? Maybe they want to sound more convincing, so they're shouting over each other? That's what kids always do to get everyone's attention, to force people to listen to them—they start shouting, blotting everything else out with their own voices. These guys, they're like kids," Pasha thinks, his eyes sliding over their faces, dried out by the cold, their unshaven cheeks, their uncombed hair. And suddenly he spots a dried strip of blood under one of the soldiers' ears—very young, about eighteen, holding a metal mug filled with something hot, warming his hands on the heated metal, not actually drinking much. And he's shouting, too, shouting into his mug. "Kid's ears don't bleed," Pasha thinks, and then he figures out what's going on. They've come under heavy artillery fire and they've all gone deaf. That's why they're shouting, like kids listening to loud music with headphones who don't realize that nobody else can hear it. Yep, they've just come from the battlefield, they're trying to figure out what's happened, what's next, trying to call whoever they have to call. "Oh, yeah," Pasha remembers. "I have service here. Have to call dad, tell him where we are, put him at ease." He takes out his phone. It's slowly nearing its demise, but it's still glowing faintly. One bar appears, then another. Gotta try it. Pasha calls his old man. Waits awhile. Calls again. The kid's standing there, patiently anticipating, knowing full well who Pasha's trying to get hold of. His old man picks up, unexpectedly. He's barely coming through. Moreover, everyone around Pasha is screaming and making so much noise. All this ruckus could make his old man very anxious. But he cuts out right away, before he can hear anything. Pasha tucks his phone away and clears a path, cautiously, so as not to attract any attention, moving from group to group and catching movements and colors out of the corner of his eye. Mud on combat boots, blood under nails, unwashed camo, voices chilled by the wind, stubble on faces—it's immediately obvious that they've spent the past several days outside in the rain, and they still don't have anywhere to hide from the rain that's encroaching upon the high-hanging January sky. Someone adjusts a stick in a fire, sparks soar, soldiers stick their hands very close to the flame. Everything smells of smoke and sweat, worn clothing, and diesel fuel. Somewhere beyond the city, in the darkness, there's a rhythmic series of blasts; the soldiers automatically turn toward them, listen tensely, yet quickly lose interest. They return to the flame, to their screaming. Clouds drift, the rain lets up again, for the *nth* time today, and a round moon materializes above a long row of apartment blocks, a golden glint gushing onto the metal of the cars. Women in down coats mill around outside one of the apartment buildings. They've brought pots filled with something edible, and they're ladling the warm, thick stew into disposable bowls, handing them to the soldiers, crying. The soldiers, slightly mistrustful, surround them, accept the hot plastic bowls, unfazed by the temperature, offer some words of appreciation, soothe the women. They eat quickly, seemingly afraid they'll soon have to drop everything and run. They swallow their hot meals whole. There's an old minibus—riddled with bullets, smashed windows, busted doors—in the middle of the sidewalk. They have to squeeze against the building to get past. The door of the bus is busted, and an elderly soldier is sitting inside. Below him on the ground a small fire is burning. He's warming himself up on the little steps without getting out of the minibus, extending his combat boots right up to the flame. He spots Pasha and the kid.

"Hey," he says, waving. "Come over here."

Pasha pretends he doesn't hear him. He pulls the kid along, wanting to slip between the minibus and the building. I just didn't hear you, there are so many people all around making such a racket, I'll be on my way, leave me alone. You can't even hear your own footsteps or the disgusting squelching of wet boots in cold puddles over all this racket. The soldier seems to think otherwise, though. He thinks very differently.

"Hey, brother," he shouts hoarsely, like he's calling to an old friend.

Pasha stops, probes. Whadaya want? The soldier waves again.

Come on over here. Pasha and the kid exchange glances, then walk over.

"All right then, brother," the soldier yells. "Got any smokes?"

Wrinkles—looks like someone's been kneading his face. Hair—gray and so short that it seems like his skull is metallic gray, made of cold iron. Appears to be about sixty, sagging camo, gut propped up by his belt. Fur coat on his shoulders. He stares at Pasha and the kid blankly. It's as though he's looking at them but seeing something only he can see. And he's yelling, his voice raspy, strained.

"Got any smokes?" he asks again.

"I don't smoke," Pasha answers.

"What?" Metal Head doesn't understand him. "I can't hear anything, brother. The shelling . . ." He's speaking a mix of Russian and Ukrainian, hopping back and forth between the languages. "Just slow down," he says. "I'll lip-read."

"I don't smoke," Pasha says. "I do not sm-o-ke."

"You don't smoke?" the soldier surmises.

Pasha shakes his head.

"Why's that?" the soldier asks, disappointed.

"It is bad for you," Pasha answers slowly.

"Bad for you?" the soldier surmises. "Sure is. What about you?" he asks the kid.

"What about me?"

"You smoke?"

The kid hesitates for a moment, glances at Pasha, then takes a step forward, pulls out his cigarettes, and proffers them to the soldier, who takes one, thinks for a second, and then another.

"Just take the whole pack," the kid yells. "I quit."

"You quit?" Metal Head surmises. "Good work. What do you

do for a living, brother?" The soldier lights a cigarette from the fire and shifts his attention to Pasha.

Pasha looks at the fire, at the cigarette in his black, somewhat metallic fingers, at the kid who's warming his hands over the flame, and he feels warm, calm.

"I'm a teacher," he says to the soldier. Then he repeats slowly. "A tea-cher."

Metal Head freezes. The cigarette's sticking out of the side of his mouth, releasing smoke, shedding ashes. His eyes narrow, as if he's looking at a bright light. His gaze hardens. Pasha gets the chills. "What's wrong?" he thinks. "Was it something I said?"

"I'm a teacher," he repeats. "We're on winter break."

But the soldier doesn't appear to be listening to him anymore. He gets up, hops down into a puddle, adjusts the fur coat on his shoulders.

"C'mon, Teach," he says. "Come on in."

"What for?" Pasha's confused.

"Just come on in," Metal Head repeats.

Pasha hesitates, glances at the kid. He seems oblivious, though, crouching there by the warm fire. Well, Pasha doesn't have anything to be afraid of. He goes around the fire, grabs the handle, puts his foot on the step. The soldier gives him a gentle push from behind, follows him into the bus.

It smells like wet wool, as though there are sheep in there, huddling together, trying to get warm. Actually, there's just a heap of clothing on the shabby seats: fur coats, sheepskin coats, down jackets. "Are they selling them or something?" Pasha thinks in surprise, keeps going. Farther back are some crates filled with ammunition, several scorched AKs, and entrenching tools on the floor.

They're all piled up, right in the middle of the aisle. They have to step over them. And they have to watch their step—there's no knowing what else could be in that pile. The soldier follows him, warily peering out the smashed windows. He isn't saying anything. Pasha just can't get himself to climb over all that prickly, burnt metal; he takes a metal container off a seat, plops down. The soldier hovers darkly over him, giving off that faint smell of wet wool. Pasha finds himself thinking that this smell has been stalking him for the past few days. It's as if wet, famished dogs are stalking him, trying to catch his scent, lurking in the darkness, moving in on him, refusing to retreat. And heaps of household items have been accompanying him for the past few days, too. Clothes, dishes, wrecked furniture, wet books that look like fallen birds left out in the rain. Other people's domestic lives just lying there, completely exposed, like someone's ripped off the decorative tiles, torn off the wallpaper, and laid the old walls bare, and now every vein, every fissure and crack has become visible. And their domestic lives look so sad, so hopeless: the clothing—worn and washed; the books—yellowed by time and unread; the dishes—cheap, unsightly, the kind of dishes made for burned or undercooked food. In their warm homes—off-limits to strangers—all of this might have had a nice, domestic feel to it, something you can call your own, something you've grown used to. But now, removed from their usual setting, tossed out into the rain, sprinkled with ashes, all these household items have immediately lost their value, and the clothes smell of poverty and disorder, and the dishes, coated with grease, glisten in the headlights, and the furniture looks like bones dug out of the wet January earth. And this smell pervades everything—there's no washing it off, no scrubbing it off.

"So, you're a teacher?" the soldier asks, for some reason.

Pasha nods wordlessly. "What's the point of talking if he can't hear anything anyway?" he thinks.

"Where's your school?" the soldier asks, bowing in Pasha's direction, like he wants to ram him with his metal forehead.

"At the St-a-tion," Pasha says in a singsong voice.

"We held the Station. The Station's ours," the soldier replies, his eyes still fixed on Pasha.

"Yeah," Pasha agrees. "It's ours, of course."

The soldier isn't saying anything more, though. He's just looking straight ahead, which makes Pasha feel uneasy, once again, like he's just said something he shouldn't have, once again. They sit there in silence for a bit. Pasha cracks first, obviously.

"It's ours," he says loudly, looking the soldier right in the eye. "The Station is ours!"

"Yep," the soldier replies, and his eyes instantly go out of focus. It's as though he's remembered something unsettling yet very important.

He takes the metal containers off a seat, tosses them onto the pile of metal, and sits down across from Pasha.

"So you're a local guy?" he asks.

Pasha nods.

"You know our mine's over there?" the soldier asks, pointing out the window.

"Yeah."

"I used to work there," Metal Head explains. "Before the war," he adds. "Ten years," he continues. "I came here ten years ago," he says, but he doesn't say where he came from.

"Where'd you come from?" Pasha asks him.

The soldier answers with an amiable smile. He can't hear Pasha. Or he's pretending he can't.

"I see," Pasha replies.

Well, what else could he say?

"Have you been back home?" Pasha inquires.

"What?" the soldier asks apprehensively.

"Ha-ve you been back ho-me? Seen your fam-i-ly?" Pasha asks slowly.

The soldier freezes. And his eyes are completely still, like tin that's been poured into a mold. "Shouldn't have asked him about that," Pasha surmises.

"Nobody's home," the soldier says. "Everyone's gone."

Where they went he doesn't say. This time around, Pasha doesn't ask.

"Everyone's gone, yeah," Metal Head repeats. "I went to a museum this morning. You're a teacher, right?"

"Yeah," Pasha says loudly.

"Take this with you," says Metal Head.

He reaches under his seat, roots around in the pile of metal, finds a gas mask pouch, pulls out a knife, hands it to Pasha, wooden handle first, and then keeps rummaging through the pouch. Pasha holds the knife, notices clumps of red blood on the blade. "What else is he gonna whip out?" he thinks. The soldier produces something heavy, wrapped in a page of newspaper filled with ads, and Pasha realizes that it could be anything—it could be a stick of dynamite, or it could be an enemy soldier's liver, cut out of his body with this very knife. Could be anything. His motions leisurely, the soldier unfurls the parcel, layer by layer, as if he's peeling bandages off a dry, scabbed-over wound, and he reveals a piece of coal coated with damp soil.

"Do you know what this is?" he yells, sticking it right in Pasha's face.

"Coal?" Pasha asks skeptically.

"Coal!" the soldier yells, as if he's contradicting Pasha. "Gimme it!"

He takes the knife from Pasha and begins scraping clumps of dirt off the rock. Then he hands it back.

"See that?" he asks.

Pasha strains his eyes in the twilight, adjusts his glasses. It's a rock. So what?

"No," he admits.

"It's a fern," the soldier yells. "It's a fossilized fern."

Pasha turns toward the smashed window, and under the thick yellow moonlight, he sees some patterns—barely noticeable, seemingly outlined with a slate pencil—imprinted on the hard surface of the rock. He touches it, feeling the cold, rocky notches, feeling the thin grooves and nicks on the rocky surface. "What bizarre patterns," he thinks. "Who could've traced them all?"

"It's a fern," Metal Head repeats. "It's a million years old. How old are you?" he asks Pasha.

"Thirty-five," Pasha answers, perplexed.

"Well, it's a million," the soldier reminds him.

"So what?" Pasha's confused.

"And it's still holding up just fine," the soldier explains, like Pasha's a little kid. "A million. It was a million years old before we were even born. We'll kick the bucket, and it'll still be lying there somewhere in the ground. That's history, you know? The two of us, we aren't history. We're here now, gone tomorrow. I took this from the museum," he explains.

"Why?" Pasha's still confused.

"What do you mean 'why'?" the soldier asks him adamantly.

"Why'd you take it? Why not leave it there at the museum?"

"The museum's gone," the soldier yells patiently. "They wiped it out. Now it's a trash heap. A heap of burned trash. The fern's still holding up, though. You're a teacher, right?" he asks, as if he's already forgotten.

"Yeah," Pasha answers, irritated.

"Take it." The soldier points at the rock. "You probably have some sort of museum there. Or a geography classroom. Keep it there. I mean, it's a million years old. It shouldn't just rot in the ground. All right?"

"All right," Pasha yells.

"You'll take it."

"Yeah."

"Well, thanks." Metal Head sighs in relief, tucks the knife under the seat, and wipes off his hands with the wet newspaper. "Thanks."

They step outside. Pasha touches the kid on the shoulder. He lifts his head, curious. Well? You have a nice chat?

"Had a nice chat," Pasha explains. "Yep."

The soldier comes over, shakes their hands. Pasha wants to say something in parting, but nothing comes to him; he tosses the rock in his backpack, places his hand on the kid's shoulder, nudges him forward. Once they get a certain distance away, the soldier yells at their backs.

"My aunt worked at the museum," he yells. "Now there's not gonna be a museum."

"That's bad," Pasha answers quietly.

"That's bad?" Surprisingly, the soldier understands him.

"That's bad."

"It's only gonna get worse," the soldier assures him.

He goes back into the bus, sits down by the window, hides his head in his fur coat. "He's sleeping," Pasha surmises. "Or crying."

The moon smears itself across the sky and moves toward the night, leaving behind black desolation. "Gotta get going," Pasha thinks suddenly. "Gotta get home." The metal spring digs sharply into his heart, goads him forward, reminds him about time—it's running out. The water in the puddles is starting to freeze, becoming coated with a sharp crust. The kid slips along the building, Pasha follows him. They walk down the street among the soldiers. There are more and more of them. Black pits under their eyes. The inflamed eyes, the parched mouths, and the screams—abrasive, loud, discontented—that they let out in an attempt to communicate. Some more vehicles pull up. Buses battered by shrapnel, cars covered in clay, trucks with military slogans on the sides. More and more soldiers climb out of cabs, hop out of truck beds, clamber through the shattered windows. The smell of smoke, the smell of sweat and gunpowder become more distinct, it becomes harder and harder to push forward, dodge the frozen figures. But Pasha pushes forward, persistently shoving his way through, realizing that he'd better get the kid some food soon, he'd better take him someplace warm, he ought to find some form of transportation and try to make it home. While Pasha may be able to hang around here, out in the wet wind, under the yellow moon, a little bit longer, there's no telling how much longer the kid will last. Better not risk it, better not push their luck. If, God forbid, it starts up again with the kid, they simply won't know where to run, who to call. So their best bet is to get out of here, find a taxi, head home, forget all this, and never think about it again. "Can someone forget all this?" Pasha asks himself. "Of course they can," he answers his own question. "Of course. I'll forget all this," Pasha tells himself. "And the kid will, too. There's no need for him to remember all this, he has no need for the smell of sulfur and raw human flesh, he shouldn't remember the dirt under fingernails. People aren't meant to keep so much fear and anger in their memories. But how do you live with this? He'll forget everything, he'll be fine, he'll forget about the orphanage, about being abandoned, about that feeling of being boxed in when you wake up in a black basement. Let him have good memories, memories that don't stir up hatred or despair. The smell of home or the smell of the trees out in the yard, or the smell of a thaw—a long January thaw that smells like a river. He'll remember a thaw," Pasha assures himself. "He definitely will. No blood, no metal." And the more passionately he's telling himself all this, the more distinctly and firmly he understands. Nope, nobody'll forget anything, nobody'll leave anything in the past, and the kid, no matter how things play out for him, will keep carrying these memories, like bags filled with rocks, and the smell of torn skin and men's salty tears will pursue him until the end of his days, and the shadow of the orphanage will linger behind him, no matter where he goes, no matter how sunny those places may be. And for the rest of his life, food will smell faintly of the orphanage cafeteria, and his dreams will be filled with orphans' voices, and women will remind him of those girls from the bunker, their tears and makeup, and he won't be able to do anything about it, and nobody will ever be able to help him with it. And all Pasha can do is drag him back home, get him all washed up, give him some hot tea, and put him to bed. Let him catch up on sleep, let him sleep as long as he can, as long as he wants, as long as his dreams stay with him. Everything'll be different tomorrow, everything'll be just the way it always is, just like it used to be. Relaxed days at home where everyone's busy doing their own thing, where everything's where it's supposed to be, where there's nothing superfluous but you have everything you need. Mornings filled with domestic tasks, a job you've gotten used to like it's one of your outfits—it's not too constricting, it doesn't get in the way, wear it while you can. Quiet evenings, dark nights. Actually, there's so much joy, so much warmth in all of this. You had to wind up here, in the middle of hell, to feel how much you had and how much you've lost. Just have to get home as quickly as possible, finally step off the circles of others' misfortune, get home fast, very fast. Pasha speeds up, noticing that the soldiers have become more lively, too; they jolt up, run, pass Pasha and the kid, warily shouting something into the black air. Panic immediately overcomes Pasha. "What's up?" he thinks. "What's going on? Where are they all going?" And he runs after them, still trying to hold on to the kid's hand. They race through the wet, unnerved crowd, shoving soldiers in the back, throwing elbows, moving forward, more and more nervously. And they run out into the square and bump into a wall of dark backs—there's nowhere to run, the square's packed with people. "The hospital," Pasha thinks. "The city hospital." A two-story red-brick building. Windows battered by shrapnel and covered with plastic sheets. The windows glow into the night, and at a distance the hospital looks like an ocean liner that's slowly, unhurriedly sinking. The crowd sways like cattails in the wind. Pasha tries to break free, but they're being pushed from behind, squeezed forward. Then, a KAMAZ truck—no windshield, open bed—pulls up, coming from somewhere off to the side, and the driver yells so furiously that the crowd parts, steps back, makes way for him. The KAMAZ crawls past the crowd, closer to the hospital building. The crowd advances again, shoves Pasha and the kid forward, right up to the truck. Four people carrying stretchers race out of the hospital and fight their way to the back of the vehicle, pushing aside people who respond by pushing, yelling, arguing, but not getting out of the way. They seem to be waiting for something important. Someone lowers a metal ramp, and it turns out that the truck is loaded with wounded people—there's no counting how many of them there are. Pasha stands nearby, examining the bent wet metal up close, the water mixed with blood, examining boots—at eye level—black, metal-lined soles, right there on the metal floor, on the cold metal. Someone hops up.

"Take it," he yells. "Take it, fuck, wake up!" And Pasha realizes that the guy's yelling at him.

"What?" he asks. "What's going on?"

"Hold him!" the guy yells from above. "Fuck! Hold him."

"How?" Pasha's panicking.

"By his legs. Fuck!"

Pasha flings his backpack off, hands it to the kid.

"Wait for me here! Got that? Wait!"

The kid nods. Okay, don't worry, I'm here. Pasha picks up the person lying closest to him, grabs him by his combat boots.

"Where you going?" the guy above yells. "Fuck! Where you going? Not him! The other one! Get the other guy! The one who's still alive!"

At first Pasha doesn't understand what he's talking about, and then it hits him. He abruptly releases the combat boots. They land on the metal floor with a hollow bang. He automatically looks at his hands—any blood? But the guy above yells at him again.

"C'mon! Wake the fuck up!"

Pasha grabs another pair of combat boots, pulls them toward himself. The guy yelling—a young chubby orderly in camo and a bulletproof vest wearing a cross made out of red tape—takes a wounded man by the shoulders. Down below, someone immediately grabs him. The body falls, into the soldiers' hands. Pasha clings to the boots, not letting them slip away. Heavy, unwieldy, cramped. The crowd wobbles, but nobody's going anywhere. They make their way toward the hospital, stepping on other people's feet. Pasha can't see the kid anymore, but he catches a glimpse of the next wounded man being lowered off the truck.

"Move out of the way!" someone yells up ahead. "Move it! Fuck!" Step by step, they move forward, advance, carrying a still living load, hastening toward the illuminated hospital steps, then go up them. Someone opens the doors. Hurry up, this way, hurry! Pasha's panting; he nearly trips on the steps. He can hardly keep up. Two middle-aged soldiers are carrying the wounded guy, holding him under his armpits. Pasha's running, bent over, holding the guy's boots from behind. The hospital hallway is also packed with soldiers. It's warm. It smells of dirty clothes and motor oil. Blood-colored clay is smeared across the wet floor. The hospital is run down, hasn't been renovated in years, handwritten posters cover the walls. Plywood over the windows, rags drying on massive radiators. Stretchers line the hallway. On the first one lies an old soldier: bare chest, dirty body, unwashed skin, bloody bandage over the heart area. Worn boots, ripped camo pants. Eyes closed. He might be sleeping. Or pretending he's sleeping. Unshaven, frigid skin. Next to the stretcher on the floor a bloody bucket, some boxes filled with supplies delivered by volunteers. It looks like they were brought inside, placed here, and forgotten. They keep carrying the body, past another stretcher. A body, partially covered with an army jacket, is lying on it. Pasha timidly tries to get a closer look. Still breathing? He can't tell. They keep moving. One of the guys up ahead kicks open a door. They carry the body into a room—six beds, all of them occupied, two wounded men just lying there, right in the middle of the room, on some blankets. Someone's moaning in the corner; a woman in a wet coat is hovering over him, whispering something, soothing him, crying.

"Keep going!" one of the guys up front yells, turning around and gripping the wounded man with his other hand. "C'mon, c'mon!" he yells furiously at Pasha.

Pasha backs up, still holding on to the man. He stumbles, can't open the door.

"Hurry up!" someone yells at him. "Hurry the fuck up!"

He turns around, releases one leg, opens the door. They charge back into the hallway. Where to now? Pasha doesn't know. He stands there, looking all around, and then someone yells at his back. Go, go! C'mon! Get your ass moving! And Pasha runs down the hallway, carrying the wounded man, feeling the furious hissing at his back, running forward, not knowing where to stop. He dashes to the next room, kicks the door open with the tip of his boot, peers inside. But there are bodies on the floor here, too—dirty, exhausted, bloody, lying on mattresses, on blankets, on peacoats, wall to wall. He keeps running, down the cramped hallway: people sitting against the wall, giving themselves shots, reapplying bandages on someone's head. Nobody's paying any attention to Pasha, so he has to stick out his chest and clear a path, clear the way. He sees a skinny little guy in a white coat up ahead. Doctor, yeah, he's gotta be a doctor.

"Hey!" he yells. "Hey, sir!"

Sir turns around, and Pasha nearly loses his balance. His white coat is covered in blood, and his overall appearance—well, it definitely doesn't befit a Sir, not even close. But Pasha keeps looking at him and says:

"Where should we put him, sir?" He's referring to the wounded guy.

The doctor is clearly exhausted, all wrung out. It's scary to think about when he last got some sleep. And he was apparently about to lie down and curl up in a corner, wait it out, take a little nap—just twenty minutes. And at first he looks at Pasha with poorly concealed irritation. Nah, it's not that he's poorly concealing his irritation; he's looking at Pasha like he's a pile of shit. And he's just about to give him a piece of his mind. Suddenly, though, it's like a switch flips inside Sir, and he starts living up to his title. He adjusts his bloody coat, wearily rubs his stubble, and asks,

"Is he in bad shape?"

"Nah," Pasha replies cheerfully. "He looks pretty fit."

"Damn it," Sir says. "I mean what's wrong with him? Something serious? Is he critical?"

"Sir!" the guys holding the wounded man by the shoulders wail. "Fuck, sir! He's almost dead! Can't you see that?! Where should we put him?!"

That catches the doctor's attention; he looks over Pasha's shoulders, sees those two other guys, and quickly thinks of something.

"C'mon!" he says. "Follow me!"

He's speaking calmly, judiciously, unlike those two guys who are carrying the body with Pasha. Seeing that he isn't throwing a fit, they quiet down, stop yelling. All right Sir, do your thing. And he walks down the hallway, and all the wounded, all the dirty and deafened men, step aside, let him through, giving Sir the respect someone with his title deserves. Sir responds with a nod, a pat on the back, and a handshake. His hand is small, bony, his bald spot is wide, shiny, groomed. Thin, nimble body, hunched back. His coat droops off him like he's a hanger. His shoes are stained with muck. All of him is stained—with blood, iodine, black earth. He looks like a passenger who's been stuck at a train station for several days, just can't escape. He's been sleeping on the benches, subsisting on fast food. But everything'll be fine once he gets home. Just wash up, clean up, catch up on sleep. But for now, he has to handle one more body, keep it from dying, try to bring it back.

Sir walks to the end of the hallway, opens a barely visible door with a thick coat of green paint on it. In here. A nod. They hastily push their way into the room and see they're in the cafeteria: several tables, chairs, the little window where the patients are given something edible. And the smell of overcooked food, stagnant, dirty dishes. "I've seen this somewhere before," Pasha thinks. "Just the other day. Feels like I keep walking around in circles—from cafeteria to cafeteria, from shelter to shelter, from orphanage to orphanage."

"Fuck, what is this?" yells one of the guys standing behind Pasha. "What is this?"

But Sir isn't listening. He's already on the phone, calling someone. "And he has service, goddammit," Pasha thinks. "And clearly, someone's been expecting his call, goddammit." He promptly begins issuing orders, talking to some lady named Lida, giving her some pointers, asking her to get right on it, telling her she can do it. Then he switches off his phone and turns toward the three of them.

"What are you holding him for?" he says peevishly, yet quietly, seemingly saving his strength for an impending outburst. "Put him down."

"Where?" Everyone's confused.

"On the tables, that's where!" Sir finally explodes. His nerves aren't made of steel, after all.

"On the tables?" one guy—short, fat, gray crewcut on his big skull—asks, perplexed. "What about the operating room?"

"There's a two-day wait for the operating room," Sir replies coldly. He's already regained his composure. "I said put him down."

They move two tables together and carefully lower the soldier onto them. Then a nurse runs into the cafeteria, holding some sheets and a metal medical thingy. The soldier is lifted carefully and a sheet is spread underneath him. Sir produces a pair of scissors and begins snipping through his sweater from his throat to his stomach, like he's making construction-paper art. At one point, he stops, looks up at the fat guy, then at his buddy, and finally at Pasha. His eyes settle on Pasha.

"You," he says firmly and dryly, seemingly delivering an unpleasant, yet inevitable message. "You, hold this."

And he points at the sweater. Pasha grips the sweater, pulls it toward himself.

"Easy, there," the doctor advises. "The blood's dry. This is gonna hurt."

He says that to Pasha, not the wounded guy, as if Pasha will be the one in pain. He keeps cutting. Then he tears the sweater out of the wound—abruptly, quickly. The soldier shrieks and jolts up.

"Hold him!" Sir yells at Pasha. "Make sure he doesn't fall off."

Pasha grips the soldier's hand and tries to avert his eyes so as not to see the dried blood and torn flesh.

"Wake up!" Sir shouts. "Hold him tighter!"

Pasha has to look then, whether he likes it or not. The soldier's just a boy, probably still in his teens. Shaved skull, nicked chin—must have been shaving in the dark. Sharp nose, dark eyes, shut in pain. Striped sleeveless undershirt beneath his sweater. Heavy military belt, camo pants, combat boots. And a wound just below the neck. He coughs violently, and blood soaks the undershirt. So he's holding his breath, like he's about to go underwater. But he bursts into coughing each time he exhales, expelling blood. And Pasha looks at the blood, mesmerized, transfixed, looks at the tender raspberry drops that seep into the fabric, looks at the dark, dry crust around the wound, at the cut flesh, as life escapes from the soldier.

"Cut his shirt," says Sir. "Get cutting!"

He gives him the scissors, takes out a syringe and some vials, starts doing something with them. Pasha clasps the fabric hesitantly, doesn't know where to start. He freezes up.

"Cut it," Sir orders dryly.

And he cuts it. Shreds the undershirt all the way down to his stomach. The soldier's skin is white, wintry. Hardly any chest hair. His body makes the pink blood look very bright. And there's more and more of it. The soldier laboriously swallows air. He's clearly having a hard time breathing; his eyes roll back, his hand grasps at emptiness. Pasha intercepts his hand, squeezes it. C'mon, c'mon, just a little longer, c'mon. Sir swings around, syringe in hand, leans in, drives the needle into his body. The soldier trembles, tries to break free.

"Hold him!" Sir yells angrily. "Hold him down."

Pasha throws his body on the soldier, yet tries not to put too much pressure on him. Sir begins working his magic on the wound, treating it with something, which makes the soldier tremble again and begin crying loudly. Pasha presses his whole body down on him, averts his eyes, looks to the side so he doesn't have to see the blood flowing out of his body. The soldier jerks. He begins pleading. Don't, don't touch that, don't. But then he bursts out coughing again. Pasha can feel how much the soldier's chest has tightened up, but he keeps holding him, not letting go. The fat guy and his buddy avert their eyes, too. They can't take it anymore. They turn around, disappear into the hallway. Sir whispers something to the nurse. She takes out a metal box, opens it, takes out some forceps, hands them to the doctor. He accepts them without even looking. He works with automatic precision, like a gardener pruning flowers. He isn't rushing, he isn't worrying. It's as if he's sure that everything will be fine, that there's a happy ending to this. His confidence should put Pasha at ease, but for some reason it doesn't. Pasha's shaking, he's freezing, and the smell of blood becomes more distinct, more intrusive. He gulps down some air, breathes deeply, and tries to calm himself.

"What's wrong?" Sir asks as he digs around in bloody flesh with the forceps.

"I'm fine," Pasha replies curtly.

"You sure?" Sir doesn't believe him.

"Yeah," Pasha assures him.

"Well, that's good," Sir says, and thrusts the forceps right into the shredded mush.

The soldier shrieks and tries breaking out of Pasha's embrace. Pasha squeezes him, realizing that he won't be able to hang on much longer. But then the soldier slumps back down, like the spirit has gone out of him.

"Sir!" Pasha yells, turning toward the doctor. "What's wrong with him?"

"Nothing," Sir answers. "Guess he's feeling better now."

"What should we do now?" Pasha's confused.

"Well, nothing," Sir replies, irritated. "Just let him lie here."

"Is he gonna live?" Pasha continues his line of questioning.

"Who the hell knows?" Sir answers bluntly. "Yeah, he will," he adds, after a moment's thought.

Then he gets a call. Sir reaches his bloody hand into the pocket of his coat, takes out an iPhone. He drags a finger across the screen, leaving a streak of blood, starts listening.

"Yeah," he says. "And?" he asks. "Is he in bad shape? Can't you do without me? All right, I'll be right there."

So he begins putting his instruments away, tossing each one into the box with a cold, metallic bang.

"Where are you going, Sir?" Pasha asks.

"To the operating room," Sir answers imperturbably.

"What about him?" Pasha starts panicking.

"Hold him," Sir advises. "So he doesn't fall off. Just hold him. I'll come back when I'm done and take a look at him." He points at the wounded guy.

He leaves. The nurse leaves, too, without even promising to come back. Pasha stands over the soldier, holding his hand, not knowing what to do. Out in the hallway, people screaming, running around. In here, there's the dusky light, the smell of the cafeteria, and this kid on the table. He's quieted down, not saying anything. The fresh bandage on his neck is soaked with blood.

Pasha scans the room. Tiled floor, whitewashed walls. Just like a morgue. And there's a faucet on the wall, wrapped in a rag, like a finger with a band-aid on it. And the water, drop after drop, dropping into the sink. Resonantly and rhythmically. Irritating, infuriating. Echoing somewhere in his skull. Pasha tries to focus on something else, but he can't. It feels like the drops are trying to drill a hole in his skull. Drop after drop, drop after drop. Methodical and deathly. Knock it off! Pasha can't take it anymore, and he jolts toward the faucet. But at that very moment, the soldier grabs Pasha's hand. His grip is firm and predatory.

"Hold on." He struggles to move his lips. "Wait, don't go."

He wants to say something else, but then he bursts out coughing, gasping for air.

"Wait," he says to Pasha after he's finally caught his breath. "Who are you?"

He's speaking Ukrainian, not mixing the languages at all. He's probably a student.

"A teacher," Pasha explains.

"From around here?"

It's hard for him to speak, but he keeps talking, straining.

"From the Station."

"What are you doing here?"

"It's a long story."

"Gotcha," the wounded guy says, even though he clearly doesn't get it. "So, Teach, what's your name?"

"Pasha," Pasha answers.

"So, Pasha, my phone's around here somewhere. Call my family."

"What for?" Pasha's confused.

"Tell them I'm doing all right."

"You tell 'em," Pasha suggests.

"Are you a complete idiot or what?" the wounded guy asks him sharply, and has another coughing fit.

He coughs hoarsely and deeply, as though his heart is lodged in his throat. Pasha holds him by the elbow, waits. The soldier catches his breath, looks Pasha right in the eye.

"Are you a complete idiot?" He repeats his question. "How'm I supposed to talk to them with my voice like this?"

"Well, just tell them you're at the hospital."

"Are you for real?" the wounded guy asks, aggrieved. "They don't even know I'm here. You have a family?" he asks.

"Yeah," Pasha answers. "A nephew."

"Okay, then," the wounded guy replies. "C'mon, call 'em."

Pasha hesitates, but the soldier's looking at him firmly. And he's holding Pasha's hand firmly, too, not letting go. Then Pasha reaches into his pants pocket and actually finds a basic Nokia right away.

"What's the number?" he asks.

"The last one I dialed," the soldier answers. "Called them right before we got hit. C'mon already."

He keeps holding Pasha's hand, but Pasha can tell that his grip is loosening—running out of strength, eyes rolling back, labored, choppy breathing. "Just don't die on me," Pasha thinks. "Where'd that doctor go?" Pasha anxiously finds the last number—"Home."

That's it. He goes for it, thinks about what to say, but doesn't come up with anything, so he just presses the button.

The soldier tenses up, listens. It keeps ringing and ringing, ringing for an eternity. Well, c'mon—Pasha encourages someone, who knows who, though—c'mon, pick up. Well, where are you? C'mon, he's gonna croak any second now. Pick up the phone, c'mon.

"No one's picking up," he says to the soldier, somewhat relieved.

"Well, what would I've told them anyway?" he thinks. "Would've had to make something up. They aren't answering, that's on them," he thinks and places the phone on the table, next to the soldier. But he squeezes Pasha's hand once again.

"Wait," he says. "Hold on, Teach."

He catches his breath, musters his strength.

"Try. One more time."

"They aren't picking up."

"It's my grandma," the wounded guy explains. "She's almost deaf. She just didn't hear it. C'mon, just call."

All Pasha can do is make the call. He presses the button, listens. And he notices that the soldier is also listening, tensing up, and it's getting harder and harder for him to keep listening. Well, and it's getting harder and harder for Pasha, too. He wants to sit down and relax. Not look at anyone, not see anything. Forget all the sounds and smells. Forget the train station, forget the bus, the crumbling road, the moonlit landscapes out the window, the hapless travelers trudging through the January fields, the black, scorched forest, the dark houses, the frightened voices, the lifeless windows, the intersections where death may be waiting for you. And all of that is sitting inside him like lead—heavy and cold, dragging him down to the bottom, making him unwieldy and vulnerable. And the drops—the drops are hitting him right on the head, echoing in his mind, drop by drop, as if someone's mocking him, as if someone's standing nearby and watching him, laughing at him, seeing him struggle, yet not doing anything about it, not rushing to help, not rushing to pick up the phone. Well, c'mon, c'mon, let's go already. Well, where are you? But nobody's answering. And the wounded guy's fading, closing his eyes, not saying anything. He merely squeezes Pasha's hand, squeezes, seemingly pleading. C'mon, one more time, Teach, c'mon. Pasha keeps calling and begins counting the drops as they smash coldly. He counts, loses track, starts counting again, skips around, starts all over, stubbornly, insistently, feeling that the metal spring isn't letting him breathe. It's pushing his heart out of his chest, not letting his heart beat, jabbing into it—sharply and implacably. Well, why aren't you picking up, huh? Why? C'mon, pick up while he's still here, while he's still alive, pick up while he can still hear you, before it's too late. C'mon already. He's about to pass, right here, right now, close his eyes, and that'll be it—you won't hear him ever again, he won't say anything ever again, he'll be here a few more minutes, you can still say something to him, he can't pass without hearing you talk—pass like this, on these two lunch tables moved together, with a slit throat.

Pasha suddenly feels someone else's presence alongside him—someone invisible, someone standing there and waiting persistently. Like someone's transparent silhouette is standing there, watching, plotting. Who's it waiting for? And who has it come for? "For me, clearly," Pasha surmises. "Clearly. It's what's been on my heels for three days now, it's what reeks so much of wet dog, it's what's been hunting me, aiming at me. And now is the perfect moment—we're here all alone, this kid won't notice anything, he doesn't notice anything anymore. Yeah, right now," Pasha thinks resignedly. "Right here."

Then the soldier squeezes his hand again. C'mon, don't give up, keep calling. And Pasha feels the silhouette behind him tense up and finally start paying attention to the kid, to its new victim, scrutinizing, considering. And as soon as he shuts his eyes, as soon as he drifts off, as soon as he releases Pasha's hand, there'll be no saving him. "Hold on," Pasha says. "This can't be, you came for me, what's he got to do with this? Hold on." And he presses the green button again. "C'mon," he repeats in despair. "C'mon, where'd you all go? Pick up. Someone just pick up! Why isn't anyone answering? Where'd you all go? Anyone there? Anyone at all? Where are you? Anyone out there? Can't hear anyone. No pity for anyone. Anyone," Pasha repeats, mouthing the words. "No pity for anyone. No pity for anyone, anyone at all." He can feel death retreating, sidestepping him, moving on to someone else. The ringing dissolves, time flows out, the air thins. There's no fixing anything, there's no saving anyone. The main road stretches out, just a series of snowy fields. There's so much white all around. It's as if all the other colors have disappeared and only white remains. It stretches as far as the eye can see, never-ending white, deep and unmoving, all the way out to the horizon. White fields and the black thawed streak of the road that he's following as he tries to escape, the road that ought to save him. He's running, shielding his eyes from the blinding, white mist all around, running, dragging all his fatigue, all his drenched torment. Just don't stop, don't stop no matter what. You'll make it, you will, you'll break free, you'll slip through. You'll pull it off, you will.

Just a little more, a little bit more. Footsteps. The asphalt echoes hollowly. Snowy fields approach, like the sea at high tide. The white, white surface of life. The white, white space where no one can help. And then he spots some movement. The white canvas sways ever so slightly; his retinas respond to a nearly imperceptible quivering. Black dots—one, two, three, four, five—emerge distinctly on the horizon, expand, move toward him, and in all this movement, he suddenly senses some sort of danger, something irreparable, something that will usher in the end of this, something that he has to escape—as fast as possible, as far as possible. And he's running, on the brink of exhaustion, down the black channel of the road. He runs and catches the cadenced, contentious movement of black dots on the white canvas, sees them expanding, throbbing, charging toward him, seemingly reacting to his body heat. "Don't look," he says to himself. "Don't look, don't, just run, run as fast as you can, until you drop, until you're out of time, run and don't look," he orders himself. And he looks. And he clearly makes out dark dogs on the white backdrop: their heavy chests sinking into the icy expanse, their paws churning scraps of snow, their throats wailing as the warm smell of their victim reaches them more and more sharply. Closer and closer, more furiously, more consumed with the hunt, realizing that their victim won't be able to escape, that he isn't going anywhere, that he's up ahead, a few strong spurts away. Almost there, one more second, and they can pounce, sink their teeth into his neck, but he's trying to escape, trying to trick fate. He's already picking up that wet dog smell, hearing the snowy crust crunch under heavy paws, deafened by their hoarse barking that shreds the surrounding silence. "How many of them are there?" he thinks. "How many?" One, two, three, four, five—he jerks forward, runs, his eyes trying to latch on to anything that could save him or simply delay his death. But the space is empty, rarified, and there's just the white light that's burning his eyes, and there's so much of this light—nothing else, nothing at all, just light, that's it, nothing more. And all he can do is run—don't stop, don't turn around—until he drops, until he's out of time. How much time does he have left? "How much?" he asks himself and begins counting:

one

two

three

four

five

six

seven

eight

nine

ten

There's more and more light; it floods everything all around. There's just so much of it; it fills up everything. It's as if life consists solely of light, as if, in this light, there's no place for death.

I've been sitting in the hallway for over an hour now—just waiting at first, then walking around, reading the posters on the wall. That gets old pretty fast, so I take out my phone. Finally have service. I think about who I should call. Nina. I can't get through, obviously. I send her a text, just in case. I'm doing fine, don't worry. But is she worried? Maybe. She's always worried about everyone. I think that's why nobody likes her.

Pasha shows up sometime around midnight. Tired, pale. He

sees me, sits down on the floor, shakes his head. "No pity for anyone. No pity for anyone," he repeats. I don't really get what he means. I sit down next to him.

"No pity for who?" I ask.

"Anyone," he repeats.

Then he turns toward me. He looks at me long and hard, like he's looking through me. He smiles in recognition. I pat him on the back.

"Want some tea?" I ask. He nods. I walk over to the soldiers, get some tea, bring it back. Pasha thanks me, holds the cup in his hand, but he isn't drinking. His fingers are shaking. His fingers have always scared me. I've never seen anything like them. But his fingers aren't what matters, obviously. Making sure he's doing all right—that's what matters. The past few days have taken a lot out of him: all slouched over, gray face, tired eyes. I carefully touch his shoulder.

"You all right?" I ask. He gives me an exhausted look, fixes his glasses the way he always does, nods.

"Everything's fine," he says. "You hungry?"

"Yeah," I answer. "Let's go home already."

We can't go out the main exit. A stretcher got stuck in the doorway when the soldiers were wheeling it in. They're arguing, pushing it forward and trying to pull it back, which has caused a little traffic jam. Can't get through. We find the back door, open it, pop out into some sort of storage area. Freshly whitewashed hallway, stains showing through the plaster. Metal staircase attached to the wall.

"Wait," Pasha says. "I wanna finally see what's up there." He points at the staircase.

"Nothing's up there," I answer. "Forget about it."

He listens, doesn't argue. He nods at me, as if he's getting rid of something nasty that's been bothering him.

We go outside, push our way through the soldiers. I'm walking up ahead, leading him, like a guide. He's following me, his hand resting on my shoulder.

"All right," he says. "Let's find the train station and take a taxi. Got any money on you?"

"Yeah," I answer.

"We'll have enough then," he replies cheerfully.

I like the way he talks now, the way he talks to me. He used to sound like he was always apologizing for something. It was awkward—for him and for me. What was he even apologizing for? He didn't have anything to apologize for. Actually, I always felt bad when I gave him a hard time. Pasha has a heart condition, shouldn't upset him. His heart could give out anytime, anywhere. That's why I was so worried about him these past few days. I didn't know if he'd make it. But he did it. So now he's speaking in a calm voice, like he trusts me, figures I'll understand what he wants. He isn't yelling or ordering me around. He's calmly explaining everything—go to the train station, find a taxi, we'll have enough money, we'll eat at home. The worst is behind us. Nothing's going to happen to us here. We'll be home soon. The soldiers aren't paying any attention to us; they're yelling to each other, carrying the wounded inside, and taking those who've already been treated out into the fresh air. We make our way out to the main road, go around a tractor, and when we're already some distance away, someone behind us suddenly yells,

"Hey, Teach!"

Pasha stops. Out of the darkness emerges a man: dark, expensive jacket, dirty boots, backpack. His outfit looks pretty sharp, but it's kind of rumpled, like he was being held in some pit for the past few days. He speaks with confidence, takes his time. He's speaking Russian, but even I can tell he's a foreigner.

"What are you doing here?" he asks, looking at Pasha with an unpleasant smile.

"Heading home," Pasha answers.

"That must be your nephew?" He points at me like I'm a dog. "Picked him up after all?" And he talks about me like I'm a dog, too.

"Yeah."

"I didn't think you'd risk it." The man keeps smiling.

"Would you have?" Pasha asks him. The man simply scoffs.

"Well, I . . . ," he says tentatively. "What do I have to do with this? Cigarette?" He changes the topic, takes out a pack of cheap, strong cigarettes, offers Pasha one.

He shakes his head. The man, still smiling, extends the pack toward me.

"I don't smoke that kind of shit," I reply.

"Sasha," Pasha says severely.

"It's all right." The man chuckles. "It's fine, no need to scold him."

"I'm not," Pasha explains. The man stops smiling, tucks his cigarettes away.

"Going to the Station?" he asks Pasha. "I can give you a ride. Let's go?"

"Okay," Pasha agrees, and gives me a gentle push forward.

The man turns around and walks down the road, past a long column of military vehicles. He walks, head down, like he's hiding from someone. And the soldiers look at him like they know that he's hiding from someone. He goes over to an ambulance—a fat guy's sleeping in the driver's seat. He drums on the door. The driver shudders, peers into the darkness, eventually discerns the man, curses. Well, I can't hear what he's actually saying, but he's obviously cursing. The man climbs inside, nods at us. Get in the back. Pasha opens the door, lets me in first, then follows.

"To the Station," the man says. He's speaking like a supervisor. One who isn't that high up, though.

The driver gives him a dirty look but doesn't say anything. "We're in odd company," I think. "Well, it is what it is."

The streets are packed with soldiers. There's no knowing where they all came from. They trudge down the sidewalks, make fires so they can get warm—in groups, by themselves. Some of them have weapons, others don't have anything. There's a big crowd outside the train station, too. A tank crawling with soldiers is parked off to the side. It's as if the soldiers are afraid to get too far away from it. We pass the central square, the railroad crossing, and then leave the city. It's dark—no lights, no movement anywhere. The man up front takes out his cigarettes and lights up.

"All right if I roll down the window? The kid won't get too cold?" he asks Pasha.

"It's fine," I reply.

Pasha merely scoffs at him.

"You call Grandpa?" I ask him.

"Yeah," he replies. "Everything's fine."

I know he isn't telling the truth. He doesn't want me to worry. He's just looking out for me. He's always looking out for me, afraid something'll happen to me. Honestly though, I'm worried about him. I might be the only person who worries about him. Maryna left him, his sister—my mom, I mean—takes no interest in his life, and Grandpa's at war with him. I love him, though. I knew he'd come get me, I was sure. I was just counting on him coming earlier, when you could still leave the city. And when he showed up two nights ago, I immediately thought to myself, "How are we gonna get out?" Well, it's a good thing everything went okay. And the fact that he isn't telling the truth—that's a good thing, too. Talk all you want, Pasha. Just don't worry about me. I simply don't understand how he's still hanging in there, after three days out in the wind and rain. When I saw him in the hospital, out there in the hallway, I thought that he'd just spoken to his death. And he was able to sway it. Or maybe he wasn't. But it wasn't able to sway him either.

"Well, so . . ." The man holding the cigarette turns toward Pasha. "When do you go back to school?"

"After break," Pasha answers calmly.

The man laughs heartily, like he's just heard an old joke.

"What do you teach again? History?" he asks.

"No," Pasha answers.

"Chemistry?" the man inquires.

"Ukrainian." The man whistles in reply.

"That's like teaching Latin," he says, chuckling.

"That's a bit of an exaggeration."

"Well, all right." The man doesn't want to argue with Pasha. He takes out another cigarette and lights it from the butt of the last one. "Just tell me this—how are you going to teach your language now? After all of this?" He points into the black night.

Pasha thinks, doesn't say anything. "He's feeling blue," I think. But no, he isn't.

"Peter," he says to the man. It turns out he knows his name. "Do your readers send you letters?"

"My readers?" The man's confused.

"Like the people who read your newspaper," Pasha elaborates. "Do they send letters to your office?"

"What?" The man's still confused.

"Basically, I'm trying to say that even if they do, you probably don't read them. You probably aren't interested in that. And you aren't interested in us either. That's what I'm trying to say."

"Uh, why would you say something like that?" The man's offended, but he's trying to speak amicably.

"That's how we talk at school," Pasha explains. "We say what we think. Otherwise, what's the point of even talking, right?" The man apparently doesn't know if he should outwardly take offense or keep his hurt feelings to himself.

"You're a strange guy," he begins softly. "I don't get you."

"That's just because you don't understand our language," Pasha replies offhandedly. "We all speak Latin around here."

"Very funny," the man replies.

"Yeah, but tell me I'm wrong."

We pass a checkpoint on the road that leads out of the city. The lights of the Station shine in the distance. The soldiers instantly recognize the ambulance. It's clearly been here before. They nod at the driver. And give Peter the cold shoulder.

"We'll drop you off at the motel," he says to Pasha stiffly.

"Thank you," Pasha says just as stiffly.

They don't say anything more. The driver turns on the radio, picks up noise.

There's a ton of military equipment by the motel. The soldiers are running from vehicle to vehicle. They scan the ambulance and spot Peter, so they lose interest. The driver stops but doesn't switch off the motor; he considers pulling up a little closer. Everyone's sitting, waiting wordlessly.

"They picked up a woman here yesterday." The driver cracks first. "Special ops guys came in. Turns out she was leaking information."

"Who was she?" Pasha asks lazily.

"A waitress."

Peter sneers.

"Name?" Pasha suddenly asks.

"Huh?" The driver's confused.

"What was the waitress's name? Anna?"

"Nah," the driver answers, flustered. "Not Anna. Definitely not Anna. Why do you ask?"

"Never mind," Pasha replies. "Get out," he says to me. "Let's go home."

In parting, Pasha hollowly shuts the ambulance door. But Peter leaps out as soon as we start to walk away.

"Teach!" he yells. "Wait."

Pasha takes several more mechanical steps but then stops. He stands in silence. Peter walks over, frostily rubs his hands, seemingly not knowing what to do with them.

"Want me to tell you the password?" he asks.

"What password?"

"It's getting late," Peter explains. "You won't get past the first checkpoint without it."

"We don't need it," Pasha says. "But thanks," he adds after a moment's thought.

"No hard feelings, all right?" Peter somewhat awkwardly extends his frozen hand.

Pasha shakes it. They stand there, not knowing what to do. Peter pulls his hand out of Pasha's just as awkwardly, tucks it into his pockets.

"You probably think I'm a real asshole," he says. "You really shouldn't, though. You don't know anything about me. All right?"

"All right," Pasha replies, smiling.

He doesn't challenge the asshole part, though.

"Why were you being like that to him?" I ask Pasha once we've walked away.

"Is there any other way to be with guys like him?" Pasha asks, surprised. "He really just isn't interested in anyone. And he isn't interested in us either. He'll leave, we'll stick around. That's all there is to it."

On the way back, it starts raining again. You don't really pay attention to that, though. Just want to get home. Service is spotty, but Mom gets through. She's speaking calmly, as if everything's fine and nothing has happened. She tells me she'll be back tomorrow. I answer in a calm tone, too. Actually, nothing did happen. Pasha calls Grandpa, tells him we'll be home soon, asks him what to pick up at the store. It feels like we just went for a hike and now we're coming home—tired, dirty, smelling of smoke. The closer we get to the Station, the more soldiers there are. A long column of heavy armor heads past us, toward the city. They were clearly coming from where the tracks are. Just disembarked. The soldiers are focused and calm. Nobody's yelling. Nobody's berating anyone. Everyone's preparing for the war that's still going on. Everyone's planning to survive, thinking about returning. Everyone wants to return home; everyone likes returning. I like returning to the Station, too, I like counting the buildings, seeing our neighbors at the bus stop, waiting for our house—looks like a half-loaf of black bread—to appear around the corner. On the trees around the bus stop, groups of birds. Drowsy, wet, motionless. It's as if they're waiting for a ride. They may've flown here from the city, come back to their flock. They feel safer here.

Rain-drenched street, black windows, low-hanging sky. I see a box by the bus stop. Something's squeaking quietly inside.

"Pasha," I yell. "Hold on."

Two puppies. Red with spots. One's cold. The other one is almost dead, too.

"Let's take him home," I say to Pasha.

"Ugh, no," he replies. "Grandpa'll have a fit."

"And then he'll deal with it," I say.

"Just leave him. He's gonna die anyway."

"Yeah, if I leave him he will." I carefully pick him up, tuck him under my shirt.

Then the puppy starts peeing, right on my sweater. But he's calmed down, stopped whimpering. "Well, all right," I think.

"He dead?" Pasha asks, now obviously interested.

"Yeah right!" I answer. "He'll be a badass when he grows up."

Pasha laughs skeptically. We turn the corner. Smooth television light shines through our windows.

At home, it smells like fresh sheets.

SERHIY ZHADAN was born in the Luhansk Region of Ukraine and educated in Kharkiv, where he lives today. He is the most popular poet of the post-independence generation in Ukraine and the author of twelve books of poetry, which have earned him numerous national and European awards. His prose works include *Big Mac* (2003), *Depeche Mode* (2004), *Anarchy in the UKR* (2005), *Hymn of the Democratic Youth* (2006), *Voroshilovgrad* (2010), *Mesopotamia* (2014), and *The Orphanage* (2017). Zhadan's books have been translated into Belarusian, Czech, English, French, German, Hungarian, Italian, Latvian, Lithuanian, Norwegian, Polish, Russian, and Swedish. He is the front man for the band Zhadan and the Dogs.

REILLY COSTIGAN-HUMES and ISAAC STACKHOUSE WHEELER are a team of literary translators who work with both Ukrainian and Russian. They are best known for their translations of Serhiy Zhadan's prose, including *Voroshilovgrad* and *Mesopotamia.*

The translators are grateful to Hanna Leliv and Yevhenii Monastyrskyi for their generous and thoughtful assistance with the text.